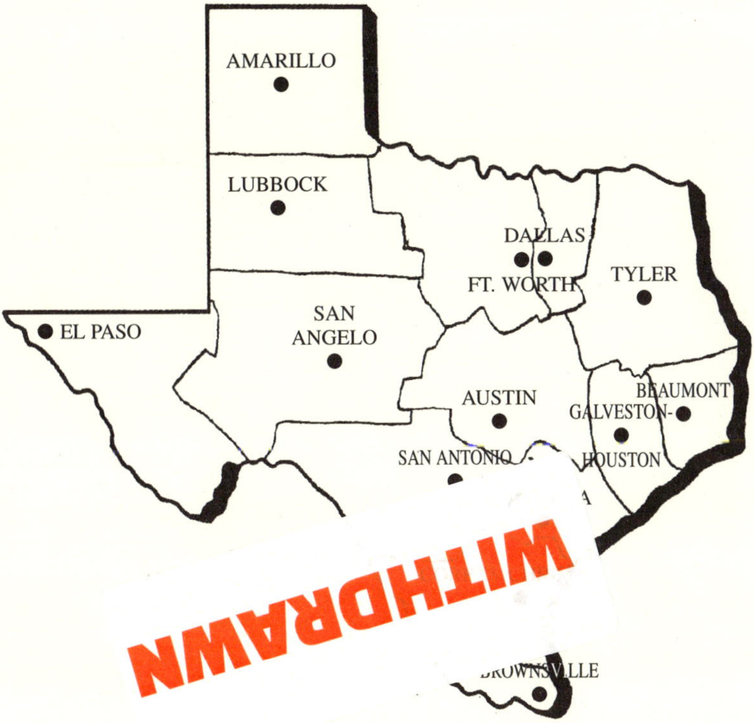

THE ROMAN CATHOLIC PROVINCE OF SAN ANTONIO
1995

Lone Star Bishops:
The Roman Catholic Hierarchy in Texas

BY

Franklin C. Williams, Jr.

Member, Texas Catholic Historical Society
Member, Texas State Historical Association

Library of Congress Catalog Card Number
97-90535

ISBN 0-87244-101-6

Printed by

Texian Press
Waco, Texas

TO MY PARENTS,

THE LATE FRANKLIN CADMUS
AND
CATHRYN LUCILLE (PESSONEY) WILLIAMS,

TO WHOM I OWE EVERYTHING.

CANON 330 — Just as, by the Lord's decision, Saint Peter and the other Apostles constitute one college, so in a similar way the Roman Pontiff, successor of Peter, and the bishops, successors of the Apostles, are joined together.

CANON 375 — §1. Through the Holy Spirit who has been given to them, bishops are the successors of the Apostles by divine institution; they are constituted pastors within the Church so that they are teachers of doctrine, priests of sacred worship and ministers of governance.

§2. By the fact of their episcopal consecration bishops receive along with the function of sanctifying also the functions of teaching and of ruling, which by their very nature, however, can be exercised only when they are in hierarchical communion with the head of the college and its members.

CODE OF CANON LAW, effective 27 November 1983.

Contents

Preface

I can not remember a time when I was not interested in history. As is true of most Texans, I have studied the heritage of my state in grade school, in high school, and at Baylor University, where my double major included history. My particular interest in the Roman Catholic saga in Texas was sparked by my reading of Carlos Castañeda's famous work, *Our Catholic Heritage in Texas*, which is being rewritten in part.

Monsignor Leo Wleczyk, VF, asked me to make a brief talk to his congregation of Sacred Heart Church in Palestine, Texas (then part of the Diocese of Galveston-Houston and now part of the Diocese of Tyler), on 4 July 1976. It stressed briefly the Catholic history of America and of Texas and was part of the local Bicentennial celebration of that year. Another monsignor, the late Anton Frank of Assumption Parish in Houston, became interested in the parish history I had written and felt I deserved some recognition. Before I knew it, I was enrolled in the Texas Catholic Historical Society by the director of the Texas Catholic Conference, John E. McCarthy, the present bishop of Austin. Monsignor Frank then persuaded the late bishop of Galveston-Houston, John L. Morkovsky, to appoint me to the parish history project of that diocese.

At length the idea occurred to me to give, within a single volume, not only complete biographical accounts of each Roman Catholic bishop serving in Texas, auxiliary as well as diocesan, but to supply the reader with an introduction, explaining what a bishop is, how he functions (specially post-Vatican Council II), and to supply historical detail with some specific relation to Texas. The result is two books in one, with the "Introduction" designed to answer questions about the office of bishop, particularly the bishop in Texas, with the biographies explaining the contribution made by each bishop who has served in Texas from 1842 through 1995.

The phrase "in Texas" means that the present work includes only those bishops who have held office within the boundaries of the Republic and the State of Texas. I am leaving out any bishops "of Texas," i.e., born within the confines of the Republic or the State who did not serve in it. Those who temporarily administered dioceses between the vacancy of one bishop and the appointment of the next are omitted if they were not themselves bishops.

While this book is meant to be inclusive, it is not put forward as an officially sanctioned history concerning which some ecclesiastical authority has made decisions or supplied funding for its issue. Nor is it a parish-by-parish or institutional account. Such works have been and will be written by those priests and scholars who dwell within the inner structure of the Church edifice. I alone am responsible for what is included in this book, and I have tried as hard as is humanly possible to make correct statements of fact and analysis.

Before proceeding, I would like to state the meaning of some terms, sometimes seemingly used interchangeably. Before Vatican Council II (1962-1965) the terms "assistant pastor" or "curate" described those in a subordinate position to the pastor. Such a priest is now generally called an "associate pastor" or "parochial vicar". For reasons explained within, the ceremony in which bishops receive the fullness of their ministerial authority was once called "consecration," but more correctly today, "ordination". The term "diocese" sometimes includes the term "archdiocese," as both entities are governed similarly internally. The word "church" as a community of believers here normally refers to the "Roman Catholic Church," unless some other distinction is made. The terms "Apostolic See," "Holy See," "Rome," and the "Vatican" generally refer to the authority of the Pope. The reader is invited to seek further explanations in such standard works as *Catechism of the Catholic Church*, *Catholic Almanac*, the *New Catholic Encyclopedia* and its supplements, and editions of the *Official Catholic Directory*.

In writing this book I have relied upon many people and would like to thank some of them. Rev. Harold P. Paulsen, pastor of Sacred Heart Church in Palestine, Texas, has supplied the Palestine Public Library with numerous works pertaining to the Roman Catholic Church. I am grateful to the staff of this library, especially to the former head librarian, Mrs. Cynthia Gray, for the use of this collection and for her assistance. I have also spent time in the University of Texas at Tyler Muntz Library, as well as the Eugene C. Barker Texas History Center and the Perry-Castañeda Library of the University of Texas at Austin. Ms. Kennon Garofalo, the former archivist of the Catholic Archives of Texas in Austin, made my visit memorable by her courtesy and helpfulness in answering my numerous questions during my visit there.

I would also like to thank Bro. Edward J. Loch, SM, archivist of the Archdiocese of San Antonio and Ms. Margaret Schattel, circulation manager for its official newspaper, *Today's Catholic*. Together they have provided much-needed help and kindly encouragement over the years. Rev. James Vanderholt, a church historian and editor of *East Texas Catholic*, has aided me with materials concerning the bishops of his diocese of Beaumont. Ms. Agnes Browne of Brownsville, Texas, and Mrs. Pamela G. Downing, Director of Public Relations of the Diocese of Brownsville, have aided my inquiries and smoothed my way more than they will ever know. I am grateful to Ms. Estelle Metzger, the archivist of the Diocese of Dallas, who provided me with information concerning Bishops Danglmayr and Tschoepe, as well as Ms. Nancy Claire of the diocesan newspaper, *Texas Catholic*.

Most Reverend John J. Cassata, DD, the late bishop of Fort Worth, took the time to write to me concerning the details of his life. Ms. Pat Behnke, Communications Office Manager of the Diocese of Lubbock, supplied useful information on the bishops of her diocese. Monsignor Maurice Voity and the staff of the *West Texas Angelus* of San Angelo, as well as Ms. Mary Louise Anderson, Secretary to the Provincial of the Southern United States Province of the Missionary Oblates of Mary Immaculate in San Antonio, supplied me with biographical details of Bishop Pfeifer. I also thank the staff of the *Catholic Lighthouse* of the Diocese of Victoria in Texas for information on their bishops.

Outside of Texas, I would like to thank the following persons for their aid:

Ms. Margaret M. Maher, librarian of the Catholic News Service in Washington, DC, for information about Bishops Herzig and Pfeifer; Very Rev. Borgia Aubespin, SVD, Provincial of the Southern Province of the Society of the Divine Word in Bay St. Louis, Mississippi; Ms. Penelope B. Powell, acting executive director of the National Office for Black Catholics in Washington, DC; and Mr. Joseph Larose of the *Clarion Herald*, the newspaper of the Archdiocese of New Orleans, for information on Bishop Guillory; Mr. Paul Joly, Maryknoll Media Relations of Maryknoll, New York, for information on Bishop Gerbermann; Ms. Mary Ann Sullivan, Administrative Assistant for the Secretariat for Clergy, and Sr. Kathleen Leary, SSJ, Subscriptions/Projects Coordinator for *The Catholic Standard and Times*, both of the Archdiocese of Philadelphia, for information on Bishop Galante; Rev. Theodore Cirone, CMF, Provincial Superior of Claretian Missionaries in Oak Park, Illinois; and Ms. Nancy Sandleback, Assistant Archivist of the Archdiocese of Chicago, for information about Bishop Rodriguez; Ms. Ann C. Bruce, Business Office Manager of *The Pilot*, the official newspaper of the Archdiocese of Boston, for information about Bishop Gonzalez; and Sr. Nancy Kazik, OSF, editor of *People of God*, the official newspaper of the Archdiocese of Santa Fe in Albuquerque, New Mexico, for information about Archbishop Sheehan.

These individuals and institutions provided me with information, which I have carefully examined and tried to relate accurately, especially in the case of dates with conflicting sources. Such matters I decided on a case-by-case basis, using the best authorities generally available. These people have in no way influenced my use of their materials and all judgements and conclusions of fact and analysis in the present work reflect those of its author alone.

F.C.W.

Palestine, Texas.
For the Sesquicentennial of the establishment of the
Diocese of Galveston, the first in Texas.

Part I: Introduction

A. The Province of San Antonio: An Overview

On 1 January 1992 the Most Reverend Patrick Fernandez Flores, fourth archbishop and metropolitan of San Antonio, might have paused to take stock of his jurisdiction, the ecclesiastical province of San Antonio. In this 150th year of the establishment of the Roman Catholic hierarchy in Texas, Archbishop Flores might have observed that his province was not a small one. It consisted of the entire state of Texas.

As archbishop, Flores is directly responsible for the spiritual needs of the Roman Catholics within his archdiocese and for the practical management of those institutions owned and operated by the Catholic Church within it. The entity he governs corresponds geographically to the Texas counties of Atascosa, Bandera, Bexar, Comal, Dimmit, Edwards, Frio, Gillespie, Gonzales, Guadalupe, Karnes, Kendall, Kerr, Kinney, that part of La Salle north of the Nueces River, Maverick, that part of McMullen north of the Nueces River, Medina, Real, Uvalde, Val Verde, Wilson, and Zavala. As constituted on this specific day it comprised roughly 27,841 square miles. When the Diocese of San Antonio was established on 28 August 1874, it had a much larger area. And it had a different composition when it was created an archdiocese on 3 August 1926.[1]

How, then, may we say that Archbishop Flores is the spiritual leader of the Roman Catholics across the entire state of Texas? Figuratively he wears two hats. As archbishop he is the superior or chief bishop presiding over one of the greater sees or jurisdictions in the United States of America. Like other bishops he has a specific territory which he governs directly. As metropolitan he is one of thirty-three heads of American ecclesiastical provinces, which contain the same number of archdioceses (sometimes called archbishoprics) or metropolitan sees.

In 1992 six archbishops and metropolitans of the provinces of Chicago, Boston, New York, Washington D.C., Los Angeles, and Philadelphia were also cardinals. These prelates had the added responsibilities of electing a pope (if necessary) and of serving in some department of the Roman Curia. The Curia is the Church's central administrative network made up of various agencies which assist the operation of the Vatican and dioceses throughout the world. The title of cardinal is awarded for life, but residential archbishops must tender their resignations from their provinces by the age of seventy-five. Nor may they vote to elect a pope or hold active curial positions after reaching the age of eighty.

The Province of San Antonio is made up of the Archdiocese of San Antonio and the other (or suffragan) sees within Texas. These are the dioceses of Amarillo, Austin, Beaumont, Brownsville, Corpus Christi, Dallas, El Paso, Fort Worth, Galveston-Houston, Lubbock, San Angelo, Tyler, and Victoria (in alphabetical order). Each diocese is headed by a bishop, assisted in some cases by his auxiliaries.

The San Antonio province is one of the thirty-one metropolitan provinces which include all fifty states, the District of Columbia, and the Virgin Islands. Yet another province (non-metropolitan) is the Archdiocese for the Military Services, U.S.A., with headquarters in Washington D.C., which is headed by its own archbishop called the military ordinary. Its primary purpose is to provide chaplains for all branches of the military.

The thirty-one American provinces just referred to practice the Latin or Roman Rite, which is the type of liturgical worship making up the Western religious heritage of Roman Catholicism. Liturgical worship is made up of forms and usages deriving originally from apostolic times and affects the prayers and ceremonies of the Mass, sacramental celebration, sacramentals, the Liturgy of the Hours, and observances of the liturgical character. The Latin Rite developed from Roman practices and the use of Latin in the third century and has been general throughout the West since the eighth century.

In addition there are Eastern Rites observed by Eastern Catholic churches, of which the principal ones are Byzantine, Alexandrian, Antiochene, Armenian, and Chaldean. A child may adopt the rite of both parents, the rite decided by the parents when they belong to different rites, or the rite of the father when mutual consent is lacking. Adoption of the rite takes place upon baptism. The baptismal candidate is free to choose any approved rite upon reaching the age of fourteen. Transfer to another rite depends upon permission of the Holy See (the Vatican) and in accordance with the provisions of canon law.

The two American provinces which observe the Eastern Rite are Philadelphia (Byzantine Rite, Ukrainians) and Pittsburgh (Byzantine Rite, Ruthenians). Each is headed by an archbishop. The Philadelphia province (not to be confused with the Latin Rite province of Philadelphia) includes the Metropolitan See of Philadelphia (Byzantine Rite) and Eparchies (Dioceses) of St. Josaphat in Parma (Ohio), St. Nicholas of the Ukrainians in Chicago and Stamford, Connecticut. This jurisdiction extends to all Ukrainian Catholics in the United States from the ecclesiastical province of Galicia in the Ukraine. The Pittsburgh province (not to be confused with the Latin Rite Diocese of Pittsburgh within the Archdiocese of Philadelphia) includes the Metropolitan See of Pittsburgh and Eparchies of Passaic (New Jersey), Parma (Ohio) and Van Nuys (California).

Completing the organizational structure of the Catholic Church in the United States are four Eastern Rite jurisdictions immediately subject to the Holy See. These are the eparchies of St. Maron (Maronites), Newton (Melkites), St. Thomas Apostle of Detroit (Chaldeans) and St. George Martyr of Canton, Ohio (Romanians). An Armenian Rite exarchate for the United States and Canada has its seat in New York and is under the direction of its own ordinary (bishop).[2]

As a metropolitan archbishop of the Latin Rite Archbishop Flores has a necessary relationship between his see city of San Antonio and the other sees which make up the Province of San Antonio. The system of naming the older and more active churches "metropolitan" existed in the West as early as the third century A.D. Bishops who headed these dioceses were known as archbishops, signifying bishops with the title of their archdioceses, by the sixth century. By the eighth century bishops subject to archbishops were known as "suffragans" because of their ability to vote (*suffragio*) in a provincial council. Metropolitans confirmed the elections of their suffragans and consecrated them, called and presided over provincial councils disciplined their suffragans and took over their ministries when necessary and acted as an appellate court from the decisions of their own suffragan diocesan courts.[3]

In the twenty-fourth of the twenty-five sessions of the Council of Trent

(1545-1563) Pius IV (1559-1565) reorganized the metropolitan system, restricting its functions but requesting continued coordination within the province by means of regularly-called provincial councils. The 1917 Code of Canon Law imposed further restrictions upon metropolitans, making clear their prerogatives. The 1983 or present code continues to simplify their rights. Canon 435 states:

> The metropolitan, who is the archbishop of the province which he heads, presides over an ecclesiastical province; this office is connected with an episcopal see which has been determined or approved by the Roman pontiff.[4]

The effect of this canon is to connect the office of metropolitan to its particular see. Internally (or within his own diocese known as an archdiocese) the archbishop has the usual powers of a diocesan bishop. Externally (or as metropolitan of his province) he has certain other powers to exercise over the neighboring dioceses which (with his own) are part of his ecclesiastical province.

The 1917 Code did not distinguish between the titles of "archbishop" and "metropolitan". Some archbishops are not metropolitans. A coadjutor archbishop is an assistant archbishop who may succeed the archbishop to whom he is appointed upon the death or inability to serve of the incumbent. A titular archbishop has the title of an archdiocese which formerly existed but does not presently. Such titles are often given to clergy in the Roman Curia or to high-ranking diplomats of ambassadorial level within the Vatican diplomatic service. The "archbishop ad personam" is a bishop given a title as a distinction without ecclesiastical jurisdiction, such as the archbishopric of Newport was conferred upon Fulton J. Sheen.

A second difference between the 1917 and 1983 codes is that the former refers to the metropolitan's "dignity" and the latter refers to his "office". This difference changes the emphasis from the privileges of the individual to the services which he provides. The metropolitan is not a "chairman of the board" or "chief operational officer" elected by area bishops. He is instead the appointee of the pope, who serves by designation or approbation and is always the metropolitan of the province.

In the case of Archbishop Flores, whose province happens to be coterminous with a state rather than with the boundaries of a country, he and his brother bishops of the United States of America are affiliated with their territorial episcopal conference. It is known as the National Conference of Catholic Bishops, established by action of the United States hierarchy on 14 November 1966. It has the approval of the Holy See and is guided by direction of the Second Vatican Council (1962-1965). Its constitution was formally ratified at its November 1967 meeting.

The National Conference of Catholic Bishops (NCCB) is an ecclesiastical body with defined juridical authority over the Catholic Church in America. It is a development of the Annual Meeting of the bishops of the United States, which was granted papal authority in 1919. Within the conference the bishops of the United States act together, officially and with pastoral authority. The bishops of Texas have served the NCCB with distinction, especially as chairmen and members of various committees. Archbishop Flores has served as chairman of the Committee on the Permanent Diaconate, along with Bishop Enrique San Pedro, SJ of Brownsville, chairman of the Committee on Hispanic Affairs.

The NCCB also sponsors the United States Catholic Conference (USCC), a civil corporation and service secretariat, which became operative in 1967. It is an outgrowth of the National Catholic War Council (1917), which became the National Catholic Welfare Council (1919) and later the National Catholic Welfare Conference (1923). These organizations were service agencies of the bishops and the Church. The present purpose of the USCC is to provide the wherewithal for public, educational and social concerns through national, regional, state, and diocesan levels in America.

The headquarters of the NCCB and the USCC are in Washington D.C., as is the Apostolic Nunciature or Vatican embassy. Since 1984 the Vatican and the United States have maintained full diplomatic relations. The apostolic pronuncio (ambassador) exercises his office to serve dioceses and bishops in such matters as the nomination of bishops aiding and counseling bishops, assisting the NCCB, advising major superiors of religious communities of the Church, and working with civil governments for peace and the good of mankind. In these activities, in addition to its general and special duties, the nunciature performs service and liaison functions, while respecting the autonomy of local dioceses and bishops. From 1893 until 1984 the Vatican maintained an American apostolic delegation, lacking diplomatic status.

Texas also maintains a state Catholic conference, in cooperation with organizations in twenty-seven other states (as of 1992). The purpose of such conferences as state agencies of bishops and dioceses is to provide programs for pastoral and welfare needs and to represent the dioceses before governmental bodies, the public, and in private sectors. The Texas Catholic Conference has headquarters in Austin. The National Association of State Catholic Conference Directors, whose executive director is the director of a state conference, maintains affiliation with the general secretariat of the USCC. Of the thirteen NCCB-USCC regions within the United States Texas (along with Arkansas and Oklahoma, together the Province of Oklahoma City) is part of their Region Ten.[5]

Having seen Archbishop Flores within the organizational structure of the Catholic Church in the United States, it remains for us to examine his authority over his suffragans and his use of the pallium as a symbol of his authority. We conclude this section by examining what it means to be the metropolitan archbishop of the Province of San Antonio in the year 1992.

Concerning the authority of a metropolitan over his suffragans, Canon 436 states:

> §1. Within the suffragan dioceses the metropolitan is competent:
>
> 1° to be vigilant that the faith and ecclesiastical discipline are preserved and to inform the Roman Pontiff of abuses if there are any;
>
> 2° to perform the canonical visitation if the suffragan bishop has neglected it, after the reason for doing so has first been approved by the Apostolic See;
>
> 3° to appoint a diocesan administrator in accord with the norm of cann. 421, §2 and 424, §3.

> §2. Where circumstances demand it a metropolitan can be invested by the Apostolic See with special duties and power to be determined in particular law.
>
> §3. The metropolitan possesses no other power of governance within the suffragan dioceses; he can, however, perform sacred functions in all the churches as if he were a bishop in his own diocese, but he is to inform the diocesan bishop if it is the cathedral church.[6]

Canon 436 of the 1983 Code of Canon Law specifically restricts the metropolitan and generally strengthens the authority of his suffragans to act within their own dioceses. The metropolitan is still charged with vigilance over faith and morals, but not as a means to extend governing power over his suffragans. He must work more closely with the Apostolic See and gather information for later decision-making on higher level than his own rather than intervene actively in all situations. He may, for instance, note the failure of a suffragan to visit within a diocese. But he may not undertake such a task without prior approval of the Apostolic See. He may appoint a diocesan administrator in a suffragan diocese if the consultors or chapter of canons of that diocese fail to elect the administrator within the prescribed time (c. 421, §2) or have elected one lacking the necessary qualifications for the position (c. 425, §3).

The metropolitan may be granted extraordinary powers within the province by the Apostolic See. These powers are to be left to particular law. Other canons relate to other duties of the metropolitan. Canon 442 mentions his role in regard to provincial councils when the consent of a majority of his suffragan bishops is given. He may convene meetings of the bishops of the province to determine various financial matters (cann. 952, §l and 1405, §3, 1°).

The metropolitan's tribunal is the court of second instance for tribunals of the suffragan dioceses (c. 1438, 1°) and the court of first instance in actions concerning the rights of a juridic person (any entity considered as a person for legal purposes, ex. a corporation) represented by a suffragan bishop (c. 1419, §2). This last situation excepts the usual manner in which bishops are judged in certain cases by the Roman Rota (c. 1405, §3, 1°).

Concerning the pallium and its use Canon 437 states:

> §1. Within three months from the reception of episcopal consecration or from the time of canonical provision if he has already been consecrated a bishop, a metropolitan is obliged personally or through his proxy to request the pallium of the Roman Pontiff; the pallium signifies the power with which the metropolitan is invested by law within his own province in communion with the Roman Church.
>
> §2. In accord with the norm of liturgical laws a metropolitan can use the pallium in any church whatsoever within the ecclesiastical province over which he presides, but not outside it, even if the diocesan bishop gives his assent.
>
> §3. A metropolitan requires a new pallium if he is transferred to another metropolitan see.[7]

The pallium is a circular band of white wool, made from the wool of lambs presented to the pope on the Feast of St. Agnes (21 January). It has front and back pendants, marked by six dark purple crosses, and is worn around the neck by the pope and archbishops of metropolitan sees on top of vestments used for Mass and in other liturgical celebrations.

Its use seems to have come from festive garb worn occasionally by nobles of the Roman Empire. Eastern bishops first adopted it and it was conferred by patriarchs on their metropolitans. Popes adopted it in the West and sent it to certain bishops as signs of esteem. Mandatory use of the pallium began in the ninth century when metropolitans petitioned it from the Pope to confirm their authority within their provinces. In the Middle Ages it became a sign of pontifical power and was considered a delegation of papal authority. By 1917 obtainment of the pallium was considered necessary before the performance of some archiepiscopal functions.

On 11 May 1978 Pope Paul VI issued a *motu proprio* (a self-initiated administrative document) concerning the use of the pallium. It became effective on 20 July 1978 and restricted use of this article to the pope and archbishops of metropolitan sees. Although the metropolitan is no longer considered to be a participant in papal authority, the pallium is still considered to be a sign of authority and it is still required that it be petitioned. The metropolitan must do so personally or through a proxy within three months of taking possession of the metropolitan see or of being consecrated. Because the pallium may be used only within the ecclesiastical province over which the metropolitan presides, it is particular to that province. A new one would have to be petitioned if the metropolitan were to be transferred to a new metropolitan see.

In 1984 Pope John Paul II decreed that the pallium would ordinarily be conferred by him on the solemnity of St. Peter and Paul (29 June). It is sometimes actually conferred by the senior cardinal deacon upon the authority of the pope.[8]

We conclude this section as we began with Archbishop Flores's imaginary contemplation of his province of San Antonio, as it existed on New Year's Day 1992. In the course of the Introduction we will consider various aspects of bishops and observe how this province developed from its inception until the present time.

On this particular day the Province of San Antonio contains the largest number of dioceses in any American state with the possibility of future additions. Coterminous with the State of Texas it contains twenty bishops (in office and retired) and three abbots. There are 1,163 diocesan priests and 945 of religious orders, including twenty-two newly ordained.

This clergy is assisted by 963 permanent deacons (all male), 252 brothers, and 3,290 sisters. Nine hundred forty-four parishes, 330 missions, and thirty-six pastoral centers exist with one new parish created during 1991. There are twenty-five Catholic hospitals assisting 1,442,609 patients annually, fifteen health care centers with 121,841 patients, forty-seven specialized homes serving 77,940, and seven orphanages with 580 children. Fifty-one day care and extended day care centers took charge of 4,517 individuals, as did thirty-eight special centers for social services, providing programs for 1,690,128 people.

Education in the Province of San Antonio this day involves five diocesan seminaries with 206 clerics and eleven religious seminaries (for the formation of priests of various religious orders) with ninety-five clerics. Seven colleges and universities enroll 17,688 students. There are twenty-three diocesan and parochial (parish) high schools with 6,315 students and twenty-four private high schools with 8,826 students. On the elementary level 207 diocesan and parochial schools instruct 52,522 boys and girls, while twenty-one private schools perform the same function for 6,316 other students. In addition four nonresidential schools for the handicapped serve 378 people. For those not attending elementary and secondary Catholic schools 238,967 students of public elementary institutions receive Confraternity of Christian Doctrine instruction in their faith, as do 69,725 students on the secondary level. All of these students are taught by 148 priests, two scholastics, sixty-eight brothers, 579 sisters, and 4,673 lay teachers.

Continuing his imaginary survey the archbishop might have contemplated other 1992 statistics on this day. During the year just past 82,869 people were received into the Church. There were 58,935 first communions, 32,319 confirmations, 16,320 marriages performed, and 19,554 deaths. Three million six hundred thirty-seven thousand and six hundred eighty-five Catholics lived within Texas out of a total population of 17,150,596. Thus 22% of Texans were Catholic, or a little more than one in five, comparable to 23% of all Americans throughout the United States.

In the hierarchy of the United States, Texas has no cardinals, a little over two percent of forty-five archbishops, and about five-and-a-half percent of 352 bishops. It also has roughly two-and-a-half percent of the 115 abbots. In addition only a few more than three percent of diocesan priests and five-and-a-quarter percent of religious priests serve Texas, in which whole counties are without their services. Of these priests about two-and-a-half percent of the total are newly ordained. Texas has about nine percent of all American permanent deacons, about four percent of religious brothers in the United States, and less than four percent of its religious sisters.

Texans have almost four-and-a-quarter percent of American Catholic parishes, nine percent of its missions, and about three-and-a-quarter percent of its pastoral centers, including slightly more than two percent of parishes created during 1991.

The state contains about four percent of American Catholic hospitals, some six-and-a-half percent of its health care centers, three percent of its specialized homes, about three-and-a-half percent of its orphanages, about five-and-a-half percent of its day care and extended day care centers, and two percent of its special centers for social services.

Texas has almost seven percent of Catholic diocesan and religious seminaries in America, almost three percent of Catholic-affiliated colleges and universities throughout the nation, a little more than three-and-a-quarter percent of Catholic high schools, about three percent of Catholic elementary schools, and four percent of the denomination's nonresident schools for the handicapped. And a little over six percent of American Catholics live in Texas, where about one in every five people is Catholic (twenty-two percent). The Catholic percentage of the population (twenty-three percent) is much the same for the entire United States.[9]

For a period of some 300 years from the sixteenth century under Spanish exploration and colonization and into the early Anglo settlement in the nineteenth century, Texas was Catholic in name if not always in practice. Even so great a transplanted Texan as Sam Houston thought it politic to announce his membership prior to his baptism into the Baptist faith by Rev. Rufus C. Burleson. In 1980 a survey of an estimated 7,781,967 members of more than sixty denominations in Texas showed Catholicism with 2,340,162 adherents compared to the first-ranked Southern Baptist Convention with an estimated membership of 2,659,894.[10]

While Catholic "receptions into the Church" include infant baptisms as well as adult conversions, Texas has a large Hispanic population and immigration into the state continues to swell the numbers. Demand for clergy continues to exceed supply and lay members, ordained deacons, and/or religious sometimes fill in for priests, who still retain the exclusive right to perform Mass and administer the sacrament of Penance. As those who preside over Catholic people and institutions, Texas bishops have their work cut out for them as their faith expands throughout the state.

B. The Foundation of the Office of Bishop

The Roman Catholic Church bases its official teaching of the institution of bishops upon the formation of the Apostles by Jesus Christ. Canon 330 states:

> Just as, by the Lord's decision, Saint Peter and the other Apostles constitute one college, so in a similar way the Roman Pontiff, successor of Peter, and the bishops, successors of the Apostles, are joined together.[1]

If we are to understand what a bishop is, we must look to the meaning of the word "Apostle" and its historical significance. In Greek *apostolos* means envoy, a messenger. Christ chose, trained, and sent out his apostles to preach the Gospel, to baptize, and to establish, direct and care for his Church as servants of God. The twelve Apostles as listed in Matthew 10:1-4 are Peter, Andrew, James the Greater, John, Philip, Bartholomew, Thomas, Matthew, James the Lesser, Jude [Thaddeus], Simon, and Judas Iscariot. Later Matthias was elected to fill the place of Judas (Acts 1:26). [2] Acts 13:2 suggests the inclusion of Paul and Barnabas as Apostles also. Paul calls himself and his fellow workers "apostles" in 1 Thessalonians 2:7.

Most of Matthew 10 details Christ's sending out the Apostles with the injunction, "Go and preach, 'The Kingdom of heaven is near!' Heal the sick, bring the dead back to life, heal those who suffer from dreaded skin diseases, and drive out demons" (verses 7-8). In Luke 6:13 Christ calls them apostles.

The number of Apostles signifies Christ's claim upon the twelve tribes of Israel (Matthew 10: 5-6). Their importance was their authority to preach the Kingdom of heaven. After the Resurrection Jesus enjoined them at the hill in Galilee, saying:

> I have been given all authority in heaven and on earth. Go, then, to all peoples everywhere and make them my disciples: baptize them in the name of the Father, the Son, and the Holy Spirit, and teach them to obey everything I have commanded you. And I will be with you always, to the end of the age (Matthew 28:18-20).

Of particular importance is Christ's selection of Peter to be the head of the Apostles, thus establishing a structure or base, upon which the bishops are sharers of authority with the pope as the visible head of the Church with Christ as its invisible head:

> And so I tell you, Peter: you are a rock, and on this rock foundation I will build my church, and not even death will ever be able to overcome it. I will give you the keys of the Kingdom of heaven; what you prohibit on earth will be prohibited in heaven, and what you permit on earth will be permitted in heaven (Matthew 16:18-19).

Thus Catholics say that the Church is founded by Christ on (and not *by*) the Apostles.

Before proceeding to the establishment of the Church office of bishop, we need to note the importance of its origin as Catholics perceive it. Foundation by

Christ on the Apostles emphasizes the function of the Apostles as witnesses to the teachings of Christ. The Church believes it has received the whole of Revelation exclusively through the Apostles (H. Denziger, *Enchiridion Symbolorum, Definitonum et Declarationum de Rebus Fidei et Morum [Handbook of Beliefs, Definitions and Declarations concerning Matters of Faith and Morals]* (31st ed., 1957, 1501) and that public revelation ceased with the death of the last Apostle (Denziger 3421). Dogma (defined doctrine) may be developed but nothing may be added to its content.

The Catholic Church recognizes that the functions assigned by Christ to the Apostles are necessary for its continuance as an institution. In particular, it views the pope and the college of bishops as a true succession of Christ and the Apostles, primarily in their ministerial service and duties in governing the Church, maintaining the purity of Revelation, and explaining its sense according to the New Testament.

In this regard these passages in the New Testament may be cited:

> So keep watch over yourselves and over the flock Which the Holy Spirit has placed in your care. Be shepherds of the church of God, which he made his own through the sacrificial death of his son (Paul to the Elders of Ephesus, Acts 20:28).

> Do not neglect the spiritual gift that is in you, which was given to you when the prophets spoke and the elders laid their hands on you (Paul to Timothy, 1 Timothy 4:14).

> For this reason [Timothy's and his family's sin cere faith] I remind you to keep alive the gift that God gave you when I laid my hands on you (Paul to Timothy, 2 Timothy 1:6).[3]

The word "bishop" comes from the Greek *episkopos*, meaning "inspector," "overseer," or "superintendent". In Late Latin the word *episcopus* becomes *bisceop* in Old English and *bisshop* in Middle English. It is used a number of times in the New Testament:

> (1) In I Peter 2:25 Peter addresses Christians in Asia Minor, calling Christ "the Shepherd and Keeper of your souls," recalling John 10:11-16, where Christ calls himself the "good shepherd".

> (2) In Philippians 1:1 Paul greets the Christians at Phillippi "including the church leaders and helpers," i.e. bishops and deacons.

> (3) In Acts 20:28 (quoted above) Paul speaks to the "elders" gathered at Miletus (20:17-18). The word for elders is the Greek *presbyteros*, which through Late Latin *presbyter*, Old English *prēost*, and Middle English *preist*, comes to us as to "priest". As we shall see, this situation has much significance for the future development of church offices.

In 1 Timothy 3:1 Paul refers to the office of bishop: "This is a true saying: If a man is eager to be a church leader, he desires an excellent work." He then describes the qualities (though not the functions) of a good bishop:

> (4) A Church leader must be without fault, he must have only one wife, be sober, self-controlled, and orderly; he must welcome strang-

> ers in his home; he must be able to teach; he must not be a drunkard or a violent man, but gentle and peaceful; he must not love money; he must be able to manage his own family well and make his children obey him with all respect. For if a man does not know how to manage his own family, how can he take care of the church of God? He must be mature in the faith, so that he will not swell up with pride and be condemned, as the Devil was. He is a man who is respected by the people out side the church, so that he will not be disgraced and fall into the Devil's trap (3:2-7).

And, finally, these two verses from 1 Timothy describe the role of "church helpers":

> (5) "Church helpers must also have a good character and be sincere; they must not drink too much wine or be greedy for money; they should hold to the revealed truth of the faith with a clear conscience" (3:8-9).[4]

From what we have seen, the New Testament suggests two theories of church leadership, based upon the words "episcopal" (relating to bishop) and "presbyteral" (relating to priest). The blending of these two orders contemplates the idea of being an apostle (the representative of Christ) in a college (authority-sharing governmental system) , deriving one's authority from the earthly Jesus. This type of apostolate is a council of presbyters in a local community at the time of Luke's gospel, and mentioned in James, 1 Peter, Titus, 1 Timothy and in Revelation.

Another is the Pauline apostolate in 2 Corinthians 8:23: "As for Titus, he is my partner and works with me to help you; as for the other brothers who are going with him, they represent the churches and bring glory to Christ." The apostle represents the risen Christ and later a single *episkopos* without a presbyter. Such a person is associated in the New Testament as a church official with deacons, as in Philippians 1:1 and 1 Timothy 3:2 above, and not as a secular official with limited duties.

With these elements in mind we may now begin to see the emergence of development in early church leadership and to draw some conclusions about it. We see a connection between *episkopos* and "shepherd" in I Peter 2:25. In 1 Peter 5:2,4 Peter calls upon fellow "church elders" to 'be shepherds of the flock that God gave you and to take care of it willingly, as God wants you to, and not unwillingly" and "when the Chief Shepherd appears, you will receive the glorious crown which will never lose its brightness." Acts 20:28 may be compared to Old Testament Numbers 27:16 where Moses invokes "Lord God, source of all life, appoint, I pray, a man who can lead the people." Peter also counsels Christians to be subject to human authority, to the Emperor and to his representatives, the "governors, who have been appointed by him to punish the evildoers and to praise those who do good" (1 Peter 2:13-14). These terms indicate the origins of a hierarchy (clergy ruling as a body and so organized that each rank is subordinate to the one above it).

The leadership pattern revealed in Philippians 1:1 shows the presence of several bishops within one community, having supervisory duties in the church. Paul's injunctions to Titus concerning the qualities of a church leader (Titus

1:6-9) closely recall those qualities listed in 1 Timothy 3:4-5. Philippians 2:19 hints the monarchical episcopate where Paul sends Timothy as his representative. Thus the local character and duties of bishops derive from a "collective" episcopate and the monarchical character from the apostolic office.

In 2 Corinthians we have one apostle for one community representing and communicating with Jesus Christ in a communion of suffering and labor. 1 Peter shows that the idea of the highest local authority is the image of Christ as the *episkopos* of the community (2:25) and its supreme shepherd (5:4). Presbyters or elders (5:1) parallel Christ's shepherding. In the "collective" form several exercise the function of the supreme shepherd. The monarchical episcopate combines the idea of *episkopos* with presbyteral order. This idea arises from the image of Christ as one *episkopos* and continues with the Pauline conception of one apostle in each community. The monarchical form was the type of authority structure in the Hellenistic area evangelized by Paul, in the mission of Timothy, in I Peter, and in the pastoral letters. Unlike the synagogue, the law, and traditional Jewish thought, Paul had no presbyteral order in his communities. But by the time of Acts churches in Lycaonia and Pisidia had elders.

In Acts 20 presbyters (verse 17) are called *episkopoi* (verse 28). The Holy Spirit decides their vocation and authority. In Acts 6:3 reference is made to the initiation of the seven deacons. Throughout Acts reference is made to the ruling system and also to the presbyteral system. Chapter One of Titus and Chapter Three of 1 Timothy show similarities to Acts 20 in this regard. The presbyteral system exists with the episcopal orders over it. In 1 Timothy 5:17 the "presbyters" are *episkopoi* representing the development underlying the preeminent episcopate. In Titus 1:5-9 Paul charges Titus to appoint elders in Crete, as he and Barnabas had in Acts 14:23. But Titus 1:7 and I Timothy 3:2 speak of *episkopos* (a bishop) in the singular. The duties of Timothy and Titus in several communities soon pass to the individual *episkopos*.

Without tracing the development of the office of bishop through twenty centuries, it is perhaps enough for present purposes to note that Catholics view the term "monarchical episcopate," as different from "collegial episcopate," holding that the direction of local communities (dioceses) rests with the superior authority of the pope and not in the hands of a group of clerics. The bishops and the pope have a common mission for the universal Church.[5]

Without discussing the individual characters of various ranks of authority within the Church we may close this section by saying that the organization and government of the Catholic Church has the pope as its supreme head. Bishops are both in union with and subordinate to him. They are successors of the Apostles in their care of the Church and in continuing Christ's mission in the world. Within their own dioceses (or particular churches) they serve their people with ordinary authority and jurisdiction. They share with the pope and with each other concern and effort for the general welfare of the entire church.

The hierarchy (or governing body) of the Catholic Church comprises order in the arrangement of ranks and orders of the clergy. This system provides for the spiritual care of the faithful, the government of the Church, and the accomplishment of the Church's mission in the world. In particular we are concerned with the hierarchy (or entire body or group) of Texas bishops.

To a Roman Catholic the Hierarchy of Order is made up of the pope, bishops, priests and deacons. These leaders are ordained to holy orders to carry out the sacramental and pastoral ministry of the Church. The Hierarchy of Jurisdiction consists of the pope and bishops (of divine institution) and other church officials (by ecclesiastical institution and mandate), who have authority to govern and direct the faithful spiritually.[6] In succeeding sections of the Introduction we will continue to examine the office of the bishop and the development of the Roman Catholic hierarchy within Texas.

C. Formative Education of a Bishop of Texas

Whatever a prospective bishop's educational experience might be, his preparation will lead him to a seminary or an institute of study (if he plans to enter a religious order). Such an education directs him toward ordination into the priesthood. For a man cannot become a bishop without first becoming a priest.

The Congregation for Catholic Education (Seminaries and Institutes of Study) is the agency of the Roman Curia controlling Catholic educational institutions. Cardinal Pio Laghi, the former apostolic delegate (lacking diplomatic status) and pro-nuncio (ambassador) from the Vatican to the United States, has headed it since 1990. Cardinals and other clergy are members of these departments. Cardinal James Hickey, archbishop of Washington, DC, is the only American of his rank serving this congregation. Cardinal William Baum (Hickey's predecessor in Washington and a native of Dallas, Texas) headed it from 1980 until 1990.

Two congregations established by Pope Sixtus V (1588) and Pope Leo XII (1824) originally carried on this work. Pope Benedict XV combined them, defined their functions, and called the new agency the Congregation of Seminaries and Universities on 4 November 1915. Popes Pius XI (1931 and 1932) and Pius XII (1941 and 1949) extended its operations. Pope Paul VI changed its title to Congregation for Catholic Education (1967) and Pope John Paul II gave its present title on 28 June 1988.

This congregation has "supervisory competence over institutions and works of Catholic education" through three offices: one office processes matters concerned with direction, discipline and temporal administration of seminaries, and with education of diocesan clergy, religious and members of secular institutes. The second office oversees Catholic universities, faculties of study and other such institutions "inasmuch as they depend upon the authority of the Church" and the establishment of Catholic centers in non-Catholic institutions. The third office concerns itself with Catholic elementary and secondary schools and their related matters. The congregation also supervises Pontifical Works for Priestly Vocations.[1]

The appointment of the first bishop and the establishment of the first diocese in the United States of America (John Carroll of Baltimore, Maryland, in 1789) soon led to the first ordination of a priest (Rev. Stephen Theodore Bazin by Bishop Carroll on 25 May 1793). Rev. Demetrius Augustine Gallitzin (Dimitri Augustin Golitzyn) became the first priest to receive his entire theological training in the United states. Bishop Carroll ordained him on 18 March 1795.[2] As of 1 January 1993 there were seventy-five diocesan seminaries and 138 religious (for priestly orders) seminaries in the United States with 4,335 and 1,556 seminarians, respectively.[3]

Excepting some foreign bishops and others who were educated abroad or in other states, many Texas bishops received their priestly formations in two major seminaries, St. Mary's in La Porte (later in Houston) and Assumption in San Antonio. There were also two minor (pre-collegiate and pre-theologate) seminaries in Corpus Christi and El Paso and Holy Trinity Seminary in Dallas, the last once a major seminary and now a college-level institution leading to major seminary studies. On 1 January 1993 these five institutions (in the see cities of their respective dioceses) had 210 students. The eleven religious [order] seminaries in Texas had seventy-six students.[4]

From his earliest days in Texas, before he became its first bishop, J. M. Odin, CM worked to provide seminarians for the then republic. As vice-prefect of Texas he began this work in San Antonio but lacked the personnel and finances to make his dream a reality. As bishop he did better in his see city of Galveston, establishing St. Mary's Seminary-College on New Year's Day 1855 with the Rev. Julian Baudre, OMI as President and Superior. The state legislature approved it as an institution of higher learning on 12 August 1856. It continued until the end of the Civil War, reopened in 1870 and closed in 1879.[5]

But Bishop Odin's dreams did not die. In 1874 Bishop Anthony D. Pellicer, the first of San Antonio, began a seminary in that city under diocesan auspices. In 1876 Jesuit priests exiled from Mexico opened a seminary in Seguin, Texas, known as Guadalupe College. In 1880 it was transferred to St. Joseph's College in Victoria. When the Victoria institution closed in 1902, pre-philosophy students were sent to what is now the Oblate School of Theology, which opened in 1903 as the San Antonio Philosophical and Theological Seminary. From 1920 until 1927 it moved to Castroville and was known as the Sacred Heart Scholasticate. Established in its present location in north San Antonio in 1927 as the De Mazenod Scholasticate in honor of Bishop Charles Eugene De Mazenod, founder of the Oblates of Mary Immaculate, it was known as the Oblate College of the Southwest from 1962 and acquired its present name in recent years. It is now the theology department of Assumption Seminary.

Meanwhile philosophy and theology students received their instruction at various American seminaries. In 1915 Bishop John W. Shaw of San Antonio reestablished the diocesan seminary in what had been the bishop's residence. His successor, Bishop Arthur J. Drossaerts, named it St. John's Seminary and moved it to a campus adjoining Mission Conception on Mission Road. The school of theology was added in 1928. The Vincentian order of priests, of whose congregation Bishop Odin was a member, operated the seminary at the invitation of Archbishop Robert E. Lucey from 1941 through 1967. But the need for expansion caused Archbishop Lucey to purchase the former Trinity University campus on Woodlawn Avenue and convert it into a major seminary under the name of Assumption of the Blessed Virgin Mary in 1952.

In 1968 decreases in enrollment forced the closing of the St. John's campus and it was combined with Assumption Seminary until 1971. Theology students began taking courses at the Oblate School of Theology in 1969. The undergraduate department was closed and the Mexican American Cultural Center was opened on the campus in 1972. This national center, which specializes in pastoral studies and language education, is now located on West French Place in San Antonio. Its special competency is the ministry among Hispanics in the United States and Latin America. It offers master-level programs in pastoral ministry, in cooperation with Incarnate Word College, Boston College, the Oblate School of Theology, St. Mary's University, and Loyola University of New Orleans. It awards a certificate of pastoralism for those attending during the summer period. The Center also distributes pastoral materials and assigns resource personnel as needed.[6]

In 1979 Archbishop Patrick F. Flores established his residence on the seminary campus and the archdiocesan chancery operates there today. The seminary physical plant consists of an administration building (containing the library), chapel, student union building (with an auditorium and book store), dormitory, dining hall, and facilities for outdoor sports and exercise. The seminary received national attention on 13 September 1987 when Pope John Paul II stayed there overnight and held an audience with 1,000 Polish Texans outside the chapel. Assumption has graduated over 500 ordained priests (including a number of bishops) and serves dioceses in Texas, Oklahoma, Arizona, Louisiana, New Mexico, and Central and Western states.[7]

Nor did Bishop Odin's other attempt to found a seminary in Galveston go entirely for naught. His successor Bishop Nicholas A. Gallagher carried out these plans with a change in location. After the Galveston flood of 1900 the bishop was able to purchase the property known as the Sylvan Beach Hotel, together with several adjoining acres, at La Porte in Harris County. The York family built the hotel in 1880 for the tourist trade. But the area failed to be promoted as a resort due to inconveniences involving poor transportation and its remote location. Speculation about the sale of the premises became a certainty after the flood, which devastated the grounds.

Bishop Gallagher completed the transaction in 1901, and that fall St. Mary's Seminary began under the direction of the Basilian order of priests. Ten years later the diocese took over for the next forty years. Then Bishop Wendelin J. Nold invited the Vincentians to direct the seminary. This they did for about thirty years before it came again under direct diocesan control.

After its modest beginnings with three priests and about a dozen students the institution did well and on 25 March 1908 added a new wing to the main building. In 1920 that building was moved to its present location and thoroughly renovated. The charter of 1856 was amended by the Texas secretary of state and on 1 May 1926 St. Mary's Seminary became St. Mary's University (not to be confused with the university in San Antonio founded in 1852). Seminarians completing their course of study were ordained in the chapel at La Porte for many years afterward. The diocese erected a church in 1927, which reverted to parish status in 1951.

Construction began on the new St. Mary's Seminary in Houston in 1952. On 1 September 1954 seminarians and their teachers made their move to Memorial Drive. On 4 November of that year Cardinal Samuel Stritch, the archbishop of Chicago, dedicated the new property, consisting of the administration building, chapel, dining hall, sisters' convent, two residence halls, and a classroom and recreation building. On 1 October 1966 Cardinal James McIntyre, the archbishop of Los Angeles, dedicated the Cardinal Beran Library and the Wendelin J. Nold Auditorium. These buildings of Romanesque style occupy about fifty acres in a setting reminiscent of the St. Anselm Monastery in Rome. In 1968 the theology department of the seminary became part of the University of St. Thomas in Houston and is now known as the University of St. Thomas School of Theology at St. Mary's Seminary.[8]

Developments within the Church and various social changes of the past thirty years have made theological studies no longer an entirely male province. The same may be said of religious education, canon law, and ministerial studies. The lack of priests and the increasing need for varied ministries and services on all diocesan levels have created a situation where advanced education plus managerial skills become increasingly important. Despite the example of the Anglican communion the door to the Roman Catholic priesthood remains firmly closed to women, however. Thus, while there are female professors, female directors within seminaries, and some female diocesan officials, no woman may be ordained or consecrated.

Working together with universities and graduate schools, seminaries remain places of spiritual formation. Unlike the situation in Texas at the dawn of the twentieth century where one entered a seminary as a child and left as a priest, most students live at home and proceed through elementary, middle, and secondary education. On reaching the college level they are free to major in a variety of subject fields. But they must have sufficient grounding in philosophy and theology (or religious studies) or, following the receipt of a bachelor's degree from an accredited university, they must make up deficiencies.

The pre-seminarian, on his way to the professional degree of Master of Divinity (M.Div.), needs to consider the educational requirements of the institution he will enter. In Texas one may seek such an education through any of the universities offering the appropriate training. A Catholic institution, ideally situated, is the University of Dallas in Irving, on the northwest boundary of the city of Dallas, about fifteen minutes from downtown and about forty minutes from Fort Worth. With roughly 3,000 students during its regular academic year, this university, sponsored by the Diocese of Dallas, is one of the few in the State with a chapter of Phi Beta Kappa. Its faculty has an international quality and its departments of philosophy and theology are complemented by its Center for Contemplative Studies and on the graduate level by its Institute of Philosophic Studies (offering the Doctor of Philosophy degree [Ph.D.] with a concentration in philosophy). The university offers the Master of Arts degree (M.A.) in philosophy and theology, as well as a Master in Theology degree (M.Th.). The Institute for Religious and Pastoral Studies offers the degrees of Master of Religious Education (M.R.E.) and Master of Theological Studies (M.T.S.).

Holy Trinity Seminary is the Dallas diocesan seminary. Founded as a major seminary in 1965, it moved to its present facilities adjacent to the main campus of the University of Dallas in 1967. It is the residence of undergraduate students preparing for the diocesan priesthood and attending classes at the University. It is thus a diocesan college and pre-theological seminary, reaching its present status in 1986. It has its own religious, dining and athletic facilities. In 1993 it had forty-one seminarians with four priests serving as rector (head of the seminary), vice-rector and director of liturgy formation, academic dean and director of the Rome (foreign study) and pre-theology programs, and director of spiritual formation. Another priest was in residence, with a layman as director of field education and counseling services and a laywoman as director of music and tutoring.[9]

College annual tuition and fees have for years outstripped the annual inflation rate (2.8% for the twelve months ending in August 1993, as measured by the Consumer Price Index). The College Board figures the rate of average annual increase in tuition and fees alone (exclusive of books and supplies, room and board, transportation, and other costs) for private four-year colleges between 1990-1991 and 1993-1994 at 20%. The same rate of increase for four-year public colleges during the same period is 30%. According to the College Board, in the 1993-1994 academic year the average cost nationwide for a resident student at a four-year private college is $17,846 (about $2,500 less for a commuter). This cost may be weighed against a student at a four-year public college where comparable costs would be $8,562 for a resident and $6,809 for a commuter.[10]

The United States Department of Education estimates that the average annual cost during 1991-1992 for a Texas resident attending a public four-year college at $1,144 and for a student at a private four-year college as $6,992.[11] While Texas higher education is generally considered a bargain, though tuition rates at state institutions are considerably higher for nonresidents, undergraduate tuition and fees at the University of Dallas for 1993-1994 were $10,180, higher than five other Catholic four-year institutions in Texas.[12]

No matter what route the student takes he makes a considerable educational investment before beginning major seminary training. Holy Trinity Seminary may charge other fees as well. But of some 150 institutions of higher learning, only three private church-related colleges in Texas (Southern Methodist at Dallas, Southwestern at Georgetown, and Trinity at San Antonio) charged more in undergraduate tuition and fees during 1993-1994 than the University of Dallas.[13]

With his bachelor's degree from an accredited institution (not necessarily Catholic) in hand, the graduate is now ready to enter one of the two major Catholic seminaries in Texas. As in any other college, standards, procedures, and requirements change periodically. Nevertheless, within recent years, these are the programs facing the average seminarian on his way to ordination.

A student attending the University of St. Thomas School of Theology at St. Mary's Seminary in Houston in early 1993 would find it staffed with nine priests, a deacon, a layman, a religious sister, and four laywomen.[14] The School of Theology is accredited by the Southern Association of Colleges and Schools (SACS) and holds membership in the Association of Theological Schools in the United States and Canada (ATS). It has academic affiliations in itself, through its faculty, and through the University of St. Thomas.

The School of Theology serves Texas and other states in the South and Southwest. It offers graduate programs at the professional (Master of Divinity) and academic (Master of Arts in Theological Studies) levels with opportunities for non-degree students. The University of St. Thomas also confers advanced academic degrees of Master of Arts and Doctor of Philosophy through its Center for Thomistic Studies. It is the Master of Divinity (M.Div.) program which provides professional theological and pastoral education to qualify candidates for ordination to the priesthood, however. The program is open to others in modified form.

The prospective seminarian must hold a valid bachelor degree, complete an application form, submit official transcripts, and furnish one academic and one personal letter of application. Foreign applicants must apply for full-time status, complete all admission requirements, and submit a passport-size photo, a physician's medical examination and personal medical history, documentation of legal status in America, and an affidavit of support and bank verification. Those for whom English is not the primary language must take the Test of

English as a Foreign Language (TOEFL) with a required minimum score of 550. This test has no failing grade, but its boundaries are 400 (poor) to 600 (excellent).

Throughout his residence his bishop, his vocation director, and the rector (head) of the seminary monitor the seminarian's grades after he signs a release complying with the Family Educational Rights and Privacy Act of 1975. In 1991-1992 minimum credit hours were raised from 116 to 120 (112 in course work and eight in field experiences [on-location training in pastoral ministry]). A thesis may be required. For the M.Div. program, twelve credit hours a semester is a full course load, with tuition as of 1989-1990 at $192 per credit hour (graduate tuition with $186 per semester hour set as undergraduate tuition for the same period). In 1993-1994 a St. Thomas undergraduate would pay $8,162 in tuition and fees (up from $7,440 in 1992-1993). Other fees, due and payable at registration time, for the 1989-1990 year were $50 for graduation (one time only), an international student fee of $60 for student visa holders, a late registration fee of $50 (if applicable), and $100 per audit hour. The University provides student aid and dioceses maintain burses (funds) to defray seminary costs.

The M.Div. program requires eight semesters of full-time study, with a grade point average of at least 2.0 (C or 73-76) required for graduation on a four-point system in which 1.0 is D or 60-65 and 4.0 is A or 94-100. Field education courses merit marks of P (passing) and no credit courses get AD for successful completion. Neither P nor AD are computed in the grade-point average (total credits divided by hours attempted; example, If a student made an A for a three-hour course, he would have a credit of twelve [4 times 3] divided by three [number of course hours] for a total of 4.0). A student average of two points per semester avoids academic probation. Since grades of D and D+ (1.3 or 66-69) are below graduation standard and unacceptable for core courses, the student may take one supplemental examination. But it must be completed and submitted to the registrar's office prior to registration the following fall. A supplemental grade may be no higher than C.

In 1991-1992 the course of study required 112 credits of academic and eight hours of field pastoral work. Core courses are fifteen hours of church history, thirteen of moral theology, fourteen of pastoral theology (exclusive of field education), eighteen of sacred scripture, and thirty-three of systematic theology (with twenty hours devoted to the study of dogma and thirteen hours to liturgy). Master of Divinity students take these thirty-five courses, though the curriculum may be adjusted for specific needs. Electives fill other hours.

Church history traces Christianity from its Jewish roots in the Christian community through modern issues in Europe and America. It includes patristics, which are the lives and works of Greek and Latin writers of Christian antiquity and their decisive contributions to the development of Christian doctrine. Electives may be about women in church and society, ecumenical councils, and Texas Catholic Church history.

Moral theology considers the function of natural law, sacred scripture as the basis of moral theology, and individual applications to moral rules and the *magisterium* (teaching authority) of the Church in regard to morality. Beyond this moral theology concerns the operation of the human will, faith, hope, and charity, civil law and moral obligation, and spirituality and growth as a Christian. It also concerns individual and social ethics and their proper applications. Electives may include medical ethics and war and peace in the Catholic tradition.

Pastoral theology involves areas of service and ministry within the Church. Counseling, preaching, teaching, and the application of canon law are important areas. Some electives may be an introduction to pastoral ministry (emphasizing the ministry of social service and social action) and social service ministry.

Sacred scripture pertains to the contemporary study of the Bible, with particular emphasis upon the New Testament. The student learns to appreciate biblical literary types and the development of scripture, its historical value, and ecclesial and scientific norms for its interpretation. There is particular stress upon the gospels and the pastoral use of the epistles of Paul. Electives include such topics as the Greek language in the New Testament and the relation of New Testament teachers, discipleship, and evangelical counsels to contemporary Christian and ministerial experience.

Systematic theology refers to dogma and liturgy. Dogma considers such matters as revelation and faith, God in the Christian tradition, the Christian view of the individual person, creation in scripture, divine providence, evil and suffering, the questions raised by immortality and the afterlife, the development of theology about Christ, the Church as a supernatural society, the scriptural and systematic treatment of Mary, and ecumenism and interfaith relations. Liturgy is the study of the public worship of the Church and includes the sacraments and holiness in historical, theological, and pastoral perspectives.

The M.Div. degree is so constructed that in four years the student, building upon his academic background, acquires the necessary skills for full-time ministry within the Church. The background needed at St. Mary's Seminary, in addition to a valid bachelor's degree, are at least twelve hours of undergraduate philosophy (especially metaphysics, epistemology, philosophical psychology, logic, and history of philosophy). Some general background in the humanities and social sciences (particularly literature and languages, history, sociology, and anthropology) is most useful. A student should have some introductory courses in theology and scripture, a reading knowledge of a classic and a modern language, and perhaps some specific training in these and other areas of learning may be required by certain ecclesiastical authorities. Priests and ministers with seminary education must complete at least two semesters of full-time study in residence or the equivalent before receiving this degree. In addition to the credits and whatever additional work may be prescribed with a 2.0 (C) average, nine hours of electives may be replaced by the writing of a thesis. This program conforms with the *Program of Priestly Formation* (3rd ed., 1981) of the National Conference of Catholic Bishops.[15]

Similar to the situation in Houston, the student who attends Assumption Seminary in San Antonio must also enter the M.Div. program (in this case at the Oblate School of Theology). Assumption requires the first degree, transcript of credits, and application form, as well as a completed medical form, a psychological assessment of academic potential and ministerial suitability, certificates of Baptism and Confirmation, and two three-by-five inch photos. The bishop or vocation director of the sponsoring diocese, the applicant's pastor, and the rector of his past seminaries or religious houses of study (if applicable) must submit letters of recommendation. The applicant must also furnish two names and addresses from his place(s) of employment or schools attended. Assumption expects its seminarians to have eighteen hours of credit in philosophy and twelve hours in theology for admittance.

As of 1 January 1993 the Seminary staff consists of a rector, a vice-rector and director of pastoral formation, a director of spiritual formation, an academic dean and director of studies and international program, and a director of development. Priests hold these positions. A religious sister directs cultural formation and admissions.[16]

Assumption Seminary prepares students for a bilingual and bicultural ministry to serve Hispanics. Its priestly formation has three principal components: (1) spiritual and personal growth, (2) academic preparation involving theoretical and practical studies, and (3) pastoral training through supervised personal experience. Its atmosphere encourages prayer and stresses the preaching of the Gospel according to Jesus Christ.

Students learn to develop communal and collaborative ministry by electing one another to committees on spiritual life, social, and physical life. Those who serve on the academic, student services, and cultural awareness committees represent the Seminary at the Oblate School of Theology.

Texas incorporated this school under its laws on 18 April 1950. The United States Office of Education lists it as an accredited institution of higher education and the Texas Education Agency (TEA) approves its training of those receiving Veterans Administration benefits under Section 1775, Chapter 36, Title 38, of the U.S. Code. The federal Immigration and Naturalization Service of the Department of Justice approves it for nonquota foreign students and, under federal law, it may enroll nonimmigrant alien students. Like St. Mary's Seminary the Oblate School is accredited by the Southern Association and the Association of Theological Schools and has other academic and professional affiliations.

The Oblate School serves Assumption seminarians, various religious orders (such as the Oblates of Mary Immaculate, Pallotines, Redemptorists, Missionhurst, Carmelites, Holy Cross, Franciscans, and Franciscan Conventuals), and the laity. Cultural awareness and sensitivity to Hispanic-American cultural values (such as family, community, hospitality, celebration, relgiosity, and music) become important to the future minister. Toward this end Spanish language studies in San Antonio and in Mexico, parish assignments in Hispanic communities, migrant ministries, tours and clinical pastoral education experiences connect the students with another culture. As a freestanding graduate school it offers the degrees of Master of Divinity, Master of Divinity for Clergy (for clergy with a seminary education but without a degree and for updating in theology and ministry), Master of Theological Studies, and the Certificate of Pastoral Studies (for special students).

Admission to the Oblate School of Theology requires completion of a valid bachelor's degree or its equivalent, or for M.Div. candidates with seminary education outside the United States or Canada, completion of all philosophical studies necessary for pursuing theological studies in their home countries. The

Dean's interview with the applicant determines his background and readiness for graduate study. When official transcripts arrive, the Admissions Committee (with the academic dean as chairperson, the registrar, and one elected full-time faculty member) reviews the application. An undergraduate major in the humanities, social sciences, or natural sciences aids theological study, as well as a basic reading knowledge of ancient and modern languages.

In 1989-1990 Assumption Seminary charged $1300 per semester for room and board plus $225 in general fees (for library use, retreats, and other costs), and $50 for transportation. For a year the expense would be $3150. For the same period the Oblate School of Theology charged tuition at $162 per credit hour ($81 per audit hour) plus some $60 in fees. This would mean $2490 per semester (assuming a normal course load of fifteen hours) plus fees of $4980 per year. Thus for 1989-1990 total expenses for residence in both institutions would mean an outlay of $8130.

Admission to the M.Div. program also requires completion of the Miller Analogies Test, a statement of goals and objectives, information about the applicant's commitment to professional ministry, and the required paperwork and interview. For those not formally admitted into a recognized formation program, three letters are necessary. They must be from one in authority within the applicant's denomination, one who knows the applicant as his/her college student, and one person of the applicant's choosing.

For the M.Div. degree the candidate must complete 107 credit hours (ninety-three in course requirements and fourteen in electives). Not more than forty-eight hours of graduate credit earned within ten years prior to admission may ordinarily be transferred. The residence requirement is two years of full-time study with the Seminar in Integration of Theological Studies and a major paper in connection with the seminar specified. On 13 December 1988 the grading system changed from D as a passing grade to C. The grade of D no longer earns one quality point, grades of A- and B- are in effect, and B is the normal or standard grade, with B- (a 2.5 grade point average) as the mark for continuance and for graduation. All courses must be completed seven years after matriculation.

The ninety-three required credit hours are taken in historical and cultural studies (eleven), scriptural studies (eighteen), theological studies (thirty-five hours of systematics, sacramental, moral and spiritual theology, and interdisciplinary studies) and pastoral studies (twenty-nine). At his option the student may choose American church history, Southwest religious history, or Mexican religious history. The remaining fourteen hours are electives. Two three-week summer sessions offer the possibility to earn a maximum eight credit hours.

Two facets of priestly formation mark the distinctive approach taken by the Oblate School of Theology in Texas: Spanish language ministry and the particular program of field supervision and pastoral internship. The student must read the Spanish Lectionary and ritual, preach in Spanish, and be able to converse. Some courses are offered bilingually and/or in Spanish in the third and fourth years of theology. University courses, work at the Mexican American Cultural Center, private tutoring and summers in Mexico are all learning options to achieve required fluency.

Because Catholic pastoral formation attempts to reflect Christ as teacher, priest, and shepherd, pastoral settings train students except for their first and last semesters of theology. Field supervisors consult each week concerning questions, problems, and reflections about the placement. At the end of each semester, the seminarian, his supervisor, and the director of pastoral formation evaluate the pastoral experience. In the M.Div. program each student must complete three field experience units (F.E.U.'s) of supervised pastoral education before beginning internship. One of the three units should be a summer clinical pastoral educational experience. Work, supervision, and the F.E.U. combine with theological reflection sessions.

Internship is a year-long required experience in the fourth year of the student's program. The Perkins School of Theology at Southern Methodist University in Dallas develops and oversees it, with the Oblate School of Theology as the administrative unit for Catholic interns. The director of internship program at the Oblate School coordinates and supervises the internship program.

Field education, internship, and the pastoral practicum all form part of the supervised M.Div. program of professional pastoral formation and ministerial training. Field education unites active ministry with theological reflection. The two-credit field education unit involves 100 clock hours and comprises the place of ministry, individual supervision in placement, and theological reflection seminars with other students and supervisors in a peer group setting. M.Div. students participate in the orientation to supervised ministry in their first year, and are required to complete three supervised F.E.U.'s. The clinical pastoral education carries the equivalent of eight semester hours of credit, but may be counted only as one F.E.U. and as three semester hours toward the degree program.

The internship program provides for full-time involvement in which the student is part of a pastoral team, consisting of a field instructor trained in pastoral supervision, a lay committee representative of the parish, and a professional consultant to aid regular growth group conferences. All members form this part of the program and share in the evaluation. The student matures as a minister and develops competence in pastoral skills through actual practice. This program normally follows the completion of three years of studies and lasts nine months after which the intern completes requirements for his degree. On completion of requirements it contains twelve semester hours of credits, of which three may apply toward the M.Div. degree. Internship may be taken after the completion of four years of studies or a one-semester internship may be negotiated.[17]

So far we have concentrated on the education of a priest. Canon 378, §l, 4° specifies that the suitable candidate for the episcopacy be "ordained a priest for at least five years".[18] The education already discussed is neccessary for ordination to the Roman Catholic priesthood. So far as further education matters, the same canon and section, 5° specifies that the candidate be

> in possession of a doctorate or at least a licentiate in sacred scripture, theology, or canon law from an institute of higher studies approved by the Apostolic See or at least truly expert in these same disciplines.[19]

As we shall see below, many factors enter into the selection process of bishops. The pope considers many facets of the candidate in making his appointment. A priest in his career or later as an auxiliary or coadjutor bishop, for example, may have become "truly expert" in the requisite disciplines. The candidate may also have advanced degrees in various academic or professional areas, earned in course. Sacred scripture, theology, and/or canon law advanced degrees, however, are particular fields of expertise suited to diocesan administration.

Faculties teach these disciplines in institutions in which instructional and research programs reflect the Catholic faith. Canon 812 states:

> It is necessary that those who teach theological disciplines in any institute of higher studies have a mandate from the competent authority.[20]

Additionally, Canon 817 provides:

> No university or faculty which has not been erected or approved by the Apostolic See can grant academic degrees which have canonical effects in the Church.[21]

In this context "university" applies to post-secondary educational institutions: colleges, universities, academies, institutes, and others. Seminaries are separately regulated by cc. 232-264 of the Code of Canon Law. "Theological disciplines" refer to dogmatics or systematics, as well as historical, moral, and sacramental theology. It may also refer to church history, liturgical studies, canon law, and sacred scripture. But catechetics, many areas of pastoral studies, comparative religions, and history or sociology of religion are not included.[22]

Most Catholic colleges and universities of the United States are related to or affiliated with the Church rather than canonically Catholic, that is, established by and under the direct control of the Holy See. Many were established by religious orders of the Church and not tied canonically to the diocese in which they reside. The total Catholic community and church authorities have been cooperative and collaborative in the maintenance of the individual institution's Catholic character and mission. In the United States many such institutions are publicly chartered, accepted by private accrediting associations and other professional agencies and by voluntary educational associations. The highest institutional authority in such institutions may be a governing board or board of trustees holding a public trust under the charter of incorporation.[23]

Another class of institution existing in thirty countries, including the United States of America, is the pontifical university. These universities are canonically erected and are authorized by the Congregation for Catholic Education. Rome has a number of such universities and institutes dating from 1398 to 1970. There are also ecclesiastical faculties in Catholic seminaries and universities in thirty-one countries (including the United States) which have the same origins of authority. These faculties award degrees, and there are other faculties of theology or philosophy in state universities and for members of certain religious orders only. Such faculties are in seven American states and the District of Columbia. The Pontifical College Josephinum at Columbus, Ohio, exists separately as a national pontifical seminary immediately subject to the Holy See.

In the United States there are three pontifical universities: Georgetown (30 March 1833) and the Catholic University of America (7 March 1889), both in

Washington, DC, and Niagara (21 June 1956) in Niagara University, New York. Although Texas bishops have been educated in many different institutions, some have attended the Catholic University of America, which deserves our further consideration.[24]

The Catholic University of America arose from a meeting of the Roman Catholic bishops of the United States in Baltimore, Maryland, in 1866. During this meeting (the Second Plenary Council of Baltimore) the bishops expressed their desire for a university under Catholic auspices in which "all the letters and sciences, both sacred and profane [secular], could be taught." At the Third Plenary Council of Baltimore (1884), they accepted a gift from Miss Mary Gwendoline Caldwell of Newport, Rhode Island, to establish a school of theology, the nucleus of a complete university. Pope Leo XIII formally approved the national university project on 10 April 1887 (Founders Day) and also appointed John Joseph Keane (1839-1918), the bishop of Richmond (1878-1888) as first rector (1888-1897). The seventeen member board of trustees incorporated the university on 21 April 1887, which undertaking was supplemented and amended by Congress in 1928.

Classes began in the School of Sacred Science on 13 November 1889, which became the School of Religious Studies in 1973. At present there are nine schools, of which Philosophy and Religious Studies make up two. Though conceived originally for graduate study and research, the university conferred its first undergraduate degree in 1897. The Middle States Association of College and Secondary Schools accredits the Catholic University of America, and it is a member of the Association of Theological Schools in the United States and Canada. We shall concentrate on the schools of Philosophy (offering the pontifical degrees of Bachelor, Licentiate, and Doctor of Philosophy) and Religious Studies (offering the pontifical degrees of Licentiate and Doctor of Canon Law and Bachelor, Licentiate, and Doctor of Sacred Theology). Advanced degrees in sacred scripture are offered by the Pontifical Biblical Institute in Rome, in course, and by the Pontifical Biblical Commission, by exams.[25]

Admission to graduate study at the Catholic University of America begins with a completed application (including an application fee), official degree transcripts from accredited institutions showing degree(s) obtained, courses completed, grades obtained, and the grading system with which the work was undertaken. The university requires two or more letters of recommendation showing the candidate's ability for graduate study and working ability (if applicable). International students, students with deficiencies, and special (non degree-seeking) students may be admitted, with the academic dean making the final determination.

General requirements for graduate study include one year minimum of full-time residence for the master's degree and three for the doctorate. During this time tuition and fees fully apply. In 1993-1994 tuition and fees are $13,644 for the academic year. In past years Catholic University has had a policy of charging the same tuition for both graduate and undergraduate study except in the schools of law and of engineering and architecture. Twelve semester hours is the normal course load for the full-time graduate student. As the general requirements for advanced degrees at Catholic University are not unlike those of similar institutions, we shall proceed to the pontifical degree programs offered by the School of Philosophy and the School of Religious Studies.

Candidates who undertake the Bachelor of Philosophy (Ph.B.) degree must fulfill a complete baccalaureate program of at least 120 credit hours. All course work taken at Catholic University, including the comprehensive examination equal to three semester courses of three hours of credit each, calls for a C average. An F in any course must be repeated and a passing grade received, as three-fourths of all courses taken need a grade of C or better. As this is an undergraduate degree, the normal course load per semester is fifteen hours. Course changes and additions must be made through the dean, but only if the student maintains a B average. The degree option called "the program of concentration" is the pre-theological sequence for those completing sixty credit hours in college. It mandates ten specified courses in philosophy plus two electives in philosophy and six additional electives in approved areas.

The student takes first History of Ancient Philosophy (prephilosophic mythology to Plotinus), unless he has already taken The Classical Mind: The Origin and Growth of Western Philosophy. In this case he can substitute it for History of Ancient Philosophy or History of Medieval Philosophy (but not for both). Other program courses is Philosophy of Being and God, Philosophy of Religion, Introduction to Symbolic Logic, Philosophy of Knowledge, Senior Seminar (in political philosophy), Senior Seminar (with different writers), History of Modern Philosophy, and Contemporary Philosophy.

Two other courses may be selected from Approaches to Morality, Contemporary Moral Issues, Philosophy of Human Nature, Philosophy of Language, and Philosophy of Science. Each of these courses is three credit hours. With most other degree prerequisites completed in the first two years of the college course, the student adds the needed electives and the comprehensive examination.

To obtain the Licentiate in Philosophy (Ph.L.) degree the student must have received a valid bachelor's degree with a minimum of eight undergraduate courses in "select philosophical disciplines," including one course in symbolic logic. The student must take a minimum of eight three-credit courses. Between 1985 and 1987 the School of Philosophy offered two introductory courses, seventeen courses to fulfill arts and sciences requirements, eighteen courses for students concentrating in philosophy, one course in symbolic logic open to all undergraduate students, three other courses involving political philosophy and theology, and fifty-nine other courses to be taken with permission of the school.

The candidate must complete two semesters of full-time study in residence or the equivalent. A dissertation must be presented for six hours of credit. The candidate then passes a written examination in French or German and otherwise fulfills the university's language requirement. Finally, the candidate must withstand an oral examination lasting one hour before four members of the faculty. (*Note:* I use the terms "student" and "candidate" interchangeably. Strictly speaking, one is a student throughout his tenure in college and a candidate only when he has completed all requirements except the dissertation and its defense.)

Concluding this series, the candidate for the Doctor of Philosophy (Ph.D.) degree must obtain the Licentiate in Philosophy degree and spend at least an additional two years in residence, earning a minimum of sixty semester hours of course work. This work includes that earned for the licentiate (excepting credits awarded for the dissertation). A maximum of two semesters of graduate work in philosophy may be transferred from another institution. In addition, the candidate must present a publishable dissertation, pass written examinations in both French and German, complete written examinations on all three sections of the Graduate Reading Program, and submit to a public oral examination (defense) of the dissertation conducted by five members of the faculty. The oral committee consists of the candidate's dissertation committee from the School of Philosophy plus a chairman and secretary from the university faculty not included in the philosophy faculty.[26]

The School of Religious Studies of the Catholic University of America administers its pontifical degrees through the Departments of Canon Law and Theology. The canon law department, a separate school from 1923 to 1973, prepares professional administrators and trains competent canon lawyers. It achieves these goals by its introductory courses in law and administrative science and by offering a curriculum covering the sources, development, and interpretation of ecclesiastical legislation. The Department of Theology seeks to train scholars and teachers in theology and ministers in the Church.

The Department of Canon Law instructs the student in the development, interpretation, and application of law in the Catholic Church. The professional practice of canon law includes diocesan and religious administration, advocacy and jurisdiction in ecclesiastical tribunals, and teaching and research. Understanding and implementation of canon law requires technical skill in legal interpretation and a grasp of the historical, theological, and sociological factors contributing to its development, with a sensitivity to its pastoral application. Admission to the programs in canon law requires a bachelor's degree with the ability to pursue graduate studies, official transcripts of post-secondary studies, two or more letters of recommendation by administration or faculty members of institutions already attended, and results of the Graduate Record Examination (GRE) or the Miller Analogies Test. Those who are to receive ordination and in religious vocations must submit a letter of assignment from their bishop or religious superior.

Those who lack a master's degree in theology or do not have the philosophical and theological courses necessary for priestly ordination must complete preparatory courses (the First Cycle) before being admitted to study for the Licentiate in Canon Law (J.C.L.). A minimum of twenty-four credit hours prepare candidates for the Second Cycle. Areas of study for the preparatory year include fundamentals of canon law, the law pertaining to parochial ministry, ecclesiology, sacramental theology, moral theology and related studies in ethics and natural law. Canonical Latin and a modern language are necessary for canonical research.

The Licentiate in Canon Law program lasts a minimum of two years or four semesters. The Catholic University has recently begun a summer program for this degree for those in full-time pastoral ministry. It is designed to be completed in five summers, with four summers for classes and the fifth for completing the dissertation and oral comprehensive examination. Before the beginning of the third semester of the Second Cycle, the student must pass a reading examination in French, German, Italian, or Spanish.

The course of study for this degree is forty-eight semester hours, thirty-six in required courses and twelve in electives in canon law or in other departments. The required courses are History of Canon Law, General Norms, Power of Governance, Sacramental Law, Official Ministry, Consecrated Life, Matrimony, Structures of the Particular Church, Matrimonial Jurisprudence, Procedural Law, Teaching Office of the Church, and Temporal Goods. The Department of Canon Law offers some twenty other courses exclusive of dissertation credits. The candidate also needs knowledge of Latin to interpret and apply the law as the official code text is Latin, interpretations and analyses are in that language, and references are often made to Latin texts.

The dissertation required for the licentiate investigates a problem to prove that the student can carry on research, master the subject matter, and exercise sound judgment and arrive at accurate conclusions. Passing a comprehensive examination on church law, at least by the second try, is necessary for reception of the degree.

To receive the Doctorate in Canon Law (J.C.D.), the student must have completed the Seminar in Sources, with readings in Gratian, the Decretals, the *Glossa ordinaria*, and the commentators before the Council of Trent. He must have the licentiate in hand and have maintained a B+ average in course work, dissertation, and comprehensive examination. Fluency in canonical Latin and two modern foreign languages is essential. The Third Cycle is a minimum year of doctoral residence in which a student completes his dissertation and four courses or seminars. In addition to submitting this document to the faculty, the candidate must defend it and pass a public examination on at least ten theses related to it or subjects of special study. Publication may be by library deposit, by microfilming, or by journal article.

The Department of Theology awards the pontifical degrees of Bachelor of Sacred Theology (S.T.B.), Licentiate in Sacred Theology (S.T.L.), and Doctor of Sacred Theology (S.T.D.). In this sequence the first degree provides the basis of a theological orientation. The degree mandates sixty-nine semester hours in academic theology with pastoral courses suggested as electives. The residency requirement is six semesters.

Admission to this department requires a valid bachelor's degree, the ability to pursue graduate studies, the GRE, two or more letters of recommendation attesting to the applicant's ability for graduate studies in this field, and a foundation in philosophy with a background in the history of philosophy, logic, metaphysics, ethics, philosophy of God, and philosophical anthropology. In addition one should have a background in religious studies in both Old and New Testament literature and a reading knowledge of Latin.

To obtain the bachelor's degree, the student first takes the proseminar in theological sources and research methodology (noncredit). He then takes the foundation series of seven courses for twenty-one credit hours, of which Introduction to History and Method in Theology and Foundations of Christian Moral Life must be taken during the first year of the program. The other five courses are Introduction to Patristic Theology, Liturgiology, Pastoral Theology, Introduction to Christian Spirituality, and Basic Principles of Canon Law.

The student chooses another forty-eight credit hours from systematic theology (fifteen), sacramental theology (six), moral theology (nine), scripture (fifteen) and church history (three). Candidates for ministry in the Roman Catholic

Church take one course in another theological tradition and are encouraged to take pastoral electives to a total of fifteen credit hours per semester.

To be admitted to the comprehensive examination for the S.T.B., the student maintains a grade point average of 2.75 (C+) or better in all required courses. He takes this examination during the sixth semester. It consists of one hour each of written examinations in systematic theology, moral theology, and scripture or one hour of oral examinations on the same material before three members of the faculty. Not more than two failures in this examination are allowed.

The next degree in this sequence is the Licentiate in Sacred Theology (S.T.L.). From 1931 to 1966 it was considered the equivalent of a Master of Arts degree in theology in the United States. Today its distinctive features are recognized. Based upon the student's familiarity of the history of Christian theology, it introduces the appropriate method of scientific investigation, specialization in one area of concentration with a dissertation, and a set of written and oral comprehensive examinations. The residency requirement for this degree is four semesters. The student chooses his area of specialization from systematic theology, moral theology, biblical theology, historical theology, or liturgical studies.

To gain full admission the applicant must possess the S.T.B. from a pontifical university or faculty with a satisfactory grade point average of at least 3.0 (B) and equivalent GRE/Miller Analogies Test results. If not, he must have either the Master of Arts in theology or a Master of Divinity with course work equivalent to the S.T.B. at Catholic University. Reading knowledge of Latin must be demonstrated by the end of the first year in the department.

The S.T.L. requires completion of the Proseminar in Research and Dissertation Methodology (for no credit) and twenty-four semester hours of course work in the areas of concentration and six credits for the approved dissertation in connection with this degree. The twenty-four credits may be selected from 700 and 800 level courses, reserved for students taking this degree, the doctorate in this sequence, and for Doctor of Ministry (D.Min.) and Doctor of Philosophy (Ph.D.) candidates in this department. With approval, the student may enroll up to six semester hours in another school or department relative to his area of concentration.

The dissertation approval, guidance, study, and writing begins in the second semester of the program and involves three semesters of work in addition to the required courses. Nine hours of course work is the first semester load, followed by three semesters of six hours each. In addition a concentration in biblical theology requires prerequisites of six hours of Hebrew and six hours of biblical Greek beyond elementary level to be taken in the first two semesters.

The purpose of the dissertation (worth six credits upon approval) is to prove one's familiarity with basic research, mastery of its subject matter, and the ability to use sound theological judgment and to formulate accurate conclusions. With approval by the director and the reader, the student may proceed to the oral comprehensive examinations. Written and oral examinations concern the chosen field of concentration. To reach this level a cumulative average of 3.0 (B) or better is needed.

These tests may be taken on completion of the language requirements and the dissertation, but not before midpoint of the final semester of residency (late

October or mid-March). The language requirements for this degree are proficiency in biblical Greek and reading ability in either French or German. The written examination lasts three hours, and the moderator and reader of the dissertation evaluate it on a scale of zero to four. The oral examination is either a dissertation defense or an examination based on a departmental list of themes and books in the area of concentration or upon a list made by the student. It must be approved by the moderator and reader under the guidance of the Pontifical Degrees Committee. It lasts one hour and takes place before a board of four examiners selected by the department chairman, and it is graded on the same scale as the written examination. The result is the average of scores given by each of the four examiners voting secretly.

The final degree in this sequence of pontifical degrees is that of Doctor of Sacred Theology (S.T.D.). Based upon the student's theological orientation and competence in one area of specialization, it shows his ability in scholarly research and publication. Seminars chosen for this degree should lead to the writing of a dissertation which contributes to the advance of theological research. The residency requirement for the degree is four semesters, unless the candidate has completed the S.T.L. at Catholic University. In that case it requires two semesters followed by extended residence for the preparation of the dissertation. Areas of concentration are systematic theology, moral theology, and historical theology.

The candidate should have his S.T.L. or its equivalent with a grade point average of 3.0 (B) or better. A letter outlining the proposed area of concentration discussing preparation and future plans is necessary, together with GRE (or Miller Analogies Test) scores and at least two letters of recommendation. Proficiency in Latin and biblical Greek, as well as French or German, should be demonstrated by the end of the first semester of the program.

The student takes the Proseminar in Research and Dissertation Methodology for no credit in the first semester, unless he has the S.T.L. from the Department of Theology. The required course work is four doctoral seminars (twelve semester hours) offered by the Department. Up to six hours of course work plus dissertation guidance may be taken each of the four semesters. Proficiency in both French and German must be shown before the dissertation is submitted for faculty approval.

Candidacy for the S.T.D. degree requires satisfaction of the language requirements, nine hours of course work and Guided Research (assessed at six hours of credit), the completion of the Proseminar, and the approval of the dissertation proposal. Dissertation guidance lasts four successive semesters beyond the twelve credit hours of required doctoral seminars. The chosen or assigned faculty adviser will guide the progress of the dissertation and award a grade of Pass or Fail at the end of each of the four terms.

The student prepares and defends his dissertation under the guidance of his major professor. Prior to this defense he must pass a comprehensive examination based on the origins, history, and contemporary status of the entire major area of his dissertation. To provide teaching experience the candidate and his adviser may use the time to prepare the dissertation with the informal benefits of a graduate assistantship.[27]

Throughout this section I have indicated the range of possibilities in the education of a prospective bishop. Each of the degrees discussed (with or without modification) is open to qualified students of both sexes. As noted before, the Roman Catholic Church does not ordain women to the priesthood nor consecrate them to the episcopacy. Such knowledge as the degrees afford is useful in teaching, research, diocesan administration, and the practice of canon law. A Roman Catholic bishop is considered a man of attainment. If he has no other advanced degree, he may place that of Doctor of Divinity (D.D.) after his name, conferred in effect as an honorary degree by the Vatican.

D. The Theology and Authority of the Episcopate

Concerning the institution and functions of the Roman Catholic episcopate, Canon 375 states:

> §1. Through the Holy Spirit who has been given to them, bishops are the successors of the apostles by divine institution; they are constituted pastors within the Church so that they are teachers of doctrine, priests of sacred worship and ministers of governance.
>
> §2. By the fact of their episcopal consecration bishops receive along with the function of sanctifying also the functions of teaching and of ruling, which by their very nature, however, can be exercised only when they are in hierarchical communion with the head of the college and its members.[1]

Section One of this canon affirms the divine origin of the episcopate and that it combines the roles of teacher, priest, and pastor within each bishop. Section Two stresses the importance of episcopal consecration and the powers to be performed only when the bishop is in union with the pope and his fellow bishops.

In order to understand the work of a Roman Catholic bishop one needs to study the idea of hierarchy, the nature and character of episcopal consecration, and the extent of the bishop's authority within his governmental system. Nor can he or she comprehend the episcopate without first understanding the institution of the Apostles by Jesus Christ.

Christ's mission upon Earth is service. He called the Apostles to work for His whole Church (cf. Mark 10:42-45 and Matthew 20:25-28). They were to baptize, to teach, and to bring the faithful to obey the commands of the Lord (Matthew 28:19-20). To accomplish this mission, the Apostles received the special gift of the Holy Spirit (John 20:21-23; Acts 1:8 and 2:2-5). Each apostle received this assignment and this grace together with the other apostles (Mark 3:14-16). When Judas betrayed Christ and committed suicide, the Apostles elected Matthias in his place, thus keeping their group intact (Acts 1:26).

This group or "college" is a unity, but not one signifying equality. Peter was invested with higher authority than the other apostles by Christ Himself (Matthew 16:16-19; Luke 22: 31-32). The apostolate did not cease with the death of those chosen by Christ. The Apostles chose helpers to preach and govern communities (Philippians 2:25 and Colossians 4:11). Helpers shared the apostles' authority (Acts 20:28). The faithful should recognize them as their rulers (Hebrews 13:7,13,24), though it is not always possible to distinguish between "elders" (Acts 11:30 and 14:23) and "bishops" (Philippians 1:1; Acts 20: 28). The Apostles charge their fellow workers not to lord their power over the faithful (1 Peter 5:3). Their office is a ministry of service. Pope Clement I (88-97) speaks of the succession in his writings, and the phrase "successor of the apostles" designated bishops from the time of St. Irenaeus, Bishop of Lyons (130-201).[2]

Lumen Gentium (Vatican II, *Dogmatic Constitution on the Church*, 21 November 1964), chapter 3, article 20, explains the existence of the episcopate:

> That divine mission, which was committed by Christ to the apostles,

> is destined to last until the end of the world (cf. Matthew 28:20), since the Gospel, which they were charged to hand on, is, for the Church, the principle of all its life for all time. For that very reason the apostles were careful to appoint successors in this hierarchically constituted society.[3]

Vatican Council II declares the college of apostles with and under Peter corresponds to the college of bishops with and under the Roman pontiff in article 22:

> Just as, in accordance with the Lord's decree, St. Peter and the rest of the apostles constitute a unique apostolic college, so in like fashion the Roman Pontiff, Peter's successor, and the bishops, the successors of the apostles, are related with and united to one another.[4]

The individual becoming a bishop is incorporated into the college through sacramental consecration and hierarchical communion with its head and members (*Dogmatic Constitution on the Church*, article 22).[5] Members are united to its head (the Roman pontiff) and to other members of the hierarchy. Thus the bishops of the world are linked with "one another and with the Bishop of Rome in a bond of unity, charity, and peace" (article 22).[6] It is a monarchical system combined with a synodal system. As article 22 states:

> The Roman Pontiff, as the successor of Peter, is the perpetual and visible source and foundation of the unity of the bishops and of the whole company of the faithful. The individual bishops are the visible source and foundation of unity in their own particular Churches, which are constituted after the model of the universal Church; it is in these and formed out of them that the one and unique Catholic Church exists.[7]

Before examining episcopal consecration and what flows from it, it is necessary to understand what is meant by hierarchy. To do this we need to know how the system developed, its theological meaning, and its place in canon law.

In its biblical sense hierarchy means the power of a sacral government or those exercising that power. It comes from the Greek words meaning holy (or sacred) origin and command (or rule). Although the word "hierarchy" itself is found neither in the Old nor the New Testament, the Bible does reveal the presence of religious rulers of various ranks, subordinate one to the other. Each sanctuary of Yahweh had its own priest in early Israelite history. But in the temple of Jerusalem there was a true hierarchy. The head priest was usually designated "the priest" (2 Kings 22:4,8). His title of "high priest" was used occasionally in postexilic times for the postexilic period (2 Kings 12:11; 22:4,8). Under the head priest was the "second priest" (2 Kings 23:4; 25:18). Over ordinary priests were chiefs of priestly families (1 Chronicles 24:4). At the bottom of the postexilic hierarchy were the Levites (1 Chronicles 23:26-28).

In the New Testament the hierarchy of the second century is visible and differs somewhat from the hierarchy of the apostolic age. The highest rank under Christ was the Apostles. Their number (twelve) was kept complete when they chose Matthias to take the place of Judas (Acts 1:15-26). Christ also placed Paul on a par with the Twelve (Galatians 1:1,17). As we have seen, Peter was at the head of the group or "college" with special authority given him by Christ.

In the apostolic age the hierarchical order below the Apostles is not entirely clear. 1 Corinthians 12:28 ranks apostles, prophets, teachers, performers of miracles, and those having healing gifts in descending order. In Ephesians 4:11-12 the ranking is apostles, prophets, evangelists, pastors, and teachers. In Acts 15:6,22 the ranking is apostles and below them elders. Acts 20:7 compared with Acts 20:28 makes no important distinction between these two terms, as "people" to "shepherds" or "elders". Only in the postapostolic period did the terms of bishop and priest come to mean what they mean today. In the lower clergy deacons are referred to in Philippians 1:1 as church leaders and helpers, and in 1 Timothy 3:1-13.[8]

That bishops are superior to priests was confirmed by the writings of St. Ignatius in the second century and defined by the Council of Trent (Denziger 1777). The same council defined the divine institution of the ecclesiastical hierarchy (Denziger 1776) and its composition of bishops, priests, and other ministers. That the ecclesiastical hierarchy is of divine institution is confirmed by Vatican II, *Dogmatic Constitution on the Church*, paragraph 27.[9] Thus an ecclesiastical hierarchy is a definitely ordered group of men endowed with sacred power or that power practiced within a system in which lower ministries are subordinated to higher ones.

If we posit a Catholic (including Eastern Orthodox and Episcopalian) theory versus a Protestant theory of hierarchy, we say that the dispute is not so much over the existence or legitimacy of sacred functions or the legitimacy of gradation among those exercising sacred ministries. Instead it is over the origin of such functions and ministries. The Protestant view is that functions and their right are made by the Christian community itself and subject to the modification or abrogation of functionaries and their rights. The Catholic view is that principal offices are determined in essential content by Jesus Christ. There is no power in the Christian community to change or abrogate them. In the Catholic Church the faithful believe leaders enjoy powers constituted in the first instance and immediately conferred by Christ Himself.

At least three questions may arise. First, "Is there any special reason why Our Lord should have chosen to determine the constitutional structure, to determine the sacred powers rather than leave this to the community itself?" Second, "To what extent is there but one hierarchical arrangement in the Church?" Third, "If some distinction can be made between a hierarchy of order and a hierarchy of jurisdiction, how are they related, and is there a discernible priority?"

The Catholic Church makes these answers. To the first question, the Church is the Body of Christ. Its life and vigor flow from its Head to its members. Its corporate powers and visible external functions should flow from Him and be determined by Him. To the second question, unity of power in the Church derives from the unity of mission received by Christ from His Father. It is communicated to the Apostles as His surrogates. In the hierarchy of order are bishops, priests, and ministers. In the hierarchy of jurisdiction are the pontificate and the episcopate. To the third question, order is sacramental power and jurisdiction is pastoral power. Sacramental power precedes and demands the pastoral power, just as human procreative power precedes and demands moral parental powers over their issue. Through sacraments the Church with Christ at the head bestows life and increases it. Through pastoral power it maintains, preserves, and protects that to which it gives life.[10]

We may look at hierarchy in the Catholic Church as the totality of power given by Christ and His Apostles and their legitimate successors. The purpose of this power is the rule of the Church and to celebrate and dispense divine mysteries. Hierarchy also refers to grades or ranks according to the degree of spiritual power or authority that they possess. Central to the discussion are the hierarchy of order and the hierarchy of jurisdiction.

The hierarchy of order involves the sanctification of men by the Church's ministry through Mass and the Sacraments. The hierarchy of jurisdiction involves governing baptized persons and directing their intellects and wills to holiness and supernatural happiness. Order is authority over the real body of Christ, while jurisdiction is authority over the Mystical Body of Christ, the Church. Order means the sanctification of souls automatically through the power of God when the human act is posited. Jurisdiction means sanctification of souls according to the value or effectiveness of the very act that is posited. The power of the ecclesiastical hierarchy is conferred only by the Church itself and not by the consent or call of the faithful or secular power. Persons in the hierarchy of order belong by sacred ordination. Canonical appointment or mission confirms the power of jurisdiction except in the case of the pope, whose jurisdiction follows upon his legitimate election and free acceptance of office.

The power of orders cannot be lost or revoked. Its use is valid until the death of the recipient, though it may be unlawful. The power of jurisdiction can usually be revoked and a later attempt to use jurisdictional power formally held is normally invalid.

The two orders are distinct but also related and united. Their distinct nature is obvious in their distinct and independent origin and existence, their clearly diverse qualities, and their entirely different proximate ends. A titular bishop has the full power of orders but not of jurisdiction. A layman elected to the papacy would lack the power of orders yet have fullness of jurisdiction due to his election and acceptance of office. Ordinarily only an ordained cleric is capable of receiving ecclesiastical jurisdiction without an apostolic indult (release from obligation). For licit use the power of orders depends upon jurisdiction and both are normally found in the same persons, the pope and the bishops.

Both hierarchies can be divided into hierarchies of divine and ecclesiastical origin. The hierarchy of jurisdiction has defined the primacy of St. Peter and his legitimate successors (Vatican Council I, session 4, capita 1-3) and the office of bishops as successors to the Apostles (Council of Trent, session 23, capitum 4). Other grades of the hierarchy of jurisdiction are of ecclesiastical origin.

The hierarchy of order (bishops, priests, and ministers) is of divine institution. Other degrees have been added by the Church (Council of Trent, session 23, capitum 6). Ministers are usually considered to include only deacons, as only the diaconate, priesthood, and episcopacy are sacraments and thus of divine institution (Council of Trent, session 23, capitum 4, part 6). Because the so-called "minor orders" of porter, lector, exorcist, acolyte, and subdeacon are ecclesiastically instituted, ordination to them (actually rites) as steps to the clerical state of the priesthood was deemed unnecessary. The Holy See began a revision in 1971. Tonsure, the rite of admission to the clerical state by the clipping or shaving of a portion of the candidate's head, was also suppressed. By an indult of 5 October 1971 the bishops of the United States were allowed to omit ordaining porters and exorcists. Three days later a second indult permitted the revised rites for ordaining acolytes and lectors. On 14 September 1972 Pope Paul VI abolished the orders of porter, exorcist, and subdeacon, decreed that laymen and candidates for the diaconate and priesthood could be installed in the ministries of acolyte and lector, reconfirmed the suppression of tonsure and its replacement with a service of dedication to God and the Church, and stated that, upon ordination, the diaconate was the entrance to the clerical state.[11]

A bishop or archbishop is often called the ordinary of his diocese or archdiocese. This term means that his jurisdiction is ordinary in that its power is automatic because it is backed by law and lasts during his tenure. Jurisdiction can be delegated when committed to a person himself. Bishops are subject to the pope, who has primacy of jurisdiction. The power of bishops is ordinary, because it is possessed in virtue of their episcopal office itself, not because it is granted to them by the pope as delegates or vicars.

Jurisdiction includes legislative authority, the power to enact obligatory norms useful or necessary for the welfare of the people. It includes judicial authority, the right to judge how the faithful observe the laws, as well as executive authority, and the right to administer goods and to assure adherence to the laws, even with punishments when necessary. The teaching authority (magisterium) of the Church is also included.[12]

Having examined the concept of hierarchy and the bishops' position within it, we come to episcopal consecration and the extent of the powers derived from it. The Apostles received the special gift of the Holy Spirit. The liturgical rite of prayer and the imposition of hands, signifying the gift of a special grace, is an early Christian tradition. A similar rite was used for the appointment of the first deacons (Acts 6:6) and of presbyters in the course of the journeys of St. Paul (Acts 14:28). In the case of Timothy (1 Timothy 4:4; 2 Timothy 1:6) the imposition of hands conferred a special spiritual gift. That gift is "power, love and self-control," like that received by St. Paul (2 Timothy 1:7,11).

Episcopal consecration manifests and brings about the adoption of a new member into the episcopal college. Ancient prayers (*Apostolic Tradition, Canones Hippolyti, Apostolic Constitutions*) entreat the power of the Holy Spirit, given by Christ to His Apostles. The prayers ask for the grace necessary to guide the Church of God, to take a certain part in governing the universal Church. The rite incorporates the bishop into the episcopal order. Ancient tradition requires all bishops present, or at least three, to impose hands on a newly elected bishop. A bishop does not just consecrate a successor. But the consecration of a new member is the concern of the entire episcopal body, represented by several members.

This rite is sacred with signs and words conferring a grace. It is a sacrament conferring the fullness of the priesthood and bestowing a grace to enable the bishop to carry out his duties. If a layman were elected pope, he would be consecrated a bishop, which would bestow complete priestly power as well as the full powers of a bishop.

The rite is always administered by a bishop, and this minister of consecration must have the required order and intention to employ the correct sign. Pope Pius XII determined by the apostolic constitution *Sacramentum ordinis* ("The Sacrament of Orders") of 30 November 1947 (Denziger 2301) that episcopal consecration is a sacrament (and not a sacramental; that is, an action or object established by the Church serving as an indirect aid to grace by producing devotion). He also stated that whatever matter and form used in the past, requirements would be the imposition of hands and the words of the Preface, "Give your priest the plentitude of your ministry and by heavenly anointing sanctify him upon whom you have conferred supreme honor."[13]

The effects of episcopal consecration, those of the special outpouring of the Holy Spirit and of the imposition of hands, are of biblical origin. It is the special outpouring producing the totality of the Sacrament of Orders, which the Catholic Church calls "the high priesthood, the acme of the sacred ministry" (Vatican II, *Dogmatic Constitution on the Church*, paragraph 21).[14]

John 20:22-23 states: "Then he [Christ] breathed on them [the Apostles] and said, 'Receive the Holy Spirit. If you forgive people's sins, they are forgiven; if you do not forgive them, they are not forgiven'." Christ also told the Apostles: "But when the Holy Spirit comes upon you, you will be filled with power, and you will be witnesses for me in Jerusalem, in all of Judea and Samaria, and to the ends of the earth" (Acts 1:8). On Pentecost, the seventh Sunday after Easter, the Holy Spirit descended upon the Apostles: "They were all filled with the Holy Spirit and began to talk in other languages, as the Spirit enabled them to speak" (Acts 2:4).

Concerning the imposition of hands, Paul says to Timothy: "Do not neglect the spiritual gift that is in you, which was given to you when the prophets spoke and the elders laid their hands on you" (1 Timothy 4:14). Again, Paul speaks to Timothy regarding the faith of Timothy and his family:

> For this reason I remind you to keep alive the gift that God gave you when I laid my hands on you. For the Spirit that God has given us does not make us timid; instead, his Spirit fills us with power, love, and self-control (2 Timothy 1:6-7).

Consecration imparts a character or in some manner transforms the sacerdotal (priestly) character. On 1 July 1964 on the occasion of consecrating bishops, Pope Paul VI stated that episcopal consecration is

> a source or grace, a gift of God, a spiritual treasure, a higher sanctification. It is not just a transmission of liturgical, teaching, and juridical power, but a perfection conferred upon the one consecrated, who before sanctifying others is himself sanctified.[15]

The functions of sanctifying, teaching, and ruling are three ministries imparted through episcopal consecration. Christ as high priest consecrates specially those He has chosen to His service for the episcopate. These bishops are viable representatives of his sovereign priesthood, as principal ministers of sacraments which the priestly action of Christ extends to us. The sacerdotal order is subordinated and dependent upon the episcopacy. Bishops give priests what is necessary for the proper function of sacraments. They bless holy chrism, the oil of catechumens, altars, churches, vestments, and sacred vessels. They are the ordinary ministers of confirmation and of holy orders. The individual bishop receives a clearly defined power over the whole Church, for the unity and growth of the mystical body, through the sacraments. Though Canon 390 prohibits the exercise of his functions outside his own diocese without the consent of the local ordinary, the Canon refers to the lawfulness and not the validity of his power.

The first duty of the Apostles was to teach all nations (Matthew 28:19). Their successors have received that inheritance in common, ratified by Pope Celestine I at the Council of Ephesus (431). Each bishop is responsible for preaching the gospel to all mankind. Through consecration he receives the special charism of truth, an illumination and force comparable to what the Apostles received at Pentecost. The assistance of the Holy Spirit makes the teaching authority of the bishops as a body infallible. The individual bishop is not infallible, but the episcopal body is, due to the collective or collegial character of the episcopate. As a body they are infallible with and under the Bishop of Rome (the pope). When the pope defines a question of faith, the whole fellowship of the bishops, which speaks through him, is included. Infallibility is a negative notion in the episcopal magisterium. It is the power of the Holy Spirit which helps positively to preach the truths of faith to correspond to each new situation of the faithful. Bishops are responsible for the study of the word of God and must be vigilant to exclude all error.

Episcopal consecration confers charism enabling the bishop to govern the faithful. Though the pastoral office is for the universal church, for order and convenience the exercise of the individual bishop's power is limited, with jurisdiction over a limited portion of the Church. Bishops are jointly responsible for the Church's good, cooperating with the pope and each other for unity and progress in charity. They are representatives and interpreters of the law of Christ. Thus Augustine in his "Epistle 217" calls the bishop the "Servant of the servants of God".

We may summarize the authority of the bishop conferred by consecration as one sacramental power divided into three offices or ministries. In the sanctifying office he mediates salvation through the sacraments. In the teaching office he is charged with preaching the gospel. In the ruling office he is pastor of his church (or diocese) entrusted him as vicar and ambassador of Christ.[16]

To conclude this section we need to examine the bishop as he exercises his authority as a member of the college established by Christ in which he is a successor of the Apostles. Through episcopal consecration he is a member of the college in communion with its head and members. He enjoys all the ordinary, proper, and immediate authority to use his office with other bishops and with and under the Bishop of Rome. He is a member of the synod of bishops and takes part in national episcopal conferences.

Vatican Council II (1962-1965) formulated and promulgated sixteen documents (two dogmatic and two pastoral constitutions, nine decrees, and three declarations) to reflect its basic pastoral orientation toward renewal and reform in the Church. It has had particular effect in those documents pertaining to the liturgy, the Church, the Church in the world, ecumenism, the renewal of religious life, the life and ministry of priests, and the lay apostolate.[17]

For bishops the Council produced some issues and related concerns about magisterial responsibilities, the exercise of collegiality, and the role of the diocesan bishop. The issues might be posed as questions. First, "Does a bishop enter the worldwide college first or is he first a particular bishop?" Second, "Is the pope the head of the Church and of the college or the head of the Church because he is the head of and acts within the college of bishops?" Third, "What does episcopal consecration confer that is more, other, or different from the ordination of a priest?" The adoption of the Code of Canon Law, a revision of the 1917 Code, and further Church teaching addresses these issues.

In other areas the encyclical *Humanae Vitae* ("Of Human Life") by Pope Paul VI (1968) concerning marriage doctrine and morality became at first a question of the use of the magisterium or the clarification of a Christian ideal. Another magisterial responsibility for bishops is the religious education of children, adaptation to local conditions contrasted with maintenance of the unity of discipline within the Church.[18]

Two organizations formed for collegiality are the Synod of Bishops and national and regional episcopal conferences. Pope Paul VI charted the Synod of Bishops on 15 September 1965. Its provisions are contained in Canons 342 to 348 of the Code of Canon Law. Among the major provisions of its charter, its purposes are

> to encourage close union and valued assistance between the Sovereign Pontiff and the bishops of the entire world; to insure that direct and real information is provided on questions and situations touching upon the internal action of the Church and its necessary activity in the world of today; to facilitate agreement on essential points of doctrine and on methods of procedure in the life of the Church.

The Synod is a permanent and central ecclesiastical institution. It is directly and immediately subject to the pope, who can assign its agenda, call it into session, and give its members advisory and deliberate authority.

The majority of Synod members are elected and representative of national or regional episcopal conferences. There are also a limited number of ex officio members and some heads of male religious institutes. The Pope can appoint the secretary general, special secretaries and no more than fifteen percent of the total membership. He is the president of the Synod. An advisory council of fifteen (twelve elected and three appointed by the pope) members provides the secretariat with adequate staff for carrying on liaison with episcopal conferences and for preparing the agenda of synodal assemblies.[19]

Episcopal conferences are organized and operate under general norms and particular statutes approved by the Holy See. They are official bodies in and through which the bishops of a given country or territory act together as pastors of the Church. In the United States the National Conference of Catholic Bishops (1966) is the national episcopal conference. Its service secretariat, the United States Catholic Conference (1967), carries out the civic-religious work of the Church in the United States of America. Canons 447 through 459 of the Code of Canon Law discuss conferences of bishops. Section Two of Canon 455 states, however:

> The general decrees mentioned in §1 can be validly passed in a

> plenary session only if two-thirds of the members of the conference having a deliberative vote approve them; such decrees do not have binding force, unless they have been legitimately promulgated, after having been reviewed by the Apostolic See.[20]

In other words such conferences are limited so that a two-thirds majority is required even to suggest from Rome that conference decisions might be given juridical status.

We conclude this section by noting the role of the diocesan bishop and the extent of his authority. Prior to 1972 bishops of the Latin Rite discussed candidates for that office at regular provincial meetings and forwarded names to Rome. The apostolic delegate (now the pro-nuncio) made secret investigations and the final decision on appointments was made at the Vatican. Since that time the Church uses a more careful system in finding episcopal candidates through broader consultation with the diocese or archdiocese involved. Representatives from all people and their needs are taken increasingly into consideration. Pope Paul VI in his *motu proprio* entitled *Ecclesiae Sanctae* ("Of Holy Church") (1966) fixed episcopal retirement at age seventy-five. In each case bishops must be willing to resign and their resignations accepted before the selection process begins.

By another document *De episcoporum muneribus* ("Concerning the Services of Bishops") of 1966 Pope Paul VI affirmed that bishops may not dispense from procedural laws, nor from laws held to be expressions of the divine or natural law. At this time the Holy See reserved to itself the power to dispense in laws touching clerical celibacy and to regulate various matters of interest to the clergy (such as the age of ordination, course of studies, certain restricted occupations). The Holy See also has authority regarding marriage (minimum age, various serious impediments) and the time required for the Eucharistic fast. Bishops are to take charge of matters involving the clergy and religious, the liturgy, marriage, ecumenicism, justice and peace efforts, and social communications.

Concerning the clergy and religious, bishops employ greater control over seminaries and the formation of students for the priesthood. They may move pastors as needed, establish and suppress parishes according to pastoral needs, attempt to provide equitable remuneration of priests, and set up retirement plans. When the episcopal conference of his nation secures the authority, a bishop may install permanent deacons, watch over their training and ministry, and determine what offices and faculties such deacons may exercise. Religious working in a diocese are subject to the bishop's pastoral directives except for the internal affairs of their community. But the bishop may determine such matters as whether a regular confessor is needed for a particular religious house and whether the community may offer coeducation in its schools.

In liturgical matters the diocese may have options for new rituals in the Latin rite. The Eucharist may be administered in both species (solid and liquid forms). He may also decide when sacramental absolution may be given, grant partial indulgences and dispense people from the obligation of confession and communion in obtaining indulgences if judging a sufficient pastoral reason. He may reduce the obligation of funded Masses (in which an offering is given as a contribution to the support of the priest for applying the fruits of the Mass according to the intention of the donor). But he may not dispense priests from the Mass for the people celebrated every Sunday or holy day.

The bishop may grant dispensation for a religiously mixed marriage and permit such marriages to take place during Mass in church. He may also permit marriages to take place outside of church buildings and with the participation of non-Catholic clergy. He has power to dispense Catholics from the requirement of the Church's canonical formalities of marriage, provided civil law is observed. He may resolve difficulties in existing marriages and recognize marital consent which was previously technically invalid. Certain nullity cases, including underage marriages, may be more easily resolved. The diocesan tribunal may try cases with a single judge instead of three. Dispensation from a mandatory appeal of an affirmative sentence of nullity may be possible and the case tried within the diocese. The bishop is also responsible for emphasis on positive pastoral attention and on Christian marriage and family life.

Catholics may be permitted to take part in various non-Catholic religious ceremonies with active participation of other Christians in baptism, weddings, and funerals of Catholics. Former restrictions on Christian burial for non-Catholics or former Catholics may be relaxed. Worship may be shared at times. A baptized non-Catholic may receive the Eucharist under certain circumstances. Diocesan bishops work on Christian unity, joining various state councils or associations of churches and establishing their own diocesan commissions.

Bishops are charged to work for justice and peace, to intervene in strikes, civil strife, and in issues where personal rights are threatened. The individual bishop may make pastoral statements and take public positions. Migrants and travelers and their problems are of particular concern, which was the case in which the pope visited Texas in 1987.

The bishop is responsible for communications of many types. He may consider radio, television, and other media inside his diocese. He also has an obligation to deal with the press and communicate with its readers. The bishop works with such constituencies as the clergy, religious, and laity through priests' senates, diocesan pastoral councils, and parish councils. He appoints episcopal vicars for his territory, its specialized population, or its particular pastoral concern. The bishop may employ a due-process system, used after 1970, in many American dioceses for reconciliation or arbitration of disputes within the Church. Finally, there is the necessity of bishops to preach the word of God and to exercise the Church's teaching authority in their dioceses. Bishops are frequently called upon to issue statements and to take stands on matters ranging from abortion to justice, war, and peace. Yet there are limitations on a bishop's teaching authority on options for sacramental preparation and celebration.

As we have seen, the powers of a bishop are far from absolute. They must be used responsibly in communion with fellow bishops and with the pope. Their authority leaves a power vacuum from inadequate assumption of power in national conferences or locally. And there is sometimes tension between bishops, their conferences, and the Apostolic See. There remain critical restrictions on the regulation of marriage tribunals and the laicization of priests. On the local level, that of bishop to his faithful, the primary pastoral concerns of the people remain.[21]

E. The Designation of Bishops

Canon 378 of the 1983 Code of Canon Law lists the qualifications for bishops of the Latin Rite of the Roman Catholic Church. Section One states the requirements themselves, while Section Two declares that "suitability" for episcopal positions rests with the "Apostolic See," which in general is interchangeable with the Holy See, the pope, and the Roman curia (Cf. Canon 361; *CIC* 300). Specifically, the candidate should be:

> 1° outstanding for his solid faith, good morals, piety, zeal for souls, wisdom, prudence and human virtues and endowed with the other talents which make him fit to fulfill the office in question;
>
> 2° in possession of a good reputation;
>
> 3° at least thirty-five years of age;
>
> 4° ordained a priest for at least five years.

Number Five of Section One of this canon concerns the educational requirements already discussed above.[1]

The 1917 Code of Canon Law required that the candidate be born legitimately and that he be at least thirty years of age. Section Two of Canon 378 implies that other judgments are relevant to the selection process and that the definitive judgment concerning the candidate may be made at a lower level of authority (such as conferences of bishops or provinces) with the Holy See ratifying the process of decision.[2]

Canon 377 describes the designation process itself:

> §1. The Supreme Pontiff freely appoints bishops or confirms those who have been legitimately elected.
>
> §2. At least every three years the bishops of an ecclesiastical province or, if circumstances suggest this, the bishops of a conference of bishops are to compose in common counsel and in secret a list of presbyters, including members of institutes of consecrated life, who are suitable for the episcopacy and send it to the Apostolic See; each bishop retains the right to make known to the Apostolic See on his own the names of presbyters whom he thinks worthy and suitable for the episcopal office.
>
> §3. Unless other provisions have legitimately been made, whenever a diocesan bishop or a coadjutor bishop is to be named, in regard to the *ternus*, as it is called, to be proposed to the Apostolic See it is the responsibility of the pontifical legate to seek out individually the suggestions of the metropolitan and the suffragans of the province to which the diocese to be provided for belongs or with which it is joined and of the president of the conference of bishops and to communicate them to the Apostolic See together [with] his own preference; moreover, the pontifical legate is to hear some members of the college of consultors and of the cathedral chapter, and if he judges it expedient, he shall also obtain, individually and in secret, the opinion of other members of the secular and

> religious clergy as well as of the laity who are outstanding for their wisdom.
>
> §4. Unless other provisions have been legitimately made, a diocesan bishop who judges that an auxiliary bishop ought to be given to his diocese is to propose to the Apostolic See a list of at least three priests who are quite suitable for this office.
>
> §5. No rights and privileges of election, nomination, presentation, or designation of bishops are hereafter granted to civil authorities.[3]

The selection procedure of the hierarchy is the subject of this section. The types of bishops, the consecration of the designate, the taking possession of the episcopal office, and their duties are subjects for the next section. Although the pope may independently designate a bishop, his participation is generally the ratification of selections made by competent authorities in a lengthy process. The method itself is like the appointment of federal judges by the president of the United States. The pope is free to appoint and to reject the names proposed by others. Due to the tremendous demands on his time and energies, the process allows his acceptance or rejection of the candidates.

Cathedral chapters, common in such countries as Germany and Switzerland, have no place in the United States. Historically the United States government, unlike some other governments, has never prevented the free choice of Roman Catholic bishops.[4] Individuals, those in religious orders, diocesan clergy, and the hierarchy are free to make direct nominations of candidates outside the general process. As one might suspect, such nominations have varying degrees of influence.[5]

As step follows step, participants attempt to move quietly along channels not so much for secrecy itself as to avoid the factions, parties, and general intrusion into orderly decision-making. It begins with a definite need, the placement of hierarchy within a diocese or archdiocese, and ends when the candidate is informed of his selection and he accepts or rejects the position offered. Time is a relative factor. On 6 April 1993 Bishop Michael J. Sheehan was named apostolic administrator of the archdiocese of Santa Fe, New Mexico. When he was named archbishop on 17 August 1993, his acceptance created a vacancy in his diocese of Lubbock, Texas. On 9 October 1993 Bishop Bernard J. Ganter died and his diocese of Beaumont, Texas, became vacant. On 5 April 1994 the pro-nuncio to the United States announced appointments for both these vacancies. We may examine how bishops are chosen by the unfolding of events.[6]

Bishop selection is deliberate and involves many people. A bishop or archbishop in office may remain until he dies or becomes seventy-five years old. In 1989 the average age of an American Catholic archbishop was fifty-three. In 1994 when auxiliary bishops Joseph A. Galante of San Antonio became bishop of Beaumont and Placido Rodriguez, CMF of Chicago became bishop of Lubbock, their ages averaged fifty-four. On becoming auxiliary bishops their average age was forty-three. In considerably more than half of the candidates for archbishop a priest becomes a bishop first and is head of a diocese before being considered for advancement. Among other standards Pope John Paul II considers maturity important.

The regular selection process begins at the province meeting. In 1994 the

Province of San Antonio hierarchy includes the archbishop of San Antonio, his suffragan bishops of Amarillo, Austin, Beaumont, Brownsville, Corpus Christi, Dallas, El Paso, Fort Worth, Galveston-Houston, Lubbock, San Angelo, Tyler, and Victoria, and two auxiliaries of the Galveston-Houston diocese. Two diocesan and two auxiliary bishops are retired and living in Texas. The province meeting chairman is the archbishop. Although these meetings must occur every three years, they may take place once a year. The province bishops may submit names of priests to be collected by the archbishop and distributed to all bishops prior to the meeting. In addition to the names of priests under consideration, information includes their educations and assignments since ordination.

Participants at the meeting share information and observations. One may speak from his own knowledge or recall what he has learned from others. While anyone may send nominations to the pro-nuncio in Washington, group discussion outside the province meeting is forbidden. The Council for the Public Affairs of the Church has taken a part by issuing a statement on 25 March 1972 entitled "Norms for the Selection of Candidates for the Episcopacy in the Latin Church." The Council is a part of the Vatican Secretariat of State, being one of two sections now called the Section for Relations with States. Pope John Paul II renamed it in 1988, and its purpose is the conduct of diplomatic and other relations with civil governments.[7]

The norms depict a worthy candidate as "a good pastor of souls and teacher of the Faith". He should also have a good reputation, irreproachable morality, right judgment and prudence, be even-tempered and of stable character, firmly hold the orthodox Faith, be devoted to the Apostolic See and faithful to the ordinary teaching of the church, have a thorough knowledge of dogmatic and moral theology and canon law, be outstanding for piety, spirit of sacrifice, and have pastoral zeal and an aptitude for governing. In addition to these personal requirements the province archbishop and bishops should consider the priest's intellectual qualities, studies completed, social sense, spirit of dialogue and cooperation, openness to signs of the times, praiseworthy impartiality, family background, health, age, and inherited characteristics.

If information on candidates is not readily available, it may be sought. Bishops are free to confer with diocesan consultors, members of the council of priests, and the general clergy and laity. There is no bar on consultation, except that the Vatican opposes groups putting forward contenders for fear that politicking and pressure will come to bear on the process. Individuals may suggest worthies to the pro-nuncio or directly to Rome. It may be that a name often recurs in various lists, indicating the popularity and ability of a priest or bishop. In the province of San Antonio this seems to have been true of Archbishop Flores, a man approved of by many.[8]

The names of priests in religious orders, as well as diocesan clergy, may be submitted. A bishop might know a priest as a seminary classmate, as a seminary professor or as an administrator. The priest chosen may himself be a professor or administrator, such as the rector of a seminary. Members of the chancery staffs (especially chancellors and secretaries to bishops) might find themselves included.

When discussion has been completed, bishops take secret ballots of yes, no, and neutral. A bishop may abstain if he does not know the candidate. In case of a neutral vote, the voter attempts to learn more about the candidate by the next vote, in which names may be added to or deleted from the original list. Further discussion may be necessary before another vote takes place.

When the province participants have finished their deliberations, the archbishop forwards the names to the pro-nuncio. His information includes the minutes of the meeting(s), the votes, the office to be filled (auxiliary or diocesan bishop), and the type or size of diocese for which the bishops believe one suitable. The form indicates the candidate's name, diocese, parents' names, schools attended and degrees received, the date and place of his ordination to the priesthood, what foreign languages he knows (in the Province of San Antonio and the United States generally, Spanish is very important), and his appointments since ordination.

There is an appraisal of the candidate in view of the above norms and the names and addresses of those (clerical, lay or religious) associates who could supply additional information. An indication of a good pastor of souls might be being the head of a large and active parish. A seminary rector might be disciplined and in contact with current thinking and trends of priestly formation. How his colleagues view a priest is very important. If the candidate is the president of a priests' council, does he play a leadership part? Do the clergy and laity with whom he comes into contact respect him? Do his age and health present problems? The general appraisal on the province level might vary from three lines to half a page.

The province sends its list to the National Conference of Catholic Bishops (NCCB), the American episcopal conference since 1966. This body has a standing committee on the Selection of Bishops, which was formed in 1972 when the Vatican issued new norms for selection. Review by the national body in the United States is more often than not a courtesy gesture. America is so large that the candidate may not be known to members of the committee. It consequently spends most of its time on the size of dioceses and whether divisions should occur. The list often includes positive votes and abstentions, but negative votes are often omitted. Black bishops tend to favor the lists as a device to consider names regularly.

After the episcopal conference takes note of the list and makes whatever additions it considers necessary, it is sent to the pro-nuncio in Washington. He is a fully accredited diplomat of ambassadorial level. In some countries he would be called the nuncio (Latin for messenger) if he were the dean or *doyen* of the diplomatic corps. Here, however, the diplomat longest accredited to the United States enjoys that distinction. He is the papal representative both to the United States and to the American Catholic hierarchy.

United States and Vatican diplomatic relations are of long standing. Consular relations with the Papal States grew out of the American mission to France in 1784 and lasted from 1797 until the absorption of the Papal States into Italy in 1871. David M. Armstrong was the last American to hold this position, and the Vatican representative Louis B. Binsse was appointed in 1850. His title was recognized until his death in 1895. Diplomatic relations began in 1847 and continued until 1867 when they ceased due to American objections and lack of funds appropriated to continue the ministry.

The Vatican sent archbishops with the rank of apostolic delegate to Washington, DC as representatives from 1893 until 1984. These diplomats were all Italian except for the Belgian Jean Jadot. Significantly all were later promoted to the rank of cardinal except Jadot, who had managed to anger various factions during his tenure. Between 1939 and 1951 and from 1970 until 1984 various American presidents sent personal representatives to the Vatican. On 10 January 1984 relations became fully diplomatic with a mutual exchange of ambassadors. In mid-1994 the American ambassador was Raymond L. Flynn, the former mayor of Boston, and the Vatican ambassador was Archbishop Agostino Cacciavillan.

Cacciavillan is a skilled diplomat with doctorates in civil and canon law. He was born in Novale, the province of Vicenza, Italy, in 1926, and ordained for the Diocese of Vicenza in 1948. He entered the Vatican Secretariat of State in 1959 and served there and in the Philippines, Spain, and Portugal. From 1969 to 1976 he was head of the Documentation and Information Office of the Secretariat of State. In 1976 he was appointed Pro-Nuncio to Kenya and Apostolic Delegate to the Seychelles. He received episcopal ordination on 28 February 1976 as Titular Archbishop of Amiternum. In 1981 he was appointed Pro-Nuncio to India and in 1985 additionally to Nepal. He received his present appointment as Pro-Nuncio to the United States and Permanent Observer of the Holy See to the Organization of American States from Pope John Paul II on 13 June 1990.[9]

The pro-nuncio takes the list and organizes it alphabetically, by province, by ethnic group, and by other classifications. Those candidates on the list may be auxiliaries, diocesan bishops, or archbishops. Just as the impetus for auxiliaries is from the bishop or archbishop, a coadjutor (a bishop sent to administer or to help a bishop administer a diocese, who often becomes that bishop's successor) may frequently have his appointment initiated by the Vatican.

If an auxiliary is sought, the pro-nuncio must be aware of the need for the diocese or archdiocese. Generally there is no problem if the auxiliary has died or been promoted. But the bishop or archbishop must make his case if he has never had one or requests a new auxiliary. At one time (before 1982) an auxiliary would be requested by a bishop, who submitted his reasons to the pronuncio. The pro-nuncio sent the request to the Congregation for Bishops and the pope. A second stage began upon a favorable response from Rome with the proposing of names, questionnaires, and a ternus (list of three). The older practice is now used, with the request and ternus being submitted together to the Congregation.

As a rule of thumb an archdiocese with over 200,000 Catholics normally has one auxiliary. Those with over one million Catholics usually have five or six. In mid-1994 the American Latin Rite archdioceses of Chicago, Detroit, Los Angeles, Newark, and New York had five or more auxiliaries, while those of Anchorage, Atlanta, Denver, Dubuque, Indianapolis, Kansas City (Kansas), Louisville, Mobile, Oklahoma City, Omaha, San Antonio, Santa Fe, and Seattle had none. In the case of San Antonio Bernard F. Popp had his resignation accepted on 23 March 1993 and Joseph A. Galante was promoted bishop of Beaumont on 5 April 1994. Bishop Popp maintains a schedule of pastoral and confirmation activities as Archbishop Flores awaits the appointment of new auxiliaries. In 1993 the Catholic population of the Archdiocese of San Antonio was over 600,000.[10] The size of the archdiocese (or diocese) and its ethnic or racial composition may be important to the pro-nuncio. A bishop who is five years from retirement does not usually get an auxiliary.

When an auxiliary bishop is needed, the bishop draws up a list of three names (called the ternus or terna) for submission to the pro-nuncio. It is said that Archbishop Furey of San Antonio was so convinced that Patrick Flores should be his auxiliary that Flores's name occupied the entire ternus. The pro-nuncio does his own investigation and sends on the names with his report and recommendation. The candidate should have the backing of the province bishops, as cases of disagreement may not lead to an appointment. The Vatican gives preference to native clergy. According to Thomas J. Reese in *Archbishop*, Archbishop Flores repeatedly tried to appoint Monsignor Virgilio Elizondo as his auxiliary, but received a "sixty-five-year-old Polish priest" instead.[11] Of course the pope may reject all choices and freely appoint his own.

The hierarchy chooses auxiliaries for different reasons. Those appointed may have excellent social and/or administrative skills necessary for governing. A great deal of care must necessarily be taken with those advancing from priest to auxiliary. At present the Vatican seems to favor such individuals for possible further promotion and not simply for past achievements on a one-way track to retirement. Bishops may prove financially incompetent or find themselves unable to work with other bishops. In such cases the Vatican may send coadjutors with present powers to govern and the ability to succeed the incumbents.

In the case of the appointment of a diocesan bishop the pro-nuncio may construct the ternus. He may seek names from the retired bishop or from the administrator, if the bishop is deceased or has moved. His concern is always the condition and needs of the diocese and the qualifications for the new bishop. The Canon Law Society of America has suggested these questions:

> 1. In your opinion, what are the three most important needs of the diocese today?
>
> 2. In the light of the needs you have listed, what do you feel are the desirable qualifications of the next bishop of this diocese?
>
> 3. Please list three persons you feel would be good choices for the next bishop and explain why.[12]

The third question is not meant for public consultation but limits itself to the state of the diocese and its needs and the qualifications desired in the bishop. Names are not publicly discussed.

Sometimes the appointment of a new bishop is announced at the resignation of the old bishop. Even when a bishop reaches the age of seventy-five his resignation may not be announced until his successor is appointed. The acceptance of the resignation must be published in *L'Osservatore Romano* to be effective. The bishop remains so without becoming diocesan administrator. A diocesan report may be sent by the administrator of a vacated see to the pro-nuncio. It contains the names of ten to twenty people from various age groups and parts of the diocese. The pro-nuncio usually contacts the heads of various administrative bodies and others in leadership positions. He also consults heads of religious orders in the diocese, lay people who are officers in diocesan lay organizations, and members of diocesan advisory committees. He asks them to give information concerning the state of the diocese and to recommend names of possible candidates. If the last bishop did not maintain contact with his people and was an authoritarian or a weak administrator, he would seek to appoint one with opposite qualities to remedy defects. He may also find that the diocese in question might have to be divided.

The pro-nuncio must know the hierarchy of the country to which he is accredited. He may meet members in his travels or through direct communications by telephone or letter. Through these methods he gains insight into individual situations across the country and begins to know the country as a whole. His duties are a combination of apostolic delegate (knowing but not interfering with the operations of the hierarchy) and ambassador extraordinary and plentipotentiary (working with civil governments and performing various diplomatic duties).

In the selection of candidates sometimes a strong representation by the archbishop helps. But an archbishop may not always be consulted concerning his own successor. The individual may not be particularly concerned about the appointments of bishops in his province. Others may not know enough about the diocese or priests within it to make a recommendation.

When the pro-nuncio consults with the president and vice-president of the NCCB, the president learns of the opening of a see or of the consideration of diocesan auxiliaries. As is always the case, he is requested to provide information on the state of the diocese and the kind of leadership it needs. The NCCB has thirteen regions which include all fifty states plus the District of Columbia and the Virgin Islands. Texas, Arkansas and Oklahoma comprise Region Ten. The standing Committee on Selection of Bishops has thirteen bishops, each elected by the region he represents.

The president of the NCCB (a bishop or archbishop) consults with the proper regional representative on the committee. He forwards his information to the pro-nuncio, who narrows the list of candidates to eight or ten names and returns it to the officers of the NCCB for a second consultation. The NCCB seeks to be consulted about names for a given diocese. The pro-nuncio asks for a list of three in descending order and the reasons for preference. The NCCB is free to put forward its own names and to give the terna and its reasons for choice. At this point the regional representative on the NCCB committee may be consulted. But this is an internal matter.

Although Archbishop Flores presides over an archdiocese where he was once an auxiliary, few enjoy the same distinction. It is more common for an auxiliary to wait about six years and then to be appointed to another diocese. Some auxiliaries are promoted after a new archbishop arrives so he can place his own appointees. For various reasons (lack of interest, health, insufficient skills, and so forth) some auxiliaries are never promoted. Some are judged too liberal in their views, thus not reflecting the ordinary teaching authority of the Church. Some clergy hope that the selection will be made from local sources so the appointee will be sensitive to their problems. Others may feel that an "outsider" would supply a healing, objective touch.

The general process to select auxiliaries, ordinaries (diocesan bishops), and coadjutors is used to select archbishops. As noted above Latin Rite archbishops of the United States function as bishops within their archdioceses and metropolitans in their provinces. Apart from the Archdiocese of Washington, which includes the District of Columbia, five Maryland counties, and the Virgin Islands, eighteen provinces consist of one state apiece, six of two apiece, three of three apiece, and two of four apiece. The Archdiocese of San Francisco includes Northern California, Nevada, Utah, and Hawaii.

The candidate for this position is likely to be a diocesan bishop at the time of his appointment. Greater care and more people are consulted at this level, including some or all of the remaining archbishops. Some observers think that cardinals John O'Connor and William Baum, both members of the Congregation for Bishops, as well as Archbishop Justin Rigali, recently appointed archbishop of St. Louis, are especially influential. Others believe increasing conservatism of candidates is a trend in episcopal appointments beginning with Bernard Law of Boston in 1984.

In gathering information to make his report, the pro-nuncio is always aware that it will be sent to the Congregation for Bishops on its completion. The preparation of a ternus may require information from twenty to thirty people who may know the priest(s) under consideration. The diocesan bishops may suggest some of the names. Other informants may be diocesan officials or people the pro-nuncio knows personally. Religious and laity may also receive a questionnaire prepared by the Congregation for Bishops and used for all episcopal appointments. The covering letter sent by the pro-nuncio indicates it serves as an orientation and asks that answers be given in a discursive manner to develop observations. The writer is not to seek further data on the candidate, and is admonished not to discuss it with anyone, especially the candidate. A model of the questionnaire reads:

Confidential Vatican Questionnaire on Episcopal Candidate[13]

Please describe the nature of your association with the candidate and indicate the length of time that you have known him.

1.	Personal Characteristics:	Physical appearance; health; work capacity; family conditions especially regarding any manifestations of hered itary illnesses.
2.	Human Qualities:	Speculative and practical intellectual capacity; temperament and character; balance; serenity of judgement; sense of responsibility.
3.	Human, Christian, and Priestly Formation:	Possession and practice of human, Christian, and priestly virtues (prudence, justice, moral uprightness, loyalty, sobriety, faith, hope, charity, obedience, humility, piety; daily celebration of the Eucharist and of the Liturgy of the Hours, Marian devotion).
4.	Behavior:	Moral conduct; comportment with people in general and in the exercise of the priestly ministry in particular; the ability to establish friendships; rapport with civil authorities; respect and autonomy.

5. Cultural Preparation:	Competence and aggiornamento [being up-to-date] in ecclesiastical sciences; general culture; knowledge of and sensitivity toward problems of our time; facility with foreign languages; au thorship of books or magazine articles worthy of note.
6. Orthodoxy:	Adherence with conviction and loyalty to the doctrine and magisterium of the Church. In particular, the attitude of the candidate toward the documents of the Holy See on the Ministerial Priesthood, on the priestly ordination of women, on the Sacrament of Matrimony, on sexual ethics, and on social justice. Fidelity to the genuine ecclesial tradition and commitment to the authentic renewal promoted by the Second Vatican Council and by subsequent pontifical teachings.
7. Discipline:	Loyalty and docility to the Holy See, and the Hierarchy; esteem for and acceptance of priestly celibacy, as it has been set forth by the ecclesiastical Magisterium; respect for and observance of the general and particular norms governing divine worship and clerical office.
8. Pastoral Fitness and Experience:	Abilities, experience, and effectiveness in the pastoral ministry; evangelization and catechesis; preaching and teaching (preparation, public speaking capability); pastoral skills in sacramental and liturgical ministries (especially in the administration of the Sacrament of Penance and the celebration of the Eucharist); the fostering of vocations; sensitivity to the needs of the missions; a spirit of ecumenism; the formation of the laity in the apostolate (family life, youth, the promotion and defense of human rights, the world of labor, culture, and the media); the promotion of human causes and of social action with particular attention to the poor and the most needy.
9. Leadership Qualities:	A fatherly spirit, attitude of service, taking initiative; the ability to lead others, to dialogue, to, stimulate and receive cooperation, to analyze and organize and carry out decisions; to direct and engage in team work; appreciation for the role and the collaboration of religious and laity (both men and women) and for a just share of responsibilities; concern for the problems of the universal and local Church.

10. Administrative Skills:	Accountability for and proper use of Church goods; abilities and performance in fulfilling administrative tasks; sense of justice and spirit of detachment; openness in seeking the collaboration of experts in the field.
11. Public Esteem:	Estimation of the candidate on the part of confreres, the general public, and the civil authorities.
12. Your Judgment of the Candidate: Suitability for the Episcopacy:	His suitability for the episcopacy in general; in particular whether he would be more apt as a diocesan or an auxiliary bishop; whether in an urban, industrial, rural, large, medium, or small see.

13. Any additional Comments:

14. Names, addresses, and qualifications of others who know the candidate well (priests, religious men and women, laity), who are truly reliable, with good sense, prudence, and calm.

Judging from this questionnaire, pastoral characteristics are more important than administrative. Orthodoxy and loyalty to the Holy See are also valuable. Reese notes in *Archbishop* that the clerical sociologist and novelist Andrew M. Greeley has observed that, in terms of religious attitudes and sexual morality, bishops are more conservative than the clergy over fifty-five. And in matters of ecumenicism and social action bishops are more liberal than the clergy under thirty-six (Chapter One, Note 44; Greeley, *The Catholic Priest in the United States: Sociological Investigations* [Washington, DC: US Catholic Conference, 1972, 126]).

After examining questionnaire responses and preparing the ternus, the pronuncio makes his report, about twenty single-spaced pages in Italian, the working language of the Vatican Congregation for Bishops, for whom he prepares his report. He summarizes the respondents' opinions and adds his own. The report describes the diocese and the pro-nuncio's system in selecting candidates for submission. He makes up the list indicating the order of his preference with descriptions of each person named. He includes all pertinent documents he has received, with perhaps twenty or more letters for each candidate. As a bishop is better known than a priest, less documentation is needed. Depending on the size of the diocese and the degree of unanimity on candidates, the process may take several months. It should be clear that, due to his position and influence, the pro-nuncio (or apostolic delegate in some other countries) is crucial to the selection process. Mediating between the hierarchy and his Roman-superiors, his word carries substantial weight.

The next stage involves the Vatican Congregation for Bishops. Its head in 1994 is Cardinal Bernardin Gantin from the Benin Republic in West Africa. A skilled curialist he is the dean (leader) of the college of cardinals as bishop of Ostia. He is also titular bishop of Palestrina, having risen through all three ranks of the cardinalate within ten years. A priest for over forty years and an auxiliary and an archbishop in his own country for fourteen years, he began curial work in 1971. He has been prefect of the Congregation and president of the commission for Latin America since 1984. In addition he is a member of many congregations, tribunals, and councils.[14]

Originally known as the Consistorial Congregation, Pope Sixtus V established the Congregation for Bishops in 1588. St. Pius X (1908) and Pius XII (1952) extended its powers. Paul VI gave its present title in 1967 and John Paul II redefined its operations in 1988. Its functions involve bishops and their jurisdictions in many nations. It also supervises the Pontifical Commission for Latin America, a non-curial institute founded by Pius XII in 1958 and attached to the Congregation for Bishops by Paul VI in 1969. John Paul II established it in its present form in 1988. Since 1985 it has contained a central coordinating office for Military Vicars.[15]

The Vatican considered the United States a mission country until its removal from this status by Pope St. Pius X in 1908. Until that time episcopal appointments from 1789 on were made through the Congregation for the Evangelization of Peoples, which has competence over the Church's mission territories of the world, now principally in Africa and Asia. At first a commission of cardinals for missions in the East and West Indies it also served Italo-Greeks and church affairs in Protestant territories of Europe in the late sixteenth century. It later became a permanent congregation when it was organized by Pope Gregory XV in 1622. John Paul II redefined its functions in 1988.[16] Ironically, Cardinal Gantin's episcopal appointments went through this congregation.

The Congregation for Bishops deals with appointments, quinquennial reports and ad limina visits. When the pro-nuncio's reports come from America, an American priest on the congregation staff examines them to see if they are complete. He usually serves five years and also takes similar care of appointments from Canada and Australia. Another priest accepts materials from all of Europe except Italy, which two priests oversee. One priest will handle Brazil and another the rest of Latin America. Mission territory and appointments from most of Africa and Asia will be governed by the Congregation for the Evangelization of Peoples. Appointments for Eastern-rite churches in union with Rome will go through the Congregation for Oriental Churches. Established by Pope Pius IX in 1862, it has jurisdiction over territories where most Christians belong to Oriental Rites. These territories include Egypt, the Sinai Peninsula, Eritrea, Northern Ethopia, Southern Albania, Bulgaria, Cyprus, Greece, Iran, Iraq, Lebanon, Palestine, Syria, Jordan, Turkey, Afghanistan, and over minority communities of Orientals worldwide.[17] Other such appointments may be made through the synods of such churches.

It is up to the staff priest of the congregation to read the pro-nuncio's report and to become knowledgable about it. He must study the entire dossier, evaluate it, and recommend follow-ups on unanswered questions, unconsulted persons, and additional information. The cardinal prefect depends upon this staffer when he communicates with the pro-nuncio concerning reports. Staff workers expedite their work with typewriters and a photocopier. As late as 1989 files had not been computerized nor were word processors available.

The Congregation for Bishops deliberates twice monthly from October through June, taking a summer break. The pope appoints all members, who have five-year renewable terms. In 1987 the membership consisted of twenty-nine cardinals (with sixteen of them permanently stationed in Rome) and seven archbishops. The secretary of the Section for Relations with States (an archbishop) and the prefects (all cardinals) of the congregations of the Doctrine of the Faith, the Clergy, and of Catholic Education are ex-officio members.

The Congregation considers a priest's appointment to bishop. When a bishop is being promoted, the appointment is usually reviewed by the archbishops but may be considered by the prefect and his staff. In the latter case the staff prepares a three-to-five-page memorandum called a *Foglio d'Udienza* (session paper) which summarizes documents for the prefect to take to the pope in private audience. Cardinal Gantin ordinarily discusses the appointments at congregation meetings before going to the pope. If the appointment is considered vital and cannot wait, the prefect may consider it with one to three members of his congregation. It is customary to let American appointments wait until resumption of business in October.

In 1992 three American cardinals, William Baum, John O'Connor, and Edmund Szoka were members of the congregation. Cardinals Baum and Szoka are stationed in Rome as curial officials. Cardinal O'Connor, though a residential archbishop of New York, takes pains to learn Italian and to be a present and effective member considering American appointments. Cardinal Pio Laghi, ex-officio as prefect of the congregation for Catholic Education, is Italian and highly skilled. He served in America as apostolic delegate and later as pro-nuncio for ten years. Earlier in his career he was in the United States as secretary of the apostolic delegation. The American archbishop Justin Rigali served four years as president of the Pontifical Ecclesiastical Academy (a training center for diplomats) followed by five years as secretary of the Congregation for Bishops. In his current position as archbishop of St. Louis he is likely to become a cardinal in the near future. His past experience makes it likely he will be given membership in the congregation.

The undersecretary of the congregation chooses a cardinal *ponente* (presenter, sometimes called a *relator* or summarizer) to review an appointee's dossier and to provide a summary of it to the other cardinals at the regular meeting. The *ponente* synthesizes, analyzes and presents the entire picture to the rest of the congregation. He needs fluency in English to read all the material as only the pro-nuncio's report is in Italian. While the position of *ponente* is rotated, many members of the congregation can read and understand English. Meetings themselves are held in Italian.

Cardinal Gantin provides a yearly schedule of meetings so participants can arrange their calendars to attend. Members receive the agenda two weeks before a meeting, which usually consists of four or five documents with appointments up for consideration. Until recently only those attending the meeting were given the pro-nuncio's report. Cardinal O'Connor receives copies of all congregation documents in New York, If he cannot attend a meeting, he telephones or mails in his vote.

From October through June meetings are usually held at the Vatican on Thursday. About fifteen cardinals attend the average meeting with the secretary and undersecretary of the congregation and no other staff members. The cardinal *ponente* gives his report and the members discuss the appointment under the chairmanship of the prefect. Some believe that if the appointee has been educated in Rome he has an advantage. In 1989 some thirty-seven percent of American bishops and half of the archbishops had studied in Rome. Some think the training they receive there more than the sum of earned degrees. The vote comes after discussion. In the large majority of cases the congregation follows the recommendation of the pro-nuncio. This is especially true if the local hierarchy concurred in the choice. The congregation may select the pro-nuncio's second or third choice. Sometimes the ternus is rejected and the pro-nuncio is told to present a new one.

If the members of the Congregation for Bishops submit a favorable recommendation, the prefect presents the pro-nuncio's, the congregation's, and his own report to the pope in a Saturday audience. The prefect's report consists of a three-to-five page staff-prepared memorandum on the appointment. The prefect summarizes the discussion of the congregation and reports dissenting opinions and votes.

The pope is able to initiate and veto appointments of bishops due to a long historical process. While he may choose any priest he wants to, practicality requires he be aided in the process of selection. In any given year he may make more than a hundred appointments. In 1993 he appointed 114 new bishops, and he ordained fourteen of them personally. Since he became pope in 1978, he has appointed over 1600 bishops.[18]

In its first three centuries of the Church, the clergy and the people of the local community had the right to choose leaders. Gradually over time and particularly after the rise of the Frankish kings in the sixth century, the people meant princes and the powerful and the clergy meant the cathedral chapter or staff. The concept of "fullness of papal power" was defined at the First Vatican Council (1869-1870) as a supreme and distinct legal power "over all the churches, shepherds and faithful, both together and separately."[19]

Gratian (d. 1160) writes in his *Decretum*, (*Distinctions* 62 and 63) (1140): "The clergy is to elect, the people to consent." In the medieval western church between the twelfth and fourteenth centuries, the centralization of power began. As early as 1180 Pope Alexander III writes to the Chapter of Bremen: "Layfolk should not be admitted to vote." By the mid-twelfth century only the clergy in a bishop's town took part in bishop selection.

As ambitions and factions divided the electors, they increasingly submitted elections to Rome for arbitration. The pope began to make his own choices. Popes Gregory IX (1227-1241) and Innocent IV (1243-1254) cited Albigensianism as a threat to church survival. This heresy, which taught that matter was evil and denied Christ's humanity, was thought to undermine papal authority. Popes started to insist that their legates approve clerical choices. Louis IX of France protested what he considered interferences with elections. Innocent IV responded in 1252 by revoking some of his own direct nominations made, he said, as a result of "improper requests".

The general trend could not be altered. In 1278 Pope Nicholas III substituted the pope for ordinary authorities (cathedral chapters or metropolitans) in the case of disputed elections, transferences, resignations, suspensions, or dismissals. In 1363 Urban V proclaimed his rights to designate patriarchs, archbishops, bishops, abbots and abbesses throughout Christendom. This effectively ended a process begun when Gregory VII (1073-1085) or his delegate would impose a choice.[20]

Curiously and possibly because the Vatican's interests in 1789 were concerned with revolutionary and post-revolutionary activities in France and their effects on the Church, the appointment of a bishop in the then mission territory of America did not seem a matter of great concern. John Carroll, a member of a prominent Maryland family, had returned to America in 1773. He did so when Pope Clement XIV (himself a Franciscan) suppressed his own Jesuit order for unsubstantiated charges due to political intrigue in Portugal, France and Spain. (The society was restored by Pope Pius VII in 1814.)

In 1776 Carroll, at the request of the Continental Congress, undertook a diplomatic mission to Canada to win Catholic support for the colonists' cause. The committee included his cousin Charles Carroll and Samuel Chase (a Maryland Protestant), and was headed by Benjamin Franklin. Though the mission ultimately failed due to the hostility of the Canadian Catholics toward America, Franklin and John Carroll became good friends. Eight years later (1784) in Paris Franklin recommended Carroll to the papal nuncio to France for the leadership of American Catholics. As Franklin recalls in his *Private Journal*:

> The Pope's Nuncio called and acquainted me that the Pope had, on my recommendation, appointed Mr. [sic] John Carroll superior of the Catholic clergy in America, with many of the powers of a bishop; and that probably he would be made a bishop *in partibus* [a titular bishop bearing the title of an extinct see] before the end of the year. . . .[21]

Though he was now "Superior of the Missions in the thirteen United States of North America, " Carroll did not become the first American bishop until five years later. Even so, the Select Body of the Clergy, the organization of American priests he founded, had wanted the Rev. John Lewis, the last superior of the Maryland Jesuits before the order was suppressed. Lewis's age and infirmity gave Carroll the position, which he accepted fearing the appointment of a foreign bishop for America.

With Anglican bishops being selected for America, Roman Catholics became less intransigent about a bishop of their own. Carroll knew without episcopal ordination he would be unable to ordain new priests nor gain significance with the Vatican. The twenty-five priests of the United States wanted to choose their own bishop and nominate him themselves. They took this position to avoid the notion that American Catholics (all 40,000 of them in a general population of four million) were under foreign control. Carroll agreed to this, as did the Roman authorities. For comparative purposes the 1993 *Official Catholic Directory* lists forty-two archbishops, 351 bishops, 50,907 priests in dioceses, and 59,220,723 Catholics in a population of 256,042,585.[22]

The American priests sent a petition for appointment of a bishop to Pope Pius VI on 12 March 1788. It was acted upon favorably two months later on 23 June. The priests voted their choice on 18 May 1789 at Whitemarsh, Maryland, eighteen days after the inauguration of George Washington as first president of the United States in New York. John Carroll received twenty-four of the twenty-five votes cast. What happened next is described by John Tracy Ellis in "The Appointment of Bishops and the Selection of Candidates in the United States since Vatican II":

> 'WE, FOR the first time only. . .permitted the said priests to elect and to present to this apostolic See.' ['The Brief *Ex hac apostolicae* of Pope Pius VI Erecting the Diocese of Baltimore and Appointing John Carroll as the First Bishop, 6 November 1789' John Tracy Ellis, ed. *Documents of American Catholic History* (Chicago 1967) I, 165.] Such were the words used by Pius VI in the bull of 6 November 1789, that designated John Carroll to be Bishop of Baltimore, the first episcopal appointment in the United States. Actually, the priests voted twice more in selective [sic] Carroll's two coadjutor bishops, but after 1795 the practice lapsed for almost a century until 1885 when the diocesan consultors and irremovable pastors were given the right to present a *terna* for a vacant diocese, a right that was cancelled by Rome in 1916.[23]

The Right Reverend Charles Walmesley, Titular Bishop of Rama and Vicar Apostolic of the Western District of England, consecrated John Carroll bishop on 15 August 1790, in the chapel of Lulworth Castle, Dorset, England. He became the first American archbishop on 8 April 1808.[24]

Currently John Paul II makes his decision after the prefect explains the vacancy and informs him of his options and what the pro-nuncio and the congregation has recommended. About five percent of the time he may wait or read all documentation or consult other advisers. He may know bishops who are candidates for office, as he is widely travelled. If his advisers, such as the prefect and the congregation or the congregation and the pro-nuncio disagree, the pope would have to choose.

The pope gives the general orientation and direction to the congregation, the pro-nuncio, and the bishops. He looks for good pastors with solid, intellectual knowledge of theology. In speaking to American bishops in Rome in 1983 John Paul II stressed unity and fidelity to the magisterium. He wants those loyal to the Church's teaching authority to teach it. He has increased the average age of appointments from about fifty-nine in 1978 to nearly sixty-four in 1988 and increased the number of religious-order bishops more than one-fourth.

When the pope has made his decision, the Congregation for Bishops notifies the pro-nuncio, who then notifies the nominee and asks for his choice. The entire process from vacancy to appointment may take four to eight months, sometimes longer. Usually the pro-nuncio telephones the candidate or his bishop. On acceptance the new bishop or archbishop often telegraphs the pro-nuncio with a coded message, such as, "Diocesan report on its way." In the event of rejection (about one out of every twenty), the candidate says something like "After having consulted with my spiritual father, I respectfully decline." The pro-nuncio notifies Rome and sets a date for the announcement (with a week or so elapsing), usually on Tuesday. The newly selected prelate may not tell anybody until the announcement.

Throughout the pro-nuncio can help or hurt the candidate's chances by drawing up the ternus for diocesan bishops or influence or veto the ternus drawn up by the diocesan bishop for auxiliaries. His report in Italian is the primary document upon which the Congregation for Bishops and later the pope act. As late as the 1950s all documents were put into Latin.

Bishops initiate the process and provide a pool of candidates by nominating priests in province meetings and drawing up a ternus for their auxiliaries. Three-fourths of all American bishops entered the hierarchy as auxiliaries, including fifty-seven percent of diocesan bishops. Their suggestions can influence the pro-nuncio's ternus. The retiring diocesan bishop or administrator determines the need for consultations on diocesan needs and qualities desired in the next bishop. They recommend names of people to be consulted about the diocese and the appointment to the pro-nuncio. The questionnaires to be filled out by various people carry weight depending upon detailed knowledge.

The Congregation for Bishops and its prefect provide a check on the work of the pro-nuncio. American members of the congregation can certainly help by attending meetings and making their preferences felt. At the end the pope can set the tone and criteria for nominations and evaluations. He works through the congregation and the pro-nuncio, but he can replace them if he disapproves their decisions. Always the process at all levels depends upon the good will of everyone in trying to bring suitable people who will build up the Church to the attention of the decision makers.

As Thomas J. Reese notes in *Archbishop,* not every quarter is pleased with every phase of the episcopal selection process. American bishops before 1893 did not have to depend upon the apostolic delegate. The bishops of the province submitted names directly to the Vatican. The NCCB Committee on the Selection of Bishops might like to meet to make recommendations when an archdiocese is vacant. In 1972 the Canon Law Society of America wanted each diocese to have a committee for the selection of candidates for the office of bishop to receive nominations from individuals and groups. They envisioned an eleven-member committee with one member to be appointed by the bishop and the rest to be elected by the diocesan pastoral council (two each from diocesan priests, religious women, religious men, laywomen, and laymen). The committee would consider nominees and the state of the dioceses and submit its report and a list of nominees to the priests' council. The council would review the report, provide additional comments, and narrow the committee's list to not more than ten names. The report and names would be given to the diocesan bishop who would make his own enquiry concerning the merits of the candidates proposed. At the spring meeting bishops in each region of the NCCB would study candidates proposed and voted on by the bishops. The results would be forwarded to the NCCB Committee on Selection of Bishops, which would finish the list of candidates for the particular office of bishop. In filling a particular office, the Holy See would limit itself to three to five names submitted by the NCCB Committee.

Others would like to see group consultations so consensus could develop. Some want the bishop elected directly by priests, a priests' council, or a body of priests and laity in the diocese with confirmation and acceptance by the pope. Priests would like to elect bishops: seventy percent of priests and twenty-four percent of bishops favor this approach. Election by the priests, religious and laity of a diocese is favored by sixty-five percent of priests and twenty-four percent of bishops. Vatican officials and most bishops oppose making the process more democratic and public, thinking there would be too much potential for politics, pressure groups, and divisive factions. Critics say the system responds to cliques in Rome.

Priests can have an impact in recommending names to bishops and the pronuncio and by filling out questionnaires on candidates. Lay participants can describe the needs of the diocese and the kind of bishop they would like. Bishops must serve their spiritual needs and be their pastoral leader. In 1974 the National Federation of Priests' Councils prepared materials on the selection of bishops to be used by them when their diocese might need a bishop.[25]

In conclusion, we may say that the selection of bishops in the Roman Catholic Church is an institutional process which yields varying results. Over time the pope may shape it by appointing his delegates, the members of the congregations for Bishops and the Evangelization of Peoples, and bishops and archbishops throughout the world. He cannot spend as much time as he would like on each appointment. Instead he establishes a cadre of suitable officials. At the present time one may only hope that enough people make evaluations sufficient to eliminate the unworthy and to advance the causes of those who will exercise their best efforts over their jurisdictions.

F. Types and Duties of Bishops

We have already seen the origins of bishop, archbishop and metropolitan in the Roman Catholic Church. We have observed the development of those offices from biblical times, education and selection processes, and the theology and authority of the episcopate. In this section we will discuss types of bishops, their duties from selection to retirement, and conclude with the way a Texas bishop spent the year 1993.

The organization and government of the Church centers around the pope and the bishops. The pope is the supreme head of the Church with primacy of honor and jurisdiction. To Catholics he is the vicar of Jesus Christ, the successor of St. Peter, and the Supreme Pontiff (bishop). From early times he has also been known as the Servant of the Servants of God. His other titles are specifically territorial. They are Bishop of Rome, Patriarch of the West, Primate of Italy, Archbishop and Metropolitan of the Roman Province, and Sovereign of the State of Vatican City. He is the head of all bishops, who are in union with and subordinate to him. As successor of St. Peter, Prince of the Apostles, he has authority over the other bishops, considered by the Church as the successors of the Apostles.

This arrangement cares for and continues Christ's mission worldwide. While the bishops serve the people in their own dioceses (local churches), they share a common concern and effort for the general welfare of the Church with the pope and one another. Subject only to the pope, Eastern Rite patriarchs are bishops and heads of their rites throughout the world.

The Council of Nicaea (325) recognized the bishops of Alexandria and Antioch in the East, and of Rome in the West as patriarchs. The First Council of Constantinople (381) added the bishop of Constantinople to the list and ranked him immediately after the pope. The Council of Chalcedon (451) seconded the action of Constantinople and acknowledged the bishop of Jerusalem as a patriarch. It established the order of precedence as Rome, Constantinople, Alexandria, Antioch, and Jerusalem. And the Fourth Lateran Council (1215) gave this ranking full recognition.

At present there is one Eastern Rite patriarch of Alexandria (for the Copts), and three of Antioch (for the Syrians, the Maronites, and the Greek Melkites, the last having the personal title of Greek Melkite patriarch of Alexandria and of Jerusalem). There are also patriarchs of Babylon (for the Chaldeans) and of Sis or Cicilia (for the Armenians). All are elected by bishops of their own rites and receive approval and the pallium from the pope.

During the Crusades (1097-1265) Latin Rite patriarchates were established for Antioch, Jerusalem, Alexandria, and Constantinople. Three later became patriarchates in name only, but Pope Pius IX reconstituted Jerusalem in 1847. Pope Paul VI abolished the Latin titular patriarchates of Constantinople, Alexandria, and Antioch as an appeasing gesture to the Eastern Rites in 1964. Titular patriarchates (in name only) of the Latin Rite include Lisbon, Venice, and the East Indies. The patriarchates of Lisbon and of Venice are held by cardinals, and the archbishop of Goa and Danao in India is the patriarch of the East Indies. The patriarchate of the West Indies has been vacant since 1963.

Cardinals are bishops or archbishops who assist the pope, acting in his name in the central government and administration of the Church and of the Roman Curia. Others are residential archbishops. In the recent past prominent theologians and patriarchs were selected. All are chosen by the pope and collectively form the College of Cardinals. The name "cardinal" comes from the Latin *cardō* (hinge) and cardinals are called Princes of the Church.

The college evolved from synods of Roman clergy with whom popes directed church affairs in the first eleven centuries. The first cardinals of about the sixth century were priests of the leading churches of Rome assigned liturgical, advisory and administrative duties with the Holy See and the regional deacons of Rome. All Latin Rite cardinals are aggregated to the clergy of Rome, signified by the assignment of each cardinal (except the patriarchs) of a special (or titular) church in Rome. The Eastern Rite patriarchs, who are eligible for college membership, are ranked after the cardinal bishops in order of precedence.

The college achieved its present form in 1150 and in 1179 selection to it was reserved exclusively to the pope. Pope Sixtus V fixed the number of the college at seventy in 1586. In 1959 Pope John XXIII set this ruling aside. There is no specific limitation currently, though not more than 120 at one time may be papal electors. The title of cardinal was reserved to members of the college in 1567. It was used previously by priests attached to parish churches of Rome and by the leading clergy of other notable churches.

The Code of Canon Law of 1917 (effective 1918) required that all cardinals be priests. Pope John XXIII required that they be bishops in 1962, and this ruling was incorporated in the 1983 Code of Canon Law.[1] Pope Paul VI in 1970 (effective 1971) decided that all cardinals cease to be members of curial departments and offices and are ineligible as papal electors on attaining the age of eighty. Thereafter they retain membership in the college with the rights and privileges of their rank.

The three categories of collegial membership are cardinal bishops, cardinal priests, and cardinal deacons. Cardinal bishops include the titular bishops of the suburban sees neighboring Rome and Eastern patriarchs (if any). The dean of the college is Bishop of Ostia, as well as his other suburban see. These sees are Palestrina, Porto-Santa Ruffina, Albano, Velletri-Segni, Frascati, and Sabina-Poggia Mirteto. These cardinals serve full-time in the central administration of church affairs within the Roman Curia. Pope Paul VI recognized the patriarchs as heads of ancient liturgies and sees of apostolic origin in 1965. Their dignity and titles antedate those of cardinals. At present patriarchs could be included as cardinals at their own requests.

Cardinal priests, formerly pastors of leading churches in Rome, are bishops whose dioceses lie outside Rome. Cardinal deacons, formerly chosen according to regional divisions of Rome, are titular bishops assigned to full-time service in the Roman Curia. The dean and sub-dean of the college are elected by the cardinal bishops from among their number, subject to the approval of the pope. The dean (or the sub-dean in the dean's absence) presides over the college as the first among equals.

The pope first selects the cardinals by announcing their names at a secret consistory which he and the other members (who approve the nominations) attend. The new cardinals receive a document called a *biglietto* (literally, a ticket). In other and more public ceremonies they receive a red biretta and a ring and concelebrate Mass with the pope and their fellow cardinals. A cardinal *in pectore (petto)* (in the chest) is selected by the pope, but his name is not disclosed. He has no title, rights or duties until such disclosure is made. Then he takes precedence from the time of the secret election.

Subject to the Holy Father and directly responsible to him for their ministries are resident archbishops and metropolitans (heads of provinces), resident bishops (heads of dioceses), vicars and prefects apostolic (heads of vicariates apostolic and of prefectures apostolic), certain abbots and prelates, and apostolic administrators. Each of these, within his own territory and according to canon law, has ordinary jurisdiction over pastors (responsible for administering parishes), priests, religious, and lay persons. Also subject to the Holy Father are titular archbishops and bishops (who have delegated jurisdiction), religious orders and congregations of pontifical right, pontifical institutes and faculties, papal nuncios and apostolic delegates.

Of these we have discussed resident archbishops and metropolitans in the first section, pontifical institutes and faculties in connection with education, and nuncios and delegates in the previous section. We may define abbot simply as the superior of a monastery for men. An abbess is a woman superior of a convent of women.

Prelates are clerics with the authority of public office in the church; that is, those having jurisdiction in the external forum. These clerics include the pope, patriarchs, residential archbishops and bishops, certain abbots, vicars and prefects apostolic, vicars general, and certain superiors in clerical exempt religious communities. Titular archbishops and bishops without ordinary jurisdiction are not prelates in the strict sense of the term. Neither are pastors, who have very little jurisdiction in the external forum. Honorary prelates belonging to the Pontifical Household are Apostolic Protonotaries, Honorary Prelates of His Holiness, and Chaplains of His Holiness. Their title is Reverend Monsignor.

Before attempting to discuss the meaning of clergy, from which such words as clergyman, cleric, clerical, and clerk derive, we should understand what is meant by "jurisdiction in the external forum". In the Catholic Church a forum is the sphere in which the exercise of ecclesiastical authority or jurisdiction takes place. A forum may be internal or external. In the internal forum the exercise of authority deals with matters affecting the private spiritual good of individuals. The administration of the sacraments takes place in the sacramental forum. Other exercises of such jurisdiction take place in the non-sacramental forum.

Those persons having jurisdiction in the external forum exercise authority dealing with matters affecting the public welfare of the Church and its members. Those with such authority because of their offices (for example, diocesan bishops) are called ordinaries. An ordinary has the jurisdiction of an office and ordinaries include the pope, diocesan bishops, vicars general, prelates of missionary territories, vicars apostolic, prefects apostolic, vicars capitular (an ecclesiastical agent in charge of a vacated see), superiors general, abbots primate and other major superiors of men Religious. Some prelates and abbots, with jurisdiction similar to diocesan bishops, are pastors of the faithful in territories (prelatures and abbacies) not under the jurisdiction of diocesan bishops.[2]

The word "clergy" comes originally from the Greek *klēros* (lot, inheritance, or share). It recalls the biblical passage in Deuteronomy 18:1-2, in which

Moses says:

> 'The priestly tribe of Levi is not to receive any share of land in Israel; instead, they are to live on the offerings and other sacrifices given to the LORD. They are to own no land, as the other tribes do; their share is the privilege of being the LORD's priests, as the LORD has promised.'

The word evolved from Late Greek *klērikos*, late Latin *clericus*, Old French *clerc* and Old English *cleric* or *clerc*, to Middle English *clerk*.

At this point in the etymology of "clergy" we observe a useful division. Old English *cleric* in Modern English means a member of the clergy or one in orders below the rank of priest. The word retains its ecclesiastical meaning. In going from Old English *clerc* to Middle English *clerk*, however, we find secular meanings as well. Scholar is an archaic meaning of clerk (which the English rhyme with lark).

Readers of English literature may remember Chaucer's Clerk of Oxenford from the "General Prologue" to *The Canterbury Tales* (circa 1390; lines 285-308). This gaunt personage studied philosophy to the exclusion or churchly or secular work. But "gladly wolde he lerne and gladly teche."[3] Restricting our inquiry to Chaucer we find the word "clerk" used variously in *The Canterbury Tales* and in *The House of Fame* (circa 1379-1380) to mean a member of the clergy, a minor cleric, a student, a learned person, an author, or a writer, as well as a scholar.[4] Of course clerk can also mean an official responsible for correspondence, records, and accounts, one employed to keep records or accounts or to perform general office work, and one who works at a sales or service counter. All of these meanings suggest an official in charge.

Going back to Old French *clerc* (clergyman), denoting one possessing knowledge, we come to Middle English *clergie*. It is similar to the Modern English word, meaning either a group ordained to perform pastoral or sacerdotal functions in a Christian church or an official or sacerdotal class of a non-Christian religion. Our meaning, then, is a group of men ordained to holy orders and assigned to pastoral or other ministries of the people and of the church.[5] In the Roman Catholic Church there are diocesan (secular) and regular (religious) clergies.

Diocesan clergy serve in parishes and in other capacities in a local church (diocese) under the direction of their bishop, to whom they are bound by a promise of obedience. Regular clergy are so-called because they observe the rule (*regula* in Latin) in their respective institutes (orders, congregations, or societies). They are committed to the ways of life and apostolates of their institutes. In ordinary pastoral ministry, they are under the direction of local bishops as well as their own superiors.

We have discussed residential archbishops (bishops with the title of an archdiocese) and metropolitans (an archbishop in an ecclesiastical province with full powers of bishop in his own archdiocese and limited supervisory jurisdiction and influence over the other [suffragan] provincial dioceses). The pallium, which the pope confers, is the symbol of the metropolitan.

A coadjutor archbishop is an assistant archbishop with the right of succession. A titular archbishop (like a titular bishop, a coadjutor bishop or an auxiliary bishop) has a title of an extinct see. Such titles are now given to curial archbishops, papal nuncios, and apostolic delegates. The titular sees were once active but were later overrun by pagans or by Moslems and were then granted *in partibus infidelium* (Latin for "in the lands of the unbelievers"). They can also be sees which no longer exist, such as Walla Walla or Natchez in the United States. A titular bishop or archbishop lacks ordinary jurisdiction over a diocese or archdiocese.

An archbishop *ad personam* is a bishop granted a title of personal honor and distinction. Like a titular archbishop he does not have ordinary jurisdiction over an archdiocese. A primate is a title given to the ranking prelate of some countries or regions. The pope is the primate of Italy. The archbishop of Esztergom is the primate of Hungary and the archbishop of Gniezno and Warsaw is the primate of Poland.

Turning our attention to bishops, a diocesan (or residential) bishop has charge of a diocese. A coadjutor is an assistant (or auxiliary) bishop to a diocesan bishop with the right of succession to the see. An auxiliary (or assistant) bishop also assists the diocesan bishop. He may or may not become a diocesan bishop in his own or another see. Both a coadjutor and an auxiliary bishop are titular bishops. An apostolic administrator is usually a bishop administering an ecclesiastical jurisdiction temporarily. But a priest might be the administrator of a vacated see until the regular appointment of a diocesan bishop. A vicar apostolic is usually a titular bishop who has ordinary jurisdiction over a mission territory called a vicariate apostolic, which is not constituted as a diocese. An exarch is an Eastern Rite bishop, while an exarch ranks below a patriarch and above a metropolitan.[6]

A prefect apostolic is a prelate having ordinary jurisdiction over a mission territory called a prefecture apostolic. A vicar general is a bishop's deputy for the administration of a diocese. An episcopal vicar is a deputy appointed by a residential bishop for a certain part of a diocese, a determined type of apostolic work, or the faithful of a certain rite or ethnic makeup. A prefect apostolic, a vicar general, and an episcopal vicar may or may not be a bishop.[7]

With these basic definitions we can examine some boundaries set upon bishops by canon law.[8] Canon law itself is not merely prescriptive but sets certain standards and conditions indicating limits of authority a prelate may possess. As we shall see below, there are other factors controlling a bishop's administration.

We have discussed earlier the qualifications and selection processes of a Roman Catholic bishop. We turn now to the diocesan bishop following his selection, in particular the scope of his authority, how he takes over his diocese, his pastoral role, his relationship to his priests, and his responsibility to foster religious vocations. After stating his teaching office, canons treat aspects of his sanctifying ministry, his obligation to say Mass for the people, his Eucharistic presidency role, and his exercise of pontificals.

A general canon clarifies the bishop's legislative, administrative, and judicial functions. He is called upon to encourage common discipline and to prevent various abuses. And he is the legal representative of the diocese. His responsibility to oversee the apostolate and to exhort the participation of the faithful is followed by obligations of residence, diocesan visitation, a quinquennial report and an *ad limina* visit. Finally two canons discuss retirement and specify provisions for the retired bishop.

The newly promoted priest receives episcopal consecration within three months from the arrival of his letter of appointment from Rome and before he begins his duties (c. 379). Prior to the 1983 Code of Canon Law one normally received consecration within three months of his nomination and was required to go to the diocese of his appointment within four months. The consecration calls for a papal mandate (c. 1013) and the law specifies the consecrating bishops (c. 1014). So serious is the requirement of the papal mandate for episcopal consecration that a bishop consecrating another bishop without it may be excommunicated (c. 1382). The new bishop cannot take canonical possession of his diocese without professing his faith and taking an oath of fidelity to the Apostolic See (i.e., the pope) with a formula approved by it (c. 380). Entering a communion of bishops requires the profession of faith (c. 833, §4) and public loyalty to the pope by the bishop-designate.

Within his own diocese a bishop possesses all requisite power to exercise his office save for those cases reserved by law or pontifical decree for its use of that of some other church authority. The Church states that bishops govern their dioceses as "vicars and legates of Christ".[9] This is held to be a divine power in its own right and is not derived from the papacy.[10] The power of the bishop is ordinary (a part of his office), immediate (exercised directly by him without an intermediary), and proper (exercised in his own name). It is operative in legislative, judicial, and administrative matters (c. 391, §1) throughout the Church's work, including the offices of teaching, sanctifying, and governing. A bishop is not granted faculties so much as powers subject to papal reservations.[11] The bishop is presumed to have all power necessary for his ministry. Although he has increased discretional powers of office, he remains within a hierarchical structure both above and below him. The pope's prerogatives grant him the ability to safeguard the unity of all the churches. The bishop must not be arbitrary, for he is the center of ministry within his own diocese. He must fulfill his mission always according to the norm of law (c. 381, §1).

The bishop has discretion to comparable authority figures presiding over particular churches other than dioceses. Such persons are territorial prelates, territorial abbots, apostolic vicars, apostolic prefects, and apostolic administrators (c. 368). The nature of the matter or a specific legal prescription might preclude such a person enjoying the same canonical status. Such a figure who is not a bishop could not ordain (c. 381, §2).

When a bishop is promoted to a diocese, he cannot exercise that office until he first takes canonical possession of it. He can exercise the offices which he already had in the same diocese at the time of his promotion. Canon 409, §2 provides that unless other provisions have been made by the competent authority when a see is vacated, an auxiliary bishop retains just those powers and faculties he had as vicar general or as episcopal vicar while the see was filled until a new bishop takes possession of that see. If he has not been designated diocesan administrator, he may exercise this same legal power under authority of the diocesan administrator who governs the diocese during the interim (c. 382, §1).

Unless legitimately impeded, the bishop-designate must canonically possess his diocese within four months from the time he receives the apostolic letter of appointment if he has not been consecrated a bishop. Or he must possess his diocese within two months if he has already been consecrated (c. 382, §2).

Before he can take possession of a diocese, the bishop personally (or through a proxy) presents the apostolic letter to the college of consultors within the diocese. This requirement must be in the presence of the chancellor of the curia who officially records the event. In the case of a newly-created diocese, he takes canonical possession as soon as he communicates the apostolic letter to the clergy and the people present in the cathedral church, with the senior priest among those officially recording the event (c. 382, §3). The act of taking canonical possession should occur within a liturgical act in the cathedral church with the clergy and the people assisting (c. 382, §4).

Unlike the code provisions of 1917, the present code differentiates between the bishop-designate who is already a bishop (two months) and the one not yet a bishop (four months) regarding the time in which to take possession. The letter of appointment is to be presented to the college of consultors instead of to the cathedral chapter. The college represents all diocesan priests and replaces the presbyteral council during the vacancy of the see. And it also replaces the cathedral chapter unless in a given area the chapter becomes the college of consultors (see c. 502, §3).

The present code distinguishes between an established diocese and one newly created regarding the method of taking possession. In presenting the letter of appointment to the clergy and the people of the diocese at the cathedral, the new bishop symbolizes the unity in diversity of the people in a diocese. Finally the 1983 Code encourages the taking possession to be celebrated liturgically at the cathedral so it may be seen as a church reality and not just as a bureaucratic formality.

As a pastor the bishop must be concerned with all the people of his diocese. These include transients, those who cannot receive ordinary pastoral care, and those no longer practicing their religion (c. 383, §1). He must provide for the spiritual needs of those of other rites with priests or parishes of that rite or by means of an episcopal vicar (c. 383, §2). He is to promote ecumenism to those not in full communion with the Catholic Church through kindness and charity (c. 383, §3). And he is to consider the non-baptized as "committed to him in the Lord" so that they not be excluded from Christian charity (c. 383, §4).

Canon 383 is based upon parts of Sections 16, 18, and 23 of Vatican II "Decree on the Pastoral Office of Bishops in the Church". It stresses the scope of the bishop's pastoral concerns and indicates groups of people who are included in his pastoral care such as migrants, refugees, tourists, the faithful of a different rite, members of other Christian communions, and those not baptized.[12]

The bishop is to attend to his priests with "special concern" and listen to them "as his assistants and advisers". He is to protect their rights and see that they fulfill correctly their obligations in their spiritual and intellectual life. The bishop must provide for their "decent support and social assistance" within the norm of law (c. 384). This injunction to listen, to take the pastoral contributions seriously as well as the protection of their rights and obligations echoes Canons

273 through 389.

Canon 384 derives from Section 16 of the "Decree on the Pastoral Office of Bishops in the Church". The responsibility to support the spiritual and intellectual development of priests is found in Canon 179 and their support through pension and health insurance in Canon 281. Priests may be listened to through the college of consultors and the presbyteral council as well as individuals. The presbyteral council is not only for issues specified in law but for all significant matters of pastoral importance (c. 500, §2).

The bishop must foster religious, priestly, and missionary vocations, as well as all ministries (c. 385). Canon 233 speaks of the special episcopal responsibility to foster priestly vocations, especially late vocations. Canon 782, §1 refers to the bishop's missionary responsibility and Canon 791, 1° to his task of fostering missionary vocations. The bishop must see all ecclesial gifts are recognized and utilized for service in the church.

Just as Canon 385 refers to Section 15 of the "Decree on the Pastoral Office of Bishops in the Church," Canon 386 summarizes certain aspects of Sections 12 through 14. As a teacher the diocesan bishop preaches and explains church doctrine and applies it to moral issues (§1). He must preserve doctrine and acknowledge the freedom of its investigation (§2). The Christian scholar also has freedom of inquiry and a basic right to express opinions in areas of his or her competency with due regard for the Church's hierarchical ordinary teaching authority (c. 218). In the 1983 Code of Canon Law the teaching authority of the bishop is expressed in Book III on the Church's teaching office and specifically in references to preaching (cc. 762-772) and catechetics (cc. 773-780).

Mindful of his need to witness for holiness, charity, humility, and simplicity in his own life, the bishop must promote the holiness of the Christian faithful and have those for which he is responsible grow in grace in the sacraments and through the risen Christ (c. 387). This canon draws upon the same section of the "Decree on the Pastoral Office of Bishops in the Church" as Canon 385 in stressing personal sanctity and that of others. In his liturgical efforts the bishop works to deepen the life of faith of his people and to enrich their understanding of Christ's resurrection. In the 1983 Code Book IV treats the Church's sanctifying office. Canon 835, §1 discusses the bishop's sanctifying function and his role as moderator, promoter, and protector of the liturgical life of the Church. Canon 838, §1 states the bishop's responsibility to issue liturgical norms within his competency. These canons frame the specific provisions of the bishop's liturgical supervisory role. In the 1917 Code the bishop's liturgical responsibility was to implement universal norms in his diocese. He was given no real discretionary authority to shape liturgical discipline in the light of his own diocesan needs.

After taking possession of his diocese, the bishop must apply a Mass for his people on Sundays and other holy days of obligation within his region (c. 388, §1). He must personally celebrate and apply Mass for the people on these days unless legitimately hindered. In this case he must apply Mass through another priest on these days or personally on other days (§2). He may apply one Mass for all dioceses entrusted to him, even under title of administration (§3). If the obligation is not satisfied timely, the bishop must apply as many Masses for the people as he has missed as soon as he can (§4). The bishop's role as high priest of the diocese implies this special obligation (c. 1246). Pastors in their parishes are bound comparably in their liturgical presidency role (c. 534). The seriousness of this episcopal obligation is like the strictness of the law on Mass offerings (cc. 945-958).

The diocesan bishop must preside frequently over the Eucharistic celebration in the cathedral or other church within his diocese, especially on holy days of obligation and other solemnities (c. 389). This canon derives from Section 41 of "The Constitution on the Sacred Liturgy" of Vatican II.[13] Canon 899, §2 addresses the central role of the bishop in Eucharistic celebrations on the diversity of roles within the celebration. Canon 837, §1 sees the Church itself as a sacrament of unity, a holy people led by the bishop. Celebrations in the cathedral further reflect the centrality of the occasions of worship.

Pontifical functions can be conducted by the bishop within his own diocese but require the express or presumed consent of the local ordinary outside it (c. 390). These are occasions which require the use of pontifical insignia, the mitre (headdress) and crozier (staff). Within his diocese the bishop has legislative, executive, and judicial powers within the norm of law (c. 391, §1). In the exercise of these powers, legislative is personal, executive is personal or delegated to vicars general or episcopal vicars, and judicial is personal or delegated to a judicial vicar and judges, all in accord with the norm of law (§2).

The bishop's norm of law is his ordinary pastoral care, the exercise of power neither arbitrary nor unlimited within a hierarchical system. Legislative power is to be exercised in accord with legal prescription. A legislator below the supreme legislator may not validly delegate it unless it is specifically provided for by law (c. 135, §2). In the revised code of 1983 there seems to be no place where such provision is made for bishops. The code does provide, however, for a diocesan synod to assist the bishop discharge his legislative responsibilities should he choose it (cc. 440-468). He must relate to consultative bodies which are mandatory (like the presbyteral council) (cc. 495-501) and optional (like diocesan pastoral councils) (cc. 511-514). The bishop might ratify the decisions of such groups and the policy determinations of a diocesan synod.

Canon 135, §2 states that a lower-level legislator can never validly pass a law contrary to the law of a higher authority. This higher authority might mean the Code of Canon Law or the policies of the national episcopal conference (NCCB). When he has issued his own diocesan legislation, the bishop may interpret, apply, abrogate, or dispense from it (c. 88). He may legislate where there is no Holy See reservation. He may promulgate such norms by synodal statute book or by diocesan newspaper or by other means. Such laws bind those affected by them one month after promulgation unless the bishop determines otherwise (c. 8, §2).

The exercise of episcopal executive authority is personal or may be exercised through vicars general or episcopal vicars (cc. 475-481). They have certain limitations on their authority and certain areas requiring a special episcopal mandate to act.[14] Vicars may be employed for property administration, education, liturgy, ecumenism, and personnel policy. The bishop has wide authority in administration, especially such areas as personnel policy, educational policy, sacramental discipline, or the administration of church property. Many conflicts are brought about by administrative discretion, such as the removal of a pastor, the dismissal of a teacher, or the imposition of a diocesan tax upon a parish. The process of administrative recourse to such actions is referred to in canons 1732-1739.

Bishops are to preclude Church conflicts and to aid their just resolution (c. 1446, §1). They may remove some difficulties by ensuring that administrative organs and administrators have reasonable and precise competencies and see that the criteria of administrative decision-making is such areas as personnel policy should be clear. Finally, bishops should insist on issuing written opinions supporting administrative decisions, especially when the rights of individuals are adversely affected.

The bishop exercises judicial authority personally (c. 1419) or through the vicar judicial (c. 1420) and the judges (c. 1421) according to the norm of law. He seldom acts alone judicially because the procedures for judicial decision-making geared mainly to resolution of conflicts of rights.[15] Although the bishop may judge cases not reserved to higher authority (cc. 1419, 1405), in practice he supports and ensures accountability from those officials he appoints to the tribunal staff.

The bishop must promote the common discipline of the Church and observe all ecclesiastical laws to protect its unity (c. 392, §1). He must not let abuses creep into ecclesiastical discipline, especially regarding the ministry of the word (cc. 756-780), the celebration of sacraments and sacramentals (cc. 840-1172), the worship of God and devotion of the saints (cc. 1186-1190) and the administration of church property (cc. 1254-1310) (§2).[16] He represents his diocese in all its juridic affairs (c. 393). And just as the bishop is the official representative of his diocese, the Code makes comparable provisions for seminary rectors (c. 238, §1) and for pastors of parishes (c. 532).

The bishop also fosters the apostolate within his diocese and coordinates all its works under his direction (c. 394, §1). He urges the faithful in their duty to exercise the apostolate and recommends their participation and assistance within its works (§2). All of the faithful are called upon to share in fulfilling the Church's mission. The Vatican II "Decree on the Pastoral Office of Bishops in the Church," 17 speaks of catechetical, missionary, charitable, social, family, educational and other pastoral undertakings.[17] Such efforts require coordination and the bishop is the key responsible figure. He might use a vicar general or episcopal vicar to help him. Canon 493 on the diocesan curia addresses various dimensions of the broad issue of coordinating different diocesan activities, pastoral or administrative. This canon refers to the possible appointment of a moderator of the curia and the possible establishment of an episcopal council of vicars to realize such objectives.

The bishop should remind the faithful of their apostolic responsibilities and to share in the Church's apostolate according to their personal status, talents, and the circumstances of place and time. There is an implication of the basic Christian duty to foster the growth of the Church (c. 210). It also recalls the basic right and duty to participate in communicating the message of salvation to all persons (c. 211). It is basic for Christians to form associations for spiritual purposes with due regard for the approval of Church authority if such an association is to call itself Catholic (cc. 215-216; and cc. 298-329 on associations of the faithful). The bishop and other church leaders must foster a climate for development of pastoral enterprises because participating in the Church and world apostolate is a meaningful activity to be taken seriously by everyone.

Of the remaining eight canons affecting the diocesan bishop most deal with the legal expectations of his office. He must reside within his diocese even if he has a coadjutor or an auxiliary bishop (c. 395, §1). He may not absent himself from his diocese for more than one month, whether continuous or interrupted. During such absences "for a just cause" he must make provision that "the diocese not suffer any disadvantage through his absence of it." Time periods excepted from this provision are his *ad limina* visit, attendance at councils, synods of bishops, or episcopal conferences, requiring his presence or time spent on another office legitimately entrusted to him (§2). Ordinarily he is to be in his diocese on Christmas, during Holy Week, on Easter, Pentecost, or Corpus Christi (§3). An illegal absence by the bishop for more than six months requires the metropolitan to inform the Holy See. If the metropolitan is absent the senior suffragan of the province is to perform the notification (§4). This canon reflects church teaching since the sixteenth century. Its purpose is to ensure the availability of the bishop to his people. He must not only be physically present but also discharge his obligations or see that they are performed.

The following three canons concern the bishop's responsibility to visit his diocese at least every five years to ensure accountability in meeting diocesan goals and objectives and to fulfill the Church's mission. Canon 396 requires the bishop to visit his diocese annually, entirely or partially, so that he visits the entire diocese at least once every four years. He may make the visit personally or, if necessary, through the coadjutor or auxiliary bishop, through a vicar general or episcopal vicar, or through another priest (§1). The bishop may choose those clerics he prefers as his companions and assistants on the visitation (§2). In case the bishop fails in this duty, the metropolitan will visit the diocese with the approval of the Holy See (c. 436, §1, 2°).

Canon 397 states that episcopal visitation within a diocese includes persons, Catholic institutions, and sacred things and places (§1). Members of religious institutes of pontifical right and their houses in those cases "expressly mentioned in law" (§2). Persons subject to visitation are secular clergy, religious filling pastoral offices in the diocese in matters pertinent to those offices, members of associations of the faithful (c. 305), and others. Institutions include schools and other educational institutions, hospitals, nursing homes, and so forth. Sacred things include sacred vessels and vestments, altars, and relics, while sacred places are churches, oratories, and cemeteries.

The second paragraph reflects concerns of the Vatican II "Decree on the Pastoral Office of Bishops in the Church," 35 and the post-conciliar "Apostolic Letter, Written *Motu Proprio*, on the Implementation of the Decrees *Christus Dominus, Presbyterorum Ordinis* and *Perfectae Caritatis*," I, 38 and 39, 2.[18] Opportunities for increased episcopal visitation of religious institutes foster; harmony of ministers in the areas of education, worship, and pastoral care.

The law distinguishes between religious institutes of pontifical right (cc. 607-709) and other institutes of consecrated life (c. 589). This distinction implies institutes established or approved with formal decree by the Holy See are less subject to episcopal supervision than other religious, regarding the internal life of the community. Canon 683, §1 says the general right of visitation embraces churches and oratories which the faithful regularly frequent, schools, and other works of religion or spiritual or temporal charity entrusted to religious. It excludes visitation where such institutions are attended only by the religious community. The bishop may correct certain abuses not corrected by the religious superior (c. 683, §2). The bishop may also visit autonomous monasteries (c. 615) and religious institutes of diocesan right in his own diocese and be concerned even in internal religious discipline matters. But this is not permitted in religious institutions of pontifical right. In completing his visitation with due diligence, the bishop takes care that no one be required to pay unnecessary expenses (i.e., the visitors bringing gifts to institutions visited) (c. 398).

The next two canons detail responsibility to the Holy See. They concern the preparation of the quinquennial report (c. 399) and the bishop's *ad limina* visit (c. 400). The diocesan bishop makes a report to the pope every five years concerning the state of the diocese committed to him, by form and at a time designated by the Holy See (§1). The report may be omitted on one occasion only, if the year set for its presentation falls entirely or in part of the first two years of the bishop's diocesan administration (§2). In most cases the bishops submit the report to the Vatican Congregation for Bishops, which has prepared the form for it.[19] In missionary territories such reports are sent to the Congregation for the Evangelization of Peoples. Other departments of the Roman Curia and the Vatican Statistics Office share this information.

During the year in which he presents his report the diocesan bishop is ordinarily to come to Rome to visit the tombs of Peter and Paul and to appear before the pope (c. 400, §1). This is a personal obligation. But in cases where he cannot appear, the bishop may send his coadjutor, an auxiliary bishop, or a suitable priest of his diocese (§2). Such an apostolic vicar may fulfill this obligation through an agent. An apostolic prefect is not bound by this obligation (§3).

Originally pertaining to the bishops of the Roman province, this duty spread through the world by the thirteenth century. It brings about closer contact with the pope and the officials of the Roman Curia. The papal legate in conjunction with the president of the national episcopal conference coordinates the details of these visits. Such a visit is made *ad limina Apostolorum*, to the threshold of the Apostles. That apostolic prefects are not required to make such visits recalls Canon 381, §2, that those presiding over particular churches comparable to dioceses are equivalent to bishops unless the law specifically provides otherwise.

Canon 401 treats the retirement of the diocesan bishop and Canon 402 his retirement status. Paragraph One of the first canon requires the bishop who has completed his seventy-fifth year of age to present his resignation to the pope, while Paragraph Two calls for him to resign when he is unable to fulfill his office. The post-conciliar apostolic letter *Ecclesiae sanctae* I, 11 implementing the "Decree on the Pastoral Office of Bishops in the Church" 21 requires that bishops voluntarily resign at age seventy five. But the pope decides whether or not to accept such resignations and how best to provide for the retired bishop.[20]

When a bishop's resignation is accepted, he retains the title of bishop emeritus of his diocese and can reside there in lieu of other provisions being made by the Holy See due to special circumstances (c. 402, §1). The episcopal conference must see that suitable and decent support is provided for such a bishop, remembering that the primary obligation for his support rests with the diocese he has served (§2). In surrendering his active authority he becomes a titular bishop in the technical sense of Canon 376. If the diocese cannot support the retired bishop, the NCCB (in the case of the United States) is to find some avenues of support for him.

The Code provisions for coadjutor and auxiliary bishops were rewritten in the light of the Vatican II "Decree on the Pastoral Office of Bishops in the Church" 25-26 and Pope Paul VI's apostolic letter *Ecclesiae sanctae* I, 13. [21] These documents enhance the status of such bishops in diocesan life. Canon 403 discusses how they are appointed, while Canon 404 considers the formalities for taking possession of office. Canon 405 clarifies their rights and obligations and their replacing the diocesan bishop who is absent from the diocese or is impeded from functioning within it. Canon 406 states the coadjutor or auxiliary bishops are to be appointed vicars general or episcopal vicars. The diocesan bishop is to consult them on various occasions and they are to function in union with him (c. 407). The law clarifies how they can help the diocesan bishop (c. 408) and articulates their status when the diocese is vacant (c. 409). Canon 410 deals with their obligation of residence and Canon 411 with their retirement. These nine canons on coadjutor and auxiliary bishops have been refashioned for several causes. They provide for the pastoral needs of the diocese, respect the integrity of the episcopal status of these bishops, and promote unified diocesan government between them and the diocesan bishop.

Canon 403 provides that the diocesan bishop may request the appointment of one or more auxiliary bishops, who do not possess the right of succession (§1). An auxiliary bishop with special faculties may be given to a diocesan bishop when circumstances demand (§2). The Holy See may on its own volition appoint a coadjutor equipped with special faculties who possesses the right of succession with such an appointment (§3). Auxiliaries may be needed because of the size of the diocese, its large population, many of the faithful being of a different rite or language, or the concern for the ministry of a certain population segment. On the other hand the auxiliary with special faculties and the coadjutor may be needed because of the diocesan bishop's age, ill health, or time-consuming responsibilities which require his absence from his diocese. These may be his office holding in an episcopal conference or membership within a dicastery (department) of the Roman Curia.

When a coadjutor bishop takes possession of his office, he personally (or through his proxy) presents his apostolic letter of appointment to the diocesan bishop and the college of consultors. This action occurs in the presence of the chancellor of the curia who officially records the event (c. 404, §1). An auxiliary bishop on the same occasion presents his letter to the bishop in the presence of the chancellor (§2). If the bishop cannot receive the letters, a coadjutor and an auxiliary bishop may present their letters to the college of consultors in the presence of the chancellor. These provisions compare to those of the diocesan bishop on the taking possession of his office (c. 382).

Coadjutor and auxiliary bishops have rights and obligations determined by canon law and defined in their letters of appointment (c. 405, §1). A coadjutor bishop and the auxiliary bishop with special faculties aid the diocesan bishop in governing his diocese and take his place if he is absent or impeded (§2). The diocesan bishop is to appoint the coadjutor bishop and the auxiliary bishop with special faculties to the office of vicar general and to commit to them those matters requiring a special mandate by law (c. 406, §1). Unless other provisions to the contrary have been made, the diocesan bishop should appoint his auxiliary or auxiliaries vicars general or at least episcopal vicars on his own authority or that of a coadjutor or the auxiliary with special faculties (§2).

The diocesan bishop, the coadjutor, and the auxiliary bishop with special faculties must consult together on matters of great importance for the good of the diocese (c. 407, §1). In such matters, especially those of a pastoral nature, the diocesan bishop is to consult his auxiliary bishops before others (§2). Coadjutors and auxiliary bishops are to fulfill their duties to proceed in harmony with the diocesan bishop in their efforts and intentions (§3). A coadjutor bishop and an auxiliary bishop must perform the functions of the diocesan bishop upon his request unless they are impeded from doing so (c. 408, §1). The coadjutor or auxiliary bishop is to be allowed the exercise of the rights and privileges of their offices and not have the diocesan bishop entrust such functions habitually to another (§2).

When a diocese is vacated, the coadjutor bishop becomes bishop of the diocese for which he had been appointed provided he has legitimately taken possession of it (c. 409, §1). In this instance and in the absence of provisions to the contrary, an auxiliary bishop retains those powers and faculties he possessed as vicar general or as episcopal vicar when the see was filled until a new bishop takes possession of it. If he has not been designated diocesan administrator, he may exercise this power under the authority of the diocesan administrator who governs the diocese (§2).

Coadjutor bishops and auxiliary bishops are bound to be residents of the diocese to which they are assigned. They may not be absent unless fulfilling some other office outside the diocese or on vacation for more than one month (c. 410).[22] Though it is not enumerated, such bishops enjoy the clerical right of vacation time (c. 283, §2). Unlike Canon 395, §4 which applies to possible residence violations by the diocesan bishop, no explicit provision is made for violation of the law on residence by auxiliaries. The appropriate penal canon (c. 1396) would still apply. Canons 401 and 402, §2 on resignation from office apply to coadjutors and auxiliaries as well (c. 411).

Before closing this section with an account of how a Texas bishop spent the year 1993, we discuss diocesan administration in the impeded see (cc. 412-415) and the vacant see (cc. 416-430). An episcopal see (jurisdiction, e.g., a diocese or archdiocese) is impeded if the diocesan bishop through captivity, banishment, exile, or incapacity cannot act as pastor in his own diocese nor communicate with the faithful of that diocese even by letter (c. 412). For socio-political reasons dating back to the invasions of the fourth and later centuries diocesan government may be so disturbed that the bishop cannot attend to his duties within his diocese.

Upon taking possession of a diocese, the diocesan bishop must draw up a list of those in succession to him. This list must be communicated to the metropolitan and renewed at least every three years. It is to be preserved in secret by the chancellor. Unless the Holy See has made some other provision the coadjutor takes charge if the diocesan bishop is impeded. If there is no coadjutor or if he is impeded, the position falls in succession to an auxiliary of the vicar general or the episcopal vicar, or to another priest (c. 413, §1). If there is no coadjutor bishop or he is impeded and the list is lacking, the college of consultors selects a priest to govern the diocese (§2). Whoever assumes governance of the diocese immediately advises the Holy See that the see is impeded and of his assuming its functions (§3).

The individual assuming the diocese exercises the pastoral care and has the obligations and power of a diocesan administrator only for the time the see is impeded (c. 414). If the diocesan bishop cannot function due to an ecclesiastical penalty, the metropolitan must immediately inform the Holy See. If there is no metropolitan or if he himself is being penalized, the senior suffragan in terms of promotion informs the Holy See (c. 415). An example of such an ecclesiastical offense is the ordination of another bishop without a pontifical mandate. Such an offense would incur excommunication reserved to the Holy See (c. 1382).

Canons 416 through 430 involve the vacant see. Canon 416 defines it. The validity of the acts of vicars until they are aware of the vacancy of the see and the transference of the diocesan bishop from one see to another concern canons 417 and 418. Canon 419 indicates who governs the diocese prior to the election of the administrator, while Canon 420 specifies those governing the church in an apostolic vicariate or prefecture during a vacancy. Canon 421 regulates the election of an administrator while Canon 422 specifies the obligation of notifying the Holy See about pertinent developments. Canon 423, §1 prohibits the election of more than one administrator while Canons 423, §2 and 425 indicate qualifications for office. Canon 424 states the rules for the election, while Canon 426 clarifies the legal status of the person governing the vacant see before the choice of an administrator. The next four canons clarify the legal status of the apostolic administrator, reaffirm the prohibition of diocesan innovations during the absence by prohibiting the prejudicing of episcopal or diocesan rights or tampering with official diocesan documents, bind the administrator's episcopal obligations of residence and Mass for the people, and describe the cessation of office by the administrator (cc. 427-430).

Three conditions causing a vacant see are the death of the diocesan bishop, acceptance of his resignation by the pope, and his transferal or deprivation of office (c. 416). Those things done by the vicar general or episcopal vicar until they receive certain notice of the death of the diocesan bishop have full force And what is done by the diocesan bishop or the vicar general or episcopal vicar have such force until they have received certain notice of pontifical actions (c. 417). Unlike the authority of vicars, which ceases with the death of their diocesan bishop, the auxiliary bishop retains his authority as vicar general or episcopal vicar during the vacancy (c. 409, §2). The same is true of the diocesan bishop until he is duly informed of the Holy See's acceptance of his resignation, his transferal, or of his deprivation of office.

Canon 418 considers the status of a transferred bishop. Paragraph One requires such a bishop to proceed to his new diocese within two months of his certain notice of transferal and take canonical possession of it. His former diocese is vacant from the day he takes possession of the new diocese (c. 418, §1). Between the reception of certain notice of transferal until taking canonical possession of the new diocese, the transferred bishop in his former diocese attains the power of a diocesan administrator and is bound by those obligations. All authority of the vicar general and episcopal vicar ceases, with due regard for the auxiliary bishop's situation in Canon 409, §2. The transferred bishop also continues to receive the entire salary proper to his office (§2, 1°, 2°).

During the vacancy of a see and before the establishment of a diocesan administrator, the diocese is governed by the auxiliary bishop or the senior auxiliary bishop in terms of promotion (if more than one). Unless the Holy See provides otherwise, government devolves on the college of consultors in the absence of auxiliary bishops. The college is convoked by whoever assumes the governance and designates the diocesan administrator (c. 419). In a comparable situation within the missionary church of an apostolic vicariate or prefecture, its governance is assumed by a pro-vicar or pro-prefect named for this purpose by the vicar or prefect immediately after taking possession (c. 420).

The interim administrator must be elected by the college of consultors within eight days of receiving the notice of the vacancy of the episcopal see. Canon 502, §3 must be given due regard (c. 421, §1). If there can be no legitimate election during this time, the metropolitan must choose. If the vacant see is the metropolitan church or that church is also vacant as well as the suffragan, it devolves upon the senior suffragan bishop in terms of promotion (§2).

Prior to the Council of Trent in the sixteenth century, the chapter of canons generally determined how the diocese was to be governed during a vacancy. It governed corporately, by its members succeeding one another in turn, or through a representative of its own. The Council required it to choose a vicar capitular to govern until the see was filled. Chosen by the chapter, the vicar capitular was independent and could not be removed by it.

The 1917 Code of Canon Law embodied the council requirement in this type of appointment. The present Code maintains the fundamentals but simplifies them. The role of the college is highlighted, but its authority is restricted. This is true particularly in its relationship to the administrator, who is independent of it. Canon 502, §3 asserts the possibility that an episcopal conference may determine that the cathedral chapter function as the college of consultors. If an auxiliary bishop has assumed the leadership of the diocese (c. 419), he presides at the meeting of the college to elect the administrator. Otherwise, it is the senior member of the college of consultors in terms of ordination.

Paragraph Two exemplifies the supervisory role of the metropolitan in the province (c. 436, §1, 3°). It provides for his choosing the administrator if the college fails to do so within the required time period. This is considered "useful time" within the meaning of Canon 201, §2. The metropolitan fulfills the requirements of law by remedying the deficiencies of the suffragan diocese. If the metropolitan's see is vacant, the senior suffragan of the province chooses the administrator of the archdiocese if its college of consultors does not fulfill its duty.

The auxiliary bishop or (if none) the college of consultors must inform the Holy See immediately on the death of the bishop. The one elected administrator does the same regarding his own election (c. 422). If one person cannot be elected diocesan administrator, the election is invalid (c. 423, §1). Because the administrator cannot also be the finance officer, if the finance officer is elected administrator a temporary finance officer must be chosen by the finance council (§2).

Canons 165 through 178 govern the election of the diocesan administrator (c. 424). Presently an absolute majority is no longer required for election. If a priest is selected administrator he must be at least thirty-five and not previously elected, nominated or presented for the same vacant see (c. 425, §1). He must be outstanding in doctrine and prudence (§2). If the administrator's election is not in accordance with the stipulations of Paragraph One of this canon, his acts are invalid. The metropolitan or the senior suffragan bishop in terms of promotion (if the metropolitan see is vacant) ascertains the truth of this situation and appoints an administrator (§3).

In Canon 425 the age of administrator is raised from thirty to thirty-five to correspond to the same age as that of a bishop (c. 378, 3°). Whoever governs the diocese in its vacancy and before an administrator is designated enjoys the power the law grants to the vicar general (c. 426). The diocesan administrator is bound by the obligations and enjoys the power of the diocesan bishop, excluding those things which are excepted by their very nature or by the law itself. Once the diocesan administrator has accepted the election he obtains power. No further confirmation is required, with the obligation of Canon 833, §4 remaining (c. 42, §§1-2).

Since the administrator takes the place of the diocesan bishop, he is normally accorded that status. But the administrator functions ad interim until the see is filled. So he is prohibited from functioning like the diocesan bishop in a number of areas.[23] And if the administrator is not a bishop, he lacks certain episcopal prerogatives, especially in the sacramental area. Canon 833, §4 requires the administrator to make a profession of faith in the presence of the college of consultors. This is comparable to that profession made by the diocesan bishop (c. 380), though this context makes no mention of an oath of loyalty to the Holy See.

There are to be no innovations when the see is vacant. Those temporarily in charge of the diocese may not do anything prejudicial to the diocese or to episcopal rights. No person or persons may remove, destroy, or alter any documents of the diocesan curia, either personally or through another (c. 428, §§ 1-2). Canon 1391 sets the penalty for these illegal actions.

The diocesan administrator must reside in the diocese and apply Mass for the people according to Canon 388 (c. 429). Canon 430 concerns the cessation of the administrator's office, which ends with the taking possession of the office by the new bishop. The Holy See may remove the administrator. Any resignation must be presented in authentic form to the college of consultors which can elect. It does not have to be accepted by this body. If the administrator dies, resigns or has been removed, another is to be elected according to Canon 421 (c. 430).

Canon law is one way of prescribing a bishop's schedule of daily activities. The canons suggest the timing and duration of various events. Although a bishop works primarily within his own diocese, official tasks occur outside it as well. Like other clergy a bishop will celebrate daily Mass. Added to his pastoral function, his administrative duties extend to the national episcopal conference (NCCB), the synod of bishops, and to the fifth-year "ad limina" visit he must make to the Holy Father in Rome to account for his stewardship. Each day cannot be spent in his chancery doing routine office work. That facility is sometimes closed for certain religious feasts and for other observances.[24] The calender of Bishop Edmond Carmody of Tyler, as reported in the bimonthly diocesan newspaper *Catholic East Texas* during the year 1993, affords an example.[25]

Installed bishop of Tyler on 25 May 1992, Bishop Carmody replaces the first bishop Charles E. Herzig, who died 7 September 1991. Between May and November 1992 he began his first round of pastoral visits to his twenty-seven parishes and fifteen missions. As of 1 January 1993 diocesan institutions include three Catholic hospitals, two health care centers, a high school, and four elementary schools. There are also two monasteries and a convent of cloistered women religious. And the diocese provides chaplains for state prison units and higher educational facilities within it. The Diocese of Tyler comprises thirty-two counties in East Texas, an area of 22,971 square miles.[26]

Bishop Carmody began his second round of pastoral visits to celebrate weekend Masses in December 1992. Between November 1992 and 10 January 1993 he said Masses in Athens, Canton, and Texarkana. The second round of visits began on the tenth of January and was to end in mid-October 1993. Some parishes would be visited twice for confirmation services.[27] The contemporary Texas bishop benefits from the technology of the modern era. Unlike his nineteenth-century predecessor, he no longer journeys by horse and stagecoach with vestments and vessels in his saddlebags. Instead he prefers to drive his own car through the interstate, national, state, and county highway system which connects one city to another. The relative certainty of air travel allows multiple events to be scheduled closely in various locations. Many obligations may be planned in advance within shorter periods of time.

During 1993 the bishop of Tyler managed to spend all or part of thirty-nine of fifty-two weekends within his diocese. Two hundred fifty-five days were scheduled with the remaining 110 allowed for travel and for the performance of administrative duties. Work must be continuously performed on a time available basis throughout the year. Although the chancery was closed for weekends and for an announced fourteen days in 1993, it managed to move into a new (and larger) location in Tyler. This event in itself signifies the growth and demanding nature of diocesan programs.

If one thinks of a bishop as a desk-bound executive attending some ceremonial functions, he is sadly mistaken. Of 365 days in 1993, Bishop Carmody spent 273 in his diocese, thirty days in other dioceses in Texas, thirty-three days in the United States (outside Texas), and twenty-nine days abroad. During this year he scheduled 203 events inside his diocese, nineteen in other parts of Texas, and thirteen in seven states and the District of Columbia, Ireland, and Italy.

And there is more involved than the number of events themselves, which may contain meetings, religious ceremonies, and various other activities as well. A Mass may be preceded by a meeting or followed by a reception. A dinner may allow for ecumenical participation or a fund-raiser for diocesan institutions. And several such happenings may very well go on within any twenty-four hour period.

Within his diocese in 1993 Bishop Carmody said ninety-nine announced Masses, attended eighty-four meetings and twelve ecumenical and/or civic events, took part in twenty-three proceedings combining meals, receptions, and fund-raisers, and held twenty-two confirmation and two penance services. Outside his diocese he attended six installations of bishops and investitures of various Catholic organizations, seven bishops' meetings, two clerical retreats, ten other meetings, conferences, and workshops, and a Mass and dinner for a fellow bishop. He also made three pastoral visits and a parish mission (which Protestants call a "revival"). He attended two ceremonies, took his vacation with family members in Ireland, and reported on the condition of his diocese during his "ad limina" visit to the pope in Rome.

As we have seen, the types and duties of a Catholic bishop are many and varied. Each year brings many opportunities for performing ministries. In the following sections we will discuss the style, vesture and heraldry of the bishop, the development of the Province of San Antonio, the administrative and financial structures of Texas dioceses, and conclude the introduction with the profile of a Texas bishop.

G. Episcopal Style: Address, Heraldry, and Vesture

We come now to the habiliments of the Roman Catholic bishop, those elements which clothe him symbolically and literally. Styles of address denote customary written and spoken forms of respect which distinguish his office. Heraldry is a pictorial representation of his status within the Church. Vesture includes his ceremonial garb and accoutrements, themselves reflections of his historical and current position. Although these forms are outward manifestations of the bishop himself, they have become intrinsic due to their close association with his person.

The term "Reverend" is the basic form of address for ordained clergy from deacon through archbishop. Cardinals are customarily styled "His Eminence" and popes "His Holiness." While cardinals (exempting perhaps some outstanding priestly theologians) and popes are themselves bishops, their special titles spring from their unique functions within the hierarchy. The Roman Catholic Church differentiates between "permanent" and "transitional" deacons, who are addressed formally as "Mister" and "Reverend Mister," respectively. Their common salutation is "Mister".[1]

The two ranks of the diaconate differ as follows:

> The diaconate is the first order or grade in ordained ministry. Its origins are in early apostolic times, when deacons preached and baptized under the direction of presbyters or bishops. Any man who is to be ordained to the priesthood must first be ordained as a *transitional deacon*. Deacons serve in the ministry of liturgy, of the word, and of charity.
>
> In 1967, Pope Paul VI, reinstituted the *Permanent Diaconate* for men who do not plan to become ordained priests. Although men ordained as permanent deacons are sometime referred to as 'married deacons,' the permanent diaconate is open to both married and unmarried men, with the understanding that after ordination, they may not marry even after the death of a spouse. Under the authority of the diocesan bishop, they perform the same functions as the transitional deacons while, at the same time, retaining their roles in society as family and business men.[2]

There is no difference in address between religious order priests and secular (or diocesan) priests, except that the religious order priest will add the initials of his particular order following his surname. Both types are called "Reverend," with the common salutation of "Reverend Father".[3]

Some secular priests are granted the honorary title of "Monsignor" by the pope. This distinction is given to the vicar general (or executive deputy) of the diocesan bishop. European bishops are also known by this name. All classes of this rank, whether papal chamberlains (chaplains), prelates of honor, or protonotaries apostolic, are addressed as "Reverend Monsignor" with the same salutation.[4]

An abbot is the superior of a male religious community housed in an abbey or monastery. An archabbot (or abbot general) is the head of some distinguished monastery or of a congregation which contains several monasteries. An abbot primate heads the Benedictine Confederation. All these are known as "Right Reverend," a title once conferred on American bishops and presently on European bishops.[5] An abbot of whatever type adds the designated letters of his order following his surname, and their common salutation is "Right Reverend Abbot".[6]

In the United States bishops and archbishops receive the title of "Most Reverend" with the personal salutation of "Your Excellency". The distinctive form for archbishops, "Your Grace," is not used in this country. If a bishop or archbishop holds the rank of cardinal, his formal address is "His Eminence" followed by his Christian name followed by "Cardinal" followed by his surname. The salutation is "Your Eminence," with that of "Your Holiness" reserved exclusively for the pope.[7] The patriarch of an Eastern church would be correctly styled "His Beatitude" followed immediately by the name of his patriarchate, with the salutation of "Most Reverend Lord".[8]

Just as forms of address signify one's rank in the Church, so does heraldry provide a pictorial representation of the individuality and authority of its bearer. Ecclesiastical heraldry begins in the sixth century when popes used seals for official documents. As the use of seals spread, so did the need for distinct achievements in arms. Blazoning, the drawing of armorial bearings, became increasingly the work of heralds, those practiced in the creating, painting, and granting of individual achievements in arms. As we shall see, heraldry for Roman Catholic clergy is a matter of custom and usage in devising the shield. Papal authority controls the external ornaments surrounding it.

Our present concern is to understand the origin and development of heraldry as it affects the Roman Catholic hierarchy and other religious, how popes have sought to direct its practice since the seventeenth century, and how insignia and ornamentation and the rules which govern them make up the finished artistic creation.[9] I conclude this subsection with the achievement in arms of a Texas bishop.

Although seals made formal documents and contracts authentic, they soon closed letters, boxes, cabinets, cupboards, doors, drawers, tombs, and reliquaries. Embossing presses or rubber stamps secured paper. A real wax seal served the second need of enclosure. The form on both types was armorial, with the seals showing emblems of ecclesiastical rank in heraldic style. Since these objects belonged to certain individuals, those who saw them recognized their origins immediately.

Pope Agapitus I (535-536) possessed the oldest existing papal seal and documents bearing seals date from the ninth century. Bishops began to enclose secular documents a century later, and in 1166 Pope Alexander III required the sealing of all documents presented at the Papal Court. Cardinals, bishops, cathedral chapters and temporal princes also used this method to validate official papers and actions.

From the eleventh century Geoffrey V, Count of Anjou, aided the graphic representation of the individual through heraldry. It eventually came to belong to families and to corporations. As an emblem of warfare through the thirteenth century and for tournaments through the fifteenth century, usage thereafter became ornamental. The knightly costume and the implements of war discarded by the wearers soon took their places on shields. The clergy continued to put on their vestments and insignia. The principles of secular heraldry are free choice, inheritance, and land ownership. In the Church heraldry depends upon the "dogmatic and in part only juridical and historical order of the Hierarchy," and "is exclusively concerned with ecclesiastical status."[10] This status derives from ordination or consecration.

It is extremely important to understand that, in speaking of ecclesiastical heraldry, heraldic considerations as well as doctrinal, liturgical and canonical factors come to bear. Risking oversimplification, the considerations apply primarily to the charges (figures) on the shields and the factors concerning church authority apply primarily to the ornaments external to the shields.

The Church has always realized that the charges upon the shield are marks of its owner's individuality expressed through family tradition. In fact prelates and bishops often marshal their personal arms with those of their diocese, territories, monasteries or chapters.[11] The Church has a long tradition of so doing, its problem being how to transfer the vehicle of representation from the ecclesiastical seal.

Knights and those engaged in warfare and tournaments first used heraldry. Clerics are forbidden arms as a profession (see cc. 285,§1 and 289,§1).[12] But by the thirteenth century the Church was using personal marks and adornments mainly as seal emblems. At first painted on banners, armorial bearings were on shields in 1263 when Guy de Rochefort, Bishop of Langres, became the first bishop to place a seal bearing his family arms upon a shield. While some other bishops, such as those of Coire in Switzerland, waited another hundred years to begin this practice, Guy had some predecessors among the lower clergy. These were Nicholas, Archdeacon of Valciennes (1236) and Hunon de la Fosse, Canon of Saint Quentin (1239). The first pope to use inherited arms was probably Boniface VIII (1294-1303).[13]

The papal arms adorn Vatican stamps and coins. They may be found over the main door of all churches in Rome, in the palaces of Roman congregations, and in pontifical institutes, nunciatures (embassies), and delegations. Cardinals' coats of arms have decorated their titular churches in Rome since 1658. In many dioceses a bishop's arms are displayed on façades of churches and above his throne in cathedrals. Arms are permitted on liturgical vestments (such as stoles) and on liturgical objects (such as chalices), whether in memory of the donors or as a mark of ownership. Since 1924 flags have been allowed in church on the condition that they not be of associations openly hostile to the Church or that they depict figures or emblems obscene or anti-religious.[14]

One attains arms in the Church by being at least a priest and in such office as the arms depict.[15] Arms bearers may be impeded, deprived, or lose the rights to display ecclesiastical insignia through loss of office by disability, retirement, death, or canonical punishments. As we have seen, archbishops and bishops have limited terms of office. Ecclesiastical punishments have historically included excommunication, interdiction, suspension, demotion, exclusion from dignities, punitive privation of office, privation of ecclesiastical dress (unfrocking), deposition, and degradation.[16]

Most countries allow complete latitude in blazoning, subject to an official authority. In England it is the College of Arms.[17] Such also is the function of the Collegio Araldico, founded in 1853, in the pontificate of Pius IX. The Church does not concern itself with the armorial bearings of papal titles of nobility, not conferred since the pontificate of John XXIII (1958-1963).

Crowns began to be used as emblems of rank in England, France, Italy, and later Germany during the fourteenth century. Princes who were bishops and abbots often placed arms on a red mantle lined with ermine, raised on both sides by gold cords and ensigned with a prince's crown. This practice was dropped about 1953. If the see had a noble title, the Church did not forbid emblems of it until 1915. At this time it ended the use by cathedral chapters with court or baron titles attached.[18]

To regulate the use of crowns Pope Innocent X began a series of papal edicts in 1644. Nineteen additional documents regulating ecclesiastical heraldry were written between then and 1969.[19] To end the marshalling of crowns with ecclesiastical insignia Innocent forbade the use of heraldic crowns to cardinals. Benedict XV applied the same prohibition to bishops (implicitly, to all prelates) in 1915. The helmet of early heraldry denoted the warrior, while the crown bespoke the noble. Neither role was suitable for priest or prelate.

With the origin and development of heraldry and how ecclesiastical insignia came under papal supervision in mind, we are ready to look at heraldic ornaments and how they are used in the blazoning of achievements in arms. Having introduced the subject of headgear with crowns, we begin with the papal tiara. In ecclesiastical apparel nothing so directly identifies its wearer as does the tiara with the pope. Because of his unique position, this object has come to symbolize his authority. Once called a *regnum*, it was a *camelaucum* or *phrygium*, a white bonnet shaped like a sugar loaf and indicating liberty. Other sources are the Old Testament high priest's headdress and the mitre.

Popes wore a special headpiece as a sign of their dignity from about the eleventh century onward. Of the three circlets, the first or lower one seems to come from the ninth through eleventh centuries and demonstrates a religious association with the Holy Roman Empire. The second crown was added to the tiara by Boniface VIII (1294-1303), the two denoting spiritual and temporal power. Benedict XI (1303-1304) or Clement V (1305-1314) added the third crown. The inventory of the papal treasury first lists the triple tiara in 1315. Two originally black ribbons were from about the thirteenth century and hung from the back, as on a mitre. The knob and small cross surmounting the tiara are from the fifteenth century.

The tiara indicates the sovereign power of the pope as Supreme Head of the Church and as the ruler of the Papal State. And, in the event he should ever lack temporal power, he is still primate of the Universal Church. The tiara can also symbolize supremacy over the church militant (on Earth), penitent (in Purgatory), and triumphant (in Heaven). It also demonstrates the pope's triple ministry as priest, pastor, and teacher of the faithful. The first pope to use it as an external ornament for his shield was John XXII (1316-1334).

Another type of clerical headdress long in favor is the mitre. The usually white headband, worn as a turban with two ribbons suspended, was used by priests in ancient Rome and called the *infula* (or fillet). The wearer implored the protection of the gods in temples, and it was also placed on the heads of sacrificial victims. The *mitra* was a banded bonnet like a turban worn by women, though men wore it in the East. In Greek the word means a band and a diadem.

It has nothing in common with the *kideria* (or *miznephet*) of the Old Testament.

The mitre comes into liturgical and pontifical use in the tenth century. It appears on seals two centuries later. Until the pontificate of Leo IX (1049-1054) only popes and cardinals wore the mitre. It was also conferred on foreign bishops. Abbot Engelsinus of St. Augustine's Monastery, Canterbury, received it from Alexander II in 1063. Leo IX presented the mitre to the canons of Besançon Cathedral, as did Nicholas II (1059-1061) to Duke Spytihnev of Bohemia. There is a tradition that Lucius II (1144-1145) presented Roger of Sicily a mitre, crozier, ring, dalmatic and sandals. But the mitre has never belonged to abbots in their own right, nor to the canons nor any sort of prelate below the rank of bishop.

At the dawn of the eleventh century the mitre was conical or hemispherical. It was later divided from front to back and from about 1125 was made up of two pointed pieces called horns. They rise from each side, slightly inclined toward each other and held together by the lining. At first it was short, rising vertically, and was bent in to a point at the top of the horns. From the fourteenth century it grew in stature and size and became more bejewelled and embroidered. At one time the mitre was adorned with solid gold and some types weighed more than fifteen pounds.

There are three kinds of mitres in ecclesiastical use, the precious (jewelled), golden (*auriphrygiata*), and the simple white. Their ground color is now always white or gold. Two *infulae* or ribbons, also white or gold with a red lining like the mitre itself, hang down the back. To Pope Innocent III (1198-1216) the mitre itself represented the knowledge of the Old and New Testaments, with the horns being the testaments themselves. The *infulae* were the spirit and the letter of the law. In heraldic use the mitre is generally restricted to the bishop. French and Italian bishops ensigned their shields with the ecclesiastical hat and cross. This usage of the hat is in keeping with Catholic custom, but the Church of England still uses the mitre heraldically.[20]

The ecclesiastical hat favored by the Roman Catholic Church is known variously as the pontifical, prelate's, or priest's hat. This pilgrim's hat of various colors has a low crown with a wide brim, pierced with two cords ending in tassels. It seem to have been first conferred upon cardinals in 1245 during the pontificate of Innocent IV (1243-1254). This papal action symbolically told the newly-appointed cardinals that they should defend the Church even at the expense of their blood and lives. When worn, it was tied under the chin or brought together with a sliding ring. The more recent version is flat and hard to wear. It was used at a cardinal's funeral and hung over his tomb. Pope Paul VI (1963-1978) abolished the hat for cardinals and replaced it with a red cap.

In its heraldic form the hat continues to be displayed. As early as the fourteenth century it appeared resting on the cardinal's shield or a little above it. Heralds have employed it since the fifteenth century. The number of tassels was a matter of dispute until the Sacred Congregation of Ceremonies fixed it at fifteen on each side in 1832.

Protonotaries apostolic (priests who are actual or honorary curial clerks) had a black hat on shields. Such a hat was worn by patriarchs, archbishops, and bishops. The green hat began in Spain. Here it was made of green silk, embellished with green cords and tassels, and worn by bishops with a processional cloak and in cavalcades. The black hat is in current use, embellished with green cords and tassels. Certain prelates have purple hats, a color associated with princes, senators, and the law. Various prelatial hats were red and violet and full hats in purple were once worn. All of these were brought under uniform control by Pius X in 1905.[21]

The last article of ecclesiastical dress used heraldically is the pall or pallium. It is the symbol of the pope's supreme pastoral power, indicating shepherding and leading the faithful and their pastors. At this rank it is depicted above, below or on the shield. Derived from the toga, it is a circular band of white wool, almost two inches in width, with black crosses. It is worn about the shoulders with two similar bands about twelve inches long hanging from it over the chest and back.

At first the pallium was a sort of wraparound cloak, later worn folded and finally as a band. By the fourth century it had become an emblem of the pope. Used earlier than this time in the Eastern Church and known as an *omphorion*, the pope began to bestow the pallium on other metropolitans. They have requested it from him since the second half of the ninth century, and it became an attribute of the metropolitan.

From the eleventh century bestowing the pallium requires an oath of fidelity to the pope. Archiepiscopal power requires its reception. Innocent III (1198-1216) forbade anyone to style himself archbishop without obtaining it. In 1978 Paul VI reserved the use of palliums to the pope and archbishops of metropolitan sees. Since 1984 John Paul II has decreed that the pallium would ordinarily be conferred by the pope on the feast day of Sts. Peter and Paul, 29 June. Palliums are issued once and for life to the recipient. He is not to lend, give, or bequeath it and, if he loses it or is transferred to another archdiocese, he receives a new one. From the fifteenth century the archbishops of Canterbury have shown the pallium as a charge within their shields.[22]

Besides the tiara the keys are the symbols most often associated with the pope. They recall immediately the words of Christ to Peter in Matthew 16:18-19 on the institution of His Church. As a symbol the keys represent the absolute authority of Christ transmitted to Peter, His vicar on earth. They symbolize full power to administer the treasures of redemption, merited by Christ, and to teach His doctrine with authority.

The keys were first depicted alone on church banners, seals and coins, then inside shields, beside the shields of popes, and, lastly, in saltire (crossed) above or behind the shields. The gold key points upward on the dexter side (left side facing the viewer and right side from behind the shield), signifying the power extending even to Heaven. The silver key points up to the sinister side (right side facing the viewer and left side from behind the shield), symbol of power over all the faithful on Earth. The keys are often linked by a red cordon as a sign of union of the two powers. The handles are turned downward, as they would be in the hands of the pope. The wards (notches in the key corresponding to a ridge of metal in the keyhole) point upwards, for the power of prohibiting or permitting concerns Heaven itself. They are cut in the shape of a cross, to recall that the pope possesses his power through the death of Christ. The authority symbolized by the keys passes to the Camerlengo (Chamberlain of the Holy Roman Church, a cardinal) on the death of the pope. He bears them in saltire beneath the pavilion, behind or above his shield.

This basilical pavilion is not properly a heraldic design, though it appears as such in the fifteenth century. Called an *ombrellino* (unbrella or canopy) it is usually represented in banners and sometimes on postage stamps during the period between the death or retirement and election of a pope. It is generally shown as a half-open parasol and its function is to be kept in a basilica to shield the pope from inclement weather during processions. The keys and the pavilion are used by cardinals, the Apostolic Chamber (the office headed by the Camerlengo), and by some pontifical institutes and seminaries.[23]

Other heraldic emblems of authority are the crozier, the prior's staff, the cross, and the sword. The crozier is an emblem of pontifical dignity and sign of jurisdiction with the symbol of the Good Shepherd. Titular bishops may carry it on suitable occasions, and it is laid down during prayer. Outside of his own diocese, the prelate who owns a crozier may use it only with the consent of the local ordinary or when authorized by the Holy See to perform ordinations or certain benedictions. The same condition is true of abbots outside their monasteries.

The crozier dates from at least the fourth century and with some abbots since the seventh century. At first it was a pilgrim's staff or walking stick for preachers of the Gospel sent out by the Church. The later staff is the characteristic sign of the high priest. At first made of wood and later of precious metals, "the hook pulls, the straight stick leads, and the point goads." Only bishops should carry it with its crook turned towards the people. It should be turned forwards, in heraldry toward the dexter side.

Like the crozier, the prior's staff can be traced to the pilgrim's staff. It is often made of silver or of wood encased in finely chased (ornamented) silver with its upper part terminating in a knob with the form of an apple, fleur-de-lys, or a little house or chapel. It is the emblem of certain chapter officials without the right to pontifical insignia, such as provosts (heads of collegiate churches or cathedral chapters), priors (monastery officials), precentors (leaders of choral or congregational singing), or first cantors (song leaders, possibly of a section of the choir or congregation). Provosts, major priors, cathedral and collegiate church administrators bear it during divine service or as armorial ornaments. It is a straight pastoral staff, not curved like that of abbots or bishops, and may be found in ancient achievements.

As a heraldic ornament the cross has been displayed by patriarchs and archbishops since the fourteenth century, first in the shield, then in front of it, and last in pale (perpendicular) behind the shield. It is not a bishop's pectoral cross but the cross carried in procession before the pope, legates, patriarchs, and archbishops, and not the ordinary processional cross It is the cross which marks the hierarchical character of these dignitaries.

Carried before the pope since the fifth century, the cross has a single transverse bar. Innocent III in 1215 allowed patriarchs the right to have the cross carried before them except in Rome when the pope or his legate was present. Clement V (1305-1314) extended this right to archbishops, even outside their own dioceses. Bishops alone have the right to make use of this cross in heraldry, and it is not part of the papal heraldic achievement. The processional cross is always simple (with one crosspiece) even when carried before the pope.

By the fifteenth century patriarchs adopted the double cross with two bars, the upper crosspiece being the panel of inscription Pontius Pilate had placed upon the cross of Christ. Since the seventeenth century, many primates have adopted this practice. At present archbishops have assumed the heraldic use of the double-transversed cross. Patriarchs, metropolitans and archbishops (including titulars) use the double-transversed cross. Bishops use the simple cross.

The temporal sword as it affects ecclesiastical character has disappeared, unless it is a part of the family achievement of the cleric bearing it. It is no longer officially employed in the Church. It once adorned the arms of bishops, abbots and even abbesses. Once placed crossed with the crozier and behind the shield, the sword indicated the power of capital punishment. Temporal sovereigns in their territories granted this right to prelates, and the prelates then placed the sword behind their shields. The secularization of ecclesiastical principalities brought this usage to an end.[24]

Other elements found about the shield and external to it are the rosary, the decorations, the motto, and the supporters. The rosary or chaplet is the heraldic sign of a religious, such as an abbot or abbess. Professed knights of the Order of Malta who are in religious orders surround their shields with a silver rosary placed on and interlaced with the Maltese Cross. This rosary itself has a small Maltese Cross at bottom in place of a crucifix. Members of certain religious orders are allowed to place their shields on a cross, while cardinals and bishops may use the orders of Malta and of the Holy Sepulchre heraldically.

Decorations not proper to armorial bearings are the motto and the supporters. The motto, appearing beneath the shield, expresses briefly the ideal, plan of life, and mentality of its bearer. It is distinctly of the person himself or of his family. It serves to encourage bravery, self-discipline and benevolence. It should sound well and be ingenious and concise. As an inscription it should be legible in capitals on a scroll of the same tincture (color) as the shield. It may be put below the achievement itself. Supporters may be real or imaginary beings, animals, or objects, placed on either side of the shield. They fill spaces and balance the designs. Their first application was on seals from the end of the twelfth century. Official arms of a prelate do not have supporters.[25]

Having discussed briefly the components of ecclesiastical heraldry, we turn now to their application affecting the ranks of the hierarchy from the pope through bishops. We should observe here that it is a fraud to use arms illegally. Such ill usage should be suppressed by ecclesiastical authority. At one time a person was thought to deserve capital punishment if he intentionally misused the pope's jurisdiction knowingly by usurping his armorial signs. Sometimes usurpation occurs unintentionally or through ignorance. For example, the patriarchs of Lisbon use the tiara and some metropolitans use the patriarchal hat. Some French and Swiss bishops use the archiepiscopal hat. Rome did not rebuke the patriarch of Lisbon but did get the archbishop of Benevento to desist in a similar situation.

The insignia of ecclesiastical dignities always depends upon apostolic privilege. If absence of such privilege is proved, the right of the present beneficiaries is not weakened. The continued use of anomalies after a century or so becomes rights. Only a formal prohibition by the Holy See or a waiver by concerned prelates abolishes them.

In this connection it is the regulation by custom or law which has made codification of church heraldry unnecessary, except for the use of seals. The heraldic law of the Church remains in force (c. 6). It is principally the Roman Curia which determines the use of arms by its rules and traditions. Since 1644 popes have promulgated rules by apostolic constitution, decrees, *motu proprios*, and curial decisions. The Church does not wish to decide matters of blazon, but instead attempts to introduce order, eliminate aberrations, avoid usurpations, and maintain simplicity by papal instructions on heraldic marks of dignity.

Pope Innocent XI in his apostolic constitution "Militantis Ecclesiae Regimini" of 19 December 1644 attempted to end the adorning of a cardinal's achievements with crowns and temporal signs. To this end he invoked *latae sententiae* (automatic excommunication) against those making such signs or causing them to be made. Pope Pius IX lifted this excommunication in his constitution "Apostolicae Sedis" (1869), as did Pope Benedict XV in the Consistorial decree "De Vetitis Nobilitatis Familiaris Titulis" dated 15 January 1915. His ruling extended Innocent XI's heraldic prohibitions on the use of crowns to bishops. It was confirmed by the Code of Canon Law (1917, 1983) and by Pope Pius XI in the apostolic constitution "Ad Incrementum Decoris" (§§ 55, 56) of 15 August 1934.[26]

We now turn our attention to the application of heraldic and juridical principles to the hierarchy from the pope through abbots and prelates nullius.[27] Papal power comes with the pope's election and acceptance of office. His election is for life and he may lose his powers to govern only through death, voluntary resignation, certification of insanity, or the practice of heresy.

The rules for the pope's coat of arms are quite simple. His shield contains only his family arms and is marked with the signs of papal dignity, the tiara and keys. The tiara appears above the shield and is colored silver and crowned gold. The keys (one golden and the other silver) are crossed and bound with a red cord or with a gold cord on a red background and placed below the tiara and above or behind the shield. No other external ornaments or decorations are added. This pattern has existed since the sixteenth century.

Down to John Paul II ninety-two popes have been armigerous (arms-bearing). Of these only four have added something to their personal arms, quartering them with those of their religious orders. These are Benedict XIII (1724-1730), Clement XIV (1769-1774), Pius VII (1800-1823), and Gregory XVI (1831-1846). Pius X (1903-1914) and John XXIII (1958-1963) retained the lion of St. Mark as a symbol of their being patriarchs of Venice before assuming the papacy.

The first authentic heraldic monument of a pope is that of Boniface VIII (died 1303) in the Cathedral of Anagni, near Rome. The arms of John XXII (died 1334) are the first ornamented with tiara and keys in saltire linked with a cord. The Roman Curia, nunciatures and apostolic delegations, and pontifical institutes use the papal insignia excluding the shield. Popes have granted charges from their own shields to certain Church dignitaries as augmentations of honor, but never the tiara and keys together. The tiara and keys are found in the arms of the Church and in the former Pontifical state. A red shield should be charged with the papal insignia on the dividing line of the papal banner (gold and silver).

Cardinals receive their appointments from the pope and are permitted thereafter to display appropriate arms. If a cardinal renounces his title into the hands of the pope, he loses the insignia of that office and the right to display it. The rulings of Popes Innocent X (1644), Pius VII (1823), and Benedict XV (1915) govern the arms of cardinals, as does the "Formula Juramenti A Novis Cardinalibus Praestandi" (1738; restated 1946). A red hat ensigns the shield, and from each side of this hat depends a red cord, fixed above by a tassel. Each cord pierces the brim of the hat and ends in fifteen tassels arranged in five rows of increasing numbers (one through five). There are to be no crowns, mantles, supporters, or decorations, except that crosses of the orders of Malta and of the Holy Sepulchre may be used if appropriate. Cardinals, if they are partriarchs, archbishops or bishops, may place the cross of their rank behind the shield in pale and may add the pallium, external to the shield, as a reigning patriarch or metropolitan. This practice is rare today.

The red hat was first conferred upon cardinals by Pope Innocent IV in 1245 and began to replace the mitre as a heraldic ornament in the fourteenth century. The addition of crowns to these hats inspired the Sacred Congregation of Ceremonies to draft a decree of 10 August 1644 for Pope Innocent X to combat this abuse. The pope decided that one should be content with his title of cardinal and Most Reverend Eminence. He commanded the removal of the crown and other secular emblems from the offending shields unless such devices were integral parts of family arms. He further forbade sculptors, painters, engravers, and patrons to represent these temporal signs in the achievements of cardinals under pain of excommunication. These penalties would keep in full force unless some succeeding pope should abolish them. Cardinals in Rome accepted these provisions on oath within ten days and those not resident there within four months.

Benedict XV reenacted the 1644 decree by Consistorial decree of 15 January 1915 and extended it to patriarchs, archbishops and bishops unless a princely title was connected with their sees. The number of tassels adorning a cardinal's hat is not specified. Since the pontificate of Pius VI (1775-1779), custom has fixed the number at fifteen per side. It was made law by a decree of the Sacred Congregation of Ceremonies on 9 February 1832. Cardinals who are bishops or archbishops or patriarchs place a cross in pale behind the shield according to their rank. This is custom rather than law. The pontifical emblems of crozier and mitre belong to all cardinals, but are not added in the interests of simplicity and charity. This was the order of Paul VI on 31 March 1969.

Benedict XV's decree of 1915 concerns the arms of patriarchs and primates. They use a green hat from which hangs two green cords, each one ending in fifteen green tassels on either side. Behind the shield they place a double-transversed cross in pale. There are no signs of nobility or secular dignities. All decorations are forbidden except the crosses of Malta and of the Holy Sepulchre. Residential patriarchs possess the pallium and may use it as an external ornament.

The green hat above the shield is the pontifical hat. A supposed decree of 3 November 1826 is said to fix the number of green tassels at fifteen on each side, which is the current system. The double-transverse cross and pallium are common to patriarchs and archbishops. The *Roman Pontifical* (1850) recognizes the use of the cross. Pius X forbids such use to protonotaries apostolic in his *motu proprio* "Inter multiplices cures" (Number 18) of 21 February 1905. Benedict XV's decree of 1915 forbids patriarchs to use emblems of secular dignity, though in the past patriarchs, archbishops, bishops, assistants to the pontifical throne, and Roman counts sometimes placed a count's coronet above their shields. The crown is a matter of honorary rank and not an hereditary or family title. Its heraldic use is a matter of toleration and not of right.

Patriarchs may ornament their arms with the orders of Malta and the Holy Sepulchre. Members of the Order of Malta have the right to place its cross on their shields, while other dignitaries place it below. Primates (bishops with precedence over others) have no special external ornaments but may use the insignia of archbishops or patriarchs. They seem more closely related to patriarchs by title and position than to archbishops and may make use of the same patriarchal external ornaments.

Archbishops and bishops are bound by Benedict XV's decree of 1915. The arms of archbishops resemble those of patriarchs except in the number of tassels. From the green hat descends a green cord on each side terminating in ten green tassels in four rows. There are no secular indications of this dignity and all decorations except crosses of Malta and the Holy Sepulchre are forbidden. Residential archbishops possess the pallium and can display it as an ornament external to the shield. Pope Pius XII, by his Consistorial decree "De Vetito Civilium Nobilarium Titulorum" of 12 May 1951, abolished the right of archbishoprics and bishoprics to bear both ecclesiastic and heraldic insignia in case such entities may have had principalities and earldoms attached to them.

Paul VI made another reform by his decree of 31 March 1969 forbidding heraldic use of mitres and croziers in addition to the hat and cross. Bishops formerly adorned their shields with mitre and crozier and put temporal swords in saltire with the crozier as a sign of their temporal power. The offense in this case was the juxtaposition of too many devices at once. But a prince-bishop might have adorned his arms with mitre, crozier, and double-transversed cross on the mantle.

A bishop places a green hat above the shield. This hat has a green cord with six green tassels in three rows on each side. A simple cross in pale goes behind the shield. All secular signs of dignity and all decorations except the crosses of Malta and of the Holy Sepulchre are forbidden. Generally bishops use the cross while abbots use the heraldic mitre and crozier. Pope Paul's 1969 decree makes this custom a matter of special instruction.

Patriarchs, primates, residential and titular archbishops, and bishops receive episcopal consecration, which allows them the crozier and the proper pontifical ornaments. They may use the episcopal hat on their shields but not the mitre, crozier, or cross. After official notification in *L'Osservatore Romano* (the official daily newspaper of the Holy See since 1890) a bishop may use the episcopal hat. He employs his arms for the administration of his diocese. Only the pope can order withdrawal of insignia as the result of ecclesiastical punishment. This penalty forbids the exercise of spiritual power and deprives the bearer of heraldic privileges.

Although it is true that those receiving only ordination belong with the lesser prelates lacking episcopal power, some of them exercise episcopal jurisdiction independently and the heraldry of their offices reflects such exercise of authority. Abbots and prelates *nullius* have jurisdiction from the Holy See over the clergy and people of their territories. These officials are equal to bishops in jurisdiction but inferior to them in holy orders. Some abbots have had jurisdiction similar to that of a diocesan bishop over the residents and institutions of districts (abbacies *nullius*) not belonging to a diocese. The only such abbacy *nullius* in the United States was that of Belmont Abbey in North Carolina. Pope Paul VI by his *motu proprio* of 29 December 1976 decreed that no more such abbacies would be established, except in cases of extraordinary necessity. Further, such abbacies with the possible exception of the historically significant (like Monte Cassino, the cradle of the Benedictine Order) would be phased out of existence.[28]

Abbots and prelates *nullius* place a green bishop's hat over their shields. This hat has pendent green cords which end in six tassels on each side. They might use a crozier with a veil upon it instead of a cross. These dignitaries may wear episcopal insignia and vestments and the ornaments of bishops, to whom they are equal in jurisdiction only. Pope Alexander VII so decreed on 27 September 1659 when he set out twenty-one rules for the use of pontifical insignia by lesser prelates.

Although Alexander VII did not mention the use of the cross in these rules, it is not used by cardinals who are not bishops. Bishops have used the cross often. The *Ceremoniale Episcoporum* (1860 edition) allows the use of the processional cross only to patriarchs and archbishops. Patriarchs, primates, and metropolitans separate the right to have it carried before them from the right to exercise acts of jurisdiction. Prelates *nullius* can not place this cross behind their shields, because they are not in the hierarchical order. As distinct from the hierarchy lesser prelates have not felt themselves explicitly compelled to conform with these decrees, though they have generally followed church custom and tradition in heraldic matters.[29]

Before concluding our discussion of ecclesiastical heraldry with the arms of a Texas Catholic bishop, we should note its use in the oriental churches in union with the Holy See. Unlike Western Europe, heraldry is not indigenous to these churches of Eastern Europe and the Near and Middle East except for what were ancient Russia and the former Austro-Hungarian Empire. Heraldic blazoning in these churches should avoid the use of landscapes, crucifixes, statues, chalices with radiant hosts, letters, machines, and any vulgar or prosaic object.

The rites of the Eastern churches are Armenian, Byzantine, Chaldean, Coptic, Maronite, and Syrian. In them mitres and croziers differ from those used in the West. In the Byzantine Rite (whether Greek, Russian, Melkite, Ruthenian, Yugoslav, Bulgarian, or Rumanian) a bishop's hat differs from the Latin Rite. Here the mitre resembles a royal or princely crown made with stiff material adorned with gold, brocade, and precious stones. Such items are otherwise embroidered with flowers, crosses and other images or icons. The pastoral staff does not curve over the top in a crook but terminates in two serpents facing each other between which there is usually (but not always) a cross.

Armenian bishops wear a mitre almost identical to Latin Rite bishops and a crozier similar to theirs. These four staves are an episcopal crozier, a patriarchal staff terminating in a globe surmounted by a cross, a patriarchal double-transversed cross, and a doctoral staff with serpents like the Byzantine crozier. Armenian priests and bishops wear a headpiece resembling a Byzantine bishop's mitre. It is a round tiara issuing from a crown flory and surmounted by a small cross. These clerics rarely use coats of arms. Syrian, Chaldean, and Maronite bishops use a Latin Rite mitre and crozier in place of (not together with) the pontifical hat, not worn in the East.

Some Byzantine Rite prelates decorate their arms in the same way as Latin Rite prelates. Others use mixed external ornaments such as a cross accompanied by two crescents. The pontifical hat and archiepiscopal cross are like those of the Latin Rite archbishop. In addition they used the Byzantine crozier and mitre with a coronet for family nobility, a method now forbidden.

The insignia of a Maronite patriarch are the mitre, crozier and pallium, like those of many Latin prelates of the past. He also uses the triple patriarchal cross, which is otherwise not used in church heraldry. But the Latin Rite ecclesiastical hat is inappropriate, as is the mantling of a continental prince-bishop. Oriental mantling is a kind of liturgical cope or cloak called the *mandyas*. Oriental prelates use the cross and Greek crozier on a shield set on the *mandyas* issuing from a Byzantine pontifical crown or mitre. This type of hat is sometimes gold or silver brocade or pinkish-violet embroidered with gold. The *mandyas* is of the same colors and is lined mostly with bright yellow silk. It should not be hitched up on both sides to resemble the robe of estate or prince's mantle. The Copts could use their mitre, the cope, and their cross and crozier, with the cross and crozier kept under the *mandyas*.[30]

The recent appointment of Placido Rodriguez, C.M.F., auxiliary bishop of Chicago (since 1983) as bishop of Lubbock (since 1994) shows how a coat of arms may be chosen and later impaled. As an auxiliary Bishop Rodriguez's charges for the upper part of his shield are a red boat on a golden background, with a sun upon the sail, and on the right an image of the Virgin of Guadalupe. In the larger part of the shield a golden cross on a red field supports two palms of martyrdom. The Holy Spirit as a dove of peace stands out above the cross.

These symbols combine the bishop's cultural and religious heritage, indicating his Indo-Hispanic descent and Catholic faith. Caravels of Christopher Columbus bring the European religion to the New World. The sun upon the sail is Tonatium, Aztec lord of the heavens. The fusion of Indian and Hispanic results in a new People of God, the Meztizos. Our Lady of Guadalupe, as Patron Saint of Mexico and the Americas, is a guiding force, under whom the Rodriguez family emigrated to the United States. The colors of red and gold are fittingly Hispanic.

The palms of martyrdom are the struggles which the Rodriguez family experienced because of their faith, especially represented by the palm branch nearest the cross. On the right the other and golden palm branch stands for St. Placido, a third century Roman martyr, the bishop's patron saint and that of his native city Celaya. The silver white dove is the Holy Spirit, upon whom the bishop prays to guide his ministry. As a dove of peace it calls to mind the name "Placido," with its meaning of "peaceful".

For his motto Bishop Rodriguez takes the Latin phrase, "Caritas Christi Urget Nos," recalling the words of 2 Corinthians 5:14, in which Paul reminds the people of Corinth that for Christ's gift of redemption to mankind we should all love Him. "The love of Christ impels us" is also the motto of the founder of the Claretian order, St. Anthony Mary Claret (1807-1870), the Spanish bishop who became archbishop of Santiago, Cuba. Claret founded the order (more formally known as the Missionary Sons of the Immaculate Heart of Mary) at Vich, Spain, in 1849. The Claretians, noted for parochial, educational, and retreat work, are primarily missionaries. This motto reminds Bishop Rodriguez, the first of his order to be a bishop in North America, that he is a missionary for Christ.

As bishop of Lubbock, Bishop Rodriguez places his charges on the sinister side of the shield and impales the charges of the Diocese of Lubbock on the dexter side. From top to bottom on each side the personal arms of the bishop occupy the second and fourth quarters of the shield, while those of the diocese occupy the first and third quarters. On the Lubbock side appear the cross of Christ encircled by a crown, signifying that Christ the King is the cathedral church of the diocese. The base of the cross is anchored in cap rock, on which the see city is built. The base color is black, indicating oil in the area. A sprig of cotton reveals the chief agricultural crop of the region.

The external ornaments of the shield, in addition to the motto, pertain to a prelate of the rank of bishop. The golden processional cross is behind the shield, above and below it. The green ecclesiastical hat called a *gallero* and worn by prelates before 1870 has a green cord with six green tassels in three rows on each side. Thus we may say that Bishop Rodriguez's coat of arms is representative of current ecclesiastical heraldry.[31]

Apart from spoken and written forms of address and the portrayal of ecclesiastical status through heraldry, nothing so bespeaks the episcopate in operation as its distinctive vesture and the occasions on which it is worn. Clothing symbolizes the office, its duties and its functions. Each article has its own particular origin and usage. Though papal ceremony and vesture is beyond our present concern, it is important to understand historical distinctions underlying lay and clerical dress and liturgical and nonliturgical circumstances.

Broadly speaking, vesture depends upon certain rituals. When a judge dispenses justice or an academic marches in a processional, he wears robes. A group activity, such as an athletic event, may require the participants to wear certain recognizable costumes. In the United States a Roman Catholic clergyman may appear in public wearing a black suit with a roman-style collar. Bishops add the pectoral cross. Permanent deacons, men in sub-priestly orders, often wear lay clothing. Beyond this the diocesan bishop may decide their correct ecclesiastical attire.

Christians in the time of Christ wore a style known as Greco-Roman. Such clothing consists of a tunic (an inner garment fastened at the back and tied at the waist with a belt) and a mantle (an outer garment wrapped around the body). By the fourth century priests used a special set of Mass vestments. With the barbarian invasion of Europe between the sixth and ninth centuries the laity adopted trousers. The more conservative clergy retained the older dress, which thus attained symbolic value.

The clergy continued to wear the tunic under a modified toga known as the chasuble. In the Middle Ages brocading made vestments more elaborate and the color system more vivid. This so-called Gothic style underwent a renewal in the nineteenth and twentieth centuries. The effect of this movement was to restore the earlier, flowing Roman style of less stiff and more ample pattern. In 1957 the Vatican left the matter to the diocesan bishop.

For the Catholic Christian the rite most often celebrated is the Mass, which is the daily symbolic memorial of Christ's Sacrifice of the Cross. As for any Christian, Christ's death and resurrection and all that it embodies for mankind is the central fact of recorded history. Therefore it is not unusual that as early as the fourth century the clergy had developed distinctive garments for this celebration.

Based upon the Greco-Roman distinction between inner tunic and outer mantle, Mass vestments consist of inner and outer clothing with undergarments of linen (amice, alb, and cincture) and outer garments of more precious material (stole, maniple, and chasuble). While priests wear all of these vestments (except the maniple, which is no longer ordinarily worn), normally only priests and bishops wear stole, chasuble, cope, and humeral veil (worn about the shoulders in Eucharistic processions and certain other liturgical ceremonies). Deacons wear the dalmatic (a tunic with stripes descending from each shoulder) in place of the chasuble.

A cassock and surplice may replace an alb, unless one wears a chasuble or dalmatic or uses a stole instead of a dalmatic ("General Instruction on the *Roman Missal* [1970]," Chapter VI, Paragraph 298, in *The Documents of Vatican II*, 196-197). A cassock is a non-liturgical and full-length robe worn by priests and other clergy under liturgical vestments. It takes the place of the clerical suit on some occasions and is black for priests, purple for bishops and other prelates, red for cardinals, and white for the pope. Priests belonging to religious orders may wear their proper habit. A surplice is a kind of shortened alb, white and with wide sleeves, worn over a cassock for some liturgical ceremonies.[32]

The alb, stole, and chasuble are the minimal vestments for priests celebrating Mass. But the complete inner vestments for Mass are the amice, the alb, and the cincture. The amice probably began as a stole designed to save an outer garment from becoming soiled. It is a rectangular piece of white linen or hemp about twenty-four by thirty-six inches, with long tapes crossed over front and back for wearing over the shoulders. The alb is the modern linen or hemp version of the Greco-Roman tunic. It is white and fastens at the shoulder. In the tenth century the hem and cuff were decorated and later embroidered. The cincture is a white cord of unspecified material about four feet long which belts the alb at the waist twice, its ends fastening the stole in place.

The complete outer vestments for Mass are the stole, maniple (not in current use), and the chasuble. All of these garments follow a color sequence linked to the liturgical year and devised by Pope Innocent III (1198-1216). The stole is a band three inches wide and long enough to show below the chasuble. It may increase in width from three to five or six inches. Although there are often crosses at both ends, either type must have an embroidered cross at the center. It is worn by a priest wearing an alb with both ends folded across his chest.

The maniple was originally a napkin or abbreviated subdiaconal stole with its traditional look developing about the eleventh century. It might be three inches wide with the width extending to five or six inches, varying in length from about thirty-eight to forty-eight inches. Between the ninth and eleventh centuries it was worn just above the left wrist. But since the twelfth century it is worn on the left arm as a symbol of work and service.

The chasuble is the outermost and best-known eucharistic vestment. Descending directly from the toga, its form was modified in the Middle Ages when heavier cloth was used. The arms were gradually cut away until they resembled two panels hanging from shoulder straps. For processions and other ceremonies priests and bishops use the cope, a mantle-like vestment worn open in front and fastened across the chest. It follows the liturgical color scheme.[33]

Liturgical colors vary with seasons of the liturgical year and the feast being celebrated. The liturgical year begins with the season of Advent. Just as Advent foreshadows the season of Christmas (the birth of Christ), so also does the season of Lent foreshadow the season of Easter (the resurrection of Christ). Violet (or purple) is the proper color for Advent and Lent as it symbolizes penance, necessary for the life of the soul and as a solemn preparation for the joyful seasons of Christmas and Easter. The color rose may be used on the Third Sunday of Advent (formerly called Gaudete [Rejoice] Sunday) and the Fourth Sunday of Lent (formerly called Laetare [Joyful] Sunday) in place of purple. The Church allows this custom to remind the faithful that even in such times of penance we may anticipate the joys of the coming seasons.

White has wide usage as a color for the seasons of Christmas and Easter, feasts and commemorations of Christ (except for those of His passion), feasts and commemorations of the Blessed Virgin Mary, angels, saints who are not martyrs, and for the feasts of the Conversion of St. Paul (25 January), the Chair of St. Peter (22 February), St. John the Baptist (24 June), All Saints (1 November), and St. John the Evangelist (27 December). White symbolizes purity and the integrity of the life of faith. It is used increasingly to replace black in Masses for the dead since this usage was approved by American bishops in their Committee on the Liturgy.

Red vestments are worn for the Sunday of the Passion, Good Friday, Pentecost, feasts of the Passion of Our Lord, the Apostles and Evangelists, and martyrs. It is symbolic of the supreme sacrifice of life for the love of God. The liturgical year ends with the season of Ordinary Time, which is the time following the feast of Pentecost. Green is the symbol of hope and the vitality of the life of faith. Thus the year may be said to begin in anticipation and end in the hope of faith, as expressed by the color system ("General Instruction on the *Roman Missal* [1970]," Chapter VI, Paragraph 308, in *The Documents of Vatican II*, 197-198).[34]

Having examined Mass vestments used daily by all ranks of the clergy, we take note of monastic attire and orthodox usage before surveying episcopal ceremony and vesture. Both men and women in religious orders wear habits. This garb consists of a tunic (or cassock), which is secured at the waist by a cincture (or girdle) worn under a scapular (in this case a short cloak derived from a Byzantine work apron). A hood for men and a veil for women completes this outfit, made of brown or black undyed coarse cloth.

Various orders make some differences in the basic pattern. Capuchins wear a rough brown tunic with a hood and a white rope cincture. A mantle covers the hands completely and leather sandals cover the feet. Dominicans use a white tunic, hooded scapular, linen surplice, and a black cloak. Eastern monks wear both the *rhason* (a long black cassock) and a *kamelaukion* (a tall, brimless black felt hat with lappets for ear plugs). Monks of the Assyrian Oriental Church (Nestorians) add a leather cincture and a blue turban, while Syrian Studites use a red cross worn over the chest.

In the fifteenth century usage in the Byzantine Rite began to differ from its Latin Rite (or Greco-Roman) source. Here the clergy employs the *sticharion* (a long alblike tunic) and the *sakkos* (a short, half-sleeved tunic). Other garments are the *epimanika* (stiff cuffs), the *epigonation* (a lozenge-shaped pendant hanging from the waist to the knee on the right side), the stole (worn on the left shoulder like the Latin Rite deacon), and the *omophorion* (like the pallium, but it is a wide scarf of embroidered silk or velvet). The miter (here made of cloth or gilded metal over a frame topped by a cross) and the crozier (here ending in a simple "T" or in a cross centered between two sides) are also in evidence.[35]

In the case of bishops of the Latin Rite of the Roman Catholic Church robes, vestments, and insignia have liturgical and nonliturgical functions. That is, their garments may be worn at sacred functions as prescribed dress (liturgically) and prelatially at sacred functions and as personal robes apart from sacred functions (nonliturgically). In the Roman liturgy bishops celebrate their ceremonies in their cathedrals surrounded by the clergy and people of the diocese. Such ceremonies are treated comprehensively in the *Caeremoniale Episcoporum* (1600) promulgated by Pope Clement VIII. The *Caeremoniale* begins with the arrival of the newly elected bishop in the diocese and ends with his death and burial. It is modeled on papal ceremonial and a new and revised edition was ordered by Vatican Council II's *Sacrosanctum Concilium* (*Constitution on the Sacred Liturgy*, §25, 4 December 1963, in *The Documents of Vatican II*, 10).

Before proceeding to the discussion of episcopal vesture, we shall examine episcopal ceremony to determine ceremonial occasions and some objects associated with them. We have described Mass vestments at some length because Mass is the chief pontifical rite performed by bishops and the single most important ceremony performed by all ranks of the clergy. The various sacred objects used in the celebration of the Mass are not peculiar to bishops. But some objects described in the Roman Pontifical are used by bishops and other higher than priestly ranks in the performance of these rites.

During ceremonies diocesan (residential) bishops have all liturgical privileges accorded to them. These privileges may include solemn reception at the church door with bells ringing, having the throne with assistant deacons, being accorded the seventh candlestick at pontifical Mass, genuflection by the clergy, and having his name read at the canon of the Mass and in the Presces [Prayer] of the Breviary.[36] At his death (which may or may not occur during a bishop's tenure) the bishop may be buried in his cathedral, its churchyard, or in the hallowed ground of a cemetery in his see city.[37]

The archbishop as metropolitan of the province is allowed all the privileges of a local bishop in his suffragan sees, with the right to a throne opposite the diocesan prelate. He may wear the pallium and have the processional cross with the image of Christ facing him. When the metropolitan has been invited to pontificate, he is given the throne while the local ordinary sits elsewhere with no assistants except his master of ceremonies.

When visiting the local ordinary, apostolic delegates or nuncios (all titular archbishops) receive the same privileges except that of the seventh candlestick. Titular bishops may have all the pontifical vestments and insignia except those reserved to the ordinary. They may use the crozier only when required by the Roman Pontifical and the faldstool when pontificating at Mass, Vespers, and other rites. There are no assistant deacons, no throne, and the celebrant does not carry the crozier.

The throne, the faldstool, the bugia, and the canon are objects associated with episcopal ceremonies. The throne is the one item which distinguishes a cathedral from a church, as the word "cathedral" derives from the word for chair or throne. And the phrase to speak *ex cathedra* (literally, "from the chair") means to speak officially. It is a noble chair about four inches higher than an ordinary chair, with a high back and arms and a large footstep in the front. Not more than three steps lead to it, resting on a dais with room for assistant priests and deacons. A baldachino (canopy) is hung over the throne and dais. The throne may not be higher than the altar and, if there is no canopy over the altar, there should be none over the throne. Its use is reserved to the diocesan ordinary and to those enjoying his privileges (the metropolitan, apostolic delegates or nuncios, or a cardinal). In addition it is allowed to an abbot in his titular church, to an apostolic vicar in his own territory, and to prelates *nullius*.

The faldstool is in the shape of a folding chair (though it may not fold) with arms but no back. It is used by all bishops and major prelates. Those using the throne may use the faldstool at the altar, but titular bishops and those without the throne pontificate at the faldstool. It belongs opposite the throne and bishops and cardinals use it when pontificating in the presence of the pope.

The bugia is a small candle in a portable candlestick with a long handle, used by domestic prelates and apostolic protonotaries. A prelate reads at an altar with the bugia on it as a reading light near the Missal. When a prelate is at the throne or faldstool, an acolyte holds the bugia. The canon is a large book containing the Ordinary of the Mass (those prayers which are said daily) and prayers before and after. Bishops use it for convenience, as well as protonotaries apostolic. Like the bugia, it is a prelatial privilege.

Episcopal robes, vestments, and insignia are worn liturgically and nonliturgically. Liturgical vestments and insignia consist of buskins, sandals, and gloves, the tunic and the dalmatic, the miter, the crozier, the ring, the pectoral cross, the pallium, the morse, the gremial, and the rational.

Buskins and sandals are footwear which follow liturgical colors but are not worn at requiem masses. Buskins are stockings reaching just above the knees, with the Roman type made of silk cloth. Roman sandals are usually made with silk on the upper part but may be entirely of leather. Silken gloves follow liturgical colors but are not black nor worn in funeral Masses. The initials "I.H.S." (in Greek, the first three letters of the name of Jesus — Iota, Eta, Sigma) are usually embroidered on a small shield applied to the gloves.

Since the simplification of the Code of Rubrics (§134. 1960), the bishop needs not wear the tunic and the dalmatic in pontifical ceremonies. The tunic was formerly worn by the subdeacon, as the deacon wears the dalmatic. These garments are made of light silk, follow liturgical colors, and are a little longer than (and worn under) the chasuble.

We have discussed the miter and the crozier extensively above. The miter is a type of hat granted by the pope to bishops, abbots, and other dignitaries since the eleventh century. It is always white and made of two similar parts back and front, coming to a point. In the nineteenth century it reached its maximum height of eighteen inches. There is a circle about two inches wide going around the bottom and the *titulus*, a vertical strip of the same width and centered back and front. It can be worn only with other liturgical vestments.

There are three types of miters: the simple, the *auriphrygiata*, and the precious or jeweled. The simple and precious varieties are both white, made of linen or white damask in the first case and white or cloth of silver in the second. The *auriphrygiata* is cloth of gold with no trim except for a gold galloon (embroidery with metallic threads) around the edge. It can also be of white silk or satin, with circle and *titulus* in cloth of silver or some other embroidered cloth. At convocations such as Eucharistic congresses it is plain cloth of gold with no ornament. The simple miter in plain linen is worn in papal ceremonies and at ecumenical councils. Silken miters are for funerals and for Good Friday. But they can take the place of cloth of gold miters in processions, church consecrations, and in other ceremonies. The precious miter has its circle and *titulus* embroidered in gold, silver, or silk. It may be enriched with semiprecious stones or some kind of embroidery.

We have discussed the crozier as an heraldic emblem. This shepherd's staff is a sign of the diocesan bishop or abbot's office. The gilt silver type is usually for cardinals. It should be light and portable. As old as the ring, it dates to at least the sixth century. Like the king's scepter, it symbolizes authority, watchfulness, and discipline.

Bishops, abbots and others wear the ring as marks of their offices. They wear the pectoral cross on chains around their necks and over their chests. This practice was put into standard effect by Pope Pius V in his edition of the Roman Missal (1570). Composed of gold or gilt silver, it may have precious stones and contain relics. When worn with the prelatial habit, it is attached to a green and gold cordon with a tassel at the back. The pallium is an ecclesiastical garment now worn exclusively by the pope and archbishops. It is discussed thoroughly in connection with the archbishop as metropolitan and in church heraldry above.

The morse is an oval ornament originally used to fasten the cope. It has a symbol of Christ or of the Holy Spirit upon it, though a special design for cardinal bishops is that of three pine cones. In general use by diocesan bishops, a simpler type is for penitential days and a silver one for solemn occasions. The gremial is a silk veil following the liturgical color scheme. It is twenty to thirty inches long, adorned with a cordon all around without a cross added to it. It is laid over the knees of a bishop when he is seated on his throne or the faldstool. The rational or superhumerale is a modern form of the ephod (a linen apron worn in ancient rites by the Hebrew high priest), a shoulder cape made of embroidered gold cloth. It is still worn mainly in Europe by some bishops in what was once part of the old German Empire.

Bishops and some other prelates also wear nonliturgical robes, vestments, and insignia. These consist of a cassock (purple for bishops and archbishops, red for cardinals, and white for the pope), with its train eliminated by Pope Pius XII in 1952. Other regalia are the silk sash with a tassel at each end, the rochet covered by the mantelletta, the mozzetta, and the *cappa magna*. Various types of headgear are the zucchetto (skull cap), the biretta, and the ecclesiastical hat. The ring and the pectoral cross also have nonliturgical use.

The newly chosen bishop receives his rochet from the pope in Rome. Pope Innocent III declared in 1215 that all bishops should wear this linen tunic in church and in public over their ordinary clothes or cassocks. Innocent's order exempted all religious order bishops who wore habits. But its use was extended to them by Pope Benedict XV (1914-1922). The rochet relates closely to the alb with its long sleeves, which are wide on the upper part and narrow at the wrist. It reaches below the knees and is three yards around, with lace at the lower part of the skirt and sleeves. The rochet is never more than a foot wide.

The mozzetta (formerly the capucium) is a short cape with a nonfunctional hood worn over the rochet. It reaches below the elbows and is buttoned in front with the pectoral cross worn over it. It has been used by popes and prelates since the twelfth century. About the same time the mantelletta came into use. This garment is a cape covering the surplice of bishops and cardinals in the presence of the pope. It is sleeveless, open in front, and fastens at the neck with an opening on either side for the arms. It should reach three to four inches below the knees and cover the rochet entirely. Both the mozetta and the mantelletta should be of the same cloth and color as the cassock eccept for religious prelates wearing the color of their orders. The mozetta is a sign of jurisdiction and should be worn by the diocesan bishop. Pope Paul VI (1963-1978) decided that bishops may wear both garments.

The *cappa magna* or large cloak is obligatory for the diocesan bishop when assisting at the throne. An assistant carries the train (except when cardinals are present and the bishop carries it himself). Covering the entire body, this shoulder cape has a large hood attached to the upper part and is covered by ermine in winter. The train is about ten feet long and is added to the back. Its use is reserved to the diocesan bishop, the metropolitan in his province, apostolic delegates and nuncios, and to cardinals. It is purple for bishops and purple or red for cardinals.

The zucchetto or skullcap, the biretta, and the prelatial hat are worn by bishops and other higher ranks. The zucchetto is now given to bishops on appointment. Originally it was a liner for the miter and still serves in this capacity. Colors follow personal rank and it is removed when the Blessed Sacrament is exposed and in the presence of the pope. It originally covered the sides and back of a bishop's head and had the shape of the papal velvet biretta. Bishops who are canons regular wear a black skull cap with a white biretta.

The biretta is a stiff, square hat with three ridges and is surmounted by a pom-pom. It is of varying colors but corresponds with the zucchetto in this regard. The prelatial hat is black with a low round crown and a large brim. Surrounding the crown is a cord with tassels at each end, green for bishops, green and gold for archbishops, red and gold for cardinals. It is worn with a plain habit (black cassock and purple ferraiola or ceremonial cloak) and purple robes. Purple stockings and black shoes with gilt buckles complete this outfit.[38]

We have seen how forms of address, heraldry, and vesture make up the outward being of the bishop. Many centuries have gone into achieving his style and appearance. But though these attributes indicate the way in which he is regarded, much as a uniform or regalia demonstrate to us the status of the wearer, it is diocesan administration and finance and their usages which best denote the modern hierarchy. After seeing how the hierarchy came to be in relation to its development within the State of Texas, we shall turn our attention to the modern bishop in his diocese and conclude with a profile of the Texas bishop.

H. How The Province of San Antonio Developed Within Texas

My present purpose is not to relate the history of the Roman Catholic Church within Texas.[1] Rather it is to show how the Province of San Antonio, the ecclesiastical jurisdiction now encompassing the entire state, came to be within the political jurisdiction of the Republic and later State of Texas. We need be aware of the Hispanic origins of both province and state and remember that both these entities were not provinces in the sense of independent units. They were, for much of their existences, provinces in the sense that both were part (and certainly for organizational purposes, subdivisions) of Spain and afterwards Mexico. Because church and state were so united in these Hispanic governments, it is not unreasonable to say that from the sixteenth century until the fourth decade of the nineteenth century Catholic history in Texas is much the history of Texas itself.

The independence of Mexico from Spain (1821) offered much promise for Anglo-American colonization of Texas. But Stephen F. Austin and other empressarios soon found the customs of the Mexicans restrictive. They were expected to become Catholics to acquire land and the Spanish language and traditions proved uncongenial for a number of the new settlers. For its part the Mexican government began to realize that such an arrangement was filling Texas with potential revolutionaries.

The Mexican Congress terminated future immigration from the United States into Texas by the Act of 6 April 1830. At this time a total of 26,280,000 acres, about one-seventh of the total area, was in the hands of private enterpreneurs.[2] American colonists found other Mexican land laws hostile to their interests. A statute of 26 March 1834 provided for the sale of public domain in tracts up to eleven leagues or 48,712.4 acres. A law of 5 April 1835 authorized the governor of Coahuila and Texas to grant land in return for militia service. Three speculators acquired 124 leagues or 549,121.6 acres of Texas land by this method.

The Revolution of Texas against Mexico brought about the Republic of Texas in 1836. For driving out the Mexican forces, every soldier of the Republic and those fighting at the Alamo, Goliad, San Antonio, Harrisburg, or their heirs were entitled to 640 acres each. These lands could not be sold nor mortgaged in the grantee's lifetime. Texas with all its public lands was both poverty-stricken and land-rich. Beginning with only $55.68 in its treasury, the Republic arranged two loans of $200,000 each in January 1836 with land scrip as security. Only $20,007 was advanced in payment. These debts were cancelled by 40,000 acres of land and 13,357 acres as a bonus. An Act of 10 December 1836 authorized President Sam Houston to issue scrip for sale at not less than fifty-five cents an acre. Sales and grants to retire debts continued until 11 January 1842 and a total of 1,329,200 acres were sold to pay the public debts of the Republic.[3]

Before it became a state Texas claimed much more area than its present boundaries. On 18 December 1836 its congress asserted jurisdiction over a large part of present-day New Mexico and Colorado and a smaller part of Kansas and Wyoming.[4] With the Texas Constitution of 1836 a General Land Office to administer the lands of the Republic was opened in February 1837.[5] The Republic of Texas issued headright certificates and bounties to soldiers of the Republic.

These certificates were issued under an act of 1839. It provided that every head of a family immigrating to Texas between 1 October 1837 and 1 January 1840 who actually resided within the Republic with his or her family was entitled to a grant of 640 acres of land. The certificate was to be held for three years and then conveyed by absolute deed to the settler. The deed was conditional upon the settler's permanent residence within the Republic and the performance of all duties required by citizens (Cannon v. Vaughan, 12 Tex. 401).

The Board of Land Commissioners issued the certificates, which were then located in the open domain. Location and survey were the responsibility of the land claimant. All grants were not located and surveyed and "relief" continued to be granted to headright claimants under the State of Texas until the 1880s. At that time the remaining public domain was conveyed to the public school system. Headright certificates and bounties eventually totaled 36,876,492 acres.[6]

Between 1836 and 1844 the Republic of Texas developed an empressario system of European immigration, chiefly from Germany and France. The British also backed American empressarios. Altogether the Republic conveyed 4,494,806 acres to settlers brought in by various empressarios.[7] Under the first homestead law of 22 January 1845 persons settled upon and improving portions of the public domain, or those doing so in the future, could locate 320 acres.

About this time Texas accepted the terms for annexation and statehood proposed by a joint resolution of the Congress of the United States on 28 February 1845. Congress required Texas to submit a state constitution, cede its public property (such as forts, barracks, and customhouses), and retain its public lands and its public debt. It could also divide itself into four additional states as well as the original State of Texas. For its part the United States would negotiate the Rio Grande boundary claim of Texas with Mexico.[8] Texas submitted a state constitution and was accepted by Congress on 29 December 1845. On 19 February 1846 the transfer of power was complete. The old republic was now a new state.

With the annexation of Texas Mexico, mainly concerned with internal matters during the Texas Republic period, rejected the claim of Texas to the Rio Grande as its boundary. This situation touched off the Mexican War (1846-1848). When Mexico concluded the Treaty of Guadalupe Hidalgo (1848) with the United States, Texas assumed her essential present dimensions. This loss represented about one-third of its former territory, but it did fix the Rio Grande as the boundary with Mexico. In return for expanded territory the United States paid Mexico reparations of $15 million. The American government also assumed claims payments of American citizens against Mexico incurred before the treaty and not to exceed $3.25 million.

The Compromise of 1850 permanently set Texas' western boundaries. Congress paid Texas $10 million to settle the claim to relinquished territory. With the money the Republic of Texas debt was paid off, a permanent school fund set up, and some money returned to individual counties for public works.[9] The land policy of Texas continued even after secession and involvement as a Confederate state (1861-1865). Although it rejoined the Union five years later (1870), its citizens did not regain effective control of the state government until 1874.

Homestead laws of 1845 and 1853 were repealed in 1854, and settlers improving the public domain were limited to 160 acres. The constitution of 1876 (Texas' present constitution) restored both homestead laws, and a total of 4,847,136 acres were granted for homestead purposes.[10] So a total of 72,498,434 acres of the public domain was disposed of under the Republic and the State of Texas.[11]

An act of 26 April 1879 granted an additional 640 acres to each indigent veteran of the Texas Revolution for a total of 1,169,382 acres. By an act of 1881 disabled Confederate veterans were awarded 1,280 acres each, unless such a veteran possessed an "estate" (real and personal property worth at least $1 thousand). This act for Confederate veterans was a land donation of 1,979,852 acres, or a total of 3,149,234 acres to benefit both classes of veterans.[12]

By the Sales Scrip Act of 1879 Texas sold public land scrip in West Texas for fifty cents an acre, while the Sales Scrip Act of 1887 set a price of two dollars an acre. The proceeds were divided equally between payment of State debt and the Permanent Public School Fund. Under the two acts a total of 1,660,936 acres were sold.[13] Under the Republic of Texas scrip was sold for payment of public debt and by the State by the Sales Scrip Acts of 1879 and 1887 for a total of 2,990,136 acres.[14]

Because Texas rivers were not easily navigable, companies to clear rafts and build canals or open stream beds were organized. The Republic of Texas authorized construction of a highway in 1844, promising 160 acres for each finished mile. Twenty-seven thousand acres were awarded in partial compensation though the road was never built. During the Civil War the State offered 320 acres for each $1 thousand of machinery installed to aid the war effort. These grants for internal improvements amounted to 4,088,640 acres.[15]

Another type of internal improvement was the building of the present state capitol in Austin. The Sixteenth Legislature set aside 3,000,000 acres of public domain for this purpose. Another 50,000 acres were set aside for incidental expenses. The State built a narrow-gauge railroad from the site to Granite Mountain near Burnet and provided granite and convict labor to repair the road from Burnet to Austin. The building was dedicated on 16 May 1888. Although the State recovered 57,836 acres in excess land from the Capitol Freehold Land and Investment Company in 1928, it had expended 3,025,000 acres of public domain in this endeavor.[16]

The State of Texas also encouraged railroad construction by voting sixteen sections of public land for each mile of railroad construction. The railroad received odd-numbered sections, while even-numbered sectional tracts were reserved for the public schools. In this 1854 arrangement the railroads were required to survey an adjoining 640 acres for the school system for each bounty section received. The Constitution of 1876 enacted a general law. All locations were made prior to 1 September 1895 and totaled 35,777,038 acres. By conflicts of recovery by the State 3,623,160 acres were lost, leaving 32,153,878 acres.[17]

Land set aside for the University of Texas and Texas A&M University use amounts to 2,329,168 acres.[18] County schools have received 4,229,166 acres.[19] State eleemosynary institutions have been allotted 410,600 acres.[20] By 1993 state public free schools have 44,494,162 acres, with 813,122 acres of unsold public land.[21] This amount brings that part of the public domain dedicated to education to a total of 52,276,218 acres.[22]

We may now summarize the 1993 figures of the public domain according to the records of the General Land Office of Texas.[23]

Grants for citizenship and immigration:	72,498,434	acres
Donations to veterans:	3,149,234	
Sale for public debts/land scrip:	2,990,136	
Internal improvements:	7,113,640	
Grants to railroads:	32,153,878	
For education:	52,276,218	
Total surveyed land:	170,181,540	acres
Less conflicts (1/2 of 1%):	850,908	
Net acreage (original surveys):	169,330,632	acres
Excess (about 1.1%):	1,862,637	
River beds/vacancies (estimate):	1,000,000	
Total land area to tidewater:	172,193,269	acres

This acreage translates into 269,052 square miles, excluding 3,997,000 of submerged coastal area beyond the tidewater to the three-league (10.36 mile) limit (or a grand total of 176,190,269 acres).[24]

Thanks to the historical situation which allowed Texas to maintain its public domain after statehood, we have at least some notion of what land it contains. We now turn our attention to the ecclesiastical province of San Antonio, which has developed within the State of Texas and has continued to establish its jurisdiction within it. For the Vatican the successive revolutions freeing Mexico from Spain and Texas from Mexico represented disruptions in communication and governance. The church in Texas could no longer be viewed as a part of the Mexican church. This situation had consequences for the development of Texas as a separate entity.

As a strictly territorial matter, the Vatican recognized the fact of the Texas Revolution and the existence of the Republic of Texas. It knew that Mexico, except in the immediate area of El Paso, no longer had ecclesiastical control over Texas. The effective control had passed to a religious order known as the Congregation of the Mission, more commonly known as Vincentians after their founder and also as Lazarists after their former home, the College of St. Lazare in Paris.

Founded by St. Vincent de Paul (ca. 1581-1660) in Paris in 1625, the Vincentians were an order renowned for educational work. The order came to the United States in 1818, and in 1840 had a resident branch in The Barrens of Perry County, Missouri. On 24 October 1839 Bartolomeo Cappellari, Pope Gregory XVI, issued letters patent erecting the Prefecture Apostolic of Texas. He left the appointment of the prefect to the Superior General of the Vincentian order, the Very Reverend C. M. Nozo, CM. Nozo in turn chose one of his priests,

John Timon, CM (1797-1867), who later became the first bishop of Buffalo, New York (1847-1867).

Father Timon received the letters patent and appointment creating him both Prefect of Texas and Provincial Superior of the American Province of The Barrens on 12 April 1840. By this appointment and acceptance the first seed was planted. Texas would now grow from a mission territory into an expanding Catholic province.

As prefect Timon could appoint another Vincentian as resident substitute in the Republic of Texas. He soon named Rev. Jean-Marie Odin, CM (1800-1870) his Vice-Prefect Apostolic. At this time Odin was Procurator and Consultant of the American Vincentian Province and professor of belles lettres in St. Mary's College of the Barrens. With almost twenty years of experience as a missionary in Missouri and Louisiana he was an excellent choice.

As Prefect of Texas Timon had the powers of a residential bishop within the prefecture and ecclesiastical jurisdiction over all inhabiting Catholics. These powers were effective for Texas as it existed under Mexico, and not with all the land area claimed by the Republic of Texas. Such an entity was now formally removed from the direct jurisdiction of the bishop of Monterrey in Mexico. Organized as a territory, it was not yet independent.[25] Timon wasted no time in consolidating his gains, however.

In company with Rev. Nicholas Stehlé, CM, he brought official greetings from Rome to President Mirabeau B. Lamar of Texas in mid-December 1840. The letter from Cardinal Fransoni, Secretary of the Sacred Congregation for the Propagation of the Faith, had two purposes. One was to introduce Timon as prefect apostolic and the other was "to cause whatever property may belong to the Church to be handed over to him as to the lawful Pastor." More importantly, continued Fransoni, "I so commend him to you that whatever benefit you may confer upon him, my eminent colleagues and I will consider as conferred upon us."[26]

This "semi-state" paper was written in Latin and addressed "To His Excellency, the President of the Texian Republic". It was translated into English and first published in the *Austin Sentinel* on 9 January 1841. It officially and publicly confirmed the erection of the prefecture of Texas, and it meant formal recognition of the Republic by the Vatican.[27] This diplomatic task done, it was necessary to receive formal confirmation of church rights to the same property held under the Spanish and Mexican governments of Texas.

Odin prepared a petition to "Honorable the Senate and House of Representatives of the Republic of Texas in Congress Assembled". Congressman William Porter introduced the petition to the House and immediately referred it to a committee of seven, of which he was a member. The petition concludes:

> Confiding on the liberality and justice of your honorable Body, your petitioner humbly solicits a decision declaring that all the churches built or donated by the former governments for the use of the Roman Catholic worship shall be reserved and maintained for the same use and end. Such a decision will be a great favor conferred on the Catholic part of this community.

Thus by 21 December 1840 both the Executive and the Congress of the Republic were informed of the Catholic request for confirmation of its land.[28]

By 18 January 1841 President David G. Burnet signed into law two acts which restored churches and missions to "the chief pastor" of the Roman Catholic church in Texas and to his successors in office in trust forever. This recognition gave Timon and those who took his place the means to "control, direct, and administer" all agencies and institutions independent of lay control.[29]

Father Odin's contribution was deemed crucial to the development of the Church in Texas. The Vatican wished to advance him to bishop of Detroit but allowed the Sacred Congregation for the Propagation of the Faith to propose an alternative. Odin would henceforth be Titular Bishop of Claudiopolis and Vicar Apostolic of Texas. Pope Gregory XVI issued the Brief *Universi dominici gregis* on 16 July 1841. This document completed the second stage in Texas' growth. No longer a prefecture (a separate mission territory within an ecclesiastical province), it was now a mission territory with its own bishop. The Province of Texas was now permanently separated from even the remote authority of the bishop of Monterrey.[30]

Texas also continued to go onward. The Republic disappeared with statehood, and the Mexican War could not change its course. And Bishop Odin proved a capable chief pastor. *The Catholic Almanac for 1847* shows that the Catholic Church in Texas was more improved than the dioceses of Hartford (1843), Richmond (1820), Nashville and Dubuque (both 1837), Little Rock (1843), Natchez (now Jackson, 1837), and the archdiocese of Oregon City (now Portland, 1846) (190f, 225).[31]

The Sixth Council of Baltimore recommended the establishment of the Diocese of Galveston. On 4 May 1847 Giovanni Mastai-Ferretti, Pope Pius IX, established it with his Bull *Apostolicae sedis fastigio*. By another Bull, this time of appointment and dated 21 May 1847, Bishop Odin was appointed bishop of Galveston. He received both documents on 21 July 1847.[32]

The bull of erection creating the diocese of Galveston did not define its boundaries. But the Treaty of Guadalupe-Hidalgo concluding the Mexican War in 1848 caused Mexico to recognize the statehood of Texas and to establish the Rio Grande as the boundary line between itself and the United States. The river became the southern boundary of Texas, and the boundaries of the State were fixed.

> From Latitude 25°50' N. at the extreme southern turn of the Rio Grande on the south line of Cameron County to Latitude 36°30' N. along the north line of the Panhandle, and from Longitude 93°31' W. at the extreme eastern point on the Sabine River on the east line of Newton County to Longitude 106°38' W. on the extreme westward point to the Rio Grande above El Paso.[33]

Although Bishop Odin's church properties were protected under the State of Texas as under the Republic, how far did the boundaries of the former Mexican Province of Texas extend? Cardinal Barnabo, as secretary of the Congregation of the Propagation of the Faith, wanted to know. So on 18 September 1851, while visiting Rome, the Bishop wrote the Cardinal a letter. He mentioned that the territory between the Nueces River and the Rio Grande and the major part of Texas was formerly a part of the Diocese of Monterrey in Mexico. The political province of New Mexico had been under the jurisdiction of the bishop of Durango, Mexico.

From independence in 1836 Texans claimed the Rio Grande from its mouth to its source as their western boundary. This area included most of New Mexico on the North and the area between the Nueces and the Rio Grande. Bishop Odin did not consider this claim "part of Texas properly speaking," but he accepted the Treaty of Guadalupe-Hidalgo as absolute because the Diocese of Galveston was formed during hostilities between the United States and Mexico settled by that treaty.

The Bishop did not visit the lower Rio Grande Valley and New Mexico east of the Rio Grande claimed by Texas until claims between the federal government and Texas were adjusted. He appealed to the Congregation in 1848 and received word in 1849 that he should exercise jurisdiction "over not only that part of the country lying between the Nueces and the Rio Grande, but also all that territory of New Mexico lying east of the Rio Grande considered by Texas to be an integral part of its territory". [34]

To the Vatican this solution seemed reasonable. But Bishop Odin knew practical governance was beyond the powers of any one man. Accordingly, he petitioned the Seventh Provincial Council of Baltimore for aid in 1849. As the Bishop explained to Cardinal Barnabo in his letter of 1851, "The Bishops gathered in Baltimore [in 1849], realizing that the Diocese of Galveston was already too large for the care of one bishop, deemed it advisable to beg the Holy See to send a vicar apostolic to look after New Mexico".[35]

This matter was settled when Pope Pius IX made New Mexico a vicariate apostolic by a Bull of 29 July 1850. He named Bishop Jean B. Lamy as the Vicar.[36] And here the story might have ended, except that the Vatican did not finish developing Texas. Not until 12 April 1983 did the Province of San Antonio at last become coterminous with the boundaries of the State of Texas. With the establishment of the Diocese of Lubbock (1983) and the Diocese of Tyler (1986) the Province of San Antonio subdivided twice more. This province will undoubtedly continue its internal division into the future.

But a single diocese, even one so large as Galveston in 1847, cannot exist independently. In its case it became a suffragan of the Archdiocese of New Orleans upon its creation by Pope Pius IX through his Bull *Ad supremum Apostolicae* of 19 July 1850. This document placed Texas with the region between the Nueces and the Rio Grande within the province of New Orleans, along with Louisiana, Alabama, Mississippi, and Arkansas.[37]

In 1872 the Bishop of Durango, Mexico, whose predecessors administered the El Paso area from 1620, was relieved from his American duties by Pope Pius IX. It was now placed within the Vicariate of Tucson, Arizona. From 1890 to 1914 its care was that of the bishops of Dallas. In 1914 El Paso became a diocese.

Since it had New Mexican, as well as Texan, counties, it remained part of the Province of Santa Fe, New Mexico, until Pope John Paul II allowed the Province of Santa Fe to include only New Mexico and Arizona and the Province of San Antonio to include only the State of Texas.[38] The New Mexican counties of the Diocese of El Paso (Doña Ana, Eddy, Grant, Hidalgo, Lea, Luna, Otero, and the remainder of Sierra), together with some others, became the new

Diocese of Las Cruces on 18 October 1982, while the now entirely Texan Diocese of El Paso became part of the San Antonio province on 12 April 1983. And on this day the State of Texas and the Province of San Antonio became one coterminous land mass.

Beginning with the Diocese of Galveston-Houston, we shall examine the formation of the Province of San Antonio by continuing its narrative history and pausing at intervals to note its present (1994) constitution. Our sources for the land area of each diocese are the 1994-1995 *Texas Almanac* (TA) and the 1993 *Official Catholic Directory* (OCD) showing current boundaries with information as of 1993. Both the almanac and the directory use square miles, the almanac listing a figure for each of the 254 Texas counties and the directory listing individual counties making up the dioceses and giving a total figure only for each diocese.

Diocese of Galveston-Houston[39]
Created Diocese of Galveston 4 May 1847
Redesignated 25 July 1959

Counties	(County Seats)	Land Area (sq. ml.)
Austin	(Belleville)	652.6*
Brazoria	(Angleton)	1,386.8
Fort Bend	(Richmond)	875.0
Galveston	(Galveston)	398.6
Grimes	(Anderson)	793.8
Harris	(Houston)	1,728.9
Madison	(Madisonville)	469.6
Montgomery	(Conroe)	1,044.3
San Jacinto	(Coldspring)	570.7
Walker	(Huntsville)	787.5
Waller	(Hempstead)	513.6
TA Total:		9,221.4
OCD Total:		9,354

*These figures exclude a total water area of 870.4 square miles for the eleven Texas counties which make up the Diocese of Galveston-Houston.

At the recommendation of the Third Provincial Council of New Orleans, Pope Pius IX (after consultation with the Congregation for the Propagation of the Faith) divided the Diocese of Galveston by the decree *Arcano Divinae Providentiae* of 27 August 1874 (effective 3 September 1874). The new Diocese of San Antonio separated from the Diocese of Galveston "that part of the State or territory of Texas which lies between the Colorado River on the east and the Nueces River on the west." North and South boundaries were unspecified, but Castañeda gives the boundaries of the Diocese on the basis of an old map in the Chancery of San Antonio as

beginning at the mouth of the Nueces River and running from this

> point on the Gulf along the river to its source, thought at that time to be near Rock Springs [sic] in Edwards County. The line on the map runs lightly southwest to the point where the Pecos empties into the Rio Grande in Val Verde County, then follows the Rio Grande to the southern boundary of New Mexico, excepting El Paso County — much more extensive then — and continues along the southern limits of New Mexico east and down to the Colorado River to the Gulf.[40]

By the Bull *In Futuram Rei Memoriam* Pope Pius IX created the Vicariate Apostolic of Brownsville on 18 September 1874. He redefined certain of its boundary lines on 21 July 1877, giving the Vicariate by decree the counties of Bee, Goliad, Aransas, Refugio, San Patricio, and part of Live Oak in the Diocese of San Antonio in compensation for which it was granted a tract north of Arroyo de los Hermanos, a tributary of the Rio Grande, and San Roque Creek, which flowed into the Nueces. Castañeda could not find the "Arroyo de los Hermanos" as a creek flowing into the Rio Grande by that name in the area. He concludes, "It probably derived the name from the friars or missionaries generally referred to in Spanish as 'hermanos'. This little creek may have marked the limits of the area visited by the Oblates from Brownsville."

Among the counties ceded to the Diocese of San Antonio were Val Verde, Edwards, Uvalde, Zavala, Dimmit, Webb, Kinney, and Maverick. The boundaries of the Diocese, about 90,909 square miles, remained without major change until the creation of the El Paso diocese in 1914.[41]

By 1925 Archbishop John Shaw of New Orleans, the former bishop of San Antonio, decided that his suffragans of Galveston, San Antonio, Dallas, and Corpus Christi should be part of a new metropolitan province within Texas. The Santa Fe Province would continue to administer the Diocese of El Paso. With the approval of the Congregation of Cardinals and recognizing the development of Catholicism in Texas, Achille Ratti, Pope Pius XI issued the Bull *Pastoris Aeterni* on 3 August 1926. This action made San Antonio an archdiocese and created a metropolitan province with sees of Galveston, Dallas, Corpus Christi, Oklahoma (later Oklahoma City), and Amarillo, leaving El Paso part of the Province of Santa Fe.[42]

Archdiocese of San Antonio[43]
Created a Diocese 27 August 1874
Established 28 August 1874
Created an Archbishopric 3 August 1926

Counties	(County Seats)	Land Area (sq. ml.)
Atascosa	(Jourdanton)	1,232.2*
Bandera	(Bandera)	791.7
Bexar	(San Antonio)	1,246.9
Comal	(New Braunfels)	561.4
Dimmit	(Carrizo Springs)	1,331.0

Edwards	(Rocksprings)	2,119.9
Frio	(Pearsall)	1,133.1
Gillespie	(Fredericksburg)	1,061.1
Gonzales	(Gonzales)	1,067.8
Guadalupe	(Seguin)	711.2
Karnes	(Karnes City)	750.3
Kendall	(Boerne)	662.4
Kerr	(Kerrville)	1,106.2
Kinney	(Brackettville)	1,363.5
Maverick	(Eagle Pass)	1,280.1
Medina	(Hondo)	1,327.8
Real	(Leakey)	699.1
Uvalde	(Uvalde)	1,556.6
Val Verde	(Del Rio)	3,170.6
Wilson	(Floresville)	807.1
Zavala	(Crystal City)	1,298.5

*These figures exclude a total water area of 136.3 square miles for these twenty-one counties.

In addition to these complete counties, the Archdiocese of San Antonio includes "that part of La Salle County north of the Nueces River" and "that part of McMullen County north of the Nueces River," including their respective county seats of Cotulla and Tilden. The whole land area of both counties is 2,601.9 square miles, with La Salle County being 1,488.9 (excluding a water area of 5.3 square miles) and McMullen County being 1,113.0 square miles (excluding a water area of 29.6 square miles). As the Diocese of Corpus Christi claims 1,409.5 square miles to make up a total of 17,294 square miles, it must be assumed that the Archdiocese of San Antonio claims the remaining 1,192.4 square miles in La Salle and McMullen counties.

TA Total:	approximately	26,470.9
OCD Total:		27,841

At the request of Bishop Nicholas Gallagher of Galveston and the other bishops of the Province of New Orleans in 1889, Gioacchino Pecci, Pope Leo XIII, in his Brief *Romani Pontificis* of 15 July 1890 erected the Diocese of Dallas. It consisted of Texas north of the counties of Lampasas, Coryell, McLennan, Freestone, Anderson, Cherokee, Nacogdoches, and Shelby. It included implicitly the El Paso district and the counties of El Paso and Culberson were included in its administration until 1914. The new diocese was estimated at 108,000 square miles.[44]

Diocese of Dallas[45]
Established 15 July 1890
Redesignated Diocese of Dallas-Fort Worth 20 October 1953
Redesignated Diocese of Dallas 27 August 1969

Counties	(County Seats)	Land Area (sq. ml.)
Collin	(McKinney)	847.7*
Dallas	(Dallas)	879.8
Ellis	(Waxahachie)	939.9
Fannin	(Bonham)	891.5
Grayson	(Sherman)	933.6
Hunt	(Greenville)	841.2
Kaufman	(Kaufman)	786.1
Navarro	(Corsicana)	1,071.2
Rockwall	(Rockwell)	128.7
TA Total:		7,319.7
OCD Total:		7,523

*These figures exclude a total water area of 228.2 square miles for the nine Texas counties which make up the Diocese of Dallas.

In 1911 at the request of the bishops of the New Orleans province and with the approval of the Sacred College of Cardinals, Giuseppe Sarto, Pope St. Pius X, in his Bull *Sapienti Consilio* of 23 March 1912 raised the status of the Vicariate Apostolic of Brownsville by making it the Diocese of Corpus Christi.[46]

Diocese of Corpus Christi[47]
Erected Vicariate Apostolic of Brownsville 18 September 1874
Elevated to a Diocese 23 March 1912

Counties	(County Seats)	Land Area (sq. ml.)
Aransas	(Rockport)	251.9*
Bee	(Beeville)	880.2
Brooks	(Falfurrias)	943.3
Duval	(San Diego)	1,792.8
Jim Hogg	(Hebronville)	1,136.1
Jim Wells	(Alice)	864.6
Kenedy	(Sarita)	1,456.8
Kleberg	(Kingsville)	871.0
Live Oak	(George West)	1,036.3
Nueces	(Corpus Christi)	835.8
Refugio	(Refugio)	770.3
San Patricio	(Sinton)	691.7
Webb	(Laredo)	3,356.9
Zapata	(Zapata)	996.8

*These figures exclude a total water area of 1,507.7 square miles for these fourteen counties.

The Diocese of Corpus Christi also includes "parts of La Salle and McMullen [counties], in the State of Texas". As the Archdiocese of San Antonio claims parts of both counties "north of the Nueces River," and the land area in both counties is 2,601.9 square miles, that part claimed by the Diocese of Corpus Christi would be 1,409.5 to total the 17,294 square miles claimed for it.

TA Total:	approximately	17,294
OCD Total:		17,294

Soon after the elevation of the former vicariate to the Diocese of Corpus Christi, the rapid growth in the southwest after 1900 led the bishops of the Santa Fe province meeting in 1913 to request that the Diocese of Tucson be limited to Arizona and that the extreme southern part of New Mexico be separated from it. The New Mexican counties of Grant, Luna, Doña Ana, Otero, Eddy, and part of Sierra were joined to the Texas counties of El Paso and Culberson ceded by the Diocese of Dallas and by the counties of Presidio, Jeff Davis, Reeves, Brewster, Terrell, Pecos, Crane, Ward, Loving, Winkler, Ector, Andrews, and Gaines ceded by the Diocese of San Antonio. Thus with the consent of the Sacred College of Cardinals Pope St. Pius X ordered this arrangement by the Bull of 3 March 1914, creating the Diocese of El Paso within the Santa Fe province.[48]

Diocese of El Paso[49]
Erected 3 March 1914

Counties	(County Seats)	Land Area (sq. ml.)
Brewster	(Alpine)	6,193.0*
Culberson	(Van Horn)	3,812.6
El Paso	(El Paso)	1,013.0
Hudspeth	(Sierra Blanca)	4,571.3
Jeff Davis	(Fort Davis)	2,264.5
Loving	(Mentone)	673.1
Presidio	(Marfa)	3,855.7
Reeves	(Pecos)	2,636.0
Ward	(Monahans)	835.5
Winkler	(Kermit)	841.1
TA Total:		26,695.8
OCD Total:		26,686

*These figures exclude a total water area of 13.6 square miles for the ten Texas counties which make up the Diocese of El Paso.

Pope Pius XI created the Archdiocese of San Antonio and the Diocese of Amarillo on the same day (3 August 1926). To form Amarillo the counties of Martin, Howard, Midland, Glasscock, Sterling, Upton, Reagan, Irion, Tom Green, Concho, Crockett, Schleicher, Menard, Sutton, Kimble, half of Mitchell and Coke, and one-eighth of Runnels came from the San Antonio archdiocese. The Diocese of Dallas furnished the counties of Dallam, Sherman, Hansford, Ochiltree, Lipscomb, Hartley, Moore, Hutchinson, Roberts, Hemphill, Oldham, Potter, Carson, Gray, Wheeler, Deaf Smith, Randall, Armstrong, Donley, Collingsworth, Parmer, Castro, Hall, Swisher, Briscoe, Childress, Bailey, Lamb, Hale, Floyd, Motley, Cottle, King, Cochran, Hockley, Lubbock, Crosby, Dickens, Yoakum, Terry, Lynn, Garza, Kent, Stonewall, Dawson, Borden, Scurry, Fisher, Nolan, and the other half of Mitchell and Coke. From the Diocese of El Paso came the counties of Gaines, Andrews, Ector, and Crane.[50] Presently there are twenty-six Texas counties in the diocese.

Diocese of Amarillo[51]
Created 3 August 1926
Erected 25 August 1926

Counties	(County Seats)	Land Area (sq. ml.)
Armstrong	(Claude)	913.6*
Briscoe	(Silverton)	900.3
Carson	(Panhandle)	923.2
Castro	(Dimmitt)	898.4
Childress	(Childress)	710.3
Collingsworth	(Wellington)	918.8
Dallam	(Dalhart)	1,504.8
Deaf Smith	(Hereford)	1,497.4
Donley	(Clarendon)	929.8
Gray	(Pampa)	928.3
Hall	(Memphis)	903.1
Hansford	(Spearman)	919.8
Hartley	(Channing)	1,462.3
Hemphill	(Canadian)	909.7
Hutchinson	(Stinnett)	887.4
Lipscomb	(Lipscomb)	932.1
Moore	(Dumas)	899.7
Ochiltree	(Perryton)	917.6
Oldham	(Vega)	1,300.7
Parmer	(Farwell)	881.7
Potter	(Amarillo)	922.0
Randall	(Canyon)	914.4
Roberts	(Miami)	924.1
Sherman	(Stratford)	923.2
Swisher	(Tulia)	900.4
Wheeler	(Wheeler)	915.3
TA Total:		25,838.4
OCD Total:	approximately	25,800

*These figures excude a total water area of 6.14 square miles for the twenty-six Texas counties which make up the Diocese of Amarillo.

Central Texas was developed by absorbing parts of the Archdiocese of San Antonio and the dioceses of Galveston and Dallas. Eugenio Pacelli, Pope Pius XII, created the Diocese of Austin by his Bull *Ad animarum bonum* on 15 November 1947. The Archdiocese of San Antonio contributed the counties of McCulloch, San Saba, Mason, Llano, Blanco, Hays, Caldwell, and parts of Burnet, Travis, and Bastrop lying south of the Colorado River. Galveston supplied the counties of Lampasas, Coryell, McLennan, Limestone, Bell, Falls, Robertson, Williamson, Milam, Brazos, Lee, Burleson, Washington, Austin, and portions of Colorado, Burnet, Fayette, Bastrop and Travis north of the Colorado River. From the Diocese of Dallas came the counties of Coleman, Brown, Mills, and Hamilton.[52]

Diocese of Austin[53]
Created 15 November 1947
Erected 1948

Counties	(County Seats)	Land Area (sq. ml.)
Bastrop	(Bastrop)	888.4*
Bell	(Belton)	1,058.9
Blanco	(Johnson City)	711.2
Brazos	(Bryan)	585.8
Burleson	(Caldwell)	665.6
Burnet	(Burnet)	995.2
Caldwell	(Lockhart)	545.7
Coryell	(Gatesville)	1,051.8
Falls	(Marlin)	769.1
Hamilton	(Hamilton)	835.7
Hays	(San Marcos)	677.9
Lampasas	(Lampasas)	712.0
Lee	(Giddings)	628.5
Limestone	(Groesbeck)	908.8
Llano	(Llano)	934.8
Mason	(Mason)	932.1
McLennan	(Waco)	1,041.9
Milam	(Cameron)	1,016.7
Mills	(Goldthwaite)	748.1
Robertson	(Franklin)	854.6
San Saba	(San Saba)	1,134.5
Travis	(Austin)	989.4
Washington	(Brenham)	609.2
Williamson	(Georgetown)	1,124.3

*These figures exclude a total water area of 252.7 square miles for these twenty-four counties.

The Diocese of Austin also includes "the part of Fayette [County] north of the Colorado River." This region contains the county seat (La Grange), excluding the entire water area of the county (9.7 square miles). The land area claimed by the Roman Catholic Church for the Diocese (19,511 square miles) is exceeded by the total land area of the whole counties (20,420.2 square miles). That "part of Fayette north of the Colorado River" is approximately half the total land area of that county (475 square miles). The addition of 475 to 20,420.2 provides an estimate of the actual land area of the Diocese of Austin.

TA Total:	approximately	20,895.2
OCD Total:		19,511

Angelo Roncalli, Pope John XXIII, made the next major change by creating the Diocese of San Angelo (about 42,000 square miles) on 16 October 1961. The Diocese of Amarillo gave up the counties of Coke, Concho, Crockett, Fisher, Glasscock, Howard, Irion, Kimble, Martin, Menard, Midland, Mitchell, Nolan, Reagan, Runnels, Schleicher, Scurry, Sterling, Stonewall, Sutton, Tom Green, and Upton. The Diocese of Austin surrendered the counties of Brown, Coleman, and McCullough. The Diocese of Dallas contributed the counties of Callahan, Haskell, Jones, and Taylor, while the Diocese of El Paso supplied the counties of Andrews, Crane, Ector, Pecos, and Terrell.[54] Presently the Diocese contains twenty-nine counties.

Diocese of San Angelo[55]
Created 16 October 1961

Counties	(County Seats)	Land Area (sq. ml.)
Andrews	(Andrews)	1,500.7*
Brown	(Brownwood)	943.9
Callahan	(Baird)	898.6
Coke	(Robert Lee)	898.8
Coleman	(Coleman)	1,272.9
Concho	(Paint Rock)	991.5
Crane	(Crane)	785.6
Crockett	(Ozona)	2,807.6
Ector	(Odessa)	901.1
Glasscock	(Garden City)	900.8
Howard	(Big Spring)	902.9
Irion	(Mertzon)	1,051.5
Kimble	(Junction)	1,250.7
Martin	(Stanton)	914.8
McCulloch	(Brady)	1,069.3
Menard	(Menard)	901.9
Midland	(Midland)	900.3
Mitchell	(Colorado City)	910.1
Nolan	(Sweetwater)	912.0
Pecos	(Fort Stockton)	4,764.1
Reagan	(Big Lake)	1,175.4
Runnels	(Ballinger)	1,054.5

Schleicher	(Eldorado)	1,310.6
Sterling	(Sterling City)	923.4
Sutton	(Sonora)	1,453.8
Taylor	(Abilene)	915.7
Terrell	(Sanderson)	2,357.9
Tom Green	(San Angelo)	1,522.1
Upton	(Rankin)	1,241.7
TA Total:		37,434.1
OCD Total:		37,433

*These figures exclude a total water area of 109.7 square miles for the twenty-nine Texas counties which make up the Diocese of San Angelo.

Giovanni Montini, Pope Paul VI, established the Diocese of Brownsville from the Diocese of Corpus Christi on 10 July 1965 by the Bull *Ad Perpetuam Rei Memoriam*.[56]

Diocese of Brownsville[57]
Established 10 July 1965

Counties	(County Seats)	Land Area (sq. ml.)
Cameron	(Brownsville)	905.5*
Hidalgo	(Edinburg)	1,569.0
Starr	(Rio Grande City)	1,223.1
Willacy	(Raymondville)	596.7
TA Total:		4,294.3
OCD Total:		4,226

*These figures exclude a total water area of 578.2 square miles for the four Texas counties which make up the Diocese of Brownsville.

On 29 September 1966 Pope Paul VI divided the Diocese of Galveston-Houston, the "mother diocese" of Texas, to create the Diocese of Beaumont. It consisted of 11,790 square miles and included the counties of Angelina, Chambers east of the Trinity River, Cherokee, Hardin, Jasper, Jefferson, Liberty east of the Trinity River, Nacogdoches, Newton, Orange, Polk, Sabine, San Augustine, Shelby, and Tyler.[58] It presently consists of nine East Texas counties.

Diocese of Beaumont[59]
Established 29 September 1966

Counties	(County Seats)	Land Area (sq. ml.)
Chambers	(Anahuac)	599. 3*
Hardin	(Kountze)	897.3
Jasper	(Jasper)	937.4
Jefferson	(Beaumont)	903.5
Liberty	(Liberty)	1,159.8
Newton	(Newton)	932.7
Orange	(Orange)	356.4

Polk	(Livingston)	1,057.3
Tyler	(Woodville)	922.9
TA Total:		7,766.6
OCD Total:		7,878

*These figures exclude a total water area of 623.8 square miles for the nine Texas counties which make up the Diocese of Beaumont.

The Diocese of Fort Worth, the last diocese established by Pope Paul VI in Texas, was formed on 22 August 1969. A western extension of the Diocese of Dallas, it consists of the counties of Archer, Baylor, Bosque, Clay, Comanche, Cooke, Denton, Eastland, Erath, Foard, Hardeman, Hill, Hood, Jack, Johnson, Knox, Montague, Palo Pinto, Parker, Shackelford, Somervell, Stephens, Tarrant, Throckmorton, Wichita, Wilbarger, Wise, and Young.[60]

Diocese of Fort Worth[61]
Established 22 August 1969

Counties	(County Seats)	Land Area (sq. ml.)
Archer	(Archer City)	909.7*
Baylor	(Seymour)	870.8
Bosque	(Meridian)	989.2
Clay	(Henrietta)	1,097.8
Comanche	(Comanche)	937.7
Cooke	(Gainesville)	873.7
Denton	(Demon)	888.4
Eastland	(Eastland)	926.0
Erath	(Stephenville)	1,086.4
Foard	(Crowell)	706.7
Hardeman	(Quanah)	695.4
Hill	(Hillsboro)	962.4
Hood	(Granbury)	421.6
Jack	(Jacksboro)	917.4
Johnson	(Cleburne)	729.3
Knox	(Benjamin)	854.1
Montague	(Montague)	930.7
Palo Pinto	(Palo Pinto)	952.9
Parker	(Weatherford)	903.5
Shackelford	(Albany)	914.0
Somervell	(Glen Rose)	187.1
Stephens	(Breckinridge)	894.7
Tarrant	(Fort Worth)	863.5
Throckmorton	(Throckmorton)	912.4
Wichita	(Wichita Falls)	627.6
Wilbarger	(Vernon)	971.1
Wise	(Decatur)	904.6
Young	(Graham)	922.3
TA Total:		23,851.0
OCD Total:		23,950

*These figures exclude a total water area of 366.2 square miles for the twenty-eight Texas counties which make up the Diocese of Fort Worth.

On 6 February 1972 Paul VI separated the State of Oklahoma from the Province of San Antonio to which it had been joined since 1926 and formed the Province of Oklahoma City. This province comprises the states of Oklahoma and Arkansas.

Karol Wojtyla, Pope John Paul II, established the Diocese of Victoria in Texas on 29 May 1982. It is a combination of counties formerly a part of the Archdiocese of San Antonio and of the dioceses of Corpus Christi and Galveston-Houston.[62]

Diocese of Victoria in Texas[63]
Created 29 May 1982

Counties	(County Seats)	Land Area (sq. ml.)
Calhoun	(Port Lavaca)	512.3*
Colorado	(Columbus)	963.0
DeWitt	(Cuero)	909.2
Goliad	(Goliad)	853,5
Jackson	(Edna)	829.5
Lavaca	(Hallettsville)	969.9
Matagorda	(Bay City)	1,114.5
Victoria	(Victoria)	882.5
Wharton	(Wharton)	1,090.2

*These figures exclude a total water area of 1,073.5 square miles for these nine counties.

The Diocese of Victoria in Texas also includes "Fayette [County] west of the Colorado River". The land area of these nine counties is 8,124.6 square miles, to which I have added 475 square miles, the remainder of Fayette County and the part not shared with the Diocese of Austin. This is an estimation of the actual land area of the Diocese of Victoria in Texas.

TA Total:	approximately	8,599.6
OCD Total:	approximately	9,609

John Paul II formed the Diocese of Lubbock on 17 June 1983 from the dioceses of Amarillo (twenty counties) and San Angelo (five counties) for an area of approximately 23,382 square miles.[64]

Diocese of Lubbock[65]
Created 17 June 1983

Counties	(County Seats)	Land Area (sq. ml.)
Bailey	(Muleshoe)	862.7*
Borden	(Gail)	898.8
Cochran	(Morton)	775.2
Cottle	(Paducah)	901.2

Crosby	(Crosbyton)	899.5
Dawson	(Lamesa)	902.1
Dickens	(Dickens)	904.2
Fisher	(Roby)	901.2
Floyd	(Floydada)	992.3
Gaines	(Seminole)	1,502.4
Garza	(Post)	895.6
Hale	(Plainview)	1,004.7
Haskell	(Haskell)	903.0
Hockley	(Levelland)	908.3
Jones	(Anson)	931.0
Kent	(Jayton)	902.3
King	(Guthrie)	912.3
Lamb	(Littlefield)	1,016.2
Lubbock	(Lubbock)	899.5
Lynn	(Tahoka)	891.9
Motley	(Matador)	989.4
Scurry	(Snyder)	902.5
Stonewall	(Aspermont)	920.2
Terry	(Brownfield)	889.8
Yoakum	(Plains)	799.7
TA Total:		23,270.0
OCD Total:	approximately	23,382

*These figures exclude a total water area of 40.1 square miles for the twenty-five Texas counties which make up the Diocese of Lubbock.

On 12 December 1986 Pope John Paul II created the Diocese of Tyler. The diocese was effectively constituted on 24 February 1987 and was composed of counties from the dioceses of Dallas, Beaumont, and Galveston-Houston. Dallas supplied the counties of Bowie, Camp, Cass, Delta, Franklin, Gregg, Harrison, Henderson, Hopkins, Lamar, Marion, Morris, Panola, Rains, Red River, Rusk, Smith, Titus, Upshur, Van Zandt, and Wood. Beaumont gave up the counties of Angelina, Cherokee, Nacogdoches, Sabine, San Augustine, and Shelby. Galveston-Houston contributed the counties of Anderson, Freestone, Houston, Leon, and Trinity. The total land area was 22,971 square miles.[66]

Diocese of Tyler[67]
Established 12 December 1986

Counties	(County Seats)	Land Area (sq. ml.)
Anderson	(Palestine)	1.070.9*
Angelina	(Lufkin)	801.6
Bowie	(Boston)	887.9
Camp	(Pittsburg)	197.5
Cass	(Linden)	937.4
Cherokee	(Rusk)	1,052.3
Delta	(Cooper)	277.1

Franklin	(Mount Vernon)	285.6
Freestone	(Fairfield)	885.2
Gregg	(Longview)	274.0
Harrison	(Marshall)	898.8
Henderson	(Athens)	874.3
Hopkins	(Sulphur Springs)	784.7
Houston	(Crockett)	1,230.9
Lamar	(Paris)	917.0
Leon	(Centerville)	1,072.1
Marion	(Jefferson)	381.2
Morris	(Daingerfield)	254.5
Nacogdoches	(Nacogdoches)	946.8
Panola	(Carthage)	800.9
Rains	(Emory)	232.0
Red River	(Clarksville)	1,050.2
Rusk	(Henderson)	923.6
Sabine	(Hemphill)	490.2
San Augustine	(San Augustine)	527.9
Shelby	(Center)	794.1
Smith	(Tyler)	928.4
Titus	(Mount Pleasant)	410.5
Trinity	(Groveton)	692.8
Upshur	(Gilmer)	592.6
Van Zandt	(Canton)	848.8
Wood	(Quitman)	650.2
TA Total:		22,972.0
OCD Total:		22,971

*These figures exclude a total water area of 747.1 square miles for the thirty-two Texas counties which make up the Diocese of Tyler.

THE PROVINCE OF SAN ANTONIO: 1994[68]
Land Area in Square Miles

Jurisdiction		TA		OCD
Archdiocese of San Antonio	approximately	26,470.9		27,841
Diocese of Galveston-Houston		9,221.4		9,354
Dioxese of Corpus Christi	approximately	17,294.0		17,294
Diocese of Dallas		7,319.7		7,523
Diocese of El Paso		26,695.8		26,686
Diocese of Amarillo		25,838.4	approximately	25,800
Diocese of Austin	approximately	20,895.2		19,511
Diocese of San Angelo		37,434.1		37,433
Diocese of Brownsville		4,294.3		4,226
Diocese of Beaumont		7,766.6		7,878
Diocese of Fort Worth		23,851.0		23,950
Diocese of Victoria in Texas	approximately	8,599.6	approximately	9,609
Diocese of Lubbock		23,270.0	approximately	23,382
Diocese of Tyler		22,972.0		22,971

I. The Bishop and His Diocese[1]

All bishops and archbishops were once priests. Their philosophical and theological training lacked a business and management orientation. In moving from parish to diocese they may have acquired administrative skills to govern their territories. Whether they have (or not), their needs and those of their faithful require them to seek and obtain competent professional assistance. Their responsibilities demand that they retain veto power over all decisions made within their jurisdictions.

Called to preach and to pray, a bishop may wish only to proclaim the gospel and increase his personal spirituality. He may view his role primarily as ceremonial, sacramental, and educational and himself as a spiritual leader. But he must organize his diocese, build facilities which ensure meaningful parish life, operate a school system, provide personnel and social services, and find the money to pay for all these enterprises.[2]

Contemporary complex diocesan administration forces the bishop to delegate his authority, though not his ultimate responsibility. He may have great interpersonal skills but few organizational ones. So he may pick and choose carefully those who aid his decision-making process. He governs through such cabinet-level officers as auxiliary bishops (in Texas, in the archdiocese of San Antonio and the diocese of Galveston-Houston), vicars general, chancellors, secretaries, moderators of the curia, and directors of finances, personnel, pastoral service, social service, and education. Each bishop has his own style of governing based upon his own strengths and weaknesses.

It may be that a bishop needs a vicar for priests to act in his behalf in staffing parishes and providing chaplains throughout the diocese. Skill in operating a priests' personnel board and in working with a priests' council may be necessary. Perhaps the diocese is so large that the bishop needs his auxiliaries to make his presence felt within parishes.

Whatever the case may be, the bishop is the ultimate authority within his diocese. There are certain matters which he can not delegate. He must communicate with the Vatican, with the National Conference of Catholic Bishops (NCCB), with other bishops (including his auxiliaries), with priest personnel problems, with budget deficits, with opening (or closing) parishes and schools, with front-page newspaper crises, and with appointments of pastors and administrators. He must also keep in mind the long-range interests of his diocese and of the entire church.

At the same time the bishop does not govern within a vacuum. He makes his decisions in the light of canon law, financial considerations, and the views of his superiors. He must keep his institutions funded while retaining their particularly Catholic character. His agencies must be supervised and coordinated and serve the faithful and other groups. Demographics and historical situations are built-in factors which may also influence decision-making.

Daily routine brings with it setbacks and opportunities. Time must be budgeted. The daily mail brings in information, requests, and complaints. Schedules control one's time and attention. There are people to see, confirmation schedules to keep, meetings with boards and councils with agendas to act upon, advice and opinions to take into consideration, and budget cycles needing review of expenditures and projections for the future. Dilemmas also intrude. Newspapers quickly act upon stories of the erring priest. Pro-life demonstrations against abortion clinics, protests in favor of the ordination of women to the priesthood, the closing of an inner-city school, and labor disputes are divisive matters upon which the bishop must take stands.

In the past thirty years changes have taken place affecting diocesan operations. Shifting standards of sexual morality, broken homes with one-parent families, the increasing use of drugs, the non-institutionalization of dependent people, ecumenism, and the necessity to reach out to all in bringing Christ to the world population make the increase of social agencies imperative. At the same time the lack of vocations for the priesthood and religious life, together with the need for expanding parishes and other facilities, pose a definite challenge. Lay ministers are not priests, and they cannot bridge the gap. And in a world constantly separating the fortunate from the poor, a Church with universal mission responsibilities must address itself not only to preaching the gospel of Christ but to such problems as overpopulation, famine, natural disasters, political dislocations, and general human want.

Thirty years have passed since the end of the Second Vatican Council with its emphasis on ministerial service to others. The episcopal style now includes consultation among all involved parties from other bishops to the faithful. In working toward consensus the accent is on unity and charity. Plans await accord or until the lack of resources (money or personnel) forces a decision. Sometimes a bishop will assign something to avoid causing conflict by direct encounter. But conflicts are inherent within the situation. Inside a school system, is it better (or not) to raise salaries by raising tuitions? How does one tell a priest that he cannot be a pastor or that he is the unsuccessful candidate when several priests want to be pastors of a particular parish? Is the pastor suited to the needs of his parish?

Bishops make sincere efforts to aid the work of their priests and chancery employees and keep them happy. Just as the bishop cannot make decisions within a vacuum, he needs these agents to carry out the mission of the diocese. Therefore he makes his time available for his priests. He does not want to tax his parishes needlessly nor overburden the pastor. He tries to make existing programs work and is careful when inaugurating new ones. He tries to coordinate the work of the various agencies, to impose rules and standardization where appropriate, and to reach objectives through general agreement if possible.

The Church is somewhat like a corporation, but it can not always alter or abolish its policies. A business examines indicators like profit, market share, efficiency, and growth. The Church is a nonprofit organization which judges things satisfactory if they seem to be going well. Thus in a parish one hopes people attend Mass, receive communion, and support it financially. A bishop may feel that Catholic Charities is doing well if it is deemed successful in its mission, can receive grants from the government and private agencies, pleases those it serves, is judged sound by its board of directors, and incurs little negative feedback from important groups, such as pastors. But the Church sponsors comparatively little research about itself as a social system or in terms of the quality of its services and the expectations of its faithful.

Just as the bishop does not wish to impede the work of his pastors and staff, the Vatican does not wish to interfere with the work of the bishop within his diocese. It nevertheless provides norms for governance and makes the bishop responsible to it. Bishops work together in a Church in which supreme authority belongs to the pope. And work goes on both inside and outside the diocesan structure.[3]

Now that we have an overview of diocesan organization, and how the bishop functions within and outside it, we need to know just what a diocese is. A diocese is a division of territory within the Church. In Texas there are thirteen such divisions (Amarillo, Austin, Beaumont, Brownsville, Corpus Christi, Dallas, El Paso, Fort Worth, Galveston-Houston, Lubbock, San Angelo, Tyler, and Victoria). The chief diocese of the province (a geographical area with an archdiocese and at least one diocese) is the archdiocese (in Texas, San Antonio). The Province of San Antonio (geographically, the State of Texas) comprises the archdiocese of San Antonio and the thirteen dioceses of Texas listed above. Each diocese has a bishop (in the case of San Antonio an archbishop) who governs as an ordinary, ruling in his own name without delegation from another, with jurisdiction over the clergy.

When governing his own archdiocese the archbishop has the same powers as any of his suffragans (or residential bishops within his province). But as metropolitan he is head of his province with some supervisory powers and influence over the other dioceses and bishops within it. Archdioceses and dioceses are also called sees from the Latin *sedes* (or "seat"). The Holy See refers to the diocese of Rome, whose bishop is the Pope.[4]

Catholics believe that divine law requires that there be bishops with ordinary power over their flocks. Territorial divisions are of human creation, however. Since authority is over people, divisions may be made not only according to domicile but also by rite or country of origin. And one territory may be within the jurisdiction of various dioceses. Passaic, New Jersey is within the Latin-rite Diocese of Paterson and the Byzantine-rite (Ruthenian) Eparchy of Passaic.

Following the Apostles, whose exercise of authority was collegial (shared equally with other bishops), local churches became established cities, each with its own bishop. Patriarchs or metropolitans formed new dioceses with the aid of their provincial bishops. Not until the sixth century, when the pope sent missionaries into Scandinavia, was papal authority involved in this process. In the eleventh and twelfth centuries the pope exclusively reserved the right to erect dioceses in the West.

First called churches, and then parishes, the term diocese was used in the fourth century. In the thirteenth century it became the exclusive term to designate territorial divisions within the Church. In the Latin rite the pope erects, changes, and suppresses dioceses. He is assisted by curial departments in the Vatican.

The Congregation for Bishops relates to bishops and their jurisdictions. Once known as the Consistorial Congregation it was established by Sixtus V on 22 January 1588 by the apostolic constitution *Immensa*. St. Pius X extended its powers on 20 June 1908 as did Pius XII on 1 August 1952 by the apostolic constitution *Exsul Familia*. Paul VI gave its present name on 15 August 1967 and John Paul II redefined its competencies on 28 June 1988. It oversees the

Pontifical Commission for Latin America (founded by Pius XII on 19 April 1958 and a part of the Congregation from July 1969) with a central coordinating office for military vicars (established 2 February 1985) and an office for coordinating *ad limina* visits (established 29 June 1988).

The Congregation for the Evangelization of Peoples was founded by St. Pius V in the sixteenth century as a commission of cardinals for the East and West Indies, Italo-Greeks, and for church affairs in Protestant Europe. After Clement VIII began a Congregation for the Propagation of the Faith (1599) which endured for several years, Gregory XV erected a permanent congregation on 22 June 1622 by the apostolic constitution *Inscrutabili Divinae*. John Paul II redefined its functions on 28 June 1988.

This congregation directs and coordinates universal missionary work. It fosters missionary vocations and assigns missionaries, establishes jurisdictions and proposes candidates for bishops and other positions to serve them, aids in recruiting and developing indigenous clergy, and mobilizes spiritual and material support for missionary activities. The Supreme Council for the Direction of Pontifical Missionary Works promotes missionary cooperation through its constituent Missionary Union of the Clergy and Religious, the Society for the Propagation of the Faith, the Society of St. Peter the Apostle for Native Clergy, the Society of the Holy Childhood, and the International Center of Missionary Animation. The United States of America was considered a mission territory until it was removed from this status by Pope St. Pius X in the apostolic constitution *Sapienti Consilio* promulgated 29 June 1908.

The Section for Relations with States (so named by John Paul II on 28 June 1988) is one of two sections of the Vatican Secretariat of State. Its business is to conduct diplomatic and other relations with civil governments. A Council of Cardinals and bishops is attached to it. Called the Congregation for Extraordinary Affairs on its establishment by Pius VI in 1793, it was restructured as the Council for the Public Affairs of the Church by Paul VI in 1967. These three departments aid the pope in the administration of Latin rite dioceses.

In the case of the Oriental (or Eastern) Churches, the pope uses this section of the Secretariat of State. It handles relations with the civil governments of those countries which contain the majority of those Christians belonging to these churches. The Congregation for Oriental Churches concerns these persons and discipline in Egypt, the Sinai Peninsula, Eritrea, Northern Ethiopia, Southern Albania, Bulgaria, Cyprus, Greece, Iran, Iraq, Lebanon, Palestine, Syria, Jordan, Turkey, Afghanistan, and minority communities of Eastern Church members worldwide.

This congregation was established by Pius IX on 6 January 1862 in the apostolic constitution *Romani Pontifices* and united with the Congregation for the Propagation of the Faith (now the Congregation for the Evangelization of Peoples). It was made autonomous by Benedict XV on 1 May 1917 in the motu proprio *Dei Providentis* and given wider authority by Pius XI on 25 March 1938 in the motu proprio *Sancta Dei Ecclesia*.

The Congregation for the Oriental Churches assists the pope in creating, changing, and suppressing eparchies. Patriarchs may perform these functions within their patriarchates with the consent of their synods or bishops for a serious reason and with the confirmation of the Holy See. The major archbishop has the same power within his province and with his archiepiscopal synod or synod of electors. Patriarchs and archbishops may do the same in regard to exarchies with their consent of their permanent synods and the knowledge of the Holy See.[5]

Canon law requires that each diocese in the Latin Church be divided into parishes. Parishes are Christian communities, each with its own church building and under the authority of a pastor (a priest in charge providing ministerial service), formed on a specific geographical basis or along national or ethnic lines. The entire diocese is divided into deaneries (districts or vicariates *forane*, or outside the episcopal or see city of the diocese, not usually constituted as a deanery). The prelate in charge of a deanery is the dean, rural dean, archpriest, or vicar forane. His work is to promote, coordinate, and supervise the common pastoral activity within his deanery or vicariate. Some dioceses, such as Galveston-Houston in Texas have a superstructure of episcopal vicariates in which episcopal vicars (priests or bishops) had a group of deaneries within each vicariate. An episcopal vicar may not only serve a territorial governing function but also be a deputy governing a group of people, a specific rite, or a type of apostolic work within the diocese.

There are other types of vicars as well. A vicar for religious is a priest appointed by a bishop as his representative to the religious communities in his diocese. While the residential bishop judges all cases of first trial in the diocesan tribunal, he appoints a priest with a graduate degree in canon law to judge cases not reserved to the bishop himself. This priest is the judicial vicar and is sometimes called the chief judge or *officialis*. His assistant (if he has one) has the title of adjutant judicial vicar. And every diocese has an official whose office smooths and unifies diocesan administration. This bishop or priest participates in the executive governance of the diocese with executive jurisdiction as the diocesan bishop's deputy. This official is a vicar general.

An eparchy in the Eastern Church is also divided into deaneries (protopresbyterates) if it is outside the patriarchate. The deanery does not function inside the patriarchate and parishes are not organized in some Eastern jurisdictions.

In the Latin Church contiguous parishes are usually grouped into provinces containing a metropolitan see and at least one diocese (suffragan see). The archbishop of the archdiocese has no direct powers over the suffragans, but as metropolitan has some limited advisory and appellate authority and obligations.

In the Oriental Churches the partriarch has ordinary jurisdiction over the faithful of his rite within and retains general supervisory authority over persons of his rite outside the patriarchate. This jurisdiction may be divided into provinces, each headed by a metropolitan, who also has general supervisory authority over his eparchies. These provinces do not function as the archbishops and metropolitans within them are titular. Some metropolitans do have power over their provinces outside the patriarchates.

When a Latin-rite territory has not become a diocese but is more than a mission, it is called a vicariate or apostolic prefecture, with a bishop usually at the head of a vicariate. These prelatures have papal-delegated (but not ordinary) power to govern. Abbacies and prelatures *nullius* contain territory not part of any diocese with an abbot *nullius* or a prelate *nullius* in charge. The Oriental Church equivalent is an exarchy, with distinct territories not erected into eparchies, and ruled by exarchs.[6]

With these basic concepts in mind, we shall now examine some environmental characteristics of a bishop governing his diocese, episcopal styles and structures, and parish and regional governance. We shall then consider some specifics of Texas dioceses with particular regard to the dioceses of Galveston-Houston and Tyler, and end this section with how some institutions external to the diocese affect it. Finance is a specialized subject and will be taken up separately.

We focus throughout on the Province of San Antonio, one of thirty-one Latin-rite provinces with 175 geographical units comprising all fifty of the United States, the District of Columbia, and St. Thomas in the Virgin Islands. The commonwealth of Puerto Rico has its own territorial structure. As an average each American see has 186 diocesan priests and 286,000 Catholics.[7] At the beginning of 1994 only the Galveston-Houston diocese exceeded this number with 190 diocesan priests with Tyler having twenty-three and San Antonio having 156 diocesan priests respectively. In terms of the Catholic population for each Texas diocese, the Archdiocese of San Antonio had 628,776 Catholics, and these dioceses exceeded the national average: Brownsville (652,214), Corpus Christi (349,500), Dallas (287,826), El Paso (499,376), and Galveston-Houston (748,781). In the dioceses of Brownsville and El Paso Catholics form the majority with 81 and 70.6 percent of their respective populations. In Texas as a whole Catholics make up 22.4 percent of the total population of 17,701,899, slightly above the average of 22 percent for the United States of America.[8] As a metropolitan see based upon these statistics, San Antonio compares with the national average of 395 priests and 695,000 Catholics with 394 as the combined total of diocesan and religious priests.[9]

With the power to govern the bishop does not receive carte blanche to act. He is not exempt from moral, civil, or canon laws. Financial and personnel resources influence his decisions, as does the particular social and ecclesial environment in which he finds himself. His faithful have their cherished traditions and expectations.

Governing depends largely upon the consent of the governed. Lay Catholics may disobey church laws and commandments, refuse financial support, or leave the Church. Prelates have no military or police powers. In fact, the bishop depends upon civil authority to aid him in such matters as trespassing and theft. The diocese or archdiocese may be sued and one may not obtain a "sanctuary" within church properties as a violator of local, county, district, state, or federal law. The bishop depends upon priests to minister to his people. He can decide who will serve in his diocese, but priests can and do leave the ministry.

On the positive side Catholics share many beliefs and have a liturgy, sacraments, and Scriptures in common. The change in attitude since Vatican II is not doctrinal. But on the diocesan and parish levels it has more to do with the ideas of service, collegiality, subsidiarity, and the pastoral role of the bishop. Lay participation is encouraged to a greater degree than formerly. The hierarchy, clergy, and faithful work together with the pope. The shift is away from an authoritarian style with priests working closely with their bishops, yet developing their own councils or senates.

Canon law has a definite effect in setting norms for the individual bishop. He cannot alter liturgical texts or ceremonies, ordain women or married men to the priesthood, or consecrate a bishop without approval by the Vatican. Nor may he contravene laws passed by the pope or by the National Conference of Catholic Bishops (NCCB).

Although the diocesan bishop is the chief legislator, executive, and judge in his diocese, he must make sure that certain institutions are in place. He must have a priests' council with about half of the members elected (cc. 495-501) and may include the laity in a pastoral council (cc. 511-514). Whenever he modifies parishes (by erection, division, or suppression), calls a diocesan synod (an advisory and consultative body meeting every ten years to recommend diocesan legislation and policies), or imposes a tax for diocesan needs, he must consult his priests' council.

Canon law requires a college of consultors (six to twelve priests from the priests' council with five-year terms) (c. 502), and a finance council (with members having five-year terms including at least three persons "skilled in financial affairs as well as in civil law") (c. 492). The college of consultors and the finance council must give their consents for the alienation of church property (conveyance to another party) and acts of extraordinary administration (c. 1277).

The residential bishop has considerable control over his diocesan policies, personnel, and finances. He may establish procedures and programs and open offices. He can appoint and fire all diocesan administrative officials. By canon law he must coordinate and arrange all matters concerning administration for his entire diocese (c. 473§1) and appoint priests or a vicar (or vicars) general to act as his deputy in pastoral and administrative affairs (c. 475).

The bishop may reserve many matters to himself (c. 479) and can appoint episcopal vicars (who may be auxiliary bishops) with geographic or functional responsibilities (c. 476). Lay people, who cannot be vicars, are often called delegates, secretaries, or directors with powers delegated by the bishop. Canon 482 provides that the bishop appoint a chancellor.[10] This official originally signed and preserved the bishop's letters. His present function is to gather, arrange, and safeguard the acts of the diocesan curia (principally the vicar general, the chancellor, diocesan tribunal officials, examiners, consultors, auditors, the promoter of justice, and the defender of the bond). It is not necessary that the chancellor be a priest.

Canon law states the chancellor is to take care of the archives and prepare certain canonical documents. He may be the chief financial officer, in charge of priest personnel, or canonical advisor to the archbishop. The chancellor was formerly considered chief of staff. The 1983 code of canon law provides an optional officer called the moderator of the curia, a priest who is normally the vicar general. Canon 473§2 states that the moderator coordinates the exercise of administrative responsibilities and sees that other members of the curia fulfill the office entrusted to them. Thus, at one time or another chancellors have combined the functions of their own office, plus those of the vicar general, moderator of the curia, priests' personnel director, and finance officer.

Canon 494 states the requirement for a diocesan finance officer who cannot be removed by the bishop during a five-year term. An exception is for a serious reason and consultation with the board of consultors. The bishop's tribunal deals mostly with marriage annulments, for which canon lawyers must be trained and an office staff maintained. Due process (or grievance) panels review the decisions of church officials. The bishop also appoints other officials, officers, and pastors. And he must maintain consultative bodies, such as the finance committee and consultors.

Although dioceses generally follow political boundaries, they differ in size, population density, and the number of Catholics they contain. Within each are political, social, and economic differences. The average American archdiocese is 17,700 square miles, or more than twice the size of the state of Massachusetts. The Archdiocese of San Antonio, for example, at 27,481 square miles exceeds the national average.[11] At the same time San Antonio is one of some nine other provinces with twenty or fewer Catholics per square mile.[12] Yet with its large metropolitan center and many faithful concentrated within it, the archbishop of San Antonio (like his brother archbishops in Boston, New York, and Philadelphia) is an important force in city affairs.[13]

Turning from the way in which canon law and the makeup of a diocese shape its institutions, we come to styles and structures bishops use to govern. If a bishop were ideal, he would be a paragon with superlative pastoral skills, a prodigy at administration, a prophetically inspiring preacher of the gospel who makes no one uncomfortable, and a provider of inexpensive social services and educational programs with a streamlined bureaucracy. This saintly priest (spiritual yet practical) would please all: the rich, the poor, priests and religious, the laity, the Vatican, and the Christian and non-Christian communities. He would also be an international figure without spending too much time outside his own diocese.

Due to human imperfections, such a composite does not exist. The bishop must try to fulfill these goals, though no one can completely. Most have working-class backgrounds, half of whose fathers have not graduated from high school. Of those only 12 percent are college graduates, with 36 percent being high school graduates. The average archbishop is fifty-three (Archbishop Flores of San Antonio was a few years younger when appointed). Ninety percent of them were bishops at appointment, with 61 percent already diocesan bishops, serving about six years in that capacity. About half of them have held top chancery positions (vicar general, chancellor, or secretary to the bishop). About 35 percent worked in a seminary, with about 30 percent holding doctorates in theology (STD) or canon law (JCD). About half have studied in Rome. As a group they tend to be more conservative on religious attitudes and sexual morality than priests and more liberal on ecumenism and social action.

Each bishop spends a long working day made up of correspondence, appointments, meetings, and engagements. Many evenings and weekends take up time devoted to parish, diocesan, and civic functions. Mail comes from the faithful, priests, diocesan officials, bishops, and civic and ecumenical leaders. Some messages receive personal answers. Besides requests for time and attention, many letters seek the intervention of the bishop in various matters. There are complaints about various aspects of parish life, other denominations wishing to use diocesan facilities, religious orders asking to minister or be assigned within the diocese, personnel to assign or to release for special duties such as graduate study, and matters before the tribunal. Such a list does not suggest the full range of mail received but is representative.

The bishop is a part of many boards, which report on various activities and finances. Changes in the city by various administrations often affect parishes. The bishop must also make time for his priests and visiting prelates. Within his parishes individual groups call upon him during their scheduled activities. His presence is welcome to dedicate buildings and to mediate personnel problems. And the contemporary bishop sometimes appears on television programs.

Bishops govern their flocks in various ways with liberality on social issues and conservatism on doctrine and morality. According to Canon 375§1 they are "teachers of doctrine, priests of sacred worship and ministers of governance". They are pastors, administrators, teachers, national leaders, or a combination of all of these elements. Depending upon the need, they are civic, ecumenical or international figures, hands-on administrators or delegators. But even those who are delegators do not delegate controversial or crisis matters demanding their direct notice.

Archbishops and bishops have spoken on local ordinances, mediated disputes between police and militants, and tackled such problems as capital punishment, public school integration, fluoridated water, abortion funding, and low-income housing. Parishes and agencies work with church groups that favor pro-life activities. National and international leaders hold offices within the national episcopal conference and meet with presidents and popes. At the end of 1994 Bishop Fiorenza was secretary of the National Conference of Catholic Bishops.

Many prelates have taught academic subjects for which they are qualified Cardinal Bevilacqua of Philadelphia is both a civil and a canon lawyer and Bishop Gracida of Corpus Christi is an architect. Preaching and writing columns for their own newspapers are communication outlets, as are articles, pastoral letters, and addresses. Various liturgies are telecast.

But most bishops are administrators. They build churches, schools, orphanages, hospitals, and other charitable institutions. When their Catholic agencies were absent, the bishops provided them without financial subsidies from the state. And the structures which operate these establishments are influenced by their missions, ministries, and environments. As we have seen, the regional vicariate organization divides vicariates (under priests or auxiliary bishops, representing the bishop or archbishop) into deaneries Another form is the department or secretariat model. As the regional vicariate model seeks to enable cooperation and coordination with parishes, the department model aids parishes by supervising and coordinating diocesan agencies. There are directors or secretaries (or vicars, if priests) for administrative, community, educational, financial, pastoral, and personnel services. A small number of key administrators (usually four to seven) oversee parts of the archdiocesan bureaucracy and report to the bishop or to the vicar general.

Diocesan structure provides administrative, educational and social services. Some dioceses have departments for ministries (liturgy, marriage preparation programs, parishes, chaplains, and lay organizations), personnel (lay ministry, lay personnel, vocations, seminary), and/or ethnic affairs. Schools and Catholic Charities have their own personnel and finance staffs.

There are pastoral, educational, and financial components to many programs. The RCIA (Rite of Christian Initiation of Adults; generally, the process of entering the Catholic Church), the diocesan newspaper, and the youth ministry are pastoral and educational. Sometimes it is hard to fit ministries into particular categories. For example, the youth ministry has educational, pastoral, and social service elements, while the family ministry is primarily pastoral and social. Because ethnic groups have their own traditions, programs which serve them, including youth and family ministries, need coordination. It is also hard to fit public relations, the diocesan newspaper, cemeteries, and the tribunal into particular groups.

How to organize these agencies into workable divisions is often a challenge for the bishop. In Boston Cardinal Law has taken fifty-four of them and put them into seven categories: social services, pastoral services, education, community relations, health care services, ministerial personnel, and central services. The Cardinal provides direction, vision, and priorities for the agencies. But priests often feel that such an organization only makes communication more difficult between them and him. Such an elaborate structure might misdirect and redirect information delaying some final decision.

While power can be delegated to geographical sections of a diocese, the bishop must coordinate and arrange matters pertaining to the administration of the entire diocese (c. 473§1). In this vicar general/moderator of the curia model of government, a bishop exercises power directly Or he may appoint a moderator of the curia, also a vicar general, to harmonize the administration and see that other members of the curia fulfill their offices (c. 473 §2). Before the moderator system was devised, the chancellor or the bishop's secretary performed these functions.

Canon 479§1 says that a vicar general "possesses that executive power in the entire diocese which belongs to the diocesan bishop in law, that is, he possesses the power to place all administrative acts with the exception of those the bishop has reserved to himself or which in law require the special mandate of the bishop." The power of a vicar general then depends upon how much power the bishop reserves to himself. A powerful vicar general hears officials report, chairs cabinet meetings, and has authority flow to him. He coordinates and supervises department heads and secretaries.

The model a bishop will choose depends upon his own personality and situation. He may wish to free his time for long-range planning, pastoral work, or work outside the diocese. Conflict and confusion may adversely affect his health. As a chief executive, some bishops prefer doing their own administrative work without a moderator of the curia. Others prefer a cabinet style of organization.

In the cabinet style there are department heads (for education, social services, finance, and pastoral concerns), the vicar general, chancellor, moderator of the curia, and secretary to the bishop. Other key officials, such as the head of the tribunal and directors of planning, minority affairs, and public relations, may be included. There may be weekly or monthly meetings, separate meetings with department heads, or no regular meetings at all. But with so many individuals involved meetings may be necessary for communication and for morale. Much scheduling, budgeting, planning, and developing of policies and procedures contribute to a smooth operation.

While an episcopal council could consist of vicar generals and episcopal vicars, lay people cannot be vicars. So bishops have consulted with their cabinets (cf. c. 473§4). Archbishop Flores and Cardinal O'Connor have met monthly with their consultative bodies. Cardinals Hickey and Law meet more frequently. In the area of diocesan organization, canon law requires the existence of certain boards. It is necessary to have a college of consultors, a priests' council, and a finance council. Most American dioceses also have a diocesan pastoral council, a board of education, and a priests' personnel board.

The college of consultors predates Vatican Council II (1962-1965). The bishop appoints six to twelve priests for five-year terms (c. 502). They must be members of the priests' council but may be chosen from elected, appointed or ex-officio membership. Some consultors are appointed to priests' councils and some are from an executive committee of the priests' council. Their primary function is to elect a diocesan administrator between the death of a bishop and the appointment of his successor (c. 421). Before 1983 consultors were sometimes an informal priests' personnel board. The college must be consulted on certain financial matters and acts of extraordinary administration. But the bishop must also consult the finance council on the same matters (cc. 494, 1277, and 1292). He may also seek advice from his auxiliaries, the personnel board, the executive committee of the priests' council and his cabinet.

The presbyteral (or priests') council comes from the Vatican Council II "Decree on the Ministry and Life of Priests [*Presbyterorum Ordinis*]" of 7 December 1965. It states bishops

> should be glad to listen to their priests' views and even consult them and hold conference with them about matters that concern the needs of pastoral work and the good of the diocese. But for this to be reduced to practice a group or senate of priests should be set up in a way suited to present-day needs, and in a form with rules to be determined by law. This group would represent the body of priests and by their advice could effectively help the bishop in the management of the diocese.[14]

Another important statement concerning this body is in the "Decree on the Pastoral Office of Bishops in the Church [*Christus Dominus*]" *of* 28 October 1965:

> Among the cooperators of the bishop in the governing of the diocese are included the priests who constitute his senate or council, such as the cathedral chapter, the council of consultors, or other committees according to the circumstances and character of different localities.[15]

The first priests' senate was organized in the diocese of Worcester in March 1965. Each diocese drew up its own statutes approved by the bishop. In 1983 the Code of Canon Law established the rules for membership and authority and changed the name to presbyteral councils. Canon 497 directs "about half" of the council is to be elected. The remainder can be ex-officio members designated by the council's statutes or appointed by the bishop. Elections may be by deaneries (geographic districts), by ordination ranks (seniority) among priests, or by a combination of these two methods. Members of the council are supposed to represent the diocese from which they are chosen.

In some cases where elections are by deaneries the representatives are made deans. They become channels between the council and priests and also diocesan administrators. They may also be leaders and coordinators in their deaneries on local issues. The vicar general, auxiliaries, and the chancellor are ex-officio or appointed members of the council. Each council ceases to exist on the death of the bishop.

Canon 500§2 requires the bishop to listen to the presbyteral council in matters of great moment. These matters concern the holiness of life, sacred science, other needs of priests, sanctification and religious instruction of the faithful, or the government of the diocese. Other topics are the aims of ministries, the proposal of more urgent subjects, the indication of ways to act, and the fostering of spiritual life. The council also concerns itself with the equal distribution of funds for clerics and with the erection, suppression, and restoration of parishes.[16] Specifically the bishop *must* consult the presbyteral council on the advisability of a synod (c. 461§1), the modification of parishes (cc. 515§2, 813), offerings of the faithful on the occasion of parish services (c. 531), norms for parish councils (c. 536), the construction of a church or the conversion of a church to secular use (cc. 1215§2, 1222§2), and the imposition of a diocesan tax (c. 1263).

Before 1983 the priests' senates elected their own officers (usually a president and a vice-president) and set their own agendas. Presently the diocesan bishop is the president of the presbyteral council and he determines its agenda (c. 500§1). The elected chairman can run meetings, which might be eight to ten times a year. The bishop and the executive committee or officers may set the agenda.

A priest has many interests and topics often before the council involve his morale, salary, stipends, health insurance, automobile expenses and insurance, pension, retirement, retreats, the process for appointing pastors (personnel boards and tenure), continuing education, due process, living conditions, and relations between a pastor and his associates.[17] The social concerns of priests nationally have focused on the subjects of abortion, racism, housing, welfare reform, nuclear weapons, and distressed areas of the world. Letters to public officials from the diocese usually come from the bishop himself or the priests' council. Generally the councils have established parish council guidelines, implemented the RCIA, and promoted liturgical reforms.

The Vatican Council II "Decree on the Pastoral Office of Bishops in the Church [*Christus Dominus*]" of 28 October 1965 states:

> It is highly desirable that in every diocese a special pastoral council be established, presided over by the diocesan bishop himself, in which clergy, religious, and laity specially chosen for the purpose will participate. It will be the function of this council to investigate and consider matters relating to pastoral activity and to formulate practical conclusions concerning them.[18]

The first such council was established in the diocese of Richmond in 1965. But such bodies exist "to the extent that pastoral circumstances recommend it" (c.

511). They vary in organization, size, procedures, and frequency of meetings. In 1989 the median size was thirty-three, with Omaha having 407 and Beaumont fifteen.

The pastoral council includes priests, religious and laity, but emphasis is on lay input. Women make up about 32 percent and men about 34 percent, or a total of two-thirds. The chair of the council may be the bishop or a layperson. Membership selection is to be representative of diocesan regions, social conditions, and professions (c. 512§2). Seventy percent are elected by deanery councils or similar bodies. Priest representatives are normally elected by the presbyteral council and religious representatives by religious communities. Lay representatives, with allowance made for minorities and young people, may be chosen from each parish. In large archdioceses regional councils often elect members to the pastoral council.

The council's responsibility is "to investigate under the authority of the bishop all those things which pertain to pastoral works, to ponder them and to propose practical conclusions about them" (c. 511). Most of them meet quarterly, but some meet annually as assemblied (with the executive committee meeting monthly). Its agenda is usually set by the executive committee, which may discuss and react to documents from the National Conference of Catholic Bishops or from Rome.

The council also deals with internal church issues such as parish councils, financial policy, lay salaries, due process, religious education, and issues concerning the wider community, such as abortion, minority programs, peace, and justice. Some are too large and act too slowly, meeting only three to eight times a year. Although members reflect the church with varied educations, backgrounds, and interests, they lack a professional theological orientation.

As a feedback mechanism, the council lets the bishop hear from a representative group of people in his diocese. His mail normally brings complaints, requests to do something, or letters from people working directly for the Church. His pastoral council tells him how well his programs serve the people. Members are enthusiastic about church activities touching themselves and their children. They react well to proposals for new programs or policies and can give the bishop an idea about how well people will react to them.

Another important church body is the diocesan (or archdiocesan) synod, which dates from the fourth century. A diocesan synod is "a group of selected priests and other Christian faithful of a particular church which offers assistance to the diocesan bishop for the good of the entire Christian community" (c. 460). It meets only when called by the bishop after consultation with the presbyteral council. The 1917 Code of Canon Law mandated synods every ten years; the 1983 Code makes no particular requirement.[19]

Ex-officio members may be auxiliary bishops, vicars general, episcopal vicars, the judicial vicar, members of the presbyteral council, the seminary rector, deans, a priest elected from each deanery, and some superiors of religious communities. Lay and religious members are chosen by the pastoral council in a manner and number determined by the bishop (c. 466). Other Catholics and non-Catholics may be invited as observers.

The *Directory on the Pastoral Ministry of Bishops* suggests ways a synod can assist the bishop for the good of the diocese. It can adapt laws and norms of the universal church to local conditions, set policies and programs of apostolic works, resolve problems of the apostolate and administration, give impetus to projects and undertakings in the diocese, and correct errors in doctrine and morals, primarily by providing authentic teaching.[20] The goals of the synod might be planned by the diocesan pastoral council. But synods involve more people and are taken more seriously than pastoral councils. Pre-preparation often begins with surveys, parish discussions, and work by commissions and committees.

Councils of various types are important in the life of the diocese. The synod sets a vision (general direction), which expresses the spirit of the diocese by enacting basic policies concerning parish liturgies, affordable Catholic schools, and effective social programs. The pastoral council implements this vision by pastoral planning over a period of time. The presbyteral council advises the bishop on the governance of the diocese and implements the pastoral plan in practice. Finally, the college of consultors and the finance council provide advice and sometimes consent to a number of financial transactions.[21]

These bodies furnish the bishop with advice and information. The quality of discussion depends upon mutual trust in which the bishop indicates his sympathetic concern. The councils in turn must rely upon good staff work and an understanding by each member of the diocesan structure and his or her role within it. And to be truly efficient they must communicate with their constituencies on the regional and parish levels. The role of the bishop as leader is more important than in the past. He recognizes the need to use his councils to the benefit of all concerned.[22]

Because a diocese is divided into parishes, it is on the parochial level that Catholics enter upon and nurture their spiritual lives through the sacraments and diocesan programs. The bishop affects parish life by training seminarians, ordaining priests, and appointing pastors. He oversees parish financial administration and writes pastoral letters and newspaper columns. His sermons and addresses to parish personnel exhort some activities and discourage others.

Parish policies and procedures are spiritual, sacramental, educational and financial. Vatican or national regulations may help decide wedding music or preparation for the sacraments. Policies develop through the consultative process and tend to become standard throughout a number of dioceses. These most detailed involve finances (budgets, construction, collections), personnel (salaries, hiring, firing), and legal obligations (contracts, taxes, insurance). They coordinate by planning through parish visitations or by feedback.

The bishop works to support, encourage, and correct (if necessary) situations in parishes. His mail contains a laundry list of real or perceived grievances. Like letters to the editor, negative comments tend to incite more negative than positive communication. Complaints have their origins in sermons, liturgies, disagreements with pastors, schools, or a priest's personal conduct. Pastoral criticisms may find their ways to the chancellor, priest personnel director, or regional vicar or dean. These officials investigate specific problems and get in touch with individual priests. Anonymous complaints are usually dropped. Those which are serious often come through the episcopal vicar. The bishop and chancery maintain a priest's innocence until he is proven guilty and try not to take sides in disputes.

Large numbers of parishes within a diocese may cause division into regional vicariates. Auxiliary bishops (especially if they are regional vicars) visit parishes to inform the bishop about the needs and difficulties within their territories. Vicariates in turn often divide into deaneries, some reflecting city and county boundaries and others the entire diocese The process of twinning involves a joining of parishes, in which the more fortunate attempts to aid the less fortunate.

A bishop usually reserves priestly assignments, large expenditures, and the closing or opening of a school or parish to himself. But he often has help in making key decisions. Vicars may sit on the priests' personnel board, the finance council, the bishop's cabinet, and other diocesan bodies. But the priests' personnel director, the superintendent of schools, and the director of finances may report to the bishop and not to the vicars. The vicar must persuade the bishop, diocesan officials, and pastors to go along with his proposals. As a facilitator, he may develop social or educational programs, communicate with the parishes and the chancery, interpret and explain policies to pastors, and try to settle disputes. Vicars try to coordinate schedules of events and liturgical services with their deans, who as full-time pastors consult them.

Some bishops like to visit their parishes and others seldom come except for reasons like confirmation. Visits can help to improve supervisory and coordinating activities. Much can be learned through observation. Can the choir sing properly? Does it do so alone or with the congregation? Do the lectors (readers) proclaim the Scriptures and prayers understandably? How is the offertory procession composed? Are there extraordinary ministers of communion? The bishop notes that, if no special preparations are taken for him, they are also unlikely to take place in his absence.

The training of acolytes (altar servers), the condition of the rectory and the sacristy, and the interaction between parish priests and staff are informative. The bishop notes the preparation of the confirmation class and the remarks made to him at the following reception. He may also meet with the parish council, visit the parochial school and its principal, and speak with other ministers and deacons. The input he receives may be crucial to his agencies and the programs they administer.

Closing parishes, especially in inner cities, may cause dislocations. Population shifts may leave them empty with the resulting loss of money and problems in staffing. Sometimes rural parishes become centralized. If the parish is still serving a congregation, where can the people go? The archdioceses of Baltimore, Chicago, Cincinnati, and Detroit have suffered these problems in recent years. Before taking appropriate action, the bishop consults priests and parishioners. He may also commission plant surveys, collect census data, examine urban planning, and take into account the annual income and expenditures of the parish in question.

But closing may not be an option when a parish might be operated by a lay administrator. Such a person would not have the priestly functions of saying Mass and hearing confessions. He or she would serve to keep the faith community together in the priest's absence. In small towns and rural areas women religious or lay catechists may be administrator. Such a person visits the sick, prepares people to receive the sacraments, and counsels parishioners. A priest may come to say Mass or the layperson will offer the Liturgy of the Word. This service is the first part of the Mass or what, prior to Vatican Council II, was known as the Mass of the Catechumens (those receiving instruction but not enjoying full communion with the Church). It consists of prayers, songs, Scripture readings, and a homily, followed by a type of eucharistic prayer (without the Consecration) and a Communion service.

Over time the lack of priestly and religious vocations has pushed lay participation to the forefront. Volunteers teach religious education to children, run social programs, and take part on various parish committees. Eucharistic ministers take Communion to the sick and shut-ins. And there are more full-time professionals working in the ministries of the Church. These workers include teachers, bookkeepers, and directors of religious education teaching catechetical programs to adults and children not in parochial schools. And others take part as music ministers, singers, eucharistic ministers, servers and lectors. Liturgical ministers may plan and organize weddings, funerals, baptisms, and Sunday liturgies. Pastoral ministers are involved in marriage and baptism preparation programs and in marriage counseling. There are youth ministers, social ministers for the poor and underprivileged, and business or plant managers.

For its professional staff and employees the diocese provides guidelines, tax coverage, contracts, and insurance. In some cases there are workshops and training programs. In some dioceses there are personnel offices for lay ministers. The applicant may be given lists of parishes for which the personnel office might draft a contract and propose a salary scale.

Besides working with parishes and through vicars, the bishop oversees a number of agencies providing programs for parishes. The liturgy office uses workshops to train lectors and eucharistic ministers. The education office might have workshops for catechists, while the social justice program may need parish volunteers. The bishop often mediates between pastors and agency heads. The offices want pastors to get involved on the parish level to fight abortion, feed the hungry, share dialogues with other faiths, improve the liturgy, and reach out to the unchurched. Priests like to be consulted and get a full range of information (encyclicals, pastoral letters, reports, newsletters, and statements) from the Vatican, the National Conference of Catholic bishops, and their local chanceries.[23]

Turning from the national model of a bishop in his diocese, we now examine some characteristics of the Province of San Antonio in early 1994. Its components vary greatly in size and makeup. From the 4,226 square miles of the Diocese of Brownsville along the Rio Grande to the 37,433 square miles of the Diocese of San Angelo in West Texas few sees are similar. While all these jurisdictions follow the system with bishops (or an archbishop), vicars general, vicars of various types, consultors, presbyteral councils, tribunals, and chancellors, there is no one form of organization.

There is a moderator of the curia in San Antonio, Austin, Brownsville, Fort Worth, and Galveston-Houston. Fort Worth and Galveston-Houston combine this office with that of chancellor and in San Antonio and Brownsville with that of vicar general. Victoria in Texas has a composite vicar general, chancellor, and judicial vicar. And in San Angelo the vicar general is also the judicial vicar and chairman of the presbyteral council. San Antonio unites the offices of chancellor and judicial vicar. In El Paso the judicial vicar is also the vicar for religious.

In Amarillo and Brownsville the chancellors are women religious, while in Corpus Christi a deacon holds this position. Corpus Christi joins the curia with an "administrative council". In Fort Worth and Lubbock the presbyteral council and the college of consultors have the same members. In Dallas one priest serves as the entire presbyteral council and Beaumont does not list such a council separately. There are reasons for uniting various diocesan offices. Chancellors and judicial vicars find a specialized knowledge of canon law useful. Others have particular experiences, interests, and capabilities which qualify them for their positions. Then, too, sufficient personnel may be unavailable to fill each office with a separate incumbent.

Just as individuals differ among themselves, so do the dioceses of Texas differ from one another. The four counties of the Brownsville diocese have the most Catholics in the general population (81 percent), while the thirty-two counties of the Tyler diocese have the fewest (4 percent). Galveston-Houston leads in diocesan priests (190), total priests (diocesan and religious order, 413), seminarians studying to become priests (43), parishes (146), high school students under religious education (16,017), and Catholics in the state (748,781 of 3,974,688). San Antonio has the most permanent deacons (225) and elementary students under religious education (36,905). Correspondingly, Tyler has the fewest diocesan priests (23), parishes (27), and high school students under religious education (780). Lubbock trails in priests (44) and San Angelo in seminarians (3). Victoria in Texas has only eleven permanent deacons, while Amarillo has just 3,694 elementary students under religious education and 36,795 Catholics in the State.[24]

Perhaps the most important consideration is the physical organization of the sees themselves. As organizational units Texas dioceses range from Brownsville (four counties of 4,226 square miles) to San Angelo (twenty-nine counties with 37,433 square miles). But the dioceses of Galveston-Houston and Tyler command our attention. Galveston-Houston (originally Galveston) was the first diocese in Texas, while Tyler is the most recent. Galveston-Houston virtually included Texas on its establishment (1847), while Tyler is derived from several dioceses and is the latest to be formed (1986). Tyler has developed its own institutions and will continue to do so.

At present the eleven counties of the Galveston-Houston diocese with its 9,354 square miles sit upon the most heavily populated area in Texas. Although the archdiocese of San Antonio (twenty-one entire counties and parts of two others with 27,841 square miles) is formidable with its seven urban and seven rural deans, only Galveston-Houston unites its thirteen deaneries under four territorial and regional vicariates. It has a diverse population and the problems of a modern metroplex with commuter cities and rural areas as well. Its complicated organization and many ministries are indications of how a contemporary diocese must serve many needs and constituencies.

In 1994 Galveston-Houston had a bishop with two ethnically diverse auxiliaries to serve an area in which about one in every five persons is Roman Catholic. With 413 priests, 218 permanent deacons, seventeen male and 570 women religious, there were 146 parishes and eleven missions. Three hospitals, two health care centers, ten specialized homes, an orphanage, and seven special centers for social services assisted almost one million persons. The diocesan educational establishment consisted of one diocesan and three religious order seminaries, a university, two diocesan and parochial and six private high schools, forty-three elementary schools (forty-two diocesan and parochial and one private), and a nonresidential school for the handicapped. There were 16,017 high school and 44,995 elementary school students under religious education programs. The teaching staff included forty-nine priests, five religious brothers, ninety-six religious sisters, and 1,450 lay teachers. In the previous year (1993), there were 14,813 infant and 874 adult baptisms and 2,360 receptions into full communion with the Church. There were 10,964 first communions, 5,333 confirmations, and 3,491 marriages performed. Three thousand and forty-seven of the faithful died.

At the beginning of 1994 the bishop was assisted by two auxiliaries, a chancellor, a vice-chancellor, and two vicars general. Four ethnic vicars (including the auxiliary bishops) served the Black, Vietnamese, Hispanic, and Filipino parishioners. There were a vicar for religious, a spiritual director for priests, a finance officer/business manager, and a diocesan tribunal. The college of consultors and the presbyteral council were in place to serve their functions. The diocese was divided into four vicariates including thirteen deaneries. Diocesan commissions and committees included the diocesan presbyteral council, the priests' personnel committee, the building commission, the board of education, the ecumenism and interreligious affairs commission, and the liturgical commission.

Secretariat directors for Christian formation, for social concerns, for family concerns, for administration and communication, and for special services divided various diocesan offices among them. These were offices for administrative support, community services for the aging, the diocesan AIDS ministry, the apostleship of prayer, the apostleship of the sea for Galveston and diocesan (port ministry), archives and records, African American ministries, boy and girl scouts, Catholic chaplains corps (hospital chaplains), Catholic Charities (divided into immigration, outreach, and direct services and further subdivided) and Catholic Charities of Galveston, Guadalupe Area social services, community relations, construction and maintenance, correctional ministries (jail chaplains), continuing Christian education, council of Catholic women, cursillos in Christianity, deaf ministry, development office, disaster relief, and the diocesan services fund.

There were also offices for the disabled persons ministry, evangelization, family life, Hispanic ministries, the Holy Name Society, the insurance director, the Legion of Mary, the media center, missions, *Movimento Familiar Cristiano*, Newman apostolate (campus ministry), *Oremus Pro Invicem*, parish accounting system, permanent diaconate, personnel office, press (*The Texas Catholic Herald*), pro-life activities, radio, risk manager, rural life activities, schools, the School of Environmental Education-Camp Kappe, special youth services (juvenile detention ministry), St. Dominic Center, Inc., St. Vincent de Paul Society, Stewardship Office, vocations to priesthood and religious life, worship, and youth ministry.[25]

Joseph A. Fiorenza, the present bishop of Galveston-Houston, implemented major changes in his diocesan structure with the vicariate system and the reorganization of his chancery to include five secretariats. His letter of 24 January 1986 addressed to all diocesan clergy named Monsignor Joseph H. Crosthwait, pastor of St. John Vianney parish in Houston, to a five-year term as vicar general (effective 1 March). Monsignor Crosthwait would serve as temporary episcopal vicar for the Central Vicariate pending the appointment of an auxiliary bishop to assume that office. The Central Vicariate would include the Central, Northeast, and Southeast deaneries.

Monsignor Vincent M. Rizzotto, pastor of St. Cecilia's parish in Houston, would be episcopal vicar for the Western Vicariate including the Western, Southwest, and Northwest deaneries. Monsignor William L. Tinney, pastor of St. Martha's parish in Kingwood, would be episcopal vicar for the Northern Vicariate with the Northern, San Jacinto, and Eastern deaneries. And Monsignor T. Joseph Culver, pastor of St. John Neumann parish in Houston (later pastor of Queen of Peace parish in La Marque) would be episcopal vicar for the Southern Vicariate comprising the Galveston-Mainland, Bay Area, and Southern deaneries. Like Monsignor Crosthwait Monsignors Rizzotto, Tinney, and Culver were to begin their new duties on 1 March, but their terms would be for three years. Bishop Fiorenza gave his new episcopal vicars the right to administer the Sacrament of Confirmation "until an auxiliary bishop is appointed". He thanked them for assuming the new positions in addition to their pastoral duties.

At this time the Diocese of Galveston-Houston consisted of seventeen counties. The Northern Vicariate had the Texas counties of Anderson, Freestone, Leon, Houston, Madison, Trinity, Grimes, Walker, Montgomery, San Jacinto, Liberty, Chambers, and parts of Harris and Waller. The Central Vicariate included the central portion of Harris County, the Western Vicariate having Fort Bend County and parts of Harris and Waller. And the Southern Vicariate contained Galveston and Brazoria counties.[26]

When the Diocese of Tyler was formed (1986) Galveston-Houston lost the counties of Anderson, Freestone, Houston, Leon, and Trinity to it and the counties of Chambers and Liberty to the Diocese of Beaumont. Later Galveston-Houston acquired Austin County from the Diocese of Austin. As of 1994 the vicariate system was somewhat altered. The Northern Vicariate now included Madison, Grimes, Walker, San Jacinto, Montgomery, and parts of Waller and Harris counties. The Central Vicariate with episcopal vicar Bishop Curtis J. Guillory, SVD still contained central Harris County. The Western Vicariate, with the addition of the Bluebonnet Deanery (1991) was composed of Austin County with parts of Waller, Fort Bend and Harris. The Southern Vicariate now had Galveston and Brazoria counties with sections of Fort Bend and Harris as well.[27]

The *Texas Catholic Herald* for 25 July 1986 announces the reorganization of the Galveston-Houston diocesan chancery. With the restructuring of the deaneries into vicariates Bishop Fiorenza divided his administration into five secretariats. The move to a "cabinet-type system" placed the chancery's twenty-eight departments and other diocesan apostolates under the new secretariat directors. In this new plan Sister Mary Grace O'Brien, CVI would be the director for Christian Formation, Wally Honeywell for Family Concerns, Monsignor Dan Scheel for Administration and Communication, Rev. Frank Rossi for Special Services, and Monsignor James A. Jamail as temporary director for Social Concerns. Bishop Fiorenza stated, "A decentralization of diocesan administration is needed because of the growth of the diocese and the Chancery departments." The paper noted that the duties of operating a diocese with state and national committee work by the bishop required the aid of episcopal vicars and secretariat directors. The directors would coordinate the departments of their divisions by "joint-planning and the sharing of information". Periodic evaluations of each department and assistance with budgets to be reviewed by the Diocesan Finance Council would help implement the new arrangement. Directors could better account for the different offices within their secretariats. Department heads would report regularly to their directors.

As planned, the Secretariat for Christian Formation would comprise the School Office, the Department of Continuing Christian Education, the Office of Worship, the Office of Campus Ministry, the Media Center, the Board of Education and the Liturgical Commission. The Secretariat for Social Concerns would include Catholic Charities, Immigration Services, Correctional Ministries, the Department of Community Relations, the St. Vincent de Paul Society, St. Dominic Retirement Center, the Charities Board and the Social Concerns Committee.

The Secretariat for Family Concerns includes the Family Life Office, Youth Ministry, Aging Ministry, Special Youth Services, the Deaf Apostolate, Catholic Ministry for Disabled Persons, Pro-Life Activities, the Youth Board and the Senior Senate. The Secretariat for Administration and Communication encompasses the Office of Finances and Accounting, the *Texas Catholic Herald*, the Office of Radio (and Television), the Parish Council Office, and the Finance Council.

The Secretariat for Special Services has the Office of Vocations, the Pontifical Mission Societies, the Hospital Chaplains Corps, the Seaman's Center, the Admissions Board, the Permanent Deacons and the Permanent Diaconate Commission. At the time the secretariats were set up Bishop Fiorenza appointed Monsignor Scheel (chancellor since 1979) moderator of the curia to coordinate the entire administrative system. The moderator also maintains the chancery buildings and allocates office space within them. A month before (June 1986) the Bishop had appointed vicars for the ethnic ministries, Bishop Enrique San Pedro, SJ for Hispanics, Rev. Charles Andrus for Blacks, and Monsignor Philippe Le-Zuan-Thoung for Vietnamese.

Bishop Fiorenza also appointed Rev. Stephen Zigrang as judicial vicar, Bishop San Pedro episcopal vicar for the Central vicariate with Monsignors Culver, Tinney, and Rizzotto for the Southern, Northern, and Western vicariates respectively. Bishop San Pedro and Monsignor Crosthwait were vicars general and Walter Leeds the finance officer.

A diagram entitled "Organizational Chart: Diocese of Galveston-Houston" is a part of this article. It shows the bishop as the source of all diocesan authority with the following consultative groups directly responsible to him: the Presbyteral Council, the Priests' Personnel Board, the Finance Council, the Sisters' Council, the Permanent Diaconate Commission, the Ecumenical Commission, and the Building Commission. On the next level and listed separately are the episcopal vicars (with the deans below them), vicars general, the judicial vicar, and the vicar of religious. Immediately under this level and directly below the bishop is the chancellor/moderator of the curia, with the vice-chancellor connected to him but to the side as his immediate subordinate. Beneath the bishop and chancellor/moderator of the curia are the financial officer and the vicars for ethnic ministries. On a lower level and directly under the bishop and chancellor/moderator of the curia are the secretariats: for administration and communication, for Christian formation, for family concerns, for social concerns, and for special services.[28]

By 1994 the reorganization plan was still in effect. During the year (for the most part effective on 1 July) Bishop Fiorenza made a number of personnel changes. Monsignor Vincent Rizzotto was promoted to vicar general (in place of Monsignor Crosthwait) and his former position as episcopal vicar for the Western Vicariate was taken over by Monsignor William M. Pickard, the pastor of St. Frances De Sales parish in Houston. Monsignor Tinney's replacement in the Northern Vicariate is Monsignor William P. Robertson, pastor of Christ the Good Shepherd parish in Spring.

Rev. Frank H. Rossi replaced Monsignor Scheel as chancellor and moderator of the curia, while the Rev. Robert Troy Gately, a parochial vicar (associate pastor) of St. Martha's parish in Kingwood, occupied Reverend Rossi's former position as vice-chancellor. In 1994 the ethnic vicars were Bishop Guillory for blacks, Bishop James Tamayo for Hispanics, Rev. Peter Chu Ngoc Tranh for Vietnamese, as well as Monsignor Seth Hermoso for Filipinos. In earlier events Monsignor Jamail held his secretariat for social concerns from its inception until 1 October 1991 when his duties were assumed by Mrs. Susan Stromatt. A stewardship office under the direction of Adam Martinez opened in 1993. On 28 June 1994 the Bishop put Thomas B. O'Toole (already finance officer and business manager) in place of Monsignor Scheel as director of the secretariat for administration and communication. Continuing to make personnel changes on a timely basis, the structure set in place in 1986 functions today.[29]

In 1994 the Diocese of Tyler was organized differently from Galveston-Houston, which began in 1847 with more than 200 Texas counties and which now contains only eleven. But Galveston-Houston's large metropolitan area, number of Catholics and need for increased services refined its development into a model for the contemporary and increasingly urban diocese. Instead of a large expanse becoming smaller and changing to meet new requirements, the Diocese of Tyler began as a composite, made up of counties from three already existing dioceses, twenty-one counties from Dallas, six from Beaumont, and five from Galveston-Houston. Tyler had to build up its own institutions

Established on 12 November 1986 and effectively constituted on 24 February 1987, when its first bishop Charles E. Herzig was ordained, the Tyler diocese had to create itself. It had thirty-two counties containing twenty-five parishes and sixteen missions. There were thirty-five priests (twenty-one diocesan, thirteen religious order, and a hermit), with twenty-seven permanent deacons, three men religious (including two hermits), and seventy women religious (including thirty-four cloistered nuns). There were four elementary, one middle, and one high schools, and two hospitals. The diocese also contained a number of state prison units, a state hospital, a state university, and two junior colleges, all needing ministers. The entire population of these counties was estimated to be 1,167,000. But the Catholic population, not fixed at the time, was estimated to be between 25,000 and 45,000 (2.14% to 3.86% of the total). It was later placed at 28,774 (or 2.5% of the total population).[30]

Bishop Herzig immediately set to work to build his diocese. He appointed Monsignor Milam Joseph his vicar general, but he did not appoint a diocesan chancellor.[31] On 27 November 1987 the first edition of *Catholic East Texas* (the diocesan newspaper) began to appear bimonthly. On the first page of that issue the editor Robert Plocheck, in an article entitled "Diocese Launches Newspaper to Serve East Texas Catholics," notes that there are now twenty-six parishes with fifteen missions, thirty-eight priests, thirty permanent deacons, two men religious, and seventy-one women religious. He also lists the diocesan schools and their locations. In the same issue (page 2) Susan De Matteo in "With A Little Help from Our Friends" notes that the chancery building, then located at 1920 Sybil Lane in Tyler, was purchased from the Rev. Paul Powell, pastor of Green Acres Baptist Church and president of the "Texas Southern Baptist Convention" (correctly known as the Baptist General Convention of Texas). The first year of existence of the Tyler diocese (1987) ended with 1,009 baptisms and 195 marriages (ninety-eight Catholic and ninety-seven interfaith), with 4,962 students under Catholic instruction in religious classes having six women religious and eighty-one lay teachers. There were 202 deaths among the faithful.[32]

By the end of 1990 basic diocesan institutions were in place in Tyler. Catholics celebrated the three-hundredth anniversary of the Church in East Texas at Mission Tejas State Park at Weches, near Crockett, in June. And in December more than 2,000 people commemorated the American apparition of Our Lady of Guadalupe (1531). Bishop Herzig ordained two more men to the priesthood, the fourth and fifth for his diocese. School population and physical plants expanded. St. Michael Hospital in Texarkana proposed crossing the Arkansas state line into Texas with construction set for the new year. The bishop continued to staff his parishes and his diocese showed an increase in net worth from $1.3 to $1.8 million. Yet with all this success a great sadness came in October. Doctors discovered a tumor on the bishop's right lung.

Though weakened by phlebitis, balance problems, and the severity of his necessary treatment, Bishop Herzig seemed to gain in overall health. But the cancer, eradicated in January, had spread to his brain by July. Strengthened by his faith and refusing to yield to adversity, he met Archbishop Flores in Tyler on 6 September and died on the following day. The diocesan consultors met three days later, selecting Monsignor Joseph to administer the diocese until the pope's next appointment.

It is a tribute to Bishop Herzig's stewardship that his diocese flourished even as his health declined. Despite a general shortage of priests, he ordained his sixth and last priest on 8 June 1991. The number of registered Catholics increased by five percent, bringing the total number to 32,000. The year also saw the beginning of a diocesan tribunal, when the bishop designated Rev. Joseph Strickland to attend a two-year canon law program at the Catholic University of America. The Diocesan Council of Catholic Women undertook a child adoption program. And the mission of Gun Barrel City was raised to the status of independent parish.

Bishop Edmond Carmody was installed in Tyler on 25 May 1992, and he blessed the new church building in Nacogdoches on 26 June. Next day he ordained five new permanent deacons. By the end of the year seven men began studies for that position. The new bishop appointed the first diocesan chancellor and the first full-time director of vocations. He began a working tribunal with a part-time secretary and canon lawyers from the Beaumont diocese and named the first women to the Diocesan Finance Council. Perhaps his biggest change was the reduction of the Presbyteral Council from forty-five priests to ten. The smaller council also replaced the five-member College of Consultors. On 12 December the ordination of Rev. Dan Gonzalez, the first Hispanic priest for the diocese, took place on the feast day of Our Lady of Guadalupe. There was an eleven percent increase in diocesan Catholics (with an increase of Hispanics of 22 percent), for a total of 35,581.

The year 1993 was one of growth with the movement of the chancery on 10 September from 1920 Sybil Lane to expanded quarters at 1015 ESE Loop 323 in Tyler. The bishop began the year by instituting a lay pension plan and issued formal employment policies in June. The diocese acquired land for church sites in Lindale, Tatum, and Whitehouse. Three priests came from India and one from Poland. Bishop Carmody met the pope twice in 1993, at Denver for World Youth Day in August and in Rome for his regularly-scheduled visit in September and October. They discussed life in the Bible Belt, increased Hispanic population, and the World Youth Day just past. In memory of his predecessor Bishop Carmody dedicated Bishop Herzig's grave marker on the second anniversary of his death (7 September 1993), as well as the monument for the priests' burial plots at Rose Hill Cemetery in Tyler. In December the bishop named six lay people, two deacons, and three priests to a new Diocesan Liturgical Commission. Plans were made for the diocese to host the thirty-second annual Southwest Liturgical Conference in January of next year.

The Conference opened in 1994 with some 500 people from fifty southwestern dioceses and from as far as Los Angeles and Chicago. Catholic communities in Lindale and Whitehouse became missions of the Cathedral in Tyler, while a new mission opened in Gilmer. And the mission in Carthage became a parish. Bishop Carmody ordained two new priests, as others took up appointments within the diocese. Enrollment in the diocesan schools surpassed 1,000 for the first time in about four years. For the first time a superintendent of schools was appointed specifically for the Tyler diocese.

Ministries gained considerable attention. The education office launched the Lifelong Individual Faith Enrichment (LIFE) program, designed to increase adult instruction in the faith. The first round of classes in English and Spanish in seven cities drew about 400 people. The Hispanic Ministry Advisory Council developed a Hispanic pastoral plan for the diocese and the new family life office offered workshops for various family issues, with ministries to the widowed and divorced. The Youth Fiesta '94 lasted three days and the Junior Youth Rally held in Tyler drew 192 young people. The youth group at St. William Church in Carthage won national recognition for its "Mountains of Food" campaign, one of 300 national projects honored by the Points of Light Foundation and *USA Weekend*, a national Sunday newspaper supplement. An AIDS task force came into being to provide a pastoral response to the disease in East Texas. Finally, the new St. Michael Health Care Center in Texarkana, owned by the

Sisters of Charity of the Incarnate Word of San Antonio, opened to join the diocese's two other hospitals in Paris and Tyler.[33]

The Diocese of Tyler continues to grow and expand its services. Its traditional system uses deaneries for organization. This is the method of the majority of Texas dioceses. The Northern Deanery of the Diocese of Tyler contains the counties of Bowie, Camp, Cass, Delta, Franklin, Hopkins, Lamar, Morris, Red River, Titus, and part of Wood. The West Central Deanery includes Cherokee, Henderson, Rains, Smith, and Van Zandt counties. The counties of Gregg, Harrison, Marion, Panola, Rusk, Upshur, and part of Wood make up the East Central Deanery. The Southwest Deanery contains Anderson, Freestone, Houston, Leon, and Trinity counties, while the Southeast Deanery contains those of Angelina, Nacogdoches, Sabine, San Augustine, and Shelby.[34]

Some situations involving church institutions outside his diocese affect the bishop (or archbishop). The chain of authority does not end with him. The Vatican, the National Conference of Catholic Bishops (NCCB), ecumenical councils, Roman synods, and Vatican curial departments all exert their own controls.[35]

An archbishop may have an ecclesiastical province coextensive with his state, as in Texas. As metropolitan he has almost no practical power over his suffragans. But he often attends their celebrations of anniversaries of ordination, their installations and burials. He is certainly not limited to functions of courtesy. Priests in a diocese tell him their complaints. The pro-nuncio may request information. The archbishop may intervene in a lawsuit concerning his personnel seeking a settlement. He frequently helps to draw up lists of episcopal candidates for papal consideration. And he may have provincial tribunals review marriage annulments.

At least yearly bishops attend a state conference usually headed by their archbishops. Here they develop a consensus on common policies and programs. A core staff (usually between one to fifteen employees) may have a lobbyist in the state capital. Chancellors, school superintendents, and Catholic Charities directors from dioceses within the state make up committees doing more staff work. Outside experts, observers, and representatives from priests' councils might attend meetings.

The agenda may include purely religious and various public policy matters. Common religious concerns might include sacramental preparation, faculties, implementation of canon law, common regulations for marriage preparations and church attendance with holidays following on weekends.

Sometimes the result of the meetings is to issue joint pastoral letters through the state conference. The bishops of Texas, for example, have written letters on such subjects as pastoral care of Hispanic immigrants and the sacrament of reconciliation (penance). On 17 November 1987 they issued a twelve-page document entitled "An Invitation to Love: A Pastoral Statement on Human Sexuality," urging the necessity for chastity.

Some conferences develop such services as health and liability insurance or retirement plans. Focus on public policy concerns causes the representation of bishops before the legislature in twenty-seven state capitals. It is no wonder that the Catholic Church closely monitors legislative activity. State laws on such subjects as zoning, building codes, bingo, tax exemptions, private education, churches, hospitals, and social agencies can directly affect church organizations. The Catholic bishops of Texas oppose casino gambling, for instance, as a possible cause of social and familial dislocation.[36]

The Texas Catholic Conference, located in Austin, is one of thirty state conferences plus one for the District of Columbia. In 1994 the head of the National Association of State Catholic Conference Directors was James M. Lago, the executive director of the Catholic Conference of Illinois. The National Association maintains liaison with the general secretariat of the United States Catholic Conference (USCC), which is located in Washington, DC. The USCC is the operational secretariat and service agency for the NCCB existing to carry out the civic-religious work of the Church in America.[37]

The executive director of the Texas Catholic Conference is Brother Richard Daly, CSC. In 1995 the 74th Session of the Texas Legislature convenes in regular session on 10 January and adjourns 29 May. During this meeting of the legislature some five to six thousand bills and resolutions are expected to be introduced. The Conference monitors their introduction and expects that approximately sixty to eighty of them will be of concern to the Church. House Bill 301 would establish sixty voucher experiments in Texas to aid "educationally disadvantaged" children. The legislature would permit 80 percent of the funds allocated for the student's education in the local district to be transferred to the school of choice. The remaining 20 percent would remain in the public school district where the student resides. Available funding of this type would enable school children to seek a private school education. And some of these children may enroll in Catholic schools.

Other areas of interest include legislation to regulate abortion in Texas. Companion bills (Senate Bill 83 and House Bill 313) require parental notification before the performance of an abortion on a minor. There have been bills to require public and private colleges and high schools to distribute condoms, mandatory coverage for in vitro fertilization by insurance policies, and mandatory sex education curricula in public schools. The Texas Catholic Conference and other advocacy groups monitor developments during the session and oppose or support measures as appropriate. The Conference provides a toll-free number to keep Texans informed on the status of bills and resolutions.[38]

Many state conferences oppose capital punishment and public funding of abortion. In addition such matters as brain death, living wills, surrogate mothers, homosexual rights, public school health clinics, sex education, welfare reform, shelters for the homeless, public housing, the farm crisis, migrant workers, prostitution, the criminal justice system, pornography, and other matters governed by legislative enactment may cause conferences to take stands concerning them. When bishops meet in this way they are able to consider such positions formally.

On the national level bishops are active in the NCCB/USCC and meet centrally at least once yearly to deal with issues of common concern. All bishops have an equal vote except on financial issues, with retired bishops and auxiliaries not voting. The president and the vice president are conference spokesmen during their three-year terms. Through the years the bishops of Texas have rendered outstanding service as members of committees and as committee chairmen. In 1994 Bishop Fiorenza of Galveston-Houston served as secretary of the

NCCB/USCC and Bishop Curtis J. Guillory, SVD, his auxiliary, headed the standing committee on African American Catholics. At the same time another Texas bishop, Edmond Carmody of Tyler, was chairman of the standing committee on Missions. In the single year 1987 Bishop Delaney of Fort Worth chaired the Liturgy Committee, Bishop Peña of El Paso chaired the Hispanic Affairs Committee, and Bishop McCarthy of Austin served on two other committees of international scope.[39]

As an organization the NCCB/USCC has issued pastoral letters on peace and on economic justice. It has issued public statements on Central America, South Africa, the Middle East, Northern Ireland, the Church in communist countries, racism, capital punishment, health care, abortion, the ERA, care for the terminally ill, food stamps, Medicaid, education, homelessness, international debt, immigration, tax reform, labor relations, and other subjects.

The national conference spends much time on church issues, such as ecumenism, Catholic education, evangelization, family ministry, catechetics, women in the Church, liturgy and sacramental practice. With the approval of the Vatican the NCCB can set policy binding on all bishops. Such matters require a two-thirds vote. Standing and ad hoc committees deal with such concerns as budget, liturgy, doctrine, pastoral practice, canon law, farm labor, Hispanics, missions, ecumenism, laity, pro-life, priestly life and formation, vocations, Latin America, the permanent diaconate, women, education, communications, social development, and world peace. In addition the administrative committee draws up the agenda for conference meetings and makes policy when the conference is not in session.

Staff based in Washington, DC aids the committee and leadership of the conference. Headed by a general secretary, it has experts on issues of concern to all bishops, such as public relations, liturgy, doctrine, church finances, education, priestly life and formation, civil and canon law, and domestic and international affairs.

On the international scene bishops support dioceses in Latin America, Asia, and Eastern Europe. They give financial assistance to poor churches around the world individually and through agencies such as Catholic Relief Services and the Propagation of the Faith. Bishop Carmody of Tyler was a missionary in Latin America before assuming his episcopal office in Texas.

Bishops acted with the pope during Vatican Council II, pushing through the decree on religious liberty. The synod of bishops meets about every three years as his advisory body. Four American bishops are usually elected by their peers to attend the synod, and the pope usually appoints two or more Americans. Archbishop Flores of San Antonio has been elected to the synod. In the past American bishops have defended their tribunals for granting large numbers of annulments and for urging a greater role for women in the church. Other bishops, such as Dallas-born Cardinal William W. Baum have served as heads of Vatican curial departments. Other American prelates have conducted visitations of archdioceses, dealt with theologians like the Rev. Charles Curran, chaired the commission on religious life, advised on finances, raised money, helped write the new catechism, and planned the pope's American visits.

Bishops take an oath of loyalty to the pope and also take seriously the pastoral needs of their people. Every five years American diocesan bishops visit Rome to meet with the pope and various Vatican officials, as required by canon law (canons 399-400). In this cycle called *ad limina* (to the threshold) visits, the last round took place in 1993 and will again in 1998.

Before the visit to Rome the Congregation for Bishops receives each bishop's quinquennial (fifth-yearly) report, which describes in detail information on thirteen areas. These are: 1) the pastoral and administrative organization of the diocese, 2) the general religious situation, 3) the economic situation of the diocese, 4) liturgical and sacramental practice, and 5) the clergy. Other areas concern: 6) religious and secular institutes, 7) cooperation with the missions, 8) seminaries and universities, 9) Catholic education, 10) the life and apostolic action of the laity, 11) ecumenism, 12) social assistance, and 13) other pastoral questions. In addition statistical data on advisory councils, the tribunal, publications, the clergy, and educational institutions become part of the report. After initial submission to the Congregation, parts of the report are distributed to the proper Vatican departments.

Individual meetings between bishop and pope last for about fifteen minutes. The bishop gives the pope an envelope containing a donation from the diocese. The pope usually asks questions based on the report, such as the number of people and priests. Some bishops bring up matters of interest to them, like ecumenism and positive things the religious orders are doing in the diocese. The pope may take up specific matters. While the meeting is the only chance the bishops have for one-on-one conversations, the pope invites them to dinner, usually in groups of twelve. During these occasions topics are unlimited and the pope addresses each bishop by the name of his diocese rather than by given name. Such meals are informal and may last from one-and-a-half to two hours. In the last part of the visit bishops as a group meet with the pope. The senior bishop briefly addresses the Holy Father on their behalf and the response acknowledges the visitors. It is not unusual for the pope to prepare his response in advance.

The pope's *ad limina* addresses to the bishops tell them his wishes for individual countries. In 1978 Pope Paul VI emphasized the sacrament of penance to some American bishops and praised other bishops for seeking to preserve life in supporting programs to aid, shelter and feed the poor, the elderly, and minorities. In his last address that year he spoke on the reception of the Eucharist as the summit of Christian life. In his short reign that same year John Paul I addressed the bishops on the Christian family, its indissolubility, and the love of the pope for married people. In 1983 John Paul II recounted all of these themes for their importance, making them more explicit and praised fidelity to church doctrine and church discipline. He advised against general (as opposed to individual) absolutions, as did Paul VI. He urged bishops to be holy, loving, compassionate, and truthful and to stress the bond of marriage and the dangers of premarital sex and homosexuality to that bond.

John Paul II affirms humanity and demands preservations of the rights of the unborn, the weak, the handicapped, the poor, and the aged. He opposes priestly ordination of women and expects priests not to engage in secular and political activity. He wants religious orders to rededicate themselves to holiness, renewal, penance, and conversion. He believes that prayer and the union with the *magisterium* (the ordinary teaching authority of the Church) are essential to religious life. He acknowledges the worthiness of married love, the worth of the family, and its mission in the Church and in the world. He expects needy families to be aided through social service agencies. And all of these things he points out, individually and entirely, to the various groups of American bishops he meets.

The pope is also a wide-ranging traveller, making his presence felt wherever he goes. His visits to America in 1979 and 1987 offered occasions to deliver his message to the bishops. At an assembly in Chicago in 1979 he urged them to live lives of personal holiness and to guard and keep church doctrine. He commended their Christian witness and referred to pastoral letters some had written on the subjects of racism and homosexuality. He stressed Christian unity, the importance of sacramental penance, the Eucharist, and the unity of local churches (dioceses) with the universal church. Although the pope addressed the bishops, he submitted advance copies of his talk not to them but to the press.

During the pope's 1987 visit to America, he met with the bishops in Los Angeles. In this "dialogue" four archbishops addressed him on four different subjects, and he replied to each. Cardinal Bernardin of Chicago began by speaking of the Church as a communion of particular churches, forming a unique Catholic Church and united with the Bishop of Rome. The Cardinal demonstrafed that the American qualities of freedom to speak, to question, to know, and to criticize did not signify disobedience. Americans maintain unity but affirm diversity, seeking a balance between freedom and order. He cited the NCCB itself as a visible expression of the principle of collegiality in church leadership. The pope responded that authority in the Church is vertical, a unity of God and of the local churches with the pope. Unity resolves tensions. Neither American culture nor a need for candor between the bishop and Rome was part of his reply.

Archbishop Quinn of San Francisco spoke on the state of moral theology. He defined moral theology as human wisdom trying to understand God's revelation about how we live. The American world role involving the military as an instrument of policy, instability in the family, the high standard of living, new medical technologies, psychological insights and the sociology of the nature of human sexuality, the sexually permissive climate of the country, the changing social status of women, and the higher level of education among American Catholics were new realities bishops must face as pastors. The Archbishop cited American bishops' pastorals on peace and economics, distinguishing universally binding moral principles from special applications and recommendations. He mentioned dialogue and discussion as effective in understanding moral questions and in developing responses. John Paul's answer was that a good Catholic does not dissent from the *magisterium* and remain in good standing. He did not comment on the "new realities" and ignored the distinction between principles and applications. But his silence on these matters was deafening. It implied that the bishops should proclaim the *magisterium* more forcefully and courageously.

Archbishop Weakland of Milwaukee's subject was the role of the laity in society and in the Church. He stressed the education and participation of the laity in American society. As a group they held the worth of an argument of more value than uncritical acceptance of the Church's teaching authority. The faithful look for spirituality to integrate their lives and wish to contribute to the life and growth of the Church. Women wish to be equal partners with men in the fulfillment of the mission of the Church. John Paul acknowledged the growing role and education of American Catholics and wondered about their impact on American culture. He thought bishops should provide the laity with sufficient religious instruction to bring the gospel's influence to bear upon the world of culture. He indicated that pastoral care to families should include the concept of natural family planning. And he commended the bishops for their work for peace and justice, stressing the equal human dignify of women and true feminine humanity.

Archbishop Pilarczyk of Cincinnati concluded the representations to the pope with remarks on lay, religious, and clerical vocations in America. The decline in religious and priestly vocations and the rise of the lay ministry were present conditions. Mandatory celibacy and the church's teaching on the ordination of women seem to have led to the decline. There is a sense of the broadening of church ministry and an increasing appreciation of prayer, Scripture, and the liturgy. Parish life is increasingly developed as a result. The pope avoided using the term "lay ministry" but spoke instead of the active participation of the laity in the mission of the Church. He stressed that the vocation of the laity resided in the world rather than the Church.

The pope concluded by reminding the bishops to be vigilant in presenting dogmatic and moral teaching of the Church faithfully and clearly to seminarians. They must see that the norms for the use of general absolution are observed. The Church's teaching should be explained to homosexuals. The virtue of chastity must be recovered. He did not mention the bishops' pastoral letters on peace and the economy and did not seem to favor the widely consultative process involved in their writings.

The 1988 *ad limina* visits were made after the pope's visit to Texas in 1987. He met with eleven groups of American bishops during the year and with a representative group the following year. Bishop Michael Pfeifer, OMI of San Angelo reported that the pope seemed to have an improved view of America. There were no demonstrations against him, and he liked the universality and catholicity in American ethnic groups. He hoped the bishops would not forget the missions.[40]

In 1988 the second group of American bishops included the Texans. In particular John Paul II recalled his recent visit to San Antonio, his welcome, and the "impressive faith of the people." He cited their 1987 statement on human sexuality as "a much appreciated pastoral effort to present the Church's teaching on chastity without fear of reticence." He also spoke on the pastoral vision for the third millennium and of the necessity of individual confession.[41]

Between *ad limina* and papal visits letters from Rome arrive in American chanceries. Reports from the laity are investigated. Tribunals are defended from being divorce mills by being better staffed with canon lawyers and secretarial staff. Papal interventions into internal diocesan affairs are extremely rare, as are attempts by Catholic pressure groups to undermine the authority of the diocesan bishop.[42] Conflicts between local needs and universal teaching are part of the process. Rome prefers that women religious live in religious communities, but some sisters live alone while serving poor, rural areas. Nor is a diocese free from making its own mistakes. When the Archdiocese of Santa Fe took over the University of Albuquerque, the school closed two years later and saddled the archdiocese with a two-million-dollar debt.

Outside his diocese the residential bishop finds the actions of his archbishop as metropolitan, his state conference, and the NCCB/USCC influence his decisions. He is also in constant communication with Rome. He spends a good portion of time (perhaps as much as twenty to thirty percent) outside his diocese. Decisions of the NCCB may be binding and Rome is the source of policies and procedures. The bishop is aware of limits to general absolution, the desirability of first confession before first communion, the indissolubility of marriage, and prohibitions on intercommunion. As an American bishop, he wins high marks for his concern for the poor, his sponsorship of such agencies as Catholic Charities and Catholic Relief Services, and his advocacy of human rights.

We now have some idea of the bishop's work within his diocese, what it is, how it is organized, and how it is governed. We have examined the national picture and included the Province of San Antonio to see how it may be alike or different from the overall pattern. We have taken particular note of two Texas dioceses (Galveston-Houston and Tyler) and we have seen how institutions outside the diocese affect it. Next we will examine the role finances play in diocesan operation.

J. Some Notes on Finances

It is almost a commonplace that a Catholic is not an especially cheerful giver to his or her church. In a recently conducted study sociologist Dean Hoge, a member of The Catholic University of America's Life Cycle Institute, reached a similar conclusion in his survey of more than 10,000 church members of five denominations and the yearly financial reports of 625 congregations across America. Results were funded by the Lilly Endowment with data from a Gallup survey and were released in Washington, DC, on 4 November 1994.

At the same time Professor Hoge and his fellow researchers delivered their reports to the annual meeting of the Religious Research Association in Albuquerque, New Mexico. They found that the typical Catholic household gives only $386 a year toward church support. This figure is less than one-fourth given by the typical Assemblies of God family. Catholics offer about one-third the amount given by Baptist and Presbyterian homes and about half as much as the average Lutheran family. Although Catholics had an average parish size of 2, 723 members (or nine to ten times that of the average congregations in the other denominations studied), the researchers did not conclude that smaller congregations have higher per-member givers than larger ones.[1]

It is somewhat paradoxical that a church supplying the spiritual, and increasingly some material, benefits in life should be treated so. Blame may be apportioned widely. Young people may think their parents and other adult gifts dispense them from similar obligations. Perhaps they are not aware that the precepts of the Church involve a moral obligation to provide for its material needs.[2] Yet in teen age a young person's thoughts heavily turn toward such things as gasoline, CDs, clothes, and dates. As one gets older and faces college and more extended education, he or she is more likely concerned with its costs. And that one commodity time, which was once so freely squandered, is now of the essence.[3]

As parishioners grow older and begin families, they find much of their life is church-centered. They are more alert to tradition and more comfortable with its value system. They would like a parish home for themselves and their children. Contribution on a steady basis now seems an acceptable option. The church is for celebrating Mass and receiving the sacraments. Thus it provides a needed source of spiritual strength. Parish membership provides more than a place for weddings, baptisms, and funerals. It offers continuing religious education, from Bible study to guest lectures to parish retreats. It affords a pleasant atmosphere in which people meet socially. The physical plant of the church and equipment supplies and other costs are expensive. And the obligation of maintenance extends to all members.

Parish schools need subsidies to reduce spending to families. Parents and others accept this expense so that students will benefit academically, morally, and religiously. On the average this is a bargain as it is less than a third of the cost per child spent by public schools. Catholics realize they have a duty to assist the work of the Church, particularly with its ministries to the poor, the sick, and the needy. The Church's worldwide missions, campaigns against world hunger, and promotion of religious vocations are worthy causes requiring financial aid. In the Catholic Church charity begins with parishes helping less fortunate parishes and priests providing food and clothing for hungry people who come to their rectories. Finally, giving maintains the church structure itself and enables the Church to carry out its programs. All of these reasons give Catholics a powerful impetus to give to their church.[4]

While laypeople support the Church on a freewill basis, the hierarchy encourages the practice of tithing and of sacrificial giving. Tithing exhorts the faithful to set aside one-tenth of income for church and charitable support. Sacrificial giving enjoins fixed funds for the Church with the faithful living on the remainder. The bishops know that if people give only at random times from available cash that longtime planning will be uncertain. They prefer to "convert" the flock from this idea to one called "stewardship".

As a united effort, American bishops began in 1988 at the annual meeting of their episcopal conference, the National Conference of Catholic Bishops (NCCB). One of their number asked the following question: "How do we develop among ourselves, our priests, our seminarians and our people a spirituality of giving, a biblical concept of stewardship?" The late Archbishop John May of St. Louis, president of the NCCB, formed the Ad Hoc Committee on Stewardship to address this problem.

Archbishop Thomas J. Murphy of Seattle became the head of the committee. He decided to present stewardship as a way of life employing three convictions. First, the baptized are called to be disciples of Christ and to implement this belief. Second, conversion to this life involves appropriate actions. Finally, stewardship expresses discipleship, with the knowledge that God is the source of life, the giver of freedom, and the supplier of the means to live. The hope is that people will turn from selfishness to generosity. The bishops incorporated these purposes in a pastoral letter in 1992. What began as an idea is now a formal policy, one to realize in all dioceses of the United States.[5]

Giving, and particularly the practice of tithing, has its source in the Bible. Biblical students have found forty-six references to it in Scripture. Malachi 3:10 states:

> Bring the full amount of your tithes to the Temple, so that there will be plenty of food there. Put me to the test and you will see that I will open the windows of heaven and pour out on you in abundance all kinds of good things.

In Genesis 14:17-24 Abram, before God changed his name to Abraham, returns from his victory over Chedorlaomer and the other kings. Melchizedek, king of Salem and a priest of God, brings Abram bread and wine, invokes the divine blessing upon him, and praises God. Abram gives the king a tenth of his loot. When the king of Sodom tells Abram to keep the loot, he refuses, insisting this is a fair share.

Abram's grandson Jacob has a mysterious dream at Bethel. When he awakes, he vows:

> "If you [God] will be with me and protect me on the journey I am making and give me food and clothing, and if I return safely to my father's home, then you will be my God. This memorial stone which I have set up will be the place where you are worshiped, and I will give you a tenth of everything you gave me" (Genesis 14:20-22).

God tells the ancient Israelites in Deuteronomy 14:22-26:

> "Set aside a tithe — a tenth of all your fields produce each year. Then go to the one place where the Lord your God has chosen to be worshiped; and there in his presence eat the tithes of your grain, wine, and olive oil, and the first-born of your cattle and sheep. Do this so that you may learn to have reverence for the Lord your God always. If the place of worship is too far from your home for you to carry there the tithe of the produce that the Lord has blessed you with, then do this: Sell your produce and take the money with you to the one place of worship. Spend it on whatever you want — beef, lamb, wine, beer — and there, in the presence of the Lord your God, you and your families are to eat and enjoy themselves."

In the New Testament we find:

> Jesus also told this parable to people who were sure of their own goodness and despised everybody else. "Once there were two men who went up to the Temple to pray; one was a Pharisee, the other a tax collector. The pharisee stood apart by himself and prayed, 'I thank you, God, that I am not greedy, dishonest, or an adulterer, like everybody else. I thank you that I am not like that tax collector over there. I fast two days a week, and I give you one tenth of all my income.' But the tax collector stood at a distance and would not even raise his face to heaven, but beat on his breast and said, 'God, have pity on me, a sinner!' I tell you," said Jesus, "the tax collector, and not the Pharisee, was in the right with God when he went home. For everyone who makes himself great will be humbled, and everyone who humbles himself will be made great" (Luke 18:9-14).

Clearly, the Pharisee's attitude was at fault in bragging about fulfilling his obligations. Jesus accepted the custom of tithing, but He warned the teachers of the law and their hypocrisy in giving in Matthew 23:23:

> "How terrible for you, teachers of the law and Pharisees! You hypocrites! You give to God one tenth even of the seasoning herbs, such as mint, dill, and cumin, but you neglect to obey the really important teachings of the Law, such as justice and mercy and honesty. These you should practice, without neglecting the others."

The early Christians understood the importance in giving to the Church as a continuation of God's work on earth. They supported the clergy, the needy and the poor, and those in authority above their pastors. As Paul says in 2 Corinthians 9:7-8:

> "Each one should give, then, as he has decided, not with regret or out of a sense of duty; for God loves the one who gives gladly. And God is able to give you more than you need, so that you will always have all you need for yourselves and more than enough for every good cause."

Paul tells us in Philippians 4:19 that God is not outdone in generosity: "And with all his abundant wealth through Christ Jesus, my God will supply all your needs." It is important to remember that giving to advance the work of God is giving to God Himself. David invited the people to give for the Temple and they responded unstintingly: "The people had given willingly to the Lord, and they were happy that so much had been given. King David also was extremely happy" (1 Chronicles 29:9).

Tithing in the Catholic Church has come to mean funds set aside for the support of the Church and charity. It is a freewill offering, though in recent years the biblical one-tenth has continued to receive a favorable response. St. Augustine (354-430) taught the tithe was a debt the Christian paid to God. Pope Gregory I, the Great (c. 540-604) condemned those who cheated on their payment. The Council of Trent (1545-1563) enjoined the faithful to make their offerings.[6]

Canon 222, Section 1 of the 1983 Code of Canon Law states:

> The Christian faithful are obliged to assist with the needs of the Church so that the Church has what is necessary for divine worship, for apostolic works and works of charity and for the decent sustenance of ministers.

No one, laity, religious, or clergy, may fail to support the Church. Clergy are encouraged but not obliged to give to the Church or to works of charity the surplus from their church income (c. 282,§2). But this does not exempt them from church support from other personal income. Although professed members of religious institutes do not have personal administration of their goods, they may, barring the law of their institutes to the contrary, determine what is to be done with the income from their goods (c. 668,§1). Canon 222,§1 seems to apply when they make this decision prior to religious profession.

In the Catholic Church the family is the fundamental unit, a sort of "domestic church" in itself. As the basic unit of ecclesial and secular society, family resources must be safeguarded. Those lacking financial resources may provide their time and talent to support the Church in its mission. In this endeavor the Christian faithful pursue holiness and aid the Church (cc. 210-211). While the Church reserves the right to demand financial support of the faithful (c. 1260), it prefers that offerings be freewill or in reponse to authorized appeals for specific purposes (cc. 1261-1262, 1265). There is a provision in canon law for the taxation of physical and juridic persons by the diocesan bishop. But he cannot impose more than a moderate tax on people and then only after consulting with his finance and presbyteral councils (c. 1263). In the United States with its long tradition of separation of Church and State, however, such taxation would lack the incentive of civil endorsement, and (if imposed) is unlikely to be collected.

The Church acquires temporal goods for limited purposes (cf. c. 1254, §2). Traditionally these purposes are divine worship, support of the clergy, and benefits for the poor. A fourth purpose provides an additional part for the bishop's work of hospitality. The Church takes part in divine worship, but also in apostolic and charitable works. Those ministers who support this mission should be supported themselves. The 1983 Code of Canon Law requires adequate assistance for those providing special services to the Church (c. 231, §2), as well as clergy (c. 281). Just wages should be paid to employees (c. 1286) but not to lay ministers such as lectors or acolytes who have no such claim (c. 230, §1).

Section Two of Canon 222 requires the Christian faithful "to promote social justice and, mindful of the precept of the Lord, to assist the poor from their own resources." It is recognized that donations, though in themselves necessary, do not change the social structure producing the conditions of poverty. During the past thirty years popes have stressed the global aspects of the problem due to interdependence of peoples. The emphasis placed on the individual is that he or she must undertake the betterment of society as a moral obligation.

The idea of charitable works allied to religion is an ancient Christian concept. Paul collected for the Church at Jerusalem and deacons were instituted to administer care for the poor. Alms have been distributed through the ages as an expression of the personal concern of the Christian community.

Social justice and Christian charity are intimately related. Justice impels charity and charity provides the ultimate end of justice. Personal involvement is a reminder to address the needs of others and to work for social justice. This precept of the Church is based upon Matthew 25:40: "I tell you, whenever you did this for one of the least important of these brothers of mine, you did it for me!"

Canon 222 states the right of the Church to seek the support of the faithful and the faithful's right and duty to offer assistance. The Church's mission in a diocese may be supported by ordinary or extraordinary taxes or by fees for certain executive acts. Collections for special needs may be sought from time to time. Permission of the local bishop is necessary to solicit funds in a diocese. The diocese is financially responsible to the Apostolic See and to the system of church benefices.

The *cathedraticum* is no longer mentioned specifically in canon law, though it may come under the general provisions of Canon 1263 (see above). Historically the term meant "a moderate tax that is paid annually to the bishop of a diocese as a token of subjection to him by all churches and benefices subject to his jurisdiction." Such a tax was established on the provincial level and approved by the Vatican so that all churches, benefices, and lay confraternities in the province paid an equal amount. It was not paid to the vicar capitular or to the apostolic administrator during the time a diocese was vacant because of the death of the bishop. It occurs in the 1917 Code in Canons 1504 and 1507, §1. But in the present 1983 Code the 1917 Canon 1504 has no counterpart and Canon 1507 comes under new Canon 1264.

The term *cathedraticum* from the Second Plenary Council in Baltimore (1866) has been extended to mean a tax "given for the support of the diocese by each church, and this tax is proportionate to the income of that church." This method was approved by the Vatican Congregation of the Propagation of the Faith and continued after 1908 when the United States became subject to what is now the Congregation for Bishops. As we have seen, it may continue today.[7]

Canon 1259 states: "The Church can acquire temporal goods by every just means of natural or positive law permitted to others." Goods may be acquired legitimately by purchase and contract, contributions, gifts, and bequests, by labor and donations-in-kind, by prescription (long-standing possession in good faith), by court order, or by fees for certain services. Canon law affirms a right in natural law. By positive law the Church means canon law first and civil law second.

By law the Catholic Church means "an ordinance or rule governing the activity of things." It recognizes four kinds: natural, divine positive, ecclesiastical, and civil. Natural law comprises moral laws corresponding to the nature of mankind, which order conduct toward God, neighbor, society, and self. Its divine origin binds those who use reason. The Ten Commandments declare and simplify natural law, the precepts of which are to do good and avoid evil. Divine positive law has been revealed by God. Its essentials are love of God and love of nature, and the Ten Commandments. Ecclesiastical law is established by the Church for the spiritual welfare of the faithful and the orderly conduct of ecclesiastical affairs. A socio-political community establishes civil law for the common good.[8]

The Church may not acquire goods unjustly, nor may it pay an unfair price in the absence of giving. It cannot, for example, deprive a family in need by seeking to influence the will of a very old or very sick person. The Church is not to acquire vast property such as land without making some commitment for sharing its wealth. But it opposes civil laws which deny or restrict its right to receive donations and gifts, to purchase and hold property, and to solicit funds from church members and others. It asserts an "innate right" to require from its Christian faithful whatever is necessary to achieve its proper ends (c. 1260). At the same time the faithful may give temporal gifts to the Church and the diocesan bishop must remind them of their obligation under Canon 222, §1 and urge it to be observed appropriately (c. 1261). This obligation is considered absolute.

Canon 1262 states: "The faithful are to contribute to the support of the Church by collections and according to the norms laid down by the conference of bishops." Canon 1263 states that the diocesan bishop has the right to impose a "moderate" tax on "public juridic persons" under his authority. The tax should be proportionate to income and imposed after consultation with the finance and presbyteral councils. Only in "cases of grave necessity" is the bishop to impose extraordinary taxes on "physical and juridic persons" and then they must be "moderate" and levied "under the same conditions with due regard for particular laws and customs attributing even more significant rights to him."

Under these conditions an annual tax or parish assessment and some form of annual diocesan fund-raising drive may be considered ordinary means of support. The context of canon law indicates that "extraordinary" is used to mean some need not contemplated in the usual scheme of things. By "moderate" it means the word must be interpreted according to traditional usage and the centrality of functions and services, within a period of changing times and situations, in each diocese.

Canon 264 suggests the possibility of a tax to support the diocesan seminary. There is also the possibility under the 1983 code of Canon Law that the diocesan bishop could tax the income of his priests on the money received from Mass stipends. A Mass stipend is "an offering given to a priest for applying the fruits of the Mass according to the intention of the donor." One may ask a priest, for example, to offer the Mass for a personal intention or for the repose of the soul of a relative or friend. The offering made prior to the occurrence of the Mass contributes to the priest's support. The benefits accrued by the Mass itself are spiritual and subject to the will of God.

In the early Church Christians made offerings of bread and wine for the saying of the Mass and their own Holy Communions. They gave also for support of the clergy and of the poor. Giving for particular intentions may have begun in the fourth century. Private Masses began to be offered in the sixth century, while the stipend practice can be documented from the eighth century. By the eleventh century the private Mass and the stipend were regular practices.

Pope John Paul II issued a decree on 22 March 1991. It provides for one offering to be accepted for a Mass. The Mass should be offered with the donor's intention. The priest accepting the offering should say the Mass himself or have another priest do so. Secondly, several Mass intentions, for which offerings have been made, can be combined for the application of a single Mass only if the previous and explicit consent of the donors is obtained. Such Masses are exceptions to the general rule. An offering for a special occasion (a baptism, wedding, or funeral) given for the support of the clergy administering the sacraments and performing other sacred rites is called a stole fee, after the vestment worn by the officiating priest.[9]

Canon 1262 implies the systematic support of the Church by the faithful. The implication is based upon the Church's right to require necessary support and the obligation of the faithful to contribute to specific appeals by church authorities. Further, this canon "appears to empower the [national episcopal] conference to set down regulations on form, style, accountability, and other such matter" (*CIC*, 866). It is now generally acknowledged in the United States that "stewardship" supplies a valid basis for giving and that regular fund-raising is an acceptable means to advance the mission of the Church.

Canon 1264 states:

> Unless the law has provided otherwise, it is the responsibility of a meeting of the bishops of a province:
>
> 1° to fix the amounts of the tax for acts of executive power granting a favor or for the execution of rescripts of the Apostolic See, to be approved by the Apostolic See;
>
> 2° to set a limit on the offerings given on the occasion of administering the sacraments or sacramentals.

The concept that a Church authority may tax those under his jurisdiction and that the faithful may make offerings in connection with sacraments and sacramentals is a valid fund-raising practice. The Latin word "taxa" may be translated "fee," as, for example, one pays driver's license fees or court costs to civil authorities. While imposition of formal taxes within a religious context may be disagreeable to some, such fees exist in many parts of the world to support priests and further the work of the Church. Canon 1264, Number One, continues this practice for executive acts in a diocese and for the execution of rescripts (written replies by an ecclesiastical power regarding questions or requests) of the Holy See. As the Apostolic See is involved in approving fees set by bishops concerning its rescripts, the approval of the Apostolic See would seem to be needed to remove them too.

Support of the clergy is not separated from ministerial occasions involving the sacraments and sacramentals. The term "offerings" for priestly support seems more palatable than considering such payments as "taxes". Under the 1983 Code bishops may dispense with offerings for such services or resort to Canon 1264, Number Two, and set appropriate limits on giving.

Canon 165 considers fund-raising by religious mendicants (beggars) in certain religious orders and its control by church authority:

> §1. With due regard for the right of religious mendicants private persons whether physical or juridic are forbidden to raise funds for any pious or ecclesiastical institution or purpose without the written permission of their own ordinary and that of the local ordinary.
>
> §2. The conference of bishops can determine norms on fund-raising, which must be observed by everyone including those who are called and really are mendicants by their foundation.

Some religious mendicants, such as the Capuchins, rely on gifts for their sustenance. They do not need written permission to beg, as do others seeking this privilege. Here the diocesan bishop exerts control to keep order. It is also desirable that private persons have approval for their actions in representing the Church. In addition persons may receive end hold offerings or bequests not publicly solicited.

Bishops may raise special collections under Canon 1266:

> The local ordinary may prescribe the taking up of a special collection for specific parochial, diocesan, national or universal projects in all the churches and oratories which are, in fact, habitually open to the Christian faithful, including those belonging to religious institutes; this collection is to be diligently transmitted afterwards to the diocesan curia.

Special collections derive from ancient church tradition, especially when for the poor, needy sister churches, and other works of charity. Paul urged support for the Church in Jerusalem (Romans 15:26-27) and commended Christian giving (2 Corinthians 8).

Canon 1267 protects the trust relationship between the faithful and church authorities who receive their gifts for specific purposes. Section Two examines the phase of the donor-donee relationship in which the donee may not wish to receive a gift. An administrator may not want to receive funds or wealth improperly acquired. Or the donor might wish his gift to exert undue influence over church policy or future decisions. The Church may not want to be indebted to certain givers. The bishop may accept or refuse gifts for just reasons, especially those given conditionally.

Canon 1268 concerns the acquiring of gifts by prescription, which is good-faith possession of something over a proper period of time to achieve legal title over temporal goods. Prescription is akin to limitation in other legal systems, and both clarify the relationship between possession and ownership. When a certain time elapses, the original owner has no legal recourse against adverse possession. Canons 197-199 explain the principles concerning prescription. Here civil law of the respective nation involved has binding canonical significance where the Code does not provide to the contrary. In the United States individual state law binds, except where certain exceptions are made in canon law, such as

Mass stipends and obligations.

Private ownership of sacred objects is covered by Canon 1269. Although such objects may be acquired privately from privately-owned sources through prescription, they may not be employed for profane uses "unless they have lost their dedication or blessing". If owned by a church entity, they can be acquired only by another such entity. A sacred object is one set aside for divine worship or blessed for that purpose. Prescription can not transfer their ownership from a public source to a private entity or person. Sacred objects belonging to a parish or diocese, for example, could not be prescribed by an individual, even by otherwise meeting civil law requirements. But a private individual may transfer ownership of such objects as a chalice or a rosary to another private individual by prescription, by fulfilling its requirements.

By Canon 1270 "immovable properties, precious movable objects, and the personal or real rights and claims" belonging to the Apostolic See are subject to a prescription period of 100 years. Those belonging to another "public ecclesiastical juridic person" are subject to a prescription period of thirty years. Personal rights or actions govern one's relationship to other physical or juridic persons. Real rights or actions pertain to real property. The rights and immovable property or movable precious objects belonging to the Apostolic See require a specific prescription time and then can be prescribed only by a public ecclesiastical juridic person. There is a separate prescription period for such properties or objects of other public juridic persons. Other movable objects of various ownership, even those belonging to the Apostolic See and to other public juridic persons, may (or may not) be prescribed depending upon operative civil law in various regions.

Canon 1271 is of such importance to all concerns that it merits quotation in full:

> In view of their bond of unity and charity and in accord with the resources of their dioceses, bishops are to assist in procuring those means whereby the Apostolic See can properly provide for its service of the universal Church according to the conditions of the times.

The Second Vatican Council (1962-1965) expressed the principle of collegiality. All bishops share responsibility for the entire Church. Pope Paul VI in his *motu proprio* (document) *Ecclesiae sanctae* of 6 August 1966 authorized patriarchal synods and episcopal conferences to assess dioceses for the needs of other dioceses or the support of special programs.

This canon recognizes the bond between the Apostolic See and the bishops of the world and requires them to respond to the needs of the Apostolic See in light of resources available to each diocese. The system seems to be voluntary, as it does not call for taxation of dioceses or others by the Holy See. Further, Canon 1274, §3 encourages richer dioceses to aid those without sufficient means.

To conclude our discussion of the way in which goods are acquired under canon law, there is Canon 1272, which deals with the subject of benefices. According to the definition of Canon 1409 of the 1917 Code a benefice is a "juridic entity perpetually constituted or erected by the competent ecclesiastical authority, consisting of a sacred office and the right to receive the income from the endowment connected with the office." Such an entity seems to have arisen either from the pension granted Roman soldiers of merit or to the Germanic feudal system of reward for special service by the grant of a life income. It is somewhat like an endowed chair in a university, especially when the holder of the chair holds tenure.

The possession of benefices is not considered a problem in the United States because, even though parishes are canonically benefices, they have not operated as such. Where they exist, originally for the purpose of ministerial support, the goal presently is to suppress them and to transfer their incomes and principals into a common fund established in Canon 1274, §1.[10]

We have introduced the subject of finances in the Roman Catholic Church in America. The discussion has included the present state of giving, its rationale among the faithful, the concept of "stewardship" in the hierarchy, the biblical basis for donations, and the canon law norms for the Church's acquisition of goods. We will now examine church spending (especially for ministerial and agency needs) and pay attention to the dioceses of Tyler and of Galveston-Houston. Our concern is the financial foundation of Tyler and information about fund-raising and spending in both dioceses. This analysis concludes with the diocesan finances of the pope's 1987 visit to Texas, showing how Texas bishops work together toward a common goal.

In the Church the diocese aids its institutions including parishes, and individuals and families contribute to parishes. The work of the Church proceeds from the parish, to the diocese, to the province, to the nation, and then to the Vatican and its universal works. While authority and jurisdiction flow from the top down, the individual Catholic plays an important role at the parish level. At the same time the priest represents the bishop, who appoints him and keeps him in office and to whom he is responsible in governing the parish assigned him. From the most humble parishioner to the Holy See, the acquisition, management, and dispersal of finances involves all Catholics.

With continual need the priest must seek funding continuously. Not educated in financial matters during his training, he must learn to manage or seek the help of those who can. Living by collection-to-collection or crisis-to-crisis is ineffective in a long-term situation. Fund-raising and endowments are better means to solutions of money problems. As we shall see, there are many reasons to spend to maintain present levels. Expansion and betterment of facilities require greater efforts.

Richard P. Garrigan of Richard P. Garrigan and Associates, a consulting firm in Omaha, Nebraska, assists pastors to plan their financial futures. He provides guidance training and educational resources to American Catholic institutions. Since 1986 the training division has had more than 1,000 pastors go through its annual seminar, including the Pastors National Development Congress. This three-day program works to raise the level of pastoral leadership and management skills. It can involve estate planning, capital campaigns, foundation grants, corporate giving, annual giving and gifts through insurance policies.

Over the past thirty years the decline in religious vocations has vastly decreased the value of contributed services. As the number of priests declines further, the faithful will need larger churches and want more suburban schools built. Presently, with Catholics giving only about 1.4 percent of their annual incomes and increased expenses, priests must exercise increased leadership and management. Garrigan suggests establishing an independent parish development committee. Failing this, he believes it could be a subcommittee of the pastoral council or act as an advisory committee. It would not confine itself to monitoring a budget like a finance committee but consider sacrificial giving, endowments, campaigns, major gifts, alumni (for the school system), the bishop's appeal, and other matters. He envisions it composed of eight to ten people, themselves steady donors, meeting on a regular basis.

Garrigan does not expect pulpit requests but supports a "communications system" providing information to individual and potential donors. Development committee members should articulate the parish "vision" and resources. Methods might be annual reporting, newsletters, special report meetings and updating donors, and visits by members to discuss wills and estates.

Individual parishioners, according to this plan, should be giving to the parish annually for a specific project, such as an endowment or building campaign. Giving might extend to an individual's will, or trust, or insurance policy. Garrigan emphasizes that about 91 percent of wealth is in assets (investments, retirement plans, insurance policies and real estate) and that about 80 percent of American wealth is held by people fifty-five or older. He concludes by urging the evangelizing of people to become committed givers who take part in the meaningful development of the parish.[11]

While Catholics give a small proportion of income to the Church, recent surveys show the overall picture, at least in terms of clergy salaries, is not significantly brighter in other Christian denominations. The Empty Tomb Inc., a Christian research organization in Champaign, Illinois, reveals a decline among twenty-nine Protestant denominations from 3.05 percent in 1968 to 2.62 in 1989.

According to the 1992 Church Compensation Report, compiled by the evangelical publishing house Christianity Today Inc. of Carol Stream, Illinois, Christian clergy salaries rose an average of only 7.4 percent from 1988 to 1991, or less than half the inflation rate. Translated into dollars and cents, this would mean a base salary of $21,940. Total compensation, including housing allowances, pension, and insurance expenses, showed a rise of 12.6 percent to $37,260. This is more than a 50 percent increase in insurance benefits due to higher health care costs. Even so, total compensation for the period fell behind the 16 percent increase in the Consumer Price Index between 1988 to 1991.

The Church Compensation Report is based upon about 4,000 of 10,251 surveys sent out. These churches reported pay packages for 10,000 employees. The average of total benefits ranged from $78,421 for a senior pastor of a church with a budget of over $1 million to $22,849 for a single pastor of a church with a budget of less than $50,000. Pastors from Episcopal, United Church of Christ, Lutheran, Presbyterian and Reformed churches received an average of $53,115 totally, or 30 percent higher than the lowest-paid Protestants. These last included Menonites, the Christian Church (Disciples of Christ), and some Baptist churches. Catholic priests received $20,892 as average total compensation. According to James D. Berkley, editor of *Your Church* magazine published by Christianity Today Inc., an episcopal rector of a large church in a metropolitan city in the south Atlantic region over age fifty and the holder of a doctoral degree is the best prospect for highest pay. The Connecticut Conference of the

United Church of Christ, on the other hand, in 1992 was considering raising minimum salaries for pastors from $16,500 to $20,000.[12]

Responding to a question about the proper donation from a layperson to Catholic clergy or religious for personal use Rev. Peter Stravinskas believes diocesan clergy "receive a subsistence salary (usually around $500 a month), in addition to room and board." He notes that clothing, cars and auto insurance come out of salary and that health and life insurance, as well as retirement, policies come from the parish or the diocese. All material needs of religious order priests are met by their communities, and these priests receive no salary. Religious order priests are not to own things or bank accounts. All gifts received are reported to superiors. For diocesan priests "stole fees" for baptisms, weddings, and funerals may go into a parish fund, become the property of the celebrant, or go into a common fund for the benefit of all diocesan priests.[13]

In Texas financial reports for 1991 show priests of the Diocese of Tyler making a salary of $6,600, with a car allowance of $3,600, both fees set by the diocesan presbyteral council. There is an average of $750 for car insurance, $2,400 for car maintenance and gas, $5,570 for health insurance, $1,200 toward a pension fund, $4,800 for food, $3,000 for utilities, and $5,100 for housing. In this case utilities include electricity, water, and gas for rectories of two to three bedrooms. The total compensation is $33,020.

The salary and the car allowance come from the diocese. The room and board, health and car insurance, and car maintenance and gasoline are part of the parish budget and missions. The Chancery pays the pension for the priest from the Diocesan Annual Appeal. Costs of continuing education and retreats for priests are borne equally between the priest, the parish, and the diocese. The bishop approves the occasions and costs for such trips in advance.

Diocesan and religious order priests engaged in parish ministry in the Tyler diocese receive much the same compensation. Funds for order priests in many cases go to the order, which then pays its priests a certain preestablished amount. The Tyler diocese allows priests to receive Mass stipends and stole fees. In the past five dollars has been suggested for Mass stipends, with stole fees ranging from $5 to $25 for baptisms, between $15 and $30 for weddings, and $25 to $100 for funerals. In 1991 "the most recent salary figures available" showed that parish priests of the Tyler diocese with a monthly base pay of $550 were within $21 of the state average of $571.

The Diocese of Dallas in its *Texas Catholic* for 19 April 1991 showed $29,900 as the average total compensation for its diocesan priests. Its estimates did not include payment of utilities. Dallas shows an associate pastor (parochial vicar) receives compensation $600 less than the figure for pastors, or $29,340 in total. The Tyler diocese does not differentiate in pay between pastors and non-pastors.

In the Dallas diocese salary is $6,600, with a car allowance of $4,200 and a continuing education and retreat allowance of $520. Clergy receive an annual average of $720 for car insurance, $3,000 for car operation and gasoline, $2,400 for health insurance, $2,500 toward a pension fund, $5,000 for food and $5,000 for housing. In the Tyler diocese medical insurance premiums cost double that in Dallas because Dallas has a larger employment base and does not distinguish premiums between laity, priests, and sisters.

In terms of base salary the Diocese of Austin pays its pastors the highest ($730 per month), while the dioceses of Lubbock and Victoria are the lowest ($450). State car allowances range from $200 to $350 per month. Housing, food and insurance compensation vary with each diocese. The Diocese of Lubbock parish priests receive an annual total of about $24,560, while those of the Diocese of San Angelo about $25,500.[14] A recent study undertaken by the Catholic University of America places the average institutional cost of a full-time priest at $26,326 at the local level plus $1,428 at the diocesan level (and $1,039 for continuing education). The equivalent rate for Episcopalians is $45,005, for Lutherans $39,059, and for Methodists $35,308.[15]

Two of the largest programs in the Catholic Church are education and social services. Schools (exclusive of various universities, colleges, seminaries, and houses of study) are attached to parishes, while social services are run independently of them. Because such programs serve the public at large (especially the poor), they now compare favorably in outreach and professionalism with state or private agencies.[16]

At the beginning of 1994 there were 7,136 elementary schools, 1,248 high schools, and 227 colleges and universities affiliated with the Catholic Church. While most colleges and universities are run by religious orders, 60 percent of high schools and practically all elementary schools are the responsibilities of bishops. There are almost two million children in Catholic elementary schools and some 693,000 in Catholic high schools. But about three million elementary and some 790,000 high school students are in parish religious programs, mostly taught by volunteers.[17] Bishops concern themselves with the governance (decisions), Catholicity, and finances (costs and payments) of education programs.

School policies affect students, faculty, and administrators in admission, expulsion, tuition, hiring, firing, salaries, textbooks, curricula, insurance, and maintenance. They involve the diocesan (or archdiocesan) board of education, the vicar for education (if any), superintendents of schools, unions, principals, pastors, parish councils, parish education committees, and teachers. Finances are usually handled by the finance office. Other staff members deal with government regulations and staff development. There is often a placement service for principals and teachers seeking jobs. Problems such as tuition, teacher salaries, hiring, book selection, and others may be parochial or diocesan.

In a centralized school system a superintendent of schools approves the hiring of principals and mandates school policies, procedures, curricula, textbooks, and testing. School office officials visit and evaluate schools. In a decentralized system pastors and principals may ignore parish school board guidelines. Decisions are made at the lowest possible and the responsibilities of the parish staff are taken more seriously.

The structure of the Church encourages centralization. Government laws and regulations and accreditation tend to make for uniform policies and procedures. During conflicts angry parents, fired teachers and principals tell the bishop about their problems. To avoid lawsuits and insurance claims it is best to have diocesan policies in place which deal with hiring, firing, contract renewal, and liability. In a time when former religious jobs are filled increasingly by the laity, the diocese involves itself in their selection, training, and supervision.

As in other systems, teaching in Catholic schools is an interactive process.

The school office oversees the choice of textbooks and materials made by curricula experts and classroom teachers. Workshops and training programs are provided for teachers of religion. Some dioceses require catechists to be certified. And teams from state or private school associations evaluate the school system and its programs.

In the process of maintaining quality the Catholicity of various programs is essential. The total school experience comprises academic instruction, the Mass and other religious services, and prayer. The principal of each school should be a practicing Catholic and the National Catholic Educational Association (NCEA) informs teachers of the purpose of Catholic schools. Some dioceses want all their teachers to be Catholic and policies may be determined (at least partially) by religious considerations.

Regarding finances, school buildings and facilities must be provided, paid for, and kept up. Afterwards salaries and additional personnel costs can take up to 75 percent of funds budgeted for the school. The decline in religious vocations in turn forces up costs which must now be paid to their lay counterparts. Even so, the pay scale may differ from other systems as much as 50 to 90 percent. Tuition raises funds for salaries but only about 43 percent of revenues. The question is often to admit more students or to increase tuition. Around the country 46 percent of Catholic schools are financed by parish subsidies. Diocesan money also helps parishes in supplying grants for general operations or capital improvements. Those who can pay the full cost of tuition and others can apply for scholarships. State and local governments have supplied such items as school lunches, secular textbooks, transportation, nurses, guidance counseling, remedial courses, bilingual education and state-ordered testing programs.[18]

The bishop must do many things to operate his schools. He needs to know the status of all programs and the problems which may arise with them. He must know all the ramifications coming from the opening, closing, and consolidation of schools. He may supply direct financial aid, raise money for endowments, and approve changes in key personnel, policies, and procedures. He must appoint a superintendent of schools whose vision is similar to his own and who can work effectively with the diocesan board of education, pastors, and principals. Finally he must be a presence, articulating his ideas on Catholic education to teachers, catechists, and parents at liturgies, commencements, workshops, and conferences. For here, and in homilies and speeches, he himself is a teacher.[19]

The Catholic Church is the largest non-governmental provider of social services in America. It underwrites programs for the poor, the sick, the hungry, the homeless, the handicapped, and the emotionally disturbed, the unemployed, runaways, unwed mothers, refugees, alcoholics, drug addicts, prisoners, AIDS victims, and the generally needy. It administers to them in hospitals, nursing homes, orphanages, and low-cost housing units. And it works in neighborhood centers, shelters, foster homes, group residences, day care centers, and parishes. Its day-to-day activities include emergency care, counseling, education, and preventative services.[20]

In 1993 in America 609 Catholic hospitals treated 53,385,630 patients, while 313 health care centers aided 2,201,855 people. There were 1,620 specialized homes for 633,714 inhabitants and 194 residential homes (orphanages) for 76,245 children. There were 995 day care centers for 136,073 toddlers and 2,135 special social service centers for the use of 19,545,247 people. And ninety-seven schools for the handicapped assisted 8,778 students.[21]

These figures give only a partial idea of the total volume and kinds of care administered. In 1986 Catholic Charities provided services to 8.7 million people including 2.6 million families. Of these the largest number (5.2 million individuals and 1.4 million families) received emergency and food services. Seven hundred thousand people and 300,000 families were counseled. Over 240,000 persons and 90,000 families received refugee resettlement and immigration services. Over 100,000 individuals and 50,000 families were helped by pregnancy services with almost 4,000 adoptions processed. Over 600,000 persons and 50,000 families received support services in the form of day care, respite care, home health care, and homemaker services. In addition over 180,000 people and 119,000 families received housing services. And there were out-of-home care services for 182,000 persons, of whom there were almost 150,000 children and almost 120,000 families.[22]

Catholic Charities USA began in 1910 as the National Conference of Catholic Charities. Founded by Most Rev. Thomas J. Shahan (then rector of the Catholic University of America) and Rt. Rev. William J. Kerby, it acted in cooperation with lay leaders of the Society of St. Vincent de Paul to promote the charitable programs and activities of the American Catholic community and social service agencies. Through consultation, information, and assistance it serves more than 1,400 Catholic agencies and institutions with their social programs. In 1991 more than 12 million people turned to Catholic Charities for its aid.[23]

The clergy and religious make up no more than 15 percent of the total individuals in Catholic Charities agencies. Seventy-nine percent are volunteers (of these over half have special training) and 15 percent are paid staff (of whom 60 percent are professionals, 12 percent are managerial, and 19 percent are clerical and support staff). The state and professional organizations certify professional staffs in such fields as refugee resettlement, health care, marriage counseling, psychological counseling, and therapy.

Part-time volunteers operate soup kitchens, shelters, day care, special youth programs, shut-in visitations, crisis centers and hotlines. With population shifting toward the elderly, programs are increasingly geared to adults, the poor, the hungry, and the homeless. Because of church involvement in advocacy of education, community organizing, and proper societal structures, service and advocacy are usually separated so that money is not lost.

Some programs such as hospitals are usually governed by boards of directors usually filled by lay people. These directors set policy, hire personnel, and are legally and financially responsible as independents. Some programs are under diocesan control, which means the boards are appointed by the bishop, who has the final approval in policy, finance, and personnel matters. In such cases the diocese is responsible for operations.

In 1986 Catholic Charities made $600 million. Of this amount 45 percent was from government fees and grants, 20 percent from church sources, 17 percent from program services, 10 percent from the United Way, and the remaining eight percent from other sources. Of the church money less than half came from diocesan grants or Catholic Charities appeals. Private funds come mainly from contributions and services. But the federal government aids in refugee resettlement and states assist the dependent, neglected, delinquent and abused children, and the mentally deficient.

Dioceses frequently provide services like shelters, soup kitchens, and some advocacy programs like Hispanic Legal Action. They also begin some projects, such as halfway houses for female alcoholics and homeless youth shelters, in hopes that others will take over the work. In San Antonio Catholic Charities funded an office so it could hire a specialist on religious education of the handicapped.

Catholic Charities serves all. And in some places aid to non-Catholics outnumbers aid to Catholics. Hiring is on a nonsectarian basis, but the Church asserts its convictions on pro-life and on Catholic adoption of Catholic children. The bishop sees that programs reflect church teachings and gospel values and aids them financially. He approves major new programs and has ultimate authority for all diocesan services.[24]

Having examined some personnel expenses and how these and programs such as education and social services impact dioceses and those they serve, we now turn to diocesan administration, particularly on the parish level. Our particular interest is the conduct of financial operations. Money goes toward basic necessities, utilities, supplies, and beyond these help in realizing the supernatural goals of the Church. Prelates are theologians and do not purport to be financial officers. Monetary matters are the province of one (perhaps an accountant or bookkeeper) who makes collections, pays bills, and manages cash flow and investments. Beyond this he or she negotiates contracts for construction, insurance, and salaries. To the bishop this person is the chief financial adviser, assisting him in concerns affecting the diocese. And duties may also include real estate transactions, investment purchases, fund-raising, buying insurance, pensions, purchasing, and the maintenance and expansion of diocesan institutions.

In the United States a diocese (or archdiocese) is either a corporation sole or a corporation aggregate. More than half comprise the first type, in which the bishop (or archbishop) is the legal owner of parish and diocesan assets without a board of directors. In the second case each parish is a separate incorporated nonprofit corporation with the bishop and/or his appointees acting as trustees or members of the board of directors. One example of the second type has the bishop as head of the parish corporation with his vicar general, pastor, and some few laypersons as trustees. All diocesan institutions and agencies, including schools, seminaries, hospitals, cemeteries, charities and others, would be separately incorporated. The bishop is president of each and all such corporations, keeping control over church funds.

On the parish level the pastor may submit a financial report to the chancery yearly. Such reporting can become the basis of the assessment by the diocese. Parish income derives from collections, tuition (if the parish has schools), bingo, and other fund raisers, such as special dinners. Expenditures are mainly salaries, utilities, insurance, and repairs. Income from and expenses of schools is separate from other income and expenses. A parish should be self-sustaining, as subsidy payments are not expected to sustain it. Nor should parishes borrow money without the knowledge of the diocese. In some cases the financial report and budget fall under the scrutiny of the parish financial council.

Increased use of technology promotes regular comparison of yearly parish budgets and finding increases and decreases for various allocations. Some dioceses have internal auditors, especially for a parish in financial trouble or after the appointment of a new pastor. Such auditors stress regularity in accounting procedures, particularly in understanding how parish financial structure relates to the diocese. If there is a particular problem, a public accounting firm may make an independent audit.[25]

When a pastor wishes to construct, renovate, or goes over a specified amount (between $3 to $10 thousand), it requires diocesan approval. Above the limit the bishop must guarantee expenses involved. Building and remodeling also require approval. A large project necessitates at least three bids with consultation and dialogue between parish and diocese.

In the Diocese of Tyler necessary land must be acquired if not already available. Increasingly such space goes considerably beyond the church building. It may also include a rectory for the priest, education, social, and sports facilities to suit the needs of the total parish community. Financing involves the diocesan finance council and building board. The board consists of five members, of which one must be a priest, with the vicar general and the business manager acting ex-officio.[26] Lay members must be contractors, architects, mechanical or electrical subcontractors, and suppliers. The board handles projects of more than $5 thousand when plans were submitted. The parish may spend up to $1,500 to have preliminary studies completed.

The Finance Council considers population growth, the level of collections, the expenses of existing parish programs, the amount of unfunded debt (if any), and the amount of parish money on deposit. The money on deposit (excluding pledges) should be at least one-third the cost of the project. The Catholic Church Extension Society assists "missionary areas" in the United States if the requests go through the local bishop.[27] The bishop may use part of the Diocesan Annual Appeal funds to cover the debt.

When the Finance Council, the architect, and the representative of the parish building board agree, the project may be considered by the diocesan building board. At this stage the preliminary building budget, topographic survey, architect's preliminary proposal, and his resumé are submitted. A $50 thousand project requires a bid bond (money put up by the contractor to assure he will not make a bid on the project and then refuse the job). A performance bond provides parish protection. At least three bids are considered before the pastor and his board may approve the work.[28]

Some dioceses maintain a central bank paying parishes interest on their deposited funds. Pooled money can bring about lower rates of interest, and the diocese may get a more favorable rate for a parish by dealing with a bank by guaranteeing the loan. Loans are normally paid back within ten years to make money available to other parishes. If the diocese decides not to make good a loan, the requesting parish borrows from a bank charging two or more points over the prime rate.[29]

A diocese may purchase property, casualty, liability, and health insurance to cover various situations. Centralized insurance programs cost less. In the Diocese of Tyler effective 1 October 1989 the George Washington Life Insurance Company raised the deductible from $100 to $200. Monthly rates went from $93.18 to $130.86 for individuals and from $203.12 to $295.87 for individuals and their dependents. At that time 145 employees were included in the group plan. These people worked for the parishes, schools, and the diocese itself.

In medical insurance the Diocese of Tyler and Arthur J. Gallagher and Company became coinsurers for the same 145 employees effective 1 November 1989. Under this plan the diocese pays about $76 thousand to Gallagher. The remainder of premiums collected are to be held by the diocese to pay off claims. The diocese is required to pay up to $220 thousand in claims yearly, which are covered beyond this amount by other carriers for Gallagher.

An individual claim of more than $35 thousand is covered by other carriers. Combined dental and medical insurance can range from $76 thousand to $296,500, with the Diocese expected to pay $176 thousand in claims during 1989-1990. Savings is expected to reduce existing costs and/or to prevent increases. But costs for the same medical services increased 25 percent per year for three years.[30]

Parishes are usually self-supporting, though those in the inner-cities and schools may sometimes need cash infusions. Where money is decentralized, the practice of "twinning" between rich and poor parishes is encouraged. In the Diocese of Tyler there are the "rich" Sacred Heart Parish of Palestine in Anderson County, without missions of its own, and the "poor" Sacred Heart Mission of Mount Vernon in Franklin County. These churches were joined in April 1989, with Palestine sending Mount Vernon ten percent of Sunday collections and equipment for the church.[31]

While parishes are one type of diocesan institution with money requirements, cemeteries, hospitals, high schools, social services, seminaries, the chancery, and other agencies also vie for attention. Cemeteries can make money by selling plots and maintaining funds for perpetual care. Schools may be funded partially through tuition, while social services may acquire money from grants. The diocese itself depends upon assessments on parishes, special parish collections, and income from investments.

Assessments are ordinarily a percentage tax on income, not including tuition (in the case of schools), but may (or may not) derive from bequests, investments, special collections, and fund-raising profits. Parishes are taxed on ordinary income (not to exceed twelve percent) with consideration for a parish school or for a parish or school with a mortgage. Support for an institution such as a seminary may also be part of the assessment, which may exclude special collections, estates, property, gifts, and stocks. There may be a surcharge on investment income if the funds are not within the diocese investment management program. Percentages benefit dioceses if parishes are rich or each parish may have a set (as opposed to a percentage) amount in assessment.[32]

While separation of church and state is a fundamental principle underlying American democracy, tax exemption for churches is not expressed in the Constitution of the United States nor in the Bill of Rights. Instead the First Amendment to the Constitution requires Congress "to make no law respecting an establishment of religion, or prohibiting the free exercise thereof." The Amendment reflects the justifiable fear of a national established church and the consequences of erecting one. States have exempted churches historically, but on the federal level there have been major challenges from the time of the Liberal League in the 1870s. Such challenges assert that, as the beneficiary of services, churches should take a part in the taxation process.

Thomas Jefferson first expressed his interpretation of the First Amendment liberties in his letter to the Danbury [Connecticut] Baptist Association on 1 January 1802, in which he mentions the concept of "a wall of separation between Church and State". Associate Justice Hugo Black of the United States Supreme Court stated Jefferson's views judicially in *Everson v. Board of Education*, 330 US 1 (1947), affirming the New Jersey statute allowing bus transportation for parochial, as well as public, school children:

> "Neither a state nor the Federal Government can set up a church. Neither can pass laws which aid one religion, and all religions, or prefer one religion over another. Neither can force nor influence a person to go to or remain away from church against his will or force him to profess a belief or disbelief in any religion. No person can be punished for entertaining or professing religious beliefs, for church attendance or nonattendance. No tax in any amount, large or small, can be levied to support any religious activities or institutions, whatever they may be called, or whatever fees they may adopt to teach or practice religion. Neither a state nor the Federal Government can, openly or secretly, participate in the affairs of any religious organizations or groups and vice versa. In the words of Jefferson, the clause against establishment of religion by law was intended to erect 'a wall of separation between Church and State.'"

For present purposes the crucial case is *Walz v. Tax Commission of New York* (1970) in which the Supreme Court upheld the constitutionality of a New York statute exempting church-owned property from taxation. The findings in the Walz decision answer the question of whether there exists a contradiction between federal constitutional provisions against establishing religion and public funds used for religious purposes when state statutes exempt church property from such taxation. In the majority opinion (7-1 with Associate Justice William O. Douglas dissenting), Chief Justice Warren Burger says that no such contradiction exists.[33]

American bishops have begun to address the basis of assessments in their meeting at the University of Notre Dame in June 1992. Proponents of a progressive tax in which richer dioceses must pay more carried the day. But there was general agreement upon reviewing the entire tax system. Individual Catholics have an indebtedness of about fifteen cents per person under the 1992 system with money going to support about one-fourth of the bishops' $40 million annual budget. Additional funds come from fees for services and government grants to support social service objectives.

One method under discussion is that of the Texas Catholic Conference which supports its work by assessments based upon Offertory income from each Texas diocese. In this way poorer dioceses (such as Brownsville) pay a lesser proportion. Brownsville gives about $90 thousand yearly in assessments to the bishops' conference (NCCB). On the other hand the dioceses might give less if assessments were income- rather than numerically-based. Collection from parishes may affect dioceses adversely and vice versa.

In the head count system the *Official Catholic Directory* is used annually to make determinations. But various dioceses use different criteria for their reporting systems. Such questions arise as the definition of a Catholic as either one baptized into the Church, or a regular attender, or one placed on the parish roster.[34]

The pressures upon a contemporary diocese require a consistent fund-raising process. Some appeals total the parish assessment and at least one special parish collection per parish. Such requests are for social services, education, and those programs with the potential to raise funds. The parish assessment is usually used for payment of insurance, utilities, the finance office, the tribunal, and the chancery. As we have seen, modern business methods call for modern information and retrieval systems, equipment, and the staff to administer work properly.

Increasingly dioceses need to plan from year-to-year. Their institutions must be kept up and, while parish programs often have their donors, bishops need the support of all in providing services for the entire diocese. Churches are often well-served by this plan as the excess is sometimes refunded for local needs. And, when funds build diocesan resources, the faithful are equally well-served.[35]

The Diocese of Tyler issues an attractive and informative brochure yearly with a message from the bishop. For the 1995 Diocesan Annual Appeal Bishop Edmond Carmody requests the aid of his 11,000 Catholic households. In this year his goal is $678,000. The first goal set for 1988 was $480,000. This figure was met and exceeded, and the Appeal is generally well-received. Contributions are appreciated and specially generous givers are often honored at special dinners in their honors.

In 1995 allocations come under five headings: aid to developing parishes, priests and lay social programs, ministries, education, and family and youth development. New programs cited for 1994 and 1995 are the Family Life Office with its marriage enrichment and preparation programs, the Religious Education Office with catechetical training, and the Superintendent of Schools Office. Parish growth proceeds with the establishment of three new stations, two newly-ordained priests for the Diocese, and three new seminarians. A station represents new development in places where there was no previous Catholic presence. These stations may eventually grow into missions (to be administered by parishes) and into independent parishes with missions of their own. The Youth Ministry plans a fiesta and a rally. The thirty-two counties of the Tyler diocese are so spread out geographically that such events give young people a much needed sense of community.

Under the 1995 Appeal $541.9 thousand would be allocated specifically with $136.1 thousand in reserve. Aid to Developing Parishes (ten this time) would receive grants ranging from $2.4 thousand to $10 thousand, with the majority receiving $5 thousand. This makes a total of $50.4 thousand. Under Priests and Lay Social Programs, the Priests' Pension is $50 thousand, the Lay Pension is $25 thousand, and continuing Education is $55 thousand, for a total of $130 thousand. Ministries Birthright in Nacogdoches and Tyler, a pro-life program, would receive equal grants of $1.5 thousand apiece, the Tribunal $5 thousand, the Diaconate (men in orders below the rank of priest) $14.5, Vocations and Seminarians $90 thousand, and Catholic Charities (the diocesan Council of Catholic Women) $1 thousand. The Ministries allocations for 1995 totalling $113.5 thousand clearly reflects the importance of attracting and maintaining priests throughout the Diocese.

Allocations for Education include *Catholic East Texas* (the bimonthly diocesan newspaper, $85 thousand), the Stephen F. Austin State University (SFA) Student Center ($20 thousand), Kilgore Junior College ($5 thousand) and the four elementary and middle schools and one high school, which comprise the Catholic Schools ($72 thousand). Under the division of Family and Youth Development, Pastoral Ministries receives $65 thousand, while Martha's Kitchen (a social service) receives $1 thousand. The Diocesan Annual Appeal (DAA) is administered by the Steering Committee composed of people from eight cities and including two priests, six laymen, six laywomen, the finance officer and the DAA director.[36]

The Diocese of Galveston-Houston (Texas's oldest Catholic diocese) calls its annual appeal the Diocesan Services Fund (DSF). Its goal for 1995 is $5,211,326, and it is divided seven ways. As in the case of Tyler and all other such appeals, contributions are freewill offerings. In Galveston-Houston half of the amount received beyond the goal is remitted to the parish, while the other half aids the poor parishes fund.

The Secretariat for Christian Formation receives $1,486,659 (or 28 percent) of the total. Its needs are educational and it supplies the Catholic Schools Superintendent's Office, the Board of Education, the Texas Marathon for Non-Public Schools, the Media Audio-Visual Library Resource Center, Catholic Student Centers on College Campuses, and High School Subsidies. It provides funds for the Office of Continuing Christian Education, the Office of Worship-Liturgical Music, and the Office of Evangelization.

The Secretariat for Special Services ($1,025,253) and the Secretariat for Administration and Communication ($1,022,995) each make up 20 percent of 40 percent of the total. Special Services includes Vocations for Priesthood and Religious Life, the Hospital Chaplain Corps, the Seaman Centers in Galveston and Houston, Holy Cross Chapel in downtown Houston, Correctional Ministries, Special Youth Services, the Office of Permanent Deacons, the Ecumenism Commission, and Rural Life. Administration and Communication funds help the Radio Office, Infirm Priests, Foreign Missions, Special Charities, the Spiritual Director for Priests, the Vicar of Religious, and the Presbyteral Council.

The Secretariat for Family concerns ($845,576 or 16 percent of the total) and the Secretariat for Social Concerns ($509,596 or ten percent of the total) make up the next categories. Family Concerns includes Family Life Services, the Youth Ministry, the Aging Ministry, Respect Life Activities, the St. Dominic Deaf Center, Camp Kappe for Youth Programs, the Catholic Committee on Scouting, and the Ministry for Persons with Disabilities. Social Concerns takes in Community Relations for Social Action, Catholic Charities Immigration Ministry, the John XXIII Residence for Retired Priests, the Santa Maria Hostel for Women, Our Daily Bread-Galveston, Catholic Charities-Galveston, the AIDS Ministry, and the San Jose Maternity Clinic and Guadalupe Area Social services.

Ethnic Ministries allots $196,695 (4 percent) for the African-American and Hispanic diocesan ministries, while the Judicial Office targets $124,053 (2 percent) for the Diocesan Tribunal. The Galveston-Houston diocesan chancellor is the director of the Diocesan Services Fund, while in Tyler a layperson occupies that office for the Diocesan Annual Appeal.[37]

In a letter of 27 January 1995 Bishop Fiorenza of Galveston-Houston addresses the Catholics of his diocese: "Your support of the diocesan Church enables us to bring the truth of Christ to more than 800,000 registered Catholics and several hundred thousand more who live in this area." This message accompanies the "Financial Report (for the fiscal year ended June 1994)," which contains a detailed accounting of diocesan, parish and school funds of the Diocese under the heading "Combining Balance Sheets," as well as diocesan funds and parishes of the Diocese under the heading, "Combining Statements of Support and Expenses." Both statements show specific details as of 30 June 1994, with comparative totals for the same period in 1993, with both statements designated "unaudited". Two tables accompany the data showing "Allocation of Revenue" and "Allocation of Funds" for fiscal 1993-1994:[38]

	Allocation of Revenue
40.2%	Parishes
16.2	Tuition
9.4	Gifts
6.8	Insurance
4.2	Diocesan Ministries
3.9	DSF
3.7	Cathedraticum [tax assessed churches]
3.2	Subsidies
2.7	Fund-raising
2.4	Interest
2.3	Miscellaneous
2.2	Collections
1.8	Nursing Home
0.8	Lease and Rental
0.1	General Diocesan

	Allocation of Funds
37.4%	Parish Ministries
19.3	School Ministries
15.6	Debt Retirement/Construction
10.7	Diocesan Ministries
5.4	Insurance Premium/Claims Expense
4.1	Diocesan Program Expense
3.1	Interest Expense
2.2	National and Diocesan Collection
1.8	Nursing Home
1.0	Miscellaneous Expense
0.3	General Diocesan Expense

When the Galveston-Houston diocese (known as the Diocese of Galveston until 1959) began in 1847, it was virtually the area of Texas. But when the Tyler diocese was established in late December 1986, there was more than the mere transfer of title of various churches and institutions to the new bishop. Financial assessments were made by each of the three dioceses — Beaumont, Dallas, and Galveston-Houston — which made up the new Diocese of Tyler.

The reader may obtain an idea of the problems involved by reading *Catholic East Texas*, the Tyler diocesan newspaper, which published its first issue for 27 November 1987. Assessments of this kind are based on the number of priests, parishioners, real estate, and other considerations. Beaumont made a contribution of $322,297.89 and Galveston-Houston $146,040, for a total of $468,337.89. Issues taken up with the Dallas diocese involved such matters as assets, the priests' pension plan, and funds from the Catholic Foundation of Dallas. The paper records that the Dallas diocese transferred blueprints of all churches, buildings, and institutions, now part of the Tyler diocese. It readied for transmission files on parishes, schools and hospitals, priests' personnel files, and records of the Dallas building board.

On 16 June 1988 Bishop Tschoepe of Dallas and Bishop Herzig of Tyler, together with their representatives, met in Dallas to clarify the amount owed the Tyler diocese by the Dallas diocese. On the following day representatives presented information to the Tyler Diocesan Finance Council. Dallas had made a contribution of $675,000 and on 21 June 1988 added its final payment of $31,303 for a total payment of $706,303. This total, together with the previous payments by the Beaumont and Galveston-Houston dioceses made a grand total of $1,174.640.89 to the Tyler diocese. The monies held by the Catholic Foundation of Dallas, a charitable organization independent from or dependent upon the Diocese of Dallas. Canon lawyers were to decide the question.[39]

Finally, we have an example of how Texas bishops work together to achieve a common financial goal; in funding the pope's one-day visit to Texas in 1987. This aid is entirely apart from the annual collection in each parish known as Peter's Pence. It supports the pope and his charitable works and was originally collected on St. Peter's day (February 22). The practice began in England in the eighth century.[40]

For the brief time of the pope's visit to Texas (13-14 September 1987), he was the guest of its Catholic bishops, generously supplied by the Catholic laity of the state. His host in San Antonio was Archbishop Patrick F. Flores, the metropolitan of the Province of San Antonio. This province with its archdiocese and thirteen dioceses makes up the entire geographical Texas. During the *ad limina* visit of the Texan bishops (11-17 April 1988) Archbishop Flores presented Pope John Paul II with $105 thousand. This amount represented the surplus after all expenses in connection with the visit were paid. The total collected was more than $2.4 million. Expenditures included catechesis (religious instruction) in all parishes to prepare for the visit, the cost of the visit itself, and a post-visit evangelization program called "Mission: Texas," headed by Paulist Father Bruce Nieli of Austin.[41]

The bishops of Texas extended their invitation in 1986, making the reception of their guest a joint venture of all dioceses. Bishop Charles V. Grahmann (then of Victoria and later of Dallas), Chairman of the Papal Visit Finance Office, reported at the bishops' meeting at the Holy Name Retreat Center in Houston on 27 October 1987 that contributions of $2,408,200 had been received. At that meeting Rev. Lawrence J. Stuebben, state coordinator, reported that bills of $2,158,000 had been received and that bills of $150 thousand were to be received. Archbishop Flores stated that he expected the total cost would be $2.3 million for a year of educational programs in Texas, the visit itself, and the follow-up educational effort. They again agreed that the pope would receive whatever surplus there might be.[42]

The bishops used a flexible system in their fund-raising effort. Surplus monies were collected which provided a cushion for unforeseeable circumstances. Assessments were made based upon each diocese's ability to pay. Goals were set as follows: $50 thousand for Amarillo, $200 thousand for Austin, $125 thousand for Beaumont, $100 thousand for Brownsville, $150 thousand for Corpus Christi, $475 thousand for Dallas, $75 thousand for El Paso, $200 thousand for Fort Worth, $650 thousand for Galveston-Houston, $50 thousand for Lubbock, $29 thousand for San Angelo, $275 thousand for San Antonio, and $75 thousand for Victoria.[43] The Diocese of Tyler coming into being formally on 24 February was not given a special goal. Nevertheless it raised a collection of more than $20 thousand to help cover expenses.[44]

By 29 August, two weeks ahead of the visit, Corpus Christi, San Angelo, San Antonio, and Victoria had exceeded their goals, making a surplus of $354 thousand plus Tyler's $12 thousand. By dividing the money in proportion to need almost all remaining diocesan debts could be satisfied with the exception of a few such as Dallas and Galveston-Houston. About $1.8 million of the total of over $2.4 million was thus raised in a timely manner.

Though consisting of only four counties Brownsville was able to obtain $49,120 in two special collections, plus $34,763 to total $83,883. Dallas, diminished from thirty to nine counties by the creation of the Tyler diocese, had only raised about $75 thousand of its $475 thousand goal by 22 August. Plans were made to make up the $400 thousand by a special collection to be taken up either 29-30 August or 5-6 September.[45]

Individual contributions and collections were not the only official means to accumulate money. The Archdiocese of San Antonio sold a "Papal Visitation Medal" two inches in diameter, made of bronze with gold plating and weighing two-and-a-half ounces. It featured John Paul II on the obverse with the Hemisfair Tower and the Alamo superimposed on the map of Texas on the reverse. A similar one-inch pendant was included with each order of two medals. The individual medal sold for $19.95 with $1.45 sales tax and $3.00 for shipping and handling per order. The medal and pendant were advertised in print. A videotape of hour length endorsed by the bishops of Texas was *John Paul II: A Pope's Pilgrimage to Texas*. It was produced by ROGO Publishing Inc. of Dallas in VHS or Beta in English and Spanish for $35.13 for one copy and $32.13 for each additional tape.[46]

For the papal visit the City of San Antonio and Bexar County requested national guardsmen armed with night sticks and handcuffs for crowd control. The fee for their services was more than $200 thousand. Although the Church did not request the guard, it was responsible with the City and the State for payment.

According to Deputy Police Chief Robert Heuck of San Antonio, the guard would help put up and later take down rope-and-barrel barriers on the papal parade route and other sites. He felt this would allow more police officers to be available for patrol duties, with one shift handling the papal visit and two other shifts working twelve hours. The City of San Antonio expected to spend up to one million dollars for the twenty-two hour visit.[47]

Father Stuebben figured the Texas share of the papal visit to America at about $3.8 million. The cost to Church (and faithful) was roughly $2.5 million, an additional $180,000 to the State for 800 of the Texas National Guard for traffic control, and $800 thousand to one million dollars to the City of San Antonio for police and emergency medical support.[48]

The official gift of the bishops of Texas to the pope was a watercolor painting of "San Antonio de Yanaguana." It was executed by the San Antonio artist G. E. "Buddy" Mullan of Shavano Park, a northwest suburb. The eighteen by thirty-six inch portrait of St. Anthony was under the name given by the Payaya Indians for the area which became San Antonio. The Franciscan order established the mission on the saint's day (13 June) and named it after him.

St. Anthony of Padua wearing Franciscan robes holds the Christ Child in his left hand and a lily in his right. The dominant color is green and represents hope and the Ordinary Time in the church year in which the pope visited Texas. Below the central image of St. Anthony and Christ is the "vignette" of the Mission San Antonio. It is flanked by the Alamo, the Spanish name for the cottonwood tree and the popular name for the Mission. In the "vignette" Franciscans preach and baptize the Indians of Yanaguana in front of the Mission by the waters of the San Antonio River.

The decorations in the picture are designed to be specific. The personal papal coat of arms is at the top center of the border. Coats of arms of the fourteen dioceses of Texas are among the squared margins. At the bottom center is the Seal of the State of Texas with the arms of San Antonio on the left and those of Bexar County on the right. In each corner and in the middle of each border is a rose, representing the Blessed Virgin Mary, the Marian Year of 1987, and Our Lady of Guadalupe.

The forty-four-year-old Mullan made 250 reproductions of this painting. Signed and numbered 1 through 22 prints were given to the active and retired Catholic bishops of Texas. Number 23 went to Father Lawrence Stuebben, the coordinator of the Texas papal visit; number 24 to Sister Charlene, Father Stuebben's assistant; and number 25 belonged to John Paul Anthony Cisneros, the infant son of the Mayor of San Antonio. Numbers 26 through 250 were sold without advertising within three weeks, before they were printed. The profits of $10 thousand from the sale were given to Archbishop Flores to help defray the costs of the papal visit. Artist Mullan kept twenty-five artist's proofs to be sold later.[49]

On balance, on this trip of 1987, we must award the palm that year to the Texas bishops, who provided wisely. Having said this, we must also realize that the pope is not only a great religious leader but also a head of state. His security involves government at all levels — city, state, and federal. In Texas the bill for the trip ran close to four million dollars, or over $180 thousand for each hour of his twenty-two-hour stay. The City of San Antonio needed one million dollars for police and emergency medical facilities due to the crowds appearing that day. And the Texas National Guard sent in a bill for $180 thousand in overtime expenses.

But to cavil is not the point. On the positive side, many people were inspired by the pope's presence and many others worked together in a notable spirit of unity. In these perilous times one may regret that the appearance of such a world leader and the crowds he draws may require such massive outlays of time and money to prevent conditions in which illness, death, assassination, and social dislocation might take place. Nor does such great preparation encourage more and longer papal visits. But, by the Grace of God, dire events did not take place. The papal visit brought out the essential goodness of the overwhelming number who labored to make it a success. That the visit was a success is a tribute to all concerned.

The purpose of this section is not to provide an exhaustive nor exhausting study of Catholic finances on the diocesan level. Instead it is meant to illustrate the importance of funding in the Church's efforts to bring the benefits of the life, teachings, and redemption of humanity by Jesus Christ to all people.

Beginning with the individual Catholic's obligation of support, we have seen how the concepts of tithing and stewardship are fostered by the hierarchy. We have examined scriptural, canonical, and specific methods of how funds are gathered and spent for diocesan work, particularly referring to the dioceses of Galveston-Houston and Tyler. At the end we have noted the financial basis of the Tyler diocese and how the bishops of Texas can work together to solve a common financial problem. We have not answered all questions. But we should now have a better idea of what finances mean to the Catholic Church.

Postscript

On 15 November 1995 the bishops of the United States replaced the per capita diocesan assessment with a new method contemplating collections, the number of registered Catholic households, and the contribution of each diocese to some national collections. The new arrangement determines contributions of each diocese to the national episcopal conference (NCCB-USCC). About 22 percent of the bishops' total operating cost presently comes from diocesan assessments.

Under the old method each reported Catholic in a diocese was taxed at a rate of 15.7 cents. Under the new plan half the assessed amount will come from net parish offertory income in each diocese. Thirty percent will be based on the number of registered Catholic households in each diocese. Twenty percent will depend on each diocese's contribution to Peter's Pence, Campaign for Human Development and overseas aid collections. The new formula results in a net increase of eleven ($11) dollars over the current 1995 assessment of $9,262,723.

Offertory income includes collections at Mass, money given at the rectory, children's offerings, less frequent than weekly offerings, checks, currency, stocks and real property, but not national or seminary collections, building funds, and endowment donations. The three collections chosen are permanent and are processed through the bishops' conference.

Under the new system dioceses in Alabama, Arkansas, Georgia, North and

South Carolina and Tennessee are expected to double their obligations. The assessment of increase on the Diocese of Jefferson City, Missouri, would be 256 percent ($13,312 to $34,017). The 1996 cap would reduce the figure to $15,974. The new assessments for the archdioceses of Baltimore, Cincinnati, Milwaukee, St. Louis, and St. Paul-Minneapolis would range from $106,661 to $154,910.

Regarding other money matters during the annual meeting (13-16 November 1995) of the National Conference of Catholic Bishops (NCCB) and the United States Catholic Conference (USCC) in Washington, DC the bishops extended the annual appeal to reduce the unfunded retirement liability of religious orders to the year 2007. The bishops set up a reserve fund from later collections to be used after the collection ends and will set up more exact reporting requirements for religious orders seeking funding from the National Religious Retirement Office. The 1995 yearly collection for this purpose was to be 9-10 December in most American dioceses.

The United States episcopal conference expressed itself against attempts to put the poor and children at possible risk due to proposed congressional budget cuts. It feared welfare reform measures would appear to represent a massive disinvestment in poor children and working families - $110 billion by some estimates." The bishops called for "genuine reform which will encourage work, strengthen families and protect human life and dignity."

Insofar as the fourteen dioceses of Texas are concerned by the new levies, there will be large percentage changes projected for twelve dioceses. The assessment in six dioceses will lessen. But the change in any given year will not exceed 20 percent of the 1995 levy. In the case of the Diocese of Tyler (a change of 38.50 percent), twenty percent will be phased in in 1996 and the remaining 18.50 percent in 1997. Brownsville and El Paso diocesan decreases will be phased in from 1995 to 1999, a four-year period.

Projected Changes in Texas Assessments

Diocese	Current Assessment	Future Assessment	Percent Change
Amarillo	6,112	7,268	18.91
Austin	39,864	40,664	2.01
Beaumont	14,391	19,820	37.72
Brownsville	108,333	31,882	-70.57
Corpus Christi	58,052	37,387	-35.56
Dallas	47,808	58,069	21.46
El Paso	82,946	20,325	-75.50
Fort Worth	29,082	39,284	35.08
Galveston-Houston	124,373	118,180	-4.98
Lubbock	7,365	10,306	39.93
San Angelo	13,097	16,127	23.14
San Antonio	104,440	88,466	-15.29
Tyler	6,301	8,727	38.50
Victoria in Texas	18,034	10,528	-41.62
Totals:	660,198	507,033	-23.20

(Source: *CET*, 1 Dec. 1995, 3)

K. Roman Catholic Bishops in Texas: A Processional

Between 1842, when the Vicariate Apostolic of Texas came into being as a mission territory separate from Mexico, and the end of 1995, sixty-three Roman Catholic bishops administered the geographical entity known as Texas. As we have seen, this territory is, ecclesiastically, the Province of San Antonio. Taken as a group, this body of men is remarkable for its singular devotion to the Roman Catholic faith and to the mission of building up the spiritual and temporal resources of the faithful and others by establishing and maintaining the institutions and ministries necessary to the governance of the Church in Texas.

The shepherds entrusted to the Province of San Antonio have distinguished themselves in many ways. Outstanding as administrators, their ranks have included an Eagle Scout, a high school football and baseball team captain, a student of Lyndon Baines Johnson and a Son of the Republic of Texas, a member of the Texas A&M University Corps of Cadets, military chaplains including a Confederate post chaplain, a decorated war veteran, a Navy war veteran, and a lifesaver, an honorary member of the Marine Corps, and a Lieutenant General in the Texas State Guard. One bishop of Texas never forgot that he was born on the anniversary of San Jacinto Day, while another was born on the same day Texas officially entered the Union. And another bishop was given a medal especially made in his honor.

Two bishops were known as distinguished citizens of El Paso and San Antonio, while another was called "Mr. South Texas". One played the harmonica, while another sang in cabarets. There have been outstanding scholars and linguists, a public school teacher, an architect, a practicing attorney, and college presidents. And in the field of religion there have been a street preacher, Vatican officials and papal nobility, the youngest archbishop in the United States, a cardinal and papal elector, the vice-president of the national episcopal conference, and the head of a worldwide religious order within the Catholic church. And this list is but a faint reflection of the talents and abilities of these men.

At the end of 1995 seventeen bishops were serving actively in Texas, two were heads of jurisdictions out of state, five had retired, and thirty-nine were deceased. Of the seventeen Coadjutor Bishop Roberto Gonzales, OFM of Corpus Christi was the youngest at forty-five, while the oldest was Bishop Leroy Matthiesen of Amarillo at seventy-four. Auxiliary Bishop Hugo Gerbermann, MM of San Antonio was the eldest of the five retirees at the age of eighty-two. Of the two active former bishops in Texas, Ricardo Ramirez, CSB of Las Cruces was the elder at fifty-nine. In Texas, between the establishment of the Diocese of Galveston (now Galveston-Houston) in 1847 through 1995, when there were fourteen dioceses within the State, the average of the average length of service of a Texas bishop for all jurisdictions was eleven years. And during this time forty-three of the sixty-three bishops performed their episcopal service entirely in Texas.

As auxiliaries, coadjutors and administrators, vicars apostolic or retirees, thirty-nine of the bishops in Texas received titular titles of bishop or archbishop. After service in Dallas, Labrador, and Newfoundland, Thomas F. Brennan was known as Titular Bishop of Caesarea in Mauretania from 1905 until his death in 1916. From his resignation of the title of Bishop of Galveston in 1892 until his death in 1895 Claude Dubuis was known as Titular Archbishop of Arca. In retirement from 1969 until 1975 Bishop Thomas Gorman of Dallas-Fort Worth was known as Titular Bishop of Pinhel. But in 1975 that title was awarded to Auxiliary Bishop Hugo Gerbermann, MM of San Antonio, who had been a bishop in Guatemala and who continues to bear it. And from his retirement in 1949 until his death in 1952 Bishop Emmanuel Ledvina of Corpus Christi was known as Titular Bishop of Pitanae.

As the word "catholic" means "universal," one could expect a diversity of the sixty-three bishops in Texas. Forty-seven bishops through 1995 have been natural-born American citizens, while the remaining sixteen were born foreigners in nine foreign countries. Of the Americans thirty were from the South or Southwest (including twenty-three native Texans), with seven from the Northeast, eight from the Midwest, and two from the West. Of those from foreign countries five came from France, four from Ireland, and one each from the Azores (Portuguese), Canada, Cuba, Germany, Mexico, The Netherlands, and Spain.

In paternal ethnic heritage the bishops in Texas have been primarily Irish and German, as well as African-American, Czech, Dutch, English, French, Hispanic, Italian, and Polish. A number of the bishops' fathers were sharecroppers, small farmers, or businessmen. Bishop Schuler's father was a miner in Colorado, while Bishop Tamayo's father was in civil service. Among the skilled occupations Bishop Herzig's father was a printer, Bishop Rodriguez's father a craftsman in woodwork, specializing in furniture and cabinetry, and Bishop Fellhauer's father was a radio engineer. Representing the professions was Bishop Morkovsky's father, a school teacher, Bishop Harris's father, a pharmacist, and Bishop Fitzsimon's father, a physician.

In thirty-six of the sixty-three families, where the size of the individual family is known, twenty-one sets of parents had more than five children. Although birth order within these families does not seem to have made a particular difference as an advantage or hinderance in pursuing a religious vocation, six children were the oldest in their families.

In a general sense the family unit was the earliest influence upon the choice of a religious vocation. In most cases the prayer life and image of the father as provider instilled early habits of piety and responsibility. The presence of the mother, her own prayer life and devotion as a parent, helped to keep the focus on the family as an evolving entity. Religious life, with church attendance and stress placed upon the nature of religious holidays, aided the selection of vocations. Brothers and sisters involved in family chores and duties aided positive notions of sharing, self-worth, and a disposition to care for family, relatives, and the entire community. Other important influences were pastors of home parishes and the religious orders who taught schools.

Devout families sometimes had more than one member who pursued a religious calling. Bishop Byrne's nephew, Leo Christopher Byrne (1908-1974) concluded his career as coadjutor archbishop of St. Paul and Minneapolis. Bishops Gerbermann and Morkovsky both had brothers who were monsignors, while Bishop Metzger's nephew also holds this title. Bishop Pfeifer's brother became a priest, while a maternal uncle of Bishop Dubuis also served in that capacity. Bishop Grahmann's older brother became a religious brother and his two older sisters became religious sisters. One of Bishop Guillory's brothers is a Franciscan brother, Bishop Carmody has a sister who belongs to a religious order, as does Bishop Rodriguez, who also has a brother in orders as a permanent deacon.

Of popular names the first name of choice for most Texas bishops is John, appearing eight times. Other popular first names are Anthony, Bernard, Edward, Joseph, Laurence, Peter, Robert, and Thomas. Joseph is the most popular middle name, also appearing eight times. Aloysius, Anthony, Edward, Louis, Michael, and Patrick are also favored. The only Texas bishops with both most popular first and middle names in correct order are Bishops Cassata and Fitzpatrick.

Of the forty nonnative bishops in Texas, the youngest to arrive was Michael J. Sheehan, born in Wichita, Kansas, who grew up in Texarkana. Adolph Marx came from Germany to Texas to study for the priesthood at La Porte at age nineteen. Of the remaining bishops, eleven came to Texas between the ages of twenty-one and thirty, four between thirty-one and forty, ten between forty-one and fifty, eleven between fifty-one and sixty, and two past the age of sixty. The oldest was Archbishop Francis Furey, who came to San Antonio at the age of sixty-four.

A number of the sixty-three bishops in Texas attended public schools at some point during their careers. Among them Mariano Garriga attended schools in Port Isabel and Brownsville, Bernard Popp attended high school in Nada and Draughon's Business College in San Antonio, Ricardo Ramirez, CSB attended the public schools of Bay City, and John Yanta went to school in Runge. Rene Gracida attended the public schools of New Orleans, Houston, and was valedictorian of Central High School in Texas City. He later received a degree in architecture from the University of Houston. Vincent Harris was a pupil of Lyndon Baines Johnson and a graduate of Sam Houston High School in Houston. James Tamayo attended Del Mar Junior College in Corpus Christi, while Bernard Ganter spent a year at Texas A&M University, where he was a member of its Corps of Cadets.

In other states Cardinal Humberto Medeiros attended schools in Fall River, Massachusetts. Joseph Lynch went to public schools in St. Joseph, Michigan. In Pennsylvania Francis Furey attended public schools in Coaldale, while Lawrence De Falco was a graduate of McKeesport High School. Joseph Delaney received the degree of Master of Education from Rhode Island College, a state-controlled institution. Edmond Carmody attended a national school in Ireland.

Twenty-five of the bishops in Texas received all or part of their educations in Texas, while the entire group of sixty-three also attended schools in twenty-one other states and the District of Columbia, as well as sixteen foreign countries. In Texas John C. Neraz attended a seminary then located at Galveston. St. Mary's Seminary in La Porte, known after its relocation in Houston as St. Mary's Graduate School of Theology of the University of St. Thomas, educated twelve future Texas bishops. Nine future Texas bishops attended those institutions known as St. John's Seminary, later as Assumption Seminary, and now as Assumption-St. John's Seminary.

Rene Gracida also attended Rice University (1942-1943). John McCarthy, Ricardo Ramirez, CSB and James Tamayo are graduates of the University of St. Thomas in Houston, while Charles Herzig attended St. Mary's University of San Antonio for two years. Bernard Popp also received a graduate degree from this San Antonio institution. Edmond Carmody, Charles Grahmann, and Charles Herzig received the degrees of Master of Education from Our Lady of the Lake University in San Antonio, while Carmody received the additional degree of Master of Social Work from that institution. Michael Pfeifer, OMI of San Angelo has received the degree of Master of Divinity from the Oblate College of the Southwest in San Antonio.

Among other institutions attended by bishops in Texas is the Pontifical College Josephinum at Columbus, Ohio, a national pontifical seminary dating from 1888, whose students include David Fellhauer, Leroy Matthiesen, and Thomas Tschoepe.

Of the sixty-three bishops in Texas sixteen have studied in Rome, nine of them resided at the North American College founded in 1859. Between them they have earned twenty-one degrees in that city, including nine doctorates. Twenty of the sixty-three bishops have earned twenty-five doctorates in the United States of America, Austria, Belgium, Canada, The Netherlands, and Italy. While the majority of degrees earned have been in theology, canon law, and philosophy, bishops in Texas have received degrees and certification in such fields as education, social work, history, and sociology. And these achievements, while impressive in themselves, do not indicate expertise in planning, organization, business, and finance learned as matters of practical application in administrative situations.

Because verbal skills are important in preaching, celebrating the sacraments, and diocesan administration, a knowledge of languages besides English becomes necessary to reach the comprehensions of ever-changing flocks. In Texas Spanish is becoming indispensable. A knowledge of the classical tongues (especially Latin and Greek) has also been important traditionally. Among Texas episcopal linguists of the past, Thomas Brennan, Arthur Drossaerts, Claude Dubuis, and John L. Morkovsky have been excellent. The most capable of them was Enrique San Pedro, who could speak English, French, German, Italian, Latin, Spanish, and Vietnamese, read biblical Hebrew and Greek, and made himself understood in some ten additional languages. Among bishops living in 1995, who speak English and Spanish, John J. Fitzpatrick adds French and Italian, while John W. Yanta also speaks German and Polish.

Thirty-five bishops in Texas have been ordained to the priesthood between the ages of twenty-three and twenty-five. The youngest was Nicholas Gallagher at twenty-two years and eleven months, while the oldest was Rene Gracida at thirty-five years and eleven months. Of fifty-two ordained diocesan priests, thirty-one were originally for Texas dioceses. Of eleven religious order priests, two have been Jesuits, with the others being Basilian, Claretian, Divine Word, Franciscan, Holy Cross, Maryknoll, Oblate of Mary Immaculate, Passionist, and Vincentian. Of these eleven the youngest ordained was Jean-Marie Odin (the first bishop of Texas and a Vincentian) and the oldest was Enrique San Pedro (bishop of Brownsville and a Jesuit). Odin was twenty-three years and two months old at ordination, while San Pedro was thirty-one.

The time spent by future bishops as priests may be considered under five headings: pastoral, chaplaincies, sponsor or directorship of ministries, administrative, and educational. Most bishops in Texas have had pastoral experience of some kind (usually as associate pastor, administrator, or pastor of a parish), with the exceptions of Peter Dufal and Sidney Metzger, who were primarily educators and had no parish experience before attaining episcopal rank. On the other extreme John Cassata had thirty-four years as an assistant pastor and pastor of Holy Name Church in Houston, while Bernard Popp had forty years of pastoral experience before becoming bishop, including five years as rector of San Fernando Cathedral in San Antonio.

Eighteen future bishops in Texas have had experience as chaplains, including five who served as military chaplains. A number of these future bishops have held directorships of ministries and of organizations, some on the national level. Emmanuel Ledvina spent fourteen years as secretary of the Catholic Church Extension Society, which collects and dispenses funds for home mission work. As priests, John McCarthy was executive director of the conference for the Spanish-Speaking and as director of the Texas Catholic Conference, while Michael Sheehan was assistant general secretary of the National Conference of Catholic Bishops/United States Catholic Conference (NCCB/USCC).

Within the central administrations of various dioceses eight future bishops in Texas have served as vicar general or administrative deputy to the bishop, six as vice-chancellor and eleven as chancellor, nine as the bishop's secretary, five as deans of deaneries with a number of churches under them, nine as judicial vicars or heads of diocesan tribunals, and eleven as diocesan consultors. A number of bishops have also held executive appointments as administrators of educational institutions.

Peter Dufal was prefect of two collegiate seminaries in France for five years, while Paul Nussbaum was vice-rector of St. Mary's Passionist Seminary in New York for three years. Francis Furey was both president of Immaculata College in Pennsylvania (1936-1946) and afterwards rector of St. Charles Borromeo Seminary (1946-1958) in that state. Stephen Leven was vice-rector of the American College in Louvain, Belgium (1935-1938). Mariano Garriga was cofounder and vice-rector of St. John's Seminary in San Antonio (1915-1916; 1919-1936) and temporary president of Incarnate Word College (1919), also in San Antonio. Sidney Metzger was a student at St. John's (1915-1922), professor of canon law and philosophy (1928-1933), and pro-rector (1933-1940). Later Charles Herzig was vice-rector of St. John's (1968-1970) and vice president of its successor, Assumption Seminary (1970-1973).

Of the sixty-three Roman Catholic bishops in Texas twenty-four received the dignity of Monsignor before the episcopal appointments. The youngest to receive this award were Adolph Marx and Leroy Mattheisen, both at age thirty-three. John Yanta was the oldest to attain this dignity at the age of fifty-eight.

Fourteen bishops founded the present jurisdictions in Texas, plus Dominic Manucy, the founding bishop of the now defunct vicariate apostolic (*not* the diocese) of Brownsville. Six other bishops, who also served in Texas, founded dioceses in Florida, Louisiana, Nevada, New Mexico, Oklahoma, and in Guatemala. Sixteen of the sixty-three bishops in Texas served in more than one Texas diocese. The youngest to be appointed was Nicholas Gallagher as coadjutor of Galveston at the age of thirty-five, while the youngest to be ordinary (or head) of his own Texas diocese was Thomas Brennan of Dallas at age thirty-seven. The oldest ordinary appointed for Texas was Thomas Drury of San Angelo at fifty-nine, while the oldest bishop (not an ordinary) appointed for Texas was

Bernard Popp of San Antonio at age sixty-five.

Peter Dufal took off two years from his duties as vicar apostolic of Eastern Bengal to serve as Superior General of the Congregation of the Holy Cross (1866-1868). Bishops are often called upon to serve on boards within and outside of their dioceses. Bishops in Texas have served on the boards of Catholic Relief Services, the National Shrine of the Immaculate Conception, and of the Catholic University of America. A bishop has also served as the president of the Texas Conference of Churches.

Seven bishops in Texas have served as spiritual director or national chaplain of Catholic organizations in the United States. And while many bishops are called upon frequently to write columns or to make other written statements, five of them have completed book-length works. The contribution of the bishops in Texas to the NCCB-USCC is especially commendable.

In addition to the work Bishop McCarthy and Archbishop Sheehan have accomplished as priests for this organization, Texas bishops have served in over forty standing and ad hoc committees, and twelve of their number have chaired one or more committees. Bishop Joseph Fiorenza has chaired more committees than any other Texas bishop and has served both as secretary and as vice president of the entire organization. The contribution of Archbishop Patrick Flores to the work of the Conference has been so profound and meaningful over the years that recently it struck a special medal, known as the "Archbishop Flores Medal," in his honor.

Ten bishops in Texas have received the title of "Assistant to the Pontifical Throne," while two have been appointed papal counts. Twenty bishops have been knights of the Equestrian Order of the Holy Sepulchre with two bishops recently grand priors of their lieutenancies. There have been three knights commanders and three knights grand cross, while Bishop Cassata received the Holy Sepulchre's Order of Palm. Two bishops have been accredited canons of cathedral chapters in France and in Mexico.

Twenty-two honorary degrees have been bestowed upon sixteen bishops in Texas by colleges and universities in Texas, Colorado, Illinois, Maryland, Massachusetts, Pennsylvania, and New York. Bishop Gracida is a member of Phi Kappa Phi, a national collegiate honor society, while Bishops McCarthy and Ramirez have been honored as distinguished alumni of the University of St. Thomas in Houston. Bishop Fiorenza was named Distinguished Alumnus of St. Anthony High School in Beaumont, while Bishop Ganter was named Outstanding Alumnus of Texas A&M University by the Catholic Student Center.

Spain honored Bishop Metzger with the Order of King Alfonso, the Wise (Grand Cross) and the Medal of Madrid in 1957. Bishop Schuler was named an outstanding citizen of El Paso in 1936, while Archbishop Flores received a similar distinction in San Antonio in 1995. Bishop Garriga was voted "Mr. South Texas" in 1959. Archbishop Furey was named an honorary member of the United States Marine Corps, while Bishop Cassata was an honorary lieutenant general in the Texas State Guard.

By the end of 1995 death came for thirty-nine of the bishops and archbishops in Texas. Of these twenty-two died in the positions to which they had been appointed. The youngest of these was Adolf Marx of Brownsville, who died at the age of fifty years and eight months, while the oldest was Christopher Byrne of Galveston, who died of a heart attack at the age of eighty-two years and eleven months in 1950.

The shortest period between retirement and death was one-and-a-half years for Anthony Schuler of El Paso, who died at the age of seventy-four years and eight months. The oldest bishop to die was Augustine Danglmayr, twenty-three years after his retirement, at the age of ninety-three years and nine months. Twenty-three of the bishops died in Texas and twenty-nine are buried in the state. Of the remaining ten, three lie buried in France, one in Italy, and one each in Alabama, Florida, Illinois, Louisiana, Massachusetts, and New Mexico.

In sum, the sixty-three bishops who have served in Texas have been remarkably faithful to the positions of trust to which they were appointed. To the end of 1995 no bishop suffered the indignity of being removed from his position in an untimely manner or died of any except natural causes. With different matters placed under their cares in different times in different years, their constant concerns have always been, as Bishop Fiorenza has so well stated them, of "teaching the faith, celebrating the sacraments and administering the diocese." It may be truly said that to be a shepherd of the flock of Christ on Earth is both a blessing and challenge. All of the bishops in Texas have confronted this challenge, and in many cases they have magnificently overcome it.

Part II:
Roman Catholic Bishops in Texas

Most Reverend Warren Louis Boudreaux, DD, JCD, LLD
Titular Bishop of Calynda and Auxiliary Bishop of Lafayette
Second Bishop of Beaumont
First Bishop of Houma-Thibodaux

Born to a Louisiana family of French descent on 25 January 1918, Warren Louis Boudreaux claims Berwick, St. Mary Parish, in that state as his birthplace. The son of Alphonse Louis and Loretta Marie (Senac) Boudreaux, he received the degree of Bachelor of Science at the early age of eighteen from St. Joseph's Seminary, St. Benedict, Louisiana.

In the following year (1937) he began his major studies at Notre Dame Seminary in New Orleans, taking the year of 1938-1939 to attend the Grand Seminary de St. Sulpice in Paris, France. His French name and education, especially in this institution, recalls the tradition of the first Roman Catholic bishops of Texas, who dominated its hierarchy into the first decade of the twentieth century.

Warren Boudreaux concluded his priestly formation at Notre Dame Seminary in 1942 and was awarded its honorary degree of Doctor of Laws in 1963. On 30 May 1942 he was ordained for the Diocese of Lafayette in Louisiana. For a year he was appointed assistant pastor in Crowley, Acadia Parish, by Jules B. Jeanmard, the founding bishop of Lafayette. But clearly marked for advancement he began graduate studies at the Catholic University of America in 1943.

In 1946 Father Boudreaux completed his formal education with the degree of Doctor of Canon Law. He took as his dissertation topic "The 'AB Acatholicis Nati' of Canon 1099." This canon concerning marriage provisions of the Catholic Church refers to that part of the 1917 Code of Canon Law now partially incorporated into Canons 1117 and 1127, §1 of the 1983 Code.

Canon 1117 of the new Code states that canonical form is required for Latin Rite Catholics baptized in the Catholic Church and those having received Christian baptism but later becoming converts to Catholicism. Canonical form, according to the 1983 Canon 1108, involves the requirement that marriages with at least one Catholic take place in the presence of the Church's official witness and two other witnesses. According to Canon 1099 of the 1917 Code those baptized but not reared in the Catholic faith were not bound by canonical form.

On 1 August 1948 Pope Pius XII solved the problem two years after Father Boudreaux completed his dissertation by abrogating the last portion of the canon ("*item. . .contraxerint*"), restoring Catholic baptism as the sole basis for binding by canonical form. Thus canonical form provides proof of consent in marriage and allows the Church to investigate more effectively and to prepare a couple for marriage.

Canon 1127, §1 states:

> The prescriptions of can. 1108 are to be observed concerning the form to be employed in a mixed marriage; if a Catholic party contracts marriage with a non-Catholic of an oriental rite, the canoni-

> cal form of celebration is to be observed only for liceity [permission]; for validity, however, the presence of a sacred minister is required along with the observance of the other requirements by law.

With his expert knowledge of canon law Father Boudreaux was immediately advanced upon return from the Catholic University to the position of Vice-Chancellor of the Diocese of Lafayette. In 1950 he came to the attention of Archbishop Joseph F. Rummel of New Orleans as President of the Archdiocesan Conference of Chancery Officials, a position he held until 1951. He later served as a member of its board of directors (1952-1955).

The position of Vice-Chancellor is a weighty one for a young man of twenty-eight. A vice-chancellor assists the chancellor in a variety of ways. He coordinates functions of the chancery, interprets diocesan and general Church law and policy as it affects diocesan operations. He also cares for the records, edits the clergy newsletter, negotiates diocesan insurance, consults and coordinates priestly matters and assignments, provides for general communication services, processes special permissions and dispensations of the bishop prior to marriage, supervises the archives, and purchases future parish sites.

In addition, as Officialis of the diocese, Father Boudreaux was called upon to examine the validity of marriages, act as canonical adviser to the bishop, consult priests, religious, and laity in programs and policies relating to marriage, assist diocesan agencies and institutions with the same information, and to provide general information upon request on all canonical matters.

From 1954 until 1971 Reverend Boudreaux continued his parish work as Pastor of St. Peter's Parish in New Iberia, Iberia Parish, and as Dean of the New Iberia Deanery. In 1957 he was appointed vicar general of the Lafayette diocese and held the position until 1961. As dean he oversaw his own and the other churches in his diocesan district. As vicar general he was administrative deputy to Bishop Maurice Schexnayder. He also served as vice-president of the diocesan newspaper *Southwest Louisiana Registry* (presently known as the *Acadiana Catholic*) from 1957 to 1975.

On 19 May 1962 Pope John XXIII recognized the efforts of the forty-four-year-old priest by raising him to episcopal rank as Titular Bishop of Calynda and Auxiliary Bishop of Lafayette. He was consecrated bishop on 25 July 1962 and awarded the Vatican degree of Doctor of Divinity that same year. As auxiliary bishop Boudreaux continued his parish and journalistic duties and expanded his obligations. He held membership on the New Iberia Community Council for eight years from 1963. He served on the United States Bishops' Liturgical Commission (1966-1970) and on the Bishops' Louvain College Commission (1970-1976). During this time he was a member of the advisory council of the United States Catholic Conference (USCC) between 1969 and 1973.

Pope Paul VI appointed the fifty-three-year-old Boudreaux bishop of Beaumont on 5 June 1971, in succession to Bishop Vincent M. Harris, who had been sent to Austin to assist Bishop Reicher. As the second bishop of Beaumont, created only five years before, Boudreaux was now in charge of an area of 11,790 square miles in fifteen southeast Texas counties. He was installed at the Cathedral of St. Anthony in Beaumont on 25 August 1971.

In the following year the new bishop began a three-year term as chairman of the liaison committee of the National Conference of Catholic Bishops (NCCB) followed by three years as a member of its canon law committee. Since 1975 he has also served as a member of its liturgy commission as well. Between 1975 and 1977 Bishop Boudreaux was State Chaplain for the Knights of Columbus of Texas and National Moderator for the Marriage Encounter in the United States of America. This program brings couples together for a weekend of programs directed by several couples and a priest to develop their communication skills as husbands and wives.

On 2 March 1977 Pope Paul VI appointed Bishop Boudreaux to the newly created Diocese of Houma-Thibodaux in Louisiana. He was installed bishop on 5 June 1977, six years to the day of his appointment in Beaumont. He has served as president of the Louisiana Catholic Conference in 1984 and he is a member or the Louisiana Interchurch Conference. He is a director of the Southwest Educational Development Laboratory, the Iberia Paris Youth Home, and the Consolata Home for Aged in New Iberia. He has served as chairman of the ad hoc committee for the Nomination of Conference Officers of the NCCB.

Retired since 29 December 1992, Bishop Boudreaux published his autobiography, *Memoirs of a Cajun Bishop*, in 1995. Attending the annual bishops' conference in Washington, DC, in 1990, it was brought to his attention that he was one of the few living bishops who attended all sessions of Vatican Council II. Louis Aguirre, editor of *The Bayou Catholic*, and Irene Michel, a retired staff writer of that publication, assisted the Bishop as editors. Bishop Boudreaux says of it, "It's the true story of a Cajun as a Cajun would tell it" (*CET*, 15 December 1995, 12).

Bishop Boudreaux lives in Schriever, Terrebone Parish, Louisiana, close to Thibodaux. An able administrator and scholar, he has lived the meaning of his family name, which in English is "messenger." He has proclaimed the message of the Gospel throughout Louisiana, Texas, and the United States. His motto is "Servare unitatem" ("To preserve in unity").

Right Reverend Thomas Francis Brennan, DD
First Bishop of Dallas
Titular Bishop of Usula and Auxiliary Bishop of St. John's, Newfoundland
Titular Bishop of Caesarea in Mauretania

Of the Roman Catholic bishops of Texas, perhaps no one ever entered their ranks with the initial abilities and enthusiasm one needs to take over a newly-created diocese as did Thomas Francis Brennan of Dallas. He seemed the right man at the right place at the right time. Yet his tenure was so brief and his later career so irregular that one wonders how a man with so many gifts could become so frustrated in his life and career.

Thomas Brennan began life on 10 October 1853 in Bally Cullen, between Cloneen and Mullinahone, County Tipperary, Ireland. The oldest of five sons born to James and Margaret (Dunne) Brennan, he settled in Pennsylvania as a child. His early education took place at St. Bonaventure's School in Allegheny, New York. He completed his education in classics at Rouen University in France in 1873. After three years he obtained the degree of Doctor of Divinity from the University of Innsbruck in Austria.

The twenty-six-year-old Doctor Brennan was ordained on 14 July 1880 in Brixen, Austria, by its Prince Bishop John de Leiss, for the Diocese of Erie, Pennsylvania. He spent the following year in Rome studying canon law before returning home. Father Brennan's remaining ten years as a priest were filled with useful endeavors. As Pastor of St. James's Parish in Driftwood, Pennsylvania, from 1881 until 1891 he built three churches. He served as Diocesan Examiner (1887 to 1891) and was appointed Papal Chamberlain with the title of Very Reverend Monsignor by Pope Leo XIII on 11 January 1888.

It was the golden jubilee of Leo XIII's priesthood, and the year of 1888 would mark that pontiff's silver jubilee as cardinal and his tenth year as pope. Bishop Tobias Mullen of Erie had sent the new monsignor to Rome as a delegate, and it was here he gained his promotion. On this trip young Monsignor Brennan met his fellow Irishman Bishop Thomas Heslin of Natchez [now Jackson], Mississippi. Bishop Heslin would remember the priest who, according to *The Catholic Herald* of Memphis, Tennessee, "speaks German as fluently as English, French like an educated Parisian, and Italian as correctly as English; as a linguist he has few superiors" (23 August 1891). His recommendation would ensure Brennan's appointment as Bishop of the soon-to-be Diocese of Dallas.

When Bishop Brennan knew Dallas, it was not the metropolis or "metroplex" it would become. Texas itself was predominantly a rural state with about fifteen percent of its people living in cities. The State had a population density of about nine people per square mile, about six times less than it is today. In its first fifty years of development Dallas was far from being the seventh largest city in the United States.

The Arkansas pioneer John Neely Bryan placed his cabin near the confluence of three forks of the Trinity River in 1841. By 1846 he had become postmaster of the bustling small city of Dallas. In 1853 French settlers, followed by those of Belgium and Switzerland, and recruited by Victor Considerant, arrived to start a new colony. As the population grew, Father Claude Neraz (later the second Bishop of San Antonio) and his assistant, Father Sebastian Augagneur of Nacogdoches, became the first priests to minister to the area.

By 1872 a parish to be named Sacred Heart was established under the initial care of a Father Perrier. He said Mass in the Odd Fellows' Hall until his new church was constructed at the corner of Bryan and Ervay Streets. It was dedicated on the first Sunday of August, 1873, and was the first of about thirty such churches in the present city. In this same year the Houston and Texas Central Railway came to Dallas, Father Joseph Martiniére was put in charge of the new church, and the Ursuline Sisters of Dallas decided to open a school. This they did near the church on 18 January 1874.

The development of the entire North and West Texas area led Bishop Nicholas A. Gallagher of Galveston to consider substantial changes in his administration. South Texas was in the care of the Diocese of San Antonio and the Vicariate Apostolic (not yet a diocese) of Brownsville, both of which had been established in 1874. This situation left Bishop Gallagher in charge of the greater part of the State. He had been in active control of the Galveston Diocese as its administrator since 1882. But he could not succeed as Bishop until Bishop Claude Dubuis, who had resigned in 1881, relinquished the title. This circumstance occurred in 1892 when Bishop Dubuis became Titular Archbishop of Arca.

The scope of the problem becomes clear when we examine a standard Milwaukee-published handbook of the period, *Hoffmann's Official Catholic Directory* for 1888 (233, 235). It describes the Diocese of Galveston in 1887 as East of the Colorado River. At this time the Diocese had a population of 39,000 Catholics, served by forty-four priests, five sisters, fifty-five churches and chapels, nine "ecclesiastical students" or seminarians, twelve academies for young ladies, one "college," actually a seminary, and three charitable institutions.

Cities developing North and West of Galveston and Houston accounted for a general population of about 210,000, with Dallas and Fort Worth making up about 94,000. Other such cities numbering from five to fifteen thousand were Denison, Sherman, Marshall, Jefferson, Texarkana, Paris, Corsicana, Weatherford, Gainesville, Clarksville (then called Saint Paul), Tyler, Ennis, and Abilene.

So Bishop Gallagher drew up a prospectus entitled "Notes on the proposed new Diocese of Dallas" and presented it to the Provincial Council of New Orleans. At this time the United States was divided into thirteen ecclesiastical provinces. The Province of New Orleans included the States of Louisiana, Alabama, Mississippi, Texas, and Arkansas. It also administered the Indian Territory, which is now the State of Oklahoma. Its headquarters was New Orleans, Louisiana, and it was presided over by the Dutch-born Archbishop Francis A. Janssens.

Resident as he was in Galveston at the southern end of his diocese, Bishop Gallagher did not see how he could effectively govern territory 800 miles distant from his See city. While admitting that the northern part of the State had few Catholics, he felt that the rapid settlement of the area necessitated the erection of a new diocese with a new bishop. He believed that such a bishop could "render much aid by personal work in preaching and visiting various parts of the diocese."

Bishop Gallagher noted that North Texas had a Catholic population of about 15,000 with twenty-five churches, seventeen priests, three hospitals, five academies for girls, three boarding schools for boys, an orphanage, and eight convents, with a total general population of over a million. He did not believe that the Baptists, Methodists, Presbyterians, Episcopalians, and Christians in that region were malicious toward Catholics. He attributed their prejudices as originating chiefly from ignorance of the Catholic faith. He also felt that a diocese would help return fallen-away Catholics to the Church and wished to reach them more effectively.

In Bishop Gallagher's opinion Dallas offered the greatest possibility as the seat of a new diocese. It had two frame churches and a third of brick was being constructed and could be occupied in six months. Of two pastoral residences he considered that the two-story, ten-room frame rectory of Sacred Heart "though not grand, would be sufficient for the present residence of a bishop."

The matter of the Diocese of Dallas was submitted to all bishops of the Province of New Orleans in 1889. These were the Archbishop of New Orleans and the Bishops of Little Rock, Mobile, Natchez [now Jackson], Natchitoches [now Alexandria], San Antonio, and Brownsville [now Corpus Christi, as the former Vicariate has no connection with the present Diocese of Brownsville]. Due to their unanimous agreement Pope Leo XIII declared in his brief *Romani Pontificis* of 15 July 1890:

> We most willingly accede, and, paying heed to what the Prelates of the Province of New Orleans have urged for the greater spiritual welfare of the faithful . . . We hereby divide or dismember the Diocese of Galveston to form a new Diocese which shall bear the name of Dallas, its See and most populous city, wherein are found two churches with adjoining dwellings.

The new diocese consisted of that part of Texas north of the Counties of Lampasas, Coryell, McLennan, Freestone, Anderson, Cherokee, Nacogdoches, and Shelby. In other words the Diocese of Dallas was an entity of 108 counties of about 108,000 square miles. In addition its erection was also meant to include in the "North Texas" portion the Counties of El Paso and Culberson, in themselves an addition of 4,199 square miles. In the Diocese itself the population was a million-and-a-half, of which 15,000 people were Catholics.

Such was the situation when the Diocese of Dallas came into existence. On 22 December 1890 its bishop was appointed by Pope Leo XIII. The episcopal consecration of Monsignor Brennan was performed by Bishop Tobias Mullen of Erie in St. Peter's Cathedral in Erie, Pennsylvania, on 5 April 1891. The consecration was assisted by the Pennsylvania bishops Thomas McGovern of Harrisburg and Richard Phelan of Pittsburgh. All four bishops were Irish-born. Bishop Brennan came to Dallas at the end of April and was installed in St. Patrick's Church on 8 May 1891.

The new bishop came to his new diocese with much to offer. His accomplishments preceded him, and he had the gifts of a forceful personality, eloquence, and zeal for his faith. A formidable linguist with a repertoire of more than seven languages he spoke English, French, Spanish, German, Italian, Polish, and undoubtedly Gaelic. But even with good will on all sides the time and place of his appointment were against him.

The local economy of Dallas, which had been expanding, chose this time to contract. Father Blum as pastor of Sacred Heart Church had bought property at the corner of Ross and Pearl Streets for $30,000. He had intended to finance the transaction by selling the old church property at Bryan and Ervay. As a result Bishop Brennan found his to-be-erected cathedral saddled with a crushing debt. Added to this sad state of affairs was the mortgage of $2,500 on the new and unfurnished orphanage which had not opened. Creditors in fear of possible default pressed for a resolution and threatened foreclosure. With an explanation to his people and a prayer to God Bishop Brennan set his shoulders to his tasks.

In the following year he tried to visit every village and every audience in his reach. He established *The Texas Catholic*, the first Catholic diocesan newspaper in Texas. He made friends of all faiths and enlisted the daily presses in his cause. As he went about to build his new cathedral the active support he received whetted his appetite to succeed and made him love his newly-adopted people of Texas.

Bishop Brennan believed with all his heart in encouraging vocations and in education for the priesthood and religious. Learning led to virtue and a strong ministry was to be the foundation and future of the Church in Texas. He very much wanted to build a seminary as he implored young people by exalting the nature of the priest: "His true office is the redeeming of souls from this wicked world to give them to God. The work of saving souls is the highest, most noble, the most praiseworthy that can to man be entrusted." And his efforts in this area bore fruit. On 5 July 1891 he ordained J. A. Hartnett in St. Patrick's Church as the first priest in the new diocese. On 14 April 1892 he ordained Thomas Blakeney there, followed two weeks later by P. M. Reagan.

Bishop Brennan was also attracted by the faith of the Mexican people. Before the end of 1891 he was in Tascosa in Potter County near Amarillo to tell the people in Spanish that he was sending Father Francisco Grau y Cruz to preach a mission or revival to them in Spanish. It would begin on the twelfth of December, the anniversary of the apparition of Our Lady of Guadalupe. He visited their parish and pleased them by preaching in their own language.

Work was carried on at fever pitch. In December of 1891 the clergy learned their bishop's intention to hold periodic conferences and to introduce the Forty Hour Adoration. This idea was a great innovation in the area and showed a great love for the Blessed Sacrament. Although instituted in Milan, Italy, in 1534, it was not practiced in the United States until Bishop (later Saint) John Neumann of Philadelphia observed it during his tenure from 1852 to 1860. The devotion consists of the solemn exposition of the Host with Masses and prayer. Its purpose is reparation for sin and prayer for God's blessings of grace and peace. It was so important to Bishop Brennan that he began its observance at St. Patrick's Church in Dallas on 9 January 1892 and concluded it in company with Bishop John J. Hennessy of Wichita, Kansas.

With this appropriate beginning to the year 1892 the bishop issued a pastoral letter to his clergy on 22 February, directing them to celebrate Columbus Day on the twelfth of October with High Mass wherever possible and with appropriate sermons in all churches. He told them, "America is the world's greatest blessing" and "God's greatest blessing to mankind since the coming of Christ was the discovery of America." It is no wonder that this Irish-born bishop was considered such a great orator. In the present day of episcopal conferences and their numerous and critical recommendations on American policies, it is refreshing to read this simple and heartfelt tribute.

It was now clear that Bishop Brennan had found a new home in Texas. On 7 March 1892 he was in Pilot Point in Denton County, the birthplace of the former bishop of Dallas. Here he dedicated the new church of St. Thomas, now a part of the Diocese of Fort Worth. On 19 March he ordained Hugo Baedenheuer. He was at Waxahachie in Ellis County on the second of April. Here he sold the old brick church and four-and-a-half acres of land to the Methodists for $1,500 in cash. On the following day he was in the now almost nonexistent town of Thurber in northwest Erath County to choose the site for a new church and cemetery. Nor did his gift of languages fail him as he preached in English, Polish, and Italian.

He early felt the call of his western territory and set out on the ninth of April for El Paso. But ten days later he was in Austin, exhorting his audience in St. Mary's Church (now Cathedral) on the history and glories of his adopted state. An editorial writer for the Austin *Statesman* gave the speaker a favorable review on the following day and observed the good bishop had reached "the highest pitch of eloquence."

Perhaps encouraged by the high enthusiasm of this trip, Bishop Brennan returned to Dallas and turned over the administration of the Oak Cliff Orphanage to the Sisters of Mercy, whose services he had secured while in El Paso. He also gave this community charge of St. Mary's Academy for young ladies, which opened on the following thirtieth of April.

Meanwhile church building continued. On 4 May the bishop laid the cornerstone of St. Mary's Church in Windthorst, Archer County. This was followed by the dedication of the Church of St. Patrick in downtown Fort Worth on 10 July. This imposing church, now painted solid white, was designed by Nicholas J. Clayton, the first professional architect in Texas. It now serves the city as its Roman Catholic cathedral.

On this last occasion excellent support was provided in the person of the metropolitan of the province, Archbishop Francis A. Janssens of New Orleans. Father J. M. Guyot celebrated Solemn High Mass. Among other clergy attending were Timothy K. Crowley of Denison, Joseph Blum of Muenster, and Henry Brinkley of Abilene. On 7 August Bishop Brennan was in Ellis County celebrating the dedication of St. Joseph's Church in Waxahachie.

Years later Monsignor Joseph G. O'Donohoe, Pastor of St. Patrick's in Fort Worth and Secretary of the Texas Knights of Columbus Historical Commission, would chronicle the activities of the first year of the first bishop of Dallas. There was much to celebrate. The number of priests in the new diocese was increased by eleven. Four new religious communities had been introduced into its institutions. Texarkana, Forney, Pilot Point, Muenster, Windthorst, Lindsay, Wichita Falls, Clarendon, Fort Worth, Waxahachie, and Denton had new churches. And of these churches five were new parishes. A Catholic newspaper was founded for the diocese, a new and important introduction in Texas.

Yet with all these accomplishments Bishop Brennan did not remain long to head the See of Dallas. On 17 November 1892 he was in Rome for his *ad limina* visit to Pope Leo XIII. Ordinarily the purpose of such a visit made by diocesan bishops and apostolic vicars "to the threshold" of the Apostles is to visit the tombs of Sts. Peter and Paul, have an audience with the pope, consult with Vatican officials, and present a report on their particular jurisdictions. Such a visit is generally scheduled for each Catholic bishop on a five year basis. In this way the Holy Father and his curial court learn in a personal manner the needs, concerns, and achievements of every Catholic bishop in the world.

There is a strangeness about this particular visit that one cannot grasp from reading the official record. It is unlikely that anything beyond the nature of a courtesy call would be expected of a bishop so recently enthroned in his diocese. It is true that Bishop Brennan would have much to discuss. In his brief administration the first seventeen priests were increased to thirty. There were twenty-five chapels with resident priests, nineteen more without, and seventy-four missions and chapels. The parochial schools in 1893 had an enrollment of 1,500, and this figure did not include the nine academies established for young ladies. Four hospitals and one orphanage operated within the diocese. And the Catholic population rose from fifteen to twenty thousand, which included 9,000 Indians. Further, the North and West of Texas were growing, and the Diocese of Dallas had every indication of success.

It is unlikely that the Pope was displeased by the outstanding work of a young man in whose career he had taken an active interest. In reading between the lines one can only suppose that Bishop Brennan's personal problem was his inability to construct his cathedral and to retire its debt. Castañeda in *Our Catholic Heritage in Texas* states that Bishop Brennan was transferred and gives no reason (7: 144). Given the facts as we have them, it is likely that Bishop Brennan himself requested the change. Pope Leo XIII granted the request and on 1 February 1893 the prelate of Dallas became Titular Bishop of Usula and Vicar Apostolic of Labrador.

Labrador today includes the Diocese of Labrador-Schefferville. This diocese in the eastern and French-speaking part of Canada encompasses a portion of Newfoundland and the northern part of the Province of Quebec. In the following year of 1894 Brennan was made Auxiliary Bishop of the Diocese of St. John's, Newfoundland, under Bishop T. J. Power. It is unlikely as Castañeda suggests that he was Coadjutor having rights of succession.

The final ten years of this outwardly enthusiastic, though perhaps inwardly melancholic, man declined in almost as spectacular a way as his first ten years as a priest gave promise of future success. Recalled to Rome in 1905 by Pope St. Pius X, he was relieved of his administrative authority in Canada and appointed to the purely honorary position of Titular Bishop of Caesarea in Mauretania.

Bishop Brennan first lived at Number 112 Via del Seminario in Rome. He later retired to the Monastery of Grottoferrata, about six miles from the City in the Alban Hills. Here he found a life of meditation in an ancient structure built by St. Nilus in the year 1004 over the remains of a Roman villa. Today it is the property of Greek Orthodox monks, though it was formerly kept by Basilian priests of Greek origin.

In this monastery Thomas Francis Brennan, the first bishop of Dallas, whose Irish name means "young raven," died on 21 March 1916 during the First World War. He lies buried at Frascati, about two-and-a-half miles from Grottoferrata and about fifteen miles from Rome, in an ornate tomb fashioned like an outdoor temple and fallen into ruin. Surely this is a strange and almost anonymous end for an ecclesiastical career which seemed to have so bright a future.

Most Reverend Christopher Edward Byrne, DD, LLD
Fourth Bishop of Galveston

Of those who have been bishops in Texas, one of the proudest to be and an important contributor to the state he served was Christopher Edward Byrne, Bishop of Galveston. An imposing six feet in stature his erect bearing and unceasing activity masked his lifetime heart trouble. Before it caused his death at eighty-two he had completed an excellent record of service. His ability was recognized in his lifetime and afterwards.

Born in Byrnesville, Jefferson County, Missouri, on 21 April 1867, Christopher Byrne as bishop liked to tell his audiences that his birthday was San Jacinto Day. He was the fifth of eight children born to Patrick and Rose (Byrne) Byrne. He received the Bachelor of Arts degree from the no-longer extant Jesuit-operated St. Mary's College in Kansas in 1886. Ten years later St. Mary's followed the ancient academic custom, still observed in England, and awarded him the Master of Arts degree.

Immediately after his graduation nineteen-year-old Christopher returned to the family farm. Here he would rest for a year on doctor's orders due to his heart condition. After recovering he decided to pursue the vocation of priest. From 1887 until 1891 he studied at St. Mary's Seminary in Baltimore, Maryland. This institution is still operated by the Sulpician priests at 5400 Roland Avenue in that city. Bishop Thomas A. Becker of Savannah, Georgia (and formerly of Wilmington, Delaware) conferred the diaconate upon the young seminarian. On 23 September 1891 Archbishop Peter Richard Kenrick ordained the Reverend Mister Byrne in St. John's Church in St. Louis, Missouri.

On the following 19 October Father Byrne became Assistant Pastor of St. Bridget's Parish in St. Louis. His next assignment from 7 June 1897 was the pastorate of Sacred Heart Parish in Columbus, Missouri. In 1898 he spent three months in San Antonio, Texas, attempting to recover from a heart ailment. At the end of this period he petitioned his superior Archbishop John J. Kain of St. Louis for reassignment.

This opportunity did not come until 8 December 1899 when Father Byrne was Pastor of St. Joseph's Parish in Edina, Missouri. At this post he showed his future promise by building a parochial school and a convent. And as Pastor in Edina he made his first visit to Rome in 1909.

By 27 January 1911 he began his last priestly appointment as Pastor of Holy Name Parish in St. Louis. He threw himself into parish work by remodelling its school, buying a convent, building a rectory and finally a new church. His work came to the attention of the Holy Father and, at the age of fifty-one on 18 July 1918, he was appointed Bishop of Galveston, Texas, by Pope Benedict XV.

His episcopal consecration took place on 10 November 1918 in St. Louis Cathedral, St. Louis, Missouri, the day before the Armistice which ended the First World War. His superior Archbishop (later Cardinal) John Joseph Glennon of St. Louis performed the ceremony, assisted by Bishop Thomas F. Lillis of Kansas City, Missouri, and by Bishop John Morris of Little Rock, Arkansas. The newly-created Bishop Byrne set off for Texas and took formal possession of the Diocese of Galveston on Thanksgiving Day, 26 November 1918.

On this day what did Bishop Byrne have to be thankful? He had just inherited a diocese of 43,000 square miles, the oldest in the State. He had the services of 105 priests with fifty-nine churches with residential pastors and sixty-one missions. It was a handsome gift, and the new bishop settled in for a stay of over thirty-one years. He took pride in his position and in his adopted state. And he showed this pride by a solid record of accomplishment, making it a better place for the Catholics of the region.

During his years as bishop Byrne consistently expanded the institutions of the Diocese and brought in workers to staff them. Figures tell the tale. By 1 April 1950 he had 240 priests. Between 1918 and 1950 he had ordained 200 and introduced the priestly orders of Missionaries of LaSalette, Passionists, Redemptorists, Felicians, Franciscans, Augustinians, and the Society of the Divine Word into the Diocese.

Needing women religious for his schools, hospitals, and other institutions, he brought in many orders of sisters. These orders included Sisters of the Blessed Sacrament, Dominicans of the Second Order, Felicians, Sisters of the Atonement, Missionaries of the Immaculate Conception, Sisters of St. Francis of Our Lady of Lourdes, Holy Cross Sisters, Servants of the Holy Ghost, Holy Family Sisters, Sacred Heart Sisters, and Sisters of Divine Providence.

In Byrne's time a bishop did not hold his office until forced retirement at the age of seventy-five. He governed alone if he had no coadjutor or administrator to affect his authority. And in that time his residence if not princely might be at least baronial. The Walter Gresham home, built by Nicholas J. Clayton between 1886 and 1888, suited the Bishop and his sisters Mary and Ellen admirably. It was bought and furnished by the people of the Diocese, and is now operated as a museum by the diocesan Newman Club. Located at 1402 Broadway in Galveston, the Byrnes moved into it in 1923. Thereafter it became known as the "Bishop's Palace." Here the Bishop lived for twenty-seven years and here he died, resisting with all his heart the eventual movement of administration to Houston. Bishop Byrne kept his ties to Galveston even after his death. He was the last Bishop of Galveston, his successors being bishops of Galveston-Houston.

Upon taking office Bishop Byrne revived the position of diocesan chancellor, which had ceased to exist under his predecessor for the past thirty-five years. He raised it to such eminence that, in the seventy years since, his chancellor and those succeeding have become bishops. Perhaps the present incumbent will continue in that tradition. The first chancellor of the new creation was Louis Joseph Reicher, who served almost thirty years until he became Bishop of Austin, Texas.

Just as Chancellor Reicher attempted to establish finances and administration on a modern basis, so did Bishop Byrne long to introduce those institutions into the Diocese which would provide programs for the religious and the laity. These institutions were many and varied. While they were not original, they did serve to unite the Texas Church with a number of national Catholic organizations.

Between 1918 and 1950 there came into the Diocese of Galveston the Priests' Eucharistic League (founded 1887) and the Society for the Propagation of the Faith (1822) with headquarters in New York City. There were the Holy Name Society, (founded by Dominicans in 1274 and in the United States in 1870-1871), Catholic Rural Life (1923) of Des Moines, Iowa, Catholic Charities (1910) of Washington, DC, and the Catholic Youth Organization, organized in Chicago in 1930 with its parish-centered diocesan programs.

There were, in addition, the National Council of Catholic Women (1920) of Washington, DC, and the Sodality of the Blessed Virgin Mary. The Bishop furthered the work of the Knights of Columbus, founded in 1882 in New Haven, Connecticut. He sponsored the Catholic Knights of America (1877) of Cincinnati, Ohio, and the Catholic War Veterans (1935) of Washington, DC. In 1946 he accepted the office of supreme spiritual director of the Catholic Knights of America.

With the introduction of men and women religious and organizations into the Diocese, 215 churches and seventy-two schools were built. The Bishop also extended spiritual and charitable facilities for Blacks and Hispanics. But the years brought interests and honors as well and the recognition that came with them.

Bishop Byrne revisited Rome in 1926 and in 1935. In 1930 he convoked a diocesan synod. St. Edward's University in Austin, Texas conferred the honorary degree of Doctor of Laws in 1927. He became a member of the Catholic Knights of America and was a Knight of the Equestrian Order of the Holy Sepulchre of Jerusalem. On 8 May 1941 Pope Pius XII appointed him Assistant to the Pontifical Throne. And the great highlight of this period was the celebration of his golden jubilee as a priest in his own cathedral of St. Mary's on 23 September 1941. His consecrator Archbishop John Glennon and his metropolitan Archbishop Robert Lucey of San Antonio came and praised his accomplishments.

After the Second World War the auspicious year of 1947 approached. The Bishop would be eighty years old and his diocese would be one hundred. For the centennial he announced plans for the construction of a new seminary and a new orphanage. Social services and work among deaf mutes would be extended. And his diocesan flock would raise one million dollars and present it during the celebrations. The plans made were worthy of the eloquent and aristocratic bishop who lived in his stone "palace" with its brocaded living room, its dining room with a massive crystal chandelier and hand-carved sideboard, its capacious fireplaces, parquet flooring, and its unusual ventilation system.

Everyone was coming. Archbishop Amleto Cicognani, the Apostolic Delegate to the United States, would celebrate Mass and Archbishop Lucey would preach the sermon. Seven other archbishops, twenty-two bishops, and 15,000 guests were to take part. On 30 March 1947 Pope Pius XII gave Bishop Byrne the apostolic benediction for the centennial of the erection of the Diocese of Galveston, to be celebrated on the twenty-ninth and thirtieth of April. One might suppose that such a festival as this would be a fitting climax for a bishop in the thirtieth year of his term. But it was not to be. On the sixteenth of April occurred the most terrible event of its kind in the history of the State of Texas.

In the nearby seaport of Texas City, about ten miles northwest of Galveston, the French steamship *Grandcamp* exploded. In this place, a center for refining and petrochemical plants, a fire raged for two days. And when it was done more than five hundred people had died, 4,000 people were injured, 539 structures were destroyed, and damage amounted to about $200 million. On 18 April the saddened Bishop cancelled the celebration of the centennial.

The losses suffered were personal and profound. When the accident happened, some thirty priests of the diocese rushed to lend aid and the sacraments of the Church to the injured and dying. Such was Father William Francis Roach, who lost his life while aiding those who needed him. His own church of St. Mary's, of which he was Pastor, was shattered by the explosion of the first day. On the twenty-fourth of April Monsignor Joseph A. Valenta celebrated a memorial Mass at the site. The Church of Our Lady of Snows was also destroyed.

And so the centennial of the Galveston Diocese passed that year without formal celebration. Its memorial lies not in pomp but in its development. On the fourth of May, 100 years from its date of erection, the diocesan area was the same as when Bishop Byrne first came upon it. Its territory gave a good accounting. There were 117 parishes with resident pastors, seventy-nine missions, 160 diocesan priests who were mostly native Texans, 103 priests who were members of religious orders, 1,272 women religious, two universities, and a seminary. There were fifteen high schools, seventy-seven elementary schools, two orphanages, twelve hospitals (including two for Blacks), and a home for the aged. Bishop Byrne had done well for his people, and he could take some satisfaction in his performance.

Still the aged man worked on. In September 1947 the University of St. Thomas opened in Houston with seventy students taught by the Basilian Fathers. Forty years later the University had grown some twenty times. But on 29 November Bishop Byrne must at last have felt his age. On that day Pope Pius XII appointed Monsignor Reicher, the diocesan chancellor, Bishop of the new Diocese of Austin. This diocese of twenty-seven counties and 22,180 square miles was formed from the Diocese of Galveston. Monsignor Wendelin J. Nold of Dallas became coadjutor with right of succession to Bishop Byrne on the same day.

Whatever his personal opinions of his own mortality and the changing situation, the Bishop did not falter. On 25 February 1948 he assisted in the consecration of Bishop Nold in Sacred Heart Cathedral in Dallas. And on 14 April he consecrated Bishop Reicher in St. Mary's Cathedral in Austin.

The day of 31 March 1950 found Bishop Byrne involved in a typical activity close to his heart. W. L. Moody, Jr., had given the gift of the Moody Memorial Home in Galveston. The Bishop was there to dedicate this facility for the care of child victims of cerebral palsy. His eloquence and grace did not fail him. The good man continued to do his good day's work.

But on the next morning of 1 April his housekeeper discovered his body in his bedroom at 9:30 A.M. His old nemesis, heart trouble, had claimed him in an attack in the night. He left behind 240 priests, 215 churches, and seventy-two schools with nearly 30,000 students. And there were more than 200,000 Catholics in his diocese.

On the fourth of April 1950 at 10:30 A.M. his successor Bishop Nold celebrated a Pontifical Requiem Mass for the repose of his soul in St. Mary's Cathedral in Galveston. Archbishop Lucey delivered the eulogy which Bishop Byrne could not hear three years before. His body was brought to Calvary Cemetery in Galveston that day, and it now rests at the foot of the cross, not far from his sister Miss Mary Byrne.

The State of Texas also took note of the Bishop's passing. State Senators Jimmy Phillips (D-Angleton) and Gus Strauss (D-Hallettsville) sponsored Senate Concurrent Resolution No. 12, adopted by the senate on 28 April 1950. After noting its subject's success as a builder and his time of service as a member of the Texas Good Neighbor Commission, the Resolution states:

> He was a mighty champion of right, fearless in his espousal of causes that he felt to be just; yet he was a man of sweet and kindly disposition, whose tolerance, understanding and magnanimous spirit made him one to be loved as well as respected.

This was a fitting tribute for a man of Irish descent, whose name means "raven," and whose motto he observed in life, "Nec Timeo Nec Sperno" ["I neither fear nor despise"].

Most Reverend Edmond Carmody, DD
Titular Bishop of Mortlach and
Auxiliary Bishop of San Antonio
Second Bishop of Tyler

In Ireland it is said that if one receives aid from a family, that person blesses his hosts by declaring, "May one of your sons become a bishop." In the case of Mrs. Mary Carmody of Tarbert, near the mouth of the River Shannon, such a blessing is literal truth. She has seen one of her sons, known to his large and affectionate family as "Eddie," become in succession an auxiliary bishop of San Antonio and later bishop of Tyler.

On the occasion of his episcopal ordination in San Antonio Edmond Carmody's mother, five of his brothers, and all three of his sisters were there. His father had died in 1977 and four brothers remained behind. Ever mindful of his family, the new bishop spent the week of 13-20 January 1989 with them in Ireland. Such an event should not surprise one acquainted with the bishop's life. If one word could characterize his ministry, it would be "family." That one word embraces all the bishop holds dear. By recalling family values and attempting to live by them, he has become a successful priest and bishop. He knows the meaning of the fatherhood of God and the brotherhood of mankind. He has throughout his life treated each assignment with the love and devotion he gives to his own people.

On 11 November 1988 Bishop Carmody said that parents should teach children the sanctity of life, respect for their own bodies, and the importance of fulfilling the purposes for which God created them. He knows that discipline "has to be reinforced in schools and churches that we cannot give in to every whim and desire."

He knows that religion serves to reinforce a strong family foundation. As he said at his ordination as bishop on 15 December 1988: "If you have a strong family you have a strong community and a strong country." This bishop has kept on his wall a gift from his native village. It is a cross of hammered brass with representations of his life and work. Pictured here is the church in which he was baptized and confirmed and the school he attended as a child. And there are Christian motifs there as well, such as the loaves and fishes, the Paraclete descending, and the bishop's miter, a symbol of his office.

Born to Michael and Mary (Stack) Carmody in Ahalane, Newtownsandes, County Kerry, Ireland, on 12 January 1934, Edmond is the second son and second child in a family of ten boys and three girls. His father bought three more farms as his family grew. These farms are now operated by the three youngest brothers. His parents believed in proper educations for their children and made sure that they received them. Of the bishop's brothers, two entered the practice of medicine, one became a teacher, one a government official, one a salesman, another a medical representative, and the three youngest are family farmers. Of his sisters one manages a savings and loan institution, another is a Sister of Mercy, and the third is a housewife.

The young Edmond worked on the family farms and at home in his early years. Growing up in Moyvane in County Kerry, he milked cows, cut turf for heating and cooking, and tended the vegetable garden. He learned English and Gaelic, the ancient language of Ireland. A natural athlete, he found soccer and Gaelic football (a combination of rugby and soccer), hurling, tennis, racquetball, and water skiing to his liking. He rode horses and would retain an adult interest in racing and racquetball. Even his non-sporting pastimes indicate a practical and active mind. In later life he would take up auto mechanics, electronics, and computer science.

The bishop's formal education began early. He attended the Newtownsandes National School in 1938. St. Brendan's College in Killarney was his preparatory school from 1946 to 1951. In this boarding school of 200 boys work included three hours of supervised study a night. His call to a vocation came, as his mother remembers, when he was on holiday from school on All Saints Day, at the age of sixteen. That call began to become a reality when he undertook priestly studies at St. Patrick's Seminary in Carlow in 1951.

Early in his stay at St. Patrick's the Seminary had a most distinguished visitor, Archbishop Robert E. Lucey of San Antonio, Texas. He awakened in the young student a missionary zeal for foreign lands, which has never left him. The Archbishop told his audience that San Antonio needed priests. Something in his message impressed the young seminarian. According to Bishop Carmody, Lucey "said Texas was a very primitive cowboy land where some parishes didn't have buildings and kids had to sit under the trees for catechism. I expected to see horses tied up at the airport, and I found it was a big city. It took me awhile to get used to that." In fact it would not be until 1984, as a missionary in Peru and Ecuador, that he would come close to seeing the kind of mission territory he envisioned.

His resolve held fast, and he was ordained in the seminary chapel by Bishop Thomas Keogh, for the Archdiocese of San Antonio, on 8 June 1957. The Carmody family was reluctant to see him leave, thinking at first that he might not return. His sister Eileen recalls: "He said if we pressured him [to stay in Ireland] too much, we might cause him to lose his vocation."

Father Carmody left Ireland at Cobh, County Cork, aboard the *RMS Mauretania* in August 1957. His thoughtful father gave him money for return air fare to Ireland in case of necessity. He arrived in New York six days later and flew to San Antonio on Eastern Airlines in company with his seminary classmate, Father Peter McKenna, also a priest of the San Antonio archdiocese.

His first assignment was Associate Pastor of St. Mary's Parish in Victoria, Texas, from 18 September to 22 November 1957. Dating back to 1824, St. Mary's is the first Catholic parish canonically erected in the Republic of Texas. The present stone church was built between 1902 and 1904.

Back in San Antonio Carmody was Associate Pastor of St. Margaret Mary's Parish in the Highland Hills area of the southwest part of the city from November 1957 to September 1960. This parish had become independent in 1955 and its pastor had built a school and chapel in 1956. He was then assigned as Associate Pastor of St. Henry's Parish in southwest San Antonio from September 1960 to August 1966. The first parish church was built-in 1902 and the second in 1929. While at St. Henry's, Carmody was assistant archdiocesan chaplain of scouts in 1965. And here he began the study of Spanish, a language which would serve him well in the years ahead.

His early training in pastoral work completed, Father Carmody now entered into the administrative work of the archdiocese full-time. He was Secretary to the Tribunal from 19 August 1966 until December 1983. From 1966 to 1968 he was also Chaplain of Incarnate Word High School in San Antonio. He served Archbishop Lucey as Secretary from October 1967 to November 1969 and was Archdiocesan Moderator of the Catholic Youth Organization from 1967 to 1968.

In addition to these duties Father Carmody was Catholic Chaplain assigned to the 36th Infantry Brigade of the Texas National Guard, with the rank of Captain. He received the degree of Master of Education in Psychology and Guidance from Our Lady of the Lake University in San Antonio in 1969 and certificates of teacher and counselor from the Texas Education Agency.

On 4 July 1972 Chaplain Carmody was at Canyon Lake near New Braunfels in Comal County. A sudden thunderstorm caused a dock to collapse as two boatloads of nuns approached it. While trying to save one boat, he broke his left leg when it was struck by one of the boats he was attempting to tow. He was nevertheless able to bring the first boat ashore and to return to two sisters in another boat despite further injury to himself. He did not rest until his rescue mission was completed.

For this gallant act he was cited by the National Guard Association of the United States for bravery in the following year. The citation noted that "Captain Chaplain Carmody continued his heroic and successful mission" despite his broken leg and torn ligaments. He was awarded the Valley Forge Cross, the Major General Berry Award, and the Silver Star Cross.

Archbishop Francis J. Furey appointed Father Carmody Moderator of the Tribunal and Vice-Chancellor of the Archdiocese. He served in these positions from October 1969 until December 1983. The Worden School of Social Work of Our Lady of the Lake University awarded him the degree of Master of Social Work in 1973. On 5 November 1974 he was made Director of the Archdiocesan Family Life program. He saw the need for developing marriage enrichment and parenting programs and devised them. He retained this position until 1980 and in that year was a delegate to the White House Conference on Families.

On 26 June 1978 Father Carmody became Director of the Society for the Propagation of the Faith and of the Holy Childhood Association for the Archdiocese of San Antonio. The Propagation of the Faith Society was founded in 1822 and has headquarters in New York City. It promotes mission awareness and generates financial support for missions in 174 American dioceses, subject to the Vatican Congregation for the Evangelization of Peoples. The Holy Childhood Association (or Pontifical Association of the Holy Childhood) was founded in 1843, with headquarters in Washington, DC. It is the official church children's mission-aid society and provides financial assistance to children in ninety-four developing countries. It produces mission and global education material. He was also Director of Pastoral Services for the Archdiocese in 1979. Pope John Paul II appointed him Prelate of Honor, with the title of Reverend Monsignor, on 24 April 1979.

Monsignor Carmody's experiences as pastor and administrator did nothing to end his desire for active missionary work in the field. He could not refuse the continuing call to farther horizons. He requested permission from Archbishop Patrick Flores in December 1982 to depart for a five-year period of missionary work. He would be a member of the St. James the Apostle Society, which is composed of diocesan priests throughout the English-speaking world. The mission fields in Peru, Ecuador, and Bolivia are assigned by the Society, which is under the sponsorship of the Archbishop of Boston.

Although he was needed at home, Archbishop Flores granted his request. He continued his training in Spanish language schools in Mexico City and Cuernavaca, plus a ten-week refresher course in Peru. With the necessary fluency in this adopted language he was assigned first to Lima, Peru, and then to Duran, in the Archdiocese of Guayaquil, Ecuador. His responsibility of a parish of 40,000 people plus forty-two villages led to encounters with more than 100,000 people in 138 parishes and forty-eight missions, often in conditions of extreme poverty.

His mission began with the New Year on 2 January 1984 in locations which could only be reached by truck, horseback, or by boat. Even in such surroundings he found the people most kind and charitable with strangers. And in cases where he was the only visitor the people saw, they wanted a priest at all fiestas, meetings, celebrations, and parades. He was a welcome guest in every home.

His heart was touched by the faith of those communities, each of which contained a lay catechist. They worked to build at least a modest chapel and kept alive prayer and sacramental lives. He marvelled at their unshakable belief in divine providence, noting: "The people of Ecuador have enormous trust in the Lord. He'll solve everything because he's the Lord of the Miracles. Their attitude is, 'He said He would work miracles, and if we believe, He will do it.'"

The village people "can't read or write, but their faith in the living God is unbelievable. They always say, 'Isn't God good, Father.' In the United States or in Ireland, you often hear people say, 'If there is a God, how could he let this happen?'" Ecuador is different. "They don't have much to save, so they have no need to hold onto things. They are not attached to things."

Some time before 27 November 1988 Monsignor Carmody invited Archbishop Flores to preach at a retreat at his mission church of Santa Marianita near Guayaquil. The Archbishop would also celebrate a confirmation. Because of changed flight schedules Carmody knew Flores would arrive too late for the confirmation.

So it was something of a surprise when Archbishop Flores called on the first of November with "good news" and "bad news." The "bad news" which the missionary requested first was that he would have to leave his mission. The "good news" was that Pope John Paul II had appointed him auxiliary bishop of San Antonio.

Carmody accepted and chose a Thursday for his ordination, remembering that Christ had instituted the priesthood and the Mass on that day. He added: "The joy of being a parish priest is fantastic — being with people when they are happy, when they are sad, in their homes and hospitals, sharing their feelings and being a sign of encouragement."

He noted the need of the priest for constant support and affirmation: "Some priests view the priesthood as a job to do — not a vocation — because other people see it that way. People who can give direction are not encouraging young people to follow religious vocations, so there are fewer vocations today." He saw the need for challenging the secular values of society:

> The world is not going to evangelize the church. We have a vocation to evangelize the world with strong values. We all must be out there as a sign of contradiction to the values of an undisciplined way of life. People also should be sad when a priest goes astray, not rejoice when he doesn't set a good example. Maybe they should have helped him confront his problem.

On 8 November 1988 Pope John Paul II formally appointed Monsignor Carmody Titular Bishop of Mortlach and Auxiliary Bishop of San Antonio. That same day Archbishop Flores held a press conference at the Chancery in San Antonio. Auxiliary Bishops Popp and Carmody stood by his side. The Archbishop had suffered inner ear trouble several years before and a heat stroke that past September. He said he had need of the new bishop whom he described as "a raw-boned, brown-eyed Irishman who is as comfortable speaking Spanish as he is English."

For his part Bishop Carmody was aware that San Antonio was his home despite his missionary duty. But immersion into missionary life had tempered him, as water tempers steel. He had a new resolve, a new purpose. He had built five churches in South America and a high school that enrolled 200 students. He would return to Ecuador after his ordination and later for other visits.

He would say at another time that Archbishop Flores and former Archbishop Bernardino Echeverria of Guayaquil were his role models. Both show tremendous capacity for compassion and willingness to be available to their flocks. The Church should aid in eliminating homelessness, poverty, illiteracy, and sickness.

Bishop Carmody at this time thanked Christ for the "great gift of the priesthood" and the Pope for naming him to his position as auxiliary bishop. He then thanked the Archbishop for submitting his name as a candidate and promised him "full cooperation" and "true brotherly affection and esteem." To friends among the priesthood and the laity he said:

> I present myself to you as servant, seeking not to be ministered to, but to minister to you, for whom I have been called to serve. I can never be your model, but I pray that I will always be your servant and an instrument of grace for you.
>
> Finally, I ask you to pray always for us priests, that we may be willing to radiate the love of the Lord Jesus Christ and that our ministry may reveal His presence in our world today. We are but earthen vessels so pray that the Lord's power, love and hope may shine through our weakness so that we may fulfill our calling to bring good news to the poor, release to the captives, recovery of sight to the blind, to set at liberty those who are oppressed and be a source of hope, joy and encouragement to all.
>
> *Que dios les bendiga* [May God bless them].

In Spanish he said:

> Today is for me a day of joy and I am glad to be here with you in

> San Antonio after an absence of five years. I worked as a missionary in Guayaquil, Ecuador, and there was satisfied but never forgot San Antonio was my home.
>
> I wish to thank our Lord Jesus Christ, the Lord of the miracles, for all the gifts that He has given, especially the gift of the priesthood.
>
> I wish to thank the Holy Father, John Paul II, a man of faith, for the soft and sweet burden that he gave for naming me Auxiliary Bishop of San Antonio.
>
> I wish to thank Archbishop Flores for presenting my name as a candidate for this ministry.
>
> And you my partners in the priesthood and the laity pray for me that Christ may assist me to be your good servant.

On 15 December 1988 Bishop Carmody's episcopal ordination took place at St. Matthew's Church in northwest San Antonio. Archbishop Patrick Flores was consecrator with Bishops Charles Grahmann of Victoria and Charles Herzig of Tyler as co-consecrators. All of these bishops had served in the San Antonio archdiocese. Among the 2,000 estimated in attendance were the Cardinal Archbishop of Boston, the papal nuncio (ambassador) to the United States, and bishops from Ecuador, New Zealand, Texas, and Oklahoma. The new bishop's mother and most of his brothers and sisters attended.

At the conclusion of the ceremony Bishop Carmody said:

> The Lord called us to feed the hungry, clothe the naked and visit the sick and imprisoned. I ask your prayers that I will never rest as long as there is a poor Lazarus at the door begging.
>
> Pray for me that I know the people of San Antonio better than I am known to them. What I want is your happiness. If there is anything you need, pray for it. May the god of peace be with you.

Ten days later, on Christmas Day 1988, the Bishop spent the holiday with his former parishioners in Ecuador. He wanted to say good-bye to them. In the next month he spent a week with his family in Ireland. One would not expect less from a man who had returned to Ireland more than ten years earlier to aid and comfort his dying father.

Bishop Carmody served his archdiocese in many ways. He was moderator of the Legion of Mary and taught marriage counseling at the Pastoral Institute at Incarnate Word College and at the Oblate College of the Southwest, both in San Antonio. Now he had new duties. As auxiliary bishop he became the Director of the Department for Research, Planning, Development, and Communications for the Archdiocese.

In this position he was required to develop a vision for the mission of the Archdiocese. He worked always to increase participation of the laity in the work of the Church. To broaden the concept of stewardship in response to faith he set up the Annual Appeal. He used cable television and the archdiocesan newspaper to spread the word of the events taking place concerning Catholics.

On 24 March 1992 Bishop Carmody was promoted to bishop of Tyler by Pope John Paul II. He continued his duties for the Archdiocese to the day of his installation. A farewell Mass and reception were held for him at St. Matthew's Church and parish hall in San Antonio at 7:30 P.M., Sunday, 17 May 1992. About 1,000 people attended. His last obligations were on 23 May 1992 with confirmations in Del Rio in three different parishes.

The day of his appointment (24 March 1992) a public announcement was made at 9:30 A.M., in the Cathedral of the Immaculate Conception in Tyler. The Archbishop was there with more than fifty parishioners and media representatives. Bishop Carmody paid tributes to Archbishop Flores and to his predecessor, Bishop Herzig, whom he was succeeding. He also thanked the vicar general, Monsignor Milam Joseph, who was acting as administrator of the diocese until the coming installation. He spoke on the family and the need to strengthen it. He recalled that in the family "people learn values, learn discipline, learn love, and learn respect for each other." The young are important, because they are "the church with us." In Spanish he said the family is the "domestic church," with the father having the role of priest in teaching his children.

The installation took place at the Oil Palace, a public auditorium, in Tyler. Three thousand people were expected to attend on the evening of Memorial Day, 25 May 1992. A twenty-foot Jerusalem cross would serve as a backdrop for the two-hour ceremony. The Herzig family had been especially invited, and two brothers, their wives, and a sister-in-law of the former Tyler bishop attended from San Antonio and Houston. The bishop's own family came from all over Ireland in the persons of his mother, three of his brothers, one of his sisters, and four sisters-in-law. The archbishops of San Antonio and Oklahoma City were there, as were nineteen other bishops, including Bishop Raymond J. Boland of Birmingham, Alabama. Bishop Boland hailed from Tipperary and would become bishop of Kansas City-St. Joseph, Missouri, the following year. Among the 108 priests from Texas there were some from Bishop Carmody's seminary in Ireland. Many well-wishers came from San Antonio.

Among the crowd there were also deacons, women religious, Knights of the Holy Sepulchre, and Knights of Columbus. Religious leaders of the area were invited, and Bishop Carmody made sure that the handicapped attending would be seated advantageously and that there would be signers for the deaf as well.

Before the installation 500 clergy, nuns, and guests from outside the Diocese of Tyler attended a buffet dinner on the Gorman Middle and High School campus in Tyler. They were entertained by a troop from Tatum, Texas, known as "La Repetida," which performed northern Mexican folk dances. It was led by Jose Luis Mireles and Father Ron Diegel of St. Jude's Parish in Henderson. A Mariachi band from Dallas would play at the Oil Palace.

Bishop Carmody met at a dinner for bishops from Texas, Oklahoma, Louisiana, Alabama, and Missouri. He read an oath of allegiance to the Holy Father in Latin, which was signed by the witnessing bishops. Afterwards, all groups converged on the Oil Palace, where pre-installation events began at 6:00 P.M. in English and Spanish. The "El Coro" group from St. Michael's Catholic Church in Mount Pleasant, the Cathedral handbell choir, St. Gregory's Elementary School Choir from Tyler, and the diocesan choir under the direction of Brian Braquet supplied music for the occasion.

There was a procession of fifty banner-bearers from every parish and mission in the diocese and various organizations, such as the nuns of the diocese, the Diocesan Council of Catholic Women, the Catholic Daughters of the Americas, and Boy and Girl Scout troops. Each banner was accompanied by four people from the church or organization it represented with a Knight of Columbus as an honor guard.

When the ceremonies began at 7:00 P.M., Monsignor Milam Joseph, vicar general and diocesan administrator, read the translation from Latin into English of the "Bull of Appointment of Most Reverend Edmond Carmody as Bishop of the Diocese of Tyler." Archbishop Flores conducted Bishop Carmody to his throne and presented him with his crozier, a symbol of his office. The bishop received welcomes from pastors, associate pastors, and two representatives from each parish.

When the bishop spoke as homilist, he paid tributes to his father and to the late Bishop Herzig of Tyler. He said of himself: "I, as your bishop, offer to you my service and leadership, my energies, my gifts, my mind, my heart, my strength and my limitations. I offer all that I am to serve you." He noted that the "church community, you and I" must deal with the problems "of poverty, illness, ignorance, injustice, aimlessness, and lack of purpose and meaning in individual lives and in society." As brothers and sisters, "We need to link together to purify our world, to make the mission of Jesus more real in our time." He also promised to visit each parish and mission in the Diocese before Christmas.

Prayers of petition were offered in English, Spanish, Gaelic, Lebanese, Ido (Nigerian), Vietnamese, and Filipino. Kenneth Herzig, brother of the previous bishop of Tyler, read the prayer in English, and Dr. Frieda Carmody, wife of the bishop's brother Dr. Paschal Carmody, read her prayer in Gaelic. When the gifts of bread and wine were presented, four couples dressed in native costumes, representing European, African, Mexican, and Vietnamese cultures of the Diocese of Tyler, offered them. Newspapers in Tyler, Longview, Lufkin, Nacogdoches, Paris, and Texarkana, cities of the East Texas area, supplied newspaper coverage, as did those in the larger cities of San Antonio, Dallas, and Houston. Two Tyler television stations made the ceremonies visible. The Associated Press spread the news to wider areas, and a videotape was prepared for posterity.

On the following morning of 26 May 1992, at 9:00 A.M. Bishop Carmody concelebrated Mass with Fathers Joseph Strickland, Peter Whitney, and Randy Martin, in the Cathedral in Tyler. Among the 150 present were fourth graders from St. Gregory's School in Tyler, people from the cathedral parish, and some of the bishop's friends from San Antonio. The Bishop recalled that like Moses, he could win his battles if his friends would keep his arms uplifted.

Edmond Carmody was now the spiritual leader of 32,094 Catholics in a thirty-two county area of East Texas containing some 22,971 square miles. Comparable figures from his homeland of the Republic of Ireland embraced 27,137 square miles with 3.5 million people. While the bishop had forty-two priests, twenty-four permanent deacons, seventy-four nuns, and no male religious to serve him, Ireland had a cardinal, five archbishops, forty-three bishops, 6,392 priests, 1,558 male religious, 11,399 women religious and 1,350 parishes in contrast to his own forty-three parishes and missions scattered throughout his diocese. Or, considering it another way, the Tyler diocese was twice the size of a mission parish in Guayaquil, Ecuador, with less than a third as many Catholics. In addition his area contained about 48,000 Hispanics. The bishop of Tyler had come a long way.

His flock was of diverse origins. Many were from the American Midwest and the Northeast. Others were of French descent who had come into the area from Louisiana. Others were Hispanic and Vietnamese, who had come in more recent years. He realized that bilingualism in English and Spanish would become necessary for his priests. He had three seminarians from the Diocese, and another would be ordained in December 1992. Two priests from India would soon see him about locating in the Diocese, to be followed later with two more from Poland. As the bishop knew well, if there are not enough native laborers for the vineyards others may be introduced as needed.

The bishop was a man of his word. He kept his appointments with all of his parishes and missions by Christmas 1992. On 23 September 1992 he appointed Father Gavin Vavarek chancellor on the recommendation of the Priests' Personnel Board. The Diocese to this time did not have a chancellor. Such an official gathers, arranges, and keeps acts of the Chancery in the archives. He is involved in catechesis (religious teaching), Catholic education, construction, administration, and dispensation in matrimonial situations. He also compiles statistics and makes diocesan reports.

The appointment of Father Vavarek was not only necessary but beneficial to the growing diocese. His background in lay life as a computer systems analyst aided his ability to keep and maintain records. He is a member of the Priests' Personnel Board and moderator of the Diocesan Council of Catholic Women. On 20 December 1994 he became vocations director for the Diocese. His studies at the Catholic University of America in Washington, DC, and his earned degree of Licentiate in Canon Law allowed his appointment in June 1995 as Defender of the Bond of the Diocesan Tribunal.

As an official of the Tribunal, the defender of the bond considers cases involving the nullity of sacred ordination or the nullity or dissolution of the marriage bond. He reviews the evidence, examines documents and witnesses, and maintains proper procedures during the ecclesiastical trial. In some situations his concern is the content of the litigations rather than with the legal procedures.

Bishop Carmody made other key appointments at this time. He named Father Benedict ("Ben") Comiskey and Deacon William H. ("Bill") Bridwell co-directors of the diaconate program and Joe and Marge Dudas of Longview co-directors of pro-life activities. Father Christopher Shackelford became chaplain to the Catholic Committee on Scouting.

In the early days of his episcopate the Bishop received $60 thousand in grants for programs and parish subsidies from the Catholic Church Extension Society of Chicago, which provides such funds for home mission work. The Society had now paid a total of $324 thousand to the Diocese of Tyler, including $25 thousand to help the Diocese begin its operations.

By February 1993, after nine months in office, Bishop Carmody had put some 30,000 miles on his car. He had met with religious and lay leaders in his every parish and mission at least once. He planned a diocesan liturgy commission and urged deacons to form Catholic communities in towns without churches. He wanted to build or occupy a new chancery building with more space, establish a diocesan office for Catholic charities, form a bishop's advisory committee composed of laity, nuns, deacons and priests, centralize the diocesan office for ministries, and recruit priests and encourage vocations. Noting growth in the communities of Tatum in Rusk and Panola counties, and in Lindale and Whitehouse in Smith County, he urged deacons to locate a chapel in every community. He named a full-time vocations director and contacted Sts. Cyril and Methodius Seminary in Orchard Lake, Michigan, to encourage seminarians to locate within the Diocese of Tyler.

By May 1993, one year after his installation he had some perspective on his flock in East Texas and praised the people's "great sound values, honesty, integrity, compassion, tolerance, acceptance and interaction between the different groups." He visited various community ministry operations: PATH, the East Texas Regional Food Bank, and in Tyler the Tyler Together sponsored events. He established the diocesan marriage tribunal and developed a marriage preparatory program for couples.

Bishop Carmody looked forward to hosting the Southwest Liturgical Conference in Tyler in January 1994. He appointed Father Randy Martin Director for Pastoral Ministries and evangelistic efforts. He expanded work among Hispanic church members and in basic evangelism. He made it mandatory that more than half of his parishes and missions have Spanish-speaking or bilingual services. Reducing the Presbyteral Council from all diocesan priests to a ten-member board meeting monthly, he began to get the necessary input and advice he would need to administer. He developed specific mission goals for parishes and missions, placed new emphasis on vocations, and dedicated a new church in Nacogdoches. He began to rebuild the church in Jefferson, which was destroyed by fire.

The Church in Tyler had grown so that the chancery building at 1920 Sybil Lane, in use since the Diocese's beginnings in February 1987, had become too small. The thirteenth building looked at and located in the Woodgate office complex near the Gorman School campus seemed to fill the bill. Situated at 1015 East Southeast Loop 323, it contained 20,000 square feet. This was four times larger than the old premises and would include a chapel, a library, a room for archives, meeting rooms, and offices. It was accessible to the handicapped and the lot contained seventy parking spaces. By 1 July 1993 a $10 thousand down payment to the Fitzgerald, Burns and McCaslin Development Partnership, owners of the building, secured the property. IBM, which occupied the building, held the lease through the end of June and would be given two additional months to vacate. The Sybil Drive chancery, to be sold with the approval of the Diocesan Building Board and the College of Consultors, would realize about $200 thousand of the $650 thousand selling price. Other funds from foundation grants and from the Diocesan Annual Appeal would make up the balance. On 13 September 1993 the Chancery opened for business in its new location.

Mothers' Day, 9 May 1993, marked the tenth anniversary of Birthright of Tyler, a crisis pregnancy center located at 327 West Houston Street. Mrs. Priscilla Kelsey, the director and a Catholic parishioner, ran the facility staffed with volunteers. She states that, during the course of its operation, Birthright assisted more than 500 women who later had babies. Mrs. Kelsey offered free pregnancy tests, aid with maternity and baby clothes, and placement in shelter homes. The service received donations and $3 thousand from the Diocesan Annual Appeal.

The Presbyteral Council at its 11 May 1993 meeting approved an employment practices handbook entitled, *Personnel Policies and Procedure Manual* to take effect on 1 June following. Drafted by Ed Luman, the diocesan business manager, and Deacon Bill O'Sullivan, the cathedral business manager, it contained sections on evaluation, termination, salary policies, and work standards. Besides Mister Luman and Deacon O'Sullivan, Monsignor Milam Joseph, the vicar general, made up an ad hoc personnel panel to deal with grievances. The scope of the work covered chancery and other Catholic employees. On 25 May more than 200 copies of the handbook were sent to all pastors, principals, and administrators in the Diocese of Tyler. It was estimated at the time that about 150 full-time employees were eligible for benefits, with most employees having ten to twenty days vacation a year.

The Council also discussed forming a committee on priestly life. It would deal with such matters as parish administration, theological studies, enrichment programs, retreats, and days of recollection for the ongoing formation of priests. It was noted that the yearly priests' retreat held in Beaumont, Texas, was a program of spiritual enrichment already in place. The question of priests' salaries and stipends (offerings) should be discussed at the September 1993 meeting.

At that meeting, held on 7 September 1993, with Father Randy Martin, chairman, it was observed that no salary change had been made since the foundation of the Diocese. The base salary was $6,600, with components for housing, food, travel, insurance, pension fund, and utilities, raising benefits to about $33,020. This compensation was found similar to the Diocese of Dallas and the Archdiocese of San Antonio. The Council noted that the average in annual salaries for priests was $7,525 in 1988. Discussion ended by recommending a plan for regular increases.

In August 1993 World Youth Day included a visit by Pope John Paul II to Denver, Colorado. Bishop Carmody accompanied several hundred young people from the Diocese of Tyler. The pope asked his audience of some 400,000 to respect life and to aid the innocent, the poor, and the helpless through Christian principles.

In Tyler on 7 September 1993 the bishop blessed a monument for priests and the permanent grave marker of Bishop Herzig, for whom this was the second anniversary of death, at Rose Hill Cemetery. Members of the Herzig family were invited and a Mass was said at the Cathedral to mark the occasion.

It was more than five years since Bishop Herzig had represented the Diocese of Tyler in an audience with the pope and toured the Lyon area of France to visit the homes of the first bishops of Texas. Now it was time for a ten-day regular visit to Rome which Bishop Carmody undertook with seventeen other bishops of his region. During such a visit it is customary for bishops to visit the tombs of Sts. Peter and Paul, say Mass and have dinner with the pope, as well as a brief private audience and a public meeting. The public meeting includes the pope, Vatican officials, and all bishops present. Such a visit normally lasts about ten days.

At his private audience on 30 September 1993 John Paul II asked Bishop Carmody, "How do Catholics get along with the other Christian denominations?" The Bishop answered affirmatively, informing His Holiness that the people of the Tyler diocese had such respect for life that there were no abortion clinics to be found within it. When the pope urged the bishop to have priests in every diocesan community and to strengthen youth ministries and families, Bishop Carmody reported that he was working to ensure these goals. His recent trip to Denver for World Youth Day found approval, and the Bishop pointed out advances made in ecumenical work, efforts to welcome immigrants and newcomers and in helping some 48,000 Hispanics with Spanish-language liturgies and priests working to learn Spanish. He said that the majority of parishes and missions had Spanish language or bilingual liturgies and that the number of registered Catholics attending Mass on any given Sunday in the Diocese of Tyler (54%) exceeded the national average (52%). John Paul closed the audience by sending his apostolic blessings to the priests, deacons, religious, and laity of the Tyler diocese.

On 8 October 1993 the celebration of "Bishop Carmody Day" took place at the Gorman Middle and High School in Tyler. Mayor Smith Reynolds, Jr. read his proclamation and the bishop dedicated a bird sanctuary on the campus constructed by the eighth graders. Bishop Carmody said Mass on the campus at 8:00 A.M. and taught theology classes throughout the day. He was treated to a luncheon hosted by the middle schoolers, and the school choir performed musical selections in his honor.

By New Year's Day 1994 there were forty-six priests in the Diocese of Tyler. A priest and two transitional deacons studying for the priesthood were ordained in 1993. There were twenty-eight permanent deacons, one male religious, and seventy-four women religious to assist the work of the bishop. Of the twenty-seven parishes and fourteen missions, the station of Tatum in Panola and Rusk counties had been raised to the status of a mission under the title of San Pedro the Fisherman on 7 November 1993. There were two Catholic hospitals assisting 91,211 patients, two health care centers assisting 35,161 people, four seminarians studying for the priesthood, a high school with 131 students and four elementary schools with 917 students. There were 6,046 students under Catholic instruction taught by eighty-one teachers. In the previous year 1,070 new Catholics were received into the Church, with 248 marriages and 269 deaths. There were 37,932 registered Catholics in the total population of 1,157,000. Recognizing the need to expand faith communities in Lindale and Whitehouse in Smith County, missions have since been established under the names of Holy Family and Prince of Peace.

At the same time Bishop Carmody had significantly increased the scope of diocesan administration to care for his flock more adequately. Since October 1992 he has replaced the business manager Ed Luman, who had died, with James R. Smith as Finance Officer. He selected a permanent archivist, established a chapter of the Campaign for Human Development to aid the poor, appointed a full-time Director of Pastoral Ministries (Father Randy Martin) and established offices for Campus Ministries, Missions, Clergy Development,

East Texas Community Services, Adoption, and Catholic Services for Immigrants. He has also founded a Diocesan Liturgical Commission and appointed a Director of Religious Education.

This list does not mean to be all-inclusive nor to suggest all plans and programs governing the Diocese of Tyler. A more comprehensive idea of its year-to-year progress may be found in that section of the Introduction entitled "The Bishop and His Diocese," together with its Note 33.

One institution, developed by Bishop Carmody, does deserve particular mention. From 1992 he had been trying to develop an independent tribunal. The Tribunal is a person or persons employing the judicial powers of the Church. Its major function as an ecclesiastical court is to decide the validity of marriages. On the diocesan level the Tribunal is a court of first impression in which a matter is tried. Appellate court cases may ultimately reach the Holy See acting as an appellate court.

The problem in Tyler was to expedite cases which took up to twenty months to decide in Dallas. When Monsignor Sidney J. Marceaux, the judicial vicar (judge) of the tribunal for the Diocese of Beaumont, took such a position in the Diocese of Tyler, cases could be decided within two-and-a-half to three months. In the period of one year (1992 to 1993) a final decision was rendered in ninety-four of 129 cases. Priests and deacons of the diocese are "advocates," presenting the cases for trial and other matters for decision. Mrs. Margaret Oppenheimer was designated administrator and aided the process greatly by her expertise. Marriages are declared null or validated with the cost of $300 to defray office expenses. No one is turned away for nonpayment of fees.

Monsignor Marceaux was eventually able to retire his position in Tyler with Fathers Joseph Strickland and Gavin Vavarek, returned from graduate study in canon law at the Catholic University of America, as judicial vicar and defender of the bond, respectively. So in June 1995 the Tribunal became self-contained within the Diocese of Tyler and fully functional as a diocesan institution.

Between 19 and 22 January 1994 the Tyler diocese hosted the Southwest Liturgical Conference meeting at the Sheraton Tyler Hotel in Tyler. The theme of this thirty-second annual event was "Come to the Table: Rites of Welcome and Initiation." The keynote speaker was Bishop Donald W. Trautman of Erie, Pennsylvania, chairman of the bishops' committee on liturgy. Bishop Ricardo Ramirez of Las Cruces, New Mexico, also spoke. Liturgy is the ceremonial means by which the clergy and faithful find expression in worship.

From 23 April to 6 May 1994 Bishop Carmody acted as chaplain for thirty members of the Southwestern Lieutenancy of the Equestrian Order of the Holy Sepulchre, whose pilgrimage included a tour of the Holy Land. The Southwestern Lieutenancy has members from the States of Texas, Oklahoma, Arkansas, and New Mexico. The pilgrims in this case were Texans. They went throughout Israel praying for peace. Married couples renewed their vows at Cana and all renewed baptismal vows at the River Jordan. They climbed Mount Tabor, made the Way of the Cross, heard Mass at the Hill of Calvary, and prayed at the empty tomb of Christ. They were granted an audience with His Beatitude Michel Sabbah, the Latin Patriarch for Jerusalem. Patriarch Sabbah invested the bishop with the pilgrim shell, a sign that he had made his pilgrimage.

Bishop Carmody was also the head of the bishop's committee on missions, a national office with international ramifications. On 23 October 1994, on World Mission Sunday, he recalled that the Society for the Propagation of the Faith remands funds to missions. Those who support with prayer and/or material assistance are missionaries too, he recalled. He noted that in Ecuador the poor give a weekly donation equivalent to fifty cents in American money, but on this Sunday, the next to last in October, they give the equivalent of three dollars. Forty percent of American donations goes to the American Board of Catholic Missions to needy American missions and nine percent to the Catholic Near East Welfare Association.

The bishop of Tyler is a citizen of the world, functioning well on three continents. He is proud of his family and his Irish heritage, but his love and his considerable abilities extend to his flocks in Texas and in South America. His coat of arms summarizes his career. It contains a green shield for his birthplace, a silver star for Texas, and an oak stump from the family crest with roots in the earth and capable of generating new life. It features a condor in gold with red beak and claws symbolizing the sacrificial nature of missionary service. The bird is a relative of the Carmody falcon. The family name derives from the Irish "O'Cearmada" meaning "right with God." And the bishop's motto speaks of his philosophy of life and ministry. It is, "With Christ All Is Possible."

On 16 September 1995 after the concelebration of Mass with nine priests before a congregation of 500 in his cathedral in Tyler, Bishop Carmody was one of 163 candidates (including eleven priests) from the Third Texas Our Lady of Guadalupe Province to be elevated to the Fourth Degree of the Knights of Columbus. The Bishop was joined by Revs. Dan L. Daugherty, Michael A. Doyle, Peter Revel, and Octavio Suarez, and forty-five laymen from Our Lady of Roses Assembly No. 1119, Tyler, in the Third Texas District. The exemplification ceremony took place at the Sheraton Inn in Tyler.

Founded by Father Michael J. McGivney in Connecticut in 1882, as of 1994, the Knights of Columbus had a membership of more than 1.5 million worldwide. Active in many apostolic works and community programs, local units in 1994 gave more than $100 million for charitable and benevolent causes and over forty-eight million hours of community service. Its headquarters is in New Haven, Connecticut (1996 *CA* 581).

Bishop Carmody brings more than his administrative abilities to his Tyler position. He views the family institution as fostering stability in the community and in the Church. He knows the people of Texas through his years of ministry. Bilingual in Spanish and English with service in South America, he builds upon the foundation begun by the late Bishop Charles Herzig.

Most Reverend John Joseph Cassata, DD
Titular Bishop of Bida and
Auxiliary Bishop of Dallas-Fort Worth
First Bishop of Fort Worth

On Saturday, the sixteenth of September 1989, John Joseph Cassata came to the Sacred Heart Co-Cathedral in Houston, Texas, to receive the final rites of his church and to be remembered for his career of thirty-four years in that city and for the additional twelve years he had spent as auxiliary bishop of Dallas-Fort Worth and then as first bishop of Fort Worth.

His see city also remembered him. Three days before the faithful of St. Patrick's Cathedral in Fort Worth heard the Office of the Dead read for him followed later by a vigil and a rosary. Next day his successor Bishop Joseph P. Delaney offered a funeral Mass for him. On 15 September others participated in a vigil and a rosary at the co-cathedral in Houston.

Now, late on the morning of September sixteenth, Archbishop Patrick F. Flores of San Antonio concelebrated the Mass of Christian Burial for Bishop Cassata, assisted by the Bishop of Galveston-Houston, his two auxiliaries, his predecessor, and the Bishop of Beaumont, as well as more than forty priests. But why had the late bishop chosen his family plot in the Garden of Gethsemane section of Forest Park Cemetery in Houston for burial over a location among his flock in Fort Worth? When the time came, the homilist Bishop Joseph Fiorenza of Galveston-Houston spoke for him:

> Although he was the first bishop of Fort Worth and served there in a very faithful and effective way for eleven years, he could not forget this diocese — where he was born, where he was reared, where he had so many close ties and friendships, where he ministered as a priest for many years before being called to the episcopacy.

John Joseph Cassata was born to Vincent and Ann (Pizzitola) Cassata into a family of four sons and four daughters on 8 November 1908 in Galveston, Galveston County, Texas. His parents were natives of Sicily. Young John attended St. Mary's Parish School in Galveston, conducted by the Ursuline sisters at 20th and Winnie Streets, in the land occupied by the cathedral. After completing these early studies, he attended St. Mary's boarding school at La Porte.

For a short time the young man worked as a bookkeeper and floor covering salesman. He then returned to St. Mary's Seminary at La Porte and began to study for the priesthood. His superiors recognized his ability and sent him to the North American College in Rome to develop his priestly life before ordination. Founded by the bishops of the United States in 1859, the North American College was granted pontifical status by Pope Leo XIII on 25 October 1884. Student residents study theology and related subjects in the universities and institutes of Rome.

The young Cassata attended the Propaganda Fide and Gregorian universities. The Pontifical Gregorian University was established in 1552 and became associated with the Pontifical Biblical Institute and the Pontifical Institute of

Oriental Studies in the twentieth century. Here the seminarian studied for and received the degree of Licentiate in Sacred Theology (STL), intermediate between the degrees of Bachelor of Sacred Theology (STB) and Doctor of Sacred Theology (STD).

The prestige of this degree has grown with the years. It requires a strong foundation in such areas as the history of philosophy, logic, metaphysics, ethics, philosophy of God, and philosophical anthropology, together with an understanding of the Bible and of Latin. The licentiate-to-be should have the background of a Bachelor of Sacred Theology. This means knowing the history of theology, Christian morals, patristic theology, liturgiology, pastoral theology, Christian spirituality, canon law, and theological research. Added to this the degree candidate should be exposed to systematic, sacramental, and moral theology, scripture, church history, and another theological tradition and pastoral ministry.

In Cassata's student days the licentiate was the rough equivalent of a Master of Arts in Theology. More recently credit and language requirements, areas of concentration, a dissertation option, and different types of qualifying examinations have added to the importance of the degree. In many respects the present degree is not unlike the doctorate in its field.

The completion of the Reverend Mister Cassata's theological studies was a prelude to his ordination. On 8 December 1932, in the Chapel of Our Lady of Humility in the North American College at Rome, Cardinal Francesco Marchetti Selvaggiani performed the rite of holy orders. This sixty-year-old Roman churchman, the Vicar General of Rome, would end his career as the dean of the college of cardinals.

Bishop Christopher E. Byrne gave Father Cassata his first permanent appointment as assistant pastor of Holy Name Parish in Houston in January 1934. The tenth oldest existing parish in that city, Holy Name belongs to the north side, east from Little White Oak Bayou to the Eastex Freeway and north from the Southern Pacific tracks to the boundary of St. Patrick's church. The fire which destroyed the church, school, and rectory of St. Patrick's was the origin of the new parish. A combination church and school was erected near the site of the burned-out buildings.

In a letter of 20 March 1919 from Bishop Byrne to Father Bernard Lee, permission was given to buy property for the building of a new church. This instruction led to the acquisition of the H. C. House block, and in September 1920 Father George Wilhelm was named pastor. Bishop Byrne blessed and opened a temporary church for the parish under the name of Our Blessed Savior on 1 May 1921. The congregation grew so rapidly that on 15 March 1925 Bishop Byrne laid the cornerstone for the permanent church. In that same year the Sisters of the Incarnate Word established the parish school.

In January 1945 Father Cassata became pastor of Holy Name Parish. Following the canonization of St. Frances Cabrini (1946), the first American citizen honored with sainthood, Holy Name became the first diocesan parish to have public devotion in her honor. After the death of Bishop Byrne in 1950 Bishop Wendelin Nold named Cassata vicar general for the Galveston diocese, a post he continued to retain under the coadjutor bishop John L. Morkovsky.

Pope Pius XII named Father Cassata a domestic prelate with the rank of

Right Reverend Monsignor in 1956. From that year until 1963 the newly-created monsignor had as his assistant pastor a young priest who would one day become Archbishop Flores of San Antonio. The former assistant thus became the head of the province in which his former superior served him as suffragan bishop.

While retaining his pastorate, Monsignor Cassata also had many other duties besides those of vicar general. Among these were diocesan consultor, synodal judge of the matrimonial court, member of the diocesan boards of examiners and of education, and chairman of the diocesan expansion program. He was as well an advisory of the Catholic Youth Organization board, moderator of the Confraternity of Christian Doctrine, and director of diocesan radio and television programming. As diocesan procurator he attended the Second Vatican Council in Rome in 1962.

Pope Paul VI appointed Monsignor Cassata Titular Bishop of Bida and Auxiliary Bishop of Dallas-Fort Worth to assist Bishop Thomas K. Gorman on 20 April 1968. Bishop Gorman performed his episcopal ordination on the following 8 June in St. Michael's Church in Houston. Archbishop (later Cardinal) John F. Dearden of Detroit and Auxiliary Bishop (later Bishop) Frank H. Greteman of Sioux City assisted as co-consecrators. In October of that year Bishop Cassata began his tenure as grand prior of the southern lieutenancy of the Equestrian Order of the Holy Sepulchre, retiring with distinction in October 1986.

In 1969 Bishop Gorman retired and Pope Paul appointed Bishop Thomas Tschoepe of San Angelo to the vacant Dallas diocese. He created a separate diocese of Fort Worth and made Bishop Cassata its first ordinary on 2 August. The first bishop of Fort Worth was installed in St. Patrick's Cathedral in his see city on 21 October by Archbishop (later Cardinal) Luigi Raimondi, apostolic delegate to the United States. Between 1971 and 1973 he served as Texas State Chaplain of the Knights of Columbus.

In his *ad limina* report to Pope Paul VI in Rome in 1973 Bishop Cassata showed an increase in his diocese from 67,690 to 72,629 Catholics. There were seven more priests since the diocese began, though no new religious brothers and sisters. Three high schools remained, though elementary schools decreased from eighteen to fifteen. But the number of students receiving Catholic instruction grew from 10,070 to 12,194.

Bed capacity increased in diocesan hospitals and outpatients numbered about 2,000 more in the four years covered by the report. Foster and retirement home care improved, as did marriage tribunal administration. The bishop backed his interest in lay involvement in diocesan matters with the founding of the lay assembly. He assisted the lay ministries program and the Catholic Renewal Center.

The Cassata tenure in Fort Worth was spent in founding the institutions of the new diocese and in providing outreach to the faithful. The bishop encouraged his seminarians to learn Spanish to broaden their service to their future parishioners and founded twelve new parishes. Two institutions continue to aid constituencies within the diocese to fulfill their goals. The Catholic Renewal Center helps prepare engaged couples for marriage and aids married couples in strengthening their unions. The Learning Center (renamed the Cassata Learning Center) assists students to achieve the high school diploma or its equivalent. The lay ministries program involves more than 100 parishioners in its two-year schedule, while All Saints Church in Fort Worth carries out numerous activities for the Mexican-American Catholics of that city.

By 1981 the diocesan population had grown to 93,500, an increase of more than 25,000. On 13 September Bishop Cassata retired with the title of Bishop Emeritus of the Diocese of Fort Worth, after a short time as apostolic administrator awaiting his successor's appointment. As a citizen of Texas, he accepted the honorary appointment of Lieutenant General in the Texas State Guard. With a current membership of over 1,500, this unit was created by the Texas Legislature in 1941 and became a part of the state military forces in 1965. It participates in local emergencies and reinforces the National Guard in state emergencies and replaces its forces when they are pressed into federal service. The governor of Texas is commander-in-chief and exercises command through an adjutant general appointed by him with the authority of Congress and the state legislature.

On 27 October 1986 Bishop Cassata retired as grand prior of the southern lieutenancy of the Equestrian Order of the Holy Sepulchre. At that time he was presented with the Palm of the Order, which he informed the present writer was "very special," being one of the three honorary decorations in its gift. One can better understand the bishop's feelings when he remembers that belonging to one of the five classes of knighthood in this order requires the pledge of an upright Christian life and loyalty to the pope. In the early years of this century the pope himself was the grand master, an office now filled by a designated cardinal. The 1949 constitution enjoins members "to revive in modern form the spirit and ideal of the Crusades with the weapons of faith, the apostolate, and Christian charity."

This bishop of Italian descent, whose name means "box," lived on Ridglea Country Club Drive in Fort Worth until his health began to fail in 1989. Heart surgery in August of that year was unavailing, and he died on Friday, 8 September, at St. Luke's Hospital in Houston, Texas. His brother Baldwin, and his sisters Katherine (Mrs. Culotta), Pauline (Mrs. Dazzio), Mary (Mrs. Saladino), and Teresa (Mrs. Musachia) survived him, as did many nieces and nephews. Secure in his family and in his devotion to his church, he chose as his episcopal motto, "Dominus Regit Me," which his colleagues translate as "The Lord Guides Me. The Lord Leads Me."

Most Reverend Augustine Danglmayr, DD, LLD
Titular Bishop of Olba and Auxiliary Bishop of Dallas

The life of Bishop Augustine Danglmayr illustrates a happy family situation leading to distinguished service in the Church with pleasant retirement among relatives and friends. It shows how one may work in his native state for the well-being of all and receive the recognition of achievement.

Born in Muenster, Cooke County, Texas, on 11 December 1898, Augustine was one of the five sons, as well as three daughters, born to Joseph and Theresa (Muck) Danglmayr. In this small dairy center in the north central part of the state, the future bishop attended Sacred Heart Parochial School from 1903 until 1911. For the next eight years (1911-1919) he studied at Subiaco College in Subiaco, Logan County, Arkansas. Here he earned the Bachelor of Arts degree in 1919. Today the former college is a private high school for boys under Benedictine auspices and is known as Subiaco Academy.

The young graduate set his mind upon becoming a priest. In September 1919 he began theological studies, which lasted until December 1921, at Kenrick Seminary in St. Louis, Missouri, known today as the St. Louis Roman Catholic Theological Seminary. Here he was admitted to the clerical state by receiving the ceremony of tonsure from Archbishop (later Cardinal) John J. Glennon of St. Louis nine days after his twenty-first birthday. Tonsure was achieved by clipping or shaving part of the head, generally the crown, of the clerical candidate. It was replaced by another form of ceremony to serve the same purpose by Pope Paul VI in an indult or dispensation of 8 October 1971 to the bishops of the United States.

Having achieved the clerical state and minor orders, the young seminarian transferred to St. Mary's Seminary in La Porte, Texas, to complete preordination studies in 1922. During the brief time of his residence Augustine taught spelling in the commercial and arithmetic in the preparatory departments. He was ordained here in the major orders of subdeacon on 2 June and deacon on the following day by Bishop Christopher Byrne of Galveston. The order of subdeacon, with its specific duties in liturgical worship, first came to notice in the third century, according to extant records. It was regarded as a minor order until the thirteenth century, when it was called a major order in the western Church.

On 14 September 1972 Pope Paul VI abolished the orders of porter (presently unimportant), exorcist, and subdeacon. He decreed that laymen, as well as diaconate and priesthood candidates, can be installed (rather than ordained) in the ministries (no longer called orders) of acolyte (server) and lector (reader). At the same time he reconfirmed the abolition of tonsure and its replacement of a service of dedication to God and the Church. He also stated that ordination to the diaconate signifies entry into the clerical state.

His priestly training completed, the Reverend Mister Danglmayr was ordained by Bishop Joseph P. Lynch in his Sacred Heart Cathedral, Dallas, for the Diocese of Dallas on 10 June 1922. Only one week had elapsed from diaconate to priesthood. Three days later Father Danglmayr celebrated his First Mass in his home parish at Sacred Heart Church in Muenster.

His career as a clergyman began in earnest with his appointment as Assistant Pastor to the cathedral parish in Dallas on the following 1 July. And with it came the additional duties of Director of the Sodality of the Children of Mary and Spiritual Director of the Catholic Girls' Athletic Club. The young priest apparently performed these obligations well because on 30 November 1923 he became First Assistant Rector of the Cathedral, Chancellor, and Secretary of the Diocese of Dallas to Bishop Lynch. The diocesan directorship of the Society for the Propagation of the Faith came in February 1926.

The fact that Father Danglmayr obtained the effective control of the day-to-day affairs of the Diocese before reaching his twenty-fifth birthday says much about his ability. As chancellor it was his duty to draw up documents for the government of the Diocese, preserve its archives in an orderly system, and record dispensations and ecclesiastical decisions. As secretary he was in daily contact with the Bishop attending to the work of the Diocese.

The Society for the Propagation of the Faith was founded in 1822 and has headquarters in New York City. Established in 174 dioceses it promotes mission awareness and generates financial support for missions. Its worldwide operations are subject to the Vatican Congregation for the Evangelization of Peoples. Another responsibility of Chancellor Danglmayr was the position of Director of the National Catholic Welfare Conference on Immigration, to which he was appointed on 17 July 1926.

In 1928 the Chancellor was fortunate enough to win a "popularity contest" in the form of a vacation, sponsored in part by the now-defunct Dallas *Post Dispatch.* His ship left Galveston on 2 July and sailed via New Orleans to Cuba and then on past the Canary Islands en route to Europe. Father Danglmayr visited France, Germany, Italy, Switzerland, and Czechoslovakia, returning to Dallas via New York on 29 September.

This travel experience came at a good time because work continued without pause. The Chancellor became a Diocesan Consultor on 4 November 1929 and the Spiritual Director of the Catholic Young Men's Association from February 1930. In his pre-episcopal days he also had charge of various missions near Dallas and was Chaplain of the orphanages, the Good Shepherd Home (no longer extant), and of the Ursuline Convent and Academy of Dallas. He conducted weekly religious education classes for adults, from which he estimated about sixty converts came into the Church for every year of instruction.

Such fidelity in so many enterprises could not be overlooked indefinitely. The Holy See took notice and gave Father Danglmayr rank equivalent to his positions. Pope Pius XI appointed him Papal Chamberlain with the title of Very Reverend Monsignor on 11 August 1934. Within three years the same pontiff made him Domestic Prelate with the title of Right Reverend Monsignor on 15 January 1937.

The letters apostolic for the last appointment stress that the honor is to "reward your fidelity to your Ordinary [Bishop Lynch], your many labors, and your great zeal and success in the matter of leading converts into the fold; and in order at the same time publicly to attest our own benevolence toward you." The document is signed by Cardinal Eugenio Pacelli in his office of papal Secretary of State. He was soon to become Pope Pius XII.

Rank may have its privileges, but it meant more work for the Monsignor.

He became actuary or clerk of the matrimonial court, a member of the diocesan finance and building commission, and in 1938 Catholic representative and director of relief. He was also Director of the Union of Catholic Youth and of the Catholic Nurses' Association. A participant in civic and charitable activity, he became Director of Catholic Charities.

St. Edward's University of Austin, Texas, took note of the accomplishments of Monsignor Danglmayr and conferred upon him the honorary Doctor of Laws degree on 28 May 1939. In December 1941 Bishop Lynch appointed him Vicar General or administrative deputy of the Diocese of Dallas. As the Second World War broke upon the United States a higher recognition was yet to come from the Vatican.

Pope Pius XII appointed the Vicar General of the Diocese of Dallas to the rank of Titular Bishop of Olba and Auxiliary Bishop of Dallas on 26 April 1942. His episcopal consecration took place in Sacred Heart Cathedral on the following 7 October. It was performed by Archbishop (later Cardinal) Amleto Giovanni Cicognani, the Apostolic Delegate to the United States. He was assisted by Bishop Joseph P. Lynch of Dallas and by Auxiliary Bishop William D. O'Brien of Chicago.

And now Bishop Danglmayr was made to realize the extent to which the hierarchy of the Church and the people of the Diocese appreciated the love and devotion he had so generously expended on their behalf. All bishops and abbots wear a pectoral cross on a chain around their necks and over their breasts as a mark of their office. Bishop Lynch presented his new auxiliary and devoted assistant of twenty years the cross which he himself had received on his own consecration as bishop thirty-one years before. It was set with pearls on a chain formerly worn by Bishop Lynch's predecessor, Bishop Edward Dunne.

Bishop Danglmayr was given a second pectoral cross set with rubies, worn by the late Monsignor Bernard H. Diamond, his predecessor as Vicar General. It had been bestowed on Monsignor Diamond by Bishop Lynch when Diamond became Protonotary Apostolic. The new bishop was then given Bishop Lynch's own amethyst bishop's ring, which he had received from the hand of Pope Pius XI while on a visit to the Vatican in 1925. The parishioners of the Cathedral presented the crosier or bishop's staff, which symbolizes his pastoral office, responsibility, and authority. It was adorned with medallions of St. Augustine for his name, of St. Theresa for his mother's name, of the Sacred Heart for his cathedral, and of the Blessed Mother and St. Joseph.

The new bishop took as his motto an expression from St. Augustine's *The City of God*, "Cor ad Cor Loquitur" ["Heart speaks to heart"]. It was noted upon his consecration that he was the fifth native-born Texan to be elevated to the episcopacy. And he was the first to work in the Diocese where he was born, reared, and labored as a priest. The City of Dallas tendered him a reception in the luxurious Hotel Adolphus.

During the war years Bishop Danglmayr served as a public member of the regional War Labor Board. He continued to serve Bishop Lynch until his death in 1954 and thereafter his successor Bishop Gorman. On 20 October 1953 the Diocese of Dallas was redesignated the Diocese of Dallas-Fort Worth. On 26 February 1954 Bishop Danglmayr was appointed founding pastor of St. Monica's Parish in Dallas. He retired as Pastor in 1962 and moved back to Muenster. On

27 August 1969 after the establishment of the separate Diocese of Fort Worth the Diocese of Dallas-Fort Worth once again became the Diocese of Dallas. In that year Bishop Danglmayr retired as auxiliary bishop. His hometown is now a part of the Fort Worth Diocese.

On the tenth of June 1982, the sixtieth anniversary of his priestly ordination, the former Chancellor of the Diocese of Dallas returned to the Chancery at 3915 Lemmon Avenue. He had now been bishop for forty years. That day he offered Mass as the Bishop Danglmayr Assembly Fourth Degree Knights of Columbus stood in attendance. Monsignor Hubert Neu, whom the Bishop had ordained, gave the first reading. Nieces of the Bishop constructed an altar banner, nephews were ushers, and great-nephews served at Mass.

At the reception following in the Sacred Heart Community Center dinner was provided for the honoree and his guests. Nieces and nephews planned and provided table decorations, while nieces served the catered dinner, designed the anniversary cake, arranged a display table of the bishop's activities, and presided at the guest book. Right Reverend Abbot Alfred Hoenig of Corpus Christi gave the invocation. Bishop Tschoepe of Dallas addressed the group, and Bishop Delaney of Fort Worth gave the closing prayer. Former Bishop Cassata of Fort Worth also attended, as did a number of clergy, religious, and other friends.

Perhaps more importantly and to make his day complete, Bishop Danglmayr greeted the living presence of his surviving brothers Joe and Albert and his sisters, Theresa (Mrs. Felderhoff), and Bertha (Mrs. Fleitman). He thanked his brothers and sisters and especially his nieces and nephews for a "job well done."

In his formal statement the Bishop remarked:

> I am grateful for a long life. . . .I am residing in a new house of my own design, on land contiguous to the old homestead where all of us eight children were born.
>
> I am surrounded by brothers and sisters, their children and spouses, all of whom are interested in and of valued assistance to an old man.
>
> So, I'm happy in my retirement, and am enjoying my home and life in the country.

Muenster was dear to Bishop Danglmayr. His grandparents immigrated here from Germany and Czechoslovakia in the 1890s. He was the second child in a family of eight children, and he attended school in a one-room country schoolhouse. For a time he continued to minister at Muenster Memorial Hospital and in area nursing homes until an accident in 1985 confined him to his home on Route 2.

Bishop Danglmayr, whose name in English means "scythe edge," died at home in Muenster on 18 September 1992. At the time of his death he was thought to be the oldest bishop in the United States. He had lived to celebrate the seventieth anniversary of his priestly ordination. Funeral Mass was said for him in Dallas on 21 September and in Muenster the following day, in his beloved Sacred Heart Church. He was buried in Sacred Heart Cemetery in Muenster. His survivors included his brothers Albert and Joe R. and his sister Mrs. Bertha Fleitman, with twenty-eight nieces and nephews. Bishop Grahmann of

Dallas said of him: "We are saddened by the death of our brother bishop. His contributions to the Diocese of Dallas were many, and his seventy years of service as a priest were a gift to all of us."

Bishop Thomas Tschoepe paid his final tribute, one that seems to fit Bishop Danglmayr: "He was a kind, loving person. He was proud that he was a priest and that he could help people." Truly, "Heart speaks to heart."

Most Reverend Lawrence Michael DeFalco, DD
Fifth Bishop of Amarillo

Born in McKeesport, Allegheny County, Pennsylvania, on 25 August 1915, Lawrence Michael DeFalco was the eldest of nine children born to Rosario and Margaret (Desmone) DeFalco. He graduated from McKeesport High School in 1933, after which he entered Saint Vincent College in Latrobe, Westmoreland County, Pennsylvania. Founded in 1846, Saint Vincent is a coeducational college operated under Benedictine auspices with a little over one thousand students.

Lawrence left Saint Vincent after two years without a degree in 1935 and enrolled in St. John's Mission Seminary in Little Rock, Arkansas, where he remained for seven years. The Reverend Mister DeFalco was ordained by Bishop John B. Morris of Little Rock, for the Diocese of Dallas, on 11 June 1942.

For the first ten years of his priestly life Father DeFalco was Assistant Pastor of St. Patrick's Parish in Fort Worth, Texas (1942-1952), and thereafter Assistant Pastor of Sacred Heart Cathedral in Dallas, Texas (1952). For the next three years he served as Vice-Chancellor and Procurator-Advocate for the Diocese of Dallas, earning the degree of Licentiate in Canon Law (JCL) from the Pontifical Gregorian University in Rome in 1955.

The degree of Licentiate in Canon Law prepares the student for the professional practice of church administration, tribunals, and in teaching and research. It provides the student with skill in legal interpretation and gives one a knowledge of historical, theological, and sociological factors in its development and the means to apply it in pastoral situations.

Admission to the degree program requires a bachelor's degree or its equivalent and a master's degree in theology or its equivalent in the course of study prescribed for priestly ordination. Otherwise about twenty-four credit hours are required in such areas as the fundamentals of canon law, parochial ministry law, ecclesiology, sacramental theology, moral theology with studies in ethics and natural law, canonical Latin, and a modern foreign language useful for canonical research, such as French, German, Italian or Spanish.

The licentiate program itself requires two years for completion and a reading proficiency examination in a modern foreign language. About thirty-six hours in required courses and twelve hours in electives are needed. The required courses consist of the history of canon law, general norms, power of governance, sacramental law, official ministry, consecrated life, matrimony, structures of the particular church, matrimonial jurisprudence, procedural law, the teaching office of the Church, and temporal goods. The student is required to use the Latin text of the Code of Canon Law.

One must also write a dissertation investigating a minor but significant problem to prove familiarity with research, technical mastery of subject matter, and demonstrate an ability to exercise sound judgment and formulate accurate conclusions. A comprehensive examination over the whole body of church law is required.

With the necessary professional education Father DeFalco quickly advanced in his chosen vocation. While continuing as Vice-Chancellor and Procurator-

Advocate in the Diocese of Dallas-Fort Worth until 1963, he now became the Secretary of its Marriage Tribunal from 1955 until 1962. He held the additional posts of Pastor of Our Lady of Perpetual Help Parish in Dallas (1956-1962), membership on the Building Commission (from 1956), Diocesan Councillor and Pro-Synodal Judge (from 1957), and Diocesan Consultor (1958-1963).

Hereafter his rise was rapid. Pope John XXIII appointed Father DeFalco Papal Chamberlain with the title of Right Reverend Monsignor in 1962 and that same year he became Pastor of St. Patrick's Co-cathedral in Fort Worth. He was appointed Bishop of Amarillo in succession to Bishop John L. Morkovsky by John XXIII on 16 April 1963. He was consecrated bishop on the following 30 May and installed in his diocese on 13 June.

Bishop DeFalco began to implement the decrees of Vatican Council II (1962-1965). He established one of the first presbyteral councils in the United States, as well as parish councils, a priests' senate, a diocesan personnel board, and the Diocesan Council of Women Religious. He oversaw the transformation of liturgical worship and the training of eucharistic ministers and permanent deacons. In 1975 Sacred Heart Cathedral was closed and St. Laurence's became the diocesan cathedral.

Illness overtook this promising bishop of Italian descent, whose name in English means "hawk," and he was forced to retire on 28 August 1979. He died soon after on the following 22 September in Amarillo and is buried there in Llano Cemetery.

Most Reverend Joseph Patrick Delaney, DD
Second Bishop of Fort Worth

This capable and scholarly addition to the Texas hierarchy comes from Massachusetts by way of Brownsville. His contributions in education and in diocesan administration have brought him to the attention of the Holy See.

Born in Fall River, Bristol County, Massachusetts, on 29 August 1934 to Joseph and Jane (Burke) Delaney, Joseph Patrick Delaney is one of four sons in a family which also includes a daughter. The future bishop attended the diocesan high school for Fall River operated by the Sisters of the Holy Union of Sacred Hearts. It is located in Taunton and was formerly named Monsignor Coyle High School, but is now known as Coyle and Cassidy High School.

Beginning his priestly studies, young Joseph first attended Cardinal O'Connell Seminary in Boston and then left Massachusetts for the Theological College of the Catholic University of America in Washington, DC. The purpose of Theological College is to prepare diocesan students for priesthood programs of theological instruction and professional pastoral training for ministry and for spiritual formation and readiness for ordination.

Under the Sulpician order of priests, founded by Rev. Jean Jacques Olier in 1641 at Paris, France, each seminarian has one of these specially trained priests as a spiritual director. Spiritual formation is based upon three dynamics. The first dynamic, as expressed by Father Olier, is "To live entirely for God in Christ Jesus," as Jesus is given us through faith and in Word and sacrament. The response to this gift is to have "that same mind which was in Christ Jesus" and to serve others in name and in spirit as the Lord would approve.

The second dynamic derives from reflection on the way priests live and minister. The focus is on the development of a personal spirituality to survive the transition from seminary to priestly ministry. The third dynamic derives from the circumstances of the Theological College with its university atmosphere and the diversity of its students and their programs.

Seminarians complete ordination requirements of scripture, systematics, moral theology, liturgy, history, and canon law. Also included are supervised ministry to the sick, preaching, and celebration.

Joseph Delaney received the degree of Bachelor of Arts from the Catholic University of America in 1956. In the following year the University conferred upon him the degree of Master of Arts. Thereafter he attended the North American College in Rome, Italy, and was ordained there on 18 December 1960, for the Diocese of Fall River.

He continued to remain in Rome after ordination and received the degrees of Bachelor of Sacred Theology and Licentiate in Sacred Theology from the Pontifical Gregorian University in 1961.

Having received his professional education, Father Delaney returned to Fall River. Between 1961 and 1967 he held a variety of positions including those of assistant pastor and high school teacher, and was Diocesan Assistant Superintendent of Schools for the Diocese of Fall River. During this period he received the degree of Master of Education from Rhode Island College in Providence in 1964.

In 1967 Father Delaney became incardinated or affiliated with the Diocese of Brownsville, Texas. For the next fourteen years he took an active part in the affairs of that diocese. He first served as assistant pastor in parishes in Pharr and McAllen in Hidalgo County, and was later Pastor of Christ the King Parish and Pastor of the Church of the Good Shepherd in Brownsville in Cameron County.

His education and experience also fitted him for a variety of posts in diocesan administration. He was a member of the Marriage Tribunal and Pro-Synodal Judge from 1968 to 1971, Co-Chancellor from 1971 to 1979, and Chancellor from 1979 to 1981. He was also Chief Judge of the Marriage Tribunal (1971-1974) and was Diocesan Consultor and Officialis or curial officer (1974-1978). In addition he was Diocesan Superintendent of Schools.

His efforts came to the attention of the Holy See, and he was appointed Bishop of Fort Worth in succession to Bishop Cassata by Pope John Paul II on 10 July 1981. He received episcopal ordination from his metropolitan Archbishop Patrick F. Flores of San Antonio at Tarrant County Convention Center in Fort Worth on 13 September 1981.

Coming directly from a Diocese in which over sixty percent of the population is Catholic to one in which only seven percent is Catholic would present a challenge to any clergyman. However, this is no burden for a bishop of Irish descent whose name in English means "challenger" and whose episcopal motto is "Praised Be Jesus Christ."

On New Years' Day 1994 Bishop Delaney had a Catholic population of 175,087 in a total population of 2,168,900 in his twenty-eighth county diocese of some 23,950 square miles. There was a total of 119 priests, forty-nine permanent deacons, fourteen male religious, and 108 women religious to assist the bishop. During the past year one seminarian was ordained for the priesthood and fourteen seminarians studied for ordination. The Diocese of Fort Worth had eighty-four parishes and three missions. There were two Catholic hospitals assisting 136,406 people and four homes for the aged with 400 inhabitants. Three residential facilities aided 360 children, and three specialized homes helped ninety people. There were four high schools and thirteen elementary schools, with a total of 25,116 students under Catholic instruction and 329 teachers in the Diocese. In the past year (1993) 4,392 were received into the Church, and there were 1,120 marriages and 954 deaths.

In June 1995 a situation occurred in the Diocese of Fort Worth that was a new experience for Bishop Delaney after fourteen years in office. A man confronted church officials of the Diocese with a problem. He alleged that in 1957, when he was twelve-years-old, Father William Hoover of St. James Catholic Church in the Oak Cliff section of Dallas had molested him. Father Hoover had been the pastor of St. Patrick's Cathedral in Fort Worth since 1987 and was now sixty-four years old.

A special committee representing the Diocese met with the man and then told his account to Father Hoover, who confirmed the accusations. He resigned his position as of 26 June and left for a time of psychological testing. His status was indefinite leave of absence.

Bishop Delaney met with about 500 of the cathedral parishioners on 2 July 1995 and read a brief statement explaining Father Hoover's resignation. The policy of the Diocese requires full disclosure. The Bishop did not know whether legal action would arise out of the situation. Meanwhile the victim discussed the matter on a broadcast over television station KXAS-TV in Fort Worth on 6 July. A standing committee in Dallas will also investigate the incident. In the Diocese of Dallas several people had sued Father Rudolph Kos, a priest of that diocese, over alleged sexual abuse said to have taken place between 1977 and 1992. Father Kos was suspended from the active priesthood in 1993.

Active in the state and national church, Bishop Delaney is a member of the Texas Catholic Conference, the Texas Conference of Churches, and has served as a board member of the National Pastoral Planning Conference. He has also been a member of the Administrative Board of the National Conference of Catholic Bishops (NCCB) and is a member of the United States Catholic Conference (USCC). In 1987 he was given the chairmanship of the NCCB Committee on the Liturgy.

Most Reverend Arthur Jerome Drossaerts, DD, LLD
Fifth Bishop and First Archbishop of San Antonio

One of the most appealing figures in the Catholic hierarchy of Texas is the Dutch Arthur Jerome Drossaerts, a quiet scholar and holy man. He was so self-effacing that he refused to accept any salary as archbishop and could not afford his own funeral. This thoughtful prelate, who loved to read and to collect clocks, spoke Dutch, English, Spanish, French, German, and Latin, and had a working knowledge of Greek and Hebrew. He loved his adopted country and state, and he was loved in return for his devotion to those he served.

Born in Breda, Province of North Brabant, The Netherlands, on 11 September 1862, Arthur Jerome was the son of Cornelius and Sophie (de Fraiture) Drossaerts. He attended St. Michael's School in Gestel and later the Diocesan Seminary of Haaren in Brandt, where he received the degrees of Doctor of Divinity and Doctor of Laws. He completed his priestly formation in the Diocesan Seminary of Bois le Duc and was ordained by its bishop Adrian Gottschalk in the Cathedral of St. John the Apostle in the provincial capital of Hertogenbosch on 15 June 1889.

In 1890 Father Drossaerts answered the call of the Dutch-born Archbishop Francis A. Janssens of New Orleans to come to America. His first assignment was Pastor of Immaculate Conception Church and Mission in Lake Charles, Calcasieu Parish, Louisiana. This parish church later became the Cathedral of the Diocese of Lake Charles in 1980.

In 1892 Father Drossaerts moved to New Orleans as the Pastor of the St. Vincent de Paul Church, which was founded in 1838. Here he remained for twelve years before becoming Pastor of Sacred Heart of Jesus Church in Broussard, Lafayette Parish, Louisiana. It was to become part of the Diocese of Lafayette in 1918.

It was in his last priestly assignment that Father Drossaerts came into his own. As Pastor of St. Joseph's Parish in Baton Rouge in 1911, he became upon acceptance Canon of the Cathedral Chapter, Rural Dean, and Archdiocesan Consultor. His church, founded in 1792, became the Cathedral of the Diocese of Baton Rouge on its creation in 1961.

He was appointed Bishop of San Antonio by Pope Benedict XV on 18 July 1918 in succession to Bishop Shaw, who left to become Archbishop of New Orleans. The fifty-five year old Dutchman, whose name in English means "throttle," took for his episcopal motto the pledge of service, "All things to all men."

His episcopal consecration was performed by Archbishop (later Cardinal) Giovanni Bonzano, Apostolic Delegate to the United States, in St. Louis Cathedral in New Orleans on 8 December 1918. He had as co-consecrators the Dutch Bishop Cornelius Van de Ven of Alexandria, Louisiana, and the Belgian Bishop Theophile Meerschaert of Oklahoma City. It was the forty-fourth anniversary of the consecration of the first Bishop of San Antonio Anthony Pellicer.

As Bishop of San Antonio Drossaerts' first important decision was to restore the Bishop's Residence on Dwyer Avenue as his home and chancery and to transfer St. John's Seminary to a temporary location on Rigsby Avenue. Plans were made for the erection of a new seminary building adjoining Mission Conception.

The following year of 1919 Bishop Drossaerts set out with vigor to make needed changes. He reorganized the chancery staff, erected two new parishes in San Antonio, and solemnly blessed San Fernando Cemetery on Cupples Road. In addition to the usual business of the Diocese he administered the Sacrament of Confirmation in sixty churches. The Sisters of Charity of the Incarnate Word celebrated their golden jubilee in the Diocese this year, while Benedictine and Dominican Sisters were welcomed into it.

The 1920s were busy years. St. John's Seminary was dedicated on 25 November 1920 in the presence of Archbishop John W. Shaw of New Orleans, who founded it and now officiated at the ceremony of dedication. Today the Assumption-St. John's Seminary is located at 2600 West Woodlawn Avenue and is the residence of the Archbishop of San Antonio.

Bishop Drossaerts convened the third Diocesan Synod in San Fernando Cathedral on 24 November 1921. Such a meeting of priests, religious, and lay people is important in the life of a diocese. Its purpose is to consider and then act upon matters affecting the life and mission of the Church. Only a bishop has power to turn synodal decrees into law. Today it is expected that a synod should be called every ten years. But at this time it was a grand and formal occasion. The fourth such meeting for San Antonio was an archdiocesan synod, presided over by Archbishop Drossaerts in 1930. The last general event in the history of the Diocese of San Antonio was the celebration of its golden jubilee on 7 September 1924, when Masses of thanksgiving were celebrated in all the churches and chapels of the area.

The Church in Texas was now coming of age. By 1915 it was organized into the Dioceses of Galveston (1847), San Antonio (1874), Dallas (1890), Corpus Christi (1913), and El Paso (1915). By 1925 there were 800,000 Catholics in the State. The Diocese of El Paso was the suffragan of Santa Fe and the other four dioceses were suffragans of New Orleans. It was time for the erection of a Metropolitan See within the State to serve the needs of the faithful of Texas.

Archbishop John W. Shaw of New Orleans believed that he could no longer effectively control an area so large as Texas. Archbishop Albert T. Daeger, OFM, of Santa Fe could continue to care only for the Diocese of El Paso. The matter was referred to the Consistorial Congregation of Cardinals, where it awaited the decision of the Holy Father.

Pope Pius XI issued the Bull *Pastoris Aeterni* on 3 August 1926. This most formal papal document, with the leaden seal or the imprint of its device called in Latin *bulla*, promoted the Diocese of San Antonio to an archdiocese and created an ecclesiastical province making the Cathedral a Metropolitan Church. The province would include the dioceses of Texas (except El Paso), the new Diocese of Amarillo created at the same time as the Province of San Antonio, and the State of Oklahoma.

Not until 6 February 1973, when Pope Paul VI created the Province of Oklahoma City for the States of Oklahoma and Arkansas, would the metropolitan of San Antonio be free to administer the dioceses in his own state alone. On 12 April 1983 Pope John Paul II joined the Diocese of El Paso (minus its former

New Mexican counties) to the Province of San Antonio. At present the Province of San Antonio contains only the State of Texas, including the Dioceses of Austin (1947), San Angelo (1961), Brownsville (1965), Beaumont (1966), Victoria (1982), Lubbock (1983), and Tyler (1986) created since the establishment of this province.

The final effect of *Pastoris Aeterni* was to appoint Bishop Drossaerts the new archbishop. When the news was received in San Antonio in September 1926, it was greeted with general approval by all. It was a vote of confidence in a shepherd who had built sixty new churches and fifty schools with a value at that time of eight million dollars.

As Carlos E. Castañeda says in *Our Catholic Heritage in Texas*: "The ceremonies attendant upon the erection of the new archdiocese and the investiture and installation of Archbishop Drossaerts outrivaled in splendor and genuine fervor any other civil or ecclesiastical function ever witnessed in the old city of the Alamo" (7:155). Although the formal erection of the Diocese of Amarillo on 25 August 1926 decreased the size of the Archdiocese by about 21,000 square miles, together with parts of the Dallas and El Paso Dioceses, there was no rain on the parade of the new archbishop.

Three days of celebration were needed to comprehend the event. On the first day of Tuesday, 15 February 1927, a civic reception was held at the Municipal Auditorium in San Antonio attended by officials of the state and city, the hierarchy of Texas and Oklahoma, representatives of the clergy, and "countless admirers of the kindly, beaming honoree," whose joy was almost inexpressible. In all about 6,000 people attended.

Reverend Mariano S. Garriga, Pastor of St. Cecilia's Parish in San Antonio and Vice-Rector of St. John's Seminary, acted as master of ceremonies. Within ten years he would become the first native Texan to enter the Texas hierarchy as Auxiliary Bishop of Corpus Christi. He introduced Lieutenant Governor Barry Miller, who represented Governor Dan Moody of Texas on this occasion. Governor Miller praised the Archbishop, declaring that he deserved his high honor "by fighting for the basic principles of democratic government and the right to civil and religious freedom." Nat Washer representing the laity commended the Archbishop's "self-sacrificing devotion."

On this august occasion four archbishops were present: Albert T. Daeger, OFM, of Santa Fe, John J. Glennon of St. Louis, John W. Shaw of New Orleans, and Peter J. Hurth, CSP, of Bosnia, India, residing at St. Edward's University in Austin, Texas. Archbishop Shaw, a former bishop of San Antonio, rose to confess he felt Texas was too big not to have its own ecclesiastical province, though he would miss the "smiling friendly faces" of the bishops of Texas at his provincial council meetings.

Bishop Francis C. Kelley of Oklahoma, founder and director of the Catholic Extension Society until 1924, offered congratulations and noted his pleasure in having Oklahoma become part of the new province. Archbishop Glennon ended his remarks with this declaration: "The Catholic Church is dedicated to justice and liberty, and its children are ready to make the same sacrifice today as the men of the Alamo made in giving their lives for the same principles."

Almost overwhelmed with thankfulness, the sixty-four year old Archbishop Drossaerts expressed his gratitude in his characteristic way: "I can say in all sincerity that I never dreamed I would someday be a bishop, much less that I would become the first archbishop of the province of San Antonio." He insisted that his happiness heretofore had been the dream of being "in a little nook with a little book" as a "country pastor." The applause was almost deafening when he concluded that the honor would bring heavy responsibilities and personal sacrifices, but "At least we are assured of home rule in Texas. Texas is too big not to have a province of its own, it is time we were paddling our own canoe."

On the following day of Wednesday, 16 February 1927, the four archbishops and fourteen bishops and a multitude of the faithful presented themselves at San Fernando Cathedral for the formal installation of the new archbishop. The procession marched into the Cathedral through streets that led to Main and Military Plazas. The *Ecce Sacérdos* ["Behold the Priest"] and the proper of the Mass was sung by exiled seminarians from Zacatecas in Mexico, from whence had come Antonio Margil, builder of San José Mission.

At this Pontifical Mass of installation Archbishop (later Cardinal) Pietro Fumasoni-Biondi, the Apostolic Delegate to the United States, brought the pallium, symbol of the archepiscopal office, from Rome. Bishop Christopher Byrne of Galveston, who preached the sermon, explained its significance. Originally reported in the special Installation Edition of *The Southern Messenger* of 17 February 1927, Castañeda in *Our Catholic Heritage in Texas* describes the Bishop's comments concerning the pallium as follows:

> The *palliums* [sic] is a band of finely woven virgin wool about two inches wide worn over breast and shoulders. It is decorated with six crosses which fall one each on breast and back, one on each shoulder and one on each of the two pendants. The *pallium* is worn over the chasuble. The wool of which the *pallium* is made comes from lambs presented (two annually) by the canons of St. John Lateran on the Feast of St. Angus [Agnes] (January 21) to the Pope who blesses and gives them to the nuns of St. Cecilia. At Easter these lambs are shorn and the wool given to the Holy Father for *palliums* [sic], which are blessed and finished and placed in a silver urn, kept near the tomb of St. Peter (7:157 n.96).

On 20 July 1978 Pope Paul VI issued the document *Inter Eximia Episcopalis* restricting the use of the pallium to the pope and archbishops of metropolitan sees. In 1984 Pope John Paul II decreed that the pallium would ordinarily be conferred on metropolitans by the pope on the solemnity of Sts. Peter and Paul.

Immediately after the Pontifical Mass Archbishop Shaw placed the pallium upon the shoulders of his former suffragan, symbolizing his new dignity and authority and indicating by this act the transfer of ecclesiastical jurisdiction. Archbishop Drossaerts was sure that San Fernando Cathedral had never witnessed such a scene when he observed:

> I see gathered around me four archbishops, fourteen bishops, a host of abbots and monsignori, including the special representative of His Eminence Cardinal Hayes [of New York], and hundreds upon hundreds of clergy, the high dignitaries of state, county, and city, in addition to my innumerable friends.

A banquet in the historic Menger Hotel followed the investiture when Governor Moody, unable to attend the reception on the previous evening, congratulated the new archbishop and the Church on its choice. Brigadier General Paul D. Malone spoke on "Our Country and Our Flag."

On the third and final day of the celebration, Thursday, 17 February 1927, Archbishop Drossaerts offered a Pontifical Mass in Municipal Auditorium for six to seven thousand school children. A choir of 1,500 voices composed of students from colleges, academies, and parish schools under the direction of Rev. (later Monsignor) James T. Lockwood sang the *Missa de Anqelis* ["Mass of the Angels"].

Archbishop Drossaerts proved to be no less effective in his new role. He made the archdiocese a haven for refugees from religious persecution in Mexico, including men and women religious, priests, and bishops. The Apostolic Delegate to Mexico, Archbishop Ruiz y Flores, was his personal guest. He saw that more than $21,000 was collected for the relief of victims of the persecution. For these activities the Archbishop was named Assistant to the Pontifical Throne and a Papal Count by Pope Pius XI on 19 August 1934.

Preservation of the old Spanish missions in the San Antonio area was another item on the archbishop's agenda. Between 1928 and 1937 the Mission of San José was restored and rededicated on 18 April 1937. On 5 March 1931 Archbishop Albert T. Daeger, OFM, of Santa Fe celebrated the bicentennial of the founding of San Antonio and of three of the historic missions with a military field Mass behind the Cathedral. Cardinal Patrick Hayes of New York presided, attended by fourteen visiting bishops, hundreds of clergy, and military guests.

Archbishop Drossaerts was also mindful of the future. On 24 November 1929 he dedicated the combined St. Peter's-St. Joseph's Children's Home. But the heroic past of his adopted state thrilled him. He seemed to relish occasions when he could combine the ceremony of the Church with the historic memory of the State of Texas. Such an event was the centennial of the Fall of the Alamo on 6 March 1936.

The Archbishop celebrated it with a pontifical field Mass before the Alamo attended by some 20,000 persons. From his point of view the day was a complete success. The entry for his daybook states:

> At night, after the flag's presentation, I was host at the St. Anthony Hotel, to the bishops and governors of Texas and Tennessee and a few of the more prominent citizens. Our celebration was an honor to Mother Church and many most favorable comments were heard from all sides.

He also arranged for the presumed bones of the Alamo heroes to be exhumed from under the main altar of the Cathedral and placed in a marble sarcophagus within it.

Nor did the Archbishop neglect current events. He was present at the St. Anthony Hotel at 300 East Travis Street at the reception for President Franklin D. Roosevelt on 11 June 1936 and at the laying of the cornerstone of the Post Office and Federal Building at 615 East Houston Street four days later.

Archbishop Drossaerts welcomed many new religious communities of men and women into the archdiocese. He built some 134 churches, some fifty schools, and forty-one new parishes between 1918 and 1940, as well as other institutions. He urged that the Holy Name and the St. Vincent de Paul societies be established in every parish.

The love of the Archbishop for the pageantry of the Church continued into his last years. He consecrated Monsignor Mariano S. Garriga Titular Bishop of Syene and Coadjutor (with right of succession) to Bishop Ledvina of Corpus Christi in San Fernando Cathedral on 21 September 1936. In this centennial year of the Independence of Texas this ceremony marked the entrance of the first native Texan into the Texas hierarchy.

The Archbishop celebrated his golden sacerdotal jubilee with a solemn pontifical Mass in the Municipal Auditorium on 18 October 1939. This occasion, marking the fiftieth anniversary of his priestly ordination, was attended by a capacity of priests, seminarians, and school students of the archdiocese.

The last ceremony of these ecclesiastical spectaculars so beloved of the Archbishop was the consecration of the Texan Sidney M. Metzger as Titular Bishop of Birtha and Auxiliary Bishop of Santa Fe in San Fernando Cathedral on 10 April 1940.

Death came at last for the Archbishop on 8 September 1940 at Santa Rosa Hospital in San Antonio, three days short of his seventy-eighth birthday. His body was taken to the Cathedral, which had played such an important role in his life. There it lay in state until it was removed to the Municipal Auditorium where Bishop Byrne performed a last office for his metropolitan by offering a pontifical requiem Mass on 12 September. Burial followed in the priests' plot in the San Fernando Archdiocesan Cemetery.

Thus lived and died the last bishop and first archbishop of San Antonio. His wish for peace and quiet as a country pastor may never have been realized. But when he was called upon to play a larger role, he mounted the stage with an enthusiasm and a sense of history. He combined love of the Church with the love of his adopted State of Texas to such a degree that he wrote a new page in the annals of both.

Most Reverend Thomas Joseph Drury, DD, LHD
First Bishop of San Angelo
Fourth Bishop of Corpus Christi

Bishop Drury was a native-born Irishman who knew the United States and Texas well. A priest of the Diocese of Amarillo, he became bishop of the dioceses of San Angelo and of Corpus Christi. He served as a military chaplain and was honored for his contributions to journalism and to education. He was successful in each and every project in which he took part.

Born in County Sligo, Ireland, on 3 January 1908 [see below], Thomas Joseph was the son of Michael and Margaret (Lannon) Drury. He came to the United States in 1926 and went to live with a sister in St. Louis, Missouri. At the age of eighteen he attended St. Benedict's College at Atchison in northeastern Kansas. Here he remained in this Benedictine institution until 1929. It merged with Mount St. Scholastica in 1971 and is known today as Benedictine College with an enrollment of about one thousand students. He received the degree of Bachelor of Arts from Kenrick Seminary in St. Louis, Missouri, in 1931. He was ordained to the priesthood by Bishop (later Archbishop) Robert E. Lucey in Sacred Heart Cathedral, Amarillo, for the Diocese of Amarillo, on 2 June 1935.

Father Drury was assistant pastor and pastor of the then Sacred Heart Cathedral in Amarillo from 1935 until 1945. In his first year he was secretary of the Matrimonial Court, a tribunal he later assisted as Promoter of Justice (1938) and Defender of the Bond (1939). In 1936 he became diocesan director of the Confraternity of Christian Doctrine and of the Society for the Propagation of the Faith. He was also involved in Catholic Action and in the Holy Name Society and was chairman of the Amarillo council of the Boy Scouts of America. He was vice-president of the Amarillo Catholic Welfare Board and in 1938 held membership on the Diocesan Administrative Board.

Between 1936 and 1938 he was founder, editor, and business manager of the Diocesan newspaper, the *Texas Panhandle Register* (now the *West Texas Catholic*). This effort was the beginning of a lifelong interest in press journalism. Father Drury exchanged his cassock for the uniform of the United States Army Air Force (USAAF) from 1945 to 1947, seeing duty in Washington, Florida, and in Guam. Upon leaving the service, he was transferred to the Archdiocese of San Antonio. He returned to active duty in the Chaplains' Corps, this time in the United States Air Force (USAF), from 1949 to 1955, attaining the rank of Major. On his tour of duty he was stationed in Greenland.

Returning from the armed forces, Father Drury was Pastor of St. Elizabeth University and Christ the King parishes in Lubbock between 1956 and 1961. On 16 October 1961 he was appointed bishop of the newly-created Diocese of San Angelo.

In his own words:

> During October, 1961, I was in the midst of a building program that, today [1985], is the Cathedral complex in Lubbock. I received, in the mail, a letter, from the Office of the Apostolic Delegate in Washington, D.C., stating that it was the intention of the Holy Fa-

> ther (Pope John XXIII) to establish San Angelo as a new See and that I was chosen to become its first bishop. The letter directed that, if I accepted, I should reply, by telegram, with a code message: 'seven years in the military Chaplaincy.' It further stated that my lips were sealed until the announcement could be made at a later date and that I was free to discuss the matter with my own Ordinary - then Bishop John L. Morkovsky [of Amarillo, to which diocese Drury had returned in 1955]. Because the Bishop was out of the Diocese at the time, I had to arrive at a decision on my own. This I did and, in the early part of November, the news was out.

The formal erection of the Diocese was performed by Archbishop Robert E. Lucey of San Antonio on 23 January 1962, assisted by Bishop Morkovsky of Amarillo. Archbishop Lucey also presided at the consecration of Bishop Drury, again assisted by Bishop Morkovsky, at the Cathedral of the Sacred Heart (a newly constructed church) in San Angelo at 10:00 A.M. on the following day of 24 January 1962.

The Diocese of San Angelo started from scratch. The chancery office was a two-story building adjacent to the Cathedral. The new bishop was given temporary lodging in St. John's Hospital, operated by the San Antonio-Based Sisters of Charity of the Incarnate Word. Some time later the Bishop received the use of a house on four acres of land, a ten-minute drive from the Chancery. It was sold during the tenure of Bishop Joseph A. Fiorenza (1979 to 1984).

On its establishment the Diocese had 42,000 square miles with thirty-four counties taken from the dioceses of Amarillo, El Paso, Austin, and Dallas. The Catholic population was 47,561 out of 600,000 people. There were thirty-one diocesan priests and thirty-two religious with thirty-five parishes and thirty-five missions attached to parish churches. Two high schools had an attendance of sixty-three students.

By 1 January 1994 the Diocese had 37,433 square miles with twenty-nine counties. The Catholic population was more than 78,000 with more than 674,000 people. There were fifty-two diocesan and twenty-three religious order priests and forty-five women religious with forty-nine parishes and twenty-four missions. The high schools were closed.

In 1962 the Diocese of San Angelo contained Franciscans, Missionary Oblates of Mary Immaculate, Redemptorists, and Immaculate Heart of Mary Missionaries. Women religious came from the orders of the Incarnate Word and Divine Providence in San Antonio and Our Lady of Victory from Indiana. The National Conference of Catholic Bishops and the Catholic Church Extension Society provided "seed money" to repair and construct buildings and to serve the needs of parishes and missions.

Bishop Drury appealed to Cardinal Albert Mayer of Chicago, Cardinal Francis Spellman of New York, and to Bishop Bryan McEntegart of Brooklyn for aid. Bishop Nold of Galveston-Houston and Bishop Thomas Gorman of Dallas-Fort Worth allowed him to administer the Sacrament of Confirmation in their areas. It is customary to provide the confirming bishop with expenses. There is no fee, of course, for the administration of the Sacrament itself.

In addition to building up the staff, facilities, and institutions of the Diocese, Bishop Drury was in Rome about two months during the years 1962 to

1965 to attend sessions of Vatican Council II. He founded the *Texas Concho Register*, now the *West Texas Angelus*, as the diocesan newspaper in 1962. On 19 July 1965 Pope Paul VI transferred Bishop Drury to the Diocese of Corpus Christi. He was installed as bishop in Corpus Christi Cathedral on the following 1 September. In his first year he founded the *Gulf Coast Catholic Register* (now the *South Texas Catholic*) in 1965.

When Bishop Drury retired on 19 May 1983 the 17,294 square miles of the Diocese of Corpus Christi contained some 180,000 Catholics with thirty schools, seventy-six parishes, forty-five missions, two hospitals, two children's homes, four monasteries, a home for the aged and forty-one convents.

After his retirement Bishop Drury was honored for his services to the Catholic press during the Southern Regional Catholic Press Association conference held at Corpus Christi between the thirteenth and fifteenth of October 1983. Rev. Norman Muckerman, CSSR, President of the Catholic Press Association and Editor of the *Liquorian* magazine, presented a hand-lettered certificate to the Bishop. He in turn recounted his experiences in founding the diocesan newspapers of Amarillo, San Angelo, and Corpus Christi.

On 2 February 1987 Bishop Drury received the honorary degree of Doctor of Humane Letters (LHD) from Incarnate Word College in San Antonio, Texas. It was in honor of his contributions to education and the Catholic Church in Texas during the twenty-fifth anniversary of his episcopal ordination.

In after years Bishop Drury moved to Sea Girt, Monmouth County, New Jersey, about fifty miles south of New York City, to be near family members. In mid-July 1992 he suffered a heart attack and died on 22 July in a New Jersey hospital. Monsignor Robert E. Freeman, a vicar general of the Corpus Christi diocese, said a funeral Mass for the Bishop and acted as homilist on 24 July. On the following day Msgr. Richard Shirley, chancellor under Bishop Drury and pastor of St. Pius X Parish in Corpus Christi, said a second funeral Mass. Later that day, after a funeral Mass in Corpus Christi Cathedral, the body of Bishop Drury was entombed in the crypt of the Emmanuel Chapel of the Cathedral.

The *South Texas Catholic* noted that when Bishop Drury came to Corpus Christi in 1965 he prohibited discussion of his age. Official documents listed his birth date as 1908. But after his death family members said his correct birth date was 1902, Father Roger Smith, who was ordained by the Bishop in 1976 and who was with him when he died, offered an explanation. According to Father Smith, Bishop Drury wanted to serve as a military chaplain but feared his age would have prevented him. So he had his birth certificate changed. As Father Smith put it, "Once that was done, there was no going back. What he did was wrong, but he had very high motives."

Joe Michael Feist, editor of the *Texas Catholic* and onetime editor of the *South Texas Catholic*, remembered the Bishop was not afraid of being controversial and had a good journalistic sense. He was a man of enormous energy, a fast driver who was always in a hurry to be somewhere. Mister Feist recalls Bishop Drury as an Irishman's Irishman, who spoke with a brogue, had twinkling eyes, and cared about Irish nationalism, the color green, St. Patrick, and shamrocks. Feist's tribute to the Bishop, "He was a human being, not perfect by any means, but faithful to his calling," fits a man whose name in English means "darling one" and whose motto was "Deo Servire Resnare" ["To Serve God Is To Rule"].

Right Reverend Claude Marie Dubuis, DD
Second Bishop of Galveston
Titular Archbishop of Arca

The French Bishop Claude Marie Dubuis belongs to an heroic period of the State of Texas. In the early days of statehood the Catholic Church in Texas became established in its present form. A bishop like Dubuis could not just serve existing institutions. He had to create them. A lesser man might have failed to preach the Gospel in the circumstances which this bishop faced daily. His story is one of mind and will overcoming adversity, and he worthily followed the founder of the Texas hierarchy, his fellow countryman John M. Odin.

Born near Teche, Coutouvre, in the Department of Loire, France, on 8 March 1817, Claude Marie was the fifth of eight children born to Francois and Antoinette (Dubost) Dubuis. Because of family poverty, young Claude was taught at home by his mother. He did not receive his First Holy Communion until the age of ten on 12 May 1827. Despite this late start when most contemporary children have received the Sacrament at the age of seven or eight, the boy showed an early disposition for the priesthood.

Fortunately, Antoinette Dubuis had a brother, the Abbe Dubost, the Vicar of Violay, who taught his nephew Latin and other pre-seminary requirements between 1827 and 1832. With this preparation the boy was able to enter the Ecclesiastical Institute l'Argentier at Rhône and later the Petit Seminaire of St. Jodard in the Loire Department from 1832 until 1840. For the next four years he studied at the Grand Seminaire in Lyon. Here he received the clerical tonsure and minor orders (1841), as well as the orders of Subdeacon (21 May 1842) and Deacon (10 June 1843).

The Reverend Monsieur Dubuis was ordained a priest by Cardinal Archbishop Louis Maurice de Bonald of Lyon in Lyon on 1 June 1844. Thereafter, for almost two years, Father Dubuis was Vicar of the Parish of St. Martin-de-Fontaine in Lyon. On the historic day of 19 February 1846, when the flag of the Republic of Texas was lowered and the American flag raised in its place, Claude Dubuis answered the missionary call of Bishop John M. Odin and set out for Texas on the ship *Elizabeth Ellen*.

Arriving in New Orleans on the following 20 March, the young missionary proceeded to Vincentian College in Perry County, Missouri. He reached this station in May and, in company with eight other priests and three future Ursuline Sisters, he studied English to prepare for his future service in Texas.

It was not until December 1846 that Father Dubuis left Missouri for Texas. He endured the collision of his steamer with a schooner and the perils of a Gulf storm before he crossed from New Orleans to Galveston. When he arrived on 4 January 1847, there were 25,000 Catholics in the State. He celebrated his first Mass in Texas in the soon-to-be See city of Galveston in a leaky wooden structure for one woman.

The first assignment of Father Dubuis was the Parish of St. Louis in Castroville, Medina County, now a part of the Archdiocese of San Antonio. The new town was settled by Henri Castro and settlers from Alsace-Lorraine in 1844. But the new church was two years in building at its location twenty-five miles west of San Antonio on the banks of the Medina River. It was dedicated by Bishop Odin on 9 November 1846, with Father Dubuis as its first resident pastor.

Today Castroville is an agricultural and tourist center atop the Edwards underground reservoir with Medina Lake in the northeast part of the county eighteen miles long and 102 feet deep when full. But in 1846 its inhabitants were subject to drought, hunger, flu, and diphtheria epidemics, as well as harassment and killing by Indians and cowboys.

Somehow the new pastor was able to master the dialect of his 1,300 parishioners in three weeks. His congregation was made up of Alsatians, Belgians, Dutch, Germans from Hanover and Prussia, Austrians, and French. He built a chapel which stands today behind Moye Military Institute and attended his mission territories in Medina, Comal, Gillespie, Llano and Travis counties. He started a free school, teaching French, English, and German to eighty children in 1848.

Father Matthew Chazelle visited Castroville in 1847 and died there of typhoid fever on 1 September. But another priest, a Father Domeneck, worked with the pastor from 1848 to 1850 building a rectory and larger church dedicated on Easter Sunday, 31 March 1850. Castroville was not the most hospitable environment for new enterprises, as the drought of 1848 was followed by a plague of locusts and then by a cholera epidemic. Nevertheless, the work of the Church flourished even in this climate.

Father Dubuis earned a temporary respite when Bishop Odin sent him to France in 1850 to recuperate and to recruit more missionaries. But due to lack of funding, Dubuis was forced to engage fourteen passages for the recruits and act as physician on board *The Queen of the Sea* on his return to Texas in 1851.

The decade of the 1850s was crucial for the Church in Texas. Bishop Odin appointed Father Dubuis Vicar General and Pastor of San Fernando Cathedral in San Antonio in 1851. Progress was made when the Ursuline Academy opened on Augusta Street on 3 November 1851 and St. Mary's University began classes the following year. The hostility and active persecution of the Know-Nothing Party, a native American and anti-immigrant group, persisted in the middle of the decade.

The ill feelings thus generated did not deter Dubuis, who laid the cornerstone of the new St. Mary's Church in San Antonio on 6 January 1856 and dedicated it on the Feast of the Assumption, 15 August 1858. On the completion of this church Father Dubuis, assisted by Rev. Michael Sheehan, was made Pastor in addition to his other duties. Rev. Alto Hoermann aided the German-speaking parishioners of St. Mary's, while Father Dubuis worked with Benedictine Abbot Boniface Wimer of St. Vincent's Abbey in Pennsylvania to restore the Mission of San Jose as a Benedictine monastery.

In June 1861 Dubuis went to New Orleans in an attempt to revive his health and later to France to recruit more missionaries for the Texas missions. During this period Bishop Odin was transferred from the Diocese of Galveston to assume new duties as Archbishop of New Orleans. On 14 May he had appointed Father Louis Chambadut (d. 7 December 1880) in his absence. As Archbishop he recommended Fathers Chambudut, Dubuis, and Peter Parisot, OMI, as candidates for succession to the See of Galveston. Odin believed the next bishop should be able to speak English and Spanish and know privation and hardships. These men knew the area, its people, and the languages.

Father J. A. Faure, who Father Dubuis left in San Antonio as acting pastor, wrote to Odin in August 1861 that he personally preferred Dubuis but that some Irish-Americans had shown a preference for Father Chambadut. Dubuis was still in New Orleans in the early part of 1862, for he wrote his colleagues in Texas that he would be leaving for France, probably on 15 April. This would make it necessary to run the federal blockade imposed upon New Orleans during the Civil War.

Whether Father Dubuis left at this time or a few weeks later with Archbishop Odin, both were in France in October 1862. At this time Dubuis was formally appointed Bishop of Galveston. Carlos E. Castañeda in *Our Catholic Heritage in Texas* accepts the date of 22 October 1862 for the issuance of the bull of appointment for Bishop Dubuis by Pope Pius IX. His basis is a copy of the Register of the Grand Seminary of Lyon showing the Act of Consecration of Bishop Dubuis, which took place on 23 November 1862. This copy with the supposed date of 22 October is in the Catholic Archives of Texas (7: 123 n.34). Although Castañeda saw the copy of the Register which gives 22 October 1862 as the date for Dubuis's bull of appointment, he neither states nor indicates that he had seen or examined the document itself. He states that Dubuis was informed by Odin at Lyon of his formal appointment as the second Bishop of Galveston (*OCHIT*, 7:123).

Monsignor Alexander C. Wangler, editor of *Archdiocese of San Antonio 1874-1974,* fixes the "date of the notification" as 15 October 1862 (13). Robert C. Giles in *Changing Times: The Story of the Diocese of Galveston in Commemoration of its Founding* says: "While in France he [Dubuis] received the news that he had been chosen second bishop of Galveston to succeed Bishop Odin, who had been promoted to the archbishopric of New Orleans. This was October 21, 1862" (25).

The matter can be easily resolved. Regardless of the date of the bull of appointment, if indeed it were 22 October, its existence was known as early as 15 October 1862. And Dubuis received notification on the twenty-first six days later. The entry in question in the Register of the Grand Seminary of Lyon was apparently written at a later date than the actual appointment, as the entry itself shows Bishop Dubuis's Act of Consecration on 23 November 1862. It would not be the first entry concerning the date of another document which was subject to the memory of its registrar. Further, in such a situation, it would not be unusual for the notification of the candidate to precede the formal announcement. It seems most logical, therefore, that the actual date of Bishop Dubuis's appointment was 15 October 1862 with his notification coming six days later.

We do know that in a chapel of the Grand Seminary at Lyon, where Bishop Dubuis had studied and heard the call to Texas, he was consecrated by Archbishop Odin of New Orleans on 23 November 1862. His co-consecrators were Archbishop Armand Francois Marie, Count de Charbonnel, the former bishop of Toronto, Canada, and Bishop Jean Paul Lyonnet of Valence. The new bishop's mother was present, as were twelve seminarians who agreed to journey to Texas. One of them, the Subdeacon John Anthony Forest, became third Bishop of San Antonio, and another one, Thomas Heslin, became fifth Bishop of Natchez (now Jackson), Mississippi.

And there were others besides the young seminarians who heard the call to Texas. Bishop Dubuis visited several convents to appeal for sisters and at Paris made arrangements for some Resurrectionist Fathers to staff Polish settlements in the State. With the encouragement of the Bishop of LeHavre, a large group of priests, seminarians, and women religious embarked on the *Sainte Genevieve* for Texas on 4 February 1863. In that year the Bishop brought the Sisters of St. Mary of Namur to his diocese.

The group of sixty returned to New Orleans of 4 April 1863 at the height of hostilities. Because the City was in the hands of federal troops, all were forced to take the oath of allegiance and promise not to take up arms against the United States. Bishop Dubuis went on with the sisters, brothers and priests to Matamoros. He crossed the Rio Grande to Brownsville and celebrated his first pontifical Mass in Texas. He then took formal possession of his diocese which he reached in May. There he found the Ursuline convent converted into a military hospital for those wounded during the siege which ended on New Year's Day 1863.

St. Mary's Cathedral was riddled with bullets. But the Bishop took the long view in a letter to Archbishop Odin on 13 May 1863, pleased with the love and respect the missionaries had gained for their work. He added, "With politics, we have no part, and on the battlefield, the Catholic priests meet with none but brothers. Catholicism, consequently, has gained respect and favor."

As in every area of society, the Civil War played havoc with the Church in Texas. In 1861 many families in San Antonio left for Mexico. Daily life was disrupted and the German settlers in Gillespie, Kerr, Kendall, Comal, Bexar, Medina, and other western counties were considered renegades because they opposed slavery. Martial law and mob violence caused them to suffer the loss of life and property.

The Benedictine priest Peter Baunach felt a particular sense of loss. He wrote to Archbishop Odin from Fredericksburg on 27 March 1862, "We have no bishop now to get advice from." Father Baunach must have felt some relief, then, when Bishop Dubuis came to bless the new church at Fredericksburg on 22 November 1863. In Victoria that same year Rev. Augustine Gardet built a new brick church for St. Mary's Parish at the corner of Bridge and Church Streets. In 1866 Father Gardet brought the Sisters of the Incarnate Word and Blessed Sacrament from Brownsville to Victoria. Shortly afterwards they opened Nazareth Academy in that city.

Bishop Dubuis returned to New Orleans on Easter Sunday in 1864 to bring back those seminarians he had left there in April 1863 to complete their educations. With them he returned overland through Union and Confederate army lines to Texas that same year.

The destruction of the Civil War was so devastating that it required the rebuilding of the Church infrastructure in Texas. New churches and schools were built and others enlarged. Hospitals and orphanages were erected and religious communities founded. At Mulberry (now Praha) Bohemian immigrants built a small church, and Resurrectionist Fathers were placed in charge of Polish parishes in Panna Maria, San Antonio, Cestohowa, St. Hedwig, and Bandera.

The Bishop had to keep busy, for his work of restoration was continuous and required his presence everywhere. He made a trip to France in 1866 to recruit staff and collect money. He found ten seminarians in Alsace who volunteered for the Texas missions and three Sisters of Divine Providence from Saint Jean-de-Basell also ready to return with him. His efforts proved successful. He procured much financial help, and three young ladies from the Cloistered Convent of the Incarnate Word and Blessed Sacrament in Lyon became Sisters Blandine, Joseph, and St. Ange, and sailed for Galveston in September 1866, forming the nucleus of the Congregation of the Sisters of Charity of the Incarnate Word. The Bishop built St. Mary's Infirmary in Galveston for them. He also introduced the Sisters of Divine Providence into his diocese in 1866.

Because of Bishop Dubuis's efforts at other times the Society for the Propagation of the Faith sent missionaries to Texas aboard the *Europa*, the *Saint Laurent*, the *Periere*, the *Napoleon III* and other ships. Before he returned to Texas, however, he had an important meeting to attend.

The Second Plenary Council, attended by the Bishops of the United States, met in Baltimore under the presidency of its archbishop Martin J. Spalding from 7 to 21 October 1866. This council drafted a condemnation of some current doctrinal errors and established norms for the organization of dioceses, the education and conduct of the clergy, the management of church property, parochial duties end general education. It met because of the instructions of Pope Pius IX, who praised its success on 2 September 1867.

Bishop Dubuis had special business before this council. He was late in arriving, due to his recent return from France, and his particular petition was denied. That petition he directed to the Holy See, requesting a division of his diocese, which included all of Texas except the immediate area of El Paso. But this did not occur until the twenty-eighth of August, 1874.

The Bishop returned to Galveston and left immediately for the Rio Grande Territory devastated by storm and flood. He went everywhere on horseback. In 1866 he wrote Archbishop Odin: "It has pleased God to give me a constitution of iron to do all the multiplied works with which I have been charged by my God-given Ecclesiastical Superior."

His work was bearing fruit. In 1867 the Diocese of Galveston had fifty-five churches and chapels (thirty-three of stone and twenty-two of wood), forty-five secular and twenty religious order priests, two colleges for young men, eight academies for young ladies, and eight schools for boys. The Bishop ordained ten young men as priests this year and had twelve students preparing themselves for the priesthood. The Vatican took note and on 17 June 1867 Pope Pius IX appointed Bishop Dubuis Assistant to the Pontifical Throne.

The year of 1868 was most auspicious for the Diocese. On 6 January St. Michael's Church in San Antonio was dedicated. A school was built at Panna Maria and a church begun at Cestohowa. Cornerstones were laid for new churches for St. Joseph's in San Antonio, for St. Louis in Castroville, and for churches at St. Hedwig and D'Hanis. Work started for the extension of San Fernando Cathedral in San Antonio. The Sisters of Divine Providence were established in September in a convent in Castroville.

One consequence of the Second Plenary Council in Baltimore was the Third Provincial Council called by Archbishop Odin in New Orleans for December 1868. Odin was concerned how he and his suffragan bishops might respond to the Decrees of the last Baltimore Council. The Archbishop was pleased to learn from Bishop Dubuis of the spread of Catholicism in Texas, which he attributed to the work of the Bishop and his priests and religious.

Matters had now reached such a state that Bishop Dubuis called a second diocesan synod to discuss the Decrees of the Third Provincial Council of New Orleans and to improve the administration of the Diocese. The synod was held in Galveston for the eastern half and in San Antonio for the western half of the Diocese. This was done to prevent unnecessarily long travel and to keep pastors from being absent from their parishes for too great a time.

The Synod in Galveston lasted from 14 to 21 December 1868. Twenty-two priests were present and nine were excused from attendance. In San Antonio the Synod met on 4 January 1869 where twenty-three priests attended and twenty-seven were excused. In the Statutes of this two-part Synod two archpriests could be appointed, one for the eastern half of the Diocese (from the Colorado River to the Sabine) and one for the western half (west of the Colorado to the Rio Grande and south to Brownsville). The Vicar General of the Diocese Rev. Louis Chambadut was named archpriest for the eastern half and the Vicar General of the San Antonio District Rev. Joseph Anstaett archpriest for the western half. Each archpriest could exercise special powers in his own district during the absence of the Bishop.

The office of Rector General of Religious was created at this time with Rev. Stephen Buffard acting as supreme director in spiritual and temporal matters of non-exempt religious. Rev. Matthew Sarry was created vicar forane or rural dean for the San Antonio district, while Rev. Augustine Gardet, supervisor of the Oblates, was dean for the Brownsville district. Four chancellors were named: John B. Bellaclos for Galveston, Louis Chaland for San Antonio, Augustine Gardet for Brownsville, and John C. Neraz for Laredo. Diocesan consultors consisted of the Vicar General, the archpriests, an archdeacon, the chancellors, and five consultors. This organization prefigured the division of the Diocese and the creation of a new diocese and a vicariate apostolic in 1874.

The archpriests of the Galveston Diocese were soon allowed to exercise their special powers. The Bishop left in company with Archbishop Odin to attend the first Vatican Council meeting in Rome in 1869. This Council was called by Pope Pius IX and consisted of four public sessions and eighty-nine general meetings attended by approximately 800 bishops and other prelates. It continued from 8 December 1869 until 7 July 1870 and defined papal primacy and infallibility in a dogmatic constitution on the Church. A separate dogmatic constitution on the Catholic faith covered natural religion, revelation, faith, and the relations between faith and reason. Bishop Dubuis attended as a strong supporter of papal infallibility.

In 1869 the Sisters of Charity of the Incarnate Word arrived in San Antonio and the Holy Cross Sisters came to the Diocese. The Church of the Annunciation was dedicated in Houston on 25 April. Santa Rosa Infirmary in San Antonio was founded on 1 December. During the Council period Pope Pius was pleased to learn from Bishop Dubuis what progress had been made in the Church of Texas. The Bishop for his part was pleased to report a Catholic population of more than 100,000 with seventy-seven priests (of whom sixty-two were diocesan), fifty-five chapels and churches (thirty-three of brick or stone and twenty-two of wood), three colleges, eight schools for boys, and nine academies for young ladies. The Holy Father imparted his blessing to the people of Texas and after the conclusion of the Council remarked upon the active involvement of Bishop Dubuis in its deliberations.

During the 1870s the Church in Texas continued to grow. Churches were built at New Braunfels, at High Hill, and at Seguin. The Holy Cross Fathers and Brothers were introduced into the Diocese in 1870. The Sisters of Divine Providence opened many schools and the Incarnate Word Sisters built an orphanage for girls. And other parishes and churches came into existence at this time: St. Joseph's Parish (1870) and Church (1876) in New Waverly, St. Patrick's Parish (1870) and Church (1877) in Galveston, St. Stanislaus' Parish and Church (1873) in Anderson, and St. Joseph's [now Sacred Heart] Church (1874) in Palestine. Jesuits from Mexico came to the Diocese in 1873 and the Sisters of Mercy in 1875.

Bishop Dubuis visited the northern and eastern portions of the Diocese on his return from Rome and arrived in Galveston on 17 March 1870. Two weeks later he visited the western portion again by horse. On these two trips he confirmed numerous children and adults. By the time of the Third Provincial Council in New Orleans (1873) he could report to Archbishop Napoleon J. Perche that the Catholic population was estimated at 180,000 and that thirty years had seen the priests in Texas increase from fewer than a dozen to eighty-seven.

In 1874 came the long-awaited division of the Diocese of Galveston with the Diocese of San Antonio including territory between the Colorado and Nueces Rivers and the Vicariate Apostolic of Brownsville that land between the Nueces and Rio Grande Rivers. In that same year the Bishop went to France and broke his arm on the ship. He returned by rail from New York to Galveston, noting the progress he himself had seen since he first arrived in Texas. He celebrated the centennial of the United States in 1876 with Masses of Thanksgiving and the Exposition of the Blessed Sacrament followed by the *Te Deum* ["Thee, God"], a hymn of praise and thanksgiving.

At last the time came for even so mighty an advocate of God as the Bishop to rest from his labors. On a visit to Rome in 1877 he asked for a coadjutor. One was appointed in 1878, but he resigned shortly afterwards. By January 1880 Bishop Dubuis left for France for the last time. He left behind forty-three priests, fifty churches, 107 women religious, seventeen educational institutions, and a hospital. Even after the division his diocese numbered 30,000 Catholics.

He formally resigned the administration of the Diocese of Galveston in Rome on 12 July 1881 and went back to his old home in France. He remained in that country for the rest of his life, seeking some relief from rheumatic pains and the various ailments brought about by his missionary experiences. Twice he had almost drowned from shipwreck. And he had fought with wild animals and been in contact with rattlesnakes, marauders, prairie fires, wind and snow storms. He was often the victim of the Comanches and was once taken captive by them. He was frequently robbed and his house was raided several times.

But he never lost his love of Texas. Perhaps feeling he could not break his ties he refused to resign the title of Bishop of Galveston until 16 December 1892. On this day he was appointed Titular Archbishop of Arca by Pope Leo XIII. He thus had the rank and status of an archbishop without the administrative duties. On 6 June 1894 he marked the occasion of the fiftieth anniversary of his priestly ordination by celebrating Mass at Coutouvre with many priests he had ordained in Texas and with representatives of religious orders. The day was also celebrated in the Dioceses of Galveston, San Antonio, and Dallas, and in the Vicariate Apostolic of Brownsville.

Bishop Dubuis died at the home for aged priests in Vernaison on 21 May 1895. Buried in Coutouvre and reburied there in the parish church of St. Denis in 1951, this bishop of Texas, whose name in English means "Bush," had an episcopal motto to fit his heroic purpose, "Pauperibus Evangelizare Misit Me" ["He has sent me to preach the Gospel to the Needy"].

The devotion Bishop Dubuis paid to Texas was the seed from which grew the Church of today with its membership of over three million, more than any other denomination in the State. That the Texas Church exists is due in very large part to the pioneer work of Odin and Dubuis. It is fitting, then, that the Bishops of Texas visited his tomb in France in April 1988. It is worthy of his successors to repay the call he made so long ago and to remember the roots from which they have sprung.

Right Reverend Peter Dufal, CSC, DD
Titular Bishop of Delcon and
Vicar Apostolic of Eastern Bengal
Coadjutor Bishop of Galveston

The strange case of Bishop Dufal belongs to the footnote history of the Catholic Church in Texas. A *rara avis* who passed across the page of history and was gone, it is impossible to say exactly what contribution he would have made had he remained.

The future bishop was born in St. Gervais d'Auvergne in the south central Department of Puy-de-Dôme, France to Pierre and Francoise (Galey) Dufal on 8 November 1822. Apparently a delayed vocation, Peter attended the Seminary and Novitiate of Le Mans in Sarthe from 1848 until 1852. He professed his final vows in the Congregation of the Holy Cross on the Feast of the Assumption, 15 August 1852. This order was relatively new. It was founded in France in 1837 and in the United States four years later. It is known for its educational and pastoral work, its home and foreign missions, and its social services and apostolate of the press.

Peter Dufal was ordained a priest of the Order in Blois, the capital of the Department of Loir-et-Cher, by Bishop Teophile Pallu de Pare on 29 September 1852. Father Dufal first taught at the Seminary of Dupasis from 1853 to 1855. From 13 December 1855 he was Prefect of the College of Ste. Crois du Mons and in the See of Orleans, Department of Loiret.

On 13 June 1860 Father Dufal was appointed Titular Bishop of Delcon and Vicar Apostolic of Eastern Bengal by Pope Pius IX. He was consecrated bishop at Le Mans, capital of the Department of Sarthe, by Archbishop Joseph Hippolyte Giubert of Tours on 25 November 1860. His co-consecrators were Bishop John James Marquette of Le Mans and Bishop Celestine Guyemes de la Hallandiere, formerly of Vincennes. He was installed in his cathedral at Dacca in Eastern Bengal, now the capital of Bangladesh, on 15 May 1861.

Apparently a capable and successful administrator, Bishop Dufal was elected Superior General of the Congregation of the Holy Cross fourteen years to the day after he had made his final vows as a member of the Order. He resigned this position and returned to Eastern Bengal on 20 March 1868, after almost two years of service.

Bishop Dufal was transferred to Galveston as Coadjutor with the right of succession to Bishop Dubuis by Pope Leo XIII on 14 May 1878. It is not known why this particular bishop was chosen as a replacement to the bishop of Galveston. Dubuis was in ill health and would soon resign the administration of his See. Bishop Dufal was a Frenchman and a successful missionary. So, too, was Bishop Dubuis. Otherwise the two bishops had nothing in common. Perhaps the Pope in making the appointment felt another French missionary was needed in this post.

Bishop Dufal arrived in Galveston on 15 July 1878 and resigned his position on 2 April 1879, effective on the following 9 December. He returned to Europe in 1880. The reason for his leaving appears to be unknown. For the last eighteen years of his life it is known that he held some other responsible positions in the Church.

From October 1882 to July 1883 Bishop Dufal was auditor to the Rota and an official of the Propaganda Fide in the Vatican. As auditor he examined the accounts of the Rota, which in Latin means "wheel." It is the name given to the tribunal of the Roman Curia which hears cases on appeal from diocesan tribunals worldwide concerning marriage, ordination, and religious professions of vows. The Propaganda Fide, known today as the Congregation for the Evangelization of Peoples or the Propagation of the Faith, directs and coordinates missionary activity throughout the world. Begun by Pope Gregory XIII in the sixteenth century, the Congregation is headed by a Cardinal Prefect. For the next five years (1883-1888) Bishop Dufal served as Procurator or manager of the Congregation of the Holy Cross at its generalate or headquarters in Rome.

Retiring to France, Bishop Dufal died at Ste. Crois, Neuilly-sur-Seine, on the outskirts of Paris, on 15 March 1898. He is buried there.

Right Reverend Edward Joseph Dunne, DD
Second Bishop of Dallas

Edward Joseph Dunne was an Irish-born Chicago cleric whose promise brought him to the Diocese of Dallas. He was able to extend the work unfinished by his predecessor Bishop Brennan and to develop projects of his own.

Born in Gortnahoe, County Tipperary, Ireland, on 23 April 1848, Edward Joseph was the son or Richard and Judith (Cooke) Dunne. He came to the United States as an infant in 1850. First educated at Old St. Mary's of the Lake in Chicago, he prepared for the priesthood at St. Francis de Sales Preparatory Seminary in Milwaukee, Wisconsin, and at St. Mary's Seminary in Baltimore, Maryland.

Bishop Thomas Andrew Becker of Wilmington, Delaware, ordained the Reverend Mister Dunne in Baltimore on 29 June 1871 for the Diocese of Chicago. The young priest was first Assistant Pastor of St. James' Parish in Chicago (1871 to 1873) and afterwards Assistant Pastor of St. Mary's Parish in the same city (1873-1875). He became Pastor of All Saints Parish in Chicago on 15 August 1875 and was Procurator fiscalis (manager of the treasury) for the Archdiocese of Chicago from 1888 to 1893.

On 24 September 1893 Pope Leo XIII appointed Father Dunne Bishop of Dallas in succession to Bishop Thomas F. Brennan, and he was proclaimed bishop on 22 October 1893. The new bishop was consecrated in his All Saints Church in Chicago by Archbishop Patrick Augustine Feehan his superior on 30 November 1893. His co-consecrators were Bishop James Ryan of Alton (now Springfield), Illinois, and Bishop John S. Foley of Detroit on 30 November 1893. Both Archbishop Feehan and Bishop Ryan were born in Ireland.

Resigning the pastorate of All Saints Church on 28 December 1893, Bishop Dunne was installed as Bishop of Dallas on 17 January 1894. He completed work on Sacred Heart Cathedral on Ross Avenue, today known as Cathedral-Santuario de Guadalupe. He established St. Paul Sanitarium (now Hospital) in 1897, as well as a number of other hospitals and churches, such as St. Patrick's. He founded Holy Trinity College in 1907, which later became the institution known as the University of Dallas (1911-1927). It has no connection with the present institution. Among the Bishop's other works was an industrial school for Blacks, the Ursuline academy, novitiate, and provincial house, and a junior college, academy, and provincialate for the Sisters of St. Mary of Namur.

While on a visit to Bishop Joseph J. Fox in Green Bay, Wisconsin, Bishop Dunne died on 5 August 1910. He lies buried in Calvary Cemetery in Chicago. At his death there were eighty-three priests and fifty-two parishes in the Diocese, with twelve academies and over 3,000 students receiving Catholic instruction out of a diocesan Catholic population of 30,000. There were also fourteen seminarians, an industrial school with fifty pupils, an orphanage with eighty-three children, and six Catholic hospitals. Bishop Dunne High School named for him is located at 3900 Rugged Drive in Dallas.

Most Reverend David Eugene Fellhauer, PhD, JCD
Second Bishop of Victoria in Texas

The well-known fictional television sleuth Jessica Fletcher on "Murder, She Wrote" has a fan in high places in Victoria. Not only does he admire Jessica's work on the weekly CBS program, but he also reads mystery and detective novels and watches "Mystery!" on PBS. When he attained his present position, he spoke at a press conference attended by Archbishop Patrick Flores of San Antonio and Bishop Thomas Tschoepe of Dallas. He said: "I am grateful for the confidence placed in me by the Holy Father. The reason I have been chosen for this office is by and large a mystery to me and will undoubtedly remain a mystery."

The speaker is David Eugene Fellhauer, the second bishop of Victoria in Texas. In this particular case the mystery is easily solved. His solid record of accomplishment, including his abilities in administration and in working well with others, brought about the favorable attention of the pope. But Bishop Fellhauer gives others credit for assisting his spiritual formation and his priestly vocation.

To begin with he had a loving family, a conscientious father, a devout mother, a younger sister Martha ("Marti") (a nurse in Dallas) and a younger brother Joseph (a television writer in Los Angeles). His father Harold was a radio engineer and a naval veteran of World War II. He married Helen Francis on 19 August 1936, exactly three years before the birth of the bishop. Anniversaries have become important to Bishop Fellhauer. The day after his episcopal ordination and installation marked the twenty-fifth anniversary of his ordination to the priesthood and the eighth anniversary of the creation of his diocese. And Harold Fellhauer, starting as a Presbyterian, became a Catholic twenty-five years after his marriage.

The father's conscientious regard for his family and his work and his respect for others was transmitted to the son. Born on 19 August 1939 in Kansas City, Missouri, young David attended St. Agnes School in Kansas City, Kansas. He regards the influence of the Ursuline Sisters from Paola, Kansas, as important in his development, as he does that of his professors at the Pontifical College Josephinum in Worthington, Ohio. By his ninth birthday he knew he would become a priest.

The Josephinum is a national pontifical seminary established in Cleveland, Ohio, on 1 September 1888. For David it would be high school, college, and major seminary. Two years after he entered (1955) his family moved to Dallas, Texas. His parents are now retired to Gun Barrel City, near Mabank, in Henderson County. Harold Fellhauer, a founder of St. Jude's Church there, has served on its finance council and is a Knight of Columbus. His wife Martha is a member of the Our Lady of the Lake Guild, a former teacher of religious education, and paints with oils.

On completing studies for the priesthood, David was ordained for the then Diocese of Dallas-Fort Worth by Archbishop (later Cardinal) Edigio Vagnozzi, Apostolic Delegate to the United States, in Washington, DC, on 29 May 1965.

Father Fellhauer's first eight years after ordination were spent as associate pastor in a number of diocesan parishes: St. Luke's in Irving, Christ the King in Dallas, St. John's in Ennis, and St. Thomas and St. Patrick's, both in Dallas. From 1968 to 1973 he was Defender of the Bond for the diocesan tribunal. With an analytical mind and an interest in graduate studies, he pursued canon law in Canada, spending the years 1973 to 1975 and 1977 to 1978 in residence in Ottawa. Here he received his doctorate in canon law (JCD) from the pontifical university of St. Paul and his second doctorate (PhD) from the University of Ottawa. Both of these institutions were founded in 1848, with St. Paul becoming a pontifical institution on 5 February 1889. Formerly known as the University of Ottawa, only St. Paul presently exists.

As a canon lawyer, Father Fellhauer became Vice-Officialis (1975-1979) and Officialis (Judicial Vicar) (1979-1990) for the Dallas diocese. He remained professionally active during this period, serving as both member (1978-1981) and chairman (1980-1981) of the Research and Discussion Committee of the Canon Law Society of America and as a member of its board of governors (1981-1983). He is also a member of the Canadian Canon Law Society.

Fellhauer held a number of academic appointments during these years. He was Instructor in Canon Law at Holy Trinity Seminary in Dallas (1975-1985), and held similar positions at the Institute on Matrimonial Tribunal Practice of the Catholic University of America in Washington, DC (1983-1990) and the Institute for Tribunal Personnel in Mundelein, Illinois (1987-1988). Among his publications are: "The Exclusion of Indissolubility: Old Principles and New Jurisprudence," *Studia Canonica* 9 (1975); "The *Consortium omnis vitae* as a Juridical Element of Marriage," *Studia Canonica*, 13 (1979) and "Marriage Legislation in the New Code" (with J. Alesandro and F. Morrisey), *CLSA Proceedings* (1980).

Prior to his appointment as bishop, Father Fellhauer served the Diocese of Dallas as a member of the Presbyteral Council, the College of Consultors, the Priests' Personnel Board, the Priests' Pension Committee, and as Censor Liborum. The Censor Liborum is someone with theological expertise chosen by a bishop to ascertain if writings, prior to their publication, present correct views on Church teaching.

On 9 April 1990 Fellhauer received a telephone call from Archbishop (later Cardinal) Pio Laghi, Pro-Nuncio to the United States, informing him that Pope John Paul II appointed him bishop of Victoria in Texas. Silence on the subject of the appointment was maintained until the public announcement on 17 April 1990 in Washington, DC. On that day the bishop-designate was in Victoria for a press conference.

In his statement the new appointee praised Bishops Tschoepe and Grahmann and hoped "to be able to listen well and to learn; to consult widely; and to urge action when it is needed." Near the end Fellhauer paid tribute to the Diocese of Dallas, his family, friends, and fellow workers at the chancery. He said of his new assignment:

> This part of the State of Texas has for a long time held a fascination for me. It is compelling for its history, its physical beauty, its strong traditions and sense of family life. It is well known that the people of European parentage, with their strong attachment to the land, have made their mark on this portion of the State, as well as have

> those of Hispanic origin, with their remarkable gifts and culture. To these people, and to those of every culture, living here, I come with a sense of admiration and a desire to be of service.

He ended with the hope of being an aid to the clergy and religious of his diocese.

Looking back on his duties in the priesthood, Bishop Fellhauer feels that helping people, having a variety of jobs, parish and office work, and the opportunity for graduate studies are the things he has most enjoyed. His plans, on becoming bishop, were to divide his time between administrative and pastoral concerns. He says of himself: "My tendency is to go slow and to think things out. . . .I am going to listen a lot. . . .I personally am a somewhat cautious person since I don't make quick decisions." Reflecting, he thinks:

> Perhaps, a bishop ought to be a down to earth, practical, somewhat normal person. He certainly is not expected to have all the talents that exist in the diocese. He may be one of the least talented persons in the diocese, but if he can respect other persons' talents and encourage them to use those talents for the good of the church, then perhaps he can do his job.

Some of those people who know him well can discern qualities that serve the bishop. His mother says of him: "He is very understanding. He has the patience of a saint." Thelma Gonzalez of the diocesan tribunal staff in Dallas calls him "very down to earth and very caring." His former secretary in Dallas, Ardith Hill, notes his "wonderful sense of humor and wit." While these are not the only characteristics supporting the position of bishop, they describe an individual who believes people and their problems are of major importance in life.

The episcopal ordination and installation of Bishop Fellhauer as the second bishop of Victoria took place there in the Cathedral of Our Lady of Victory, at 4:00 P.M., on 28 May 1990. Archbishop Patrick Flores was his consecrator and Bishops Tschoepe of Dallas and Grahmann (coadjutor bishop of Dallas and former bishop of Victoria) were his co-consecrators. The clergy received formal invitations and each pastor was asked to send ten representatives from each parish. Aired by KAVU-TX (Channel 25) in Victoria, the two-hour-and-twenty-minute ceremony was made available for purchase on videotape. The ceremony was also covered by Station KTXN-FM 99 in Victoria.

Those attending, a number estimated at about 1100, included sixteen Texas bishops, the archbishop of Oklahoma City, bishops from New Mexico and Mexico, and Msgr. Rino Passigato, charge d'affaires of the papal nunciature in Washington, DC, representing the Vatican. The bishop's family and friends also attended. Near the end of the liturgy, remembering his love for golf, Bishop Fellhauer said:

> I feel like professional golfer Ben Crenshaw. Two weeks ago, after winning the Colonial tournament in Fort Worth, he said, 'It's been so long since I won I don't know how to act.' With such a short time I've been ordained a bishop, I'm not sure how to act, either.

And on a more serious note, he observed:

> I am humbled and proud to be here and to add my ministry to the

> call we have all received. That is, to do our best to be disciples of the Lord, to live our faith and to do our very best to pass it on.

At the National Conference of Catholic Bishops' meeting in New Orleans in 1993, Bishop Fellhauer was appointed a member of the newly-created ad hoc Committee on Sexual Abuse. This committee, consisting of seven members, is headed by Bishop John F. Kinney of Bismarck, North Dakota. Its function is to offer to pay for mental health care of the offender and to protect victims from abusing clergy by reassigning such clergy elsewhere.

As of 1994 Bishop Fellhauer's diocese consisted of an area of approximately 9,609 square miles with a Catholic population of 108,573 in a total population of 255,276. In addition to the bishop there were sixty-nine priests and eleven permanent deacons, two men religious, and 130 women religious. The diocese contained fifty-one parishes, twenty-one missions, a Catholic hospital, a home for the aged, three high schools, twelve elementary schools, and 13,906 students under Catholic instruction by 210 teachers.

Finally, we turn to the coat of arms of this bishop of German descent, whose name in English may be rendered "hide cutter." The shield's purple field combines the red of the Diocese of Dallas representing the Sacred Heart of Jesus and the blue of the Diocese of Victoria representing the Blessed Mother. The color purple symbolizes deep reflection, restrained judgement, and wise leadership.

On the upper portion there is a silver label with three pendants from the family coat of arms denoting the eldest son. The bishop, his father, and his mother were each the firstborn in their respective families. In the bottom part of the shield two staffs are crossed with a cross, representing Christ's call to His followers to walk in His steps, over a shepherd's crook, representing the Shepherd King David in the Old Testament. It signifies the bishop's desire to be a just and caring pastor.

Bishop Fellhauer's motto "To Witness the Charity of Christ" is the injunctive duty of a bishop to be found in Canon 383, Number 4, of the Code of Canon Law. All familiar with the bishop and his record would agree that he is the living and literal embodiment of the symbols which represent him.

Most Reverend Joseph Anthony Fiorenza, DD
Fourth Bishop of San Angelo
Seventh Bishop of Galveston-Houston

Anyone seeing Joseph Anthony Fiorenza for the first time would regard him as a figure of authority. A tall man with dark, piercing eyes, he speaks out frequently with clarity and directness, and all the authority of his office. A former athlete, the Bishop of Galveston-Houston meets life with the urge to resolve problems and to clear obstacles in his way. He is the kind of bishop whose abilities have made him a national, as well as a regional, leader in the Church.

During halftime of the Homecoming football game of Monsignor Kelly High School in Beaumont, Texas, when Monsignor Kelly was playing St. Pius X High School of Houston, a visitor returned to his hometown to be honored this day of 16 October 1987. Bishop Fiorenza of Galveston-Houston was named 1987 Distinguished Alumnus of the Class of 1947 of St. Anthony High School in Beaumont by the Blue and Gold Alumni Association.

So strong was the force of young Joseph Fiorenza upon St. Anthony High School that an anecdote told by Father James Vanderholt, editor of the *East Texas Catholic* diocesan newspaper for Beaumont, indicates the student's vitality. According to Father Vanderholt, the future bishop earned the nickname "Foots," because "Joe was known to trip over his feet in fielding baseballs." His football coach Wiley Grinnell said of him, "The dream football team would be to have eleven Joseph Fiorenzas on it."

The former left end of the St. Anthony Bulldogs and outfielder on the diamond was captain of the football and baseball teams. He received the John Gray Athletic Award as best student athlete upon graduation. He found time to work in a position on the basketball team and, when he is able, expresses an interest in golf and tennis.

Athletics are only part of the story. Joseph Fiorenza was also senior class and student body president, member of the "A" Association, and editor of both the student newspaper (*The Barker*) and the yearbook (*L'Antoine*). But even then he gave a hint of the future as Prefect of the Boys' Sodality [Confraternity] of the Blessed Virgin Mary, a devotional organization.

Born in Beaumont, Jefferson County, Texas, to Anthony and Grace (Galiano) Fiorenza on 25 January 1931, Joseph Anthony was the second of four sons in a family which also included a daughter. The young Joseph attended St. Anthony Elementary and High School in Beaumont and after graduation in 1947 attended the University of Notre Dame in Indiana for a semester. He returned to Texas to enroll at the diocesan seminary at La Porte in 1948. Monsignor Andrew B. Deslatte taught philosophy and the late Bishop Vincent M. Harris taught canon law in a course of study that included one year of college, two years of philosophy, and four years of theology.

The seminary years were filled with study and varied activities for the young seminarian. Joseph was appointed student prefect and was often head of the Academic Society, which raised money for the missions. He played end in touch football and also baseball at the Seminary. At home in Beaumont during summers he taught catechism.

Ordained a priest by Bishop Wendelin J. Nold of Galveston in St. Mary's Seminary Chapel in La Porte on 29 May 1954, Father Fiorenza celebrated his First Mass at St. Anthony's Cathedral in Beaumont on 30 May the following day. His first assignment sent him to Houston as Assistant Pastor of Queen of Peace Parish in 1954, with the added duties during 1957 to 1959 of Chaplain of St. Joseph's Hospital and professor of medical ethics at Dominican College.

As Administrator of Sacred Heart Parish in Houston from September 1959 to June 1967, Father Fiorenza was one of four priests from the Diocese of Galveston-Houston to join Dr. Martin Luther King, Jr., in the March on Selma, Alabama, in 1965. Around this time he served as Chairman of the Aid to Poor Parishes Committee and as a judge on the diocesan Marriage Tribunal. In 1966 he was named Diocesan Director of the Society for the Propagation of the Faith and director of the diocesan Guatemala mission. In April 1967 he was elected Chairman of the diocesan Senate of Priests.

He was Pastor of St. Augustine Parish (1967-1969), of St. Benedict Parish (1969-1972), and of Assumption Parish (1972-1973), all in Houston. While Pastor of Assumption Parish, Father Fiorenza was also vice-Chancellor of the Diocese of Galveston-Houston from 1 June 1972 until 7 March 1973. On 7 November 1972 he was appointed diocesan director of the missions and diocesan director of Social Action and the Campaign for Human Development.

The Campaign for Human Development was begun by the United States Catholic Conference (USCC) in November 1969. Its purpose is to battle injustice, oppression, alienation and poverty in the United States by funding self-help programs begun and implemented by the poor and non-poor working together. It seeks to promote "a reevaluation of the priorities of individuals, families, the Church and the civic community with respect to the stewardship of God-given goods" (1995 *Catholic Almanac* 581). With national headquarters in Washington, DC, the Campaign has disbursed approximately $200 million to more than 3,000 self-help projects from 1970 to 1995.

On 7 March 1973 Joseph Fiorenza was appointed Chancellor of the Diocese of Galveston-Houston. On his appointment Bishop John L. Morkovsky said: "Father Fiorenza has my deepest respect and confidence. And I know too that he has the respect of the clergy, Religious, and lay people of the diocese."

Father Fiorenza was appointed Prelate of Honor with the title of Reverend Monsignor by Pope Paul VI on 5 December 1973. Soon thereafter he was given a series of positions in the Diocese commensurate with this new status. These included Diocesan Director of Catholic Relief Services and of the Diocesan Relief Fund, Diocesan Consultor, First President of the Provincial Senate of Priests, membership in the Senate of Priests, the Diocesan Finance Board, the Priests' Personnel Board, and the chairmanship of the Diocesan Loan Committee. He also became a member of the Board of Trustees of St. Mary's Seminary (now in Houston), of the St. Elizabeth Hospital Foundation, of St. Mary's Orphanage, and of the advisory boards of Catholic Charities and of the Sisters of the Incarnate Word, and a member of the Diocesan Pension Board.

As Chancellor Monsignor Fiorenza welcomed Mother Theresa of Calcutta to Houston in 1976 and appeared before the Houston City Council in 1977. Here he requested its members to enforce existing laws and to support new legislation against pornography. He was also Treasurer of the Catholic Clerical

Student Fund, a pro-synodal judge of the Diocesan Tribunal, and Chairman of the Department of Chancellors of the Texas Catholic Conference.

On 4 September 1979 Monsignor Fiorenza was appointed Bishop of San Angelo in succession to Bishop Stephen A. Leven by Pope John Paul II. In a statement recounting his activities to this time, Bishop Fiorenza said in part:

> I am in tune with the Church today; I am thoroughly supportive of the documents of Vatican [Council] II, and I will work very hard to see that they are fully implemented in the life of the Church today.
>
> I have two concerns which I share with the Church; they are those of social ministry and social action. The social ministry flows out of the teaching of the Church on social justice. To be involved in the ministry of social justice is to be involved in the mission of the Church. This is not an easy doctrine to proclaim, but we must proclaim it if we are going to present the full social teaching of the Gospel as the Church interprets it.
>
> The difference between social action and social ministry is that social action is involved in trying to bring the judgment of the Gospel on those complex difficulties of human conflict and human disagreement.
>
> Social ministry usually refers to the ministry of charity, in the traditional sense. Social action means taking some positive action to see that the Church's teaching on justice is applied to a particular situation. Both are needed; both are important.

At this time he added:

> The divorced especially need to know that the Church still cares about them. Such a group ["Divorced we care," the first diocesan program for the divorced, which he organized] gives them not only support, but spiritual programs to help them deal with the trauma of their situation.

The episcopal ordination of Bishop Fiorenza was performed by Archbishop Patrick F. Flores of San Antonio in Sacred Heart Cathedral in San Angelo on 25 October 1979. His co-consecrators were Bishop John L. Morkovsky and Auxiliary Bishop John E. McCarthy, both of Galveston-Houston, in the presence of Archbishop Jean Jadot, Apostolic Delegate to the United States.

When Bishop Fiorenza took charge of the Diocese of San Angelo, it consisted of thirty-four counties or 42,000 square miles. It had thirty-five diocesan priests, twenty-five religious order priests, sixty-three permanent deacons, thirty-seven women religious, fifty parishes, thirty-one missions, five elementary schools, and a general hospital. The Catholic population was 65,393 in a total population of 556,961.

On 1 January 1985 of the year Bishop Fiorenza left for Galveston-Houston, the Diocese of San Angelo consisted of twenty-nine counties of 37,433 square miles, the Counties of Stonewall, Haskell, Scurry, Fisher, and Jones having been lost to it on the formation of the Diocese of Lubbock in 1983. It had thirty-seven active diocesan priests, thirty-four religious order priests, fifty permanent deacons, forty-eight women religious, forty-eight parishes, twenty-five missions, three elementary schools, and a general hospital. The Catholic population was 72,000 in a total population of 604,958.

As Bishop of San Angelo Fiorenza stressed diocesan unity. He "initiated a program of clustering the priests from the different religious orders in parishes that were next to each other." He felt that this would keep their "basic identity and unity and encourage them to stay in parishes longer in the diocese."

One of his major projects was the construction of the $1.6 million Christ the King Retreat Center on the Concho River. According to Bishop Fiorenza:

> That [center] was desperately needed. We had absolutely no place to bring people and priests together. We had to work around a small-town attitude — 'We're small and few and we're not able.' We had to go around and say, 'This is needed and we can do it.' It helped us realize that we can do large projects.

Bishop Fiorenza was appointed Bishop of Galveston-Houston by Pope John Paul II on 18 December 1984 and installed publicly at The Summit in Houston by Archbishop Patrick F. Flores on 18 February 1985. As a member of the National Conference of Catholic Bishops (NCCB) and of its operational secretariat and service agency the United States Catholic Conference (USCC), he has served at various times on their committees. He has been chairman of committees on the Permanent Diaconate, Missions, and Campaign for Human Development, on the Administrative Committee of the NCCB and the Administrative Board, Missions Committee, and Bishops' Advisory Council of the USCC. He has been a member of committees for Vocations, for African-American Catholics, for Science and Human Values, and for the Selection of Bishops. He has been on the Ad Hoc Committee for the Revision of the Guidelines for Sexuality Education of the USCC. On 11 February 1992 he was named a member of the NCCB Ad Hoc Committee of the Mission and Structure of the NCCB.

As Secretary of the NCCB/USCC he was a member of the executive-level Executive Committee, the Committee on Priorities and Plans, the Committee on Budget and Finance, the Committee on Personnel, and serves on the Administrative Board. He has also held the positions of trustee of Catholic Relief Services, of the National Shrine of the Immaculate Conception, of the Catholic University of America, of the Pope John XXIII Center for Medical-Morals Research, and of the Catholic Near East Association. In Houston he has served on the board of the University of St. Thomas, of Catholic Charities, and of the United Way.

After his first five years as Bishop of Galveston-Houston, he reflected upon his experience and planned ahead. Bishop Fiorenza recalled that after his service as Bishop of San Angelo, conditions had changed since his chancellorship. He discovered in 1985 that the Galveston-Houston area had grown, and that there was a huge increase in the Catholic population and a much greater Hispanic presence. The demand for services had increased the size and scope of the Chancery, diocesan priests had replaced Vincentians at the Seminary, and pastoral councils were more firmly established in most parishes.

In addition he observed that the role of the bishop had changed in the past twenty years from 1970. The number of requests and demands upon time fought for his attention. In order to accept a commitment for a meeting or event, other meetings and events had to be declined. Many people wished to see him personally on various matters, and he found it hard to return telephone calls and to answer mail promptly because of the sheer volume involved. In addition talks and his usual informative article for the diocesan paper needed advance preparation. But the basic role of the bishop was unchanged. This was "teaching the faith, celebrating the sacraments and administering the diocese."

Bishop Fiorenza felt some of the significant developments of his administration were the reorganization of the diocese into four vicariates with an episcopal vicar for each and the reorganization of the Chancery offices into five secretariates [See the Section of the Introduction on "The Bishop and His Diocese," together with Notes 27 and 28]. He also noted the amalgamation of the Dallas and Houston seminaries, Hispanic and Black auxiliary bishops, an office for disabled persons, and the Capital Fund drive of $8 million, with $2 million of it going to begin an inner-city school fund. He mentioned the Office for worship and the indications of the growth of "faith and holiness in the diocese." In all these endeavors he praised the cooperation of the clergy, religious, and lay people.

The Bishop found encouragement in the hard work and dedicated ministries of his "brother priests." He felt their contribution and that of the Presbyteral Council had been outstanding. He praised the work of the permanent deacons, the men and women religious, the Chancery and newspaper staffs, the lay ministers, and the number and quality of the seminarians with their high percentage of Vietnamese and Hispanics. He called the Anglos, Hispanics, African-Americans, and Asians, who make up the Diocese, "a true reflection of the family of God's people."

He admitted his disappointment of "a lingering racism in some Catholics" and that more people were not actively involved in the Pro-Life movement. He regretted that all teachers of the Catholic faith did not seem to profess what the Church believes and teaches. He was sorry that "a couple of Religious Orders have withdrawn from the diocese" and that there were not more major donors for the Capital Fund drive.

As Bishop Fiorenza saw it, there were a number of long-term challenges facing his diocese. One need was "to hand on the faith to succeeding generations so that they will believe the teachings Christ revealed to the apostles as the Church understands and proclaims them." "To live daily life as a faithful and courageous witness to faith" would require outstanding religious education programs. The Bishop wanted to see an effective ministry to the minorities of the diocese. He hoped that richer parishes would work to assist poorer parishes, that the number of Catholic schools could be maintained and increased, and that each parishioner would "work and pray for vocations to the priesthood and Religious life."

His priorities for the next five years were evangelization, promotion of vocations to the priesthood and Religious life, the formation for lay ministries, a diocesan-wide stewardship program, and greater assistance to poor parishes in the twinning program [in which two parishes are joined together for a beneficial effect]. In answer to the difficulties posed by the shortage of priests, the Bishop noted moderate success in recruiting men and women. He expressed the need to attract more religious order priests to staff more parishes, the combination of parishes or the provision for parishes without resident pastors. He noted that schools and hospitals were changing to lay administrations and teachers with some success.

When asked to envision the world of the Twenty-first Century with increasing hostility toward religion, the Bishop recalled his motto, "Thy kingdom come," and its description in the Preface of the Feast of Christ the King as "a kingdom of truth and life, of holiness and grace, of justice, love and peace." The Church proclaims the truth of the gospel and defends human life. It promotes holiness of its members while working for justice and love.

Bishop Fiorenza observed that the Church's role is always to proclaim truth and to promote justice. He and his auxiliaries were asked to be part of civic committees (on such matters as drugs, AIDS, public school problems, hunger, housing, sexuality, and so on) because the city fathers knew that the Church has a vital and continuing role to play in daily society. The Church is the best hope for sanity and peace. It defends human life, with humanity itself ennobled by the Incarnation of Christ. It wars against self-gratification, greed, injustice, selfishness and permissiveness. "God alone is the source of human happiness and peace." Nothing can replace God in human life "The truth of Christ is the wisdom of God and that love of God is the only source of lasting fulfillment and happiness."

On 25 June 1992 Bishop Fiorenza wrote a letter to "The Catholic People of Galveston" concerning changes in their city which would occur effective August first of that year. In view of eight Galveston churches serving at most 15,000 people and that changes in population and an the deaths, retirements, and resignations of priests continued, a process of reorganization was being set in motion.

From 1 August 1992 St. Mary's Cathedral Basilica would continue to have a daily Mass with a Sunday vigil Mass and Saturday confessions. It would be non-parochial and staffed by chaplains at the University of Texas Medical Branch living in the Cathedral rectory. Our Lady of Guadalupe Parish would merge with St. Patrick's Parish, with priests at Our Lady of Guadalupe residing in St. Patrick's rectory. Our Lady of Guadalupe would become known as Guadalupe Catholic Center and house social agencies, such as youth programs, RCIA [Rite of Christian Initiation of Adults] and adult education programs, Catholic Charities, a food pantry, and possibly a clinic and other social service agencies. Holy Rosary Church would continue as long as Josephite priests confined to staff it and Reina de la Paz [Queen of Peace] Mission would continue to serve the Spanish-speaking.

Sacred Heart Parish boundaries would run from the east end of Galveston Island to the east side of 27th Street. St. Patrick's Parish boundaries would go from the west side of 27th Street to the east side of 61st Street. And St. Peter the Apostle Parish would now proceed from the west side of 61st Street to the west end of the Island. The consolidation of Galveston Catholic schools had already occurred in 1986, reducing four schools to Galveston Catholic School with its several hundred students.

It was fitting that parish consolidation would begin in Galveston, the original see city. By 1992 some Houston parishes contained as many Catholics as were in Galveston. And several others had nearly 10,000 parishioners. The Diocese of Galveston was created by Pope Pius IX on 4 May 1847. St. Mary's Cathedral was dedicated on 26 November 1848. Because of its historic importance to Texas, Pope John Paul II made it a Minor Basilica on 11 August 1979. It was now nonparochial, but it was still a center of worship.

Territorial parishes were now reduced from five to three. Two parishes continued to serve the Spanish-speaking and African-Americans. The Star of the Sea mission church continued to be served by St. Peter the Apostle Church. Sacred Heart, St. Patrick, and St. Peter had new parish boundaries. Our Lady of Guadalupe merged with St. Patrick and Reina de la Pas Mission continued to serve the Spanish-speaking Catholics, while Holy Rosary Church serves African-Americans. Our Lady of Guadalupe Church became a Catholic Center.

On 4 October 1992 the bishops of Texas gathered at St. Mary's in Galveston to celebrate the 150th anniversary of the consecration of Bishop Jean Marie Odin, CM, as first bishop of Texas. The Mass at 4:00 P.M. on this Sunday in 1992 recalled Odin's consecration on 6 March 1842 in St. Louis Cathedral in New Orleans, Louisiana. Bishop Fiorenza remembered how this event had come to pass.

In August 1837 President Sam Houston of the Republic of Texas wrote to Charles Comte de Farnesé, seeking the establishment of an archbishopric in Texas. Houston knew that this step would aid in establishing diplomatic relations in Europe and would result in trade agreements for Texas. Fathers John Timon, CM, and Juan Llebara, CM, set out to assess the number of Catholics and the state of the Church in Texas. They arrived in Galveston on 26 December 1838. In three weeks the two Vincentians visited San Antonio, Goliad, Victoria, and Refugio. They reported to Bishop Anthony Blanc of New Orleans concerning the establishment of a diocese.

Bishop Odin was assigned to Texas on 2 May 1840. He and his companion priests travelled through Texas facing raging rivers, heat, heavy rain, Indians, and snakes. They said Mass, baptized children, and performed or validated marriages. Always they instructed in the Catholic faith. The Diocese of Galveston began in 1847 with thirteen priests and Ursuline nuns. St. Mary's Cathedral cornerstone was laid on 14 March 1847. In 1861 when Odin left to become archbishop of New Orleans he had established forty-six priests and forty-five parishes in Texas. As Bishop Fiorenza, his successor put it, "We would be ungrateful indeed, if we would not remember and honor Bishop Odin and the many priests, religious and laity who planted the seed of faith deep in the Texas soil years ago with untiring labor and unlimited love."

In 1993 Bishop Fiorenza and his two auxiliaries made the official *ad limina* visit to Rome. "In the private meeting with the Pope, it was evident that he was aware of Houston's importance as one of the largest cities in the United States." The Bishop remarked that evangelization teams in each parish planned to implement the *Catechism of the Catholic Church.* He stated the need for more, especially Hispanic, vocations. The Pope felt young people responded well during World Youth Day in Denver that year, but the national press tended to belittle and diminish the moral authority of the Church. He asked that the people, clergy, and religious of the Galveston-Houston diocese be given his love. He spoke of his new encyclical [*Veritatis Splendor*], his desire to visit the Holy Land, and

Russia. He spoke favorably of Houston spontaneously three times during an hour-and-a-quarter lunch.

As of 1 January 1995 the Diocese of Galveston-Houston is composed of an eleven-county area of 9,354 square miles, having lost the Counties of Freestone, Anderson, Leon, Houston, and Trinity to the Diocese of Tyler on its formation in 1986. In addition to its bishop and two auxiliary bishops, it has 193 diocesan priests, 219 Religious Order priests, 232 permanent deacons, 15 male and 580 women religious. It has 94 parishes with nine missions, three Catholic hospitals, a health care center, three homes for the aged, a residential care facility for children, seven specialized homes, and seven special centers for social services.

The Diocese has a diocesan seminary, three religious seminaries, a university, eight high schools, 42 elementary schools, and 85,744 students under Catholic instruction taught by more than 1,300 teachers. There were 777,340 Catholics in a total population of 4,052,706. Bishop Fiorenza celebrated the tenth anniversary of his installation as bishop of Galveston-Houston with a Mass at 11:30 A.M., Sunday, 19 February 1995, at Sacred Heart Co-Cathedral in Houston.

This bishop of Italian descent, whose name means "flowering" in English, lives by his episcopal motto, "Thy Kingdom Come." In September 1979 he said in explanation:

> I chose that [motto] because one of the most important missions of the Church is to bring about the kingdom. Our Lord inaugurated the kingdom when He was on this earth, and He committed the spirit of that kingdom to the Church.
>
> We continually pray for the coming of that kingdom, so I thought that would be a good motto for my episcopal service — to try to work to make the kingdom of Jesus more a reality in our own personal lives and in the lives of the communities in which we live.

Bishop Fiorenza is a man of commanding presence, who is well-known in the councils of the Church. For most of 1995 he served as secretary of the NCCB/USCC and was also chairman of the NCCB's Ad Hoc Committee on Nomination of Conference Offices. On 14 November 1995, during the annual meeting of the NCCB/USCC in Washington, DC, Bishop Fiorenza was elected to succeed Bishop Anthony M. Pilla of Cleveland as vice-president of that body. Perhaps his high school classmate Father Salvador Culotta has said best of him: "He was always very calm and very stable. My mother has an Italian saying about Bishop Fiorenza, 'the wind does not blow him; the rain does not wet him; he is imperturbable.'"

Most Reverend John Joseph Fitzpatrick, DD
Titular Bishop of Cenae and Auxiliary Bishop of Miami
Third Bishop of Brownsville

Controversial because of his advocacy of the sanctuary movement in South Texas, Bishop John J. Fitzpatrick has long been a defender of the Spanish-Speaking and those who have come as refugees to the United States. He has steadfastly maintained his position despite the active opposition of the federal government. Yet his early life gives little indication of the course he would take.

Born in Trenton, Hastings County of Ontario Province, Canada, on 12 October 1918, John Joseph was one of four children (two sons and two daughters) born to James John and Lorena (Pelkey) Fitzpatrick. His late brother Robert J. became a Jesuit priest. Young John attended a Catholic grammar school in western New York and the diocesan preparatory seminary. He was a student at Propasanda Fide College and the Pontifical Urban Seminary in Rome from 1937 until 1940. He took up residence in Our Lady of Angels Seminary, Niagara Falls, New York, and received the degree of Bachelor of Arts from Niagara University in 1941. This institution, operated by the Vincentian order, was founded in 1856 and has a current enrollment of about three thousand students.

John J. Fitzpatrick was ordained for the Diocese of Buffalo, New York, on 13 December 1942. In the following year of 1943 he worked in Florida and returned that same year to New York. For the next five years he served as pastor of parishes in Buffalo and in Jamestown. He was assigned to Italian parishes because of his facility in Italian, which he learned as a student in Rome.

Father Fitzpatrick returned to Florida in 1948 as a diocesan priest of Archbishop *ad personam* Joseph P. Hurley of St. Augustine. He served this diocese for the next ten years until the formation of the Diocese of Miami in 1958 and later the Archdiocese in 1968 for Bishop and Archbishop Coleman F. Carroll. Knowing French and soon acquiring Spanish, Fitzpatrick became Diocesan Director of the Spanish-Speaking Apostolate working with Cuban refugees in 1961 and Assistant Chancellor and Director of the Spanish Chancery in 1962. He started the Cursillo movement in Miami and attended a Cursillo in Spanish in July 1963.

The Cursillo Movement is "an instrument of Christian renewal designed to form and stimulate persons to engage in apostolic action individually and in the organized apostolate, in accordance with the mission which individuals have to transform the environments in which they live into Christian environments" (1987 *CA* 561). It began near Palma, Mallorca, Spain in 1949 and was introduced into the United States in 1957. It involves a three-day weekend called a *cursillo* and a follow-up program known as the post-*cursillo*.

This weekend is Christ-centered and built around ten talks by laymen and five by priests, with active discussions and the celebration of the liturgy. Follow-ups called *ultreyas* concentrate on small weekly reunions in which three to five persons and larger group reunions share experiences and insights from prayer life, study and apostolic action. At present the cursillo movement is active on diocesan and parish levels in more than 160 American dioceses under the direction of the bishop.

Of his ministry in Florida Bishop Fitzpatrick has said:

> The American Catholic needs to make an effort to appreciate the culture of the Latins. Listening and talking with them helps us to understand.
>
> Wherever we've been, we have tried to use Spanish in the Liturgy. We have learned Spanish here in Miami working for and with the people, sort of on-the-job training.

In the early 1960s he visited all migrant camps in South Florida and later participated in archdiocesan drives to seek funds on behalf of migrant farm workers. He became Chairman of Clergy Dialogue, sponsored by the Florida chapter of the National Conference of Christians and Jews (NCCJ). On the interfaith dialogue, he said: "If we are not looking for some kind of unity of thought or action, we're wasting our time."

Father Fitzpatrick was appointed Titular Bishop of Cenae and Auxiliary Bishop of Miami by Pope Paul VI on 24 June 1968. Episcopal ordination followed on 28 August. The new bishop was appointed Vicar General, Chancellor, and Vicar of the Clergy for the Archdiocese of Miami. He was executive editor of *The Voice* for the Archdiocese of Miami and of *The Florida Catholic*, which now serves the Dioceses of Orlando, Palm Beach, Pensacola-Tallahassee, St. Petersburg, and Venice. The Director of the Archdiocesan office of Education, he was also Episcopal Vicar for the Implementation of Vatican II Decrees and a member of the Liaison Committee of the National Conference of Catholic Bishops. He conducted a number of Sacramental rites in Spanish during this time.

Nevertheless, the subsequent appointment of Bishop Fitzpatrick as Bishop of Brownsville by Pope Paul VI on 21 April 1971 was not greeted with elation in all quarters. Rev. Ralph Ruiz, then national chairman of PADRES [*Padres Asociados para Derechos Religiosos, Educativos y Sociales*], expressed disappointment over a "non-Chicano" bishop of Brownsville. This organization was formed by fifty-five Mexican-American priests in the American Southwest in February 1970. Its purpose is to promote the pastoral, social, economic and educational needs of the Spanish-speaking. Similar feelings were expressed by Sister Dorothy Donnelly, the head of the National Coalition of American Nuns, a women's activist group formed in 1969. They need not have worried, for by 1988 there were two Hispanic archbishops, six bishops, and twelve auxiliary bishops in the American Church.

Archbishop Thomas McDonough of Louisville, Kentucky, took a more confident position:

> Bishop Fitzpatrick is superbly qualified for the fullness of the sacred priesthood. He brings to his office [of bishop] a vast experience coupled with the innate ability to serve without distinction of preference the People of God.
>
> He has acquired the unusual faculty of being able to work effectively for others while preferring no personal recognition.

Bishop Fitzpatrick arrived in Brownsville on the afternoon of Wednesday, 26 May 1971, and was driven from the airport to the Chancery Office, where he gave a press conference at five o'clock in the afternoon. At the same time on the following afternoon he presented his letter of appointment to the Diocesan Consultors and was led to his Chair and given his crozier or staff by Archbishop Francis J. Furey of San Antonio.

The public ceremony and Mass of Installation was held at six o'clock P.M. on Thursday, 27 May 1971, at Jacob Brown Auditorium in Brownsville. Bishop Fitzpatrick was principal celebrant and homilist of the Mass in English and Spanish. He was joined by Archbishops Furey and Medeiros of Boston (his immediate predecessor), four monsignors, and eight priests, the last representing religious orders. In addition the bishops of Texas and Florida, other American bishops, and Bishop Sabás Magaña Garcia of Matamoros, Mexico, attended. Heads of the member denominations of the Texas Conference of Churches, state and local religious and civil officials, and about 125 priests and laity from Miami made up a congregation which numbered about 3,000 in all.

The Spanish-speaking of this four-county diocese of 4,226 square miles at the southern tip of Texas had found a friend in the new bishop. On its formation in 1965 there were forty parishes, forty-six missions, and twenty-two stations, served by fourteen diocesan and sixty-seven religious order priests, of whom the majority were Missionary Oblates of Mary Immaculate. There were twelve brothers and 165 sisters.

By 1 January 1992 there were sixty-one parishes and forty-four missions, with fifty-six diocesan and fifty-five religious order priests, forty-eight permanent deacons, thirteen brothers, and 147 sisters. There were two high schools and seven elementary schools, with one health care center, three sanatoria, two day care and two special centers. These people and facilities served a Catholic population of 567,046 in a population of 701,888.

Bishop Fitzpatrick continued his ministry in various ways. Under the direction of Father Ivan Rovira he developed special programs for the religious education of *campesino* or migrant farm-worker children. The Bishop traveled North with priests, sisters, and seminarians to ensure religious services and assistance for the workers.

The Bishop developed the Senate of the Bishop, the Pastoral Council (with strong lay participation), the Council of Religious Sisters, and individual parish councils. Boards assist many diocesan departments in their work. The *Cursillo de Cristiandad* continues, as does the Christian Family Movement with its *Encuentro Conyugal* and the Marriage Encounter (in English and Spanish). And the Legion of Mary, the Serra Club International, the Knights of Columbus, and the Catholic Daughters of America have been active in the diocese. Campus ministries at Texas Southmost College in Brownsville and Pan American University in Edinburg provide religious activities for the college communities.

Believing that the future of the Diocese lies in its own resources, the Bishop worked diligently to increase priestly vocations, the number of permanent deacons, and to make sure the proper reception of the sacraments. Chaplaincy teams of priests and sisters work with medical staffs in McAllen, Weslaco, Harlingen, and Brownsville to provide patients with spiritual guidance, counseling, and the sacraments.

In particular Bishop Fitzpatrick is associated with the sanctuary movement. It was begun in 1981 in Arizona to assist, feed, and house refugees from

El Salvador and Guatemala and was supported by a number of denominations. In 1984 churches in California and Arizona announced they would provide sanctuary for undocumented aliens from Central America. It attempts to provide support, shelter, food, medical care, employment and legal help, even in opposition to the United States government.

Bishop Fitzpatrick made his views on this subject generally known in an address delivered at the Cathedral-Basilica of St. James in Brooklyn, New York, on 28 April 1985. The first part of the address deplores the action of the United States in attempting to stem the flow of refugees away from its borders. In support of his viewpoint he quotes the words of God to Moses concerning aliens (Lev. 19:33-34) and of Isaiah (Isa. 16:3-4).

He cites Article Three of the Geneva convention of 1955 in that "no government that signed that document can expell (sic) or return a refugee, in any manner whatsover, to the frontiers or territories of a country where his life or freedom will be threatened on account of race, religion, nationality, membership in a political or social group, or political opinion." He also mentions the Refugee Act of 1980, adopted under the 1967 protocol relating to the status of refugees. It defines a refugee as "any person who is outside any country of such person's nationality. . .and who is unable or unwilling to return to. . .that country because of persecution or a well-founded fear of persecution on account of race, religion, nationality, membership in a particular social group or political opinion." He adds, "We simply cannot in faith allow our compassion to be limited by national origins or territorial boundaries." Throughout, Bishop Fitzpatrick seems motivated by his belief that the refugees are victims of persecution which may lead to their deaths upon being returned to their countries. About his own diocese he says in part:

> The Diocese of Brownsville, where most of the refugees come before attempting to find refuge in other parts of the States and Canada, opened Casa Oscar Romero about three years ago [1982] for the same purpose. It was named for the martyred archbishop of San Salvador. Many thousands have gone through it. For many it is the first and last American place that shows any compassion or gives any hope. Many refugees, unable to maneuver around immigration checkpoints, are picked up, jailed in the Corralon (the detention center in Bayview, Texas), and deported. I hope that they will forever be spared seeing a photograph of the Statue of Liberty and its message, 'Give me your huddled masses yearning to breathe free.'
>
> Then our small Casa Romero staff was singled out for persecution, tried, and found guilty of conspiracy and illegal transportation and fined. It was my privilege to bail both Jack Elder and Stacy Merkt [the director of Casa Oscar Romero and a volunteer] out of jail pending their trials. They were not allowed to plead that they were helping refugees who were here under the Refugee Act of 1980, only that they had broken a law — not even made by the U. S. Congress — but made by an agency of the executive branch, the INS [Immigration and Naturalization Service], which apparently can disregard American laws, whereas U. S. citizens cannot. Ap-

> parently Americans are not allowed to run their own lives under the protection of the first Amendment of the Constitution, which protects them in the free exercise of their religion. Our staff members thought that to give a ride in a car five or six miles to a bus station, located much nearer to the INS center, a bus station that was always patrolled by the border patrol, would be both American and Christian. More recently others have been arrested in Arizona on the same charges.

Bishop Fitzpatrick quotes the statement of the Center for Constitutional Rights in New York as expressing his position:

> 'We believe that international law mandates the U. S. to protect people fleeing war crimes, human-rights violations, persecution. If the U. S. were performing its obligations under the principles recognized in the Geneva conventions or international humanitarian law, the refugee would not be here illegally. The charge of abetting an illegal presence in the United States is at the heart of the prosecution of sanctuary workers. Since we reject that charge of illegality, we believe that the indictments against sanctuary workers should be dismissed on that ground alone. Moreover, we believe religious sanctuary workers such as Elder are protected by the First Amendment which supports the free exercise of religion. In providing sanctuary they are acting in accordance with religious doctrines which do not conflict with U. S. laws.

The Bishop concludes:

> Those of us who are Christian or American or both must decide very soon whether we are committed to the moral obligations imposed upon us either by Christ or by our American legal system. The blood being shed in El Salvador is blood on our hands. We are fostering and paying for their civil war. We have taken sides — for that government and against that people. Our refusal to accept Salvadoran refugees as refugees and our sending them back to be fodder in that civil war is another page of shame in our American history.

On Sunday, 13 December 1987, at 3:00 P.M. Bishop Fitzpatrick celebrated the forty-fifth anniversary of his priestly ordination with a Eucharistic Celebration held at the Shrine of Our Lady of San Juan del Valle in San Juan, Texas. He celebrated Mass with his brother bishops of Fort Worth, Galveston-Houston, Corpus Christi, Matamoros, the former bishop of Austin, and his diocesan and religious order priests. The bishop of Fort Worth, his former chancellor, served as homilist. Some 300 priests and community and religious leaders attended, the total comprising more than 5,000 people.

The Lieutenant Governor of Texas came, as did the state attorney general and the state treasurer. The Rev. Marcello Zago, OMI, Superior General of the Missionary Oblates of Mary Immaculate, came from Rome. They remembered that Bishop Fitzpatrick founded the program called Valley Interfaith to improve life in the Valley region of Texas in 1981.

It was a time to reflect and also to look ahead. To the Bishop Valley Interfaith "is a major hope. It teaches people how to look at their problems and study and discuss how to solve them." He was pleased at the Church's efforts in aiding some 25,000 refugees in Central America. He felt the need for expanded medical care for indigents and hoped that the Hispanic people would remember their historic discipline, respect for elders, and the teachings of their faith. But he feared that "Many people, instead of living with their customs, are going all out to accept the other [Anglo] culture."

Between 16 and 18 February 1990 the Texas Conference of Churches' Assembly of Representatives met in Brownsville. The thoughts of some 190 Texas church leaders were upon economic and political troubles which forced immigration. The Assembly was aware that the Diocese of Brownsville was 80% Hispanic with 25% of its people living below the poverty line.

At the time of the meeting some 2,000 Central Americans were being detained indefinitely after being caught crossing the border into the United States illegally. Less than two weeks earlier Immigration Commissioner Gene McNary announced that $11 million would be spent for extra agents to stem the flow of those seeking asylum. The Representatives at the meeting discussed the situation with Valley church workers, United States immigration officials, and area residents. Those attending included Bishops Tschoepe and Grahmann of Dallas, Sheehan of Lubbock, and Delaney of Fort Worth.

It was noted that the winter freeze in Texas caused work to become unavailable for migrant workers, who suffered from lack of money to travel North in the spring in an attempt to find work. The workers needed money to make payments on their homes and at work facilities for field sanitation. There was general concern that American firms doing business in Mexico should be placed under Occupational Safety and Health Administration and Environmental Protection Agency requirements, At this time Casa Oscar Romero, run by the Diocese of Brownsville, served as a temporary refuge for those fearing capture by the U.S. Border Patrol and others released from federal immigration detention centers in the Valley. There seemed to be a definite need for American-Mexican government partnerships to improve the economic development for both countries.

On 30 November 1991 Bishop Fitzpatrick retired as bishop of Brownsville, to be succeeded by his coadjutor Bishop Enrique San Pedro, SJ. Many remembered that when Bishop Fitzpatrick was installed in Brownsville he had said that a bishop "must carry in his heart the hardship, bodily and mental distress, sorrow, longings and hopes of all the people entrusted to him." They remembered his strong support for developing small Christian communities at the parish level. He had fostered parish-based social action groups sponsored by the Campaign for Human Development. And his beleaguered Casa Oscar Romero still attempted to discharge its functions. Sr. Esther Dunegan, IWBS, the diocesan chancellor, stated that Bishop Fitzpatrick would make his retirement home in the Brownsville area, still close to his flock.

After the conviction of its director and a volunteer for conspiring to transport illegal aliens, Casa Oscar Romero would provide food, clothing and temporary housing to Central Americans. But it no longer attempted to transport them. The Shelter was raided in 1990 by federal immigration officials, who apprehended thirty-four illegal aliens. At this time Bishop Fitzpatrick was quoted in an interview with the CNS [Catholic News Service] as saying: "I think it's in the best traditions of America to feed the poor. We have served almost two million meals in the last seven or eight years, mostly rice and beans. . . .I think it's a very Christian thing to do."

Casa Oscar Romero finally closed in late July of 1992. Peace accords between the government and dissident troops in El Salvador and calm in Nicaragua helped end its stormy ten-year existence. In 1986 it closed temporarily after a dispute between the Bishop and immigration officials over processing procedures. It had facilities for 200 and offered food, medical assistance, English classes, and recreational activities. It would continue as a shelter for the homeless.

Bishop Fitzpatrick has served on the committees on the Church in Latin America, the Ad Hoc Spanish-Speaking, Administrative, Social Development, and World Peace of the National Conference of Catholic Bishops. He has been a member of the United States Catholic Conference Committee on Joint Action in Community Service. His affiliations include the Texas Catholic Conference and the Valley Service Project and a directorship of the Texas Conference of Churches.

This Canadian-born bishop of Irish descent, whose name in English means "noble," has taken as his episcopal motto "Mihi Vivere Christus" from Philippians 1:21, "For me to live is Christ and to die is gain." This motto expresses his spirit, ideal, and program of life. As he himself says of it, "This is such a thrilling concept [the indwelling of Christ in us] that I know of no other that can give such inspiration."

Most Reverend Laurence Julius Fitzsimon, DD
Third Bishop of Amarillo

Born in San Antonio, Bexar County, Texas, on 31 January 1895, Laurence Julius Fitzsimon was the son of John Thomas, a physician, and his wife, Theodora (Okelmann) Fitzsimon. The family moved to Castroville a year after Laurence's birth. At the age of twelve he returned to San Antonio to receive his preparatory education at St. Anthony's Colleye, the high school seminary, where he graduated in 1911. He received the degrees of Bachelor of Philosophy from the North American College in Rome in 1914 and Bachelor of Sacred Theology two years later.

Laurence served in the United States Navy during World War I as a pharmacist's mate aboard the minesweeper USS *Heron* from 1917 until 1919. In 1920 he entered St. Meinrad Seminary, conducted under Benedictine auspices, in southern Indiana. Here he was ordained on 17 May 1921 for the Diocese of San Antonio.

For the first four years following his ordination Father Fitzsimon was a professor at St. John's Seminary in San Antonio. He then became a Pastor in Karnes County, Texas, of St. Anthony's Parish in Runge, of St. Cornelius' in Karnes City, and of Our Lady of Peace in Kenedy, between 1925 and 1932. Part of the Floresville Deanery, this area lies in the south central part of the archdiocese from Bexar County in the North to the middle of McMullen County in the South, with Atascosa, Karnes, and Wilson, and portions of Bexar, DeWitt, Gonzales, and McMullen counties. DeWitt was lost to the archdiocese on the formation of the Diocese of Victoria in 1982.

St. Anthony's Parish at Runge dates from 1901, as a mission of what is now Holy Cross Parish in Yorktown (now part of the Diocese of Victoria) until 1913. It was enlarged by Father Fitzsimon about 1930. The Parish of St. Cornelius in Karnes City was established in 1904. The original church was built in 1917 and was a mission of the church at Runge from 1917 to 1924 and again from 1929 until 1931. Our Lady of Peace Parish in Kenedy was established in 1904, and its church was built in 1912. It became a mission of the Church of St. Cornelius in Karnes City in 1924.

From 1932 until 1941 Father Fitzsimon was Pastor of St. James's Parish in Seguin, Guadalupe County, Texas. This parish, a part of the Seguin Deanery covering Comal, Guadalupe, and parts of Bexar and Wilson counties, was established in 1873. Its second church was built in 1914, and Fitzsimon built the shrine of Our Lady of Lourdes between the church and the rectory.

His pastoral work was noted by the new Archbishop of San Antonio Robert E. Lucey, who appointed him Chancellor of the Archdiocese in 1941. In that same year he was appointed Bishop of Amarillo by Pope Pius XII on 5 August to succeed Archbishop Lucey. A native Texan, who had labored all his priestly life in Texas, Bishop Fitzsimon received episcopal consecration from the hands of Archbishop (later Cardinal) Amletto Cicognani, the Apostolic Delegate to the United States, in San Fernando Cathedral in San Antonio on 22 October 1941. He was installed Bishop of Amarillo in St. Laurence Cathedral there by Archbishop Lucey on 5 November 1941.

During his administration Bishop Fitzsimon created four new parishes from Sacred Heart Parish. Other new parishes were established in the larger towns, and old parishes replaced their churches and built rectories and parish halls. Fifty churches were built, reconstructed, or replaced, and fourteen schools were built. A children's home opened in Panhandle and Price College (no longer extant) was expanded. There was a great increase in parishes in the Lubbock area of the Diocese as well.

Bishop Fitzsimon's particular interest was in preserving the records of what is now the Catholic Archives of Texas. His farsightedness has kept together for the future what is today the only statewide historical archive of its type in the United States. The Bishop was a Knight of the Equestrian Order of the Holy Sepulchre of Jerusalem and was made a Canon of Honor of the Cathedral Chapter of Lyon, France, by its archbishop in 1951. Proud of his wartime service the Bishop held membership in the American Legion, the Veterans of Foreign Wars, and the North Sea Mine Force Association.

Bishop Fitzsimon suffered a stroke in May 1954 and Monsignor John L. Morkovsky was appointed as his auxiliary. After an administration of seventeen years as Bishop of Amarillo, Bishop Fitzsimon, whose Irish surname means "one who hears" in English, died at St. Anthony's Hospital in Amarillo, Texas, on 2 July 1958. He is buried in that city.

Most Reverend Patrick Fernandez Flores, DD, LLD
Titular Bishop of Itolica and Auxiliary Bishop of San Antonio
Third Bishop of El Paso
Fourth Archbishop of San Antonio

The contribution of Patrick Fernandez Flores, both to the Church in Texas and to the Church in America, is so vast that it will be assessed by historians for many years to come. If he had done nothing but be the first Mexican-American Roman Catholic bishop of the United States in 1970 and the one Hispanic archbishop in 1995, his name would be remembered. He has always been a champion of the poor and the oppressed, and his presence shows what one man trying to help others in the name of God may accomplish. He is the living witness of his episcopal motto, "I will work not for myself but for all."

The occasion of Archbishop Flores's twenty-fifth anniversary of consecration as a bishop on 5 May 1995 caused Pope John Paul II and President William J. Clinton to reach agreement on at least one subject. Both leaders know the worth of the Archbishop. At this time the Pope praised Flores's leadership and fidelity to the Church and imparted his apostolic blessing to him. President Clinton said in part: "You can be proud of the impact you've made on the lives of those around you, and the way you have used God's gifts to help others." Former President Jimmy Carter wrote of the Archbishop's years of service to the Church and his inspiration for others.

Patrick Fernandez Flores is a younger child in a family of six sons and three daughters born to Patricio and Trinidad (Fernandez) Flores in Ganado, Jackson County, Texas, on 26 July 1929. His parents were farmers and migrant workers for many years. For a young Hispanic such a life was not an easy one. Economic necessity often broke the pattern of the education of one whose language was not that of the majority culture. He was a migrant worker and a school dropout and might have remained so save for the intervention of Sister Benetia Vermeersch. She introduced the young man to Bishop Christopher Byrne of Galveston. Bishop Byrne saw a quality in Patrick which he wished to cultivate. If the student would stay in school and maintain his grades, the Bishop would ensure his education. Given a challenge and a trust, Flores rose to the occasion and became an honor graduate of Kirwin High School in Galveston.

Soon afterwards he entered the diocesan seminary at La Porte. Completing his studies at the age of twenty-six, the Reverend Mister Flores was ordained by Bishop Wendelin J. Nold in St. Mary's Cathedral in Galveston, for the Diocese of Galveston, on 26 May 1956. Father Flores's first assignment was as Assistant Pastor of Holy Name Parish in Houston. This parish was founded in 1919 and is the tenth oldest existing in the city. On the one hundred and twenty-fifth anniversary of the Diocese of Galveston-Houston in 1972, it was that area known as the North Side, extending eastward from Little White Oak Bayou to the Eastex Freeway and northward from the Southern Pacific tracks to the boundary of the new St. Patrick's Church. Here he remained until 1963.

His next assignment took him to nearby Pasadena where he was Pastor of

Guardian Angel Parish until 1967. This parish was established in 1954 as a mission of Our Lady of Guadalupe Parish, Baytown. Father Flores was second pastor of a parish in which its frame church building, dedicated eight years before, was forty by eighty feet. The new pastor completed classrooms for the school in 1965 and erected a convent in 1967. In 1971 the Flores Community Fund to help the needy was established in his name.

From 1967 until 1970 Father Flores was the Pastor of St. Joseph's and St. Stephen's Parish in Houston. This combination of one parish with two churches four blocks apart was the union in 1967 of St. Joseph's Parish (1881) and St. Stephen's Parish (1932). The church of St. Joseph's is located at 1505 Kane Street and that of St. Stephen's at 1910 Center Street. In 1967 St. Joseph's School was closed and became used for the Confraternity of Christian Doctrine program as a parish center. During this time the Pastor in this predominantly Mexican neighborhood was Director of the Cursillo Movement and diocesan director of the bishops' Committee for the Spanish-Speaking and of the Christian Family Movement.

Once again providence intervened in the form of Archbishop Francis J. Furey of San Antonio. This Pennsylvania-born churchman, who had been bishop of San Diego, California, was aware of the future of his church. This scholarly priest, the product of Roman education with its advanced canonical degrees, foresaw the rise of an Hispanic hierarchy in which Hispanic culture and numbers would play an ever more important role. When asked by Rome to reconsider his first choice for auxiliary bishop and to submit three names for approval, Furey repeated that first choice and added twice more the name of Patrick F. Flores. Under such insistence Pope Paul VI named Flores Titular Bishop of Itolica and Auxiliary Bishop of San Antonio on 18 March 1970. By this appointment the first Mexican-American in the history of the Roman Catholic Church in the United States of America entered the ranks of the hierarchy. Another change became evident at this time. In the future bishops would be appointed not so much for their achievements in foreign universities but for their closeness to and understanding of the people they were to govern based upon their own pastoral experiences.

Bishop Flores was ordained bishop in the San Antonio Convention Center on 5 May 1970 by Archbishop (later Cardinal) Luigi Raimondi, Apostolic Delegate to the United States. His co-consecrators were Archbishop Furey of San Antonio and Coadjutor (later Bishop) John L. Morkovsky of Galveston-Houston. That year he became Vicar General for the Archdiocese and Pastor of St. Patrick's Parish in San Antonio. A parish from 1895, the present church was built in 1923. In Bishop Flores's time it was made up of about 850 families. The new bishop was honored by the conferral of the degrees of Doctor of Laws by Our Lady of the Lake University in San Antonio in 1972 and by St. Edward's University in Austin in 1973.

During these years in San Antonio Bishop Flores became a part of two new organizations with national and international outreach. He was national chairman of PADRES [*Padres Asociados para Derechos, Religiosos, Educativos y Sociales*], founded by fifty-five Mexican-American priests in 1970 to promote the needs of the Spanish-Speaking and to foster leadership development of Hispanics. From modest beginnings it has grown into a national organization now known as the National Association of Hispanic Priests of the USA (or in Spanish, ANSH, for *La Asociacion Nacional de Sacerdotes Hispanos, EE.UU.*). PADRES was originally concerned with such matters as the formation of the first National Hispanic Encounters and the naming of the first Hispanic Bishops. In 1985 PADRES began the four-year process of consolidation with ASH (or *La Asociacion de Sacerdotes Hispanos*) from the eastern United States, which ultimately produced ANSH in September 1989. Representing some 2,400 Hispanic priests in the United States, it works with laity and bishops in implementing the National Plan for Hispanic Ministry and in working toward a more meaningful ministry.

Bishop Flores was also Chairman of the Board of the Mexican American Cultural Center (MACC) with national headquarters in San Antonio. Founded in 1972 the Center is noted for pastoral study and language education. Programs aid ministry among Hispanics and personnel working with them in the United States and in Latin America. It offers courses in culture, faith development, Scripture, theology, and praxis (customary practice or conduct). The Center conducts workshops to develop leadership skills and a better understanding of Hispanic communities. Faculty members serve as resource personnel and offer master's degrees in pastoral ministry in cooperation with Incarnate Word College, the Oblate School of Theology, and St. Mary's University in San Antonio, Boston College in Massachusetts, and Loyola University of New Orleans, Louisiana. The Center also distributes pastoral materials in the United States and for Latin America. Those enrolled for pastoral study in summer can earn a *Certifcado de Pastoralista.*

From 1973 until 1978 Bishop Flores was Pastor of Immaculate Conception Parish in southwest San Antonio. It began as a mission of Immaculate Heart of Mary parish and became independent in 1939. The Bishop found it composed of over 3,000 families of almost 5,000 people. He was also Chairman of the Texas Advisory Board to the United States Commission on Civil Rights and the Founder of the National Foundation for Mexican-American Vocations.

Bishop Flores was directly involved in the legal defense of Mexican Americans accused of crime. On one occasion he donated his episcopal ring to raise defense funds. He has visited migrant farm-worker camps in Idaho, Wisconsin, South Dakota, and other midwestern states, living with the workers. He helped found COPS (Communities Organized for Public Service) in 1974 and gave it his strong support. He served as Chairman of the National Conference of Catholic Bishops Committee on the Church in Latin America. As archbishop he was a member of a group of American bishops who visited Cuba in January 1985 to determine the future of the Church there. Here again he was effective in seeking ways for the Church to flourish under adverse conditions.

As his influence grew, Bishop Flores became a consultant on the Pontifical Commission for Justice and Peace, a member of the Commission for Mexican-American Affairs, the Ecumenical Center for Health and Religion, the National Committee of the Campaign for Human Development, and the San Antonio Committee for the 1976 Bicentennial Celebration of the United States. He was also an archdiocesan consultor. Cardinal Terence Cooke of New York and President Jimmy Carter sought his support on advisory committees.

On 4 April 1978 Bishop Flores was appointed bishop of El Paso by Pope Paul VI and was installed there in St. Patrick's Cathedral on the following 29 May. Within a year Archbishop Furey died. On 28 August 1979 Flores was appointed archbishop of San Antonio by Pope John Paul II. Archbishop Flores was installed in San Fernando Cathedral in San Antonio with the farm labor leader César Chavez and some 10,000 Mexican-Americans in attendance on 13 October 1979. On 25 May 1982 he received the pallium, the symbol of his office, from the hands of Cardinal Umberto Mozzoni in the Matilde Chapel of the Vatican.

Archbishop Flores has served as Chairman of the Texas Catholic Conference, as a member of the board of Incarnate Word College, and on the Administrative Committee and Administrative Board of the National Conference of Catholic Bishops (NCCB) and the United States Catholic Conference (USCC). In 1989 he was elected head of the NCCB Committee on the Permanent Diaconate and in 1990 of its Ad Hoc Committee on Aid to the Church in Central and Eastern Europe. This Committee, formed at the request of the NCCB Administrative Committee, works with the Holy See, the Church in Western Europe, the Catholic Relief Services, the Catholic Near East Welfare Association, and other groups.

In late November 1994 Archbishop Flores called for an archdiocesan synod. Simply put, a synod is a meeting of representatives summoned by the bishop or archbishop to recommend action on matters affecting the life and mission of the Church. As a diocese San Antonio had held synods in 1879, 1906, and in 1921. All of these were in Latin and involved only the priests of the diocese. In 1930 Archbishop Drossaerts held a synod, for the first time in English. The synod or 1994 would involve religious order priests and the laity of the Archdiocese for the first time.

Archbishop Flores clearly wanted his synod to be more inclusive of opinion, though he would have the final say in acting upon the various recommendations put forward. As he observed: "Every so often, it's imperative to look at ourselves to see where we are and where we need to be." The Archbishop issued the call during Sunday Mass because he felt it important to seek the guidance of the Holy Spirit throughout the entire undertaking in an attitude of prayer. He added: "As we enumerate our problems and needs, we'll have to prioritize and determine the areas most urgent and where we have the financial and talent ability to respond."

At the outset it was expected that more than 100 representatives of religious and ethnic groups would take part in the process. Synod coordinator Sr. Janet Marie Abbacchi said the Archdiocese would train delegates from each parish to lead discussions. Information received would be presented to her office to become the basis for reflections, more discussions and the writing of working drafts for the synod assembly, a gathering of 700 church leaders and lay people to make recommendations to the Archbishop on identified needs. In December 1994 the Archbishop called together a council of some twenty-five to thirty people to set the pace of a process which could last as long as from two to four years. Although all major Catholic institutions, societies, and ethnic groups would have their say, Flores hoped that more could be done for those with AIDS, prisoners, ex-convicts, and their families.

As the year 1994 drew to a close, the Archbishop could be glad to receive the assistance of Auxiliary Bishop John Yanta, even though his other auxiliary, Joseph Galante, was leaving to become bishop of Beaumont. In addition, the archdiocesan school system led the nation in Catholic school enrollment gain for the second year in a row, adding 729 students. It was the fifth annual increase in enrollment. Our Lady of the Atonement Parish opened a new school and many schools added new classrooms.

The most bizarre event of the year to befall the Archdiocese was the opening of an art exhibit entitled "Spiritual, Sensual, Sexual," by the Houston artist Donell Hill at the ReBarn on the 10 September 1994. The ReBarn was a Center for Catholic Spirituality and Art located on the grounds of the Incarnate Word Motherhouse and Retirement Center in San Antonio. The artist's vision was that the paintings should depict the mental agonies of those suffering with AIDS. Programs of an educational nature concerning AIDS were to have been a part of the exhibit. The medium of expression was graphic sexuality, in one picture a naked angel seeming to be actively engaged in sexual union upon an altar. This picture came to a wider audience by way of television and the local newspaper.

Due to public outrage, the exhibit closed three days after it opened. Archbishop Flores judged the work pornographic and an improper way to express sympathy for those who were stricken with AIDS. The exhibit reopened on 9 December 1994 at ARTESANantonio after the artist had filed a lawsuit unsuccessfully seeking the reopening of the exhibit at the ReBarn. Its director, Sr. Alice Holden, CCVI, resigned in late December 1994.

By New Year's Day 1995 the Archdiocese of San Antonio had its archbishop, an auxiliary bishop, 154 diocesan and 240 religious order priests, 226 permanent deacons, 117 men religious and 1,080 women religious. These people served 142 parishes, forty-two missions, five Catholic hospitals, four health care centers, seven homes for the aged, an orphanage and child care center, six nurseries, three specialized homes, and four social service centers. There is an archdiocesan seminary, seven religious seminaries, four colleges and universities, three archdiocesan and parochial high schools, six private high schools, thirty-eight archdiocesan and parochial elementary schools, four private elementary schools, and one institution for the disabled. On this particular day there was a Catholic population of 639,236 in a total population of 1,766,574.

Even at this time the Archbishop was working to add to archdiocesan services. Around the turn of the year he was attempting to raise $400 thousand so that Catholic students at the University of Texas at San Antonio might have a Center to use as a place of worship. He would make funding available from the Annual Appeal and started a letter-writing campaign to get the project underway.

On 5 May 1995 Archbishop Flores had something to celebrate, the silver anniversary of his episcopal consecration, at the Municipal Auditorium in San Antonio. About 1,500 saw the Archbishop receive the City of San Antonio Distinguished Citizen Award. Thirteen active and retired bishops from Texas, Oklahoma, and Wisconsin, and 175 priests came. The Archdiocesan Choir and Incarnate Word College provided an hour of music before Mass, as well as music for the liturgy. Behind the altar table was a cross and a painting of Our Lady of Guadalupe.

In addition to the praise of dignitaries quoted at the beginning of this article, Bishop Yanta said that God made Archbishop Flores "to suffer educational disadvantage, poverty, prejudice and injustice so he could become an effective instrument of change to promote education, the greatest gift one can give to the young." Bishop Ricardo Ramirez of Las Cruces, New Mexico, and formerly an auxiliary bishop of San Antonio, called the Archbishop "an energizer whose very presence gives life. . . .He's given me an example of patience, faith, believing in people and trusting that, no matter how enormous our problems, we must put them in the hands of God."

That afternoon Archbishop Flores was the guest of honor at an afternoon reception at Mission San José. The evening before about 1,500 people attended a reception in the Marriott Hotel Rivercenter ballroom. At this time he noted, "The highlight of these twenty-five years has been the blessing the Lord gave me to love people and to be loved in return."

Between 23 and 25 June 1995 "Hispanic Convocation '95" took place at Incarnate Word College in San Antonio. It recalled the fiftieth anniversary of the founding of the Office for Hispanic Ministry in 1945. The American bishops' Committee for the Spanish-Speaking was also formed and later became the Committee on Hispanic Affairs. The national office for Hispanic Ministry moved from San Antonio to Washington, DC, in 1970, when it became the Secretariat for Hispanic Affairs. And in 1987 the bishops of the United States approved the National Pastoral Plan for Hispanic Ministry. It called for small ecclesial communities, parish renewal, youth ministry, promotion of family life, and leadership formation adapted to Hispanic culture. Now there were twenty active Hispanic bishops and a number of Church organizations actively promoting Hispanic values.

Cardinal Keeler of Baltimore attended in his capacity as President of the National Conference of Catholic Bishops and the United States Catholic Conference. Coincidentally and appropriately he was a native of San Antonio. Cardinal Law of Boston also attended, as did the Pro-Nuncio to the United States, together with some thirty other bishops and archbishops and hundreds of priests, sisters, and lay ministers.

The Conference was dear to the Archbishop's heart. It called for attention to the needs of the poor and their right to express themselves through appropriate liturgies. It was both a call to unity and a recognition of cultural diversity. It urged aid for the poor and avoidance of consumerism, materialism, and extreme individualism. During this conference the Archbishop received a medal, commissioned by the National Conference of Catholic bishops, and named for him. On this occasion there were twelve recipients, including four from San Antonio. The Flores Medal bears the bishops name and motto: "I will work not for myself but for all."

Archbishop Flores of San Antonio is an unusual man for unusual times. Called by some the "Mariachi Bishop" for the spirited music of Mexico which he sings so well, he is a force for good throughout the state and nation. A stalwart and capable defender of Hispanics, he is a dynamic advocate for his people and for the Church, But no one acquainted with his life and ministry can doubt that his love for all people and for his God is all-encompassing.

As metropolitan of the Province of San Antonio he claims all the bishops of Texas as his suffragans. He unites all Catholics of his state within a single ecclesiastical jurisdiction. On 13 and 14 September 1987 he had the singular distinction of being host to John Paul II, the first pope in history to visit Texas and San Antonio. His Spanish surname means "flowers," and his legacy continues to flourish.

Right Reverend John Anthony Forest, DD
Third Bishop of San Antonio

The last of the French bishops who came to Texas and established its hierarchy, John Anthony Forest, was one of that pioneer mode who saw his duty and performed it well. His record as a builder is impressive, and the results of his achievements are with us yet. He came to Texas during the Civil War and remained to labor in the vineyards of the Church for almost fifty years.

Born in Saint-Martin-La-Sureté, Department of the Loire, France, on Christmas Day in 1838, to Jean and Marie (Thollet) Forest, John Anthony was a Subdeacon in the Grand Seminary of Lyon on 23 November 1862. On this day Claude Dubuis was consecrated bishop of Galveston. Heeding his call for young missionaries, John Forest and eleven other young seminarians made the commitment to come to faraway Texas. He left France on 3 January 1863, in company with about fifty others, and completed his religious studies at the Seminary in New Orleans, Louisiana. Here he was ordained by Bishop Dubuis for the San Antonio area of the Diocese of Galveston on 12 April 1863. He later journeyed to San Antonio by foot and by ox-cart and remained there about one month.

Father Forest's first assignment came in August 1863 as Assistant Pastor to Rev. Charles Padey of St. Mary's Parish at Smother's Creek, Lavaca County, Texas. This parish was a part of the northwest section of the Archdiocese of San Antonio until 1982, when it became a part of the new Diocese of Victoria. Settlement of the area began in 1823, with religious development coming seven years later when the Smother's Creek area was inhabited by some Irish families from Kentucky and Missouri. Catholic settlers constructed a log church about three miles west of Hallettsville and named it St. Mary's after their church in Missouri.

Incredibly Father Forest was able to master English and Czech from scratch in three months after his arrival. He eventually became Pastor of St. Mary's Parish and used it as his headquarters until 1882, when he became Pastor of Sacred Heart Parish in Hallettsville. St. Mary's Parish then assumed mission status from 1882 until 1905. As Pastor Forest served Hallettsville, Brushy (now Yoakum), and Yellow Bank (now Koerth), all in Lavaca County, and Mulberry (now Praha) in Fayette County.

He built a stone church closer to Yoakum than the log church built in 1850 about three miles east of that town and known as Brushy Church. Forest called the new church St. Joseph's and dedicated it in 1876. Lay teachers opened a private school next to it and the first parish school was established in 1891.

Koerth (formerly known as Yellow Bank, Antioch, and Karney), a few miles south of Hallettsville, had been settled about 1833. About 1865 the first Catholic church was built of logs and covered with handmade split oak by Irish, German, and Czech settlers. A frame church was built in 1878 and 1879, and the present frame church in 1888. It was dedicated to St. John the Baptist and, until 1909, was a mission of St. Mary's Parish in Hallettsville.

As Pastor of Sacred Heart Parish in Hallettsville from 1882 until 1895, Father Forest completed the original stone church in his first year as pastor. In that same year Sisters of the Incarnate Word and Blessed Sacrament came here from their motherhouse in Victoria to occupy their convent near the church and to open a children's school. Land was purchased in 1882 and in 1890, when the first parish hall was erected. Forest built a sacristy, choir loft, and steeple, enlarging St. Mary's at Hallettsville. When the present church was finished in 1896, he dedicated it on 28 October.

Father Forest continued to expand. He completed the church for St. Joseph's Parish at Moulton in 1888 and finished its rectory in 1890. The parish was a mission for a time, with its parish school built in 1894 and conducted by the Sisters of Divine Providence until 1965. On 31 May 1891 he dedicated the church at Shiner as Sts. Cyril and Methodius, formed from parishes of Yoakum, St. Mary's, and Moulton. The Shiner church became a mission of the parish at Moulton from 1892 until 1912. Its parish cemetery was established in 1892 and a rectory was built in 1895.

From about 1860 pioneers of old Sweet Home attended churches at Yoakum, Hallettsville, St. Mary's, or Koerth. A dance hall was remodeled into a church and dedicated as Exaltation of the Holy Cross. The present church was built and rededicated as Queen of Peace in 1919.

The prodigious labors of Father Forest in developing the Hallettsville area were at last recognized by Pope Leo XIII with the appointment as Bishop of San Antonio on 27 August 1895. On 28 October Bishop Forest was consecrated by Archbishop Francis Janssens of New Orleans in San Fernando Cathedral in San Antonio. His co-consecrators were Bishops Edward Fitzgerald of Little Rock, Arkansas, and Nicholas Gallagher of Galveston.

In 1895 a combination of four priests made up the Bishop's Council, examiners of the Clergy, and Officials of the Bishop's Court. By 1910 there were a vicar general, a chancellor, a Bishop's Council composed of six members, Synodal Examiners, a *Procurator Fiscalis* (Steward of the Treasury), an *Actuarius* (Clerk), Secretary, *Defensor Matrimonii* (Defender of the Matrimonial Bond), a Director of the Priests' Eucharistic League, and the Bishop himself acted as Director for the Propagation of the Faith.

The fifteen years of Bishop Forest's tenure are filled with accomplishments. A true missionary, he worked as long and as hard as his health permitted. Shortly after he assumed his office, on 20 and 21 November 1895, he dedicated the present church of the Assumption of the Blessed Virgin Mary Parish in Praha and offered the first Mass in the remodeled St. Patrick's Church in San Antonio. On 10 December he blessed the cornerstone of the motherhouse and academy being built by the Sisters of Divine Providence. At his suggestion the name was changed from St. Mary's of the Lake to Our Lady of the Lake. It has grown into the present university of that name.

The next year of 1896 began with a brief respite while the new bishop welcomed Archbishop (later Cardinal) Francesco Satolli, the first Apostolic Delegate to the United States, to the Diocese of San Antonio. In that year the Incarnate Word Sisters purchased St. Mary's Sanatorium in Boerne and devoted it entirely to the care of tubercular patients. On 9 July the Sisters of Divine Providence completed their motherhouse and academy with a small convent chapel. Bishop Forest was on hand to bless their undertaking. He also saw the building of the first church of St. Anthony's Parish in Elmendorf. At this time the diocesan Catholic population was about 66,000, with thirty-eight diocesan and seventeen religious order priests. There were four academies for boys and five for young ladies, with twenty-six parochial schools. Students under Catholic instruction or care numbered 5,200.

In 1897 the first church of St. Mary's was built at Nada. The Sisters of Charity of the Incarnate Word purchased the property of Colonel Brackenridge in Alamo Heights and lived in his house until the completion of their new convent. Sisters of Our Lady of Charity came to San Antonio and established Our Lady of Victory School as a center for the rehabilitation of delinquent and neglected girls. Immaculate Conception Academy in San Angelo, which was built in 1888, was replaced by a large frame building equipped to serve day and boarding students. Sacred Heart Church in Campbellton was built. On 12 May Sacred Heart of Jesus Church in Sabinal was dedicated and on 21 November the Union of Czech Catholic Women of Texas (K.J.Z.T.) was established to provide insurance for members and to support seminarians.

The school at St. Michael's Parish in San Antonio began in 1898 and continued until 1965. On 25 August the Catholic State League of Texas was organized by German-Americans in Castroville to work for Church, school, and good citizenship in state and nation. On 27 October the first church of St. Ann in Kosciusko was dedicated. The year 1899 was notable for the establishment of Sacred Heart Parish in San Antonio and St. Joseph's Parish in Dilley. The Ursuline Sisters in San Antonio completed a new academy. In 1900 the motherhouse of the Sisters of Charity of the Incarnate Word was completed and Incarnate Word Academy established.

The Diocese of San Antonio ushered in the Twentieth Century with the rededication of Our Lady of Refuge Church in Eagle Pass on 13 January. The Church of St. Boniface was dedicated in Hobson on 9 April. The Fourth of July was celebrated with the dedication of the new Church of St. Anthony in Runge. During that year a Home for the Colored Poor was established under the supervision of Father John A. Dumoulin. It became the nucleus of Holy Redeemer Parish. Our Lady of Perpetual Help in Selma built its first school and staffed it with the Sisters of Divine Providence. A new and larger school building was constructed in Sts. Peter and Paul Parish in New Braunfels in the pastorship of Rev. Joseph M. J. Wack. And the third Church of St. Luke's at Loire was built.

Sts. Peter and Paul Church was built at El Campo and on 18 September 1902 Claretian Missionaries were introduced into the Diocese by Bishop Forest for parish work and given charge of San Fernando Cathedral. In 1903 Archbishop (later Cardinal) Diomede Falconio, the Apostolic Delegate to the United States, came to San Antonio to lay the cornerstone of San Antonio Philosophical and Theological Seminary, now St. Anthony High School Seminary. The new institution was operated by the Missionary Oblates of Mary Immaculate, and it marked the beginnings of the Oblate College of the Southwest. The second rectory of St. Mary's Church in San Antonio was built and St. John Berchmans Parish was established in that city. On 15 May 1903 the first Knights of Columbus Council in San Antonio was founded and on 19 August the Sisters of the Sacred Heart of Jesus came to San Antonio. The mission church of St. Andrew was built at Pleasanton.

The Sisters of the Incarnate Word constructed Sacred Heart Academy close to Sacred Heart Church in Del Rio in 1904 and students began to enroll in 1905. And in the latter year Nazareth Academy in Victoria was rebuilt and enlarged by the Sisters of the Incarnate Word and Blessed Sacrament, the Church of Holy Trinity in Falls City was built, and the first church in honor of St. Andrew in Hillje was dedicated on 20 November.

Our Lady of Guadalupe Parish in Del Rio was established in 1906. In that year Bishop Forest prevailed upon the provincial superior of the Society of Mary, Rev. George Meyer, to reopen St. Joseph's School in Victoria (closed since 1902) as a high school for boys. In the San Felipe District the Parish of Our Lady of Guadalupe was established under the direction of the Oblate Fathers. A parish school staffed by Incarnate Word Sisters opened almost immediately.

On 17 May 1907 Bishop Forest blessed the St. Francis Home for the Aged and did the same service on 30 May for the convent chapel of Incarnate Word Academy in San Antonio. In 1908 Our Lady of Guadalupe Parish was established in Helotes, and a church of the same name was dedicated at Seguin on 12 December.

The institutions of the San Antonio Diocese flourished as never before under its French bishop. Czech and German immigrants had stabilized themselves into parishes and took pride in providing places of worship. In the age of Bishop Forest many older parishes like Assumption in Praha and St. Mary's in Fredericksburg replaced smaller churches with larger ones. Frame mission chapels were being supplanted by permanent stone parish churches.

And like the institutions of his diocese, the Bishop himself had now become old and he knew, at age seventy, that he would soon need to be replaced. In 1909 he called for a coadjutor with rights of succession. Still he worked on. On 31 January the Chapel of the Mission San Juan Capistrano in San Antonio was rededicated. On 10 August St. Anthony's Parish in Harper was established. The Society of Mary added a new chapel and dormitory to St. Mary's University and Incarnate Word Sisters opened Our Lady of Guadalupe School for Our Lady of Refuge Parish in Eagle Pass.

In 1910 Holy Redeemer Church in San Antonio attained parish status and more buildings were added to Ursuline Academy. St. Mary's Parish in San Antonio completed a large parochial elementary school, conducted by the Sisters of Divine Providence. It was the first free parochial school in the State of Texas.

On 7 February 1910 Rev. John William Shaw of Mobile, Alabama, was appointed coadjutor bishop of San Antonio. He was consecrated in Mobile on 14 April and came to San Antonio on 11 May. One week later Bishop Forest welcomed Bishop Shaw to San Antonio officially in San Fernando Cathedral. At that time the old bishop conferred upon his successor the government of the Diocese and retired to Santa Rosa Infirmary, where he had lived for the past two years.

Incarnate Word College began to award degrees. In November St. John's Sanatarium, named in honor of Bishop Forest, opened its doors. In the following month its training school admitted the first student. By 1911 the Catholic population of San Antonio was about 95,000. Fifty-four diocesan and thirty-five religious order priests served the Diocese. There were five academies for boys with nineteen for young ladies, and thirty-six parochial schools in 1910.

Seven thousand six hundred and seventy-two young people were cared for under Catholic auspices.

The day of Bishop Forest was done. For forty-seven years he had labored, and it was now time to rest. He suffered a stroke in February 1911, and on 11 March he died at Santa Rosa Infirmary in San Antonio. Four days later Bishop Shaw celebrated a pontifical requiem Mass, and Bishop Morris of Little Rock preached the eulogy. Burial with ecclesiastical and military honors followed in San Fernando Cemetery. The venerable French bishop, whose name means the same in English as in his own language, took for his episcopal motto, "My hope is in the cross."

On the seventy-fifth anniversary of the Diocese of San Antonio (1949) Rev. Matthew Gilbert wrote of this last "Apostle from Lyon":

> The French missionary lifted up the cross where it had fallen to the ground after the Spanish Franciscan Friars were removed across the Rio Grande; what could be saved from the ruins of the Spanish and Mexican Church they incorporated into plans for a new and larger and more resplendent edifice (Wangler 24).

Most Reverend Francis James Furey, STD, PHD
Titular Bishop of Temnus and Auxiliary Bishop of Philadelphia
Coadjutor Bishop and Apostolic Administrator of San Diego
Second Bishop of San Diego
Third Archbishop of San Antonio

One of the most learned and accomplished hierarchs of Texas, Francis James Furey represents the flowering of the American Church. A prelate of solid attainments and honors, he reached his full potential after the Second Vatican Council and the era following it. This period stressed not the scholarly intellectual so much as the pastor and the man of the people. Being a faithful churchman and aware of what was to come, Furey aided the clerical revolution and ushered in the age of the minority hierarchy to serve their ministries in the Church in a specially meaningful way.

Born in Summit Hill, Carbon County, Pennsylvania, on 22 February 1905 to John F. and Anna (O'Donnell) Furey, Francis James was educated in the public and St. Michael's schools of Coaldale. He attended the Theological Seminary of St. Charles Borromeo in Overbrook Station Philadelphia from 1920 until 1924. He spent the next six years in Rome earning the degrees of Doctor of Philosophy in 1926 and that of Doctor of Sacred Theology in 1930 from the Pontifical Roman Seminary. He was ordained in Rome for the Archdiocese of Philadelphia on 15 March 1930.

From 1930 to 1936 Father Furey was private secretary to Cardinal Dennis Dougherty and master of ceremonies for the Archdiocese of Philadelphia. He was then President of Immaculata College in Immaculata, Pennsylvania, from 1936 until 1946. This women's college was founded in 1920 and is conducted by the Sisters, Servants of the Immaculate Heart of Mary. Its current enrollment is over 2,000 students. During his presidency Furey was awarded the honorary degree of Doctor of Laws by La Salle University of Pennsylvania in 1944 and by St. John's University of Jamaica, New York, in 1946. He was a trustee of the Catholic High School in Philadelphia, a member of the Catholic Educational Association of Pennsylvania, of the National Catholic Educational Association, and of the Association of College Presidents of Pennsylvania.

In 1946 President Furey became the nineteenth Rector of St. Charles Borromeo Seminary in Philadelphia. As Vice-President of the Board of Trustees and Prefect, he raised over one million dollars for repairs and served simultaneously as the Moderator of Priests' Conferences in the Archdiocese. He sat on the Board of Directors of Misericordia Hospital, of Rosenhill Academy, and of St. Joseph's Hospital, all in Philadelphia.

On 22 April 1947 Pope Pius XII appointed Father Furey a Domestic Prelate, with the title of Right Reverend Monsignor. Villanova University made him a Doctor of Laws in 1947, as did St. Joseph's University in Philadelphia in 1949. After twelve years as Rector and Moderator, Monsignor Furey received his first parish assignment. In 1958 he became Pastor of St. Helena's Parish in Philadelphia and the Director of the archdiocesan Catholic Charities' Appeal.

In this last position he raised millions of dollars for the Archdiocese. Rome took note of Monsignor Furey and on 24 August 1960, Pope John XXIII appointed him Titular Bishop of Temnus and Auxiliary Bishop of Philadelphia. He was consecrated on 22 December of that year.

In 1962 Bishop Furey was appointed to the administrative tribunal of the Second Vatican Council. In the following year he severed his ties of thirty-three years with the Archdiocese of Philadelphia and with his pastorate of St. Helena's. Pope Paul VI appointed him Coadjutor Bishop and Apostolic Administrator of the Diocese of San Diego, California, on 25 July 1963. He was installed in St. Joseph's Cathedral there on the following 11 September. On 6 March 1966 Bishop Charles F. Buddy died and Bishop Furey became Bishop of San Diego.

Three years later on 4 June 1969 Pope Paul VI appointed Bishop Furey Archbishop of San Antonio. He was installed in San Fernando Cathedral on 6 August by Archbishop (later Cardinal) Luigi Raimondi, the Apostolic Delegate to the United States. Archbishop Furey received the pallium in Rome from Pope Paul VI on the following 15 December.

For the remainder of his life Archbishop Furey would be joined to the development of his archdiocese. On New Year's Day 1978, the last full year of his administration, the Archdiocese had 202 diocesan and 227 religious order priests, fifty-eight permanent deacons, 142 men religious, 1,523 women religious, and 163 parishes with a Catholic population of 583,744. There were 2,281,929 Catholics in Texas on that date. Among the institutions of the archdiocese were four universities and colleges, sixteen high schools, and fifty-six elementary schools. During the year just past the archdiocese witnessed 15,128 infant baptisms and 572 conversions to Catholicism.

Between 1969 and 1979 the Diocese of Fort Worth was created on 22 August 1969 and the State of Oklahoma left the San Antonio Province on 6 February 1973. Fathers Patrick Flores in 1970, Hugo Gerbermann, MM, in 1975, and Raymundo Peña in 1976 were appointed auxiliary bishops to the Archbishop. Father John E. McCarthy was appointed Auxiliary Bishop of Galveston-Houston in 1979. The following priests were appointed bishops of dioceses in Texas: Thomas Tschoepe (Dallas), Stephen Leven (San Angelo), John Cassata (Fort Worth), Vincent Harris (Austin through succession), John Fitzpatrick (Brownsville), Warren Boudreaux (Beaumont), John Morkovsky (Galveston-Houston through succession), and Bernard Ganter (Beaumont). Bishop Flores became Bishop of El Paso (then outside the Province) in 1978. In 1969 alone Archbishop Furey installed Bishops Tschoepe, Cassata, and Leven.

In December 1969 Archbishop Furey received authority from the Holy See to designate laymen as extraordinary ministers of Holy Communion. In the following month he began the permanent diaconate program which would yield 166 such deacons eighteen years later.

Of particular interest was the ordination of Patrick Flores on 5 May 1970. At the particular insistence of the Archbishop this priest of the Diocese of Galveston-Houston became the first Mexican-American bishop in the United States of America. An era had ended and another had begun. Texas had been administered by Mexican bishops until the days of the Republic. For over a century the Anglo influence had prevailed under foreigners and natives. Now history began to reassert itself as such bishops gained an increasing constituency of their people. Rather than bowing to an inevitability the Archbishop embraced the future course of the Church. Further, a Commission for Mexican-American Affairs was established in March 1970 to coordinate religious and social programs among the Spanish-speaking in the archdiocese.

Also in 1970 a new pension plan for priests of the archdiocese began in June, Finance and Building Boards were set up with lay participation, and the Diocesan Administrative Council was enlarged. In December the Archbishop Francis J. Furey Award was instituted to honor "loyal and devoted laity of the archdiocese" by means of a bronze medal and a certificate of merit. By 1 December 1974 1,040 men and women were so honored.

In 1971 a three million dollar loan was negotiated with a banking firm to consolidate archdiocesan debts under a monthly amortization plan. Archdiocesan priests were honored in April with an "appreciation night" in which Cardinal John Wright was guest speaker. In that month eleven priests were invested as prelates of honor with the title of Reverend Monsignor. The diocesan clergy were placed in charge of Antonian College Preparatory School in June of that year.

The Archbishop began to comply with the Second Vatican Council (1962-1965) and enlarged lay authority within the Archdiocese. Rev. John W. Yanta was appointed archdiocesan director of lay activities to coordinate the lay apostolate on New Year's Day 1972. He formed a steering committee representing various lay organizations which studied and discussed the Scriptures, as well as the documents of the recent Vatican Council. A series of retreats was held that December for diocesan leaders with the designation of "Movement for A Better World." At the close of the first retreat the Archbishop announced that 1973 would be "a year of renewal, prayer and sacrifice" in preparation for the Centennial Year of the Archdiocese in 1974.

Fourteen Christian Community retreats were conducted by the "Better World" team in deaneries and quadrants of the Archdiocese. On 8 April 1973 at a convocation at Antonian High School fifty-six members of a provisional Archdiocesan Lay Board were chosen. Later Father Yanta and other priests, religious, and lay people attended a training session in New York State to form a local retreat team.

At the Archdiocesan Centennial Assembly in San Antonio fifty-two persons were elected and installed as the Archdiocesan Lay Board. On 20 January 1974 Al Notzon became President. His purpose and that of the Board was to form a Christian community in the Archdiocese, according to the teaching of the Gospels and the documents of Vatican Council II, through the encouragement, assistance and promotion of the functions of the Church. These functions are proclaiming, preaching, teaching, exhorting, dialoguing, consulting, encountering, witnessing, acting, and praying.

The Archdiocese began various apostolic movements for the laity in the Years after 1965. These included the Christian Family Movement (a dialogue to improve family relationships), the Marriage Encounter (weekend retreats to improve communication between spouses), Search and Discovery (weekend experiences for youth to develop an awareness of themselves, others, and Christ), *Nova Cor* (the relation of college students to life through a dialogue on love), Charismatic Renewal (charismatic prayer and instruction), and *Comunidades de Base* or Basic Christian Community (a search to explore one's place in the Church and the means to build a better world).

In 1972 the Mexican American Cultural Center was established with national headquarters in San Antonio. It has become an international center for research, education, leadership formation, and publication of literature for the liberation and development of the Hispanic-American. In August of that year the former archdiocesan newspaper *Alamo Messenger* was restyled as *Today's Catholic*. The Archbishop wrote weekly letters and Bishop Flores submitted columns. In December the Archives Department was set up in the Chancery to sort and catalog documents, papers and records of more than two centuries.

On 22 January 1973 the Archbishop took a strong stand against the United States Supreme Court decision of Roe v. Wade allowing legalized abortion. He also supported the national boycott of Farah slacks in behalf of the unionization of the workers. In February the Archbishop Furey Charities Fund began to provide the Archbishop with money for emergency use at his own discretion, outside the archdiocesan budget. It was financed with dinners and dances and continues to bear his name to the present day. In this same year forty-one members of the archdiocesan laity received the papal medal Pro Ecclesia et Pontifice for service to church and papacy, and fifteen men were invested as Knights of St. Gregory for personal character and reputation and for notable accomplishment. Thirteen knights received promotions within the order.

In the first five years of his administration Archbishop Furey saw eleven new parishes built, including five in San Antonio and its environs. Major construction projects of four million dollars were undertaken. Between 1972 and 1974 an expert appraisal system of all archdiocesan properties was conducted. Beginning on 1 September 1971 a uniform fiscal year was established to conform to the United States Catholic Conference system.

Between 1969 and 1973 Archbishop Furey was actively involved with the Archdiocesan Arbitration Board, and he received an award from the National Conference of Christians and Jews in 1969. In the National Conference of Catholic Bishops he was a member of the Administrative Committee and Chairman of its Region Ten (a five-state area including Texas), Chairman of the Committee on the Lay Apostolate, and a member of the Committee on the Permanent Diaconate. He was Chairman of the Campaign for Human Development, Chairman of the Texas Catholic Conference, and vicar delegate for Region Six (Texas and Louisiana) of the Military Ordinariate. In 1977 he directed plans for the restoration of San Fernando Cathedral in San Antonio, received the Order of Aaron and Hur from the USA Jewish Chaplains, the Presidential Medal of Immaculata College, and the St. Joseph the Worker Award from the Texas AFL-CIO.

Archbishop Furey was a Knight of Columbus and of the Holy Sepulchre, a member of the John H. Newman Society, and the Legion of the Cedars of Lebanon. He was an honorary member of the United States Marine Corps and wrote poetry as an avocation. He received additional honorary degrees from Mount St. Mary College in Maryland and from Our Lady of the Lake University in San Antonio.

The Archbishop was a strong defender of law and order. His Irish surname in English means "bushy eyebrows." For his episcopal motto he chose "Ipsam sequens non Devias" ("With Mary, we cannot go astray"), which was the official motto of the centennial year of the Archdiocese (1974). Archbishop Francis J. Furey died in San Antonio, Texas, of cancer on 23 April 1979 and is buried in that city in Holy Cross Cemetery.

Most Reverend Joseph Anthony Galante, DD, JCD
Titular Bishop of Equilium and
Auxiliary Bishop of San Antonio
Fourth Bishop of Beaumont

"To have the mind of Jesus" is the sense of what Paul said in Philippians 2:5. What the great missionary strictly enjoined this ancient people embodies the philosophy and purpose of Joseph Anthony Galante, the fourth bishop of Beaumont. It is also his episcopal motto. When he adopted it as auxiliary bishop of San Antonio, he put his feelings into words:

> I am convinced that we need to keep talking about Jesus. Unless we can bring people to know Jesus, to understand Jesus and to love Jesus more, all the other things we do don't make much sense. We need to develop a relationship with Christ. I believe that through Jesus moral behavior will be influenced. Social justice or sexual morality or whatever is only going to come about when people have a relationship with Christ that leads them to be responsible. For me I believe that whatever else I am called to do here [in San Antonio] — whatever the archbishop wants — fundamentally what I am to do is to try to live Christ — to have the mind of Christ for others and to try to form others to Christ.

He noted the influence of this scripture upon him and said, "I see my energy, my orientation, to try to help others be Jesus."

Bishop Galante is an enthusiastic man who enjoys football, motion pictures, and trips to the beach. Like his fellow bishop and canonist, David Fellhauer, he is a fan of mystery, spy, and detective stories, with Tony Hillerman, Tom Clancy, and Robert Parker being three of his favorite authors for recreational reading.

Those who know him say he is a good listener, loyal, trustworthy, and God-centered. He is committed to and understands the universal church. And he wants to be involved. The bishop is well-prepared to lead. He has exercised authority on several levels within the Church and he knows that his motto ("Have the mind of Jesus") indicates that humility must temper authority and that service to others requires the devotion of the shepherd to his flock.

Joseph Anthony Galante was born in the Holmesburg section of Philadelphia, Montgomery County, Pennsylvania, to Leonard J. (died 1983) and Edith (Cocci) Galante, on 2 July 1938. Leonard Galante operated a butcher shop and delicatessen at Rhawn and Bustleton Streets in Philadelphia. A second generation Italian with parents born in the United States, the future bishop grew up on Frankford Avenue near Pennypack Creek, in St. Dominic's Parish. He speaks some Italian and Spanish and is the oldest of four sons.

Joseph's brother Francis (born 1941), a funeral director, and his wife Marie have two grown daughters. Brother William (born 1944) and his wife Mary Anne have a daughter in grade school and live in Yardley, Pennsylvania. The youngest brother Paul (born 1945) and his wife Aleta have four children and live in New Town, Pennsylvania. Their mother Edith shares her home with her sister Rose in Yardley in nearby Bucks County.

Young Joseph began his education at Saint Dominic Elementary School and continued at Saint Joseph Preparatory School, both in Philadelphia. He seemed to be inclined to the priesthood at an early age. He liked to play the part of the priest after attending Mass, reciting the sermon he had heard and acting out the ceremony. Between 1954 and 1964 he attended Saint Charles Borromeo Seminary, where he was a student of the future archbishop Francis J. Furey of San Antonio. He graduated with a Bachelor of Arts degree in philosophy and was ordained for the Archdiocese of Philadelphia by Archbishop (later Cardinal) John Joseph Krol. The ordination took place in the Cathedral of Saints Peter and Paul in Philadelphia on 16 May 1964. He was then appointed associate pastor of Our Lady of Consolation Parish.

Between 1965 and 1968 Father Galante attended the Lateran University in Rome. There he received his doctorate in canon law (JCD). His dissertation concerned clerical celibacy, especially the church law and administration related to this teaching. In 1968 Bishop (later Cardinal) Humberto S. Medeiros requested a canonist from Cardinal Krol in Philadelphia to help with the newly-formed Diocese of Brownsville in South Texas. The Cardinal suggested Father Galante and Bishop Medeiros issued his invitation.

For four years (1968 to 1972) Joseph Galante was head of the diocesan tribunal (which he founded), the editor of the diocesan newspaper, the bishop's secretary, and master of ceremonies of liturgies. During this time he served on the priests' senate and the diocesan liturgical commission. He was also the director of the diocesan World Justice and Peace Commission and was the chaplain of the Catholic Lawyers' Guild. And, although he was a secular priest, he served as Vicar for Religious, replacing Rev. Eugene Canas, OMI, who had received another assignment. The experience he gained would be important in his future development as an administrator.

He returned to the Archdiocese of Philadelphia in 1972 and was assigned to Good Shepherd Parish (until 1973). He was Assistant Vicar for Religious (until 1979) and served under Msgr. James H. Meehan and Defender of the Bond (until 1974) on the archdiocesan marriage tribunal. Between 1974 and 1977 Father Galante was Professor of Canon Law at Saint Charles Borromeo Seminary. From 1975 until 1978 he also taught at Mary Immaculate Seminary at Northampton, Pennsylvania, in the Diocese of Allentown. In Philadelphia he was chaplain for the Catholic Home for Girls (1973-1981) and the Convent of the Handmaids of the Sacred Heart of Jesus. From 1981 until 1987 he aided the St. Raphaela Mary Retreat House in Haverford, Pennsylvania.

Father Galante was a member of the National Conference of Vicars for Religious, and served as President of that organization for two two-year terms (1976-1980). He succeeded Sr. Rose McDermott, SSJ, in the position of Episcopal Vicar for Religious in the Archdiocese of Philadelphia and remained in that position until 1987. As a member of the Canon Law Society of America (CLSA) he served on its Religious Affairs committee.

He maintained his interest in scholarship, with publications in the periodicals of the CLSA and the National Conference of Vicars for Religious. And he particularly relished retreat work, spiritual direction, programs and workshops, and lectures for Religious. Pope John Paul II recognized his efforts by appointing Galante an Honorary Prelate (with the title of Monsignor) on 24 April 1982.

His work as Vicar for Religious was of particular interest. It was to affect both his past and future endeavors. Sr. Charlene Wedelich, CDP, remembered Monsignor Galante in 1972, when he was in Brownsville and she was Superior General of the Congregation of Divine Providence. She met him again in Rome in 1986 when she was serving as Co-Vicar for Religious in the Archdiocese of San Antonio. The two served at this time in a panel discussion on religious orders.

On 9 December 1986 Monsignor Galante was named Undersecretary of the Vatican Congregation for Institutes of Consecrated Life and Societies of Apostolic Life. At this time it was known as the Congregation for Religious and Secular Institutes. He served with the Spanish Claretian Rev. Jesus Torres Llorente under the prefect (Belgian Cardinal Jean Jerome Hamer, OP) and the secretary (Italian Archbishop [now Cardinal] Vincenzo Fagiolo).

Founded by Pope Sixtus V on 27 May 1586 with the title of Congregation for Consultations of Regulars, it was confirmed by the apostolic constitution *Immensa* on 22 January 1588. It was made part of the Congregation for Consultations of Bishops and other Prelates in 1601. Pope St. Pius X made it autonomous as the Congregation of Religious. Pope Paul VI changed its name in 1967 and Pope John Paul II renamed it on 18 June 1988.

The Congregation has two sections dealing with institutes (orders or associations) of Religious, secular institutes, societies of the apostolic life, and third (secular) orders. It has authority concerning the establishment, general direction and suppression of these institutes. It governs them according to their rules and constitutions, their functions in contemporary life, and establishes and encourages councils and conferences of major religious superiors. In the United States the organization for sisters is called the Leadership Conference of Women Religious. Its corresponding version for men religious is the Conference of Major Superiors of Men.

As undersecretary Monsignor Galante hoped to resolve tensions existing between the Congregation and the Leadership Conference of Women Religious. In this capacity he acted as the Congregation's spokesman in a 1988 dispute between the Diocese of Paterson, New Jersey, and a group of Discalced Carmelite Sisters. These sisters had locked themselves within their monastery's infirmary to protest what they considered the modernization of their contemplative life. The Vatican recommended that two of the sisters be permitted to live out temporary vows at home or in another monastery. They would then be allowed to request a transfer. Meanwhile, two other sisters would be assisted in finding another monastery. During his time in Rome Monsignor Galante received the degree of Master of Arts in Spiritual Theology, which he earned at the Pontifical University of St. Thomas Aquinas, known as the Angelicum.

On his return from summer vacation on 30 September 1992 he heard of his appointment as bishop from his prefect, Cardinal Eduardo Martinez Somalo. A letter from Cardinal Bernardin Gantin, Prefect of the Congregation for Bishops, made it official. As Bishop Galante put it: "It took me a couple of minutes to catch my breath, then we went into the chapel and prayed, and that was it. That was a Wednesday. I had to write a letter [of acceptance] to His Holiness." The official date of the appointment was then announced on 13 October 1992.

The ordination of the Titular Bishop of Equilium and Auxiliary Bishop of San Antonio took place in St. Matthew's Church in San Antonio, Texas, on 11 December 1992. Archbishop Patrick F. Flores of San Antonio acted as Consecrator, while the bishop's Co-consecrators were Archbishop Francis B. Schulte of New Orleans and Auxiliary Bishop (and later bishop of Honolulu) Francis X. Di Lorenzo of Scranton. Both co-consecrators were Philadelphia natives, graduates of Saint Charles Borromeo Seminary, and former priests of the Archdiocese of Philadelphia. Cardinal Anthony Bevilacqua, Archbishop of Philadelphia, and his predecessor, Cardinal John Krol, attended.

On this occasion, followed by a reception at St. Matthew's, some 1,500 people attended, including about eighty relatives and bishops from Texas, Louisiana, New Mexico, Oklahoma, Pennsylvania, Maryland, the District of Columbia, Connecticut, and the Vatican. Msgr. Patrick J. Murray read the Apostolic Mandate, referring to Bishop Galante as "a man properly knowledgeable in doctrine and well practiced in priestly virtues." Archbishop Flores took his text from Matthew 9:35-38, concerning the necessity for compassion for the poor and needy. The references to "sheep without a shepherd" and Christ's injunction to request the owner of the harvest to "send out workers to gather in his harvest" were not lost upon Bishop Galante.

When he spoke, the new bishop said: "I want to be the family of Jesus to you. . . .I ask you to pray with me that all of us may grow more and more in Jesus and that together and individually we may have the mind of Jesus." He affirmed his commitment to guard the Catholic faith, to remain loyal to the pope, to show compassion to people in need and to gather lost sheep back to the Christian fold. He received the laying-on of hands by each bishop, was anointed with oil by Archbishop Flores, and received his miter, crozier, and ring.

As a person Bishop Galante brought to his new duties a charming personality, with a ready smile and a happy laugh, and an interest in cooking. Considered by some to be somewhat shy, he admitted a preference for small groups. His grounding in spirituality found an outlet in preaching and teaching. As he says: "I like giving spiritual direction-doing retreats-and giving conferences." Archbishop John P. Foley, a fellow Pennsylvanian and president of the Pontifical Council on Social Communications says of him: "[He] has always given an excellent priestly example of prayerfulness and of apostolic zeal."

As auxiliary bishop of San Antonio between 1992 and 1994 Bishop Galante was in charge of Assumption Seminary, the Casa de Padres (priests' retirement home), the Catholic Consultation Center, the Permanent Diaconate Program, the Office of Pastoral Leadership, Continuing Education for the Clergy, the Vocation Office, and the Priests' Personnel Board. While he remained in San Antonio, he was in residence at St. James the Apostle Parish, where his successor as auxiliary bishop, Rev. John W. Yanta, was pastor. Looking back on his time in San Antonio, he said: "I am especially pleased that the Pilgrim Center of Hope became established and I am certain it will be of great service in the evangelization and spiritual formation of the people of the archdiocese."

He was informed of his appointment as bishop of Beaumont on 28 March 1994. It was announced officially on 5 April, eight days later. At the press conference that day in Beaumont conducted by Msgr. Martin N. Enderle, the diocesan administrator elected following Bishop Ganter's death, the new bishop introduced himself as "Joseph, your brother." He told the assembly that his prayer for "a people to love and serve" had been answered in San Antonio and now in Beaumont. "I come with an open heart to love you and open hands to serve you. I am eager to learn from you." To the clergy, permanent deacons, religious, and laity, he remembered the youth of the Church, non-Catholics, the sick and the dying, and paid a tribute to Bishop Ganter.

But first he had to leave San Antonio. There was a farewell Mass and a reception for him at St. James's Church on the evening of 3 May. On the following day, the Chancery staff held a luncheon in his honor. The mood was kept lighthearted, yet there was some nostalgia as well.

It says much for Bishop Galante's sense of humor that he let remain throughout his tenure in San Antonio a sticker which he found on his office door on his arrival. It read: "I wasn't born in Texas, but I got here as quick as I could." Bishop Galante had served in Texas before he came to San Antonio. As Father James Vanderholt of the Beaumont diocese has recalled, the contribution of Pennsylvania to the Catholics of Texas is distinguished. Galante's seminary professor Francis J. Furey was archbishop of San Antonio. Father John Timon, CM, the founding bishop of the Diocese of Buffalo, New York, was Prefect of Texas. Bishops Nussbaum of Corpus Christi, Schuler of El Paso, and DeFalco of Amarillo were Pennsylvanians. Bishop Thomas F. Brennan, though Irish-born, was associated with the Diocese of Erie before he became bishop of Dallas.

Bl. Katharine Drexel (1858-1955), the Philadelphia heiress who founded the Sisters of the Blessed Sacrament (1891), spent her life in good works. She staffed schools in Beaumont, Port Arthur, and Orange, and constructed convents to house the sisters who taught in them. In more recent times Sr. Evelina Belfiore, OP, another Pennsylvanian, has served Beaumont as director of the Diocesan Office of Religious Education and as head of the Diocesan Catholic Biblical School.

Speakers at the Chancery luncheon recalled Bishop Galante's "Joseph, your brother" introduction at Beaumont. Bishop Popp advised him that he would not be the next pharaoh of Beaumont, but instead "an extraordinary ordinary," punning upon the ordinary (or sufficient in themselves and not delegated) powers of a residential bishop. Msgr. Lawrence Stuebben, the director of administration for the Archdiocese, observed that the Biblical Joseph had wealth and power, and added: "When we come to Beaumont asking for money, we hope you'll remember you're Joseph our brother." Archbishop Flores thought of a popular Spanish song, the refrain of which says, "You say you're leaving, leaving, leaving — but when?" The bishop's secretary Janie Montez recalled his interest in the mail he received, that he favored written responses, and that he kept and updated his calendar of appointments.

When it was his time to speak, Bishop Galante told his friends, "I keep leaving pieces of my heart in so many different places. I don't know how many more pieces are left." It was certain that the Diocese of Beaumont would be different from the Archdiocese of San Antonio. The Diocese was less than one-third the area with a Catholic population less than one-sixth that of the Archdiocese. Of his new flock nearly 17% were African-Americans. But many claimed in various percentages heritages of French, Italian, German, Polish, Vietnamese, Korean, and Mexican.

Bishop Galante was installed bishop of Beaumont in that city at Montagne Center on the campus of Lamar University on the evening of 9 May 1994. The facility is ordinarily a basketball stadium with a seating capacity of 10,000. On this evening the Installation and Mass began at 7:00 P.M. The Papal Nuncio to the United States, Archbishop Agostino Cacciavillan, was there and Archbishop Patrick Flores presided. The archbishops of New Orleans and of Santa Fe, New Mexico, came, as did bishops of Texas, Arkansas, and Pennsylvania. The Bishop of Lake Charles, Louisiana, sent his representative. Clergy came from Philadelphia, as did the bishop's mother and aunt, his brothers and their wives, and a niece. The family of Bishop Ganter was represented by the late bishop's brother Paul and his wife, his niece Rachel representing his mother, and his nephew Stephen.

On their entrances the bishop, his mother, and Monsignor Enderle were especially well-received by the audience. Banners of parishes, schools, ministries, and youth groups made their colorful display to the assembled priests, ecumenical ministers, and deacons. There were appearances by parish and ministry delegates, school children, Mexican heritage dancers, Vietnamese, and Cajuns (Louisianians descended from the French-speaking immigrants of Acadia). There were African-American liturgical movement groups, Fourth Degree Knights of Columbus, and Knights of Peter Claver. The Knights served as an honor guard for the entrance procession of liturgical ministers, ecumenical ministers, deacons, clergy, the diocesan college of consultors, visiting bishops, the clergy, and the pro-nuncio.

As Archbishop Flores presided, the pro-nuncio read a translation of the official papal letter naming Bishop Galante to head the Church in Southeast Texas. He presented the letter to the College of Consultors, and afterwards the two archbishops accompanied the Bishop to his chair and gave him his crozier. Here he was welcomed by priests, permanent deacons, religious, the diocesan pastoral staff, and ethnic communities. Then followed welcomes by representatives of civil, religious, and professional communities.

During the ceremony English, French, Spanish, and Vietnamese languages gave responses to the general intercessions. The Vietnamese prepared the altar for Mass. Bishop Galante spoke the homily. He said in part: "We are called to empty ourselves, to open ourselves to become more like Jesus. Jesus Christ is Lord and we are his people. . . .We are called to be a community of faith, hope, and love. . . .I want us to be God's people, to have the mind of Jesus, to faithfully, unswervingly follow Jesus."

As of 1 January 1995 the Diocese of Beaumont consisted of 7,878 square miles, consisting of nine Southeast Texas counties. It had eighty priests, three religious brothers, seventy-one religious sisters, and thirty-two permanent deacons, who served forty-three parishes and ten missions, two pastoral centers, two Catholic hospitals, one health care center, three day care and extended day care centers, a specialized home, a special center for social services, and a residential care for the disabled center. There were a high school and seven elementary schools with 12,470 students under Catholic instruction with 198 teachers. There were 86,420 Catholics in a total population of 541, 534, or sixteen percent.

Bishop Galante quarters his personal arms with those of the Diocese of Beaumont. From a blue field in honor of the Blessed Virgin Mary, at the upper center (honor point) there is a silver cross with a gold ring (roundel) interlaced within the arms of the cross. This symbol signifies the bishop's service to consecrated life (the religious and secular institutes). The gold ring signifies the band worn by those in consecrated life committed to Christ by the profession of the vows of chastity, poverty, and obedience. The ring is intertwined around the cross, indicating that all take up the cross and carry it daily. At the bottom center (nombril point) is a gold carpenter's square to honor his patron Saint Joseph. In the center on the left are the crossed keys of Saint Peter for service to the Holy See and the Holy Father. The silver star from the arms of the Archdiocese of Philadelphia signifies Texas and San Antonio. His motto, as we have seen, is "Have the mind of Jesus," for his belief that all minds, attitudes, and lives of Christians should be lived in conformity with Christ.

Bishop Galante's surname has many meanings, among which are splendid, stately, spirited, brave, chivalrous, and self-sacrificing. It suggests one accustomed to courtly manners, as befits the first bishop of Texas to come to its hierarchy directly from the Vatican. It also has a touch of the knightly, one whose announced quest is for everyone to know and love Jesus Christ.

In 1995 Bishop Galante served as chairman of the Bishops' Committee on Religious Life and Ministry.

Right Reverend Nicholas Aloysius Gallagher, DD
Titular Bishop of Canopus and Administrator of Galveston
Third Bishop of Galveston

Born in Temperanceville, Belmont County, Ohio, on 19 February 1846, Nicholas Aloysius Gallagher was the son of John and Mary Ann (Brinton) Gallagher. He was educated at Mount St. Mary's Seminary of the West in Cincinnati and received the tonsure and minor orders from its archbishop John Purcell on 21 September 1867. Nicholas became a Subdeacon on 21 December 1868 and a Deacon on the following day. Three days later, on Christmas Day 1868, he was ordained in Columbus, Ohio, for that diocese by its bishop Sylvester Horton Rosecrans. Until he was appointed bishop, Father Gallagher would spend his entire priestly service in the city of his ordination.

Nicholas Gallagher was Assistant Pastor of St. Patrick's Parish in Columbus, Ohio, from 1869 to 1871 and Pastor from 1876 to 1878. In between he was President of St. Aloysius' Diocesan Seminary in Columbus from 1871 to 1876. Upon leaving the pastorate of St. Patrick's Father Gallagher was administrator of the Diocese of Columbus (1878-1880). He returned to his former parish as its pastor for the second time and was, in addition, Vicar General of the Diocese from 1880 to 1882.

On 19 January 1882 Pope Leo XIII appointed Father Gallagher Titular Bishop of Canopus and Administrator (with rights of succession) of the Diocese of Galveston. He was consecrated the following 30 April in St. Mary's Cathedral, Galveston, by Bishop Edward Fitzgerald of Little Rock. His co-consecrators were Bishops Dominic Manucy of Brownsville and John Neraz of San Antonio.

As Administrator Bishop Gallagher had effective control of the Diocese of Galveston. Bishop Claude Dubuis had returned to France, but he refused to relinquish the title of Bishop of Galveston for the next ten years. Meanwhile the new bishop found himself possessed of an administrative area of 150,000 square miles with forty-three priests, fifty churches and chapels, two seminarians, three parochial schools, one college for boys and two academies for girls, an orphanage, a hospital, 107 women religious, and a Catholic population of 30,000.

Extending facilities for Black parishioners, the Bishop and the Sisters of Saint Dominic opened a school in a cottage on the corner of Twelfth Street and Avenue K in Galveston. It was the first Catholic school in Texas for Black students when it opened in October 1886. It expanded into a new building two years later. The Bishop often visited the school, always sending a basket of fruit as a gift in advance of his arrival.

Holy Rosary Parish developed from this school in 1888, with Rev. Philip L. Keller becoming the first priest in the American Catholic Church in 1889 to labor in the Black apostolate. Reverend Thomas Hennessy of the Church of the Annunciation cared for Black Catholics also. It was not until 1913 that the Josephite Order of priests began to staff Holy Rosary Parish.

On 17 October 1887 Bishop Gallagher dedicated a school for Black children named for Saint Nicholas at the corner of Chenevert and Lamar Streets in Houston. It was conducted by the Sisters of the Incarnate Word. Father Hennessy and Monsignor Roche, the President of St. Thomas College in Houston, invited the Josephite Fathers to take charge of St. Nicholas Parish in October 1901.

At the request of Bishop Gallagher the Diocese of Dallas was established on 15 July 1890. On 16 December 1892 Bishop Dubuis formally resigned his title of Bishop of Galveston and Bishop Gallagher took his place. In 1901 the Bishop bought the Sylvan Beach Hotel in La Porte and opened his own seminary, known as St. Mary's, and staffed it with Basilian Fathers. He added an administration building in 1908 and placed the diocesan clergy in charge of it in 1911. It continued to operate there until it closed in 1954 and moved to Houston.

In October 1911 the Missionary Oblates of Mary Immaculate were invited to establish a church in the East End Community in Houston to serve Mexican-Americans. Today it is the Church of the Immaculate Conception. During his tenure Bishop Gallagher invited the Jesuits to take over St. Mary's University in Galveston, the Basilian Fathers to establish St. Thomas High School in Houston, the Paulists, and the Dominicans, who founded the Church of the Holy Rosary in Houston. He introduced the Sisters of Charity of St. Vincent de Paul, the Good Shepherd sisters, Sisters of the Holy Family (who were Black and who conducted the St. Nicholas School), and the Dominican Sisters.

By 1918 there were 105 priests in the Diocese serving fifty-nine churches and sixty-one missions, with a Catholic population of 70,000. In that year on 21 January Bishop Gallagher died in Galveston. A solemn requiem Mass was celebrated by Bishop Theophile Meerschaert of Oklahoma in St. Mary's Cathedral in Galveston three days later in the presence of 112 priests of Galveston and other dioceses, with eight other bishops from Texas, Kansas, Mississippi, Arkansas, and Alabama. Bishop Lynch of Dallas, who delivered the eulogy, called Bishop Gallagher "a model priest, a zealous bishop, a loyal citizen." Bishop Nicholas Gallagher, whose Irish surname means "foreign benefactor" and whose episcopal motto was "Deus Est Caritas" ("God is love"), is buried in St. Mary's Cathedral-Basilica in Galveston, Texas, the only bishop of his diocese to be so honored.

Most Reverend Bernard Jacques Ganter, DD, JCD
First Bishop of Tulsa
Third Bishop of Beaumont

Some people would be pleased if their lives were monuments to record the good works they accomplished. In the case of Bernard Jacques Ganter, the founding bishop of Tulsa and the third bishop of Beaumont, his monuments are many and active. They are the institutions and ministries he established in his dioceses. And it was not enough for him to fulfill a need. The Bishop insisted upon excellence, and he received it. But not only was he a good provider for his flock. His spirit for good will and the provisions he made for everyone in his area outlived him. When a shepherd passes, his loss is felt by his people. For Bishop Ganter an interfaith service in his cathedral in Beaumont, four days after his death, brought together seven ministers of the Baptist, Presbyterian, Episcopal, United Methodist, Christian, and Jewish faiths. He had spent his life in trying to include all, helping each person achieve his fullest potential. One may suppose that the Bishop would have taken comfort in this gesture.

Born in Galveston, Galveston County, Texas, to Bernard Jacques and Marie (Boska) Ganter, on 17 July 1928, young Bernard Jacques attended St. Patrick's Grade School in Galveston. He graduated from Kirwin High School in that city in 1944. For a year afterwards he attended Texas A&M University at College Station, where he studied engineering and was a member of the Corps of Cadets. In 1982 as bishop of Beaumont he returned to the campus at the invitation of the Catholic Student Center to say Mass and to preach. On being introduced during the football game on the twentieth of November, the Center voted him its Outstanding Alumnus and the alumni magazine wrote a feature about its distinguished ax-student. Though he attended it for only a year, Texas A&M showed its pride in him by its significant participation in his funeral services.

Bernard Ganter entered St. Mary's Seminary in La Porte, Texas, in 1945. He was ordained in the Seminary Chapel by Bishop Wendelin J. Nold of Galveston for that diocese on 22 May 1952. The new priest enrolled that year in the Catholic University of America in Washington, DC. He received the degree of Doctor of Canon Law (JCD) in 1955, with a dissertation on "Clerical Attire." For the *New Catholic Encyclopedia* (1967) he would write articles on canon law and marriage, on the convalidation of marriage, and on the Pauline Privilege. The Pauline Privilege refers to a statement by Paul in 1 Corinthians 7:12-15, wherein Paul says that a legitimate marriage of unbaptized persons, even if consummated, can be dissolved if one of them later receives the sacrament of baptism.

In order for the Pauline Privilege to take effect, 1) the marriage must take place prior to the baptism of either spouse, 2) one spouse must have received baptism, and 3) the unbaptized person refuses to live in peace with the baptized person without interfering with his or her freedom to practice Christianity. If the unbaptized person agrees to these conditions, the privilege does not apply (1995 *CA* 133).

Returning to the Diocese of Galveston, Father Ganter held a number of positions. He was Administrator of Sacred Heart Parish in Conroe (1955-1956),

Assistant Pastor of Sacred Heart Co-Cathedral in Houston and Secretary to Bishop Nold (1956-1958), Officialis of the Diocesan Tribunal (1958-1966) and Chancellor of the Diocese of Galveston-Houston (1966-1973). Pope Paul VI appointed him a Papal Chamberlain with the title of Very Reverend Monsignor in 1964. Between 1969 and 1973 he was Rector of Sacred Heart Co-Cathedral. During his service to the Diocese he was also first chairman of the Diocesan Senate of Priests, a Diocesan Consultor, a member of the Diocesan Pastoral Council and of the Diocesan Development Fund Board, a member of the Post Cana Club of Houston, and the cofounder of Pre- and Post-Cana marriage pastoral programs in the Diocese.

Pope Paul VI appointed Monsignor Ganter Bishop of Tulsa on 19 December 1972. He was ordained and installed in Holy Family Cathedral in Tulsa by Archbishop (later Cardinal) Luigi Raimondi, the Apostolic Delegate to the United States, on 7 February 1973. In his sermon Bishop Ganter recalled that Benedictine priests from France ministered to the people of Oklahoma and that in their monastery Bishop Gallagher of Galveston ordained four monks to the priesthood on 22 August 1887. He also remembered three native sons of Oklahoma who became bishops, Stephen A. Leven of San Angelo, Charles A. Buswell of Pueblo, and John J. Sullivan (born in Kansas but who served in Oklahoma) of Grand Island (and later of Kansas City-St. Joseph).

In charge of a diocese with forty-nine parishes in a thirty-one county area with 51,000 Catholics, Bishop Ganter set about maintaining some institutions and ministries and establishing others. He chose as his episcopal motto "*In Corde Jesu*" ("In the Heart of Jesus") for his seventeen years of association with two churches under the patronage of the Sacred Heart. He said, "I have chosen this motto for it sums up everything about our life and faith."

Among the activities of the Diocese of Tulsa was its cosponsorship with the Archdiocese of Oklahoma City of a Central American mission. During this period Bishop Ganter was member of the Board of Regents of Conception Seminary, Missouri and of St. Gregory College in Shawnee, Oklahoma. He was on the Board of Directors of the Tulsa Chapter of the National Conference of Christians and Jews and was the 1975 honoree of the National Jewish Hospital of Denver at its annual banquet that year in Tulsa.

Throughout his episcopal ministry Bishop Ganter was active in the National Conference of Catholic Bishops He served on its Liaison Committee with officers in the Leadership Conference of Women Religious, the Liaison Committee with priests, religious, and laity, the Pro-Life Affairs Committee, the Ad Hoc Committee on Nominations to Conference Offices, and committees on seminaries and on health affairs. He was also a representative for Region X (which includes Oklahoma, Texas and other states) on the Administrative board.

In 1977 during an interview for the *Eastern Oklahoma Catholic* Bishop Ganter recalled his establishment of departments, staff, budgets, and all organizations in the Diocese. In October of that year his letter in this publication, supported by thirty-six priests, spoke out for better prison conditions. It suggested probationary sentences, restitution to victims, community service, fines proportionate to crimes, and daily employment with continued incarceration on weekends.

The Bishop of Tulsa was appointed bishop of Beaumont by Pope Paul VI on 3 October 1977. He was installed in St. Anthony's Cathedral in Beaumont by Archbishop Jean Jadot, the Apostolic Delegate to the United States, assisted by Archbishop Francis J. Furey of San Antonio, on 13 December 1977. During the homily Bishop Ganter expressed his interest in serving the unchurched and disillusioned, in addition to his own flock. He expressed concern about family life and broken homes. He asked his listeners to note three paradoxes: 1) We die to live eternally, 2) We grow by spending life, and 3) We serve in order to become great.

The Diocese of Beaumont had been in existence for only eleven years. The bishop's predecessor Bishop Boudreaux had established the churches of St. Peter the Apostle in Groves, Queen of Vietnam in Port Arthur, and St. Martin de Porres in Cheek, as well as the Diocesan Board of Reconciliation and Mediation, the Diocesan Council, and an independent tribunal. Before his appointment as Bishop of Houma-Thibodaux in 1977 he had named Father William Manger director of the Diocesan Resettlement Office for immigrants and refugees in June 1975 and awarded several hundred bishop's medals to lay people of the Diocese to mark its tenth anniversary and that of the American bicentennial in 1976.

In February 1978 Bishop Ganter appointed Msgr. Francis H. Burlton director of the Diocesan Office of Parish Boundaries to establish boundaries for existing parishes if none were set, to realign boundaries if necessary, and to determine the need for new parishes and/or boundaries. In the course of his tenure in Beaumont Bishop Ganter established St. Jude Thaddeus Parish in west Beaumont and St. Francis of Assisi Parish for north Orange and Little Cypress. He raised St. Joseph in Livingston to parish status in 1978 and St. Maurice in Mauriceville in 1989. He established Holy Spirit Mission in Kountze with a Dominican sister as administrator (1986) in the Infant Jesus Parish in Lumberton. In 1991 he established Holy Trinity Mission in Mont Belvieu with a permanent deacon as administrator in the Our Lady of Light Parish in Anahuac.

Over the years the Bishop put in place the mission church of St. Martin de Porres in Corrigan, and built new churches for Our Lady of the Assumption Parish in Beaumont, St. Therese Parish in Center, and St. Martin de Porres Mission in Corrigan. He provided new church buildings for Our Lady of the Assumption Parish in Beaumont, St. Therese Parish in Center, St. Martin de Porres Mission in Cheek and new parish halls for Our Lady of Guadalupe in Diboll and St. Mary's in Fannett. And he constructed new rectories for St. Joseph's Parish in Livingston and St. Mark the Evangelist's Parish in Silsbee. In 1986 he broke ground for a new church building at St. Helen Parish in Orangefield, a new church for Our Lady of La Salette Mission in Kirbyville, and a new addition to St. Catherine of Siena Parish in Port Arthur.

In May 1978 the Bishop changed priests' tenures to seven-year terms with possible three-year extensions. This policy was later changed so as to be in conformity with the Vatican terms of six years for pastors and three years for associates. Sr. Lauren Beck, CVI was appointed Director of Religious Education. She would later become Director of Diocesan Development and Vicar for Women Religious. In July 1978 Richard Kraft became Diocesan Music Director. He taught organ, piano, liturgical music, basic courses in liturgies of the western church, basic conducting, and elementary music theory.

Bishop Ganter appointed a full-time staffer for the Diocesan Office of Worship. He inaugurated a parish renewal program in the Diocese with Rev. Daniel A. Shanahan, OP in charge. Incarnate Word Sister Rose Mary Cousins became diocesan superintendent of schools in the Summer of 1978. She had degrees in education and business and was fully certified in educational administration. Sister Cousins with Sr. Jo Dederichs of the Diocesan School Office published a booklet on the history of Catholic schools in Texas.

In September 1978 the Bishop sent Msgr. Sidney J. Marceaux to study for a doctorate in canon law. His successful completion of graduate studies enabled him to become canonist for the Diocese and to head the marriage tribunal. His expertise later enabled the Diocese of Tyler tribunal to become proficient in its duties and finally to become independent of the Beaumont diocese. Rev. Michael A. Jamail also obtained a doctorate in canon law, together with another doctorate in education, and served on the tribunal and as director of the Holy Family Retreat Center in Beaumont.

Monica LeBlanc, a teacher at Bishop Byrne High School in Port Arthur, developed "Media Now," the first packaged and systematically organized media course in the country. Although the Bishop was forced to close this high school in 1983 due to declining enrollment and finances, he was able to establish a trust fund from the sale of its property for day schools in South and Mid-Jefferson County. The remaining diocesan high school, Monsignor Kelly in Beaumont, has been cited at least twice by the United States Department of Education for the excellence of its programs.

Charles and Elizabeth Balsam of the Diocesan Pastoral Office wrote a book on natural family planning published by Liguorian Publications in Missouri. Mr. Balsam later became the director of the Family Life Office with Mrs. Balsam in charge of Natural Family Planning for the Diocese. The Family Life Office grew out of the work of the Christian Life Center, headed by Rev. William Manger to 1976, and afterwards by Dr. Andre Van Chau, then head of the Resettlement Office. This organization, which began to resettle Vietnamese in the Diocese after the Vietnam War, accomplished its purpose so well that it became known to the Immigration and Naturalization Service. Its activities were the source of favorable comment by *The New York Times* and by *Texas Monthly*.

Father Manger, Pastor of St. Mary's Parish in Orange and later of St. Anne's in Beaumont, was elected to the board of directors of the National Hospice Organization. He helped organize an ecumenical hospice in Orange. The Christian Life Center started the Pro-Life Force, which established four Birthright offices to provide counseling and material aid for pregnant women. These offices were located in Beaumont, Port Arthur, Lufkin and Nacogdoches. Birthright is an ecumenical group which believes human life exists from the moment of conception. It coordinates pro-life activities held each year. It organized marriage Pre-Cana conferences and Engaged Encounter pastoral programs for the Diocese.

The first ordination of permanent deacons for the Beaumont diocese took place on 26 May 1979 with five ordained. Trained in a Diocese of Dallas program for one weekend a month in Longview for several years, by late 1993 two more classes had been trained locally and ordained. By early 1995 the Diocese had thirty-two permanent deacons. Three Franciscan sisters came from their motherhouse in Little Falls, Minnesota. Of these Sr. Antoinette Ahles, RN, visited people in hospitals and homes and translated for patients to doctors. Bishop Ganter also recruited Franciscan and Benedictine religious sisters to come to the Diocese of Beaumont to assist its Mexican-Americans.

In May 1979 the Bishop formed the Diocesan Finance Board, consisting of three lay persons and two clergymen, to advise him on financial affairs concerning parishes and the Diocese. The following month he established and promulgated guidelines for parish and mission councils to promote more active lay leadership on the parish level. In 1980 Bishop Ganter visited all parishes in the Beaumont diocese. On the 29 March he held the first march for non-public school education in the Cardinal Stadium at Lamar University in Beaumont. This ecumenical effort raised a total of $45,000.

In May 1980 the Bishop announced a $20 million expansion and renovation program for St. Mary Hospital in Port Arthur, a new five-story addition. All patient bedrooms from the original 1930 wing were to be replaced in the new wing, with the old one to house administration and business offices. On 17 May 1980 Cardinal John P. Cody of Chicago presided at the Jubilee Mass celebrating the Golden Anniversary of the hospital. Bishop Ganter was the celebrant for the Mass at St. James's Church, which was followed by a reception in Kirwin Hall. Ground-breaking for the wing took place in the following December with its dedication scheduled almost two-and-a-half years later on 1 May 1983.

St. Mary Hospital houses a family residency program in conjunction with the University of Texas medical school in Galveston. In 1986 it had five residents. It is affiliated with Lamar University for the education of students in health care skills. This hospital concentrates on preventive measures to sickness. Southeast Texas Hospice, Inc. cares for the terminally ill.

A division of St. Mary, called the Bishop Byrne Regional Wellness Center, opened on 1 May 1985. Bishop Ganter blessed and dedicated the building. It provides ambulatory care for the retired and active-duty personnel of the military and their dependents as well as classes in health education for the community and support groups for stroke, heart attack, diabetes, and cancer patients and their families. The facility is located at Ninth Avenue and Texas Highway 73 in Port Arthur.

The State of Texas granted a certificate of need to Southeast Texas Hospice in December 1978. Through its facilities the terminally ill may remain at home, cared for by a team of doctors, nurses, social workers and volunteers provided by the Hospice to ease emotional difficulties. Ministers provide spiritual advice. Its headquarters are at 912 Cherry Avenue in Orange and it is licensed to serve Jefferson, Orange. Hardin, Jasper, and Newton counties, where patients are referred by private physicians.

Another type of facility within the Diocese also had to have a certificate of need to operate. The Bishop's dedication to closing it was aided by his testimony before the Texas Health Facilities Commission on 15 August 1980. The abortion clinic, denied its certificate, had to cease its functions. In contrast, the dedication of a new building for the Queen of Vietnam Parish by Cardinal Cody was a joyful event. It complements a social center and park, dedicated to Our

Lady, Queen of Peace, which also serves the Vietnamese community.

In May 1981 St. Elizabeth Hospital in Beaumont announced a $27 million expansion to bring its capacity to 467 beds, 419 of which were to be private with the rest being semiprivate. Additional floors were added atop the south wing, with construction of a new four-story wing on the east side of the hospital. It was dedicated on 20 May 1984, to complement the intensive care unit (1966) and the coronary care unit (1967). A five-story west wing completed in 1973 gave the hospital a 271 bed capacity. In November 1981 St. Mary Hospital in Port Arthur received the "Lifeline" emergency communication service, giving each subscriber a portable transmitter and telephone attachment. St. Elizabeth Hospital received "Lifeline" in 1982.

On 10 August 1984 ground was broken for a $3.6 million outpatient center at St. Elizabeth for the people of Southeast Texas. Called the Mamie McFaddin Ward Cancer Treatment Center, it was a 10,000 square foot unit, connected to the hospital by a corridor, with a new high-energy 20 MEV linear accelerator and a radio therapy simulator.

The Diocese of Beaumont made effective use of its media. The *East Texas Catholic* diocesan newspaper began in 1982. There were four Spanish radio shows, and Beaumont was the only Texas diocese to sponsor a television program on a network-affiliated channel. A two-year adult education program for formation in ministry originated from the Office of Renewal under the direction of Sr. Rita Norris, OP. The Office of Religious Education began the Catholic Biblical School in 1985, which later led to the diocesan adoption of the RENEW adult education program in 1992.

The Diocesan Office of Catholic Charities began under the leadership of Rev. Thomas E. Phelan, a graduate of the Worden School of Social Work of Our Lady of the Lake University. Its ministries include such programs as marriage preparation, the divorced and widowed, and natural family planning. It has undertaken the resettlement of refugees and immigrants and has provided for the homeless and the ill. In the year 1992-1993 it had a budget of more than $5 million for its work.

Catholic Charities underwrites such programs as Hospitality Center, Inc. in Port Arthur, which supplies meals on a daily basis to the needy. The Hamlet in Orange is a residential facility for the care of the AIDS-stricken. The Garth House in Beaumont administers the Mickey Mehaffy Children's Advocacy Program for abused children. Beaumont and Port Arthur have Child Development centers providing day care. Port Arthur also has the Beaumont Advantage Learning Center. And there are diocesan programs for crisis counseling, parish social ministry, and RESPITE, a program for health-care providers of elderly and frail people.

The Catholic Youth Ministry sponsors the annual Catholic Youth Organization (CYO) convention and several diocesan-wide activities, plus six Quest weekends for the youth of the diocese. In 1984 it took part in a summer camp for junior high school students at Confrontation Point in Tennessee. In 1989 Bishop Ganter and four other bishops took part in a summer forum of the National Federation for Catholic Youth Ministry, Inc.'s western conference.

One project begun by Bishop Ganter became a source of special satisfaction because of its usefulness. Construction and development of the Holy Family Retreat Center, one of twelve such facilities in Texas, began in 1983 on a fifty-five acre tract in Beaumont. Four million dollars was collected for the facility, with funds left over for an endowment for maintenance. A facility for spiritual exercises and conferences within a pleasant, informal atmosphere, Holy Family consists of three guest houses, each with sixteen double rooms with private baths, a meeting room, a kitchenette, and a screened porch. There is an office building with a chapel, a residence for staff members, and a residence for the caretaker with a workshop. For the benefit of visitors a Way of the Cross has been landscaped into part of the wooded area so that each person may follow it for prayer and meditation on the Passion and Death of Christ. This extensive complex contains a central dining and meeting hall. The Center was dedicated by Archbishop Patrick Flores in 1985 and hailed as one of the best retreat houses available. To 1993 more than 40,000 people have visited it.

Bishop Ganter was a Fourth Degree Knight of Columbus, a Knight of the Equestrian Order of the Holy Sepulchre, and a member of the Canon Law Society. From May 1991 to May 1993 he served as Texas State Chaplain of the Knights of Columbus. In addition he was a member of the board of directors of the Catholic University of America and of the governing board of St. Joseph Seminary in Covington, Louisiana. His affiliations also included membership on the Board of Governors of St. Elizabeth Hospital, of the twenty-six member Beaumont civic commission to choose an item to be named for Dr. Martin Luther King, Jr., of the Beaumont Downtown Rotary Club and its education committee, and he was an honorary member of the board of the Three Rivers Council of the Boy Scouts of America.

The Bishop freely offered his time and efforts in causes he considered worthy, and he urged his staff to assist others in situations where their expertise might prove useful. He began the Diocesan Office of Worship and Renewal and addressed local businessmen on business ethics at the John Gray Institute in Beaumont. He spoke to political science classes at Lamar University on the bishops' letter on the economy. By 1986 he established a scholarship fund for students in local diocesan schools to be used for tuition and he made St. Anne's School tri-parish (with St. Pius X and St. Jude) to improve its financial status.

Bishop Ganter hosted the Southwest Liturgical Conference meeting in Beaumont through the Diocesan Office of Worship. He worked to implement his fellow bishops' 1989 pastoral letter on evangelization. In 1992 he attempted to stop the execution of an Amarillo man convicted of killing a seventy-six-year-old nun. On 10 September 1992 the Bishop, together with fifty-four of his priests, issued a statement protesting racial discrimination in public housing assignments in Vidor. He supported girls and women as altar servers and was against the ordinations of women or married men.

The creation of the Tyler diocese lost the Beaumont diocese the counties of Angelina, Cherokee, Nacogdoches, Sabine, San Augustine, and Shelby. It regained some land in 1989 when it was allotted the western halves of Chambers and Liberty counties from the Diocese of Galveston-Houston. The nine counties remaining are now divided into five vicariates for administrative purposes. By 1993 the Diocese of Beaumont consisted of 7,878 square miles with seventy-eight priests, thirty-two permanent deacons, four male religious, sixty-three women religious and had forty-three parishes, ten missions, and two stations, with seven elementary schools, one high school, two hospitals, and a Catholic population of some 89,000 in a total population of over 528,000. Despite the loss of six churches and four missions, a convent, and a Newman Center, the remaining institutions of the diocese were greatly strengthened and, as we have seen, improved in many ways, particularly in health care and in social services.

On 24 August 1992 Dr. Mark J. Kubala reported that Bishop Ganter had undergone surgery at St. Elizabeth Hospital in Beaumont on 21 August for the removal of a tennis ball-sized brain tumor. The Bishop was given radiation and chemotherapy treatment and was released from the hospital on 9 September. He tried to resume his daily routine of Mass and work and at first took daily walks. As his health continued to deteriorate Vicar General Monsignor Marceaux assumed the administrative and executive duties of the Bishop, while Vicar General Monsignor Enderle handled his liturgical, social, and ceremonial responsibilities.

On 28 June 1993 a magnetic resonance imaging scan showed the regrowth of the tumor, which was now inoperable. In July Bishop Ganter removed to his brother's home in Santa Fe, Texas, where he died on 9 October 1993. His survivors included his mother Marie of Galveston, his sisters Patricia (Mrs. Warren) of Merkel, Texas, and Barbara (Mrs. Swann) of Hutchinson, Kansas, his brother Paul, six nephews, three nieces, four great-nephews and six great-nieces.

The Bishop's body was returned to his cathedral in Beaumont, where Knights of Columbus and Knights of Peter Claver in full regalia stood as a guard of honor. Memorial services were held there and at the Church of St. Francis of Assisi in Orange. On 15 October at noon Bishop Joseph Fiorenza of Galveston-Houston said the funeral Mass and spoke the homily. Archbishop Flores, who was to have said the Mass, Cardinal Bernard Law, who was to have given the homily, and four Texas bishops were prevented from attending while fog shrouded Jefferson County Airport. There were eight Texas bishops and one each from Louisiana and Kansas present The administrators of the Lubbock and Tulsa dioceses came, as did the Benedictine Abbot of St. Benedict Abbey in Covington, Louisiana. In all a congregation of about 500 people paid their last respects.

Pallbearers were Msgrs. Martin N. Enderle and Sidney J. Marceaux, Fathers Kevin Badeaux, Telesforo R. Blanco OSA, Francis X. Conroy, Timothy Deeter, Michael Jamail, Steven L. Leger and Bennie J. Patillo. Honorary pallbearers were the diocesan clergy, Sr. Lauren Beck, CVI, James Carter, Mary McKenna, Bro. Bernard Palmeri, CSC, and Deacon Joseph Scheurich.

It is said that the Corps of Cadets of Texas A&M University never forgets one of its own. As Bishop Ganter's coffin was lowered beside the grave of Bishop Vincent Harris in the Bishops' Garden on the grounds between St. Anthony's Cathedral and the Cathedral Center, a Corps of Cadets honor guard sounded Taps in his memory.

Bishop Ganter, of French and Czech descent, has for his personal arms a gloved hand wearing a gauntlet. This symbol indicates the name "Ganter," which means "glovemaker" in French. The hand holds a red heart representing his work of Christian charity and commemorating his pastoral ministry in two churches dedicated to the Sacred Heart of Jesus. A silver star on a blue field comes from the state flag of Texas and pays tribute to Mary in her title of Morning Star.

In his eloquent homily at Bishop Ganter's funeral Mass, Bishop Fiorenza recalled the late bishop's motto, "In Corde Jesu," He said in part, "For him the Heart of Jesus was the dramatic symbol which led to the cross. It was his intention to love those he served as Jesus loved. He saw in the heart of Jesus the model for a shepherd's love." He closed by saying, "Now his good and loving heart is at rest in the 'heart of Jesus.'"

Most Reverend Mariano Simon Garriga, DD, LLD
Titular Bishop of Syene and
Coadjutor Bishop of Corpus Christi
Third Bishop of Corpus Christi

Mariano Simon Garriga was the first native son of Texas to enter its hierarchy. An outstanding priest and bishop, he loved the traditions of his state and served it well in war and in peace. His duties took him to South Texas, and he was loved and respected by its people.

Born to Frank and Elizabeth (Baker) Garriga in Port Isabel, Cameron County, Texas, on 30 May 1886, Mariano was educated in the schools of Port Isabel and Brownsville. He completed his early education at St. John's Orphanage in San Antonio under the instruction of the Sisters of the Incarnate Word and later attended St. Mary's College in Kansas City, Kansas. He completed his priestly formation in St. Francis Seminary in Milwaukee, Wisconsin, where he received the degrees of Doctor of Divinity and Doctor of Laws.

Ordained in Incarnate Word Chapel in San Antonio for the Diocese of San Antonio on 2 July 1911, he celebrated his first Mass in the College there. For the first year of his priesthood he was Assistant to the Chancellor of the Diocese and from 1912 to 1915 he was Assistant Pastor of St. Mary Parish in Marfa and its missions in Presidio County. Back in San Antonio he cofounded St. John's Seminary with Bishop Shaw and was its Vice-Rector. He filled the position again between 1919 and 1936. His peacetime routine was interrupted by service as a military chaplain for the 4th Texas Infantry, Texas National Guard, in 1916. From 1916 to 1919 he was chaplain of the 144th Infantry, 36th Division, of the United States Army at Camp Bowie, Texas, and later for the Allied Expeditionary Force in France during World War I.

On his return to San Antonio Father Garriga was briefly President of Incarnate Word College before reassuming the vice-rectorship of St. John's Seminary. During his stay at St. John's he was also founding Pastor of St. Cecilia's Parish in San Antonio from its erection in November 1919. This parish was formed from St. Mary's and St. Gerard's and began with forty families. The first Mass was celebrated in an improvised chapel on 28 November 1919. A combination church and school opened on 19 September 1921, with the school staffed by Sisters of Charity of the Incarnate Word at the corner of South Presa and Whittier Streets. Father (later Monsignor) Gus P. Staff became assistant pastor in 1930.

Father Garriga was active in diocesan and archdiocesan administration in San Antonio. He was a Synodal Examiner and member of the Diocesan and Archdiocesan School Board from 1921 to 1936 and the Administrator of the Tribunal from 1923 to 1936. He was a member of the Matrimonial Court for ten years from 1926 and on 18 November of that year was appointed Historian for the Archdiocese. He had the satisfaction of personally overseeing the reconstruction of San Jose Mission in San Antonio. He was an Archdiocesan Consultor from 1928 and Spiritual Director of the Holy Name Society from 1935 to 1936.

As the silver jubilee of his priesthood approached, Father Garriga began to receive appointments commensurate with his positions. He was appointed Papal Chamberlain, with the title of Very Reverend Monsignor, by Pope Pius XI on 25 October 1934. On 21 September 1935 Pope Pius XI appointed him Domestic Prelate, with the title of Right Reverend Monsignor. He was invested with that honor on 26 November 1935. Higher honors came in the Centennial year of Texas. Monsignor Garriga received the honorary degree of Doctor of Laws from St. Edward's University in Austin in 1936, and on 20 June of that memorable year Pope Pius XI appointed him Titular Bishop of Syene and Coadjutor (with right of succession) to Bishop Ledvina of Corpus Christi. The first native Texan to enter its hierarchy was consecrated by Archbishop Drossaerts in San Fernando Cathedral in San Antonio on 21 September 1936.

On his appointment as bishop Garriga became Pastor of St. Peter's Parish in Laredo until 1948 and Vicar General, a Diocesan Consultor, and a member of the Matrimonial Court of the Diocese of Corpus Christi until 1949. In 1941 and 1942 the Bishop was Vicar Delegate of the Military Ordinariate for military and naval forces in Texas and Louisiana. From 1942 until 1949 he was Dean of the Laredo Deanery.

On 15 March 1949 Bishop Ledvina retired and Bishop Garriga became Bishop of Corpus Christi. On 15 October 1950 he dedicated the new Church of the Immaculate Conception in McCook in Hidalgo County. During his tenure the Shrine of San Juan de Los Lagos was begun. Until 1949 San Juan in Hidalgo County was a mission of St. Margaret's Parish in Pharr. In that year Father Jose M. Azpiazu became its first pastor. Father Azpiazu ordered a replica of the statue of Our Lady of San Juan to be made in Guadalajara for the new shrine. The original statue of Our Lady of the Immaculate Conception was placed by Spanish missionaries in the church of Lagos Moreno in Jalisco, north of Guadalajara, in 1623. Bishop Garriga dedicated the shrine before an estimated crowd of 60,000 on 2 May 1954. Sacred Heart Church, founded in 1927, became the principal parish church in Edinburg. Its former mission of St. Joseph's (also in Edinburg) became an independent parish.

Bishop Garriga also established Corpus Christi Academy with a residential seminary program to encourage Texas vocations for the priesthood. It is known today as Corpus Christi Minor Seminary. Pope Pius XII appointed the Bishop Assistant to the Pontifical Throne on 14 April 1951. He was voted "Mr. South Texas" at the George Washington Birthday celebration at Laredo on 22 February 1959.

Bishop Garriga, whose Spanish surname means "oak forest," was as sturdy in devotion to his church and state as his name implies. He was a Fourth Degree Knight of Columbus, a Knight Grand Cross of the Equestrian Order of the Holy Sepulchre of Jerusalem, and Supreme Chaplain of the Order of the Alhambra. This last organization is a fraternal order which benefits mentally deficient children. He was also a member of the American Legion, the Veterans of Foreign Wars, and the Texas Historical Commission. He died in Corpus Christi on 21 February 1965 and was buried in the Crypt of Corpus Christi Cathedral in Corpus Christi, Texas.

Most Reverend Hugo Mark Gerbermann, MM, DD
Titular Bishop of Amathus and Prelate of Huehuetenango
First Bishop of Huehuetenango
Titular Bishop of Pinhel and Auxiliary Bishop of San Antonio

Born in Nada, Colorado County, Texas, on 11 September 1913, Hugo Mark Gerbermann is one of nine children of John Jerome and Matilda (Hiltpold) Gerbermann. His brother, the late Monsignor John J. Gerbermann, VF, also had a religious vocation. Nada is near the Wharton County border close to the Colorado River, in that section of the State known as the Coastal Plains. It was a part of the old Victoria deanery of the San Antonio Archdiocese until 1956, when it became part of the El Campo Deanery.

In 1882 Czech Catholics from Frelsburg in the north part of Colorado County moved into the present Nada area. Mass was celebrated there in 1883, and Germans and Austrians came in 1885. The Nativity of the Blessed Virgin Mary (St. Mary's) Church in Nada was first built in 1897. It was soon after destroyed by a storm, as was the church of 1898, which was destroyed in 1900. Nada became a parish in 1901, and the rebuilt church served until 1930. The first parochial school was staffed by the Congregation of Divine Providence Sisters and opened in 1904. The Sisters remained until 1930 when the school was taken over by Sisters of the Incarnate Word and Blessed Sacrament. The present mission style brick church was completed in 1931 and renovated in 1963 and 1964, with the installation of art glass windows in 1971. The present school was built in 1955.

The people of Nada kept the faith through adversity, and such faith must have provided good training for a future missionary. Young Hugo was fourteen years old when he entered St. John's Seminary in San Antonio and remained until 1939. He completed his studies at Maryknoll Seminary, Maryknoll, New York, and was ordained on 7 February 1943. As a missionary in the Maryknoll Congregation, he had joined the Catholic Foreign Mission Society of America. The Society was founded in 1911 and serves twenty-seven countries in Asia, Africa, Latin America, and the Pacific Islands. As a missionary Father Gerbermann built several churches in Ecuador between 1943 and 1948 and was stationed in Guatemala from 1948 to 1962. He was Maryknoll Regional Superior for Guatemala in 1956 and received the Hermano Pedro Award in 1959. As an aid to his work, Father Gerbermann speaks Spanish and German as well as English.

He was appointed Titular Bishop of Amathus and Prelate of Huehuetenango by Pope John XXIII on 6 June 1962 and was consecrated bishop on the following 22 July in Guatemala City, Guatemala. Huehuetenango is a small city about 100 miles northwest of Guatemala City, with an estimated population of about 10,000 in 1973. Food and medicine are important to the native Indians, as access is available by horseback and jeeps. Here Bishop Gerbermann began an experimental farm and built a school in Ixtahuacan.

On 30 September 1962 Bishop Gerbermann returned to St. Mary's Church in Nada where he celebrated his first Solemn Pontifical Mass in the United States since his consecration as bishop. His brother, Monsignor John J. Gerbermann, VF, served as assistant priest, while Monsignor (later Bishop) Bernard F. Popp was a deacon of honor, Monsignor Aloysius A. Leopold was deacon, and Monsignor Alois J. Morkovsky, VF, was subdeacon. Monsignor Julius A. Retru, VF, preached the sermon, and Mass was followed by dinner and a reception.

Bishop Gerbermann became Bishop of Huehuetenango when it was raised to the status of a diocese by Pope Paul VI on 23 December 1967. He remained in this position until he resigned in 1975 due to the trend toward appointing natives to serve as bishop and his own ill health. He was appointed Administrator of St. Agnes Parish in Edna, Jackson County, Texas, by Archbishop Furey of San Antonio on 21 March 1975.

Priests from Victoria and El Campo had come to the Edna area in 1880, but the first church was not erected until 1892. The first resident priest came in 1912. The church was destroyed by fire in 1925 and a new one built. In 1958 the school was established and the third church was dedicated in 1966. By 1974 St. Agnes Parish served about 500 families.

Bishop Gerbermann was appointed Titular Bishop of Pinhel and Auxiliary Bishop of San Antonio by Pope Paul VI on 24 July 1975 and, concurrently, Pastor of St. Agnes in Edna, Vicar General of the Archdiocese of San Antonio, and a member of the Archdiocesan Board of Consultors by Archbishop Furey.

On 22 August 1977 Bishop Gerbermann was assigned to St. Mary's Parish in Fredericksburg in Gillespie County. In the north central part of the Archdiocese, Fredericksburg is in the "hill country" with hills up to 2,400 feet. Ranches and fruit orchards dot the landscape and hunting for deer, turkey, and other game is available. In this part of Texas are the former homes of President Lyndon Johnson and Admiral of the Fleet Chester Nimitz. Streams and caves share the area with camps and dude ranches. German settlers arrived here in 1846 and the first Mass was said in 1847. The first church was built in 1848 and the second in 1863. The parochial school dates from 1856 and the present church was built in 1908.

Bishop Gerbermann became Pastor of St. Joseph's Parish in Yoakum in Lavaca County on 30 January 1980. A part of the old Hallettsville Deanery there was a Mass station here as early as 1847. In 1850 a log church was built about three miles East of the present town and a stone church completed in the early 1870s. The first resident pastor came in 1895 and the present church was dedicated in 1912. It was remodeled in 1955 and renovated in 1972.

Before retiring Bishop Gerbermann "helped out" in St. Anthony's Parish in Columbus, Colorado County, and at Sacred Heart Church in Rockne, Bastrop County. Shortly after his retirement he took a vacation trip with his old friend Monsignor Aloysius A. Leopold, who was struck and killed by a truck as the two men crossed the street together.

Bishop Gerbermann, whose German surname means "tanner," first resided in St. Mary's in Nada from 23 March 1982. On 29 May of that year it became part of the new Diocese of Victoria in Texas. He resigned his duties as auxiliary bishop on 30 June 1982, pleading age and poor health. On 3 July 1983 the Bishop returned to Maryknoll in New York where he celebrated a Mass of Thanksgiving at the Maryknoll Center Chapel in honor of the fortieth anniversary of his ordination with members of his ordination class. In 1995 he resided at the Czech Catholic Home on Route 3 in El Campo, Texas.

Most Reverend Rudolph Aloysius Gerken, DD
First Bishop of Amarillo
Seventh Archbishop of Santa Fe

Rudolph Aloysius Gerken was born in Dyersville, Dubuque County, Iowa, on 7 March 1887, one of thirteen children of William and Elizabeth (Sudmeir) Gerken. He was educated at Pio Nono College in Milwaukee, Wisconsin, and received the degree of Bachelor of Arts from St. Joseph's College in Rennselaer, Indiana, in 1910.

Rudolph Gerken taught in the public schools of Scotland in Archer County, Texas, from 1910 to 1912 and was an instructor in the old University of Dallas in Dallas, Texas, from 1912 to 1913. For the next four years he was both student and teacher of languages in Kenrick Seminary in St. Louis, Missouri. He was ordained for the Diocese of Dallas by Bishop Joseph Lynch in Sacred Heart Cathedral in Dallas on 10 June 1917.

For the next ten years following his ordination Father Gerken was Pastor of Sacred Heart Parish in Abilene, Texas (1917-1920), now a part of the Diocese of San Angelo, and of St. Rita Parish in Ranger, Texas (1920-1927), now in the Diocese of Fort Worth. Pope Pius XI appointed him Monsignor in 1924 and Bishop Lynch made him a Diocesan Consultor, a Dean, and a Pro-Synodal Examiner for the Diocese of Dallas between 1925 and 1927.

In Abilene Father Gerken had his parish responsibilities plus those of its missions in six counties. In 1918 he built a church and parochial school for the Mexicans in that city. Between 1918 and 1920 he founded missions at Ranger and Cisco and built two new churches. As pastor in Ranger he opened a parochial school there in the Fall of 1921, which offered instruction through high school. In three years he established Sacred Heart Church in Breckenridge, St. Francis Xavier Church in Eastland, and a mission at Pioneer dedicated to the Little Flower of Lisieux before her canonization. In 1924 he built a parochial school for Mexicans in Ranger and a rectory in Breckenridge in 1925. In that last year he was made dean of the Colorado River Deanery of the Diocese of Dallas.

Appointed Bishop of the new Diocese of Amarillo, made up of parts of the Archdiocese of San Antonio and the Dioceses of Dallas and El Paso by Pope Pius XI on 25 August 1926, Bishop Gerken was consecrated by Bishop Lynch of Dallas in Sacred Heart Cathedral in Dallas on 26 April 1927. His co-consecrators were Bishop Byrne of Galveston and Bishop Francis Kelley of Oklahoma, while Archbishop Drossaerts of San Antonio delivered the sermon. Bishop Gerken left Dallas on the next day in a private railroad car furnished by F. E. Clarity, Vice-President and General Manager of the Fort Worth and Denver City Railway Company. He was formally invested and installed in Sacred Heart Cathedral in Amarillo on 28 April 1927.

At the time of Bishop Gerken's installation there were thirteen diocesan and twelve religious order priests in his diocese. There were forty-four churches in the diocese of which nineteen had resident priests and the others were considered as missions. There were thirty-one stations, five chapels, nine schools, and three academies, with a total of 1,545 students. There were two hospitals and two nurses' training schools, with a total Catholic population of 19,450. In the Amarillo area there were eighteen churches and missions, two Catholic schools, and one Catholic hospital, with fewer than twelve priests.

Bishop Gerken attempted to locate parishes and schools to serve the Spanish-speaking. He founded Price Memorial College (no longer extant) in Amarillo in September 1928 as a boys' school in hopes of producing vocations for the new diocese. He also founded the Catholic Welfare Bureau, the precursor of the Catholic Family Service, and was aided in his efforts by the Catholic Church Extension Society. By 1933 there were twenty-four diocesan and thirteen religious order priests, with fifty-eight churches, thirty-three stations, ten parochial schools, a boys' institute, and three academies, with a total of 1,373 students. There were four hospitals with one nurses' training school, with a total Catholic population about the same as in 1927.

Pope Pius XI appointed Bishop Gerken Archbishop of Santa Fe, New Mexico, on 2 June 1933. He was installed in Santa Fe on the following 23 August and received the pallium on 11 April 1934. He opened new parishes and schools and introduced new religious communities into the Archdiocese. The first Presidium of the Legion of Mary in America was established at Raton. The teachers' college opened by the Franciscan Sisters at Albuquerque later became the University of Albuquerque. The Archbishop founded the Seminary in Albuquerque in September 1935, which is now located in Santa Fe. Some of his institutions have not endured. These are the Nazareth Sanatorium at Alameda, the hospital at Taos administered by the Holy Family Sisters, and Our Lady of Guadalupe Seminary for Mexican seminarians, which the Archbishop purchased from the Montezuma Hotel in Las Vegas, New Mexico, in September 1937.

Archbishop Gerken was a Knight of Columbus. He administered the Archdiocese of Santa Fe until his death in Santa Fe, New Mexico, on 2 March 1943. He is buried in that city.

Most Reverend Roberto Octavio Gonzalez, OFM, DD
Titular Bishop of Ursona and Auxiliary Bishop of Boston
Coadjutor Bishop of Corpus Christi

To see the Church of the future in Texas is to examine the life and career of Roberto Octavio Gonzalez. Ordained as a very young bishop, he has made his presence felt among the hierarchy. Hispanic and bilingual, he is at home with his flock through pastoral and ministerial experiences. A professional scholar, he has the ability to weigh causes and results and then to act upon them. These qualifications fit the crucible in which Texas Church leadership may well be formed for the Twenty-first Century.

Roberto Octavio Gonzalez was born in Elizabeth, Union County, New Jersey, the eldest of nine children of Jesus and Frances (Nieves) Gonzalez, on 2 June 1950. His parents soon returned to Puerto Rico and Roberto received his early education there. He graduated from the Academia Santa Monica in Santurce in 1964 and completed his preparatory studies at St. Joseph's Seraphic Seminary at Callicoon, New York, in 1968. Christ House in Lafayette, New Jersey, accepted him as an affiliate of the Franciscan order in 1970, and he professed his first vows at St. Francis Friary in Brookline, Massachusetts, two years later.

The Franciscan order, properly known as the Order of Friars Minor, was founded in 1209 by St. Francis of Assisi as a family of the First Order. It became a separate jurisdiction in 1517 and was established in America in Cincinnati, Ohio, in 1855 with its St. John the Baptist Province. The general headquarters of the Order is in Rome. Its ministries are preaching, missionary, educational, parochial, and charitable work.

Roberto graduated from Siena College in Loudonville, New York, with the degree of Bachelor of Arts in English in 1972. This Franciscan coeducational institution was founded in 1937 and has a student body of about 3500. As a Franciscan Roberto's first assignment was bilingual teacher at the Charles Street Jail in Boston, Massachusetts (1972-1973). Thereafter he was a community organizer for the United Farmworkers Union in Washington, DC (1973-1976). He made his solemn profession of vows in the Franciscan order, as a member of the Most Holy Name of Jesus Province in New York City, on 20 August 1976. Also that year he began his deacon internship at Holy Cross Church in Bronx, New York.

Roberto Gonzalez received the Master of Arts degree in theology from the Washington Theological Coalition in Silver Spring, Maryland, in 1977. His thesis was "The Anthropological Dimension of Karl Rahner's Theology of Prayer." On 8 May 1977 Deacon Gonzalez was ordained to the priesthood by the late Bishop Lawrence Graziano, OFM, the former bishop of San Miguel, El Salvador. His first parish assignment was in residence as a part-time staff member of St. Pius V Parish in Bronx (1977-1982). Between 1977 and 1981 he joined these professional organizations reflecting his various interests: Asociacion de Sacerdotes Hispanos of the Archdiocese of New York, the American Sociological Association, the Association for the Sociology of Religion, the Instituto de Liturgia Hispana, and the International Sociology Association.

While at St. Pius, Father Gonzalez had a number of other duties and obligations. He was a consultant for the social ministry Pueblo *En Marcha* at the Community Center in Bronx (1978-1988) and the coordinator of the Liturgical Committee, Comité de Ciudadanos de la Fiesta de San Juan Bautista, for the Hispanic Apostolate of the Archdiocese of New York (1978-1988). He also served as Instructor in the South Bronx Pastoral Center (1979-1980), Research Associate of The Parish Project of the National Conference of Catholic Bishops in New York City (1979-1982), Consultant for the Office of Pastoral Research for the Archdiocese (1979-1988), part-time chaplain of Lincoln Hospital in Bronx (1981-1982), and coordinator for Comité Nuestra Senora de la Divina Providencia for the Hispanic Apostolate of the Archdiocese (1981-1988).

Father Gonzalez continued his education, this time in sociology, at Fordham University in New York City. This independent institution under Jesuit auspices was founded in 1841 and enrolls about 15,000 students. He received degrees of Master of Arts in 1980 and Doctor of Philosophy in 1984 with a dissertation entitled "Ecological, Ethnic and Cultural Factors of Church Practice in An Urban Roman Catholic Parish."

During his years in the Archdiocese of New York Father Gonzalez also had a number of affiliations, which activities were a part of his priestly ministry. He was the Treasurer of the Pueblo *En Marcha* Community Center in Bronx (1978-1988), Spiritual Director of the Organizacion Catolica Puertoriquena of New York City (1978-1988), a member of the South Bronx Pastoral Center (1979-1988) and of its Executive Committee of the Board (1981-1988), a member of the South Bronx Catholic Baseball League (1980-1985), and of Aspira of New York, Inc. (1981-1987).

He became Associate Pastor of Holy Cross Church in Bronx in 1982 and Pastor four years later, having joined the Presbyteral Council of the Archdiocese of New York in 1983. While completing his graduate studies at Fordham, he was Adjunct Instructor of Sociology in its School of General Studies from 1982 until his graduation. As Pastor of Holy Cross he was Director of Pastoral Research for the Northeast Catholic Center of Hispanics in New York City (1986-1988) and a member of the New York City Civilian Review Complaint Board (1987-1988). Together with Rev. Joseph P. Fitzpatrick, SJ he published *Hispanic Americans and the Church in the Northeast: Response to a Survey* (1977). His study *The Hispanic Catholic in the United States: A Social and Religious Profile* appeared in 1985.

Perhaps the leading authority on Hispanic Catholics in the United States, Roberto Gonzalez was appointed Titular Bishop of Ursona and Auxiliary Bishop of Boston by Pope John Paul II on 19 July 1988. At this time he became the youngest Roman Catholic bishop in the country. Cardinal Bernard F. Law expressed gratitude to the Pope for the appointment. The fact that the young man was of Puerto Rican descent, had pastoral experience, was an active researcher on the Hispanic Catholic presence in the United States and had supervised a study on the Hispanic Apostolate in the Archdiocese were important qualifications. That Bishop Gonzalez was, in addition, a Franciscan was an extra positive accomplishment. The Franciscans are well-known historically for their pastoral work and outreach to the poor.

The consecration of Bishop Gonzalez took place in the Cathedral of the Holy Cross in Boston, Massachusetts, on 3 October 1988 at 2:00 P.M. His Consecrator was Cardinal Law of Boston, with Cardinal Luis Aponte of San Juan, Puerto Rico, and Cardinal John J. O'Connor of New York as Co-consecrators. Archbishop (later Cardinal) Pio Laghi, the Vatican Pro-Nuncio to the United States attended as did Cardinal James A. Hickey of Washington, DC, and the Archbishop of Hartford John F. Whealon. There were thirty-six bishops from six New England states and New York, New Jersey, Florida, Illinois, New Mexico, Puerto Rico, and missionary bishops who had served in the Virgin Islands, Tanzania, and El Salvador. Of these bishops four were Hispanics.

The more than 2200 seats in the Cathedral echoed the voices of the seventy members of the Hispanic Choir from New York and those of its own choir. The liturgy was in English, but it reflected the Bishop-Elect's Hispanic heritage. Honor guards of the Knights of Columbus, of the Holy Sepulchre, and of Malta kept their vigils. And the Bishop's late brother José, who died while studying for the priesthood, was given special attention.

Then as now the Archdiocese of Boston encompassed an area of 2,465 square miles, including the counties of Essex, Middlesex, Suffolk, Norfolk and Plymouth, excepting the towns of Mattapoisett, Marion, and Wareham. There were about 200 thousand Hispanics in the greater Boston area, 85% of them Catholic. When Bishop Gonzalez came to Boston, there were five auxiliary bishops in place, with four regional bishops and the fifth as Vicar General and vicar for Administration. The regions were the Central with headquarters in Dorchester, Suffolk County; the North with headquarters in Lynn, Essex County; the South with headquarters in Brockton, Plymouth County; and the Merrimack, with headquarters in Lowell, Middlesex County.

The new West Region with headquarters in Weston, Middlesex County, consisted of the Newton Vicariate with seventeen churches, the Natick Vicariate with eleven churches, the Framingham Vicariate with fifteen churches, and the Marlboro Vicariate with eleven churches. It covered the area from Waltham, Weston and Wellesley to Framingham and Marlboro. The Bishop's office was in the Pope John XXIII National Seminary in Weston, specializing in delayed priestly vocations for men aged thirty to sixty. He was also to act as liaison to the Boston Hispanic community and to move through the Archdiocese saying Mass and bringing the sacraments, especially Confirmation, to the people.

During his time in the Archdiocese of Boston Bishop Gonzalez served his appointed functions. He became a Vicar General and was active in the National Conference of Catholic Bishops. By 1995 he was the Chairman of the Hispanic Affairs Committee and had seats on the Administrative Committee and the Administrative Board. He was also a member of the Welfare Emergency Relief Committee, a consultant to the Committee on Liturgy, and had served on the Committee on Communications.

At his press conference upon entering the Archdiocese on 19 July 1988, Bishop Gonzalez said in part: "I am acutely aware of my own sinfulness and limitations. Yet during this singular moment of grace in my life, my heart is also filled with joy, and I am deeply grateful to God." He closed by asking for the prayers of everyone.

In 1988 the Hispanics of the area were the recipients of a social-service agency begun for them in 1957 by Archbishop (later Cardinal) Richard J. Cushing of Boston. He assigned a priest to serve the Puerto Ricans concentrated around

Holy Cross Cathedral. On his arrival Bishop Gonzalez found the situation greatly improved thirty-one years later. Some twenty-eight parishes offered Sunday services in Spanish and fourteen priests worked full-time with Hispanic communities. Another fourteen priests served part-time, along with sixteen women religious and fourteen Hispanic permanent deacons. The new bishop now spoke of "pluralistic integration" rather than "assimilation" into the larger archdiocesan community. At the time of his episcopal ordination he was the twentieth Hispanic and the second Puerto Rican bishop to be named in the United States. He then went to Ireland with Cardinal O'Connor and other New York Catholics on a pilgrimage to the shrine of Our Lady of Knock, to pray for peace in Northern Ireland.

The Bishop's national survey of Hispanic Catholics, conducted with the facilities of Michael J. LaVelle's Diversified Research, a private firm in Irvington, New York, found that the traditional religious commitment of Hispanics remained strong but less so among those born in the United States and among those younger, better-educated and affluent. In all he performed his tasks so well that on 16 May 1995 Pope John Paul II appointed Bishop Gonzalez Coadjutor of the Diocese of Corpus Christi, with the right of succession to Bishop Rene H. Gracida.

Bishop Gonzalez issued a most gracious statement in English and Spanish on his new appointment, which he looked upon "with a grateful and joyful heart." He thanked the Pope "for this further sign of confidence he has placed in me" and renewed his pledges of love and loyalty. He thanked Bishop Gracida saying "I pledge my loyalty and service to him." But he acknowledged a "heavy heart" and "much sadness" at his impending departure. He addressed Cardinal Law as "my spiritual father, brother and friend" and referred to "my brother auxiliary bishops," brother priests, and brother deacons. He noted with regard the lay men and women, and the youth and children he had served as bishop, as well as the Hispanic community and the bishops of New England. Looking forward to his new assignment in Corpus Christi, he hoped to serve all, and the civic, ecumenical, and interfaith community of Corpus Christi in itself and as a part of the Province of San Antonio. He closed with prayer requests to all.

For his part Cardinal Law admitted "mixed emotions" in regretting the loss of an able auxiliary and simultaneous pleasure that his good work had won him advancement. He called the Bishop "an effective collaborator" and praised his "generosity of spirit" and his "effective" leadership in the National Conference of Catholic Bishops. Bishop Gonzalez celebrated a Mass of Farewell at the Cathedral of the Holy Cross in Boston on the evening of 1 June 1995.

Some three weeks later, on 26 June 1995, Bishop Gonzalez was formally welcomed into the Diocese of Corpus Christi. A two-hour Eucharistic Liturgy was followed by two hours of greeting and posing for pictures. Observing the occasion and his presence in Corpus Christi Cathedral, the Coadjutor addressed the assembly in English and Spanish. When he thought of Corpus Christi (the Body of Christ), he considered both the consecrated host and the Mystical Body of Christ, which is the Church. The reception of Christ in the Sacrament of the Holy Eucharist and the position one occupies as a member of the Mystical Body brings about an interpersonal communion, in which Christ is physically and spiritually a part of the People of God.

At this ceremony greetings were given in Polish and in Vietnamese. Jesus and Frances Gonzalez attended from Puerto Rico, bringing their son Miguel, the Bishop's brother, with them. The new coadjutor said, "I've been very moved by the outpouring of affection and love. I hope I can return it in a worthy fashion."

A bishop's personal coat of arms presents his history in a brief graphic fashion. The arms of Bishop Gonzalez portray an image of Our Mother of Divine Providence, the patroness of the Puerto Ricans, on a field of the Pentecostal color red. The color blue is for perseverance and two golden Tau Crosses represent the Franciscan Order. A dove bearing the olive branch of peace is a special symbol of the Gonzalez family. Its attitude of "rising" to fly shows its readiness to carry the gospel message of the Prince of Peace. The silver or white border of the coat of arms symbolizes the joy of redemption surrounding all. Red, white, and blue are the colors of the Puerto Rican and of the American flags. His motto is "*Vita Per Jesum*" ("Life through Christ").

With such a background and the future before him, it is perhaps not too much to say that the future of Bishop Roberto Octavio Gonzalez may well come to mean that of the Catholic Church in Texas. If his record to date foretells events to come, the Church will continue to be well-served by its hierarchy.

Most Reverend Thomas Kieley Gorman, DD, DScHist
First Bishop of Reno-Las Vegas
Titular Bishop of Rhasus and
Coadjutor Bishop of Dallas-Fort Worth
Fourth Bishop of Dallas-Fort Worth
Titular Bishop of Pinhel

Born in Pasadena, Los Angeles County, California, on 30 August 1892 to John Joseph and Mary (Kieley) Gorman, Thomas Kieley Gorman was educated at St. Patrick's Seminary, Menlo Park, California, from 1910 until 1914. He received the degree of Bachelor of Sacred Theology from St. Mary's Seminary at Baltimore, Maryland, in 1917.

The Reverend Mister Gorman was ordained in Fall River, Massachusetts, for the Diocese of Monterey-Los Angeles, on 23 June 1917. In 1918 he earned the degrees of Bachelor of Canon Law and Licentiate in Canon Law at the Catholic University of America in Washington, DC. The second of these degrees is somewhat beyond a master's degree but not a doctorate. From 1918 to 1922 Father Gorman was Assistant Pastor of Santa Clara Parish in Oxnard in Ventura County and St. Vibiana's Cathedral Parish in Los Angeles. For the following three years he completed his graduate study at the University of Louvain in Belgium and was awarded the degree of Doctor of Historical Science in 1925.

From 1926 until 1931 Father Gorman held the dual appointment of professor of history at Mount St. Mary's College and Immaculate Heart College in Los Angeles and was editor of *The Tidings*, the diocesan newspaper for Los Angeles-San Diego. He was appointed Bishop of the newly created statewide Diocese of Reno, Nevada, by Pope Pius XI on 24 April 1931, consecrated in Los Angeles on 22 July of that year, and installed in St. Thomas Aquinas Cathedral in Reno on 19 August 1931.

In 1931 Nevada was still much of a mission territory. Franciscans had passed through on the way to California in 1774. It was not until 1860 that the first parish, serving Genoa, Carson City, and Virginia City, was established. Two years later Rev. Patrick Manogue became pastor of Virginia City. He began a children's school, an orphanage, and a hospital. A church was erected in Reno in 1871.

Sixty years later the new bishop began to organize the institutions of his new diocese. That he did his job in a creditable fashion is attested by his being named Assistant to the Pontifical Throne by Pope Pius XII on 4 May 1942. From 1942 until 1951 he was episcopal chairman of the press department of the National Catholic Welfare Conference and became its chairman from 1951 until 1957.

Bishop Gorman was transferred to Dallas as Titular Bishop of Rhasus and Coadjutor Bishop of Dallas (with right of succession) by Pope Pius XII on 8 February 1952. He was installed in Sacred Heart Cathedral in Dallas on 8 May 1952. On 20 October 1953 the Diocese became the Diocese of Dallas-Fort Worth. Bishop Gorman succeeded as Bishop of Dallas-Fort Worth on the death of Bishop

Lynch on 19 August 1954.

As Bishop of Dallas-Fort Worth Gorman established a number of parishes and schools. He began the University of Dallas as an institution of higher learning in 1956 and served as its first chancellor. Drawing upon his own journalistic experiences in California, Nevada, and in Washington, DC, he revived the *Texas Catholic* diocesan newspaper, the idea of the first Bishop of Dallas Thomas Brennan. The Bishop established Holy Trinity Seminary in Dallas and founded St. Jude Chapel for the downtown business community. Holy Trinity is now located in Irving and serves as the collegiate seminary for St. Mary's Seminary in Houston. The Councils of Catholic Women, Men, and Youth were effectively developed. The Confraternity of Christian Doctrine and the founding of catechetical centers strengthened opportunities for the religious education of Catholic children attending public schools.

In 1954 the Diocese of Dallas-Fort Worth had eighty-three parishes with 185 priests with 14,619 students in Catholic schools. Eleven Catholic hospitals had 60,000 patients annually. By 1963 there were 140,906 Catholics in a total population of 1,958,400 with ninety-five parishes, thirty-six missions, 267 priests, twenty-one brothers, and 712 sisters. There were eleven high schools, fifty-nine elementary schools, seven general hospitals, two schools for nurses, three orphanages, and a home for the aged. And this was after the formation of the Diocese of San Angelo in 1961, which decreased the size of the Diocese. By 1969 there were over 250 priests with close to 45,000 enrolled in the diocesan parochial school system with the Catholic population close to 175,000 people.

Bishop Gorman was active in the affairs of his diocese until his retirement on 27 August 1969, five days after the establishment of the Diocese of Fort Worth. Appointed Titular Bishop of Pinhel by Pope Paul VI, the title was later given to Bishop Gerbermann when he became Auxiliary Bishop of San Antonio in 1975. Afterwards Bishop Gorman, whose Irish surname means "blue-eyed," was known as the Former Bishop of Dallas. He was a Knight Grand Cross of the Equestrian Order of the Holy Sepulchre of Jerusalem and a Knight of the Cross of Merit with Star of Gold. He died in Dallas, Texas, on 16 August 1980 and was buried in Calvary Hill Diocesan Cemetery in that city. His name lives on in the institutions of Bishop T. K. Gorman Middle School and Bishop T. K. Gorman High School on Loop 323 in Tyler, Texas. Once belonging to the Dallas diocese, since the Bishop's death they have become parts of the Diocese of Tyler.

Most Reverend Rene Henry Gracida, DD
Titular Bishop of Masuccaba and Auxiliary Bishop of Miami
First Bishop of Pensacola-Tallahassee
Fifth Bishop of Corpus Christi

Bishop Rene Henry Gracida is a decorated war veteran who advocates the abolition of capital punishment. An architect and a private pilot, he is a forceful pleader for Hispanic rights and lends his support to many causes. Born in New Orleans, Orleans Parish, Louisiana, to Enrique J. and Matilde (Derbes) Gracida on 9 June 1923, Rene was educated in the public schools of New Orleans, Houston, and Texas City, Texas. He was class valedictorian at Central High School in Texas City in 1941.

At Rice University, Houston (1942-1943), Gracida was next in the Army Air Force from 1943 to 1945. As a flight engineer who helped bomb Dresden, he was decorated with the Air Medal with two oak leaf clusters. After World War II he resumed his studies and taught in the School of Architecture of the University of Houston from 1948 until 1951. From 1949 to 1951 he was with the firm of Donald Bartheline and Associates in Houston and received the degree of Bachelor of Science in Architecture from the University of Houston in 1950.

Gracida began postgraduate studies in philosophy and theology at the University of Fribourg in Switzerland that same year. In the following year he enrolled at St. Vincent College, conducted under Benedictine auspices, at Latrobe, Pennsylvania, and transferred to its Seminary School of Theology in 1953, remaining until 1960. Ordained a deacon in 1958, the Reverend Mister Gracida was ordained a priest for the Diocese (later Archdiocese) of Miami, Florida, on 23 May 1959.

That year Father Gracida became Assistant Pastor of Holy Family Parish in North Miami, Florida, and began service on the Liturgical Conference (1959-1972). He was secretary (1962-1965), a member (1964-1973), and chairman (1967-1973) of the Diocesan/Archdiocesan Building Commission. Meanwhile he was Assistant Pastor of St. Coleman Parish in Pompano Beach (1962-1963), St. Matthew Parish in Hallandale (1963-1964), and Visitation Parish in North Dade (1964-1965). Father Gracida was Administrator of St. Ambrose Parish in Deerfield Beach (1964) and St. Ann Parish in Naples (1965-1967).

The next period was crucial in the development of the young priest as he began to show his skills in administration. From 1965 to 1967 he was Chairman of the West Coast Deanery Human Relations Board. In 1966 he was a member of the steering committee of the biennial Congress of Worship (to 1968) and a director of the Community Action Fund (to 1972). In 1967 he began a two-year tenure as Pastor of Nativity Parish in Hollywood, Florida, and as a senator in the Priests' Senate. He was chairman of the Broward Deanery Human Relations Board from 1969 to 1972.

Father Gracida became an archdiocesan consultor of the Archdiocese of Miami in 1967 and was its chancellor from 1968 until 1972. From 1969 until 1971 he was Rector of St. Mary Cathedral Parish in Miami and Pastor of St. Patrick Parish in Miami Beach from 1971 until 1972. In 1969 he became treasurer (until 1972) and Vicar General (until 1975) of the Archdiocese. Pope Paul VI appointed him Titular Bishop of Masuccaba and Auxiliary Bishop of Miami on 6 December 1971. Episcopal ordination followed on 25 January 1972.

As Auxiliary Bishop of Miami Bishop Gracida became involved in the work of the bishops' conference (NCCB). He was a member (1972-1977) and chairman (1977-1978) of the Liturgy Committee, a member of the Policy and Review Committee (1973-1977), and chairman of the Ad Hoc Committee on Migration and Tourism (1975-1980). He was also on the Dade County Human Relations Board (1972-1975) and archdiocesan superintendent of schools, as well as Pastor of St. Kiernan Parish in Miami (1973-1975).

Pope Paul VI appointed Bishop Gracida first bishop of the Diocese of Pensacola-Tallahassee on 1 October 1975. He was installed at Pensacola on 6 November. Since 1975 he has been a member of the episcopal advisory board of PADRES and of the Word of God Institute. That year he became national episcopal promoter of the Apostleship of the Sea (until 1989). During the North American Maritime Ministries Conference held in Houston, Texas, on 26-29 September 1988 Bishop Gracida received an award for his services from Rev. Elmo Romagosa of New Orleans, director of the International Council of Seamen's Agencies.

The Apostleship is an international Catholic organization serving the moral, social and spiritual welfare of seafarers and those in the maritime industry. It was founded in Glasgow, Scotland, in 1920 and formally instituted by the Holy See thirty-two years later. The Pontifical Council for Migrants and Itinerant Peoples promotes and directs it internationally, while the American component is an affiliate of the National Conference of Catholic Bishops and the United States Catholic Conference. Established in 1947, it serves port chaplains in sixty-three American ports on the seacoasts and the Great Lakes. It offers welcoming and counseling programs through individual port chaplains in six states, with interfaith clubs in seven states, and has a national director, Robert Mario Balderas, a permanent deacon.

As bishop of Pensacola-Tallahassee Gracida was also vice-president of the American Immigration and Citizenship Conference (1977-1982), a consultant for the Pontifical Commission for the Pastoral Care of Migrants and Tourists (1978-1983), and a member of the board of directors of Catholic Relief Services (1981-1988). An activist bishop, he opposes the death penalty and nuclear weapons and supports women in some church roles, but opposes abortion. He is known as an advocate for Hispanic and farm-worker rights.

On 18 April 1980 Bishop Gracida delivered an address entitled "Capital Punishment and the Sacredness of Life" at the Cathedral-Basilica of St. James in Brooklyn, New York. In the address he notes his interest in the subject of capital punishment was awakened when Governor Robert Graham of Florida signed the death warrants for two convicts on 18 May 1979, after which one was executed. Bishop Gracida issued a pastoral letter, "Capital Punishment and the Christian Conscience," written because of his concern.

After an historical summary he notes that the Church has not condemned the application of the death penalty by the State. A young Italian, Cesare Beccaria, opposed the penalty in his essay *Of Crimes and Punishment* (1764). As of 1980 thirty-five states have effective death penalty statutes, while fifteen do not. Capital punishment is nonexistent in sixteen countries. The Bishop finds lethal injection as an execution method "complicated, especially when one considers the question of euthanasia and the necessary involvement of physicians in the execution of people."

Bishop Gracida believes in the sanctity of human life. He does not discuss what one should do in a war in connection with such life, however. He finds that "the use of the death penalty is itself a morally unjustifiable attack upon human life" because he maintains that "the good end of just punishment cannot justify the bad means of killing a person." The Bishop summarizes his argument against capital punishment as follows:

> I claim that the *theoretical possibility* exists that the use of the death penalty is *in principle* morally unjustifiable, and that Catholic teaching might eventually develop in such a way as to make clear that this is the case. Further, I claim that the *use* of the death penalty is morally unjustifiable. If the use of the death penalty cannot be shown to be absolutely necessary for such purposes, then the use of this penalty in the United States is morally unjustified. Finally, on the basis of all the evidence concerning the inability of our penal system and our judicial system to mete out punishment fairly and equitably, it seems to me that if the death penalty cannot be imposed and executed fairly, then it should be abolished.

Pope John Paul II transferred Bishop Gracida to Corpus Christi as its fifth bishop on 19 May 1983. He was installed in Corpus Christi Cathedral by Archbishop Pio Laghi, then Apostolic Delegate to the United States, and by Archbishop Patrick Flores of San Antonio on the following 11 July. As of 1 January 1984 Bishop Gracida had one abbot, sixty-eight diocesan and eighty-nine religious priests, thirty-six permanent deacons, eighteen men religious, and 358 women religious in the Corpus Christi diocese. There were seventy-seven parishes, forty-eight missions, sixty-two seminarians, and 17,099 students under Catholic instruction with 314,812 Catholics in a total population of 596,393. The Diocese was composed of 17,294 square miles.

Bishop Gracida has served as a trustee of the National Shrine of the Immaculate Conception in Washington, DC, and as a member of the advisory council of the South Texas Eye Foundation from 1984. In 1985 he became an honorary member of the Board of Directors of Stop Child Abuse and Neglect, Inc., a member of the Board of Directors of Catholic Telecommunications Network of America (to 1988), and a member of the Governor's Task Force on Border Economic Development (to 1986). During 1985 he was a member of the South Texas Regional Studies Center in Kingsville, Texas, and began a three-year term as member on the Bishops' Committee on Social Development and World Peace.

In 1986 the Bishop was a member of the board of Directors of the Institute of Religion and Democracy, the statewide advisory committee on the Texas State Aquarium, the episcopal liaison for education on the Texas Catholic Conference, and a director of Station KEDT-TV, KKED-FM. In 1987 he became a member of the Executive Committee Gulf Coast Council of the Boy Scouts of America and in the following year was a director of the Catholic Communications Foundation. The year 1989 found him a trustee of the Catholic Mutual Relief Society and of the Texas A&I University Foundation, Inc., and a member of St. Gregory Foundation Latin Liturgy Episcopal Advisory Board. In that same year he began a three-year term on the Bishops' Pro-Life Committee and has served as a consultant on the Bishops' Hispanic Affairs Committee since 1992. Since 1991 he has also served as a director of the Catholic Campaign for America and as a member of the National Advisory Board Youth Evangelization Project.

On 16 May 1990 Bishop Gracida announced that he was one of two Texas bishops refusing to sign a statement on withdrawing nutrition and hydration from comatose patients. Neither the Texas Catholic Conference nor the Texas Conference of Catholic Health Facilities would identify the signers. The Bishop said at the time that the document gave higher priority to relieving individuals and families of burdens than to a sick individual's right to life.

Early in 1992, in a pastoral letter in *South Texas Catholic*, the diocesan newspaper of Corpus Christi, the Bishop protested the "massive amounts of money and resources" he said were being spent to convince Americans that abortion is a morally acceptable means of birth control. He added, "The cultural traditions of Native American, Hispanic American, Asian American and African American women find the abortion-on-demand mentality to be reprehensible and repugnant." He concluded that the "real purpose" of abortion providers is "to control and stop the population growth of the black, brown, red and yellow minorities."

By 1 January 1995 the Diocese of Corpus Christi had an abbot, 126 diocesan and sixty-two religious priests, sixty-eight permanent deacons, twenty-eight men religious, and 336 women religious. Eighty-four parishes and fifty-nine missions, twenty-four seminarians, and 27,173 students under Catholic instruction were in the Diocese, which had a Catholic population of 350,500 in a total population of 759,800, or 46 percent. The institutions included ten pastoral centers, four Catholic hospitals, two special care homes, an orphanage and child welfare center, two homes for the aged, three day care and extended day care centers, eight special centers for social centers, two general-use institutions, three high schools, and twenty-three elementary schools.

On 16 May 1995 Pope John Paul II appointed Most Reverend Roberto O. Gonzalez, OFM as Coadjutor Bishop with right of succession to Bishop Gracida. Bishop Gonzalez was welcomed to the Diocese in Corpus Christi Cathedral in ceremonies on the following 26 June.

Bishop Gracida is a member of Phi Kappa Phi, a national honor society for high academic achievement, and the Guild for Religious Architecture. Some of his important architectural works are the remodelling of St. Vincent Archabbey Basilica in Latrobe, Pennsylvania, the Church of the Nativity in Hollywood, Florida, and St. Ambrose Church in Deerfield Beach, Florida. A Knight Commander of the Equestrian Order of the Holy Sepulchre, he was named Grand Prior of its Southwestern Lieutenancy in 1986. On 22 October 1995 in St. Michael Church in Houston, the Bishop invested 118 Catholics from Texas. New Mexico, Arkansas, and Oklahoma into the Order. One of these was Auxiliary Bishop John W. Yanta of San Antonio. More than 1,000 bishops, priests, knights, ladies and guests attended this Sunday afternoon investiture. Of the thirty-one lieutenancies of the Order worldwide the Southwestern Lieutenancy contributes more financial resources to the Holy Land than do the other thirty. Houston has many members, of whom a number hold nearly half of the council positions.

A talented and concerned man, Bishop Gracida found time to offer prayer before the 1988 Republican Party National convention in New Orleans, Louisiana. His name means "pleasing" and he has taken as his episcopal motto, "*Abyssus Abyssum Invocat*" ("The deep calls to the deep").

Most Reverend Charles Victor Grahmann, DD
Titular Bishop of Equilium and
Auxiliary Bishop of San Antonio
First Bishop of Victoria in Texas
Coadjutor Bishop of Dallas
Sixth Bishop of Dallas

Concerning Bishop Charles Grahmann of Dallas, his fellow bishop Leroy Matthiesen of Amarillo says: "He is a good organizer, administrator, and finance man. And he is active in matters of spiritual development. He is energetic and has a good record on education and support of Catholic schools." He adds that "he is a Texan." Helen Parmley, the former Religion Editor of the *Dallas Morning News*, has called him a moderate with "finely honed" administrative skills and an active interest in ecumenical affairs. Some others have said he is "competative. . .a scrapper. . .determined. . .a man who hates to lose. . .restless . . .driven." Joe Michael Feist, the former editor of the *Texas Catholic*, the Diocese of Dallas newspaper, says he is like the South Texas Gulf breezes, "driven, purposeful, refreshing, and in harmony with nature."

The Bishop has described his role, his purpose in ministry and the Church. He believes as a bishop he should "proclaim Jesus Christ, to evangelize." He can not solve all problems, nor can others: "Life is a mystery to be lived, not a problem to be solved." But he has made his commitment to do all that he can to serve Christ and His people and, in doing so, the Church.

He sees the Church as a "big table" with Christ at its head. We come to the table with our gifts, what we can do to serve God. All have a seat there and it is from our "diversity" that "unity" comes. "If we all brought our gifts and humbly placed them at the service of the body of Christ [the Church], we'd have a marvelous church." He prefers to share the burdens of others and has a special love for Hispanic people, of whom he has said the Church must become "sensitive to the presence of Hispanics, their language and their culture."

These cherished beliefs reflect the values of a man who grew up with love and respect for his heritage, his family, and his neighbors, whom he assisted from an early age. His paternal grandparents came from Ankum in Westphalia, Germany. His father Nicholas A. Grahmann married Annie B. Grafe on 14 October 1924. The couple had eleven children, six sons and five daughters, the first born in 1926 and the last in 1950. Nicholas Grahmann was a sharecropper, living on a succession of farms, which he worked with his family, rendering a portion of his income to the landowner. He bought his own farm in 1950.

Charles Victor Grahmann was born on 15 July 1931 in Hallettsville, Lavaca County, Texas. He was the fourth child and second son. Farm life involved growing cotton, corn, molasses sorghum and hay. There were cows, chickens, hogs, and a family garden to tend. Each farm in which he grew up was much like the last. As a child he had no running water. What was needed was brought up from the well. The outbuildings were an outhouse, a chicken shed, a cattle shed, and a feed barn. Annie Grahmann used a fifteen-gallon cast iron pot for washing clothes, making lye soap, and during hog killing time, when many relatives and neighbors came to share the work, for cooking soup. Nicholas taught his sons the skills of carpentry and the family helped build churches and other large buildings in Hallettsville, Schulenburg, and Lockhart. With her husband and sons away, Mrs. Grahmann plowed the land with mules and later an old John Deere tractor.

The future bishop took an active part in the work of his family daily and later during holiday breaks and summers until the time of his ordination. He helped rotate the crops and set goals for himself. He remembers chopping and picking as much as 411 pounds of cotton in a single day and, later, picking as much as 807 pounds "with hulls and everything." For recreation he played dominoes and taroky (a Central European game with special cards), rolled in tires and on barrels, and childhood games such as hide-and-go-seek. He was a fisher and hunter, sometimes selling the hides of opossums, rabbits, and raccoons. As an adult he has taken up deep sea fishing and duck and geese hunting each January. Country music is also a favorite.

If the Grahmanns were poor in worldly goods, they were rich in spiritual life. Family members prayed together daily and recited the rosary. Holidays such as Thanksgiving, Christmas, and Easter were greeted with prayers, scripture readings, and song with all taking part. It is not surprising that such a home revolved around participation in the Church, in this case Sacred Heart Parish in Hallettsville. The parish school, taught by sisters of the Incarnate Word and Blessed Sacrament, opened in 1882, the year the stone church was built. Its high school began in 1937 and went to four years in 1948. Five years later it was accredited by the Texas Education Agency. The present school was completed in 1950, and the old school was remodeled in the late 1950s. The eleven young Grahmanns attended it from 1933 until 1968.

Settlement of the Hallettsville area began in 1823, with Irish, English, and Germans coming from Alabama, Tennessee, Kentucky, and Missouri. About 1830 Irish families from Missouri and Kentucky settled on Smothers Creek, three miles west of Hallettsville. Priests came into the area in 1839 and two years later the settlers built a log church called St. Mary's, the first such church in the area.

Hallettsville became a parish in 1882. That year Sacred Heart acquired cemetery properties, added to them in 1890, and enlarged them in 1947. The first parish hall was finished in 1890, with a later one built in 1936. The church was enlarged in 1932, with a new rectory in 1960, and a brick building replaced the 1882 church on 23 November 1969.

So completely devoted were the Grahmanns to church life that James, the eldest child, became a Christian brother and the next two children Mildred and Alice Marie both became Incarnate Word and Blessed Sacrament sisters, the same order which taught them as children. Charles went on to become a bishop.

But in 1940 he started as an altar boy. He remembered the kindness of the young assistant pastor Father (later Monsignor) Victor Schmidtzinsky. He also recalled the preaching of the Redemptorist priests, who presented yearly missions, sermons and spiritual exercises to renew and enrich religious life. In school he belonged to the Sodality of the Blessed Virgin Mary and took part in high jumping, baseball, basketball, and football. He graduated from Sacred Heart School in Hallettsville in 1945.

With a solid determination to become a priest at age fourteen, Charles enrolled in St. John's Seminary in San Antonio in the Fall of 1945. His pastor Father (later Monsignor) Alois J. Morkovsky, the brother of Bishop John L. Morkovsky, drove him the hundred miles west to San Antonio. It would serve him as high school, college, and seminary. He would later receive the Master of Education degree from Our Lady of the Lake University in San Antonio in 1968.

There were thirty-eight men in his class at St. John's, where he took an active part in choir and musical productions, and played basketball, baseball, and football. He became known as a student who could absorb knowledge quickly and be well-prepared for recitations. Charles particularly enjoyed courses in economics and sociology, but his Spanish professor Rev. Thomas Kavanaugh, CM, made a particular impression. Father Kavanaugh required an openness of his students in understanding Hispanic culture. He also required them to preach and prepare parish bulletin announcements in Spanish. The young man found this study agreeable and added it to the German he could already speak and read. At home during holidays and breaks he assisted Father Morkovsky by working with the youth of his parish and by preaching on Sunday or holy day Masses.

The Summer of 1955 was unusual. In that year he toured Britain, France, Spain, Italy, Portugal, The Netherlands, and Germany with his classmates Emil Wesselsky and John W. Yanta. The young men made their way across Europe by bicycle, train, and bus, staying in monasteries along the way. They pooled their resources at one point, buying a small car and selling it before returning home. Charles's visit to Ankum, his ancestral home in Westphalia, was a high point of the trip and nurtured lifelong associations with his family in Germany.

In 1956 some members of the graduating class received early ordination to help during Holy Week services. Along with his friends Wesselsky and Yanta, who would later become a bishop, together with Alton Rudolph and Louis Fritz, the Reverend Mister Grahmann was ordained for the Archdiocese of San Antonio by Archbishop Robert E. Lucey in San Fernando Cathedral in San Antonio, Texas. It was 17 March 1956, St. Patrick's Day, a curious beginning for these young seminarians of Czech, Polish, and German descent. On the following day (18 March 1956) Father Grahmann celebrated his First Mass in Sacred Heart Church in Hallettsville. His youngest brother Nicholas Jr., a six-year-old, served as chalice bearer.

From April to September 1956 his first assignment was associate pastor of St. James's Parish in San Antonio. This duty led to his appointment as associate pastor of St. Joseph's Parish in Yoakum on the boundary line of Lavaca and DeWitt counties, with its mission of St. Ann in Hochheim, DeWitt County. Here he remained until June 1961, teaching religion, Spanish, and speech in St. Joseph's elementary and high schools. He coached the high school basketball, baseball, track, and girl's volleyball teams. He led the basketball and baseball teams to the playoffs. His football team had only fourteen players the first year and had a 1-9 season. But Coach Grahmann encouraged the team from the sidelines. His facility in Spanish proved useful in his mission with some 300 Hispanic families.

In June 1961 he returned to San Antonio as second associate pastor at St.

Paul's Parish. Here he continued his youth work as the director of the Confraternity of Christian Doctrine. These catechesis programs begin in parishes, where they are sometimes known as Religious Education or Catechesis. Parish boards or commissions develop policy and administer programs. On the national level this effort is part of the United States Catholic Conference in Washington, DC. At St. Paul's Father Grahmann increased membership from 150 to 450 elementary students and from 35 to 300 high school students within four months.

In 1964 Archbishop Lucey called the young priest into his office. He was to prepare for his new position with courses in grammar, composition and typing at San Antonio College and with bookkeeping and accounting at a local business college. Father Grahmann would then report on 24 August as the Archbishop's secretary, to become his administrative assistant and liaison. He later served as secretary to successor archbishops Francis Furey (1969-1970) and Patrick Flores (1979-1980).

Archbishop Lucey advocated organized labor, fair housing laws, rights for minorities, and was a member of President Lyndon Johnson's national advisory council on the War on Poverty. Father Grahmann was impressed by his support of social justice. The appointment as secretary coincided with another as associate pastor of St. Gregory the Great Parish in San Antonio. Grahmann was now serving on the archdiocesan level. He also became Archdiocesan Director of Catholic Relief Services (CRS) (until 1969) and Archdiocesan Director of Cemeteries (to 1981).

Catholic Relief Services is the official overseas aid and development agency of American Catholics. It is a separately incorporated organization of the United States Catholic Conference (USCC) with headquarters in Baltimore, Maryland. Founded in 1943 by bishops of the United States to help European and North African civilians in World War II, it expanded its work to Asia, Africa, and Latin America. It provides disaster relief, helps refugees, and is active in reconstruction and in rehabilitation. The agency concentrates on long-term projects to help people. Funding comes from its annual appeal, donors, and a program called Operation Rice Bowl. Father Grahmann devised a "rice bag" which was passed hand-to-hand in each parish for contributions. On behalf of CRS he went to Latin America in 1969 and made a return trip in 1972.

Project Equality was originally planned by the National Catholic Conference for Interracial Justice in 1960. Archbishop Lucey made it operational in his archdiocese in 1965. As a part of the Catholic Relief Services effort Father Grahmann used the purchasing power of the Archdiocese to help end discrimination in hiring, promoting and other employment practices in the firms with which the Archdiocese did business.

He became Archdiocesan Director of the Campaign for Human Development when it was begun by the USCC in November 1969. The agency funds self-help programs to combat injustice, oppression, alienation and poverty in America. It started funding with a collection taken up in all Catholic parishes on 22 November 1970. Seventy-five percent of this money and other annual collections went to the national fund to start self-help programs and for educational purposes. Twenty-five percent of the money remained in the diocese from which it was collected. From 1970 more than $200 million has been distributed by the Campaign. It has funded more than 3,000 self-help projects. The San

Antonio archdiocese founded its Human Development Office in 1975.

Father Grahmann became pastor of St. Gregory the Great Parish in San Antonio in March 1970, succeeded Msgr. James Boyle, PA. In 1974 over 1400 families made St. Gregory their spiritual home. It had a church building and rectory and an eighteen-classroom school with an office, assembly hall, science laboratory, library, cafeteria, and a Scout hall and baseball diamond. Parishioners had a Parish Advisory board, a Parish Education Board, the Confraternity of Christian Doctrine religious education program, Parent-Teacher Club, Holy Family Guild, St. Vincent de Paul Society, Athletic Association, youth groups, and a federal credit union. During this period Father Grahmann made efforts to help support a diocese in Northern Honduras and started a program for second-career vocations, yielding five ordinations.

Pope Paul VI noted Father Grahmann's achievements and created him a Prelate of Honor with the title of Monsignor in 1971. In 1979 Monsignor Grahmann helped found COPS (Communities Organized for Public Service). This is an organization which was part of Industrial Areas Foundation (IAF), a national network of citizens' organizations to train and develop leaders among poor and working-class families. It promotes education finance reform and indigent health care in Texas. It has affiliates in Austin, Fort Worth, El Paso, Houston, and the Rio Grande Valley. In Dallas it is called Dallas Interfaith, endorsed by Greater Dallas Community of Churches and by the Diocese of Dallas. It deals with poverty, discrimination, and political disenfranchisement. It works to develop housing, streets, libraries, and schools.

In January 1980 Monsignor Grahmann was appointed Vicar General for the Archdiocese of San Antonio and Pastor of St. Joseph's Parish in San Antonio. He established the Fatima Center in an Eastside barrio for a social center and an outreach to poor residents. Always trying to assist those in need, he made sandwiches, bought bus tickets for travelers and paid utility bills.

On 30 June 1981 Pope John Paul II appointed Monsignor Grahmann Titular Bishop of Equilium and Auxiliary Bishop of San Antonio. Before his episcopal ordination the Bishop-Elect attended a retreat given by Benedictine monks at Belmont Abbey in Belmont, North Carolina. He asked the opinion of a monk on how to be a good bishop. The advice came back: "Be humble, be simple, be poor, point the way to the Lord for your people, then get out and walk in their midst." That Grahmann took this advice to heart may be seen in the choice of his motto: "To Walk Humbly With Your God." Archbishop Patrick Flores of San Antonio ordained him at La Villita Assembly Hall in San Antonio on 29 August 1981.

Within a year Bishop Grahmann received his own diocese of Victoria in Texas by appointment of Pope John Paul II on 14 April 1982. Archbishop Flores installed him at La Villita Hall in San Antonio, assisted by Bishop Thomas Drury of Corpus Christi and Bishop John Morkovsky of Galveston-Houston, on 29 May 1982, the same day the Diocese of Victoria in Texas was established and created.

The Diocese of Victoria in Texas was composed of the counties of Calhoun, DeWitt, Goliad, Jackson, Lavaca, Matagorda, Victoria, Wharton and Colorado west of the Colorado River from the Archdiocese of San Antonio and the dioceses of Corpus Christi and of Galveston-Houston. It consisted of 9,105 square miles. On 2 October 1989 the Vatican ceded that part of Colorado County belonging to the Diocese of Austin to the Diocese of Victoria in Texas, by which Victoria in Texas gained parishes in Eagle Lake, Frelsburg, and Mentz, as well as territory to give the Diocese a total area of 9,609 square miles.

The Spanish explored the area in 1519. Beyond naming Espiritu Santo and Matagorda bays, they left missions in Goliad and a lighthouse at Pass Cavallo. LaSalle established his colony of Fort St. Louis some thirty miles from present-day Victoria in 1684 in a brief attempt to claim the region for France.

In an effort to unify the people of the Victoria in Texas diocese and give it a character of its own, Bishop Grahmann began by recognizing the different ethnic backgrounds and diverse needs of his 115,000 Catholics. He feared that the institutional church had grown so massive that existence as a prayer community depended primarily on the realization that the Church is based upon Christ's commandments to love God and one's neighbor as oneself.

The road to unity, he believed, lay through a process involving clergy, Religious, and lay people of the Diocese in a series of "town hall" meetings to examine regional demographics and identify strengths and weaknesses. This process would in turn lead to an understanding of the Church and of prospective goals. After the initial series of meetings convocations met annually to assess progress and to redefine aims. The Diocesan Pastoral Institute, begun in 1987, graduated its first lay leaders in 1990. These leaders were trained to become family life, youth and liturgical ministers, catechists and evangelizers. In addition the Institute teaches deacon candidates before they begin their training.

Not only was it necessary to set in place a governmental system for institutions to grow. It was also essential to establish a means of funding for them. Under the Archdiocese of San Antonio area parishes were taxed to meet archdiocesan expenses. Money came from weekly collections, and most parishes did not issue financial statements to parishioners. The Diocese of Victoria in Texas went directly to its people and began to publish its needs. By 1990 forty-three of sixty-two parishes paid less from their own treasuries by using a yearly appeal method of funding.

The first diocesan financing effort was a special appeal called The Founders' Fund. It began in 1982 and ended in 1985. Its purpose was to construct a chancery and a Spiritual Renewal Center. The chancery was formally dedicated in September 1985 with three floors of offices, conference rooms, a chapel, a library and resource center, archival storage, and a museum. It stands on 25,000 square feet next to the Cathedral at a cost of $2 million. It was made possible by the O'Connor family and by The Founders' Fund drive.

The Spiritual Renewal Center was dedicated in September 1988. It is a log cabin village, similar to nineteenth-century settlements, situated some twenty miles South of Victoria on the San Antonio River. Bishop Grahmann wanted the chancery and the Center to express the historical faith of the people of the Diocese. It displays, in addition, the ministry needs of Hispanics and of social justice. For both projects The Founders' Fund raised $3,572,926 and 10,795 gifts. These figures represent a contribution of about half of the Catholic families in the Diocese.

The annual appeal, known as the Diocesan Services Appeal, began in 1987.

Its theme is always "'Sharing Christ Together" and it seeks to raise $1 million yearly. It attempts to relieve parish incomes from diocesan assessments and to develop a base of voluntary support. It pays the cost of diocesan operations. Services and ministries maintained by the Appeal include the youth department, religious education, schools, family life, the reflection process, vocations, evangelization, and administrative costs including the bishop's Office. Staff salaries are paid those in charge of programs and ministries. Other costs go to the diocesan newspaper and to the Spiritual Renewal Center. Under this system funds not raised are assessed to parishes. Other income comes from private donations, grants, investments, and rental fees. In 1987 more than 90% of the Appeal goal was reached with 28% of Catholic families with more than 7,000 donors. More recent efforts have been largely successful as well.

During his stay in Victoria Bishop Grahmann held a number of important positions. He was National Chaplain of the Catholic Daughters of the Americas from 1984 to 1986 and was elected to Region X (Arkansas, Oklahoma, and Texas) of the Administrative Board of the national bishops' conference in 1985. In June 1985 the Texas Commissioner of Agriculture appointed him to the Farm Crisis Committee for the State of Texas.

On 26 October 1986 he had the honor of investment as a Knight of the Equestrian Order of the Holy Sepulchre of Jerusalem in Corpus Christi Cathedral in Corpus Christi, Texas. From 29 July to 8 August 1987 he had a tour of duty with the United States Navy aboard ships in the Mediterranean "to experience first hand the ministry of naval chaplaincy."

Bishop Grahmann presented a plan to give priests and bishops naval chaplaincy experience. The response was an invitation extended by Chief of Naval Chaplains Lieutenant-Commander Rev. Eugene Gomulka, Chc. USN. Chaplain Gomulka accompanied the Bishop on his tour, flying from Philadelphia to Naples, and from there to the ship. Videotapes of this tour were made to be used in chaplain recruitment by the Navy.

Also in 1987 Bishop Grahmann acted as state treasurer for the bishops of Texas to underwrite costs of the Pope's visit to San Antonio and other expenses. His successful handling of this matter is described in detail in the "Introduction" to this work. In March 1989 the Bishop was elected President of the Texas Conference of Churches, made up of Catholic, Protestant, and Orthodox denominations.

On 1 January 1989, at the start of his last full year as bishop, the Diocese of Victoria in Texas had a total of seventy-two priests, twelve permanent deacons, one Religious brother, 149 Religious sisters, and forty-six parishes. There is a hospital and a home for the aged, three convents, and twenty-two missions. In 1988 2,071 baptisms and 109 conversions brought new members into the Church. There were four high schools with 464 students and twelve elementary schools with 2,335 students. There were 115,000 in a total population of 233,100 or 52 percent.

On 19 December 1989 Pope John Paul II appointed Bishop Grahmann Coadjutor Bishop of Dallas. He was to succeed Bishop Thomas Tschoepe, the bishop since 1969. At a press conference in the Cathedral in Dallas, the new bishop mentioned the ''table of the Lord" and hoped "there is room for all of us" at it. In a diocese 40 percent Hispanic, he was the first bishop in modern times to speak fluent Spanish there. He expressed an obligation to the poor, the sick, and the homeless. He said, "Each person to me is an unrepeatable image and likeness of God." The Bishop pledged to continue the work with the poor of Dallas, gratitude to the clergy, deacons, and religious and thanks to the lay people and staff of the Diocese.

Bishop Grahmann's Farewell Message to his Victoria diocese appeared in its newspaper, the *Catholic Lighthouse,* on 16 February 1990. Addressed to "My Beloved People," he offered "my deepest thanks," recalling the "pilgrim journey" taken together "to build the kind of Church we envisioned, focused upon ourselves as the body of Christ. We wanted our Church to include everyone." He added, "It has been a marvelous, God-filled experience for me. I am humbled at the way God has led all of us. Thanks for being the Body of Christ." He concluded, "May God bless you! I love you all very deeply!"

Two days later, on Sunday 18 February 1990, at 4:00 P.M., the Diocese of Victoria in Texas gathered in Our Lady of Victory Cathedral in Victoria. Its people attended a Mass of Farewell celebrated by their bishop. There were people of Czech, Polish, German, Mexican, Irish, Italian, and Lebanese descent. And they held a reception following Mass. Just before the Bishop processed down the aisle, Al Hessler, manager of the Texas Lumber Company of Victoria, handed Bishop Grahmann a very special gift on behalf of them all.

It was a crozier, specially selected of South Texas Red Cedar, which Hessler had located on his family ranch. About seventy inches long and an inch-and-a-quarter in diameter, it could be taken apart into four pieces for travel. It had taken almost two years and twenty coats of lacquer to provide its beautiful finish. And it was a gift to be especially treasured.

On 21 February 1990 at the Cathedral-Santuario de Guadalupe in Dallas, the Coadjutor Bishop was installed. He had started church service as an altar boy fifty years before at Sacred Heart Church in Hallettsville. He was now a part of a Cathedral formerly known as Sacred Heart. Archbishop Patrick Flores of San Antonio was there, as was Archbishop Pio Laghi, the Pro-Nuncio to the United States. Bishop Thomas Tschoepe presided.

At 7:00 P.M. the installation began. There were three deacons, two lectors, and a Master of Ceremonies with his assistants. Seminarians acted as Assisting Ministers, with Deacons as Ministers of the Cup. Representatives of the parishes of St. Rita, Cistercian Abbey, St. Andrew Kim, St. Pius X, St. Peter the Apostle, St. Elizabeth Seton, St. Luke and Holy Cross made intercessions on behalf of the congregation. Diocesan youth from the churches of St. Rita, Holy Cross, Blessed Sacrament, and St. Andrew Kim made the Presentation of the Gifts. Joel Martinson was organist, Carly Mayers the cantor, and Juan Saenz was psalmist. The Dallas Diocesan Chorale and the Festival Brass Quintet with tympani provided music for the occasion sponsored by the Cathedral and the Diocesan Liturgical Commission .

Archbishop Laghi read the papal letter of appointment in Spanish and in English. The two archbishops led Bishop Grahmann to his chair. There were readings and proclamations in both languages. At the Homily Bishop Grahmann told his people, "There is room for diversity of color, creed, language, heritage and culture while striving for unity in the one Lord." He extended the concern of the Church to AIDS victims, the homeless, and the immigrants. He stated that ministry to Hispanics and their inclusion in the Church would be a priority.

He thanked the Pope, Archbishop Laghi, his fellow bishops of Texas (mostly in attendance), and praised Bishop Tschoepe, offering his services to him. He wanted to overcome the pain and sufferings due to division, separation, loneliness, isolation, oppression, racism, and violence. He deplored division and confusion. He greeted priests, deacons, Religious, the representatives of other denominations and faiths, and spoke in Spanish, receiving applause. There were intercessions in Hungarian, Korean, Chinese, Malayan, Polish, Vietnamese, Spanish, Filipino, English, and Sign Language. The Cathedral was filled with relatives and friends. Afterwards, there was a reception in Bishop Grahmann's honor in the Grand Ballroom of the Plaza of the Americas Hotel.

Bishop Tschoepe's seventy-fifth birthday occurred on 17 December 1990. Many believed that at that time his resignation would be accepted and Bishop Grahmann would automatically become bishop of Dallas. Instead, Bishop Tschoepe planned his resignation to take effect five months earlier on 15 July 1990. He chose this date because it was the one-hundredth anniversary of the establishment of the Diocese of Dallas and Bishop Grahmann's birthday. But the fifteenth of July fell on Sunday, a day on which *L'Osservatore Romano,* the daily newspaper of the Holy See, did not have an issue and could not print the notice which would make such a change official. So Bishop Grahmann became the sixth bishop of Dallas on 14 July 1990, one day earlier than originally planned.

Committed to spreading Hispanic ministry throughout his diocese and doing so, one very significant appointment by Bishop Grahmann is that of Rev. Ramon Alvarez, his chancellor, a procurator-advocate on the tribunal, a diocesan consultor, a member of the presbyteral council, and a director of vocations. Yearly issues of the *Official Catholic Directory* show this work in progress.

In the fall of 1992 Bishop Grahmann launched a $22 million fund drive with an executive committee, chaired by former Dallas County Judge David Fox. It included $10 million for the bishop's endowment fund, $4 million to build and maintain a new diocesan retreat and conference center, $2 million to buy and renovate a new chancery office building, $2 million to renovate the Holy Trinity Seminary, and $4 million to renovate the Cathedral.

The new chancery at 3725 Blackburn Street is a five-story building across from Holy Trinity Church on Oak Lawn Avenue designed to hold most diocesan offices. The Diocese of Dallas purchased the site from Employee Plans Management Company, an insurance company, which moved into the Catholic Charities building at 3845 Oak Lawn. Catholic Charities split its offices between the new chancery and its older location at 3915 Lemmon Avenue. The cost of the move was $2 million, including purchase of the 43,000 square foot Blackburn Street property, repairs, and renovations.

From around 1991 Bishop Grahmann participated in Dallas Pro-Life Action Network (PLAN) by attending group protests at clinics and hospitals. On a rainy 9 January 1993 he stood outside the North Dallas home of Dr. Norman Tompkins, reciting the rosary and leading prayers in an an attempt to make the doctor stop performing abortions. Surveillance of the doctor and his family with protests and distribution of fliers with his picture went on in the doctor's neighborhood, at his workplace, and at his church.

At this point Doctor Tompkins had been a focus of PLAN's attention for about three months. Its members met outside his home at least one morning each weekend. They did the same each weekday outside his office or at Presbyterian Hospital. The group effort persuaded Dr. Clay Alexander to give up elective abortions, as did three other doctors.

On 18 May 1993 two unnamed men filed a suit in District Court in Dallas seeking damages against the Diocese of Dallas and one of its priests, Rev. Rudolph Kos. They alleged that Kos sexually abused them when they were boys. They charged that "Church officials failed to inform law enforcement authorities that Rev. Kos had sexually abused a minor." According to state law, each separate offense of child abuse is a Class B misdemeanor, punishable by a maximum sentence of 180 days in jail and/or a $1,000 fine.

National Conference of Catholic Bishops' guidelines adopted in 1988 call for quick response on the part of a diocese to allegations of sexual abuse and that the priest so accused be relieved of his duties if there is sufficient evidence to warrant his removal. Such incidents are required to be reported, in Texas to state Child Protective Services officials. If an investigation follows, a diocese is to cooperate in it.

Father Kos had been assigned to All Saints Parish in Far North Dallas (1981-1985), to St. Luke's Parish in Irving (1985-1988), and to St. John's Parish in Ennis (1988-1992). Attorney Randal Mathis, representing the Diocese of Dallas, stated that a church official notified Child Protective Services of allegations against Father Kos while he was pastor in Ennis on 1 October 1992. Kos was removed from his duties on that day and reported the next day to a treatment center in Jemez Springs, New Mexico.

The lawsuit alleged that sexual abuse occurred while the plaintiffs were minors in Irving and in Ennis. Attorney Mathis stated that a diocesan investigation had started several months prior to to the filing of the suit, that Father Kos was no longer in the Diocese and was undergoing treatment in New Mexico, and that the investigation was continuing. Attorney Windle Turley, representing the plaintiffs, claimed that the Diocese knew early of Father Kos's alleged criminal activities. The Diocese filed a legal denial to these charges and requested a jury trial.

Child Protective Services officials said their agency received a complaint and notified Ennis police, a statement which the Ennis Police Chief Dale Holt denied. Chief Holt also denied a statement by Elaine Thieroff, support director for a child-welfare agency in Arlington, that records showed that her agency referred a complaint against Father Kos to Ennis police.

On 27 May 1993 Bishop Grahmann stated that the Diocese of Dallas "followed to the letter" its policies and state law in reporting allegations of a priest sexually abusing two boys. He said that the allegations caused "deep sorrow" and added that "our highest priority is helping such victims find healing and wholeness." He said, "I am committed to a complete and full investigation of the claims so that the full truth of the matter can be revealed. I have instructed my staff to cooperate fully with all officials." He offered that he had not spoken sooner because of the investigation by the Diocese of "some months" and because of the privacy and rights of both accuser and accused.

As of 1 January 1995 the Diocese of Dallas had an abbot, ninety-seven diocesan priests and eighty-three Religious order priests, five male religious, and 195 women religious. There were sixty-one parishes, seven missions, a Catholic hospital, a health care center, a home for the aged, five day care and extended day care centers, seventeen special centers for social services, a seminary, a university, seven high schools, thirty-four elementary schools, a non-residential school for the disabled and over 800 teachers. The Catholic population was 294,125 in a total population of 2,682,302 or 11 percent.

Bishop Grahmann's coat of arms is a summary of his life. On a field partitioned diagonally in red and black, the colors of Germany, there is at the top an open hand colored silver, representing the Bishop's desire to reach out to the poor and needy. It indicates a commitment to causes of justice, equality, and human dignity. On the bearer's right is a red rose, with green barbs and gold seeds. It signifies Mary, the Mother of God, especially in her title of Our Lady of Guadalupe, Patroness of the Americas. Near the bottom of the shield is a silver horse, a charge of the Westphalia district of the Rhine, in northern Germany, his ancestral home. It stands for strength, nobility, and intuition. On the bearer's left is a gold star for Texas, the place of the Bishop's birth, rearing, education, and priestly service. His motto, "To Walk Humbly With Your God" is from Micah 6:8: "No, the Lord has told us what is good. What He requires of us is this: to do what is just, to show constant love, and to live in humble fellowship with our God."

Most Reverend Curtis John Guillory, SVD, DD
Titular Bishop of Stagno and
Auxiliary Bishop of Galveston-Houston

Curtis John Guillory of the Society of the Divine Word has deep foundations in his native Louisiana. He is the fourth native of the Diocese of Lafayette and the twelfth African American priest to become a bishop of the Catholic Church in the United States in the twentieth century. As a Louisianian he can appreciate jazz and soul music and speak the French patois of his region.

In the Province of Orléanais in seventeenth-century France Francois Guillory married Isabeth Thomas. Their son Simon migrated to Quebec in 1664 and married Louise Bouchard there three years later. Simon, who was a gunsmith and a trader in guns, had a son named Francois (born 1691), as well as nine other children. Francois moved to Mobile Bay in the first decade of the eighteenth century and married Jeanne Montfort. He left his mark on the land, for Pointe Guillory on the eastern end of Dauphine Island and Guillory Pass, a small island, are named for him. Francois and Jeanne had a son named Simon, whose son Gregoire married Marie Jeanne La Casse in 1739. In 1764 they moved to Louisiana, where Gregoire received 544 acres of land and had eight children.

The Bishop's mother, the late Theresa Jardouin (who died in 1983) traced her ancestry from the Isle of Dominique. Her father Victorian married Victoria Bello and took up farming in Louisiana. Theresa married Wilfrid Guillory, the Bishop's father. The couple had twenty children, seven boys and thirteen girls, between 1943 and 1967. Wilfrid Jr., Victoria, Theresa Marie, and Catherine died in infancy. Kerry (born 1947), a Franciscan brother, is the bishop's only sibling to follow him into religious life.

Born in Mallet, St. Landry Parish, Louisiana, on 1 September 1943, Curtis John Guillory lived in Chatagnier, ten miles North of Mallet on a fifteen-acre farm until 1945. At the age of eight he helped his father by picking cotton, pulling and shucking corn, and feeding hay to mules and cows. He picked up eggs at night on one eight-acre tract and dug sweet potatoes on five acres of a fifty-acre tract sharecropping farm in Mallet, North of Lafayette. Mrs. Charley J. Quantity, who owned the farm, made a one-third profit.

Young Curtis got up at 4:00 A.M., did his chores, attended school, and then worked until eight at night in the fields. His father also worked at a cotton gin at Swords, Louisiana, to provide for his growing family. His parents were deeply religious practicing Catholics, and the young student learned his lessons through the first two years of high school at St. Ann's parish school three miles from his home. It was staffed by the Sisters of the Blessed Sacrament, an order founded in the United States in 1891 for the care of Native and African Americans. Here the sisters encouraged him to pursue a religious vocation.

In this endeavor the young man found positive role models in his pastors Rev. John B. Burnett, SSJ and Rev, George Strype, SSJ, the latter being especially noted for his friendship, good humor, and personal example. The Guillorys attended church Tuesdays, Fridays, and Sundays. Long, hard work hours did not deter them from the nightly recitation of the rosary. The Bishop says of this time: "Reflecting back over my life, I guess my vocation was probably due to the deep faith and prayers of my parents."

Recruiters from the Divine Word Fathers came to the Guillory home. Curtis worried that his absence in religious study would leave his father short-handed. But Wilfrid Guillory told him, "God will provide." Later when both his parents were ill and the seminarian questioned continuing his preparation, his mother kept him on his course.

Having decided upon his life's work, Curtis entered St. Augustine's Seminary of the Society of the Divine Word in Bay St. Louis, Mississippi. This seat of the Southern Province of the Order was founded in 1940. The Order itself was founded in 1875 in Holland by Blessed Arnold Janssen, and in the United States in 1897 at Techny, Illinois. Young Curtis completed high school at the Seminary and in 1964 professed his first vows in the Order.

An able student Guillory earned the Bachelor of Arts degree at Divine Word College at Epworth, Iowa, in 1968. He returned to St. Ann's Church in Mallet to be ordained by Bishop Carlos Lewis, SVD of Panama, on 16 December 1972. He said his First Mass there the following day. The next year he earned his Master of Divinity degree at the Catholic Theological Union at Chicago, Illinois, and the Master of Arts in Christian Spirituality degree from Creighton University at Omaha, Nebraska in 1986.

Father Guillory began his priestly career as Associate Pastor of St. Augustine Parish in New Orleans, Louisiana, from 1973 until 1976. He became Pastor of this parish founded in 1841 in 1976 and remained until 1982. In 1982 he was the founding director of the Augustine Tolton House of Studies, the New Orleans formation house for Divine Word seminarians. The following year he became the Director or Coordinator of the Black Ministries Office for the Archdiocese of New Orleans and, in 1984, the Assistant Provincial of the Southern Province of the Society of the Divine Word in the United States.

This period was one of intense activity. In New Orleans Father Guillory was a member of the Executive Committee of National Black Catholic Administrators and the Black Energy Caucus, a board member of the Louisiana One Church/One Family adoption program, a member and chaplain of the Knights of Peter Claver (of which he was National Chaplain in 1995), and chaplain of the New Orleans Chapter of the NAACP. He somehow found the additional time to serve on the archdiocesan presbyteral council and on the board of the Spirituality Center, working with local clergy and Religious.

Just beck from his appointment as a Fellow of the Carl Jung Psychiatric Conference in Küsnacht, Switzerland, in 1987, Guillory was the local coordinator for the meeting of Pope John Paul II with African American Catholics in New Orleans on 12 September of that year. He had come now to the direct attention of the Pope. But he was already on the short list of Bishop Joseph A. Fiorenza of Galveston-Houston, who requested him as his second auxiliary.

Appointed Titular Bishop of Stagno and Auxiliary Bishop of Galveston-Houston on 29 December 1987, Curtis Guillory came to Houston that day for a press conference. On this occasion Bishop Fiorenza said of him:

> In the appointment of Auxiliary Bishop-designate Guillory, the Holy See recognizes the importance of the Diocese of Galveston-Houston in the South and Southwest, and the very significant contribution

which Catholics have made to the life of the Church in these parts.

At the time Bishop Fiorenza revealed the selection process by which Bishop Guillory came to Houston.

On 6 January 1987 Bishop Fiorenza mentioned the need for an African American auxiliary bishop for his diocese to Archbishop Pio Laghi, the Apostolic Pro-Nuncio to the United States, while they were attending an episcopal ordination in Rome. On 25 March 1987 Fiorenza made his formal request for the appointment to the Holy See. He first saw Father Guillory while attending the National Black Catholic Congress in Washington, DC in May of that year. On 21 December 1987 Laghi notified Guillory and Fiorenza of the impending appointment to be announced eight days later.

Guillory learned of the appointment at 4:30 on the afternoon of 21 December, then went to his chapel and prayed. He spent the following night in prayer and reflection but could not tell his family of the news before the formal announcement. In his response at the Houston press conference Bishop Guillory expressed thanks for the honor of his appointment and spoke of Houston as a symbol of hope for the future. He added, "I will be working very hard with all people and together we will experience the deep love of God." He paid tribute also to his family who "taught me how to love and be generous."

Although Bishop Guillory is the first African American Roman Catholic bishop in Texas, African Americans are among the earliest inhabitants of the State. They came with Cabeza de Vaca in 1528. In the Diocese of Galveston-Houston these Catholics number about 70,000 of 777,340 in a total population of 4,052,706. At the time of his appointment seventeen parishes were predominantly or entirely African American.

The importance of Bishop Guillory's appointment was underscored by three activities in Houston during January 1988. All were sponsored by the Diocesan Office of African American Ministries. The first was the annual diocesan observance of Dr. Martin Luther King's birthday on Sunday, 17 January in Sacred Heart Co-Cathedral. The speaker on this occasion was Rev. Charles Andrus, SSJ consultor general of the Josephite Fathers and Brothers in Baltimore, Maryland.

The second event was a workshop based on the Afro-American Catholic Hymnal, "Lead Me, Guide Me," held on Saturday, 23 January at St. Mary's Parish Hall. It was conducted by Auxiliary Bishop James P. Lyke, OFM of Cleveland, Ohio, the coordinator of the Hymn Project. The third event was the presentation of a Day of Reflection on the National Black Catholic Congress Plan by the Diocesan Congress Implementation Team on Saturday, 30 January. It was held at St. Peter Claver Parish Hall and conducted by Sr. Patricia Haley, SCN.

In addition the second annual national consultation of Black Catholic organization met at the Marriott Hotel at the Houston Intercontinental Airport on Tuesday and Wednesday, 26 and 27 January 1988 to provide "an opportunity for dialogue and support as well as time to discuss major issues which impact Black Catholics."

In this promising atmosphere Bishop Guillory's episcopal ordination took place in Sam Houston Coliseum in Houston on 19 February 1988, his mother's birthday. Mrs. Guillory was certainly there in the spirit of the Bishop, his family and friends, as Bishop Fiorenza acted as Consecrator. Co-Consecrators were Archbishop Philip Hannan of New Orleans and Auxiliary Bishop (and later Bishop of Memphis) J. Terry Steib, SVD of St. Louis, Missouri. Archbishops Pio Laghi representing the Vatican and Patrick Flores of San Antonio were there, as was Auxiliary Bishop Joseph A. Francis, SVD of Newark, New Jersey, the homilist. Officials of the Divine Word Order attended, but it was very much a family day. The Bishop's brother Kerry carried the crozier and his sister Margaret (Mrs. Henry Armendariz of San Antonio) read the lesson. The Bishop's father watched the proceedings from his wheelchair, along with more than 6,000 people. On the same day as his ordination Bishop Guillory was appointed Vicar of African American Catholics in the Diocese of Galveston-Houston.

Bishop Guillory visited the Holy Father in Rome in 1988 and again in 1993, in company with his fellow bishops of Texas. In ceremonies held at St. Matthew's Church in San Antonio on 22 and 23 October 1988 he was invested as a Knight of the Equestrian Order of the Holy Sepulchre of Jerusalem. As a bishop Guillory strives to break down barriers of prejudice. One such effort was his support of a statewide referendum on bringing water and sewer services to impoverished communities in the Rio Grande Valley.

He spoke to the fifth annual Texas Press Meeting held in Dickinson, Texas, on 15-17 January 1993, to Catholic journalists from eleven Texas dioceses. He took as his text Ephesians 2:14: "For Christ Himself has brought us peace by making Jews and Gentiles one people. With His own body He broke down the wall that separated them and kept them enemies." Here at the Christian Renewal Center with the *Texas Catholic Herald* as host newspaper he told his listeners that Catholics are all one in Christ and should pray and worship together. To see the image of God in one another and to understand how cultures provide gifts to the Church was his theme.

On 31 August 1993 the Bishop's beloved father Wilfrid Guillory died in Mallet, Louisiana, at home. He was buried in St. Ann's Cemetery there. Bishop Guillory was celebrant and homilist, assisted in the concelebration of Mass by Bishop J. Terry Steib, SVD of Memphis, Tennessee, and by auxiliary bishops Dominic Carmon, SVD of New Orleans, Leonard J. Olivier, SVD of Washington, DC and Joseph A. Francis, SVD of Newark, New Jersey. Bishop Harry J. Flynn of Lafayette and Auxiliary Bishop James A. Tamayo of Galveston-Houston also took part.

Wilfrid Guillory was survived by his sixteen surviving children, six sons and ten daughters, of whom the Bishop is the oldest, by thirteen grandchildren, a great-grandchild, and by nieces and nephews. The Guillorys are a close and loving family, eight of the children living in Mallet and four others living in other cities in Louisiana.

In November of 1993 Bishop Guillory's colleagues in the National Conference of Catholic Bishops elected him Chairman of the Committee on African American Catholics. He defeated Auxiliary Bishop L. J. Olivier, SVD of Washington, DC by a vote of 148 to 85. He was chosen to serve for three years, replacing Bishop J. T. Steib, SVD of Memphis, Tennessee. The decisions he makes in that position affect approximately three million African American Catholics in the United States.

Bishop Guillory continues to serve as Vicar of African American Catholics. He is also a Vicar General and Episcopal Vicar for the Central Vicariate of the Diocese of Galveston-Houston, which includes the supervision of forty churches including the Co-Cathedral in Houston. And he is a member of the diocesan presbyteral council and a diocesan consultor. Fond of the zydeco, the French-style popular music of Louisiana, his leisure reading includes current events and works on Christian spirituality and psychology. Once a hunter, he tries to find time for swimming, jogging, and walking for exercise.

The Bishop whose French name means "little William" and "lively" has chosen for his episcopal motto words which he lives by from Romans 8:28, "Diligentibus Deum Omnia Cooperantur" ("For those who love God all things work together for good"). A man who knows where he came from and where he is going, an eloquent speaker and an effective administrator, the Bishop's coat of arms combines the cotton boll of the family farm, the acacia tree of Africa, and the Society of the Divine Word emblem.

Most Reverend Vincent Madeley Harris, DD, LHD
First Bishop of Beaumont
Titular Bishop of Rotaria and Coadjutor Bishop of Austin
Second Bishop of Austin

Vincent Madeley Harris exemplifies the life of one devoted to his religious vocation and to his native state. Whether he served as educator or as administrator, he gave his energies to the betterment of both. His devotion found its response in the lives of those who affected his own, and he was loved by many for his essential goodness and for his gifts of piety and kindliness.

Born to George Malcolm and Margaret (Madeley) Harris in Conroe, Montgomery County, Texas, on 14 October 1913, the future bishop's religious life owed much to his devoted mother. It was Andrew Madeley who in 1898 invited Rev. Joseph I. Klein of St. Mary's Parish in Plantersville to visit Conroe and to offer Mass in his home. The town became a mission and Rev. George Wilhelm, who succeeded Father Klein, visited it in 1906. The congregation built a frame church in 1912 and in the following year, that of Vincent Harris's birth, Bishop Gallagher of Galveston named the church St. Mary of the Woods. By 1931 it was a mission of St. Joseph's Parish in New Waverly, about the time a brick church was built. St. Mary's became a parish in 1947, and the present church was rededicated in March 1972 as Sacred Heart Parish.

Despite the family connection with the church in Conroe and the protestantism of his pharmacist father, who later became a convert, the Harrises moved to Houston about 1925. The first church of St. Christopher's Parish had been constructed in 1924 in southeast Houston, and Vincent grew up as a parishioner, attending Park Place Elementary School and later Albert Sidney Johnston Junior High School. Here he became acquainted with the church's pastor, Rev. Louis J. Reicher, the Chancellor of the Galveston Diocese, who would influence him to become a priest and whom he would follow as Bishop of Austin.

At Sam Houston High School Vincent Harris had a most unusual speech teacher, a man destined for greater achievements named Lyndon Baines Johnson. While impressed with the driving force of LBJ, Harris was undeterred in his choice of a religious vocation. After graduation from high school in 1931, he attended St. Mary's Seminary, then in La Porte, Texas. In 1934 he was sent to the North American College in Rome for further studies. He was granted the degrees of Bachelor of Sacred Theology by the Pontifical Gregorian University in 1936 and Bachelor of Canon Law in 1939.

The Reverend Mister Harris was ordained priest in the North American College chapel in Rome by Bishop Ralph L. Hayes, then Titular Bishop of Hieropolis and Rector of the North American College, for the Diocese of Galveston, on 19 March 1938. As war clouds gathered in Europe, he was recalled by Bishop Byrne of Galveston. He completed his studies with the degree of Licentiate in Canon Law, awarded by the Catholic University of America in Washington, DC, in 1940.

A Roman education in those days marked a priest for advancement in the Church. Father Harris immediately became Secretary of the Diocesan Tribunal and served until 1949. He concurrently became a professor at St. Mary's University at La Porte, teaching a wide variety of subjects including canon law, systematic theology, church history, Latin, and algebra. He held this appointment until 1951, serving summers at St. Joseph's Parish in Beaumont during the pastorale of Father Viola, who vacationed in his native Italy.

In 1948 Harris became Chancellor of the Diocese of Galveston, a position he held until 1966. During the first three years of his tenure he commuted daily from La Porte to Galveston and back again for his 5:00 P.M. class. He moved to Galveston in 1951, residing in the Bishop's Palace and assisting with Masses at Sacred Heart Church there on weekends. When the Chancery building was completed in Houston, he moved there to a fourth floor apartment.

His seminary appointment was replaced with that of Diocesan Consultor in 1951. Until his appointment as bishop, a period of fifteen years, he was also diocesan director of the Confraternity of Christian Doctrine, a member of the diocesan administrative council, pro-synodal examiner, diocesan director of the Legion of Decency, secretary and treasurer of St. Mary's University seminary, and Vice-President of the Catholic Clerical Student Fund. On 22 September 1956 Pope Pius XII appointed him Domestic Prelate, with the title of Right Reverend Monsignor. During the Second Vatican Council (1962-1965) he attended a session in Rome as companion for the blind Bishop Nold of Galveston-Houston. He also met Pope John XXIII while accompanying Bishop Nold on one of his official visits.

But it was Pope Paul VI on 4 July 1966 who made Monsignor Harris the first bishop of the newly-created Diocese of Beaumont and the first native priest of the Galveston-Houston Diocese to be named a bishop. His episcopal ordination was held in the Church of St. Vincent de Paul in Houston on 28 September 1966, with Bishop John L. Morkovsky of Galveston-Houston as consecrator. Bishops James Hogan of Altoona-Johnstown, Pennsylvania, and Leo Christopher Byrne of Wichita, Kansas, the nephew of the late Bishop Christopher Byrne of Galveston, acted as co-consecrators.

On the following day Bishop Harris was installed in St. Anthony's Cathedral in Beaumont by Archbishop Robert E. Lucey of San Antonio in the presence of thirty-eight bishops and archbishops and about 1,000 others, including the Bishop's mother and brothers. Archbishop Lucey gave a talk on social justice, and welcoming receptions were held in Beaumont and Port Arthur. Mayor Jack Moore of Beaumont presented Bishop Harris the keys to the city.

Historically the Beaumont area was the home of the Attakapa, Orcoquisa, Bidai, and Karankawa Indian tribes. Our Lady of the Light mission was established near present-day Wallisville in Chambers County, at the intersection of Interstate 10 and the Trinity River. Indians killed two Franciscans and two Dominicans. Fr. Antonio Margil established missions in Nacogdoches and in San Augustine counties and a third at Robeline, Louisiana. On 8 September 1863 Dick Dowling defeated Union troops at Sabine Pass.

The area is also Catholic with diverse traditions. There is a Czech community in Eastgate in Liberty County. Seven parishes are predominantly African American. The Vietnamese have a shrine called Our Lady of Peace in the southern part of Jefferson County. Many Mexicans and Central Americans have come North in the 1930s and again from the 1960s and beyond. The

French-Cajun-Creole influence may be found in Jefferson, Orange, and in Chambers counties.

The Diocese of Beaumont was created entirely from the Diocese of Galveston-Houston. On its establishment in 1966 it consisted of the Texas counties of Angelina, Chambers east of the Trinity River, Cherokee, Hardin, Jasper, Jefferson, Liberty east of the Trinity River, Nacogdoches, Newton, Orange, Polk, Sabine, San Augustine, Shelby, and Tyler, in all 11,790 square miles. The loss of the counties of Angelina, Cherokee, Nacogdoches, Sabine, San Augustine, and Shelby, to make up partially the Diocese of Tyler reduced the Diocese to 7,191 square miles. Vatican cession of other parts of Chambers and Liberty counties to the Diocese of Beaumont has resulted in nine complete counties of 7,878 square miles.

In 1966 the Diocese of Beaumont had forty-six diocesan priests and thirty-one Religious order priests, one male religious, 115 women religious, thirty-two parishes, sixteen missions, twenty-two seminarians, three high schools, twenty grade schools, three hospitals, with 2,187 infant baptisms and 270 conversions in the previous year. It had a Catholic population of 83,605 centered in Jefferson and Orange counties, due mainly to the influx of Cajuns and Creoles from southern Louisiana.

Hotel Dieu (later known at St. Elizabeth Hospital) in Beaumont and St. Mary Hospital in Port Arthur had nursing schools and trained more than 1,000 nurses. The former St. Anthony High School in Beaumont won national awards for selling war bonds and for collecting scrap metal in World War II. St. Vincent de Paul societies operated by parishes helped launch community cooperative social agencies in Orange and Jasper. Community bazaars and festivals were in some instances outgrowths of parish bazaars.

Bishop Harris appointed four monsignors and three priests as diocesan consultors. Rev. Frank Schanzer became diocesan director of women, Rev. George Rabroker (a diocesan consultor) the parish priest consultor, Msgr. Ernest Michalka (a diocesan consultor) director of cursillos, and Rev. James Quinlan chaplain for the Holy Name societies. Rev. Louis Catrone and Incarnate Word Sister Anastasia Thibodeaux headed the diocesan religious office. Msgr. Nester Engerle was chaplain to St. Vincent de Paul societies, Rev. Marvin Enderle was director of vocations, and Rev. William Manger was put in charge of Newman collegiate societies within the Diocese. Rev. Francis Burlton (a diocesan consultor) was named chancellor, while Msgrs. H. A. Drouilhet and Ernest Michalka (both diocesan consultors) were named co-vicars general.

Bishop Harris continued the diocesan newspaper, at first as part of the *Texas Catholic Herald*, and also the Diocesan Stewardship Fund. He established the Family Life Office and began the accreditation process for diocesan schools. He established the churches of St. Maurice in Mauriceville, Orange County, St. Francis of Assisi in Buna, Jasper County, and St. Joseph in Livingston, Polk County.

The Chancery or Diocesan Pastoral Office was originally a convent for St. Anthony Parish. It was dedicated on 16 April 1967 and was later expanded to add approximately 4,800 square feet of office space. In May 1967 the first Priests' Senate consisting of eight members was formed. On 25 May of that year Bishop Harris ordained Revs. Kenneth Greig and Bennie Patillo, both of whom have since served their diocese as chancellors. Bishop Harris served as Texas State Chaplain for the Knights of Columbus (1967-1969) and on the bishops' national Committee on the Liturgy.

On 27 April 1971 Pope Paul VI appointed Harris Titular Bishop of Rotaria and Coadjutor Bishop of Austin. He succeeded the aged Bishop Reicher as Bishop of Austin on that bishop's resignation on 16 November 1971. And now the wheel of his personal history had swung full circle. He had followed Reicher into the priesthood, into the chancellorship of Galveston, and as Bishop of Austin. It must then have been a sad irony for this quiet and kindly man to have had to sue for the return of trust funds established by the former bishop and belonging to the Diocese of Austin. Although the issue was ultimately decided in his favor, the way to settlement was troublesome and undoubtedly trying to a man of Bishop Harris's sensibility.

Despite this controversy the tenure of Bishop Harris was one of growth and he made a most positive contribution to his new diocese. He was elected by the Catholic bishops of Texas, Oklahoma, Arkansas, New Mexico, and Arizona to serve on the NCCB-USCC Region 10 Administrative Board and Committee, which included those states, in 1973. He served in this capacity until 1975. A stroke caused a resulting eye condition which led to his retirement on 19 December 1985, effective by Christmas Day of that year.

The Bishop retired because he felt his effectiveness was diminished, and thereafter lived in Houston. Here he maintained an interest in genealogy, photography, and computer systems. St. Edward's University at Austin awarded him the honorary degree of Doctor of Humane Letters in 1982. But the best tribute to his leadership is the account of the Diocese of Austin as it was on 1 January 1986. On that day it had eighty-seven active priests, fifty-nine religious Order priests, thirty-six permanent deacons, thirty-five male religious, 131 women religious, eighty-six parishes, thirty-one missions, thirty-five seminarians, a university, two high schools, fifteen elementary schools, 24,212 students under Catholic instruction, six hospitals, a special hospital, two homes for the invalid and aged, and a Catholic population of 138,640 of a total population of 1,335,464.

On 8 February 1988 Bishop Harris suffered a heart attack. He spent three weeks in St. Joseph's Hospital in Houston before being transferred to St. Anthony's Hospital in that city. Here he died on 31 March 1988. He was survived by his brother, George Malcolm Harris, Jr. (b. 1 March 1909-d. 20 June 1991), a pharmacist since 1932 and the owner of Park Place Pharmacy in Houston, until his retirement in 1987. George left his wife, the former Frances Beauregard, three sons, four daughters, eleven grandchildren, and four great-grandchildren.

On 4 April 1988 the Bishop came home. Bishop Joseph Fiorenza of Galveston-Houston said a Mass of Christian Burial for him in St. Christopher's Church in Houston that morning and delivered the homily. Bishops Ganter of Beaumont, Tschoepe of Dallas, Sheehan of Lubbock, and Grahmann of Victoria concelebrated Mass with Bishop Fiorenza. The former bishop of Fort Worth, Bishop Cassata, was there, as were the auxiliary bishops of Galveston-Houston and San Antonio. More than 120 clergymen, as well as Knights and Ladies of the Order of the Holy Sepulchre also came. Altogether 300 mourners attended in the church of Bishop Harris's childhood.

In his homily Bishop Fiorenza noted that Bishop Harris was a friend and his professor at the seminary. He also said, "Bishop Harris, truly, was a man of faith and dedication; a good man; a gracious man." A second Mass of Christian Burial was celebrated that day at Beaumont by its bishop Bernard J. Ganter at St. Anthony's Cathedral. And here in the grounds of that cathedral Bishop Harris was laid to rest.

Proud of his church and of Texas Bishop Harris was both a Knight Grand Cross of the Equestrian Order of the Holy Sepulchre of Jerusalem and a member of the Sons of the Republic of Texas. This quiet man with his self-effacing sense of humor was a capable administrator who viewed himself as a simple minister. His English name means "estate ruler" and he chose for himself words from Luke 22:26-27 as his episcopal motto: "Sicut Qui Ministrat" ("As One Who Serves").

Almost twenty-two years before his body was returned to St. Anthony's Cathedral in Beaumont, he had stood before its altar as its newly-installed bishop and told his congregation, by way of explaining that motto:

> I have come to you as one who serves. With your help, with your prayers, this area of East Texas may become a place where we shall live and work in a communion of love.
>
> I promise you, that with God's help, your new bishop will be one who serves, one who works to bring us all into the communion of love.

Whether as bishop of Beaumont or of Austin, Vincent Harris kept that pledge.

Most Reverend Charles Edwin Herzig, DD
First Bishop of Tyler

From nineteenth century Switzerland to twentieth century East Texas the Herzigs have made their ways from the Alps to the borders of the Texas Hill Country to the piney woods in the East of the State. The story of Charles Edwin Herzig, the first bishop of Tyler, begins more than fifty years before his birth with that of his paternal grandfather, John Herzig, in Wynauo, near the principal city of the Canton of Bern, in Switzerland, on 4 March 1871.

Intent on becoming a minister, John Herzig entered the Lutheran Missionary Institute of St. Crischona. Upon graduation he joined the Palatinate Missionary Society and emigrated to Victoria, Texas, in 1897. Here he sought a cure for a chronic throat ailment and spent his time in efforts to convert Indians. He met Miss Selma Bauer in the Rio Grande Valley and married her in 1898. The couple settled in the Valley where John took up farming in addition to preaching. Their son John Carl was born while his parents were on a visit to Switzerland on 17 July 1902. But the marriage was short-lived. Mrs. Herzig died of tuberculosis in 1907. Her widower husband remarried the next year, moved to California, and died in 1958.

As a young man John Carl enlisted in the army and was stationed at Fort Sam Houston in San Antonio. He met Miss Theresa Schneider, a member of Sacred Heart Parish, whose father was the founder and owner of Schneider Printing Company. This establishment was located on Market Street, across from the present Hertzberg Library. John Carl and Theresa married in her parish church on 2 June 1926, and the groom converted to Catholicism.

John Carl and Theresa had five sons born between 1927 and 1939, of which the future bishop was the second, born on 14 August 1929. John Carl worked for his father-in-law and later became part-owner until the sale of the business. In the early 1930s the young couple moved to near west side San Antonio, in the Prospect Hill district, to the old Schneider home at 2806 Buena Vista Street.

Charles Edwin was baptized and confirmed in Sacred Heart Church in San Antonio. Just as his mother had, he attended Sacred Heart School between 1935 and 1942. All of the Herzig boys attended this school and were altar boys in the Church. Their parish, originally German-American and presently Mexican-American, was founded by Bishop John A. Forest in 1899. The original frame church was dedicated on 22 October 1901. A new brick church opened a block away on property where Ursuline Nuns opened an academy in 1899. The new parish church also served as a chapel for the Sisters. Dedicated in 1906, it was converted into a gymnasium, its interior beautified, three large bells hung, and a two-story rectory built during the pastorate of Rev. Joseph Jacobi (1916-1954).

At the age of twelve Charles went to work as a bicycle delivery boy for ten cents an hour. "I had the job until somebody stole my bicycle," recalled the Bishop later. In 1941 he entered Central Catholic High School, an institution dating back to 25 August 1852 and founded by the Marianist Brothers. At the time of Charles's attendance it was located on North St. Mary's Street in San Antonio from 17 January 1932. The young student joined Rev. James McKnight's boy scout troup in the Alamo Area Council of the Boy Scouts of America and achieved the rank of Eagle Scout. He remembered, "Through the Scouting program, I achieved and developed some initiative and sense of satisfaction."

In the matter of a religious vocation, he was not pressured by his parents. No others in his family have been called to serve in this way except his grandfather. But his upbringing, his church life and school attendance, and possibly the devotion of his mother made him seriously consider it. At first, thinking of becoming a Marianist and a teacher, he attended St. Mary's University in San Antonio. This institution started in 1852 under the auspices of the Society of Mary. Here as a scholarship student he pursued a program in business administration from 1946 until 1948.

Having decided upon his vocation, Charles Herzig arrived at St. John's Seminary in San Antonio in September 1948. He wore the required dark suit and hat. At that time Vincentian Priests conducted the Seminary. Needing more land for increasing post-war vocations, Archbishop Lucey purchased the former Trinity University campus in 1951. He converted it into a major facility the following year and dedicated it as Assumption Seminary. Returned to diocesan priests in 1967, St. John's closed in 1970.

The Bishop's beloved mother did not live to see her son become a priest. She died of pneumonia on 19 January 1949. Some time afterwards John Carl Herzig met Miss Agnes Plick of Philadelphia at a church function. They married and eventually had three children, two sons and a daughter. Bishop Herzig baptized the last child, Mary Ann, as a priest. John Carl moved to the Hollywood Park district of San Antonio. He received the first Holy Communion given by his son as a priest and was present with his wife and family for Charles's episcopal ordination in Tyler.

John Carl Herzig died in San Antonio on 15 April 1988, while his son was in Europe to visit the Pope. He was survived by two sisters and a brother, all living in California, and by his wife and six children, two sons having predeceased him. Bishop Herzig celebrated the Mass of Christian Burial for his father, together with the Archbishop of San Antonio and his auxiliary, on 19 April at the Church of St. Mark the Evangelist. Mr. Herzig was buried in San Fernando Archdiocesan Cemetery in San Antonio.

The Reverend Mister Charles Herzig was ordained in San Fernando Cathedral in San Antonio by Archbishop Robert E. Lucey on 31 May 1955. Five days later he celebrated his First Mass at St. Mary Magdalen's Church at 1710 Clower Street in San Antonio. Bishops John Morkovsky of Galveston-Houston and Bernard Popp of San Antonio were pastors here. The priest's chalice was formed in part of his mother's jewels, thus commemorating her in a special way. Father Herzig gave his First Benediction that afternoon and a reception followed in the parish assembly hall.

The new priest's first assignment was the downtown parish of St. Joseph's on Commerce Street. Here he was Assistant Pastor from June to September 1955. He then became Financial Secretary to Archbishop Lucey from 1955 until 1967. From 1955 until 1959 he was Assistant Pastor of St. Cecilia's Parish in San Antonio. Bishop Mariano Garriga of Corpus Christi was founding pastor of this church in 1919. The present church was built in 1950 and was the first air-conditioned Catholic church in that city. In the first year of his priesthood

Father Herzig was appointed to the Bexar County Historical Survey Committee and served as Chaplain of the Knights of Columbus Council Number 786 until 1961.

His next major career assignment was Chaplain of St. Teresa's Academy from 1959 until 1963. Founded by Teresian Sisters from Mexico in 1910, the present plant on South Presa Street opened in 1921. Now a day school, it is coed in the elementary section with a high school department for girls. From 1962 until 1968 Herzig was Spiritual Director of the Archdiocesan Union of Holy Name Societies.

Upon leaving St. Teresa's Father Herzig became Chaplain of Holy Cross High School in San Antonio from 1963 until 1966. Founded by the Archdiocese in 1957 Holy Cross was staffed by Holy Cross Brothers and a lay faculty. It was intended for boys from grade seven through grade twelve. As Archdiocesan Director of Old Spanish Missions (1964-1967), he was Pastor of St. Joseph's Parish in Honey Creek from 1966 until 1967.

On his first assignment outside San Antonio the Pastor journeyed to the extreme western part of Comal County between Boerne and New Braunfels. The first log chapel was completed in 1876 and became a parish fifteen years later. In 1892 a new frame church was dedicated on the present site, where the present stone church of 1912 stands today.

Back in San Antonio Father Herzig was assigned to St. Pius X Parish until September 1967. The parish was founded and the church built in 1957 in the northwest section of the City. It had lost about forty per cent of its families on the establishment of St. Thomas More Parish in 1964. But ten years later it had increased to nearly 1,100 families.

The years as financial secretary now over, Herzig conducted a study of the Archdiocese for Archbishop Lucey from September 1967 to 1968. At this time he was assigned to St. John's Seminary as Vice-Rector, a position he held until that institution closed in 1970. A disagreement with the Archbishop over involvement in labor protests led Herzig and fifty other priests of the Archdiocese to sign a letter to Pope Paul VI and four other highly-placed churchmen seeking the Archbishop's removal. This request was seconded by Archbishop (later Cardinal) Luigi Raimondi, the Apostolic Delegate to the United States. Archbishop Lucey resigned on 4 June 1969.

Archbishop Francis Furey assigned Father Herzig to Assumption Seminary as its Vice-President from 1970 until 1973. As Vice-President he enrolled in the graduate school of Our Lady of the Lake University and was awarded the degree of Master of Education in 1972. From 1971 to 1973 he was Chairman of the Priests' Senate and was a member of the Board of Governors of St. Peter's-St. Joseph's Home from 1972 until 1974. This last institution is a consolidation of two children's homes in 1929. From that time it was under archdiocesan control with Sisters of Charity of the Incarnate Word in charge. From January 1970 its programs, policy, and financing were placed under the Board. Licensed by the Texas State Department of Public Welfare, it cares for about sixty children between the ages of six and fourteen.

Continuing under Archbishop Furey, Herzig next became Pastor of St. Stephen's Parish in San Antonio from 12 December 1973 until 30 September 1980. This mission of St. John Berchman's Parish had grown from 1953 into its present church dedicated in 1960. It became a separate parish in 1965 and was staffed from 1955 to 1973 by Immaculate Heart Mission Fathers. It had over 1,000 families in 1974. And in that year its pastor visited Russia and Spain. A member of the Priests' Personnel Board (1976-1980) he was Moderator of the Southwest Deanery Council of Catholic Women from 1977 to 1980.

Twenty-five years of clerical experience were leading to something as the decade of the 1980s approached. San Antonio had a new archbishop in Patrick Flores and the assignments kept coming. The first four years were a prelude to future service. From 1 October 1980 to 1 January 1984 Father Herzig was Pastor of Holy Name Parish in San Antonio. Its first church was dedicated in 1959, and it became a parish in 1961. By 1974 it had over 1,300 families. He filled other positions in this period, as Chaplain of the Bexar Caravan of the Order of the Alhambra from 1980 until 1984 and as Dean of the Southwest Urban Deanery from 26 October 1981 until 1 January 1984. He was an Archdiocesan Consultor from 1981 until 1985, and Vice-Chairman (1982-1983) and Chairman (1983) of the Presbyteral Council.

With the new year of 1984 Father Herzig entered the "fast track" road to the episcopacy. On 2 January he moved into the rectory of Our Lady of Grace Church in San Antonio and remained until 31 May 1986. Stephen Leven was Pastor of this parish as auxiliary bishop of San Antonio and remained until he became Bishop of San Angelo in 1969. For Father Herzig archdiocesan work now reached a new intensity. On the same day he entered Our Lady of Grace Parish he became Vice-Chancellor of the Archdiocese of San Antonio, Director of the Tribunal, Head of the Department of Pastoral Services, and Archdiocesan Director of the Propagation of the Faith and of the Holy Childhood Association. The day began at 6:30 A.M. and ended by 11:00 P.M., a round of appointments, meetings, counseling sessions, hospital visits, classes, telephone conference calls, reading, and letter writing.

With these new duties came the appropriate rank. Father Herzig was appointed Adjutant Vicar on 30 April 1984 and Pope John Paul II made him a Prelate of Honor, with the title of Monsignor, on 4 November 1984. From 1 June 1986 until he took up his duties in Tyler Monsignor Herzig resided at St. Ann's Church in San Antonio. Until 9 December 1986 he had no idea he was being considered for the new diocese being formed from the Dioceses of Dallas, Beaumont, and Galveston-Houston.

On 16 December 1986 Pope John Paul II appointed Charles Herzig Bishop of Tyler. He was given five hours to accept.

As he expressed it:

> Under the pressure of a deadline to signify my acceptance of this call, and with other affairs clamoring for my attention at the same time, I had but a little while to seek from the Lord guidance and direction as to my response. In the chapel [at the Chancery in San Antonio] all I could do was focus my attention on the three statues, which were recently placed there. To Jesus I said, 'You called the apostles, simple people such as I, and they responded; so must I.' To Joseph I said, 'You are the patron of the Church; protect that portion that is given to my charge.' To Mary I said, 'You have always shown yourself a mother; be that to me now. . . hold my hand.'

> Those few moments gave me the strength to say, 'Yes!'

In less dramatic fashion, he reflected:

> You don't easily turn it down, because you recognize the decision as the will of other prudent people who are interested in the good of the church. For them to have called me, it must be an indication it's God's will.

He also said, "I really had no ambition, dreams about being a bishop."

Thirty-one years as a priest had lent some perspective to his decision. He reflected on his ministry:

> What I enjoy the most about the ministry is people, involvement in the lives of people, trying to direct their lives in view of the Gospel, being with people in their joys and sorrows, celebrating the good things, being compassionate when things don't go well, reminding them by word, example and work of the love, mercy, joy and presence of God.

Archbishop Patrick Flores of San Antonio said of him on the day of his appointment:

> Bishop-Elect Herzig is a very dedicated individual with a clear and incisive mind. He is a good moral person reflecting the virtue of poverty in his lifestyle. He is dedicated to continuing education, especially updating himself after Second Vatican Council. He has a great rapport with his fellow priests and is loved by us all. His health is in excellent condition and he has always been a hard worker.
>
> He is a very pastoral person who has given himself totally to his people as a pastor in the parishes he has served. He is a most capable administrator. He proved this not only as a pastor but also as the Secretary to Archbishop Lucey. In his last assignment he clearly demonstrated his acumen and expertise as Director of Pastoral Services Department and as Director of the Tribunal. In the midst of all these virtues, he is a very humble person and will make an excellent shepherd to priests, religious and laity of a new diocese.

Of his own experience the Bishop-Elect noted:

> When I was a youngster, probably inspired by the good example of a good pastor, I dreamed of being a priest. I never thought of being a bishop; I wasn't subject to nightmares. I, like many others, have often expressed my thoughts about what I would do if I were the bishop, but that was always a judgment about a decision, not an expression of ambition. All I have ever wanted was to be a good priest. Now all of a sudden I am called to be a good bishop. When I protested to the Archbishop that there are many other more capable and talented priests in Texas than I, he said, 'We know that, but you are the one being called.'
>
> I have never experienced such a turning point in my life as I will experience now. Like Abram I am being called to leave my

> land, my kinsfolk, and my father's house for the land which he will show me. Scripture tells us that 'Abram went away as the Lord commanded him.' Obedient and trusting, I will go away to the land which he will show me.

After expressing his devotion to God, the Pope, Archbishop Flores, the bishops from whom his diocese was formed, the religious and laity he knew as a priest, and his family and friends for their love and support, he added also in fluent Spanish:

> I have accepted this call to be bishop.
>
> I give thanks to God for His constant love, for His care, and for this sign of His mysterious wisdom. Now I have become a bishop, and the anticipation of the responsibilities gives me fear. Because of this, I have asked for the presence of God to me and to the people of this new church.
>
> I express my gratitude to our Holy Father, John Paul II, for his confidence, and for giving me this opportunity to serve the Lord and his people in this new way.
>
> I give thanks, too, to our beloved archbishop, not only for his concern, but in addition for his good example. It would be a miracle, but I have desires to be a bishop like him.
>
> To all the others whom I have served, and with whom I have served [in] the churches during thirty-one years as a priest, I express my gratitude for your holiness and your generosity. The Archdiocese of San Antonio is a model for others, and I hope that God shares these blessings with the Diocese of Tyler.
>
> During all the years of my life I have been blessed with a good, loving and supportive family and friends. I am separated from them by distance, perhaps I shall be even closer to them in spirit. I ask of all of you your constant love, and, with more pressing need, your prayers.

The thirty-two counties of the Diocese of Tyler were officially erected on 24 February 1987 by the reading of the Pope's Apostolic Letter Creating the Diocese of Tyler, the Decree of Execution of the Apostolic Letter, and the Apostolic Letter appointing the Bishop of the Diocese of Tyler. These events occurred at 3:00 P.M. that day in the Cathedral of the Immaculate Conception in Tyler.

The new diocese consisted of thirty-five priests (twenty-one diocesan, thirteen religious order, and a priest with the status of hermit), twenty-seven permanent deacons, three male religious (including two hermits), seventy women religious (including thirty-four cloistered nuns), four elementary schools, one middle and high school, and about 40,000 Catholics in an area of 1,167,000 total population. The area of the Diocese was given as 22,971 square miles. The Diocese had nine convents, two hospitals, a monastery, twenty-five parishes, and sixteen missions. There were four prison units in Anderson County, a university student center in Nacogdoches County, and the Eastham State Farm in

Houston County. All these facilities required the services of chaplains.

Bishop Herzig received his episcopal ordination at the hands of Archbishop Patrick Flores of San Antonio. His Co-consecrators were Bishop Thomas Tschoepe of Dallas and Bishop Patrick Sheehan of Lubbock. The ordination took place in the Oil Palace Auditorium in Tyler on 24 February 1987 at 7:00 P.M.

After one year as bishop of Tyler Herzig had made great strides in building up his diocese. He had traveled by car some 22,000 miles in visits to parishes and missions. The Chancery functioned at 1920 Sybil Lane in Tyler and a financial council, a building commission, and a Diocesan Council of Catholic Women were in operation. *Catholic East Texas*, the diocesan newspaper, began publication on 27 November 1987. The Bishop had begun the necessary transfer of titles to diocesan property, fixed an income level, and conducted his first annual appeal for sustaining funds.

Still he saw his role as a bishop/pastor and not just as a bishop/administrator. His mission was to unify the entire diocese as a community of faith. He had celebrated a Marian Year, helped welcome the Pope in San Antonio, and presided at two church groundbreakings.

On 6 April 1988 Bishop Herzig, together with his fellow bishops of Texas, left home for their regular *ad limina* visits to Rome. These visits would take place between the tenth and the seventeenth of April. But first they would make a tour of the Rhône District of France. Specifically they would visit the towns of Ambierle and Coutouvre to visit the tombs of the first two bishops of Texas, Bishop Odin and Bishop Dubuis. They also visited Sury le Comtal, the birthplace of Archbishop Antoine Blanc of New Orleans, whose response to a request by President Sam Houston set the creation of the Texas Catholic hierarchy in progress. They met with the civil dignitaries of Lyon and with its cardinal-archbishop Albert Decoutray, the president of the council of French bishops.

The visit of the Texas bishops to France delighted, captivated, and intrigued the French by turns. As Bishop Herzig put it, "The French people were very impressed, and the French church was very pleased, with what we did because it brought them to a recognition of their own importance." The enthusiastic people and especially the children swarmed around the bishops who, unfortunately and collectively, could speak about as much French as the natives they encountered could speak English. The *Lyon Figaro* ran a photograph of Bishop Grahmann of Victoria (and later of Dallas) wearing a big (but noncowboy) hat and speaking to a little girl. The headline read "Dieu *Benisse Les Cow-Boys*" ("God Bless the Cowboys").

The bishops placed a placque on Bishop Odin's grave and presented the pastor of Coutouvre with a stone placque commemorating their visit to the grave of Bishop Dubuis. They also visited Saint Martin la Sauveté, where Bishop John Forest of San Antonio was born. It was Bishop Forest who had married Bishop Grahmann's great-grandparents. Summing up, Bishop Herzig said of the visit:

> They [the French bishops in Texas] came to us and got us started. We, their successors, have continued that work, have embellished it, have enlarged it, and now as a, not as a finished product, but as a

> much developed product, now we go back to them to say 'thank you.'

In a sense the Texas bishops were thanking France for the gift of its bishops, clergy, and Religious, without whom the development of the Catholic Church in nineteenth-century Texas might not have been possible.

Although it was not necessary that Bishop Herzig visit the Pope at this time, he wanted to thank him for coming to Texas, for creating the Diocese of Tyler, and for spending his time with the Texas bishops. The Pope asked the Bishop how was the "climate" of East Texas. By this question he meant not the weather but the situation in which the Church found itself as a minority there. The Bishop cited a number of cooperative acts by people of other denominations and assured John Paul that the atmosphere was a friendly one involving many people of good will. The Pope was also interested in learning about Tyler. For his part Bishop Herzig was impressed by the intense interest the Pope afforded him, realizing that this quarter-hour was one of many in an already busy day.

It was 16 April 1988. When the Pope learned that Bishop Herzig's father had died the day before in San Antonio, he gave an audible gasp and seemed visibly shaken. He insisted that the two immediately pray for the repose of Mister Herzig's soul and imparted a blessing for the Bishop's family. During the stay in Rome the bishops asked their colleague of Tyler to say Mass while they concelebrated with him.

In early October 1990 Bishop Herzig felt discomfort in his right arm. Early tests revealed a tumor in his right lung. Outpatient tests made on 8 October at Mother Frances Hospital in Tyler revealed small cell carcinoma. On 10 October Bishop Herzig declared: "The future is uncertain, but I am content to leave it in the hands of the Lord. The only miracle I ask for is His continued presence and love. I ask everyone to pray for me."

The following day he underwent a three-day round of chemotherapy at the Hospital. Weakened but still in control, he continued his duties, attending the seventy-fifth anniversary of the beginnings of Assumption Seminary as St. John's in San Antonio from 16 to 19 October. Msgr. Milam Joseph, the Vicar General of the Tyler diocese, returned from a sabatical retreat in Canada to assist him. On 19 October Bishop Herzig tried to allay the worries of his flock: "Since my condition has become known to others, I have been inundated with signs of love, concern and thoughtfulness." He said he appreciated prayers offered on his behalf and left Tyler on 21 October for a meeting of Texas bishops in Tulsa, following a regional church meeting there.

Mid-November 1990 brought with it daily radiation treatment at the East Texas Cancer Center and continued chemotherapy at Mother Frances Hospital, both in Tyler. Bishop Herzig had given up smoking the day after his initial diagnosis. He joked that he had no loss of appetite, energy or spirit, only hair. For a while Dr. John J. Reuland, his oncologist, prescribed one full day of chemotherapy with a partial day prior and afterward spent in the hospital. He also recommended three days of treatment with a before and after hospital stay to control nausea. The radiation continued daily except for weekends and holidays until the first or second week of January 1991.

On 11 February 1991 Doctor Reuland pronounced Bishop Herzig in complete remission of lung cancer and in excellent physical health, though he continued monthly chemotherapy as a precaution. The Bishop continued to plan ahead, hoping to start an independent tribunal for his diocese by 1993 or so. He completed churches in Clarksville and in Mount Vernon. He looked forward to the construction of a new church in Nacogdoches and the expansion project on the church building in Mount Pleasant. The Appeals Office announced that it had collected $500,105 or 90% of the $557,552 set for the 1990 Diocesan Annual Appeal. He expected excess funds to be deposited in some of the Diocese's permanent funds, such as the priests' pension plan, the infirm priests' fund, the seminary burse fund, and the continuing education of the clergy fund.

He was pleased to open a permanent Catholic schools trust fund with a balance of $20,000. He had already established a continuing education and formation committee of the priests' council. He wanted his churches to reach out to the inactive, to the poor, and to the estranged, the civic community, and to ethnic minorities. He noted that registered Hispanic households in the Diocese numbered 2,551. He praised Sr. Sara Dwyer for doing "amazing" work as head of the Office of Ministries. He felt there were a significant number of Catholics in Elkhart in Anderson County and wanted to form a faith community there without a resident pastor. And he realized "We have to preach more on the centrality of Jesus in the Catholic faith. Our lives do center on Him. He is the focal point of our faith."

But in May 1991 Bishop Herzig developed thrombophlebitis in his lower right leg. From the sixth to the sixteenth of that month he remained in Mother Frances Hospital. An embolism developed in his lung because of a breakaway from the blood clot causing the phlebitis in his leg. The blood clot and the embolism were dissolved with anticoagulants, which he continued to take for two months thereafter. While he continued to take chemotherapy, the phlebitis was not related to it. He had lost fifteen pounds and was told not to drive far. In fact he never again left East Texas.

On 1 July 1991 a CAT scan revealed brain cancer. On 3 July he began a series of twenty-eight daily radiation treatments to combat the cancer. On 15 July Bishop Herzig's radiologist, Dr. Dale Lakomy, reported that the Bishop had widespread "tumor lumps on his brain." By now the Bishop was having trouble concentrating. He endured more chemotherapy between 18 and 26 August. He returned to the hospital on 29 to 31 August. He was dizzy and fell twice, after which he used a walker to aid his movements. He still continued to work in his office at the Chancery, which he did from 3 to 6 September, being driven to and from work by Ed Luman, the diocesan business manager.

By now Archbishop Flores had become greatly concerned about Bishop Herzig's health. He decided to see for himself and, with Vicar General of the San Antonio archdiocese Msgr. Lawrence Stuebben, flew from San Antonio to Tyler on 6 September. It was Flores's first visit to Tyler since he had ordained his friend bishop. The Archbishop and his vicar general conferred with the Bishop, with Doctor Reuland, and with Monsignor Joseph. Bishop Herzig seemed to be in satisfactory condition. He and his visitors had dinner at the cathedral rectory and went on tours of the Chancery and the Bishop's residence. They left with no particular sense of dread. Monsignor Joseph stopped by the Bishop's home that evening and thought him in "terrific spirits." Bishop

Herzig planned to celebrate Mass the following morning at the Cathedral for the nuns of the Diocese of Tyler.

At 10:30 A.M. the next morning of 7 September 1991 Judy Green, a chancery employee, arrived at the residence to take the Bishop to the Cathedral. When he did not answer the door, she telephoned him from a nearby house. He told her that he could not get out of bed but needed no help. Mrs. Green immediately drove to the Cathedral to seek assistance. She encountered Jeff Wallace and Michael Mahfood there. Wallace, who had once driven the Bishop, had a key and found him in the bedroom, awake but having labored breathing. He insisted he did not want aid but asked for a glass of water. Mahfood came a few minutes later, and the men called Doctor Reuland.

On the ambulance ride to Mother Frances Hospital, Bishop Herzig lapsed into unconsciousness, from which he never awakened. It was now 11:30 A.M. in the Emergency Room, to which Doctor Reuland arrived ten minutes later. Around noon the aged hospital chaplain Fr. John Przydacz administered the last rites of the Church, anointing, absolution and the papal blessing for the seriously ill. Monsignor Joseph, who had celebrated Mass for the Bishop in his absence, was reached at the cathedral rectory. At 12:45 P.M. he was admitted to the Intensive Care Unit, as the others left. It was already too late. "I closed his eyes, anointed him, prayed and cried." Doctor Reuland returned and pronounced Bishop Herzig dead at 1:00 P.M. of congestive heart failure.

It seems no accident that Bishop Herzig as a young man achieved the highest rank conferred by the Boy Scouts of America, that of Eagle Scout. In addition to meeting all requirements specified by the traditional Scout Law, he received the St. George Emblem in 1971 for his support of that organization. Those who knew him well considered him a friend, kind, generous, truly interested in others with a special concern for Hispanics and the poor, like a member of the family. The editor of his diocesan newspaper assigned him the qualities of integrity, honesty, loyalty, and steadfastness.

The Bishop's family requested that memorials be made to the Charles E. Herzig Development Fund for Developing Parishes. But it is not difficult to believe that the Bishop would have been proud to know that in mid-1995 Seminary Burses to educate clerical students for the Diocese of Tyler had in the case of "Bishop Herzig" reached the sum of $12,927.09 and that of the "John C. Herzig Memorial" for that purpose had reached $19,100.

Bishop Herzig was survived by his stepmother Agnes Luck Plick Herzig, and his brothers Kenneth J. of San Antonio, Ronald J. and Edward C. of Houston, Francis X. and his sister Mary Ann, both of San Antonio, eighteen nieces and nephews, and twenty great-nieces and great-nephews. The Bishop lay in state in the Cathedral in Tyler from 9 to 11 September. Nightly prayers were said from 7:00 to 7:30 P.M. and a vigil until midnight. The Knights of Columbus of Tyler stood guard. On the evening of 10 September a rosary was said for the repose of the Bishop's soul. On the evening of 11 September Archbishop Flores officiated at a Vigil Service. The funeral Mass followed on the morning of 12 September. In honor of the late bishop Catholic schools in Tyler closed on the twelfth and thirteenth of September, as did St. Joseph's School in Marshall on the day of the funeral.

The Funeral Mass began on Thursday, 12 September 1991 in the Cathedral of the Immaculate Conception in Tyler, at 10:00 A.M. Archbishop Flores was the principal celebrant. More than 1100 people came to pray and to view the Bishop at his lying-in-state. Now there were more than 700 present, with Archbishop Charles Salatka of Oklahoma City, seventeen bishops from Texas and neighboring states, and at least 100 priests among their number. Many came from San Antonio to bid a last farewell. The overflowing crowd in the basement and on the portico watched the service through television.

Monsignor Joseph, Rev. Randy Martin, and the Cathedral worship directors Brian and Dianna Braquet devised the funeral liturgies. Three cathedral choirs provided music for the occasion. Archbishop Flores, who had known Bishop Herzig for many years, praised his friend's "organizational skills" and spoke of his life as "a blessing to all who knew him." He helped the poor and needy and comforted the sick and the aged. Though his doctor had given the Bishop a prognosis of four to six months to live, the Archbishop recalled, "Our loss is Heaven's gain. We don't lose, because God wins. But it is hard to surrender even to the Lord, because we know we will miss him."

Monsignor Milam Joseph mentioned Herzig's "dedication and commitment" to his diocese and his faithfulness. The Bishop's brother Kenneth Herzig remembered his standing "for goodness" and his commitment to his church and loyalty to his family. "What a blessing he has been. . .what a beautiful life. . . he was our pride and joy and now he is our glory." Press commentators felt that Bishop Herzig's concerns as bishop were evangelization, increasing lay involvement in the Church, and welcoming and assisting Hispanic immigrants in his diocese.

Bishop Herzig is buried in Tyler, as his will requests, in Rose Hill Cemetery, between South Broadway and Donnybrook avenues. It is part of the diocesan plot, a part of forty-five plots in the southwest corner of the Cemetery reserved for its priests and bishops. It was bought by the Diocese of Tyler in September 1989. On 10 September 1991 the diocesan consultors met. They elected one of their number, Msgr. Milam Joseph, the Vicar General, to serve as Administrator of the Tyler diocese pending appointment of the next bishop. Bishop Herzig's pallbearers were Monsignor Lawrence Stuebben, Vicar General of the San Antonio archdiocese, and the five remaining diocesan consultors of the Tyler diocese. These priests who performed this last service for their bishop were Revs. John Brennan of Longview, Maurice Linehan, MS of Lufkin, Harold Paulsen of Palestine, Gerald Priest of Marshall, and James Young of Nacogdoches.

Smith County Judge Larry Craig probated Bishop Herzig's will in Tyler on 6 November 1991. In it the Bishop said: "I ask pardon of all whom I have offended, thank God for the wonderful gift of life and accept death joyfully as God in His loving providence has decreed it." He required that all cash from his personal accounts, certificates of deposit and insurance policies be placed in the permanent development fund of the Diocese of Tyler so that the interest will be used for diocesan parishes, missions, and institutions. The total of nearly $145,000 including $24,000 in life insurance would have subtracted from it funeral, legal and medical expenses. He left his blue Chevrolet sedan to the cloistered Dominican nuns at the Monastery of the Infant Jesus in Lufkin and his white GMC Jimmy to his nephew David Herzig. The Bishop's chalice went to the diocesan archives and his vestments to the Cathedral in Tyler for use or distribution by the Rector. His brother Kenneth Herzig was to dispose of his other possessions. Monsignor Milam Joseph as Vicar General was named executor, charged to pay all taxes, debts, and funeral expenses. The sum of $1,000 was to be distributed as stipends for Masses for the Bishop.

Just as Bishop Herzig sought to provide for the future of his diocese, so also did he remember its historical past. He renewed annual pilgrimages to the replica of the Mission San Francisco de Los Tejas near Weches in Houston County, the first East Texas mission founded by the Spanish in 1690. And he made sure that this, and every other diocese-wide occasion, would be bilingual in English and in Spanish. And in death his flock did not forget him.

For six months preceding the second anniversary of his death, his successor Bishop Edmond Carmody and a committee met to determine what type of permanent markers would be installed in Rose Hill Cemetery. They decided upon two, one five-and-a-half foot monument for the diocesan burial plot and a permanent marker for Bishop Herzig's grave. These white marble monuments were simply inscribed. The diocesan monument had a cross and the words "Priests, Diocese of Tyler," flanked by the diocesan shield and diocesan stole. Bishop Herzig's headstone contained his name, dates of birth and death, his personal coat of arms and the legend, "First Bishop, Diocese of Tyler." The Herzig family was invited to attend the blessing of the markers at 6:00 P.M., Mass at the Cathedral at 7:00 P.M., and a reception following Mass, all on 7 September 1993.

On that date some forty-five people came to the Cemetery for the dedication and about twice that number to the memorial Mass which followed at the Cathedral. Bishop Carmody noted: "Charles Herzig looked at God as his guide, his protector. God was a real person to him. He loved his God, he loved his people, and he loved his world. His life was very inclusive." Bishop Carmody observed that Bishop Herzig tried to involve everyone in ministry. He added: "His ministry was with others and for others. The seeds he planted will continue to grow. The lives he touched are truly better lives because he loved his God, other people and the world."

While the Knights of Columbus color guard from Fourth Degree Assembly 1119 in Tyler stood at attention, members of the chancery staff, priests and deacons of the diocese viewed the markers dedicated and sprinkled with holy water. Edward and Nancy Herzig of Houston represented the late bishop's family. Leon Triana of Tyler, a member of the Knights of Columbus color guard, said of Bishop Herzig: "We came to pay respects to a very great man. He was humble, but strong."

Bishop Herzig was possessed with a sense of humor, as befits a man who listed loafing, watching television, and walking in the woods as his hobbies. His total absorption in his work is indicated by the guests he wanted to invite to his fantasy dinner: John Fitzgerald Kennedy, Francis of Assisi, Thomas Aquinas, and an ancestor of the Herzig family living in the time of Christ. This bishop, whose name means "charming" in English took for his motto, "To Build Up The Body of Christ." No one can doubt this is just what he did.

Most Reverend Emmanuel Boleslaus Ledvina, DD
Second Bishop of Corpus Christi
Titular Bishop of Pitanae

A missionary bishop of the older type, Emmanuel Boleslaus Ledvina came to Texas from the Midwest. Here he aided a young diocese as a builder of churches and institutions. Noted for his humility, he was unfailingly kind to the religious and laity, upon whom he looked as co-workers in a common goal.

Born to George Emmanuel and Mary (Kiefer) Ledvina in Evansville, Randolph County, Illinois, on 28 October 1868, Emmanuel received his early education in the parochial schools of St. Louis, Missouri, and Evansville, Illinois. He completed his clerical studies at St. Meinrad College Seminary (1883 to 1888) and Theological Seminary (1888 to 1893) in St. Meinrad, Indiana.

The Reverend Mister Ledvina was ordained for the Diocese of Vincennes (now the Archdiocese of Indianapolis), Indiana, by its bishop Francis S. Chatard on 18 March 1893. His first assignment was Curate of the Church (now Pro-Cathedral) of the Most Holy Trinity in Evansville, Vanderburgh County, Indiana, from 1893 to 1894. He was then appointed Curate of St. John's Parish in Indianapolis from 1894 until 1895. He ended his parish career as Pastor of St. Joseph's Parish in Princeton, Indiana, serving from 1895 until 1907.

In 1907 Father Ledvina joined the Catholic Church Extension Society, first as Secretary, then as General Secretary (1907 to 1921), and briefly as First Vice-President (1908). The Society was the dream of Rev. Francis C. Kelley, who made it a realization. This Canadian-born priest, who was to become Bishop of the Diocese of Oklahoma in 1924, was once the Pastor of the Catholic Church in Lapeer, Michigan.

Impressed by the ability of his protestant neighbors to build churches, Father Kelley wanted to establish such an organization as the Methodist Extension Board, the Baptist Home Mission Society with its Church Extension Board, and the Congregational Church Building Society within his own church. He particularly wanted to build churches in the South and West of the United States. Unable to enlist the patronage of the archbishops of Santa Fe, New York, Philadelphia, and Detroit, Father Kelley next approached James E. Quigley, the Archbishop of Chicago.

The young priest's earnest entreaties won over the Archbishop. At a meeting at Archbishop Quigley's residence in Chicago on 18 October 1905, Archbishop Peter Bourgade of Santa Fe suggested that the new society should aid in a broader way than simply building churches. Father Kelley was elected temporary president and a second meeting was held on 12 December 1905. By 28 December the Society was incorporated under the laws of the State of Michigan.

The broadened vision of the Extension Society was to erect parish buildings where needed, to contribute to the support of priests for their missions, to supply poor missions, to circulate Catholic literature, to educate students as missionary priests, and to direct Catholic colonists to suitable residences.

In April 1907 Father Kelley was given a full-time assignment as President of the Extension Society. He moved its headquarters from Lapeer to Chicago, where it has since remained. As the need arose to find a new General Secretary, he came to Princeton, Indiana, as a lecturer for the Lyceum. Here he encountered Father Ledvina, in whom he found all the qualities he sought for the position. Father Ledvina proved to be a godsend in his possession of the qualities of order, fair play, and boundless energy. As Bishop Kelley said of him in later years:

> His services to Church Extension were of the kind that never can be forgotten. I can really claim only the credit of striking the first blow. . . . Father Ledvina was like a quartermaster-general, who gets his supplies in bulk, but arranges and dispatches them in such a way that each unit of the army is properly fed, clothed and otherwise supplied at the right moment.

In the first year of its existence the Society collected $1,934 to aid the home missions of the United States. In the fiscal year 1993-94 it disbursed more than twelve million dollars for seventy-six designated mission dioceses throughout the country.

With its worthy objectives papal approval for the Society came quickly. During the first sixteen years of its existence (1905 to 1921) it brought into being 2,074 churches, schools, rectories, and convents for teaching Sisters. Because of its policy to aid local congregations in building, the Society did not completely finance any one work. It was thus enabled to assist in many more projects. In the same sixteen-year period, the Society gave a total of $1,255,599.03 to build new churches, while local congregations contributed $3,766,797.09. Thus 1,932 churches and chapels, ninety-eight new schools and convents, and forty-four rectories came into being.

In this time in Texas alone 313 new chapels were built with Society funds to aid the Mexican refugees of the Revolution of 1910. All of Texas benefited in every way, for the Society also helped furnish churches and rectories, educate mission students for the priesthood, and maintain mission schools. In the Diocese of Corpus Christi from its inception in 1913 through 1950, the Catholic Church Extension Society aided in major ways. In contributed to the building of 101 churches at a cost of $139,172.95, seven rectories for $3,875.00, nine schools for $20,287.84, three other buildings for $7,550.00, $142,399.00 for Mass intentions, and $277,677.74 in addition, for a total of $590,962.53.

From 1887 through 1950 the Commission for Catholic Missions Among the Colored People and the Indians contributed to the Diocese of Corpus Christi and its predecessor the Vicariate Apostolic of Brownsville the sum of $219,650.00. And from 1925 through 1950 the American Board of Catholic Missions contributed $292,866.00 to the Diocese of Corpus Christi.

As General Secretary of the Catholic Church Extension Society, Father Ledvina kept close attention upon the work of the Church in Texas. In 1918 Pope Benedict XV appointed him Domestic Prelate, with the title of Right Reverend Monsignor. And he was made an Honorary Canon of Our Lady of Guadalupe Basilica in Mexico City in 1919 for his missionary efforts.

Monsignor Ledvina was appointed Bishop of Corpus Christi by Pope Benedict XV on 30 April 1921. He was consecrated in the Chapel of the Sisters of Providence, St. Mary of the Woods, Indiana, on 14 June 1921 by Bishop Joseph Chartrand of Indianapolis, with Bishops Cornelius Van de Ven of Alexandria, Louisiana, and Joseph Lynch of Dallas as co-consecrators. On the following 12 July he was enthroned in St. Patrick's (now Corpus Christi) Cathedral in Corpus Christi.

Bishop Ledvina was well-acquainted with the South Texas area, having made a number of trips there to distribute Extension Society funds. In August 1921 he toured the Lower Rio Grande Valley administering Confirmation. His trip led to the building of a new church for Our Lady of Mercy Parish in Mercedes completed the next year. By 1926 the Parish had a new shcool. In 1924 the new parish church of St. Joseph's in Alamo was finished. A second parish for Mercedes, Sacred Heart, was readied in 1930. The Bishop also established Sacred Heart Parish in McAllen, and the parishes of Sacred Heart (1927) and St. Joseph's (1942) in Edinburg.

Because his clergy and Religious had many missions, schools, and institutions to visit with the parishes as home bases, the Bishop concerned himself with their health and welfare. He did his best to make their living conditions more comfortable by furnishing rectories and convents for their use. Bishop Ledvina's love and concern for his people led to his appointment by Pope Pius XI as Assistant to the Pontifical Throne on 30 May 1931. And from 1933 until 1952 he was the Pastor of St. Patrick's (renamed Corpus Christi in 1940) Cathedral in Corpus Christi.

Because of failing health and the increasing work of his diocese, Bishop Ledvina requested a coadjutor to assist him in 1936. Shortly thereafter Mariano S. Garriga of the San Antonio archdiocese was appointed to this position. On 15 March 1949 Bishop Ledvina resigned the administration of the Diocese and was appointed Titular Bishop of Pitanae by Pope Pius XII. He died in Corpus Christi on 15 December 1952 and was buried in the Crypt of the Cathedral in that city. The apostle from the Midwest had at last found rest among those he loved and served.

Most Reverend Stephen Aloysius Leven, DD
Titular Bishop of Bure and Auxiliary Bishop of San Antonio
Third Bishop of San Angelo

Stephen A. Leven was a preacher, scholar, and administrator who succeeded in each endeavor to which he turned his hand. Born near Blackwell, Kay County, Oklahoma, to Joseph J. and Gertrude (Conrady) Leven on 30 April 1905, Stephen was educated at St. Gregory's College in Shawnee, Oklahoma, and St. Benedict's (now Benedictine) College in Atchison, Kansas. In 1921 he studied for a year at St. Mary's Seminary in La Porte, Texas, and then attended the Catholic University of Louvain, Belgium, until 1928.

The Reverend Mister Leven was ordained in Ponca City, Oklahoma, for the Diocese of Oklahoma City, on 10 June 1928. At first Assistant Pastor of St. Mary's Parish in Ponca City, he was transfered that same year to St. Joseph's (Old Cathedral) in Oklahoma City. While there he became Secretary to Bishop Francis C. Kelley of Oklahoma City, the former President of the Catholic Church Extension Society, in 1930 and remained in the capital city until 1932.

Between 1932 and 1935 Father Leven was Pastor of St. Joseph's Church in Bristow and St. Mary's Church in Drumwright, both in Creek County, Oklahoma. These churches are now in the Diocese of Tulsa and, at the time of Bishop Leven's death, missions of Sts. Peter and Paul Parish in Cushing, Payne County, Oklahoma. In 1932 he began his career as a street preacher for the Catholic Evidence Guild in Oklahoma City. In the Summer of 1939 and thereafter he was Director of the Institute of Street Preaching. He used these evangelizing experiences as the title of his autobiography, *Go Tell It in the Streets* (1984).

Father Leven was Vice Rector of the American College in Louvain, Belgium, from 1935 until 1938. This college was founded by the Catholic bishops of the United States in 1857 as a house of formation for American seminarians and as a residence for graduate priest students pursuing courses in theology and related subjects at the Catholic Universities of Leuven and Louvain-la-Neuve. Today the College is administered by an American rector and staff and operates under a special committee of the National Conference of Catholic Bishops. Leven received the degree of Doctor of Philosophy (with great distinction) from the Institut Superieur de Philosophie of the University of Louvain (founded in 1425) in 1938.

On his return to the United States Father Leven became Pastor of St. Joseph's Parish in Tonkawa, Kay County, Oklahoma, where he remained until 1948. In addition to these duties and as Director of the Institute of Street Preaching, he was Dean of the National Center of the Confraternity of Christian Doctrine from 1939 until 1940. From 1943 until 1945 during World War II he was the Vatican's official visitor to inspect nine prisoner of war camps and a prisoner of war hospital in Oklahoma.

During Father Leven's pastorate of St. Francis Xavier Parish in Enid, Garfield County, Oklahoma, between 1948 and 1956 Pope Pius XII appointed him successively Papal Chamberlain (with the title of Very Reverend Monsignor) in 1949 and Domestic Prelate (with the title of Right Reverend Monsignor) in 1955. The same pontiff appointed Monsignor Leven Titular Bishop of

Auxiliary Bishop of San Antonio on 7 December 1955. He was consecrated bishop in Oklahoma City on 8 February 1956.

Bishop Leven was Pastor of Our Lady of Grace Parish in San Antonio from 4 June 1956 until 4 June 1969. This church was originally a chapel of St. Mary's Church in downtown San Antonio. Built to serve Catholics in the Laurel Heights area, it was constructed of native stone on property acquired from the Oblate Fathers' St. Anthony Seminary at the corner of North McCullough and Summit avenues. The church was dedicated on 23 October 1938 and a rectory, a gymnasium, and a meeting complex were added in 1951. The church achieved parish status on 30 July 1952 with its present title. Its two missions of Our Lady of Sorrows and St. John's are now independent parishes.

While in San Antonio Bishop Leven was awarded the honorary degree of Doctor of Laws by St. Edward's University in Austin in 1957. He attended all four sessions of Vatican Council II in Rome between October 1962 and December 1965. His tenure was marked by growth in his parish's religious education program and enlargement of its plant by the addition of five classrooms for the program. The sanctuary was completely refurbished in December 1963.

Bishop Leven was appointed Bishop of San Angelo by Pope Paul VI on 22 October 1969 and installed there on the following 25 November. At the time of his resignation on 16 April 1979 the Diocese of San Angelo consisted of thirty-four counties comprising 42,000 square miles. It had thirty-five diocesan priests, twenty-five religious order priests, sixty-three permanent deacons, thirty-seven women religious, fifty parishes, thirty-one missions, five elementary schools, and a general hospital. The Catholic population was 65,393 in a total population of 556,961.

Following his retirement Bishop Leven served as Chaplain of Blackwell General Hospital in Blackwell, Oklahoma, from 1979 until 1983. He died in St. Anthony Hospital in Oklahoma City, Oklahoma, on 28 June 1983, and his body was returned to San Angelo for burial. This kindly man, whose hobby was fishing, and whose name means "smooth" after the River Leven in the East Riding of Yorkshire, took for his motto, "Teaching and Preaching Jesus Christ." He did no less during the fifty-five years of his ministry.

Most Reverend Robert Emmet Lucey, STD
Second Bishop of Amarillo
Second Archbishop of San Antonio

The story of Archbishop Robert Lucey is classic. It tells about a Roman-educated powerful individual whose concentrated authority made him answerable only to the Pope within the Church. In Lucey's day a prelate expected to die on the job. He once said, "Priests can no longer afford to grow old gracefully; they must burn themselves out in a relentless dynamic drive for Christ and souls." And again:

> Priests are the standard-bearers in the army of Christ; they are the captains of God's people. And when many of the laity march backward, as they have been doing for a long time, there is something wrong with the captains.

Lucey was a great "captain," an authority on labor problems and social justice. But as the laity and clergy began to march forward, the spirit of the Second Vatican Council negated the spirit of the past. As groups within the Church wished to have a greater say about its present and future, another process was in the works. Canon 401 of the *Code of Canon Law* (1983) now requires that bishops and archbishops present their resignations to the Pope at the completion of their "seventy-fifth year of age." These resignations are generally accepted. And Archbishop Lucey being of the old order did not resign his office willingly.

The future archbishop Robert Emmet Lucey was born in Los Angeles, Los Angeles County, California to John Joseph and Marie (Nettle) Lucey on 16 March 1891. He was educated at Sacred Heart Parish School and St. Vincent's College, both in his native city. He completed his collegiate work at St. Patrick's Seminary in Menlo Park in 1912. For four years thereafter Robert pursued graduate studies while attending North American College in Rome. He was awarded the degree of Doctor of Sacred Theology by the University of the Propaganda in Rome in 1916 during World War I.

The Reverend Doctor Lucey was ordained by Archbishop Cepetelli, Patriarch of Constantinople and Vice Regent of Rome, in the Church of St. Apollinaris in Rome on 14 May 1916. The young priest returned to Los Angeles where for the next five years he was Assistant Pastor of St. Vibiana's Cathedral, Immaculate Conception Parish, and Immaculate Heart of Mary Parish, all in Los Angeles.

From 1921 until 1925 Father Lucey was Chaplain of the Newman Club at the University of California at Los Angeles and Diocesan Director of Catholic Charities. From 1923 until 1924 he was President of the California Conference of Social Work. Between 1924 and 1934 Lucey was Director of Catholic Hospitals for the Diocese of Los Angeles-San Diego. Also in 1924 the governor of California appointed him a member of the Executive Board of the California State Department of Social Welfare, a position he held until 1930. He ended his California ministry as Pastor of St. Anthony's Parish in Long Beach from 1929 to 1934.

On 10 February 1934 Pope Pius XI appointed Father Lucey Bishop of Amarillo. He was consecrated by Archbishop (later Cardinal) Amleto Cicognani, Apostolic Delegate to the United States. Bishops John Cantwell of Los Angeles-San Diego and Thomas Gorman of Reno (and later of Dallas) acted as his co-sponsors in St. Vibiana's Cathedral in Los Angeles on 1 March 1934. Bishop Lucey was installed in Amarillo on 16 May of that year.

He came to this northwest Texas city as a figure of established authority. His program began with study clubs to increase knowledge of the faith and he established the *Texas Panhandle Register* (now the *West Texas Catholic*) to foster better communication within the diocese. He stressed the work of Catholic Action or the Lay Apostolate to provide Christian witness in the life and work of the individual. The Diocesan Council of Catholic Women was organized, a parish in Amarillo opened for black Catholics, and ten churches built.

Appointed Archbishop of San Antonio by Pope Pius XII on 23 January 1941, Archbishop Lucey was installed in San Fernando Cathedral on the following 27 March by Archbishop Amleto Cicognani, from whom he received the Pallium on 22 October in San Antonio. The new archbishop hit the ground running. He immediately moved out of the combination residence and chancery at 230 Dwyer Avenue and had it remodeled into an archdiocesan headquarters building. He organized the Catholic Welfare Bureau, the Catholic Action Office, and the Archdiocesan Council of Catholic Men.

The Council was established to coordinate various activities in men's organizations. It sponsored an archdiocesan census, an industrial conference, the Summer School of Catholic Action, the expansion of the Laymen's Retreat League, and other projects. The Archbishop then became a member of the Bexar County chapter of the American Red Cross.

The rest of the year 1941 brought other improvements. The Vincentians came to staff St. John's Seminary in San Antonio. In August 1941 the Archbishop sponsored a summer school of social justice for the clergy of the Southwest to initiate a program of clergy and lay institutes to be conducted in succeeding years. The San Jose Mission was designated a National Historical Site through an agreement among the Archdiocese, the National Parks Board, the Texas State Park Board, the Conservation Society, and the County of Bexar. Many thousands of dollars were spent to preserve the missions.

In January 1942 the Confraternity of Christian Doctrine began its existence on an archdiocesan basis. The *Alamo Register* (now *Today's Catholic*) began publication as the official archdiocesan newspaper on 5 June 1942. On 20 February 1943 Archbishop Lucey appointed Rev. John L. Morkovsky archdiocesan superintendent of schools. At the time of his appointment there were 13,225 students enrolled in archdiocesan schools. Morkovsky organized the school office with 4,095 students in eighteen parish schools in San Antonio, 3,692 in thirty-six parish schools outside the City, 4,055 in eighteen private schools in San Antonio, and 1,113 in eight private schools outside of San Antonio.

When Morkovsky was succeeded by Auxiliary Bishop Stephen Leven in 1956, enrollment was 28,311 (19,248 in forty-five schools in San Antonio and 9,063 in forty schools in the rest of the Archdiocese). Reverend James Brunner became superintendent in 1960 when enrollment was 34,975. After 1963 enrollment declined from 36,442 to 25,458 when Brother Edwin Goerdt, SM, became superintendent in 1969, the year Archbishop Lucey retired.

Also in 1943 the boundary commission of the Archdiocese was organized to unravel the overlapping of national and territorial parishes. A decree of the Holy See for 6 April 1947 expedited this work in which all national parishes were given territorial limits or annexed as missions to existing territorial parishes and all parishes with clearly defined limits were given canonical status.

The Sodality of Our Lady was established as the official youth organization in 1944. Thereafter the Archdiocesan Council of Catholic Women organized to federate women's activities. A seminar of problems of the Spanish-Speaking led to the formation of the Catholic Council for the Spanish-Speaking. Archbishop Lucey was named executive chairman of the Bishops' Committee for the Spanish-speaking among bishops of the entire Southwest from 1945 until his retirement. During World War II he was a trustee of the National Catholic War Relief Service.

During the postwar period Archbishop Lucey was Episcopal Chairman of the Department of Lay Organizations of the National Catholic Welfare Conference (1946 to 1951) and a member of its Administrative Board. He also developed San Fernando Cemetery with a water well, mains and a sprinkling system, and landscaped the grounds. Irish priests came to the Archdiocese from Irish seminaries until, by 1974, they made up almost one-third of the total archdiocesan active clergy.

The year 1947 was memorable for the founding of the Archdiocesan Council of Catholic Youth. It led to the establishment of these branches of the lay apostolate in later years: the Council of Catholic Nurses, the Catholic Lawyers' Guild, the Catholic Physicians' Guild, the Catholic Public Relations Council, the Federation of Catholic Parent-Teacher Clubs, and the Archdiocesan Rural Life Conference. In October of that year the first regional Inter-American Congress of the Confraternity of Christian Doctrine met in San Antonio. More than 6,000 persons attended including five archbishops and twenty bishops from the United States, Mexico, and Central America. St. John's Seminary now had St. Mary's hall with auditorium and classrooms. Three more structures provided a new dining hall, a study hall and classrooms, and an alumni chapel, dedicated on 10 April 1962.

The erection of the Diocese of Austin in 1948 with its 22,000 square miles reduced the San Antonio Archdiocese by 7,000 square miles from its north central part, leaving the total area with 33,000 square miles. It lost the counties of Bastrop, Travis, Caldwell, Hays, Blanco, Llano, Mason, San Saba, and McCulloch, South and West of the Colorado River. The loss involved twelve parishes and St. Edward's University in Austin. This reduction in no way affected the Diamond Jubilee of the Archdiocese. This event was celebrated with a pontifical field Mass offered by Bishop Metzger of El Paso for school children in Alamo Stadium and another pontifical Mass celebrated by Archbishop Lucey on the following day. Rev. Matthew J. Gilbert compiled a 324 page volume of archdiocesan history for the occasion.

The 1950s began with President Truman appointing the Archbishop to the Truman Commission on Migratory Labor. In 1951 Archbishop Lucey purchased the former Trinity University campus on West Woodlawn Avenue as a site for the new Assumption Major Seminary, dedicated by Cardinal Samuel Stritch of Chicago on 24 September 1952. In later years the Archdiocese built residence and dining halls, classroom buildings, a student union and administration buildings, and a chapel. The year 1953 brought an end to the racial segregation of all archdiocesan schools. This order prompted the School Districts of San Antonio, El Paso, and Corpus Christi to follow suit.

The expansion of archdiocesan endeavors by the mid1950s required the services of an auxiliary bishop. Stephen A. Leven served in this position from 1956 until 1969, when he became Bishop of San Angelo. In 1956 the Third Order of Mt. Carmel was established in San Antonio and Bishop Forest High School opened that year in Schulenburg. The year 1957 was noted for the organization of the first chapter of the Serra Club in the Archdiocese. This organization which began in 1938 with headquarters in Chicago, Illinois, involves business and professional men in working and praying for vocations to the religious life. Holy Cross and La Salle high schools opened in San Antonio in September. And the archdiocesan newspaper the *Alamo Register* merged with the *Southern Messenger* to produce the *Alamo Messenger.*

The year 1959 was a particular high point in the career of Archbishop Lucey. He commemorated his Silver Jubilee as a bishop with a pontifical Mass in Municipal Auditorium. The speaker that day was his old North American College classmate, Cardinal Francis Spellman of New York. On 29 April Pope John XXIII appointed the Archbishop an Assistant to the Pontifical Throne. The second archdiocesan chapter of the Serra Club began in Victoria and the Cursillo Movement was organized in the Archdiocese. Its purpose was to emphasize the place of the individual in the Mystical Body of Christ and the presence of Christ in the whole Christian community.

The Archbishop made much progress in developing medical facilities. The twenty-one bed Yorktown Memorial Hospital in Yorktown opened in 1951 and the Czech Catholic Home for the Aged adjacent to St. Andrew's Church in Hillje near El Campo started in 1954. Between 1954 and 1974 the Huth Memorial Hospital in Yoakum (1922) expanded twice to include a coronary care unit, a computerized electrocardiac system, new X-ray diagnostic equipment, an automatic cell counter, a new infant resusciator and transport system, and incorporated the latest surgical and medical techniques.

Mercy Hospital between Jourdanton and Pleasanton, a sixty-five bed general hospital serving Atascosa and surrounding counties, opened its doors in January 1957. Floresville Memorial Hospital in Floresville began service in 1960 and had a forty-four bed capacity by 1970. The Otto Koehler Radiation and Therapy and Research Unit of South Texas Medical Center began in 1962. By 1964 St. Benedict Hospital and Nursing Home had more than a 150 bed capacity. Twenty-nine clinics in the Outpatient Clinics building dedicated in 1969 serve approximately 39,000 medically indigent patients of San Antonio and southwest Texas every year. The Villa Rosa Rehabilitation Annex and part of Santa Rosa Hospital in San Antonio has a 284 bed capacity, while another branch, the Children's Hospital, treated about 10,000 children annually in 1974.

Ever active in social justice Archbishop Lucey supervised the founding of the Patrician Movement in the Archdiocese by Rev. Dermot N. Brosnan in 1959. The Movement was to recruit volunteers to assist in rehabilitating delinquent youths, particularly drug abusers. It was incorporated in 1963 and funded by local, state, and federal agencies from 1966. The Archbishop established Project Equality in the Archdiocese in 1965. Conceived by the National Catholic Conference for Interracial Justice, it is now a national inter-religious program to eliminate discriminatory employment practices.

During the Second Vatican Council Archbishop Lucey attended all four sessions held in Rome between October 1962 and December 1965. Still he continued to work. A new chancery building opened in September 1963 at 9123 Lorene Lane, as did Antonian High School in San Antonio in 1964. On 20 January 1965 the Archbishop was present at President Lyndon Johnson's request to give the inaugural invocation.

The seventy-eight-year-old Archbishop retired as Archbishop of San Antonio on 4 June 1969. Grown old in the service of his archdiocese, he had ironically come down on the wrong side of a series of labor disputes. His priests disagreed with his leadership and the Vatican told him his day had come. Looking back on twenty-eight years of labor in his own assigned vineyard, the laborer had acquitted himself well.

It was true that, because of the establishment of the Austin Diocese, the thirty-nine counties of 40,000 square miles had decreased to thirty-one counties with about 33,000 square miles. But the fewer than 200,000 Catholics who greeted his arrival in 1941 now numbered 533,000 in 1969. Despite a four-year construction ban imposed during World War II he had seen the completion of nearly 400 building projects. One hundred thirty-five churches were built or renovated and about eighty parish school buildings erected were new or enlarged. There were seventy-eight more rectories, four high schools and thirty-six Sisters' convent buildings. Other buildings had been built on two seminary campuses with new buildings for the chancery and the newspaper. Many improvements were made to the old Spanish missions and to the Cathedral.

Between 1941 and 1969 forty new parishes were established within the Archdiocese. Eight religious congregations of men and more than twenty of women were brought there to aid the laity. The Archbishop saw the Dioceses of Austin, San Angelo, Brownsville, and Beaumont created within his province. He had also served at various times as a governor of the Catholic Extension Society, as a Trustee of the Catholic University of America, as a member of the episcopal committee of the Confraternity of Christian Doctrine, as vice-president of the Catholic Association for International Peace, and as a member of the Board of Trustees of the National Catholic Community Service.

Archbishop Robert Lucey, whose Irish name means "light" and who took for his motto "The Lord is our King," continued to live in San Antonio after his retirement. A master planner and builder of institutions, he prepared well for the future. In 1958 he acquired 160 acres of farmland in northeast Bexar County for cemetery property. Today the City has expanded to meet it. It is landscaped, paved, and curbed, and has an automatic sprinkling system and a private well. A 1,243 crypt mausoleum and chapel was dedicated there in 1971. Known as Holy Cross Cemetery, it also serves as the last resting place for its former archbishop, who died in San Antonio on 1 August 1977.

Most Reverend Joseph Patrick Lynch, DD, LLD
Third Bishop of Dallas

One of the more colorful figures of the Texas hierarchy and the only attorney to distinguish it, Joseph Patrick Lynch was born to John V. and Veronica (Botham) Lynch in St. Joseph, Berrien County, Michigan, on 16 November 1872. Educated in the public schools of St. Joseph, he was a graduate of St. Charles College in Ellicott City, Maryland, in 1891, and of St. Mary's Seminary, Baltimore, Maryland, in 1895. Admitted to the Illinois Bar in 1895, he practiced law in that state until 1899.

Apparently successful in his legal career, young Joseph yearned to complete his priestly studies. He entered Kenrick Seminary in St. Louis, Missouri, in 1899 and was ordained there, for the Diocese of Dallas, by Bishop George Thomas Montgomery of Monterey-Los Angeles, California, on 9 June 1900. He first became Associate Rector of Sacred Heart Cathedral in Dallas from 1900 to 1902 and then Pastor of St. Stephen's Parish in Weatherford, Parker County, from 1902 until 1905.

In 1905 Father Lynch was appointed Pastor of St. Edward's Parish in Dallas where he remained until 1913. His rise was rapid. As Manager of the diocesan treasury from 1905 to 1910, he built St. Rita's Church in Handley (1909) and became Vicar General of the Dallas diocese on 19 June 1910. Pope Pius X appointed him Apostolic Administrator of the Diocese on 6 August 1910 and its Bishop on 8 June 1911.

On 12 July 1911 Bishop Lynch was consecrated in Sacred Heart Cathedral, Dallas, by Archbishop James H. Blenk, SM, of New Orleans. His co-consecrators were Bishops Nicholas Gallagher of Galveston and John Morris of Little Rock, Arkansas. The new bishop built St. Edward's Church school and rectory in 1911 and continued to serve as pastor there until 1913.

A very large diocese in 1911 Dallas was reduced in size by the formation~df the Dioceses of El Paso (1914), Amarillo (1926), and Austin (1948). From 1953 until 1969 the remainder was known as the Diocese of Dallas-Fort Worth. The Bishop had eighty-eight priests in the Diocese in 1916, with 168 parishes and missions and fifty-one schools.

During his forty-three years as Bishop of Dallas, Bishop Lynch constructed over 300 diocesan buildings and ordained almost 200 priests. He built 150 churches, which were erected in sites previously without a church. Approximately 15,000 students were educated in Catholic schools and eleven Catholic hospitals served 60,000 patients annually. Bishop Lynch appointed the first religious education director and insisted that all parishes have an organized Confraternity of Christian Doctrine. He was a member of the Board of Governors of the Catholic Church Extension Society and interested himself in all pending legislation pertaining to education, the media, and abortion.

Like his contemporary Bishop Byrne of Galveston, Bishop Lynch was a noted orator. He was recognized for his achievements by the Church in a number of ways. St. Edward's University conferred the honorary degree of Doctor of Laws upon him in 1930. But the best honors came in his Silver Jubilee year of 1936. On that 13 May he was appointed Assistant to the Pontifical Throne by

Pope Pius XI. Two months later on 12 July that pontiff made the Bishop a Vatican noble under the title of Count of the Lateran. At this time, short of being created a cardinal, this was the highest honor a bishop could receive.

Due to his declining health Pope Pius XII appointed Bishop Thomas K. Gorman of Reno, Nevada, Coadjutor Bishop of Dallas on 8 February 1952. Bishop Lynch, whose Irish name means "sea dweller," died in Dallas on 19 August 1954 and was buried there in Calvary Hill Cemetery. A high school in Dallas bears his name.

Most Reverend John Edward McCarthy, DD
Titular Bishop of Pedena and Auxiliary Bishop of Galveston-Houston
Third Bishop of Austin

John Edward McCarthy is a good representative of the contemporary bishop. He achieved his present office without a Roman education with its various canonical degrees. Instead he was a local man who kept active on the state and national levels while serving in various administrative positions. His priestly career indicates that the pastor and administrator with "hands-on" experience is, in recent years, increasingly preferred over the scholarly Romanist with few opportunities to govern.

Born in Houston, Harris County, Texas, of midwestern parentage, on 21 June 1930, John Edward McCarthy is the son of George Gaskell and Grace Veronica (O'Brien) McCarthy. He was educated in St. Mary's Seminary in La Porte and Houston between 1949 and 1956. In 1956 he received the degree of Bachelor of Arts in economics from the University of St. Thomas in Houston. He earned the degree of Master of Arts in Theology from his alma mater in 1979, and it conferred an honorary degree upon him in 1991.

The Reverend Mister McCarthy was ordained for the Diocese of Galveston in St. Mary's Cathedral in Galveston by its bishop Wendelin J. Nold on 26 May 1956. He spent his first eight years as a priest in pastoral duties. His first assignment was Assistant Pastor of St. Pius V Parish in Pasadena, Texas, from 1956 until 1961. Father McCarthy participated in the building and dedication of its present limestone church in 1959. From 1961 until 1963 he performed as assistant at St. Cecilia's Parish in Houston. A relatively new parish, St. Cecilia's was erected on 9 July 1956 with 600 families. The First Mass in its new church was celebrated on 25 May 1958. In 1963 Father McCarthy became Administrator of All Saints Parish in Houston. The Parish was organized in 1908 with 650 families. Its present church building was completed during the administration of Rev. Robert C. Frei (1926 to 1943).

Between 1964 and 1973 Father McCarthy became active in the work of the lay apostolate. At various times during this period he was National Chairman of the Catholic Center of Urban Ministry, a board member for the National Center for Urban Ethnic Affairs, the Mexican American Cultural Center in San Antonio, and was Diocesan Director of the Campaign for Human Development for Galveston-Houston. In 1966 he became Executive Director of the national bishop's conference (NCCB) for the Spanish-Speaking for two years. Also in 1966 he was Chairman of the Catholic Council on Community Relations, a two-year appointment. The United States Catholic Conference (USCC) appointed him Assistant Director of its Social Action Department (1967 to 1969) and Director of its Division for Poverty Programs (1968 to 1979). From 1968 to 1969 Father McCarthy was Director of the Social Action Office for the Galveston-Houston diocese.

Reverend McCarthy became pastor of St. Theresa's parish in Houston in 1969. Founded in 1946 the present church was dedicated in 1959. When the Pastor left it in 1972 it had 1,400 families. Also in 1972 McCarthy won the first

Clergyman of the Year Award presented by the National Conference of Christians and Jews. He was appointed Executive Director of the Texas Catholic Conference in 1973. This agency of bishops and dioceses was founded in Texas in 1964. It functions in twenty-nine other states and in the District of Columbia. It develops and sponsors programs to meet pastoral and common welfare needs. Its members are diocesan representatives within each state including bishops, clergy, and lay persons. It also represents the dioceses of its state or district before governmental bodies, the public, and in private sections. An example of its work in Texas is given in the "Introduction" to this work. While executive director Father McCarthy also served the Conference as chairman of its Division for Church and Society.

Pope John Paul II appointed McCarthy Titular Bishop of Pedena and Auxiliary Bishop of Galveston-Houston on 23 January 1979. He was ordained by Bishop John L. Morkovsky of Galveston-Houston on the following 14 March 1979 in the new bishop's former church of St. Theresa's in Houston. In the first year of his appointment Bishop McCarthy was Diocesan Director of the Diocesan Services Fund and the Catholic Council on Community Relations, as well as a member of the board of St. Edward's University in Austin.

Bishop McCarthy served on the Board of Directors of St. Thomas University (1980 to 1985), of St. Elizabeth's Hospital (1980 to 1984), of the SCH Corporation (1981 to 1984), and of the Sisters of Charity of the Incarnate Word (1981), all in Houston. He was also a board member of Covenant House's Houston branch in 1985. This last organization is a nonsectarian shelter for youth with headquarters in New York City. It has branches in the United States, Canada, Honduras, Guatemala, and Mexico, serving the homeless, and the exploited under the age of twenty-one.

The Bishop was National Episcopal Advisor for the Theresians from 1983 to 1985. Founded in 1961 for the spiritual, educational, and ministerial purposes of Christian women, the Theresians numbered 5,000 members in 1987. It has headquarters in Colorado Springs, Colorado. The Theresian World Ministry founded in 1971 is centered at Phoenix, Arizona. Bishop McCarthy has served the NCCB as a member of the International Section of the Committee on Social Development and World Peace. He received an award from the Union of American Hebrew Congregations on 11 November 1983 for the NCCB's pastoral letter on war and peace. While in Houston he was also president of the Deans of the Galveston-Houston Diocese.

Pope John Paul II appointed Bishop McCarthy bishop of Austin on 19 December 1985. He was installed by Archbishop Patrick Flores of San Antonio in the Frank Erwin Activities Center at the University of Texas at Austin on 25 February 1986. The Diocese of Austin at this time consisted of a twenty-seven county area of 22,180 square miles. It had eighty-seven diocesan priests, fifty-nine Religious order priests, thirty-six permanent deacons, thirty-five male Religious, and 131 women Religious. The Diocese had eighty-six parishes, thirty-one missions, a university, two high schools, fifteen elementary schools, six hospitals, one special hospital, and two homes for the invalid and aged. There were 24,212 students under Catholic instruction with a Catholic population of 138,640 in a total population of 1,335,464.

Bishop McCarthy has served as Episcopal Advisor for the American Catholic

Correctional Chaplains Association. Founded in 1952 it has 220 members in 300 institutions nationally. He has served on the NCCB Administrative Committee and on the USCC Advisory Board for Region X which includes Arkansas, Oklahoma, and Texas, and as Chairman of the NCCB's Ad Hoc Committee on the Economic Concerns of the Holy See.

In this last capacity the Bishop asked the bishops of the NCCB to meet new diocesan goals for contributions to the annual Peter's Pence Collection given to the Vatican. To 1990 proceeds from this collection have been used to pay the Vatican deficit rather than for charitable and mission work. In 1990 there was a deficit of $86 million.

Because of the historic nature of this fund to enable the Pope to advance charitable and missionary work throughout the world rather than as a means of reducing the Vatican deficit, the Committee came into being. Consultant Thomas Flatley of Philadelphia said that goals were about 13 per cent higher than over 1989 contributions. Assessments based on collections between 1986 and 1990, the size of the individual diocese, and "economic parameters within the diocese" would determine future assessments. The goal for 1990 was set at a 25 percent increase. At that time Vatican expenditures were about $152 million a year. In 1989 the worldwide collection of Peter's Pence was $48.4 million down from nearly $53 million in 1988.

In 1991 Bishop McCarthy received the University of St. Thomas's Rev. Vincent J. Guinan Distinguished Alumnus Award. He was cited for his work as coordinator of the Galveston-Houston Diocesan Mission Council in 1964 and for his work for the Spanish-Speaking in 1965. It was recalled that he was one of the co-founders of the Campaign for Human Development. His response to being named Alumnus of the Year was: "I'm very proud of this. UST has produced a large number of colorful graduates. I consider this to be a very real and personal honor."

The Bishop has also faced temporary setbacks. On 24 May 1988 he was living away from his residence in Austin while minor alterations were being made. That morning a fire destroyed his home and many of his possessions. Characteristically pleasant and efficient he determined to rebuild at that site. He observed, ''Photographs of a lifetime, letters, awards, gifts and especially books are gone. But life-real life- goes on." And, although he had no previous history of heart problems, he underwent quadruple-bypass surgery at Seton Medical Center in Austin on 6 August 1993. He was released after about a week.

In early 1995 the Diocese of Austin contained 19,511 square miles after an administrative adjustment involving the loss of some land to another diocese to regulate boundaries. It had 120 diocesan priests and fifty Religious Order priests, seventy-eight permanent deacons, forty-eight men Religious and 110 women Religious. There were eighty-seven parishes with forty-four missions, four Catholic hospitals, three health care centers, two homes for the aged, one facility for residential care of children, three day care and extended day care centers, a specialized home, a special center for social services and one other institution. There was a university, two high schools, eighteen elementary schools, and 34,651 students under Catholic instruction. The Catholic population of the Diocese numbered 240,100 in a total population of 1,638,245 or 15 per cent.

Bishop McCarthy has a strong record in social justice matters and sits high in the councils of American Catholic bishops. Of Irish descent, his name means ''loving one," and he puts his life and ministry within the context of his episcopal motto, "Lord, I Come To Do Your Will."

Right Reverend Dominic Manucy, DD
Titular Bishop of Dulma and Vicar Apostolic of Brownsville
Third Bishop of Mobile
Titular Bishop of Maronea and Vicar Apostolic of Brownsville

Dominic Manucy was the descendant of Minorcan islanders from the Balearic Islands off the East Coast of Spain. Although they came to Florida shortly after the British conquest of 1763, the atmosphere of their new home remained predominantly Spanish. The future bishop was born in St. Augustine, Saint Johns County, Florida, on 20 December 1823 to Pedro and Maria (Lorenzo) Manucy. His father was of Italian and his mother of Irish extraction, while his maternal grandmother was Spanish.

Young Dominic studied at nearby Spring Hill College in Mobile, Alabama. Founded by the Jesuits in 1830, he taught there in 1848. He was ordained in that city for the Diocese of Mobile by its bishop Michael Portier on 15 August 1850. For the first three years of his priesthood he was assigned to the mission at Warrington, Escambia County, Florida, now a part of the Diocese of Pensacola-Tallahassee. He built a church and rectory where three parish churches exist today. His second assignment took him to the same district at St. Patrick's Parish in Apalachicola, Franklin County, Florida, in 1853.

Father Manucy returned to Mobile in 1855 as Assistant Pastor of the Cathedral of the Immaculate Conception. Religion came early to this Gulf Coast city. Within a year after its founding in 1702 the Bishop of Quebec established it as the first parish on the Coast. In 1704 the Church of Fort Louis de la Louisiane (Mobile) began. The City of Mobile relocated on its present site and a parish church was built near the Tensaw River in 1711. The Church was rebuilt as Our Lady of Mobile and given its present name in 1781. The first church on the present site was built in 1828, just in time for the establishment of the Diocese of Mobile in the following year. The parish was officially designated as the Cathedral. The present structure was built between 1835 and 1850, with the front portico finished in the 1870s. Since 1980 it has served as the seat of the Archdiocese of Mobile, serving the states of Alabama and Mississippi.

During the years of the Civil War (1861 to 1865) Father Manucy was Pastor of St. Vincent's Parish in Mobile. Thereafter he was Pastor of St. Peter's Parish in Montgomery and became a member of the Bishop's Council in 1865. Pope Pius IX appointed him Titular Bishop of Dulma and Vicar Apostolic of Brownsville on 17 September 1874. On the following day Pius issued the official documents *In Futuram Rei Memoriam* creating the Vicariate Apostolic and *Dilecte Fili Salutem* appointing Manucy Vicar Apostolic.

Archbishop Napoleon J. Perche of New Orleans consecrated Bishop Manucy in the Cathedral of the Immaculate Conception in Mobile on 8 December 1874. Bishops William Elder of Natchez (now Jackson), Mississippi, and Claude Dubuis of Galveston, Texas, acted as his co-consecrators. On the following 14 February Bishop Dubuis installed Bishop Manucy in Immaculate Conception Church (now Cathedral) in Brownsville.

The new bishop came to an area about one-eighth the size of the State of Texas. The territory was first defined as lying "between the Nueces River to the east and the Rio Grande River on the west." On 21 July 1877 Pius IX limited his bishop's jurisdiction to

> the area lying south and east of the Arroyo de los Hermanos and San Roque Creek, and south of the Nueces River to include Cameron, Hidalgo, Starr, Zapata, and Webb Counties and part of Dimmit County along the Rio Grande; Encinal, Duval, and Nueces Counties to the north of those preceding; that part of La Salle and McMullen Counties, together with Live Oak County, south of the Nusces River; and San Patricio, Bee, Refugio, Goliad, and Aransas Counties, north of the Nueces River.

The reception of the people of the area was more than cordial. They built a triumphal arch and city officials conducted the Bishop to his cathedral. Bands, bells and a ceremonial salute added to the honors. This sensitive man worried, perhaps unduly, at the reaction of Freemasons who had not received a personal invitation to the festivities. This group printed a circular expressing the opinion that the new clerical establishment was somehow undemocratic.

Manucy attempted to counter such criticism by preaching and by making a confirmation tour. He left Brownsville on 6 April 1875 in company with two Missionary Oblates of Mary Immaculate. The order of Oblates, which came to the Lower Rio Grande Valley in 1849, also needed winning over. They feared that the new bishop favored the Jesuit order to their possible exclusion.

Actually the Bishop was in great need of the Oblates in ministering to the 42,000 Catholics in his care. Most of them were Mexican Americans in possession of their land from the mid-eighteenth century. Many ranching communities were located in Cameron, Willacy, Hidalgo, and Starr counties, the present day Diocese of Brownsville. For the past quarter-century the Oblates had ministered to these communities on a weekly basis on horseback. Their work flourished over a 3,600 square mile territory, for they knew the land well.

With the Oblates laboring so faithfully in the South, the Bishop eventually decided to locate the seat of the Vicariate in Corpus Christi. On the 1875 trip he stopped at Encantada, Santa Maria, Capote, Lomita, Davis, and Roma. After a two-day rest stop he pressed on to San Ignacio. Here he met Father Lagier, the Pastor of Laredo. After a stay in Laredo the Vicar came to San Antonio for a visit with his cousin Bishop Pellicer. He came at last to Corpus Christi by way of Victoria and Indianola. He was back in Brownsville by 27 July, but controversy still dogged his footsteps.

Rumors of his move from Brownsville to Corpus Christi angered a number of his supporters, and a subscription to buy him a new home was dropped after reaching the sum of three thousand dollars. But Manucy's mind was made up. He announced his leaving in September and on the twentieth of that month preached a farewell sermon. He noted the good works and devotion of the Oblates, to whom he was most grateful.

The Bishop's sadness seemed to melt away when he came among his people. He would travel any distance to hear confessions, and to visit and instruct. In an 1879 tour with the Oblate Reverend Peter Parisot he visted more than eighty ranches from Corpus Christi by way of Brownsville to Roma and Laredo. On this trip he confirmed almost 3,000 children and adults. But though he found the cares of administration distasteful, he did not neglect his work.

Beginning with six secular priests and about twelve Oblates, Manucy ordained five priests and built nine churches. The Sisters of the Incarnate Word came to Corpus Christi and Brownsville, Ursuline Nuns to Laredo, and Sisters of Mercy to San Patricio and Refugio. The Sisters of Mercy established academies and free parochial schools for girls and in some cases for young boys. The Oblate College was established in Brownsville and a school for boys in Laredo. The Society of the Propagation of the Faith in France aided all these endeavors.

The 1882 yellow fever epidemic took the life of Rev. Florencio Vanderberghe, the Oblate superior and pastor of Immaculate Conception Parish in Brownsville. It also killed three Incarnate Word Sisters. In 1883 St. Patrick's Church in Corpus Christi was replaced, as was that of St. Mary, Star of the Sea in Port Isabel. The new Sacred Heart Church was completed in Edinburg. The Brownsville district extending to Rio Grande City had a population of 16,200. Five thousand of these lived in Rio Grande City. Three or four Oblates had charge of 110 ranches in Hidalgo, Starr, and Webb counties, with a population of 9,100. In the Vicariate there were twelve churches, twelve chapels, twenty-one priests, a school for boys, three academies for girls, and five convents. There were about 40,000 Catholics, of whom at least 37,500 were Mexicans.

Pleading ill health, Bishop Manucy requested a less strenuous assignment. Pope Leo XIII answered his request by appointing him Bishop of Mobile on 9 March 1884. He was installed there on the twenty-seventh and took charge three days later. He resigned the administration of that diocese on 3 September 1884. In a letter of 9 October he was informed that his resignation was accepted as of 27 September 1884.

Bishop Manucy attended the Third Plenary Council of Baltimore, Maryland, in his capacity of administrator of the Mobile Diocese. He arrived on 30 October 1884 and attended the sessions from 9 November to 7 December. This council ordered the preparation of catechisms for religious instruction, required the building of elementary schools in all American parishes, established the Catholic University of America in Washington, DC, and fixed six holy days of obligation (required attendance at Mass) for observance in the United States.

The dying man still yearned to return to Texas. Pope Leo XIII granted his wish by appointing him to his former position on 1 February 1885. Nine days later he received the additional title of Titular Bishop of Maronea. But it was too late for the missionary to resume his duties. Bishop Manucy died in Mobile, Alabama, on 4 December 1885, without returning to his vicariate in Brownsville. He was given a splendid funeral in the Cathedral of the Immaculate Conception in Moblie three days later. It was attended by the archbishops of New Orleans and Baltimore, and by the bishops of Mobile, Galveston, and Natchez. Following these ceremonies his body was entombed in the Cathedral crypt.

Most Reverend Adolph Marx, DD, JCD
Titular Bishop of Citrus and
Auxiliary Bishop of Corpus Christi
First Bishop of Brownsville

In fifty short years Adolph Marx lived a quarter-century as a priest and spent one-third of those years as a bishop. Although he died before reaching his full achievement in the hierarchy of Texas, his nine years as an auxiliary bishop indicate his potential success in a leadership role among his adopted people.

This German-American bishop, whose name means "warrior," chose for his episcopal motto, "Plenitudo Legis Dilectio" ("With The Full Levy Of The Law"). Adolph Marx was born to Peter and Elizabeth (Olck) Marx in Cologne, North Rhine-Westphalia, Germany, on 18 February 1915. He first studied in the schools of his native city and came to the United States in 1934. After six years of study in St. Mary's Seminary at La Porte, Texas, he was ordained in Corpus Christi for that diocese on 2 May 1940. The scholarly young priest was sent to the Catholic University of America in Washington, DC, for graduate study. Here he earned the degree of Doctor of Canon Law with his dissertation, "The Declaration of Nullity of Marriages Contracted Outside the Church" in 1943.

On his return to Corpus Christi Father Marx became Bishop Ledvina's secretary. He was sent to Refugio in 1944 and returned to Corpus Christi in 1945. The young curate became an American citizen in 1947 and Pastor of Holy Cross Parish in Corpus Christi from 1948 until 1950. The year of 1948 was crucial in the development of Father Marx. Bishop Ledvina made him Diocesan Chancellor and Pope Pius XII appointed him Papal Chamberlain, with the title of Very Reverend Monsignor. In 1950 Monsignor Marx gave up parish work in return for the diocesan directorship of the Apostolate for Vocations and Pope Pius XII named him a Domestic Prelate, with the title of Right Reverend Monsignor.

On 6 July 1956 Pope Pius XII appointed Monsignor Marx Titular Bishop of Citrus and Auxiliary Bishop of Corpus Christi. He was consecrated on 9 October by Bishop Mariano Garriga of Corpus Christi, assisted by Auxiliary Bishops John Krol of Cleveland, Ohio, and Charles Maloney of Louisville, Kentucky. Bishop Garriga appointed him Vicar General of the Diocese in 1957. Bishop Marx later became Officialis of the Diocesan Tribunal in 1962 and a Diocesan Consultor in 1964.

On 6 July 1965 Pope Paul VI appointed Bishop Marx the founding bishop of the new Diocese of Brownsville. Four days later he issued the Bull, *Ad Perpetuam Rei Memoriam,* establishing the Diocese, It consisted of the Texas counties of Cameron, Hidalgo, Starr, and Willacy, an area of 4,226 square miles. Archbishop Lucey installed the new bishop in Immaculate Conception Cathedral in Brownsville on 2 September 1965.

Bishop Marx appointed the Oblate priests Emanuel Ballard Chancellor and Harry Schuckenbrock Director of Religious Education for the Diocese. He soon left to attend the fourth and final session of the Second Vatican Council in Rome, which had begun on 14 September 1965. While visiting his family in his native city of Cologne in West Germany, Bishop Marx died suddenly on 1 November 1965. His body was returned to Brownsville for burial and now rests there in the courtyard of the Cathedral of the Immaculate Conception.

Most Reverend Leroy Theodore Matthiesen, DD, LittD
Sixth Bishop of Amarillo

Known today primarily for his opposition to the Pantex plant near Amarillo, Leroy Theodore Matthiesen was born to Joseph A. and Rosa (Englert) Matthiesen in Olfen, Runnels County, Texas, on 11 June 1921. He was educated at the Pontifical College Josephinum in Columbus, Ohio. This national pontifical seminary was established in 1888 and is immediately subject to the Holy See. Matthiesen received the degree of Bachelor of Arts there in 1942.

After four years of theological study Leroy Matthiesen was ordained for the Diocese of Amarillo on 10 March 1946. He attended the Register School of Journalism in Denver, Colorado, from 1946 until 1948. The School awarded Father Matthiesen the honorary degree of Doctor of Letters in 1962. On his return to Amarillo in 1948 he became the Editor and a columnist for the *West Texas Register* (now the *West Texas Catholic*), the Amarillo diocesan newspaper. Since becoming bishop of Amarillo he has served as Publisher.

The year he began his editorial duties Father Matthiesen became Associate Pastor of St. Mary's Parish in Amarillo. From 1952 until 1961 he was also Diocesan Director of Vocations. Pope Pius XII appointed him Papal Chamberlain, with the title of Very Reverend Monsignor, in 1954. Monsignor Matthiesen became Pastor of St. Lawrence Parish in Amarillo in 1955 and remained until 1961.

The degree of Master of Arts in Secondary School Administration, which he received from the Catholic University of America in 1961, served the Monsignor well. He became Rector of St. Lucian Minor Seminary in Amarillo (1961 to 1967) and was later principal of Alamo Catholic High School in Amarillo (1969 to 1980). During these years he was chaplain of St. Francis Convent for the Franciscan Sisters of Mary Immaculate of the Third Order of St. Francis in 1971 and Pastor of St. Francis's Parish in Amarillo in 1972.

The death of Bishop De Falco in 1979 added to Monsignor Matthiesen's duties as editor, principal, chaplain, and pastor. He now became Administrator of the Amarillo diocese. Pope John Paul II appointed him bishop of Amarillo on 25 March 1980, and he was ordained by Archbishop Patrick Flores in the Amarillo Civic Center on 30 May 1980. His co-consecrators were Bishop John Morkovsky of Galveston-Houston and Bishop Thomas Drury of Corpus Christi.

The Diocese of Amarillo was divided in half to form the Diocese of San Angelo in 1961 and divided again to form the Diocese of Lubbock in 1983. It now consists of twenty-six counties with approximately 25,800 square miles. Bishop Matthiesen carried out two of his predecessor's plans with the establishment of a convent of cloistered nuns and the Bishop De Falco Retreat Center in Amarillo.

In 1986 the Bishop appointed Sr. Celine Thames, OSF to be diocesan chancellor. The first woman to occupy such a position in Texas, Sister Thames was put in charge of the Holy Childhood Association and of the Society for the Propagation of the Faith, which are missionary organizations. In 1988 Sr. Hilary Decker, OSB, was the "Campus Ministry Contact Person" for the Newman Club, the college ministry. A Sister of Mercy administered a parish. In later years Sr. Christine Jensen, FMI, became chancellor of the Diocese of Amarillo and a number of women serve on the Diocesan Pastoral Council.

Bishop Matthiesen is nationally noted for his opposition to the Pantex Plant operated by the United States Department of Energy (DOE) just East of Amarillo on US Highway 60 on 10,300 acres. The plant assembled nuclear weapons and at one time employed 2,700 workers, second only as an area employer to the Amarillo public school system.

In August 1981 President Ronald Reagan wanted to go forward with the production of the neutron bomb. Pantex was the final assembly for all such weapons. The Bishop urged workers involved in the production and stockpiling of these armaments to consider other pursuits. In 1983 the United States Catholic Conference issued a pastoral paper on the use of nuclear weapons questioning but not condemning outright a national policy of nuclear deterrence. It did seek the elimination of nuclear weapons. Protestors sometimes camped outside the gates of the plant and attempted to block incoming traffic.

A demonstration to commemorate the dropping of an atomic bomb on Nagasaki, Japan, occurred in August 1987. In such matters the Bishop took part, generally by leading a worship service at the gates. Fear of escaping radioactive waste has prompted public concern, especially in the transport of assembled weapons from the plant. A Department of Energy report released in December 1988 identified Pantex as one of the two worst DOE areas of environmental risks in the nation. According to the report, damage was caused by two underground gasoline tanks and a pit used to burn off industrial solvents. Groundwater contamination under such conditions was a possibility.

Bishop Matthiesen stated that the DOE's self-monitoring system keeps the public unaware of the seriousness of its contamination:

> If they [the DOE] say it is a problem, one has to suspect there is a serious problem. I had a woman come to me who works at Pantex. She was angry. She said she would quit working there because she felt they were not reporting cancer cases honestly.

Private monitors, he added, should investigate the hazard potential to the environment.

A 702-paged draft inspection report compiled by a thirty-five-member special inspection team spent October 1989 studying environmental practices, worker safety issues and management practices at the Pantex plant. The report concluded that the plant did not meet federal radiation protection standards for its workers since at least mid-1985. It did not foresee a solution to the problem. The report concluded that not enough qualified radiation protection technicians were available and that employees were not adequately trained.

While it was revealed that radioactive tritium was accidentally released on 27 May 1989, the report indicated no immediate threat to public, workers, and environment. But it did list fifty-seven environmental problems and 161 occupational safety violations. Some safety employees were found not to be qualified for jobs and others did not have security clearances to enter sensitive work areas. More money was needed to be budgeted and more qualified professionals employed at the plant. In recent years, since the end of the perceived military threat by, and the dissolution of, the Soviet Union, the Pantex plant now dismantles nuclear weapons and the Bishop does not presently speak on the subject.

At the start of the 1990-1991 school year the Amarillo Catholic School System was reorganized. Alamo Catholic High School was relocated at the St. Joseph School campus. Two middle schools were consolidated on the campus of St. Mary's School in Amarillo. Four elementary schools continued to operate in sections of Amarillo. Changes were made to give greater access to more students following a process involving school system boards, parish councils, administrative staffs, and the public. Gerken Hall, part of the Alamo School, was given to the St. Clare Capuchin Sisters, while the Administration building went to the Our Lady of Vietnam Community for a social and cultural center. Although a $25 thousand deficit was projected for July 1990, it was believed that there would be a yearly savings of $100 thousand annually under the reorganization plan.

At the start of 1995 the Diocese of Amarillo had sixty diocesan priests, and eight Religious order priests, thirty permanent deacons, one male Religious, and 167 women Religious. There were thirty-four parishes and thirteen missions, a Catholic hospital, a health care center, a home for the aged, five day care and extended day care centers, two specialized homes, four special centers for social services, and one other institution. There was a high school and nine elementary schools with 7,180 students under Catholic instruction. There were 38,148 Catholics in a total population of 386,574 or 10 percent.

In 1984 Bishop Matthiesen received a porcine heart valve during an operation in Amarillo. On 15 December 1995 the valve was found leaking when the Bishop complained of feeling tired and listless. He released a statement on 19 December stating: "I would like to thank all who prayed for me and have been concerned about me these past few days." Dr. Patrick McCarthy, a Cleveland heart specialist, performed a two-hour procedure, implanting a new porcine heart valve on 19 December. Although the Bishop was to be released from the Cleveland Clinic on Christmas Eve, there were no immediate plans for him to return to the Diocese of Amarillo or to resume his duties. Under normal circumstances the Bishop would be required to submit his resignation to the Vatican on 11 June 1996, when he reaches the age of seventy-five.

Bishop Matthiesen traces his descent from Munster in Westphalia, Germany. His name means "gift of God" and he takes for his motto "Fiat voluntas Tua" ("Thy will be done"). He is a member of the Catholic Press Association, the National Catholic Educational Association, and the Knights of Columbus. He received the Father David H. Dunn award of the Catholic Historical Society of Amarillo in 1982, an organization he had helped found in 1976, for his services to Amarillo. He is a man of strong faith who keeps his commitments.

His Eminence Cardinal Humberto Sousa Medeiros, STD
Second Bishop of Brownsville
Fourth Archbishop of Boston
Cardinal Priest under the Title of Santa Susanna

The first bishop of Texas to rise to the dignity of a Prince of the Church, Cardinal Humberto Sousa Medeiros twice exercised his function as a papal elector. He was born in Arrifes, Sao Miguel, the Azores, to Antonio Sousa and Maria de Jesus Sousa Massa (Flor) Medeiros on 6 October 1915. Christianity was introduced to this island group in the North Atlantic 750 miles west of Portugal in the second quarter of the fifteenth century. But even at this early time Portugal, of which the Azores form a part, had been a Christian nation for more than a thousand years. The faith of its people has been tested many times. Yet even today more than ninety per cent of the Portuguese are Catholic.

Young Humberto was educated at the Candido Alfonso School in Arrifes and came to the United States in 1931. He continued his education at the Border City and Danforth Street schools in Fall River, Massachusetts, and graduated from B.M.C. Durfee High School in Fall River in 1937. Afterward he attended the Swaim School of Design in New Bedford and became an American citizen in 1940. He earned the degrees of Master of Arts in 1942 and Licentiate in Sacred Theology in 1946 from the Catholic University of America in Washington, DC.

On 15 June 1946 Medeiros was ordained for the Diocese of Fall River, Massachusetts. He began his clerical career as Associate Pastor of St. John of God Parish in Somerset in 1946 and held the same position in St. Michael Parish (1946 to 1947) and in Our Lady of Health Parish (1947), both in Fall River. He was Chaplain of St. Vincent de Paul Health Camp in Westport (1948 to 1949) and Associate Pastor of Our Lady of Mount Carmel Parish in New Bedford (1949).

Father Medeiros was given a year in Rome to attend the North American College from 1949 to 1950 and was Associate Pastor of Holy Name Church in Fall River from 1950 to 1951. He was Secretary, Assistant Chancellor, Chaplain of Sacred Heart Academy, and Vicar for Religious in the Diocese of Fall River from 1951 to 1953. In the meantime he completed requirements for the degree of Doctor of Sacred Theology from the Catholic University of America in 1952 with a dissertation on "The 'De Mysteriis' and 'De Sacramentis' of St. Ambrose."

Recognition now came to Father Medeiros. He was Vice-Chancellor and Chancellor to Bishop James L. Connolly of Fall River from 1953 to 1966. Pope Pius XII appointed him Domestic Prelate, with the title of Right Reverend Monsignor, in 1958. And he received the honorary degree of Doctor of Laws from Stonehill College in North Easton, Massachusetts, in 1959. From 1960 to 1966 he was Pastor of St. Michael's Parish in Fall River.

Pope Paul VI appointed Monsignor Medeiros Bishop of Brownsville, Texas, on 14 April 1966. On the following 9 June his former bishop James L. Connolly ordained him in Fall River. Auxiliary Bishops James J. Gerrard of Fall River and Gerald V. McDevitt of Philadelphia were his co-consecrators. The times favored changes and the new bishop acted with haste to meet new challenges.

On his arrival at the International Airport of Brownsville Bishop Medeiros announced he was well aware of the violent situations affecting *braceros* (farm laborers) and farm owners which occurred in Starr County near Rio Grande City. While he intended to use his office for mediation and conciliation, he would demand just wages and amenities for the workers and their families. His installation took place in Immaculate Conception Cathedral in Brownsville on 29 June 1966.

Bishop Medeiros believed it was necessary to meet the needs of the working people in his care. He invited Msgr. George G. Higgins of the National Catholic Welfare Conference in Washington, DC, to assist in formulating a position on labor and management. Because thousands of Mexican American families migrated to northern states to harvest crops, the Bishop requested his brother bishops to provide field ministries along the highways. He organized the Migrant Apostolate which sent out teams of priests, religious and laity. These teams baptized children, blessed marriages, celebrated Mass, and visited the sick. The Bishop himself located and ministered to his people while they travelled.

Bishop Medeiros dedicated St. Martin de Porres Church in Weslaco on 13 October 1966, making it the third parish in that city. He also worked to provide missions with parishes and permanent pastors. He approved opening St. Teresa's and Our Lady Queen of the Universe Parishes in San Benito in 1967. In July of that year he raised the Prince of Peace (formerly Our Lady of Guadalupe) Church in Lyford to a parish with missions in Sebastian and Santa Monica. In September 1967 Holy Family Church became the third parish in Edinburg.

The first diocesan census of 1967 provided guidelines to form home visitation programs. It also indicated needs for religious education and social services. The Bishop increased the number of Confraternity of Christian Doctrine Centers and appointed Rev. Robert Peña, OMI, Director of Catholic Charities and Social Action. Another interest was the formation of Catholic and Protestant ministers into the Texas Conference of Churches in Austin. This ecumenical movement earned strong support from the Bishop of Brownsville. Pope Paul VI appointed Bishop Medeiros Archbishop of Boston on 8 September 1970. Thousands of people bade him farewell as he flew from Harlingen International Airport to Massachusetts. He was accompanied on this trip by his Vicar General Msgr. Victor Ralph and other Brownsville clergymen and was installed Archbishop of Boston in Holy Cross Cathedral in Boston on 7 October 1970.

Knowing the Archbishop's worth, Pope Paul VI created and proclaimed him a Cardinal Priest in the consistory of 5 March 1973. As Cardinal Archbishop of Boston he was given the Church of Santa Susanna for his use while in Rome. This magnificent building stands on the north side of the Piazza San Bernardo. Rebuilt in the early sixteenth century, its baroque facade is the work of the master architect Carlo Maderno (1556-1629). Fresco paints on the side walls illustrate the life of its patron saint, while the high altar has a picture entitled "Death of St. Susanna" and the apse features a depiction of the Assumption of the Virgin Mary.

In addition to his *ad limina* visits to inform the Pope of the state of the archdiocese, Cardinal Medeiros was present at the Vatican in 1978 during the elections of Pope John Paul I and Pope John Paul II. He was assigned to the

Congregation for Bishops and the Congregation for Catholic Education, presently known as the Congregation for Catholic Education (for Seminaries and Institutes of Study).

The Congregation for Bishops was established by Pope Sixtus V in 1588. Formerly called the Consistorial Congregation it establishes and changes ecclesiastical jurisdictions, identifies suitable candidates for bishops and other prelates, studies bishops and their activities, provides for their care when they leave office, receives and studies reports on the conditions of dioceses, supervises the holding and recognition of particular councils and conferences of bishops, and publishes pastoral norms and guidelines through episcopal conferences. As in Cardinal Medeiros's time it continues to supervise the Pontifical Commission for Latin America, though it no longer has competency over the former Pontifical Commission for Migration and Tourism. It is now autonomous and is known as the Pontifical Council for Pastoral Care of Migrants and Itinerant Peoples since 1988. Presently the Congregation for Bishops directs the work of a central coordinating office for Military Vicars (established 1985) and an office for coordinating *ad limina* visits (established 1988).

The Congregation for Catholic Education (for Seminaries and Institutes of Study) received its present title in 1988. It continues the work of two other congregations begun by Pope Sixtus V (1588) and by Pope Leo XII (1824). Formerly known as the Congregation of Seminaries and Universities, it has supervision over institutions and works of Catholic education. One of its offices directs, disciplines and administers seminaries, the education of diocesan clergy, and religious and members of secular institutes. A second office oversees Catholic universities, faculties of study and other institutions of higher learning as they depend upon the authority of the Church. It encourages cooperation and assistance among Catholic universities and the establishment of Catholic hospices and centers on campuses of non-Catholic institutions. A third office is concerned with all Catholic elementary and secondary schools, with general questions of education and studies, and with conferences of bishops and civil authorities in educational matters. The Congregation supervises Pontifical Works for Priestly Vocations.

As Archbishop of Boston Cardinal Medeiros was also Metropolitan of the Boston Province, a four-state area which includes the Archdiocese of Boston and the dioceses of Fall River, Springfield, and Worcester in Massachusetts; the Diocese of Portland, Maine; the Diocese of Manchester, New Hampshire; and the Diocese of Burlington, Vermont. The Cardinal, whose Portuguese name means "wood" took for his episcopal motto "Adveniat Regnum Tuum" ("Thy Kingdom Come"). In the last year of his administration the Archdiocese of Boston covered a five-county area of Massachusetts of 2,465 square miles.

In that year of 1983 the Archdiocese of Boston had six auxiliary bishops, an abbot, 907 diocesan priests and 975 Religious order priests, 142 permanent deacons, 183 male Religious, and 4,464 women Religious. There were 408 parishes, thirteen missions, ninety-one stations, and seventy-seven chapels.

The Archdiocese had two diocesan seminaries with 249 seminarians, sixteen Religious seminaries or scholasticates with 215 Religious students, four colleges and universities with 20,172 students, thirty-eight diocesan and parochial high schools with 12,069 students, twenty-three private high schools with

12,089 students, 140 parochial elementary schools with 44,341 students, and twenty-six private elementary schools with 3,782 students. There were 345,359 students under Catholic instruction taught by 3,809 Religious and lay teachers.

The Archdiocese also had eight general hospitals treating 729,084 patients annually, four sanatoria with 51,401 patients, two schools for nurses with 795 student nurses, five homes with 899 dependent children, and nine homes for the invalid and aged with 1,884 guests. There were 1,936,146 Catholics in a total population of 3,657,659.

After an administration of almost thirteen years, Cardinal Humberto Medeiros died of a heart ailment in Boston, Massachusetts, on 17 September 1983. He lies buried in Fall River, Massachusetts. As bishop, archbishop, and cardinal he did all in his power to advance the Kingdom of God in every position to which he was summoned.

Most Reverend Sidney Matthew Metzger, STD, JCD
Titular Bishop of Birtha and Auxiliary Bishop of Santa Fe
Coadjutor Bishop of El Paso
Second Bishop of El Paso

There must be a special quality in the air of the City of Fredericksburg, Gillespie County, Texas. This beautiful part of the Hill Country is known for its ranches, fruit trees, abundant game, and clear springs. It produces stalwart citizens, clear in their convictions with the ability to lead others. Its most famous citizen Admiral of the Fleet Chester W. Nimitz was such a figure.

Another German American son of this city, also destined to become a leader, was Sidney Matthew Metzger. Born on 11 July 1902 to Francis and Ida (Dietz) Metzger, he was the inheritor of a tradition of piety which flourished here along with his native state. Catholicism came to Fredericksburg with German immigrants from the Society for the Protection of German Immigrants in Texas in 1846. The first Mass was said there in 1847 and by 1849 the people had constructed their first church building. The third and present stone church was dedicated in 1908. Young Sidney attended St. Mary's School from 1910 until 1915.

The future bishop left home to attend St. John's Seminary in San Antonio in 1915. In 1922 he went to the North American College in Rome, where he earned the degree of Doctor of Sacred Theology four years later. On 3 April 1926 he was ordained in Rome for the Diocese (and soon-to-be Archdiocese) of San Antonio by Cardinal Basilio Pompili, the Vicar General of Rome, in the Basilica of St. John Lateran. He stayed in that city to earn the degree of Doctor of Canon Law from the Pontifical Institute of Canon and Civil Law in 1928.

The scholarly Father Metzger pursued an academic career on his return to San Antonio. He was Professor of Canon Law and Philosophy at St. John's Seminary from 1928 to 1933 and Pro-Rector of that institution from 1933 until 1940. During this period he was a Regent of St. Mary's University Law School in San Antonio from 1935 until 1940. St. Edward's University in Austin, Texas, conferred upon him the honorary degree of Doctor of Laws in 1936.

Pope Pius XII appointed Father Metzger Titular Bishop of Birtha and Auxiliary Bishop of Santa Fe, New Mexico, on 5 January 1940. This first native of the Archdiocese of San Antonio to become a Catholic bishop was consecrated there in San Fernando Cathedral by Archbishop Arthur Drossaerts on 10 April 1940. Archbishop Rudolph Gerken of Santa Fe and Auxiliary Bishop Mariano Garriga of Corpus Christi were co-consecrators. On 26 December 1941 Pius XII appointed Bishop Metzger Coadjutor Bishop of E1 Paso with right of succession. He was installed in St. Patrick's Cathedral in El Paso on 4 January 1942. When Bishop Schuler resigned, Metzger succeeded to the See of El Paso on 29 November 1942 and was installed as bishop on 1 December two days later.

Bishop Metzger's thirty-five year administration of the Diocese of El Paso was marked by his interest and positive contribution toward the betterment of field and factory workers, whom he felt deserved a decent living wage. This brilliant scholar, whose name oddly means "butcher" in German, received substantial awards from many sectors attesting to the quality of his leadership.

Pope Pius XII appointed him a Knight Commander of the Equestrian Order of the Holy Sepulchre in 1952. The government of Spain conferred its Grand Cross of the Order of King Alfonso X, the Wise, and the Medal of Madrid upon him in 1957. While participating in the Second Vatican Council in Rome from 1962 through 1965, the Boswell Society awarded him the rank of *Doctor Mundunae Sapientias* [Doctor of Worldly Wisdom] in 1963 and Pope Paul VI made him an Assistant to the Pontifical Throne in 1965.

The year of 1973 was particularly notable for recognition of the Bishop's efforts on behalf of labor. The Texas AFL-CIO presented him the St. Joseph the Worker Award. The Catholic Labor Institute of Los Angeles gave him the John Casey Labor Man of the Year Award. And the Amalgamated Clothing Workers of America honored him for his part in the arbitration of wage demands to benefit the workers of the Farrah Company, who manufactured clothing.

Nor was this the extent of Bishop Metzger's interests. The Catholic Church Extension Society gave him its Lumen Christi (Light of Christ) Award for his work in promoting home missions in 1982. The Bishop was active in the National Conference of Catholic Bishops, serving on its committees for the Spanish-Speaking and for the Confraternity of Christian Doctrine (now called Hispanic Affairs and Doctrine).

When its bishop retired on 29 May 1978, the Diocese of El Paso consisted of ten counties in West Texas and seven counties and part of an eighth lying South of the Thirty-third Degree of north latitude in New Mexico. This was an area of 57,303 square miles with a Catholic population of 231,563 in a total population of 800,000. There were eighty diocesan priests and seventy-five Religious order priests, twenty-nine permanent deacons, twenty-two male Religious, and 374 female Religious. Among the institutions of the Diocese were seventy-seven parishes, four high schools, nineteen elementary schools, a home for aged women in El Paso, and a natural family planning program.

Bishop Metzger died in El Paso, Texas, on 12 April 1986, and is buried there in Mt. Carmel Cemetery. Among the last of the Roman-educated bishops without pastoral or chancery experience of any kind, he was an idealist faithful to his duty and mindful of his charges.

Most Reverend John Louis Morkovsky, STD
Titular Bishop of Hieron and Auxiliary Bishop of Amarillo
Fourth Bishop of Amarillo
Titular Bishop of Tigava, Coadjutor Bishop, and Apostolic Administrator of the Diocese of Galveston-Houston
Sixth Bishop of Galveston-Houston

Bishop John Louis Morkovsky was a Roman-educated scholar and pastor who used his zeal for Christian living, his love for others, his gift for languages, and his administrative abilities to unify diverse groups within the Church in Texas and to advance the work of the Church through the application of its teachings and by his own ecumenical efforts.

Born in Praha, Fayette County, Texas, on 16 August 1909, John Louis was the seventh of ten children born to Alois Joseph (a school teacher) and his wife Maria Theresa (Raska) Morkovsky. John graduated from St. John's Seminary in San Antonio in 1930 and then attended the North American College in Rome from 1930 to 1936. He also attended the Pontifical University for the Propagation of the Faith from 1930 to 1932. The Urban University in Rome awarded him the degree of Bachelor of Sacred Theology in 1932, and he proceeded immediately to further graduate study.

Monsignor Moses E. Kiley was the spiritual director of the North American College. Soon to be appointed Bishop of Trenton and later Archbishop of Milwaukee, he ordained the Reverend Mister Morkovsky for the Archdiocese of San Antonio in the College chapel on 5 December 1933. Morkovsky remained in Rome until he graduated from the Pontifical Gregorian University with the degree of Doctor of Sacred Theology in 1936.

At first Assistant Pastor of St. Michael's Parish in Weimar, Texas, from 1936 to 1939, he briefly served in the same position in St. Ann's Parish in San Antonio in 1940. From 1940 to 1941 he was Professor of Canon Law in St. John's Seminary and then attended the Catholic University of America in Washington, DC. Appointed Archdiocesan Superintendent of Schools by Archbishop Robert E. Lucey on 20 February 1943, he received the degree of Master of Arts in education from the Catholic University that same year.

The position proved to lead to advancement, as Father Morkovsky was an excellent administrator. He organized the school office and kept accurate records of enrollment and other school statistics. Thirteen thousand two hundred twenty-five students enrolled in 1943. There were 4,095 students in eighteen parish schools in San Antonio and 3,962 students in thirty-six parish schools outside the city. Four thousand fifty-five students enrolled in eighteen private schools in San Antonio with 1,113 in eight private schools outside that city. Thirteen years later the enrollment was 28,311 with 19,248 students in forty-five schools in San Antonio and 9,063 students in forty schools in the remainder of the Archdiocese. And this growth occurred despite the diminution of the Archdiocese caused by the formation of the Diocese of Austin in 1947.

Pope Pius XII appointed Father Morkovsky Papal Chamberlain with the title of Very Reverend Monsignor in 1944. He became Pastor of St. Leo's Parish in San Antonio in 1945, enlarging the parish hall by eight classrooms and adding six more in 1953. A cafeteria-gym replaced the parish hall in 1954. As Pastor he completed the present church at South Flores and Tommins Streets in 1952.

Archbishop Lucey appointed Monsignor Morkovsky a judge of the Archdiocesan Tribunal in 1944 and a member of the Board of Consultors in 1947. Pope Pius XII created him a Domestic Prelate with the title of Right Reverend Monsignor in 1954, the year in which Monsignor Morkovsky became Pastor of St. Mary Magdalen Parish in San Antonio. He first built a new convent and added a three-story classroom structure to the parish school. In an expansion move territory from St. Mary Magdalen's helped form the new parish of St. Gregory.

Pope Pius XII appointed Monsignor Morkovsky Titular Bishop of Hieron and Auxiliary Bishop of Amarillo on 22 December 1955. He was consecrated by Archbishop (later Cardinal) Amleto Cicognani, the Apostolic Delegate to the United States on the following 22 February. Bishops Mariano Garriga of Corpus Christi and Sidney Metzger of El Paso were his co-consecrators. As Auxiliary Bishop of Amarillo, Morkovsky became Vicar General and Chancellor of the Diocese in 1957 and received the honorary degree of Doctor of Laws from St. Edward's University in Austin, Texas, in 1958.

Shortly after the death of Bishop Fitzsimon Pope Pius XII appointed Bishop Morkovsky Bishop of Amarillo on 22 August 1958. His installation took place in St. Laurence Cathedral five days later. The new bishop opened St. Lucian's Minor Seminary in 1962 and built a home for the aged at Panhandle. He began *cursillos*, a weekend experience in Christian community living, and purchased buildings for campus ministries for colleges at Lubbock and Canyon. During his administration the Diocese was divided in half to form the Diocese of San Angelo in 1961.

In 1962 Bishop Wendelin J. Nold of Galveston-Houston became completely blind and could no longer perform all of his duties. Pope John XXIII appointed Bishop Morkovsky Titular Bishop of Tigava, Coadjutor Bishop with right of succession, and Apostolic Administrator of the Diocese of Galveston-Houston on 16 April 1963. He was installed in Sacred Heart Co-Cathedral in Houston by Archbishop Robert Lucey on 11 June 1963. For almost twelve years following his installation he would be, in effect, the acting bishop of the Diocese, with all powers to act but without the title of the incumbent.

Plunging immediately into his new work, Bishop Morkovsky confirmed 53,000 persons. He also confirmed inmates in the Huntsville, Goree, and Clemens units of the Texas Department of Corrections. In July he instituted the annual Heritage Day celebration in Houston to commemorate the feast day of Sts. Cyril and Methodius, bringing together Czech, Polish, and Ukranian Catholics. In 1964 he established the Diocesan Building Commission to oversee designing, financing, and construction of new facilities. The new Diocesan Liturgical Commission directed the liturgy and sacred music and art within the Diocese, made up of priests, women religious, and lay people. On 4 May 1964 the Bishop founded *The Texas Catholic Herald* as the official newspaper of the Diocese and established the Diocesan Development Fund supporting those projects and agencies not financially supported by parishes in 1965.

Bishop Morkovsky made plans to honor Cardinal Josef Beran of Czechoslovakia, a victim of persecution in his homeland, sponsoring his visit to the Diocese in April 1966. The Bishop oversaw the erection of the Cardinal Beran Auditorium and Bishop Nold Library for St. Mary's Seminary in Houston. Cardinal James McIntyre of Los Angeles dedicated the facilities on the first of October.

The Bishop was particularly interested in the education of priests. To this end he established a theology program at the University of St. Thomas in Houston so that college students might earn Bachelor of Arts degrees there and proceed to St. Mary's Seminary to earn the Master of Theology degree.

Once again under diocesan staffing, the Seminary offers Master of Arts and Master of Religion degrees. The Southern Association of Colleges and Schools, the Council of Southwest Theological Schools, and American Clinical Pastoral Education accredit it. Bishop Morkovsky made his retirement home on its grounds, believing that the place of a bishop is among his priests.

Believing also in the importance of diocesan missionary work, Bishop Morkovsky established the first mission to Guatemala City, Guatemala, and assigned two missionaries to it by June 1967. Closer to home he agreed with other religious bodies to provide low-cost housing for the underprivileged. Pleasantville Village was one result of this effort. In December 1967 he completed and dedicated the St. Augustine Newman Center for Texas Southern University in Houston. By 1972 there were Newman centers on every secular campus in thc Diocese.

On 25 May 1968 the Diocese of Galveston-Houston reached a milestone in the ordination of the Reverend Mister Clifton Ransom, Jr., as its first black priest. He was placed in charge of St. Raphael mission church. Two other black priests, Revs. Elbert Harris, SSJ, and John LaBauve, SVD, became pastors of the parishes of St. Peter Claver and St. Mary of the Purification.

Bishop Morkovsky also provided low-cost housing for the underprivileged in Oxford Place and established Hospital Chaplains Corps at Texas Medical Center in Houston and John Sealey and St. Mary's hospitals in Galveston. Between 1963 and 1968 he erected nine parishes, five new missions, and a chapel, while elevating sixteen missions to parish status. The Bishop authorized the building of eighteen churches, eight parochial Confraternity of Christian Doctrine buildings, three new schools, two new convents, and eleven special institutions (hospitals, retreat centers, high schools, and Newman centers) during this period. In 1969 he provided additional low-cost housing at the Houston Home Ownership Corporation. By 1972 he recommended seventeen diocesan priests to be monsignors and invested thirty-six of the laity with papal honors. By 1986 thirty-eight active diocesan priests held the rank of Monsignor while the laity continued to be honored.

Although the establishments of the Diocese of Beaumont in 1966 and the Diocese of Victoria in 1982 diminished the diocesan area, they did not stop the Bishop's progress and implementation of the decrees of the Second Vatican Council. By November 1981 there were some eighty councils, boards, pastoral offices, social service groups, and lay associations in the Diocese of Galveston-Houston. And the Diocese continues its foreign missions commitment.

Between 1970 and 1972 Bishop Morkovsky became the first Catholic bishop to serve as the President of the Texas Council of Churches. He succeeded as Bishop of Galveston-Houston on the resignation of Bishop Nold for age on 22 April 1975. During his administration in Houston (1974) Bishop Morkovsky was set upon and severely beaten by thugs invading his home. Although the beating cost him the use of an eye, it in no way lessened his effectiveness. When he reached the mandatory time, he retired on 16 August 1984 and served as Apostolic Administrator of the Diocese until Bishop Joseph Fiorenza assumed leadership on 19 February 1985.

The accomplishments of Bishop Morkovsky are so many and varied that all may never be recorded. Known as a "man of the people," he has influenced many lives. His biographer Robert C. Giles calls him "humble, warm-hearted and close to his people and priests." Just before relinquishing the keeping of his diocese to his successor his record of attainment told of his abilities and application.

On 1 January 1985 there were 188 diocesan priests active in the Diocese of Galveston-Houston, thirteen priests active outside the Diocese, and twenty-one priests retired, sick or absent. An additional diocesan priest worked in foreign missions. Two hundred religious order priests were in the Diocese with four others in foreign missions. There were also thirty-five priests from other dioceses, five temporary deacons, 171 permanent deacons, twenty-three male religious plus one in foreign missions, and 615 women religious plus sixteen in foreign missions.

One hundred forty-three parishes had resident pastors, and there were fifteen missions, six stations, and seventy-one chapels. Among the diocesan institutions were a diocesan seminary, a diocesan university, nine high schools, fifty elementary schools, and a total of more than 75,000 students under Catholic instruction. Four hospitals with 1,381 bed capacity treated 136,483 patients annually. Two special hospitals cared for 106,593 patients, while a nursing school trained 112 student nurses. And there were five homes for the invalid and aged with 577 guests. In this seventeen-county area with 13,952 square miles 612,915 Catholics lived in a total population of 3,642,231.

Always an active man, Bishop Morkovsky retired, but only in the sense that retirement allowed him to continue to pursue his interests as he wished. His wish was to be among and to help people. He continued to live in his Spanish-style house on the grounds of St. Mary's Seminary located at 9845 Memorial Drive in Houston. When at home he began his day with a private Mass, prepared light breakfasts and suppers for himself, and ate lunch in the seminary refectory. He sometimes offered home Mass for church organizations, planted spring and fall vegetable gardens behind his house and a flower garden in the courtyard.

Once a month the Bishop would journey to Hallettsville, Texas, to offer Mass at the bedside of his brother Msgr. Alois J. Morkovsky. He also celebrated Mass monthly for the Vietnamese Carmelite Sisters of the Houston Vietnamese Community, in the Czech language for the Texas communities of Praha and Moravia, and annually for the Boy Scouts Retreat at Camp Strake near Conroe. During 1989 he led a pilgrimage to the Shrine of San Juan in South Texas in September and to Rome for the canonization ceremony of Bl. Anne of Bohemia in November. He continued his involvement as a member of the Knights of Columbus and of the Order of the Holy Sepulchre.

Bishop Morkovsky had many interests. As a parish priest in San Antonio he took up bowling and found it congenial. He enjoyed playing tarok, an old card game popular in Central Europe. His languages included Czech, English, Spanish, Italian, and Latin, and he could read German, French, Portuguese, and Polish. A particular favorite author was James Michener, especially his books on Texas, Alaska, Chesapeake, and the Holy Land. He enjoyed stamp collecting, photography, fishing, hunting, and games of Scrabble. He broadcast weekly fifteen-minute radio programs in Czech to Wharton on Saturday and to Hallettsville on Sunday. He was interested in the fortunes of the Church in Czechoslovakia. He often carried a harmonica with him and especially enjoyed teaching it to senior citizens at the Third Age Learning Center in All Saints Parish in Houston and at the Sacred Heart of Jesus Parish in Manvel.

He expressed his ideas on his interests as follows:

> One should never be bored with life. If one has an interest and develops that interest, there is so much to be done in the world. It's good to have a priest or a Religious in the family. They are the ones who hold families together. Family reunions are usually promoted by a priest or Religious in the family.

On 11 April 1988 Father John Folquera, OFM, appointed Bishop Morkovsky vice postulator in the United States of the cause of beatification and canonization of Venerable Anthony Margil, OFM (1657-1726), founder of Texas missions. In this position the Bishop had authority to promote this cause for sainthood in all Catholic dioceses throughout the United States.

Bishop Morkovsky was always active in affairs of the Church. In 1964 as the first Catholic bishop to speak before the Texas Methodist Conference, he told the delegates that despite doctrinal disagreements Catholics and Methodists should "give each other credit for good faith in what we believe." When the schismatic Archbishop Marcel Lefebvre came to say Mass in Dickinson without Bishop Morkovsky's approval in July 1977, the Bishop was there to rebut him. In that year Bishop Morkovsky visited St. John Neumann's home in Czechoslovakia and was instrumental in placing a chapel in his honor in the National Shrine of the Immaculate Conception in Washington, DC.

While attending a celebration in honor of the fortieth anniversary of the ordination of his cousin Fr. Victor A. Cloquet, pastor of St. Joseph's Slovak Church in Tacoma, Washington, Bishop Morkovsky suffered two strokes. Father Cloquet administered the last rites of the Church and the Bishop died there on 24 March 1990. His body was returned to Houston and lay in state on 27 and 28 March in Sacred Heart Co-Cathedral.

During this period a number of services were held. Among them were Masses in Spanish, English, and Vietnamese, Polish-speakers offered Memorial Prayers for the Dead, the Czechs held a Vigil, and Indians conducted an Office of the Dead. The Diocese of Galveston-Houston auxiliary bishops presented their tributes at Mass on 27 March. Bishop Guillory called the deceased a person of joy and peace and a priest and bishop who led by example. Bishop San Pedro remembered the late bishop as one who held priests in high esteem, kept busy, and exhibited zeal for God.

At the Vietnamese Mass on 28 March Fr. Peter Chu Ngoc Tranh praised the Bishop for helping to bring about the Vietnamese Catholic Community, especially for aiding the growth of the Carmelite and Dominican Sisters. He referred to him as humble, goodhearted, and instrumental in aiding ethnic unity in the Diocese, and praised his good priestly life. At the Czech Vigil Fr. Paul Chovanec, pastor of St. Mary's Parish in Texas City, called him loving and hospitable. Fr. Joseph Kalladan observed during the Office of the Dead that the Bishop helped to found the Indian Catholic Community in the Diocese of Galveston-Houston in 1981.

During the Wake Service on 28 March Bishop Fiorenza said, "Whatever was the Will of God he tried to make his will conform." His acceptance was total and "He was willing to be a servant of the Church in whatever the Church asked of him." On 29 March 1990 Bishop Fiorenza concelebrated a Mass of Resurrection for Bishop Morkovsky with sixteen bishops and more than 250 priests. As homilist Archbishop Patrick Flores of San Antonio said in part:

> He was sensitive to the diversities of our ways. I saw how he related to the Hispanic community and to every culture that came into the diocese and he saw each as sacred and important. . . .He was convinced of the importance of meeting people at their cultural events and of using their language.

After Mass Bishop Morkovsky was entombed with appropriate services in the Holy Cross Cemetery Mausoleum in Houston.

On 13 April 1990 the *Texas Catholic Herald* carried Bishop Fiorenza's remarks on his predecessor as bishop. They are as follows:

> The death of Bishop Morkovsky brings deep sadness to the Catholic people of this area and throughout Texas. He was a very zealous and indefatigable servant of the gospel of Jesus Christ. As a priest for 56 years and a bishop for 34 years he served the Church with enormous energy and uncommon dedication. He was a man of the people and a friend of the poor. He was a leader in the ecumenical movement and interfaith relations. A gifted linguist, he had a special interest in ethnic cultures and promoted the celebration of national and racial customs and values.
>
> Bishop Morkovsky had a profound but uncomplicated trust in God. This unshakeable trust was the theme and guiding influence of his life and ministry.
>
> He led the Diocese of Galveston-Houston during a period of rapid growth and during the years of church renewal following the Second Vatican Council. His kindness and accomplishments as a bishop in the Panhandle of Texas and later in the Galveston-Houston area are testimony to this generous and courageous heart and his unshakeable faith in God. His memory will live in the hearts of those who knew him as a kindly and dedicated priest and bishop, and a wonderful servant of God and the Church.

Bishop Morkovsky would be remembered for many accomplishments among them his help in founding the Texas Catholic Conference, the Diocesan Development Fund, the St. Dominic Center, the offices of African American and of Hispanic ministries, the Texas Conference of Churches, and the *Texas Catholic Herald*. His motto was "Pax Diligentibus Legum" ("Peace Through Law By Means Of Diligence"). He expressed his personal philosophy in this way:

> I believe my guiding principle has been the basic Christian (or Judeo-Christian) and American conviction of the dignity of each person: God loves me, and He loves each person I deal with: I ought to act on that conviction (*WWA*, 45th ed., 2:2206).

Right Reverend John Claude Neraz, DD
Second Bishop of San Antonio

A French pioneer bishop who came to Texas with Bishop Odin, John Claude Neraz began work in what was mission territory and built many churches and institutions. Born in Anse, near Lyon, Rhône, France, to Jean and Marie Anne (Bottet) Neraz on 12 January 1828, he was first educated at the Seminary of St. Jodard in Anse and received his training in philosophy and theology in the Seminary of Alix. He was attending the Grand Seminary of Lyon when he heard the call of Bishop John M. Odin, CM, to come to Texas as a missionary.

Together the bishop and the seminarian came to Galveston around the end of 1852 and Neraz enrolled in the local seminary. Bishop Odin ordained him for the Diocese of Galveston on 19 March 1853. At first assigned to Nacogdoches in East Texas, he also served its missions Our Lady of the Pillar and St. Ferdinand, the second of which was located in Liberty County. Becoming familiar with South Texas after a tour in 1864, he was assigned to San Antonio from 1866 to 1868.

His next station was the border city of Laredo, where he built St. Augustine's Church and later the Ursuline Convent. Recalled to San Antonio, he became Pastor of San Fernando Church, which became a cathedral the following year when San Antonio was raised to a Diocese. An able administrator Father Neraz became Vicar General of the Diocese in 1874 and was named Chaplain of Santa Rosa Hospital two years later. After the death of Bishop Pellicer in 1880, Father Neraz became Administrator of the Diocese. Pope Leo XIII appointed him Bishop of San Antonio on 18 February 1881.

Bishop Neraz was consecrated in San Fernando Cathedral, becoming the first bishop to be so distinguished, on 8 May 1881. Bishop Edward Fitzgerald of Little Rock, Arkansas, was his consecrator, with Bishops Dominic Manucy of Brownsville and Claude Dubuis of Galveston as co-consecrators. As Bishop Neraz oversaw a growth in the Catholic population and in new churches, schools, and religious institutes. He continued his duties as Pastor of the Cathedral, as Chaplain of Santa Rosa, and became the Chaplain of St. Joseph's Orphanage.

For the rest of his life Bishop Neraz undertook the expansion of the Diocese of San Antonio. He blessed the new churches of Sacred Heart in Hallettsville, St. James at Gonzales, and Sacred Heart in Floresville. German Carmelites began a church and monastery in Marienfeld (now Stanton). When a smallpox epidemic ravaged Texas in 1883, the Bishop visited and blessed the sick just outside San Antonio.

The year 1884 brought new duties and responsibilities on a larger scale. That summer Bishop Neraz made the first recorded *ad limina* visit from the Diocese of San Antonio to Pope Leo XIII. He went in company with Rev. Henry Pefferkorn, Pastor of St. Joseph's Parish in San Antonio. Apparently he found Father Pefferkorn useful because that priest served as his theologian when they attended the Third Plenary Council of Baltimore in November and December. Due to Bishop Manucy's resignation as Vicar Apostolic of Brownsville, Bishop Neraz assumed its administration until the appointment of Bishop Peter Verdaguer in 1890.

The mid- and later 1880s saw the development of diocesan institutions. Bishop Neraz blessed the new church in Marienfeld and the Sisters of Divine Providence opened a school near St. Joseph's Church in San Antonio in 1885. This was the first attempt at a parochial school in the Diocese. St. Edward's College, founded in Austin by the Holy Cross Fathers as St. Edward's Academy in 1881, received its charter from the State of Texas in that year.

As a partial result of the Third Plenary Council of Baltimore, Bishop Neraz appealed for aid for black Catholics in his diocese in 1887. Rev. Richard J. Maloney, OMI, appealed for aid in St. Mary's Church and later acquired a site on Nolan Street. Here he began to build St. Peter Claver Church, the first so named in the United States. It was completed the following year and blessed by the Bishop. After desegregation the parish became affiliated with St. Joseph's and has ceased to exist separately.

Mrs. Margaret Healy Murphy heard Father Maloney's plea for support and formed the community of the Sisters of the Holy Ghost to work with blacks. The Healy-Murphy Center became a day and night school for high school students, operating as an alternative to the regular school system.

In 1889 men of Czech ancestry formed the Czech Catholic Union of Texas (K.J.T.) in Bluff (now Hostyn), Fayette County. Laymen and clergy intended to strengthen members against anti-Catholic and irreligious propaganda, to preserve their language and culture, and to provide mutual help for those in distress. With headquarters in La Grange it publishes the weekly *Nasinec* and *K.J.T. News* monthly for a membership of 17,500. That same year St. Joseph's Church in Moulton was completed and, in 1890, Incarnate Word Sisters built St. John's Orphanage and named it in honor of their bishop.

In 1890 the Diocese of San Antonio had forty-eight priests, 195 churches, forty-eight stations, eight chapels, a seminary with nine seminarians, three colleges, three academies for young ladies, twenty-nine schools and two asylums, serving a Catholic population of 60,000. The Vicariate Apostolic of Brownsville, also governed by Bishop Neraz, had twenty-one priests serving ten churches, twenty-five chapels, with four academies and six parochial schools. There were 45,000 Catholics in the Vicariate Apostolic.

In that same year Rev. C. J. Smith, OMI, began the *Monthly Review of St. Mary's Church.* This precursive Catholic publication later became *St. Mary's Weekly Review*, *The San Antonio Messenger* in 1892, and *The Southern Messenger* in 1893, publishing under that title more than a half-century.

The 1890s proved to be a period of growth for the Diocese of San Antonio. Sts. Cyril and Methodius Church in Shiner opened in 1891. In 1893 the Sisters of Divine Providence built St. Henry's School in San Antonio and started another school in Moulton. The Incarnate Word Sisters opened Incarnate Word Academy (later known as St. Patrick's) on Crosby Street. And the Society of Mary furnished additional property at the west end of Cincinnati Avenue in San Antonio and began construction of the main building of St. Louis College, now St. Mary's University. The Bishop formally approved the new congregation of the Sisters of the Holy Ghost and the Sisters of Mercy opened a new school in Stanton in 1894.

Bishop Neraz's health now began to fail. He moved to St. John's Orphanage to be near Santa Rosa for medical care. Help was unavailing, and the Bishop died in San Antonio on 15 November 1894. Two days later Bishop Nicholas Gallagher of Galveston celebrated a Pontifical Requiem Mass for the repose of his soul. Archbishop Francis Janssens of New Orleans preached a sermon in English, as did Bishop Peter Verdaguer of Brownsville in Spanish. Bishop Neraz, whose name means "summer" and whose episcopal motto was "The cross is my hope," was buried at his own request in San Fernando Cemetery in San Antonio.

Most Reverend Wendelin Joseph Nold, STD
Titular Bishop of Sasima and Coadjutor Bishop of Galveston
Fifth Bishop of Galveston-Houston

This native Texan bishop of German descent is one who served into a time of transition. He was Roman-educated with chancery and pastoral experience and attended the sessions of the Second Vatican Council. Serving two dioceses well, he became the victim of total physical blindness. Despite this affliction he carried on and, though curtailed in his activities, refused to resign until his age made it mandatory.

Wendelin Joseph was the second of three children and the only son born to Wendelin Joseph and Mary Elizabeth (Charles) Nold in the North Texas city of Bonham in Fannin County on 18 January 1900. His distinctive first name is of British derivation and means "fair." He received his high school and college education at St. Mary's Seminary at La Porte, Texas, and graduated with the degree of Bachelor of Arts in 1921. He afterward received the degree of Doctor of Sacred Theology from the North American College in Rome in 1925. He was ordained in Rome for the Diocese of Dallas on 11 April 1925.

As Assistant Rector of Sacred Heart Cathedral (1925-1941) and Pastor of Christ the King Parish (1941-1948) in Dallas, Father Nold held a number of diocesan offices as well. He was *promoter fiscalis* [keeper of the treasury] and Officialis of the Tribunal in 1930. In 1934 he was appointed a Diocesan Consultor and a synodal examiner and judge of the Tribunal in 1935. His duties in Dallas over the years included those of censor of books and the directorships of the Confraternity of Christian Doctrine and of Catholic Action.

Pope Pius XII appointed him Domestic Prelate with the title of Right Reverend Monsignor in 1942, Pronotary Apostolic in 1946, and Titular Bishop of Sasima and Coadjutor Bishop of Galveston with right of succession on 29 November 1947. He was consecrated by Bishop Joseph Lynch of Dallas in Sacred Heart Cathedral on 25 February 1948. Bishop Christopher Byrne of Galveston and Auxiliary Bishop Augustine Danglmayr of Dallas were his co-consecrators.

Bishop Christopher Byrne of Galveston knew that his coadjutor bishop would bring changes. But just as the onset of such a helper insures the succession of authority, the old bishop was not quite ready to surrender it. Giving Bishop Nold office space and a residence in Houston, Bishop Byrne announced that "your new bishop will build the new seminary" from his pulpit in St. Mary's Cathedral in Galveston at Holy Thursday services in 1949. When Bishop Byrne died on 1 April 1950, Bishop Nold immediately became his successor. For a time thereafter he continued to live in Houston and commuted twice a week to Galveston.

The aristocratic Missouri-born Bishop Byrne could not bring himself to leave his island city and the "Bishop's Palace" he called home. The job of moving the administration of the Diocese to Houston was left to Bishop Nold. The new bishop began by inviting the Congregation of the Mission (Vincentian Fathers) to staff St. Mary's Seminary in La Porte, which had been staffed by diocesan clergy for the past forty years.

He then launched a diocesan financial campaign for the building of a new seminary in Houston. Construction began in 1952 and the new facilities were occupied on 1 September 1954. On 4 November, two months later, Cardinal Samuel Stritch of Chicago dedicated the classrooms, dormitories, and the chapel.

Committed to education, Bishop Nold began plans to finance the construction of St. Pius X, Mt. Carmel, and Marian high schools, the first three co-ed high schools in Houston. Houston was to figure importantly as a center of diocesan power. Just how much so would become apparent in about five years.

In 1959 Bishop Nold appealed to the Vatican to change the name of the Diocese to include Houston. On 25 July Cardinal Marcel Mimmi, secretary of the Sacred Consistorial Congregation, issued a decree changing the name of the Diocese from Galveston to Galveston-Houston, canonically erecting Sacred Heart Church in Houston as the co-cathedral. The name change became official when the decree was executed by Archbishop Robert Lucey, the metropolitan of the San Antonio Province, on Christmas Eve. That year Bishop Nold decided to build the chancery in Houston, the largest city in the South and the seventh largest in the United States.

Bishop Nold now began to lose his eyesight due to detatched retinas. This condition resulted in total blindness on 8 September 1962. He attended meetings of the Second Vatican Council in Rome but had to relinquish the administration of the Diocese on 11 June 1963 to Bishop John Morkovsky. He continued to retain the title of Bishop of Galveston Houston until his resignation took effect on 22 April 1975. Bishop Nold refused to surrender to his ailment and continued to do as much as his health permitted. He kept current on all important events.

In his active administration of the Galveston-Houston Diocese Bishop Nold erected forty-seven parishes, fourteen missions, the new seminary, and three high schools. He became a Knight Commander of the Equestrian Order of the Holy Sepulchre of Jerusalem in 1953 and also received the honorary degree of Doctor of Laws from St. Edward's University in Austin,Texas. The Bishop whose surname means "hill" had for his motto "Serviam" ("I shall serve"). This he did to his dying day on 1 October 1981 in Houston, Texas. He is buried in Holy Cross Cemetery in that city.

Right Reverend Paul Joseph Nussbaum, CP, DD
First Bishop of Corpus Christi
Titular Bishop of Gerása
Fifth Bishop of Marquette

Born in Philadelphia, Philadelphia County, Pennsylvania, on 7 September 1870, Paul Joseph Nussbaum was the son of Bernard and Louise (Erne) Nussbaum. He was educated at St. Peter the Apostle Parochial School in Philadelphia, then operated by the Christian Brothers and now by the School Sisters of Notre Dame.

Paul professed his vows in the Congregation of the Passion at St. Paul of the Cross Monastery in Pittsburgh, Pennsylvania, on 24 July 1887. This priestly order was founded in 1720 by St. Paul of the Cross (1694-1775) in Italy. Its headquarters are in Rome with American provinces in South River, New Jersey, and in Chicago, Illinois. After study in the scholasticates of his order and in Europe, the young seminarian was ordained at St. Michael's Monastery, Hoboken (now in Union City), New Jersey, by Archbishop John Ferdinard James Eberard of Rio de Janeiro, Brazil, on 20 May 1894.

After spending ten years in Argentine missions, Father Nussbaum returned to the United States as Vice-Rector of St. Mary's Passionist Seminary in Dunkirk, New York. Between 1904 and 1907 he was Pastor of the mission of St. Mary's in Dunkirk and of St. Michael's in West Hoboken, New Jersey. After an assignment to St. Ann's Passionist Monastery in Scranton, Pennsylvania (1907-1908), he returned to St. Michael's Church in West Hoboken and served two terms as second consultor of the Eastern Province of the Passionist Order in South River, New Jersey (1908-1913).

While Father Nussbaum served as a consultor of his order, Bishop Peter Verdaguer's twenty years of service as Vicar Apostolic of Brownsville, Texas, were coming to an end. Now in 1911 the Vicariate had sixteen diocesan and sixteen religious order priests, fifteen churches with resident pastors, and sixty chapels and stations. Among its institutions were St. Joseph's College for Boys in Brownsville and five academies for young ladies throughout the Vicariate. Nine parishes had parochial schools with an estimated enrollment of more than 1,200 students.

The death of Bishop Verdaguer on 26 October 1911 brought matters to a head. The bishops of the Province of New Orleans decided the Vicariate should be elevated to a Diocese, a decision approved by the Sacred College of Cardinals. Pope Pius X issued the Bull *Sapienti Consilio* abolishing the former Vicariate of Brownsville and replacing it with the Diocese of Corpus Christi on 23 March 1912. The Church of St. Patrick (later Corpus Christi Cathedral) became the cathedral for the new diocese.

The Pope ordered diocesan records transferred from Laredo, the former seat of Bishop Verdaguer. But on examination none were found. Not until 1918 did various documents belonging to him come to light. Mysteriously they arrived by post from Chicago to Corpus Christi. No one has revealed how these records came to be in Chicago or why they were returned five years later.

Pius X authorized Archbishop James H. Blenk of New Orleans to delegate someone to erect the new diocese. He chose his Vicar General Francis Racine as his representative to execute the provisions of the Bull of Erection. Racine arrived in Corpus Christi on 9 May 1913 to perform this duty.

Meanwhile Father Nussbaum was appointed Bishop of Corpus Christi by Pope Pius X on 4 April 1913. He was consecrated in St. Joseph and St. Michael's Church of the Passionist Community by Archbishop (later Cardinal) Giovanni Bonzano, the Apostolic Delegate to the United States, in Union City, New Jersey, on 20 May 1913. Bishops Charles McDonnell of Brooklyn and John O'Connor of Newark were his co-consecrators.

Bishop Nussbaum set out for Texas and arrived by train in San Antonio on the morning of 7 June. He was taken to Santa Rosa Hospital to say his first Mass in Texas. Curiously he was assisted at Mass by Father Mariano Garriga, who would eventually become Coadjutor Bishop and Bishop of Corpus Christi himself.

Next day the Bishop reboarded the train and arrived in Corpus Christi that afternoon. Here he received a warm welcome and went immediately to the Cathedral to offer thanks to God for his safe arrival and to pray for grace and guidance in his new office. Monsignor Claude C. Jaillet, the former diocesan administrator, conducted him to a local hotel for a reception and dinner in his honor. That evening he was formally installed in his cathedral.

Bishop Nussbaum thus became the head of a Diocese which then combined the present Corpus Christi Diocese with that of Brownsville. The only other Texas dioceses then were Galveston (1847), San Antonio (1874), and Dallas (1890). Of a total population of 158,000 some 83,000 persons were Catholic. Of these 70,000 were Hispanic.

The Bishop believed in being a presence among his flock. On 13 August 1913 he began his first Confirmation tour of the Diocese, confirming almost a thousand people in Brownsville in four-and-a-half days. He confirmed 500 more in San Benito. In Mercedes, Mission, Rio Grande City, and Roma he preached missions, lectured and provided Christian instruction. He began a second tour in March 1914 which took him to Rockport, Lamar, Aransas Pass, and Port Aransas. He then went to Tivoli to dedicate the Church of Our Lady of Guadalupe, where he preached in English and in Spanish.

The quality of the lives of his people concerned the Bishop. By the end of summer in 1913 he organized the Sodality of the Blessed Virgin Mary with 100 members in Corpus Christi. He founded the Corpus Christi Catholic Club so the youth of the parish might have a more active social life. The Society of St. Ann's for married women, later the Altar Society, began in his parishes. In August 1914 he established Court No. 246 of the Court of Isabella and the senior and junior branches of the Holy Name Society for men and boys in 1916.

The need for churches was very important. To this end St. Benedict's Church in San Benito began to serve missions and chapels until 1927, when the Church of Our Lady of Guadalupe opened in Raymondville. In June 1916 the Bishop performed the solemn blessing of the new church of St. Joseph in Donna. But churches in themselves were not enough without becoming important as centers of worship for the faithful of the communities.

Bishop Nussbaum thought spiritual growth was imperative. He introduced the Holy Hour and congregational singing, pacing up and down church aisles singing to encourage the more reticent in the congregation. He firmly believed in retreats and missions to stimulate faith. Particularly anxious to begin the Forty Hours Devotion to the Blessed Sacrament in this diocese, he used this spiritual exercise to make reparation for sin and to invoke God's blessings of grace and peace.

In 1915 he wanted to expand this devotion in such a way that exercises would start each Sunday in one of his parishes. He began with the Cathedral in January of that year and assigned June as the month for those churches dedicated to the Sacred Heart of Christ. On the fifth of August he wrote to Father E. B. Ledvina, the secretary of the Catholic Church Extension Society then and his successor later: "I am trying to get the Forty Hours Adoration going in this diocese, but many missionaries have not the necessary equipment."

Travels throughout the Diocese convinced the Bishop that ignorance was the worst enemy of his flock, which would be vulnerable to proselytizers and mentally and spiritually weak. Education was the answer. In 1912 Harlingen Catholics opened their first parochial school and parishioners of Our Lady of Mercy Church in Mercedes started their first school in September 1915. Bishop Nussbaum appealed to the superiors of the American Passionists of his order and to the Pope for more men. He needed more priests in the Diocese and did all in his power to encourage vocations. He regretted the lack of a school for boys in Corpus Christi, saying: "If, when I arrived in Corpus Christi, I had found not a Cathedral, no place of worship. . .but had found a college for boys, I would have been thoroughly satisfied." He managed in his seven years of service to increase the number of parochial schools from nine to eighteen. From 1,150 students in 1913 there were more than 2,600 in 1920.

In droughts, epidemics, and hurricanes the Bishop supported his people. But on 25 January 1918 he was injured in a railway accident to such an extent that it permanently impaired his health. While in Rome in 1919 for his *ad limina* visit to the Pope he offered his resignation and made it formal in February 1920. One of his last projects was the creation of a fund for a more adequate cathedral. On his leaving the Diocese, there were forty-six priests, thirty-one churches with resident priests, and eighty-three missions and chapels. There were 99,580 Catholics in the Diocese of Corpus Christi, about seventy per cent of whom were Mexican Americans.

Pope Benedict XV accepted Bishop Nussbaum's resignation on 26 March 1920 and created him Titular Bishop of Gerása on 22 April 1920. Pope Pius XI appointed him Bishop of Marquette on 14 November 1922 and he was enthroned in St. Peter's Cathedral in Marquette, Michigan, on 6 February 1923. In this Diocese of 16,281 square miles comprising the Northern Peninsula of Michigan he labored for twelve years in good times and bad. The problem of a priest shortage still worried him. He concentrated on native vocations and his own Congregation of the Passion temporarily assigned ten priests to supplement the diocesan clergy. He was successful even in an era of depression and decreased population.

Bishop Nussbaum of German descent, whose name means "walnut tree," died at his post in Marquette, Michigan, on 24 June 1935. At first buried among fellow members of his order in Union City, New Jersey, he now rests in the imposing Crypt of Corpus Christi Cathedral in Corpus Christi, Texas. It is a fitting tribute to this missionary bishop that the Crypt has been transformed into a place of worship where Mass and the sacraments are offered on a regular basis by the present bishop of Corpus Christi and the cathedral clergy.

Right Reverend Jean-Marie Odin, CM, DD
Vice-Prefect of Texas
Titular Bishop of Claudiopolis and Vicar Apostolic of Texas
First Bishop of Galveston
Second Archbishop of New Orleans

To write the history of Archbishop Jean-Marie Odin even in outline is to write the basis of modern Catholic ecclesiastical history in Texas. A true missionary, his purpose was to restore the Church and make it flourish. Though governed by the Pope, the relationship of the Texas Church under Mexican jurisdiction was swept away by revolution and war. It was replaced by an indigenous hierarchy begun under French bishops. The loving care of Odin renewed and developed the sporadic labors of more than three hundred years. Not only a capable prelate and administrator his personal influence extended into the second decade of the twentieth century. But the influence of this first bishop of Texas resides in and beyond his own works and continues to endure as his personal legacy.

Born in Ambierle Parish, Department of the Loire, France, on 25 February 1800, Jean-Marie was the seventh of ten children born to Jean and Claudine (Seyrol) Odin. He studied in the schools of Roanne and Verrière and with a priest uncle in Nosilly. Advancing through the Colleges of L'Argentiere and Alix, he came to the Grand Seminary of St. Irenaeus in Lyon. Here as a student he first heard of Bishop Louis William Dubourg, SS, needing priests in Louisiana.

Jean-Marie came to St. Mary-of-the-Barrens Seminary in Perryville, Missouri, as a subdeacon in 1822. In this Vincentian institution founded by Revs. Felix de Andreis and Joseph Rosati of the Roman Province, the young seminarian completed his studies on 25 April 1822.

Bishop Dubourg of New Orleans ordained Odin a priest of the Congregation of the Mission (better known as Vincentians or Lazarists) on 4 May 1823. St. Vincent de Paul (ca. 1581-1660) founded the Congregation in Paris, France, in 1625. The order came to the United States in 1818. Its Southern Province in the United States has been in Houston, Texas, since 1975. But in the early days of Odin Texas was a remote mission to the Vincentians.

After ordination the young priest taught logic and theology under the supervision of Father Rosati, who ultimately became Bishop of St. Louis, Missouri. Eager to become a missionary, Odin visited Texas as early as 1824 in company with the young seminarian John Timon. Timon became Prefect of Texas and finally the founding bishop of Buffalo, New York.

Together they visited the settlers and the Quapaw Indians near Arkansas Post on the Arkansas River. When Timon was ordained in 1826, the two priests went as far south as Texas and as far north as Illinois, about a 250-mile radius from The Barrens.

Father Odin accompanied Bishop Rosati to the Second Provincial Council at Baltimore as his theologian in 1833. He then took the Council decrees to Europe for papal approval. After a brief reunion with his family in France he met Pope Gregory XVI, who gave him every encouragement in his missionary endeavors. After more than a year in Europe he was able to return to Missouri with fifteen missionary recruits and sufficient funds to bring them to America.

Returning as Visitor to the American Province of the Congregation of the Mission in the United States, Father Odin was Pastor in the parish of Cape Girardeau, Missouri, in 1836 and 1837. At The Barrens he was Professor of *Belles-Lettres* and also Procurator and Consultor of the American Vincentian Province.

Pope Gregory XVI made Texas a prefecture apostolic under the control of the Bishop of Monterrey, Mexico, on 24 October 1839. Father Odin's old friend, the Very Reverend John Timon, the Superior of the American Vincentian Province, was appointed Prefect of Texas on 2 May 1840 with Odin as Vice-Prefect. The Pastor soon said farewell to many old friends in Cape Girardeau and sailed down the river on the *Meteor* with the Spanish Vincentian priests Eudaldus Estany and Michael Calvo and Brother Raymond Sala.

They reached Natchez, Mississippi, on 7 May, just after it had barely escaped destruction by a hurricane. Stopping to aid the injured, the group proceeded to New Orleans and arrived on 12 May. They waited here and attempted to raise funds for their missionary labors. Sailing on the *Henry* with two-thirds of the ninety-three passengers being Catholics, they arrived at Lynnwood, near Victoria, Texas, on 12 July. Leaving Father Estany in Victoria to care for the sick during an epidemic there and for a few Mexican families nearby, Odin and the others left 21 July. They came to San Antonio with merchants, Mexicans, and Germans on 30 July.

The trip from Victoria to San Antonio was interesting if uneventful. Everywhere on land travel was by horseback or carriage. But bands of Comanches and Tawakonis still roamed the 150-mile area. Settlements were far apart on the open and arid prairies. Heat and the possibility of sickness were present. As Odin wrote of the trip, "We were happy if we found a little hole where we disputed with the frog for a few drops of dirty and disgusting water." En route he passed Goliad, stopped at some ranches, and visited a Lipan village with 160 Indians.

Father Odin found the situation in San Antonio appalling. While still under control of the Bishop of Monterrey, Mexico, no bishop had visited the area for thirty years. Father Refugio de la Garza was in charge of San Fernando Church, assisted by Father Jose Antonio Valdez. Damage caused by the fire of 1828 had not been repaired. Half of the roof was gone, and the building housed swallows and bats. Spiritual care of the people was virtually non-existent. One Mass was said on Sunday without a sermon and weekday Masses were negotiated for the highest bidders. Fathers Garza and Valdez neglected their duties and had taken up lives of lechery and dissipation.

As Father Odin said Mass in San Fernando Church on 2 August, preaching in English with Father Calvo preaching in Spanish, only the large attendance and grateful welcome he received gave him the stomach to do his duty. Odin had been warned by Father Timon about the character of Father Garza, a political priest who had served in the State Legislature and the national Congress in Mexico. Garza had also acquired much property in San Antonio. But Garza and Valdez had made enemies of such powerful families as the Seguins and the

Navarros. Whatever their political sins, their personal lives were a sacrilege and a reproach to the pastoral offices they held.

The state of such unworthy shepherds was reflected in the corrupt atmosphere which pervaded the city at that time. Garza and Valdez were not challenged as they did nothing for their church and people. Nor did they care for the missions of the area. The Alamo stood in ruins, as did San Juan Capistrano and San Francisco de la Espada. La Purisima Concepcion and San José were used to stable cattle, horses, and sheep.

On 3 August Odin showed Garza Timon's letters authorizing Odin to remove him as pastor and to end his priestly faculties. He describes his words to Garza in letters to Bishop Anthony Blanc of New Orleans (24 August 1840) and to Rev. Jean Baptiste Etienne, the Vincentian Procurator General (11 April 1841) as follows:

> Seeing that the people are totally uninstructed in their faith and ignorant of their moral responsibilities, that the children have been taught no catechism and are undisciplined in Christian habits, and that the dying are deprived of the comforts of religion, my duty obliges me to assign to this town a younger, more active, and more zealous pastor.

The shaken Garza obeyed and was told to hand over the parish records and church keys.

On 6 August Garza was made to surrender church property in his keeping. On 7 August Odin suspended the priestly faculties of Father Valdez. This action by the Pope's representative in Texas brought an end to Spanish and Mexican ecclesiastical jurisdiction in Texas.

Garza was arrested by the Government for writing to General Arista, Commander of Mexican troops in Mexico, for assistance. Tried in Austin and found guilty, he was given a severe reprimand for meddling in Mexican politics. Though he and Valdez continued to live off the land they had acquired in Texas, they were no longer a threat to Church authority.

Spiritual renewal brought about a much more wholesome atmosphere to San Antonio. Father Odin restored the custom of tolling church bells only as a call to worship and during funeral services for the faithful. Repairs to San Fernando began immediately. In September he toured the missions, finding Espada and Capistrano beyond repair and too distant from San Antonio. But San José and Concepcion were within five miles of the City and in better condition.

The Vice-Prefect could no longer restrain his desire to visit Texas settlements. He set out with friends on 9 November to visit the Coast. The company passed through Seguin and Gonzales and arrived in Victoria on 13 November. After surveying the good work of Father Estany and the Lavaca settlements, Odin set out for Austin on 26 November and arrived three days later. Here he was the guest of Alphonse Dubois de Saligny, Chargé d'Affaires of the French Court to the Republic of Texas. Saligny proved a good host and faithful supporter, presenting a few acres of land for a church, convent, and school and helping his guests buy several lots within Austin.

Fortunately the Vice-Prefect's presence in Austin coincided with that of

Prefect Timon. Timon came to present greetings from Rome to the Republic of Texas. The Prefect also wished to make a report on the needs for reorganizing and developing the Church there. Timon came with Rev. Nicholas Stehlé, CM, who planned to work among German immigrants to Texas. In Galveston Timon began a pledge drive for St. Mary's Parish. In Houston he promised to begin a new church for St. Vincent's Parish.

Stopping to deliver Roman greetings to President Lamar in Independence, the two priests arrived in Austin on 21 December. On the following day Timon said Mass and sent Father Stehlé on a tour of German settlements on the Colorado and the Brazos rivers. While the prefects received a most gracious greeting in Austin, their particular mission was to secure recognition of the right to retain all Church property owned in Texas under the Spanish and Mexican governments. To this end Odin wrote a petition which Congressman William Porter presented to the House of Representatives on 21 December 1840. Senator James Miller presented a similar petition to the Senate and requested that Father Odin act as chaplain for that body in the absence of its regular chaplain.

The Vatican greetings which Timon had brought to President Lamar requested the protection of the Executive for the Prefect and that property owned by the Church in Texas be returned to him. Acting President David G. Burnet favored the granting of the request. Former President Sam Houston took a positive view of the petition and on 14 January 1841 President Burnet signed a bill granting Odin's claims.

Timon and Odin did not learn of their success until April 1841, having left Austin on New Year's Day. The two came to Houston on 8 January and were in Galveston on the twelfth. Despite poor weather in the winter season they were in Nacogdoches on 30 January. Here Charles Chavalier donated a city lot and 400 acres in the county to build and maintain a church. In San Augustine Major George Nixon made a gift of half a league of land and others donated five or six sites for a church.

When Timon parted from Odin on 8 February, it would be the last time they would tour Texas together. Odin returned to San Antonio through Central Texas and arrived on 12 March 1841. In the past four months he had travelled over 2,000 miles saying Mass and administering the sacraments. He now estimated that there were 10,000 Catholics in Texas.

In his report of 11 April 1841 to the Procurator General of his order he noted:

> From August 1, 1840, to March 1, 1841, we [he and Timon] have heard 911 confessions, administered 411 Communions, and 281 Baptisms, performed 24 marriages, conducted 45 burials, given 31 First Communions, confirmed eight, and baptized 21 converts, six of them adults. We have constructed a small chapel on Don Carlos' ranch and repaired the building in Victoria, as well as that in San Antonio. The good of our Religion demands that churches be built in Galveston, Houston, Nacogdoches, San Augustine, Lavaca, and the Capital of the country, Austin, but where can the money be secured?

Only six priests including Odin cared for the people of Texas in 1841.

Meanwhile Timon had journeyed through Louisiana on his way back to The Barrens in Missouri. In April 1841 he learned that the Pope had appointed Odin Titular Bishop of Claudiopolis and Coadjutor Bishop of Detroit in December 1840. The Bulls of appointment would soon reach New Orleans. In fact Bishop Blanc received the official documents by 14 March. Timon decided to exert his influence to prevent the appointment because the presence of Odin in Texas was of crucial importance.

Bishop Blanc notified Odin in San Antonio to come to New Orleans immediately. Odin received the Bishop's letter on 30 March and left Galveston on the *Savanna* on 13 April. He received the Bulls on 16 April and was staggered by the news. Begging leave to consult Timon, he left New Orleans on 22 April aboard the *Maid of Kentucky*. Timon convinced him to return the Bulls and to give up the appointment.

In New Orleans on 9 May Odin returned the Bulls to Blanc with regrets. Next day Timon appealed to Cardinal Fransoni, Prefect of the Congregation of the Doctrine of Faith, to save Odin for his indispensable work in Texas. Back in Texas by the end of May Odin awaited the result of the Detroit appointment. War with Mexico seemed possible, money was scarce, and the church in Galveston developed slowly. Conditions were even less favorable in Houston.

On a missionary tour to the Lavaca settlements in July Odin contracted malaria but continued to travel. In Victoria Father Estany accompanied him to San Antonio. On 12 December he rededicated San Fernando in San Antonio and proclaimed Mary Immaculate the patroness of Texas. Everywhere he travelled he noted improvements and also the increasing needs of the people for priests and institutions.

Timon left the United States for Europe on 8 June 1841. He arrived in Paris in mid-July. Here he learned the welcome news that Pope Gregory XVI had on 16 July separated the Province of Texas from the Bishop of Monterrey in Mexico and erected it into a Vicariate Apostolic with Odin as Titular Bishop of Claudiopolis and Vicar Apostolic of Texas.

The Bulls of appointment arrived in New Orleans on 11 October 1841. Bishop Blanc did not notify Odin, however, until the return of Timon from Europe on 17 January 1842. Odin arrived in Galveston on 4 February and soon after received notice of his appointment and to come to New Orleans. Pleading "feebleness" and being "unworthy of the honor" and "incapable of bearing so heavy a burden," he promised nevertheless to set out by the next boat. On 17 February he left Galveston on board the *Neptune* and arrived in New Orleans two days later. Timon came back from Missouri on 26 February to be present for Odin's consecration.

Bishop Anthony Blanc of New Orleans consecrated Bishop Odin in St. Louis Cathedral on 6 March 1842. Bishops Michael Portier of Mobile and John Chanche, SS, of Natchez assisted as co-consecrators. Father Timon was present with two other Vincentian priests, John Boullier and John Burlando. Alphonse de Saligny also attended.

Texas was no longer part of the American Vincentian Mission of the Barrens in its overall world program. It was now a separate jurisdiction, and it would have to become independent. Odin was fearful, due to Mexican incursions into Texas. Though counter measures were carried out by the Government, it was the conservative policies of Presidents Sam Houston and Anson Jones that kept Texas free from fullfledged wars with the Mexicans and the Comanches.

Mexican incursions into Texas were threatening enough to keep the Bishop in New Orleans. He left there on the *New York* for Galveston and arrived on 13 May 1842. He had an agreement that the Society for the Propagation of the Faith would provide funds for the development of the Galveston-Houston area. Increases in manpower would have to wait. After providing some non-military provisions for Texas soldiers in the field, the Vicar turned to improvements. He added a sacristy to the church, bought a home for a residence, and converted a drugstore into a school, all for $1,200.00 His new "palace" was a single story frame house with a kitchen, four rooms, and a large porch.

By the end of the summer the school had twenty-two students, one-third of whom were non-Catholics. James P. Nash was sacristan and sexton and now a teacher. Odin gave catechism instruction and completed the church in Houston by mid-July. It measured fifty by twenty feet and cost $1,100. The Vicar supplied $950.00 from the French Society for the Propagation of the Faith and dedicated it to St. Vincent de Paul. About this time General Alexander Somervell donated ten acres in Richmond to defray expenses for building a church there. Odin donated fifty dollars to the fund but could give no more.

San Antonio was threatened by Mexican troops in September 1842, causing many families to abandon the city. Corpus Christi was at the mercy of destructive volunteer soldiers. Even in Galveston such troops pillaged in search of forage. Crops were ruined by drought and heavy rains. Despite these and other problems, immigration continued.

The Mexican invasion restored Garza temporarily as parish priest in San Antonio. About this time a storm destroyed St. Mary's Church in Galveston. A new one with a steeple and bell was finished by 21 March 1843. But Odin's decision to attend the Provincial Council in Baltimore on 14 May yielded few results. Recurrent headaches, nausea, and bouts of malaria weakened him. Still he pressed on with his council theologian Rev. John Boullier, CM, to visit New York. After a brief hospital stay in Louisville, Kentucky, Odin proceeded to The Barrens in Missouri. Illness detained him on his way to New Orleans. He arrived in Galveston on 16 December after being absent more than six months.

Odin's conference with Timon at Portland, Kentucky, on the return trip to Galveston yielded plans to send more men to Texas. By the end of the year Fathers Schneider and Ogé came to take up missionary work. A second discussion with Timon in New Orleans in December 1842 brought a tentative commitment to establish a Vincentian house in Galveston. The Vicar decided to visit San Antonio with Father Ogé and place him in charge of the Colorado River settlements. Father Schneider would serve the Galveston-Houston area.

In April 1844 Father Timon made good the commitment to establish a Vincentian house in Galveston. He sent Father Joseph Paquin as vicar-general and superior of the Vincentians there. Father John Brands, a native of Holland, also came. The two priests arrived in Galveston on 11 May 1844, bringing with them $2,000, the balance of funds allocated to the Texas Mission from the Society for the Propagation of the Faith.

At this point many Catholics from Europe and America still came to Texas.

The desire of the Vicar to provide more churches, schools, and personnel to staff them required a trip to Europe to secure funding. But he disliked being away even a brief time. Father Schneider's resignation from mission work required a German-speaking priest. And Odin needed to name a vicar-general before setting out to visit the San Antonio area. He named Father Paquin his vicar-general and lodged him and Father Brands in his residence, which he planned to enlarge.

Bishop Odin set out for San Antonio by way of the Lavaca, the Colorado, and the Brazos rivers. Paquin remained in Galveston in charge of about 500 German, French, and Irish faithful, with instructions to visit the Houston church once a month. But the climate weakened the priests, who suffered from fever and respiratory ailments. The yellow fever epidemic in July 1844 killed almost 200 people in a month, many of whom were Catholic. Busy among the sick and dying, priests contracted the fever. Father Paquin died of it on 13 August 1844. Curiously Father Brands made a complete recovery and improved his general health.

Meanwhile the Bishop arrived in San Antonio on 25 July. He visited the missions and organized catechism classes in German, French,English, and Spanish. His presence brought about a spiritual revival, in which he reported to Bishop Blanc of New Orleans that 2,774 people had gone to confession and that 2,507 had received communion. He laid the cornerstone for the new church of St. Louis of France in the new city of Castroville on 12 September. The increased German immigration which would shortly lead to the establishment of New Braunfels and Fredericksburg pointed up the need for a German-speaking priest. The Archbishop of Strassburg refused to release Father Ogé for work in Texas. Bishop Odin needed at least a dozen priests and additional churches.

Again in Galveston in October 1844 Odin found that the loss of Paquin and the departures of Schneider and Ogé had left him short-handed. Father Timon agreed to visit Texas to survey Vincentian activities and to determine the property rights of that order. He found in January 1845 the prospering work of the Church and that Texans of all religions felt affection for the Bishop. In 1844 the Texas missionaries had absolved 3,150 penitents and had given communion to 2,850. Father Calvo in San Antonio reported he had heard over 5,000 confessions and given communion to more than 4,000 people in a five-year period.

Visitor Timon knew that Texas would eventually become a Diocese. There were churches in Galveston, Houston, San Antonio, Refugio, Victoria, Castroville, and soon others in New Braunfels and Fredericksburg. More churches were on the Lavaca River, at Fort Bend, and in St. Augustine and Nacogdoches. Ten new churches had been built and four more started. Father Edward Clark built a school at Brown's Settlement in Lavaca County and Father James Miller built another in Brazoria County. San Antonio had 1,600 Catholics in a population of 2,000. There were several hundred Catholics in Houston and 600 in Nacogdoches. The population of Texas was 200,000.

Timon understood that diocesan organization would enforce Vincentian communal discipline and wished to make no present requirements. His more important task was to determine what property belonged to the Vicariate of Texas and what belonged to the Vincentian order. From Odin's account Timon estimated he had spent $13,000 of Propagation funding in Texas.

Odin had acquired the French Legation and nine lots in Austin, a house and lot for the Vincentians in San Antonio, a tract of about thirteen acres of land near San Antonio, eighty-five acres in the vicinity of Mission Concepcion, a lot in Houston, and two houses and lots there. One house and lot in Houston was rental property earning $200 a year. Timon decided to wait for Vatican confirmation of ownership and complimented Odin on his purchase of property. He returned to New Orleans on 8 January 1845.

Bishop Odin also felt that Galveston would soon become a Diocese. To this end he made preparations for a trip to Europe to secure the missionaries and resources to help make this possible. In August 1844 he purchased a lot for a future cathedral in Galveston and in February 1845 received a donation of seven adjacent lots from the Galveston City Company. In Europe he acquired bricks and had them transported free by a friendly sea captain. He made a will in favor of Fathers Timon and Brands, leaving them the entire Vicariate property. He also instructed Brands in his duties as Vicar-General.

Bishop Odin left Galveston on 26 February 1845 for New Orleans. Here he conferred with Timon. After visits to Washington, Baltimore, Philadelphia, and New York, he embarked for Europe from Boston on 1 April with Bishop Francis P. Kenrick of Philadelphia and by 24 April arrived in Dublin. By the end of the month he had left London for Paris. Here he was presented to the French Queen, who promised to favor his cause. He acquainted the Society for the Propagation of the Faith with his needs. It told him decisions for new grants were made in Lyon. He preached in the Cathedral of Notre Dame and was humbly grateful to the Sisters of Charity, who presented him with a new wardrobe.

Learning of increased Swiss immigration to Port Lavaca, he was in Lyon in mid-June. There the Society for the Propagation of the Faith told him that the Texas Mission was a separate cause and funds for it should be requested from the Superior of the Vincentian Order. Visiting the Grand Seminary of Lyon the former seminarian urged the young men there to volunteer for mission work in Texas. He did not try to hide the perils of such an assignment, but instead told them it would try their courage and endurance to the limit.

In Turin Father Marcantonio Durando was his host. Here Odin proposed a college for San Antonio, to which Durando offered to supply personnel subject to the approval of his superiors. He also wished to minister to the Indians of Texas. But this appeal to the Vincentian Superior Étienne was doomed to failure.

After Turin Odin was in Genoa, Lucca, Pisa, and Florence. In Florence he met the Duchess and the Archduchess and later the Grand Duke of Tuscany. His description of the needs of Texas won him many donations and gifts. Arriving in Rome on 9 September he met twice with Pope Gregory XVI by the twenty-third. On application to various curial officials, he found that no diocese in Texas would be formed without recommendation by the Council of Baltimore. The Pope met him again on 27 September and he left Rome for Vienna on 2 October.

First he went to Bologna and then to Modena to visit the Duke. After journeying through Ferrara and Padua he reached Venice on 17 October. Proceeding to Trieste, he came to Vienna on 24 October for a visit of three weeks. His reports to the Leopoldine Association of the Austrian Empire (*Leopoldinen*

Stiftung) and to the Most Reverend Prince-Bishop Vincent Edward Milde had gone before him.

German immigration to Texas had involved the Society and Odin hoped to find German-speaking priests he needed. He stressed the poverty of the immigrants and their lessened condition due to revolution and war. He explained he had had to seek donations from associations and private donors, chief of which was the Society for the Propagation of the Faith. Such donations would build eight wooden chapels, repair San Fernando in San Antonio, and assist the missionaries in their duties.

In particular he needed the vessels and vestments necessary for Mass celebration and sacrament administration. More priests could staff churches and work among the Indians. He declared he had twenty-two priests and ten nuns to follow him if he could pay their travelling expenses. The Leopoldine Association granted him $1,406, considerably less than the award of the French Society for the Propagation of the Faith.

He left Vienna on 11 November for Munich to visit the *Ludwigs-Missions-Verein*, another German missionary society. Throughout the month he was in Munich, Augsburg, Stuttgart, Carlsburg, and Strassburg, in search of priests, funds, and the creation of interest in the Texas Mission. In Belgium he obtained a gift of 500,000 bricks for his cathedral which he arranged to have transported without charge. Once again in Lyon and after making a circuit through Belgium he saw fifteen missionaries sail for Texas from La Havre aboard the *Elizabeth-Ellen* on 20 March 1846. Among them was Rev. Claude Marie Dubuis, who would succeed him as Bishop of Texas. After a trip to Ireland he persuaded the superior of the Vincentians in Ireland to allow Rev. John Lynch to travel to America. In time the young priest would become the first Bishop of Toronto and found Niagara University in New York. Odin himself sailed from Liverpool on 11 April.

Returning to New York on 28 April 1846, Odin had been successful. He had obtained both money and recruits. The Ursulines would come to Galveston in January 1847 and found a school under the auspices of Mother St. Arsene of New Orleans. It would be the first Catholic religious community of women to come to Texas. Revs. James A. Miller and Anthony Lienhart, both German-speaking, sailed from Antwerp with some young men from the Seminary of St. Irenée in Lyon. Richard Hennesy and John Lynch, Irish Vincentian priests, had gone to New Orleans. Four other Irishmen would set out after Easter. Of the young seminarians he had seen off at La Havre, six had gone on to The Barrens in Missouri to learn English and four to St. Louis to finish their theological studies. And in 1847 three priests would come from Rome.

Bishop Odin was now transformed into the capable administrator Father Timon knew he must become. Though still a Vincentian, Odin understood his responsibilities as a bishop and how to make independent decisions. Fathers Brands, Hennesy, and Lynch would follow the Vincentian Rule of communal living in Galveston, while Fathers Calvo and Estany and Brother Sala would do the same in San Antonio.

Before returning to Texas, Odin attended the Sixth Provincial Council in Baltimore, which opened on 10 May. Texas was now a state and part of the American Vincentian Province. The Superior of that order commissioned the

Bishop to make an inspection of Vincentian houses in the United States. After travels of fifteen months Odin reached Galveston.

With the Mexican War beginning far to the South, the Bishop set about improving facilities in Galveston. He found New Braunfels in good shape. But Fredericksburg suffered from epidemics of malaria, dysentery, and bilious fever. Despite the loss of twenty per cent of her people, the citizens soon arranged through Baron Otto von Meusebach for the construction of a church built with mission funds. The Association granted a lot to be deeded to the Bishop without conditions.

In January 1847 ten churches were in use in Texas: St. Mary's in Galveston, St. Vincent's in Houston, San Fernando in San Antonio, Our Lady of Refuge in Refugio, Our Lady of Guadalupe in Victoria, St. Mary's in Brown's Settlement on the Lavaca River, St. Louis in Castroville, St. Joseph's in Refugio County, Santa Gertrudis in Victoria County, and St. Peter's in Austin County. There were eleven Mass-stations including Brazoria and Velasco in Brazoria County, Live Oak Point in Refugio County, San Patricio and Corpus Christi in San Patricio County, Cuero and McHenry settlements in Victoria County, Brushy Creek Settlement in Lavaca County, Gonzales and Seguin in Gonzales County, Richmond in Fort Bend County, Spring Creek and Morgan's Point in Harris County, Liberty City in Liberty County, Nacogdoches and San Augustine in East Texas, and the San Antonio missions of San José, San Juan Capistrano, and San Francisco de la Espada.

Six Vincentian and four secular priests served these churches and their Mass-stations. Five recruits would soon take up their duties and three young seminarians from France would finish their studies within a year. The Ursuline Academy in Galveston would shortly be constructed and there were schools for boys in Brown's Settlement and Brazoria. Texas was more developed in its facilities than the Dioceses of Hartford, Richmond, Nashville, Dubuque, Little Rock, and Natchez, and the Archdiocese of Oregon City.

Among the other recommendations of the Sixth Provincial Council of Baltimore in 1846 was the elevation of the Vicariate of Texas to the Diocese of Galveston. Bishop Odin arrived in Texas in June and set out to visit the State from Houston to West Texas.

On 4 May 1847 Pope Pius IX issued the Bull *Apostolicae Sedis Fastigio*, which established the Diocese of Galveston in place of the Vicariate of Texas. Odin's Bull of appointment was issued on 21 May, and the two documents reached Galveston on 21 July 1847. The limits of the Diocese were the limits of the State, with the Catholic population set at about 20,000. The Bishop received less than four dollars a month for governing this immense territory.

In Rome in 1851 Bishop Odin informed Cardinal Barnabo, secretary of the Congregation for the Propagation of the Faith, of his difficulties in determining his jurisdiction. Texas and the territory between the Nueces and the Rio Grande had been part of the Diocese of Monterrey, Mexico, and the political Province of New Mexico was under the jurisdiction of the Bishop of Durango. After 1836 Texans claimed the Rio Grande from mouth to source as the western boundary of the State.

By the Treaty of Guadalupe-Hidalgo ending the Mexican War in 1848, Mexico ceded to the United States all territory East of the Rio Grande claimed by Texas, all of Upper California, and left Texas boundaries open for arbitration. The Congregation in Rome urged Odin to include as his territory "not only that part of the country lying between the Nueces and the Rio Grande, but also all that territory of New Mexico lying east of the Rio Grande considered by Texas to be an integral part of its territory."

Odin presented the problem to the Seventh Provincial Council of Baltimore meeting on 5 May 1849. In his letter to Cardinal Barnabo of 18 September 1851 he explained:

> The Bishops, gathered at Baltimore, realizing that the Diocese of Galveston was already too large for the care of one bishop, deemed it advisable to beg the Holy See to send a vicar apostolic to look after New Mexico. The Holy Father saw fit to accede to the request and placed Bishop John B. Lamy in charge of the said Vicariate Apostolic.

This provision left the area between the Nueces and the Rio Grande within the Diocese of Galveston. Reduction of claims by Texas omitted portions of the present states of Wyoming, Colorado, Kansas, Oklahoma, and New Mexico, reducing the Diocese by more than 104,000 square miles.

As Vice-Prefect, Vicar Apostolic, and Bishop of Galveston, Bishop Odin depended upon Bishop Anthony Blanc for guidance and support. This relationship became official on 19 July 1850 when Pope Pius IX issued the Bull *Ad Supremum Apostolicae.* This document raised New Orleans to an archiepiscopal see with Blanc as Archbishop. As metropolitan of the Province of New Orleans his suffragans were the Dioceses of Mobile, Natchez, Little Rock, and Galveston, including the States of Louisiana, Alabama, Mississippi, Arkansas, and Texas. Odin was away on a visitation and did not learn of his old friend's elevation until December 1850.

The cornerstone of St. Mary's Cathedral in Galveston was laid on 14 March 1847 and the Cathedral was consecrated on 26 November 1848. The Bishop travelled constantly on horseback, preaching everywhere including Protestant churches to all types of people. He brought the Missionary Oblates of Mary Immaculate into the Diocese in 1849 and the Brothers of Mary in 1852. He built another convent in San Antonio and the Incarnate Word Convent in Brownsville. For their part the Brothers of Mary opened a school in San Antonio and at Brownsville, Laredo, and Brazoria.

On his return to Texas in 1849 Odin made an official inspection tour of the area between the Nueces and the Rio Grande for the first time. He set out on 22 April 1850 for San Antonio and came eventually to Eagle Pass on the border with Mexico. He had stayed at military camps along the way and reached Eagle Pass under the protection of Texas Rangers. There was constant danger of attack by the Comanches.

Crossing the Rio Grande, Odin came to Presidio del Rio Grande as the first bishop to visit there in forty-five years. He proceeded eastward along the border to Brownsville. On the Mexican side of the River he confirmed 2,200 with the permission of the Bishop of Monterrey. After a successful stay of three weeks in Brownsville he left on 28 August for Corpus Christi. To avoid Indians he made the northward trip through Padre Island. He arrived in Corpus Christi on 4 September 1850. San Patricio was much reduced in population since 1836 and Refugio had been ravaged over the years. Finally he returned to Galveston in December 1850. On his seven month tour he visited the area West and South of San Antonio for the first time.

The 1850s were years of growth and progress for the Diocese of Galveston. Bishop Odin was in Rome in 1851 to report on his diocese. He accounted for thirty-three priests he had brought to Texas and stated that there were more than 40,000 Catholics, Spanish and Indians, and Americans of Irish, German, French, and Italian descent. He had repaired churches in San Antonio and Laredo and built a Cathedral of 120 by 60 feet in Galveston and stone churches at Castroville and Fredericksburg. There were wooden churches or chapels at Brazoria, Houston, Lavaca, Nacogdoches, Frelsburg, New Braunfels, Victoria, Rancho de San Carlos, Fagan, Refugio, Brownsville, and Santa Rita.

He pointed with pride to the Ursuline Convent and school for young girls and of a similar institution soon to be opened in San Antonio. His visit to the Rio Grande Valley resulted in the confirmation of more than 1,100 souls. Twenty additional priests were needed immediately and money for new churches and chapels and equipment of all kinds for the spread of religion. Because the Bible Society of New York provided salaries large enough to provide free education to Mexicans and Indians, he asked for two new convents for the Valley to instruct and to care for the faithful. To meet this challenge he borrowed 20,000 francs ($4,000) and built two schools in San Antonio, one of which was to be staffed by some "French Sisters." He estimated the total cost at about 50,000 francs ($10,000).

Bishop Odin wanted to build churches in Rio Grande City, Roma, Eagle Pass, D'Hanis, Vandenberg, Seguin, Cibolo, Austin, Corpus Christi, San Patricio, Washington-on-the-Brazos, Liberty, Woodville, Beaumont, and Clarksville. There was no end to his work. A biographer, Brother William H. Dunn, CSC, describes him as "a busy pastor, circuit rider, preacher, recruiter of missionaries, promoter of education, catechism teacher, reformer, fund-raiser, and builder," in addition to his ordinary activities as bishop.

His visits and confirmation tours are remarkable in themselves. Coming off the 1850 tour of South Texas, he had confirmed over 11,000 persons. He confirmed 150 persons in Nacogdoches in 1851 and travelled 2,000 miles in Texas over five months. In an 1854 visit of four months to South Texas he gave a retreat at Laredo and confirmed 1,123 in the Rio Grande Valley and 287 more in New Braunfels, Austin, and Houston. In 1858 he visited Houston, Frelsburg, San Bernard, Hallettsville, Victoria, Goliad, Refugio, Lamar, l'Amita, l'Arkansas, San Patricio, Corpus Christi, Port Isabel, Santa Rosalis, Arenal, San Raphael, Suez, and Brownsville. On this tour he confirmed 3,415 people. In 1860 he confirmed more than 200 people.

By 1852 Bishop Odin reported twenty churches and chapels built with four churches building. There were seventeen priests, four schools, and two academies for young ladies. The Ursuline Young Ladies Academy at Galveston required $160.00 a year or $40.00 per quarter for full-time boarders, half for half-time boarders, and twenty dollars per annum or five dollars per quarter for "day scholars." There were extra charges for such items as washing and mending. Many mission stations existed throughout the State. Centers of activity were at Galveston, Houston, Brazoria, Victoria, San Antonio, Castroville, Brown's Settlement, Cummings Creek, and Nacogdoches.

The tireless bishop continued his travels to the eastern United States and to Europe. He would continue to seek funding from the French Society for the Propagation of the Faith, the German Leopoldinen Foundation and the Ludwig Mission Society. In 1851 he called upon the Society in Lyon,as well as the Convent of the Sisters of the Incarnate Word and the Seminary for volunteers. He asked Bishop Eugene De Mazenod, the founder of the Oblates of Mary Immaculate, to send more missionaries, and he reported his general progress and plans to Pope Pius IX in Rome.

On 28 June 1852 six Oblate priests landed at Galveston aboard *La Belle Assise* (*The Good Foundation*). They came in company with eighteen seminarians, three Brothers of Mary, four Sisters of the Incarnate Word and Blessed Sacrament, four Ursuline Sisters and three postulants. The Oblates came to begin a college in Galveston and for missionary work in the Valley. The Brothers of Mary went to San Antonio to found the present St. Mary's University. The Incarnate Word Sisters came to Brownsville to found a convent and an academy. And one of the seminarians, John Claude Neraz, became the second bishop of San Antonio.

In the sixteenth and seventeenth centuries the Spanish came to Texas with de Piñeda, blacks with De Vaca, Italians with Coronado, and the French with La Salle. In the pre-Civil War era German immigration began with Prince Karl of Solm-Braunfels. There was a great influx of Belgians, Netherlanders, Hanoverians, Prussians, and Austrians. Johannes Nordboe pioneered Norwegian immigration, while Sir Svante Palm led the Swedes into Texas. A Czech priest brought Czechs in 1850, and the Franciscan priest Leopold Moczygemba led the first organized Polish migration to America in 1854.

Prejudice reared its ugly head in the form of nativism. In 1854 the Know-Nothing Party elected city officials in San Antonio. In the following year it sent five senators and twenty representatives to the state legislature and influenced the election of the Mayor of Galveston. It spread dissension among churchgoers, especially the Germans. In 1855 Bishop Odin wrote, "It takes true courage to declare oneself Catholic today." In 1856 he felt the success of the missionaries "saddened all enemies of religion, who, alas, were only too numerous!" But by 1859 the Know-Nothings were no longer a force in Texas politics. They may have strengthened the faithful in their beliefs by making them better known through discussion. Religious houses and schools began to win acceptance. This condition did much to end hostility toward the Church in Texas.

In good times and bad Bishop Odin pressed on. He attended the First Plenary Council at Baltimore on 9 May 1852. The bishops of the United States regulated parochial life, matters of church ritual and ceremonies, the administration of church funds, and the teaching of Christian doctrine. In 1853 he lost five priests and a deacon to yellow fever within six weeks. But he built a seminary in Freslburg, Colorado County, under the direction of Rev. V. Gury. In 1855 he announced that Texas had forty priests and "one poor bishop" and lost seven priests that year to yellow fever.

The Bishop was mindful that Texas was a state of great promise and potential. He wanted to build up native vocations among people he felt were of special character. He began St. Mary's Seminary-College in Galveston on 1 January 1855. It was approved as an institution of higher learning by the Texas Legislature on 12 August 1856. Reopened after the Civil War in 1870, it began again in La Porte in 1901 and presently exists in Houston, fulfilling its original function.

In 1858 St. Mary's Church opened in San Antonio as did Immaculate Conception Church in Brownsville. By 1860 the Bishop had brought Christian Brothers, Benedictines, and Franciscans into the Diocese. And in that year the Ursuline Sisters opened a convent at Liberty. By 1861, the year of his appointment as Archbishop of New Orleans, he had established forty-five churches with forty-six priests, and forty-four chapels. There was a college, four academies for young ladies, and four schools for boys.

An event that gave the Bishop particular satisfaction was the First Diocesan Synod in St. Mary's Cathedral in Galveston. It took place from 13 June to 20 June 1858, and it meant that the Diocese had grown to such an extent that it was necessary to call together its active clergy for consultation and discussion.

Bishop Odin began the first session with the celebration of a Solemn Pontifical Mass in the Cathedral. He opened the proceedings with a reading of the Decrees of the Council of Trent. Only sixteen priests were absent and those present made their Profession of Faith on bended knee and received the solemn blessing of the Bishop. June fourteenth through sixteenth were spent in retreat under the direction of Rev. Michael McDonnell. The second session began with a Solemn Pontifical Mass celebrated by the Vicar General, Rev. Louis Chambadut. The Bishop himself opened the third and last session on 20 June.

The Synod recommended the strict observance of the decrees of the seven Provincial Councils of Baltimore and of the First Provincial Council of New Orleans, which had been held between 1829 and 1858. The Blessed Virgin Mary under the title of The Immaculate Conception was recognized as patroness of the United States of America. Fathers Chambadut, Claude M. Dubuis, and Augustus Gardet were appointed Diocesan Consultors, with Chambadut as Chancellor, and Vice-Chancellors Dubuis for San Antonio, Gardet for Brownsville, and James Giraudon for Laredo.

Various regulations governing the customs and apparel of the clergy, the erection of new churches and establishment of new parishes, and proper parish record keeping were adopted and publicly read. Nine statutes covered the administration of the sacraments. The Synod recommended that the clergy instruct the young people in their faith and that the faithful should furnish the means for the education of men for the priesthood. Annual collections were ordered for the annual support of the seminary and for the obligations of the Diocese.

The Bishop ordered the statewide establishment of the Society for the Propagation of the Faith to support the Diocese and spread the faith and that the Confraternity of the Immaculate Heart of the Blessed Virgin Mary be organized on the same basis to pray for the conversion of sinners. The constitution and bylaws of the Synod were to go into immediate effect on their reception by the clergy throughout the Diocese. Each priest was instructed to say one Mass yearly for all deceased diocesan clergy and three Masses for every brother priest upon receipt of his obituary notice. The conclusion of the Synod was signalled by the singing of the *Te Deum* in thanksgiving and the imparting of the episcopal blessing upon the assembled clergy and people.

By the end of 1858 the statewide Society for the Propagation of the Faith contributed $833 to the headquarters of the Society as the Diocesan contribution. As the total raised in the United States that year was $29,221.83, Texas contributed almost three percent of the total. The Society allocated $5,984 to Bishop Odin that year and $2,251.25 to the Texas Oblates. These two gifts exceeded the largest single grant made by the Society to the Vincentians in 1858. In this one year the Society granted $111,745.75 to dioceses and religious communities in the United States for the spread of the faith.

On 20 June 1860 Archbishop Anthony Blanc of New Orleans died. As senior suffragan of the Province Bishop Odin asked his fellow suffragans of Little Rock, Natchitoches, Natchez, and Mobile, as well as the Archbishops of Baltimore, Cincinnati, New York, Oregon City, St. Louis, and San Francisco to choose his successor. Most of them favored Odin. On 28 July the Bishop of Texas wrote to the Archbishop of Baltimore:

> I am already sixty-one years of age and begin to feel the infirmities of age. New Orleans needs a younger and more active Bishop. The material interests of Texas will suffer by my departure.

But as Archbishop John B. Purcell of Cincinnati pointed out to Bishop Odin on 6 August, the new archbishop should be of French origin to understand the French people and the particular problems of New Orleans.

Those who knew Bishop Odin well knew that he disliked leaving Texas, of which he had become so much a part. By 1861 he had established forty-five churches, had forty-six priests, a college, four academies for young ladies, and four schools for boys. There were forty-four chapels and over 100 localities with Catholic populations. He had built up Texas from the ruins of revolution and war and filled the vacuum left by the Spanish and Mexicans. The modern church in the State, in terms of its revival and institutions, was due in extremely large part to his unremitting efforts over many years.

Nevertheless the Bull of appointment as Archbishop of New Orleans was issued by Pope Pius IX on 15 February 1861 and reached the new archbishop on 19 April. At last he accepted with heavy heart and left for New Orleans at the end of May 1861. His hurt was real as he bade farewell to his clergy:

> How painful it has been to us, to separate ourselves from a people to whom we had consecrated all our affections! What a heart-rendering sacrifice. . .to leave the land of Texas to which we had devoted our life, and in which we hoped our ashes would find a resting place!

Before Archbishop Odin left Texas he appointed Rev. Louis Chambadut his administrator. He later suggested three priests as candidates to succeed him. One of them, Rev. Claude Marie Dubuis, was chosen. The Archbishop himself consecrated Bishop Dubuis in the Chapel of the Seminary in Lyon on 23 November 1862. The ceremony of consecration so inspired the seminarians that more than a dozen volunteered to go to Texas. One of them was a young subdeacon, John Anthony Forest, who would become the third bishop of San Antonio.

By 1 May 1862 federal troops occupied New Orleans. The position of the Archbishop required great diplomacy and skill as he carried out his duties as the intermediary of the Pope in the South. He continued to hold synods and issue pastoral letters indicating he allowed no abuses of church discipline. Infractions were dealt with promptly. Nevertheless the Union occupation was detrimental in disrupting religious and educational work in Thibodaux, Convent, Plaquemine, Grand Coteau and elsewhere. The cities of Pointe Coupee and Donaldsonville were damaged by the opposing federal forces.

On his return from Europe the Archbishop brought with him nearly fifty priests and seminarians to work in Louisiana and Texas. Chartering their passage on the *Ste. Genevieve*, all arrived in New Orleans on Good Friday, 3 April 1863. In that year Odin brought Marist Fathers to Louisiana.

After the War the Oblate Sisters of Providence came to the Archdiocese in 1867. They were Black nuns from Baltimore who began a home for dependent children. The Little Sisters of the Poor opened a home for the aged. Brothers of the Sacred Heart came to New Orleans from Mobile in 1869. In that year Sisters of Mercy visited the civil parish prison, the city workhouse in New Orleans, the boys' house of refuge, and the insane asylum. German Benedictines came to the Parish of Holy Trinity in the See City and nuns from Covington, Kentucky, established their motherhouse in Covington, Louisiana.

Because former slaves were made to feel somewhat unwelcome at services, the Archbishop asked religious communities to assign men and women religious to minister to them and to educate their children. But not until 1867 did St. Joseph's School in Convent, Louisiana, open under the auspices of the Religious of the Sacred Heart. And the diocesan seminary in Faubourg Boligny closed because it lacked funds.

The Archbishop accepted the invitation of Pope Pius IX to attend the eighteenth centenary of the martyrdom of St. Peter in Rome in 1867. At the Third Provincial Council of New Orleans in December 1868 he heard of the progress of Texas from Bishop Dubuis and was much gratified. Pius IX called the First Vatican Council in Rome from 8 December 1869 to 20 October 1870. The Catholic bishops of the world attended. Always cautious the aged archbishop had asked for a coadjutor before the beginning of the Council. On 1 May 1870 Napoléon Joseph Perché, the archdiocesan vicar general, was consecrated coadjutor in St. Louis Cathedral in New Orleans. The orderly succession was assured.

Archbishop Odin attended the Council in Rome. He returned to his home in France suffering from neuralgia. There in Ambierle Parish, where he was born, he died on 25 May 1870, intending to return to New Orleans. First buried in a tomb in the chapel of the Blessed Virgin, he is now buried under the stone floor of the right transept of the village church, which was built in the sixteenth century and was formerly the conventual church of a Benedictine monastery.

Such was the life of the servant of God, Jean-Marie Odin. A humble man of simple tastes, he was devout in his personal life, obedient to his superiors, and compassionate to those for whom he cared. His life was one of service and complete devotion to duty. The seventeen active bishops of Texas who visited his tomb in 1988 may well owe their positions to this one man.

At the time of his death the Catholic population of Texas was more than

100,000 in a population of 818,579. There were seventy-seven priests, fifty-five chapels or churches, three colleges, eight schools for boys, and nine academies for young ladies.

But the monument and legacy of Archbishop Odin is the Catholic Church in the State of Texas. In 1988 his beloved Diocese of Galveston, which he was compelled to leave upon his promotion, had become the fourteen dioceses of the Province of San Antonio. It extended to the boundaries of the State of Texas and was governed by an archbishop, thirteen bishops, and assisted by four auxiliary bishops. There were 3,227,019 Catholics in a total 1988 population of 16,621,406. Two thousand and thirty-seven priests, 777 permanent deacons, 240 male religious, and 3,434 women religious, were a part of 932 parishes. Seven Catholic colleges and universities instructed 14,700 students, fifty high schools had 15,057 students, and 234 elementary schools had 56,050 students. There were two major seminaries in the State and facilities and institutions designed to protect life before birth to entombment after death.

And all these things came to pass because of the labors of one devoted man who loved his adopted state. Like a patient gardener who stoops to replant a crushed acorn, with his care and that of his successors, the seed has now become a mighty oak which continues to spread its branches.

Right Reverend Anthony Dominic Ambrose Pellicer, DD
First Bishop of San Antonio

Anthony Dominic Ambrose Pellicer, the first Catholic bishop of San Antonio, was born to Francisco and Margarita (Juanada) Pellicer in St. Augustine, Saint Johns County, Florida, on 7 December 1824. Francisco Pellicer was a descendant of the Minorcans of the Balearic Islands in the western Mediterranean. As such he was of Spanish extraction. Anthony's mother died in giving birth to him and his twin brother. He was reared by Pedro and Maria Manucy, who were the parents of his third cousin Dominic Manucy. Dominic would become Vicar Apostolic of Brownsville during the time Anthony was Bishop of San Antonio.

Anthony and Dominic were boyhood students in St. Augustine and left there to attend Spring Hill College in Mobile, Alabama. Anthony taught there in 1849 and also attended St. Vincent de Paul's Seminary in New Orleans, Louisiana. Both cousins were ordained in the Cathedral of the Immaculate Conception in Mobile by Bishop Michael Portier on 15 August 1850.

Between 1850 and 1861 Father Pellicer was Pastor of St. Peter's Parish in Montgomery, Alabama. During this time he ministered at Wetumpka, Tuskegee, White Creek, and Laundesborough. In 1856 he built the mission church of St. Joseph in Camden and also Our Lady Queen of Peace in Selma. Besides constructing a rectory and schools, he found time to visit Mexico and Cuba. While in Mexico on a fund-raising expedition, his stagecoach was robbed by twelve men. Two Americans and an Irishman routed them, but he had lost his money.

During the Civil War Father Pellicer was Post Chaplain for the Confederate forces, winning 300 converts. After the conclusion of hostilities in 1865 he was assigned to the Cathedral of the Immaculate Conception in Mobile. He was a member of Bishop John Quinlan's Council until 1869. In 1867 Pellicer became Rector of the Cathedral and Vicar General of the Diocese of Mobile. He served in these two capacities until he was appointed Bishop of San Antonio. In these years he built a boys' orphanage for Mobile and contributed to the North American College in Rome.

At the recommendation of the Third Provincial Council of New Orleans and with the consultation of the cardinals involved, Pope Pius IX issued the decree *Arcano Divinae Providentiae* on 27 August 1874. Effective on 3 September 1874 the decree separated from the Diocese of Galveston "that part of the State or territory of Texas which lies between the Colorado River on the east and the Nueces River on the west." The See City was to be San Antonio and the Diocese was to be a suffragan of the Archbishop of New Orleans.

While nothing in the decree of erection specified the northern and southern boundaries of the Diocese, the southern boundary was apparently the Gulf of Mexico. An old chancery office map for the San Antonio Diocese shows a boundary beginning at the mouth of the Nueces River and running along the River to its source, thought to be near Rocksprings in Edwards County. The map line runs southwest to the confluence of the Pecos River with the Rio Grande in Val Verde County. Then it follows the Rio Grande to the southern boundary of New Mexico. Leaving out El Paso County, it continues along the southern limits of

New Mexico east to and down the Colorado River to the Gulf.

The papal Bull *In Futuram Rei Memoriam* created the Vicariate Apostolic of Brownsville on 18 September 1874. Its territory was redefined on 21 July 1877, giving the Vicariate the counties of Bee, Goliad, Aransas, Refugio, San Patricio and that part of Live Oak in the Diocese of San Antonio in compensation for which the Diocese was granted a large tract lying north of Arroyo de los Hermanos. This arroyo (creek) was a tributary of the Rio Grande. The tract included San Roque Creek, which flowed into the Nueces River. The San Antonio Diocese obtained the counties of Val Verde, Edwards, Uvalde, Zavala, Dimmit, Webb, Kinney, and Maverick. The El Paso area had been assigned to the Vicariate Apostolic of Arizona in 1869. The Diocese of San Antonio from 1877 until the creation of the Diocese of El Paso in 1914 had an estimated 90,909 square miles.

Reconstruction was ending. San Antonio had more than 12,000 inhabitants. Indian tribes north and west of the City were pacified. And in the late 1870s a railroad line extended from San Antonio to Houston. Trail drivers drove cattle from Texas to Abilene and Dodge City, Kansas.

On 2 September 1874 Pope Pius IX chose Father Pellicer as the first bishop of San Antonio. He was consecrated bishop by Archbishop Napoléon J. Perché of New Orleans in the Cathedral in Mobile on 8 December 1874. His co-consecrators were Bishop John Quinlan of Mobile and Bishop Claude M. Dubuis of Galveston.

Bishop Pellicer arrived in San Antonio on 23 December 1874 and four days later was solemnly installed in San Fernando Cathedral. The *Galveston News* reported that day that ceremonies began with a parade from St. Mary's Church to the Cathedral. The Hon. Joseph E. Dwyer was Grand Marshal. The Bishop heard an address of welcome at the cathedral entrance. He celebrated a solemn pontifical high Mass and Rev. Cornelius Moynihan, Pastor of St. Peter and St. Paul Parish in New Orleans, delivered the sermon in English. At the end of the Mass a Father Astola preached in Spanish. The Rector of the Cathedral at that time was Rev. John Claude Neraz, who succeeded Bishop Pellicer. Sisters of the Incarnate Word held a banquet for the Bishop, the clergy, and their guests in Santa Rosa Hospital opposite Military Plaza.

The Bishop set out on horseback with Father Felix X. Zwiardowski to tour his diocese in 1875. Ceremony was set aside and the two men rode by day and slept out under the stars at night. This tour was a prelude of the problems and journeys with their difficulties which soon weakened the health of the Bishop.

At the end of 1875 Bishop Pellicer sent a report to the Paris headquarters of the Society for the Propagation of the Faith. Thirty thousand Catholics were served by thirty-three missionaries and one native-born priest. Father Thomas J. Johnston. There were forty-one churches, seven chapels, forty-four missions, and eighteen schools. San Antonio had one seminary, one college, one hospital, and one orphanage. The episcopal residence was at St. Mary's Church in San Antonio. Parishes were "national" with St. Mary's for the Irish, St. Joseph's for the Germans, San Fernando for Hispanics, and St. Michael's for the Polish. In this way were the parochial needs of the City's 13,000 churchgoers served.

The Sisters of Charity of the Incarnate Word had their motherhouse in San Antonio, while the Sisters of Divine Providence had headquarters in Castroville.

The Society of Mary conducted St. Mary's College. The Ursuline Nuns staffed an academy for girls, while Resurrectionist Fathers served parishes inside and outside the See City. Jesuit priests from Mexico served the old Spanish missions and had a seminary in San Antonio and later in Seguin (1876 to 1881) before they returned to Mexico. So was the San Antonio diocese upon the advent of the first bishop.

Fortunately Bishop Pellicer was no stranger to hard work. In 1875 he ordained the first of ten priests, Rev. Thomas Korbulowcks. He asked the Incarnate Word Sisters to open a school in San Fernando parish and brought them postulants from Alabama and Louisiana. In September he visited Victoria and found St. Mary's Parish serving missions of Meyersville and Garcitas. He dedicated the new church of Our Lady of Lourdes for the German-speaking, appointing Rev. Jean B. Teiten its first pastor. Rev. Augustus Gardet had built a brick church in Victoria, organized Nazareth Academy for girls with the Sisters of the Incarnate Word and Blessed Sacrament, and built St. Joseph's Academy for boys in 1867 and 1868.

Churches outside of San Antonio and Victoria served a number of missions. St. Louis in Castroville had Quihi, D'Hanis, Uvalde, Haby Creek, and Sauz Creek. St. Mary in Fredericksburg provided for Ben Ficklin, Fort Concho, Fort McKavett, Menardville, and Fort Mason. Sts. Peter and Paul in New Braunfels aided Blanco, Honey Creek, San Marcos, Walzem and Wenzel. Immaculate Conception in Panna Maria supported Yorktown, St. Hedwig, and Bandera. St. Joseph in Indianola benefitted Port Lavaca, Cuero, and Texana. St. Mary in Austin took care of Taylor, Temple, and the stations between those towns. Our Lady of Refugio looked after Don Carlos Ranch, Fagan Station, Fulton, Rockport, St. Mary's on Copano Bay, Lamar, and Goliad. St. Mary's at High Hill sustained Cistern, Columbus, and Sandy Creek. San Patricio ministered to Aransas, Beeville, Gussettville, and Papalote.

Parish churches had to be flexible. Besides missions churches like the one at Fredericksburg served some "localities." Father M. Perier at Fort Stockton had as his charges the area military posts and "a number of distant stations." And Father Emilium Chapolard was assigned Las Gallinas "with several missions."

Central to the development of the Diocese were its educational institutions. Various religious communities of women operated them. The Incarnate Word Sisters taught orphan girls at St. Joseph's Orphanage. The Congregation of Divine Providence had a school at St. Joseph's, as well as in Castroville, Fredericksburg, and New Braunfels. The Sisters of the Immaculate Conception had a school at St. Michael's and in Panna Maria and St. Hedwig. Sisters of the Incarnate Word and Blessed Sacrament were in Victoria. Sisters of the Holy Cross had a parish school in 1874 that would become St. Mary's Academy in Austin. In 1875 the Sisters of Mary made their first permanent Texas foundation in Refugio. But the Sisters of the Immaculate Conception (Blue Nuns) later discontinued work in the Diocese. There were six other congregations whose work led to future developments.

Of present importance were the churches and missions of the Diocese. In 1875 St. Mary's Parish at High Hill in Fayette County erected a new church. The old one was turned into a school. At Indianola in Calhoun County the

Church of St. Joseph's was damaged by a storm. It was rebuilt and a private school was opened by Incarnate Word Sisters in 1878. But storms of 1882 and 1886 led to the abandonment of the church and the town.

In 1876 the new church of the Assumption of the Blessed Virgin Mary was built at Praha. Missions were founded at Meyersville, Cuero, and Bandera. The Immaculate Conception Church in Panna Maria was damaged by lightning in 1877 but rebuilt and dedicated on 10 February 1878. Bishop Pellicer also dedicated the new Church of the Nativity of Our Lady of Cestohowa in Karnes County.

Bishop Pellicer went to Rome to visit Pope Pius IX in 1876. The frugal prelate had done good work and gave the promise of doing more. His eventual successors were already well-placed. Rev. John C. Neraz was Rector of San Fernando Cathedral, Vicar General of the Diocese, and chaplain to Santa Rosa Infirmary. Rev. John A. Forest was Pastor of St. Mary's Parish near Hallettsville. He had built St. Joseph's Church at Brushy Creek before 1875 and spent time in the mission at Yellow Bank while constructing a new church in Hallettsville.

Father Augustus Gardet was in Victoria and Father Johnston was Chancellor of the Diocese. The Bishop's Council in 1877 included the Vicar General, the Chancellor, and Fathers Nicholas Feltin, Stephen Buffard, Peter Richard, Henry Pefferkorn, and X. S. Wojciechowski.

On 19 February 1877 the Southern Pacific Railroad came to San Antonio. It expanded commerce and communication and eased the restrictions of missionary travel. On 30 November 1877 Bishop Pellicer sold that part of the Alamo mission known as the ''convent building," where many Alamo heroes had died. The buyer was Honoré Grenet and the sale price was $19,000. Bishop John Claude Neraz sold the rest of the property to the State of Texas in May 1883.

Bishop Pellicer, whose name means "shovel maker" and whose motto was "I live in faith," was not a man of robust health. He suffered from diabetes, which became worse in 1879. He sought treatment in Waukesha, Wisconsin, but it did not avail. He died in San Antonio on 14 April 1880. His body lay in state in St. Mary's Church and his funeral was attended by religious and civic leaders and citizens of all faiths. His requiem Mass was celebrated by his cousin, Bishop Dominic Manucy of Brownsville. He was buried in the nave of San Fernando Cathedral in San Antonio, under the floor before the main altar.

The founding bishop established at least twenty-five churches and twenty-seven schools in his diocese. At his death there were thirty-eight priests and six seminarians to minister to fifty churches, eight chapels, and a Catholic population of 47,000. There were two colleges, two academies, twenty-five parochial schools, St. Joseph's Orphanage for girls and Santa Rosa Infirmary.

In 1988 the area of the Archdiocese of San Antonio had shrunk from 90,909 square miles to 27,841. The Archbishop had one auxiliary bishop with another being assigned to him. There were 386 priests, 166 permanent deacons, 125 male religious and 1,094 female religious to serve the Catholic population of 577,721. There were 135 parishes, forty missions, and three pastoral centers. The institutions of the Archdioceses included three Catholic hospitals, five dispensaries, six homes for special care, an orphanage and child welfare center, five nurseries, two protection of life and family centers, a special social center, a diocesan major seminary, four colleges and universities, ten high schools, and fifty elementary schools. Such is the legacy of Bishop Pellicer.

Most Reverend Raymundo Joseph Peña, DD
Titular Bishop of Trisipa and Auxiliary Bishop of San Antonio
Fourth Bishop of El Paso
Fifth Bishop of Brownsville

Raymundo Joseph Peña is a bishop who rose to the episcopal rank through his ability to work well with others to achieve significant goals and his experience in a wide variety of duties. He continues to play an important role through his activity in the national bishops' conference.

The future bishop was born to Cosme A. and Elisa (Ramon) Peña in Corpus Christi, Nueces County, Texas on 19 February 1934. He grew up in nearby Robstown and attended its schools. Graduating from St. John's and Assumption seminaries in San Antonio, Texas, he was ordained to the priesthood for the Diocese of Corpus Christi in Corpus Christi on 25 May 1957. His first assignment was assistant pastor of St. Peter the Apostle Church in Laredo, Webb County, one of fifteen parish churches in this border city with Mexico, from 1957 to 1960. He was then assigned to St. Joseph-Our Lady of Fatima Mission Church in Alamo, Hidalgo County, from 1960 to 1963. This parish, founded in 1926, is now known as Resurrection, and it has been part of the Diocese of Brownsville since 1965. His third assignment was Sacred Heart Parish in Mathis, San Patricio County, from 1963 to 1967. Here he was the founding president of the Mathis Community Action Agency.

Between 1967 and 1969 Father Peña was assistant pastor of Christ the King and Our Lady of the Pillar parishes. He was also diocesan youth director (1967-1970), a diocesan consultor (1968-1976), and a member of the Corpus Christi Economic Development Corporation Board (1968-1974).

As Pastor of Our Lady of Guadalupe Parish in Corpus Christi from 1969 to 1976, which he helped found, Father Peña was Vice-President of the Nueces County Child Welfare Board (1969-1972) and the Associate Editor of *Texas Gulf Coast Catholic* (1970-1975), now the *South Texas Catholic*. He became Vice-President of the Diocesan Senate of Priests in 1970 and Director of the Department of Mexican-American Affairs and Prosynodal Judge in 1971. During 1972 he was a member of the Goals for Corpus Christi Committee. Next year he became a member of the Liturgical Commission and the Corpus Christi Seminary Clergy Board. In 1974 he joined the board of the Nueces County Mental Health-Mental Retardation Community Center and became a member of the National Committee of the Campaign for Human Development.

This record of accomplishment impressed the Vatican. Father Peña was appointed Titular Bishop of Trisipa and Auxiliary Bishop of San Antonio by Pope Paul VI on 16 October 1976. His episcopal ordination took place on the following 13 December. Under Archbishop Francis J. Furey of San Antonio Bishop Peña was Vicar General, an archdiocesan consultor, and Executive Director of the Office of the Laity from 1977 to 1980. He was also a member of the board of the Ecumenical Council of Churches for the Archdiocese of San Antonio and a charter member of the advisory council of the Family Life Center at St. Mary's University and of the advisory council of Villa Rosa Hospital. He was Vice-Chairman (1977) and Chairman (1978) of the Region X office for

Hispanic Affairs of the National Conference of Catholic Bishops (NCCB)-United States Catholic Conference (USCC). In 1979 he was Vice-President of the Texas Conference of Churches (until 1981) and a member of the Ad Hoc Committee on Evangelization of the NCCB (until 1984). Following the death of Archbishop Furey on 23 April 1979, Bishop Peña's fellow consultors elected him administrator of the Archdiocese of San Antonio. He remained in this position until the installation of Archbishop Patrick F. Flores on 13 October 1979. Peña followed Flores as bishop of El Paso when Pope John Paul II appointed him to that position on 29 April 1980. Archbishop Robert F. Sanchez installed Bishop Peña in St. Patrick's Cathedral in El Paso on 18 June 1980. The NCCB elected the new bishop a member of committees on the Parish and on Vocations, and he was a member of the board of the National Shrine of the Immaculate Conception in Washington, DC, from 1981 to 1984.

At the requests of Archbishop Sanchez of Santa Fe and Archbishop Flores of San Antonio, the New Mexican counties of Doña Ana, Eddy, Grant, Hidalgo, Lea, Luna, Otero, and the part of Sierra lying South of the 33° of the north latitude, an area of 30,617 square miles, were separated from the Diocese of El Paso. All of these counties plus those of Lincoln and Chaves in New Mexico now make up the Diocese of Las Cruces, established on 18 October 1982, an area of 44,483 square miles. The remaining Texas counties of El Paso, Brewster, Culberson, Hudspeth, Jeff Davis, Loving, Presidio, Reeves, Ward, and Winkler, an area of 26,686 square miles, are now a part of the Province of San Antonio.

Continuing active in the NCCB Bishop Peña became the Chairman of the Committee for Hispanic Affairs and a member of the Committee on Migration (1987-1990). He was also a member of the Pastoral Response to the Challenge of Proselytism Committee (1988) and served a three-year term as Chairman of the Committee on the Church in Latin America to 1994. He was also on the USCC Committee on Communications, the State Chaplain for Texas of the Knights of Columbus, and became a member of PADRES (*Padres Asociados para Derechos Religiosos Educativos y Sociales*). He was President of the board of the Mexican American Cultural Center in San Antonio from 1983 to 1987. And on 25 October 1987 he was invested as a Knight of the Equestrian Order of the Holy Sepulchre in St. Michael's Church in Houston, Texas.

No stranger to controversy, Bishop Peña is resolute in behalf of programs and policies which he believes will best aid the people of his diocese. He does not seek confrontation but to involve constituent groups in the process which concerns them. Thus he opposed the United States Border Patrol Chief Sylvester Reyes in El Paso when Reyes supported "Operation Hold the Line," in which border patrol agents would stand along the El Paso area border 400 yards apart in an effort to prevent illegal immigration. The Bishop felt this plan would adversely affect those crossing the border daily for their employment. He urged a boycott on United Way contributions, because he felt that organization's support of Planned Parenthood might indirectly fund abortions. He endorsed publicly the El Paso Interreligious Sponsoring Organization (EPISO), an ecumenical association thought by some people to be too radical.

The El Paso and Ciudad Juarez border dispute was an especially troubling one. Bishop Peña wanted a moratorium for up to a year starting in October 1993 on the Immigration and Naturalization Service efforts while officials would work to ease immigration controls. He was joined by Bishop Ricardo Ramirez, CSB and by Bishop Juan Sandoval Iniguez of Ciudad Juarez. They felt that curtailing crime would be vastly overshadowed by the damage to workers.

At this time Bishop Peña reiterated a statement he had made in 1985: "Our concern is not to support any particular effort that assists immigrants or refugees, but to help people in need in the tradition of the church's ministry." This stance means that the Church should help immigrants with their physical and spiritual problems regardless of their origin or political beliefs.

Emotions descended from opposition of policies to personalities when Sr. Rose Michael Jbara, SL, a Religious stationed in El Paso began to accuse the Bishop of incompetence in his clergy appointments and in his financial handling of the Diocese. When the Bishop at length ordered her to leave the Diocese, she left temporarily but defied his authority by returning. Nevertheless the Bishop, as a national leader whose programs affect many people worldwide, continued to have the full support of the Vatican. And his record as bishop of El Paso is one of superior achievement, to such a degree that he has been advanced to bishop of Brownsville.

As bishop of El Paso Peña reorganized the diocesan clergy to provide greater service to parishioners. He established eleven new parishes, constructed six new churches, erected nine parish halls, and provided seven catechist and parochial school centers. He restored three historic missions and five historic parish churches. His Tepeyac Institute has been nationally acclaimed for its training of lay people in church leadership. He oversaw a major expansion of Cathedral High School and instituted the concept of long-range planning in parishes. In his fifteen years as bishop of El Paso he put the Diocese on a better financial footing and raised the level of annual contributions from $200 thousand to $2 million.

At the beginning of 1995 the Diocese of El Paso had sixty-eight active diocesan priests and forty-seven Religious order priests, eighteen permanent deacons, fifteen male Religious, and 245 women Religious. There were fifty-eight parishes, twenty-two missions, a health care center, two homes for the aged, two day care and extended day care centers, a specialized home, and five special centers for social services. There were two religious seminaries, three high schools, twelve elementary schools, and 21,116 students under Catholic instruction. There were 516,725 Catholics in a total population of 725,242 or 71 percent.

On 23 May 1995 Pope John Paul II appointed Bishop Peña bishop of Brownsville. That day in a press conference at the Valley International airport in Harlingen, Texas, the Bishop said: "I am grateful to Pope John Paul II for his recognition of the work the clergy, religious and parishioners have accomplished with me in the Diocese of El Paso." He added that serving in Brownsville would be a challenge but one that he was eager to undertake. "I am happy to come home to South Texas. I feel singularly blessed to be the first South Texan to serve as your bishop." On 12 June 1995 Pope John Paul II announced that there would be a Pan American Synod of Bishops, in which bishops from fourteen countries in the Western Hemisphere and two Vatican officials would participate. Bishop Peña was named to a pre-synodal council to prepare for this event.

Coming to the Diocese of Brownsville, the Bishop could anticipate his new situation. El Paso has a population of some 650,000 people, of whom about

72 percent are Hispanic, compared to Brownsville with some 117,000 people, of whom about 91 percent are Hispanic. Almost half of Brownsville's residential families make less than a level of $8,076 for a family of two and $9,885 for a family of three, poverty levels defined by the Greater Washington Research Center. And there are immigration problems common to both border cities and *colonias,* poor districts in each city.

At the Virgen de San Juan del Valle Shrine in San Juan, Hidalgo County, Archbishop Patrick F. Flores presided over the installation of Bishop Peña on 6 August 1995. This ceremony would officially establish him as the fifth bishop of a diocese created on 10 July 1965. It is 4,226 square miles in area and consists of the Texas counties of Cameron, Hidalgo, Starr, and Willacy. But it contains one of the largest concentrations of Catholics in the United States.

Archbishop Agostino Cacciavillan, Apostolic Pro-Nuncio of the Holy See to the United States, was there. So were two cardinals, nineteen bishops of Texas and other states, and 200 priests. There were about 5,000 onlookers. Bishop Peña praised the Pope for allowing him to serve people "with whom I grew up, the people who nurtured my young priesthood, the people whom I love almost as much as I love the people of El Paso." He had said that his first goal would be to enhance "the quality of our faith and the quality of life in our beloved Valley." Brownsville Mayor Henry Gonzales and United States Magistrate Reynaldo Garza hoped that it could be possible. Certainly the relationship between Bishop Peña and Bishop Fitzpatrick, the only surviving former bishop of Brownsville, was cordial. A high point of the ceremony was the Bishop's introduction of his parents, who lived with him in El Paso and who accompanied him to Brownsville. He thanked them for his life and support and said, ''I am privileged to introduce them to you as your *abuelitos* [grandparents]."

The Diocese of Brownsville in early 1995 had a retired bishop, thirty-eight active diocesan priests, fifty-four Religious order priests, eighty-three permanent deacons, fifteen male Religious, and 146 women Religious. There were sixty-one parishes with forty-seven missions, a health care center, two homes for the aged, a day care and extended day care center, three special centers for social services, two other institutions, a high school, seven elementary schools, and 40,982 students under Catholic instruction. There was a Catholic population of 669,605 Catholics in a total population of 829,359, or 81 percent.

On 7 August 1995 nearly fifty priests from El Paso, San Antonio, Corpus Christi, and the Rio Grande Valley came to Immaculate Conception Cathedral in Brownsville to attend the new bishop's first Mass. Many people came to get a look at Bishop Peña, who had written to his new parishioners, "I am committed to build up the Kingdom and transform this valley into a magic valley for all its residents."

In one sense this new assignment was the homecoming of a man expressing a fond wish for his people. But no one acquainted with Bishop Peña's record of achievement would imagine it was beyond his ability. A quiet, soft-spoken man who rarely has time to read a book, watch a film, or listen to *ranchero* music, he likes to fish, garden, and collect nativity scenes, of which he has more than seventy-five. Bishop Peña, whose Spanish surname means "peak," takes for his motto "*Haz Todo Con Amor*" ("To Do All Things In Love"). And this he tries to do always.

Most Reverend Michael David Pfeifer, OMI, DD
Fifth Bishop of San Angelo

Before the appointments of Francis E. George to Yakima, Washington, and Roger L. Schwietz to Duluth, Minnesota, in 1990, Michael David Pfeifer of San Angelo alone represented the Missionary Oblates of Mary Immaculate in the hierarchy of the United States of America. This order was founded by Bl. Charles Joseph Eugene de Mazenod in France in 1816. Its headquarters are in Rome, with the United States Consulate of the Order in Oakland, California. The first Oblates came to Texas in 1849. There are five American provinces, of which the Southern Province was established in San Antonio, Texas, in 1904. The other four provinces are in Washington, DC, New Hampshire, Minnesota, and in California.

Michael David Pfeifer was born to Francis and Alice (Savage) Pfeifer in Alamo, Hidalgo County, Texas, on 18 May 1937. He was the eighth of nine children in a family of two sons and seven daughters. His only brother Frank Theodore is a priest of the Oblates of Mary Immaculate. After attending St. Joseph's School in Alamo, Michael studied at St. Anthony High School Seminary in San Antonio.

St. Anthony's was founded by the Oblate Fathers as San Antonio Philosophical and Theological Seminary in the Laurel Heights area of the City in 1903. It also served diocesan seminarians until 1915. A minor seminary department was added in 1905, with the last of the lay students leaving after 1915. In 1920 the Oblate major seminarians were transferred first to Castroville and then to the new De Mazenod Scholasticate on the northern outskirts of San Antonio. New construction in 1936 and in 1949 expanded facilities. In 1961 a new chapel and separate classroom building were completed. In 1959 college level seminarians took courses at St. Mary's University in San Antonio, but continued to live on campus until 1972. At this time a residence hall was established on the campus of the University of Dallas in Irving, Texas.

After completing the course of study the young seminarian made his first profession of solemn vows as an Oblate of Mary Immaculate at St. Peter's Novitiate in Mission, Texas, on 30 May 1957. He afterward completed further studies at the De Mazenod Scholasticate in San Antonio, known since 1962 as the Oblate College of the Southwest.

This institution had its beginnings in the St. Anthony High School Seminary. It was moved to Castroville in 1920, when it became known as Sacred Heart Scholasticate. It was established in its present location on 285 Oblate Drive in north San Antonio in 1927. It is also for Claretian and Holy Spirit religious congregations. It offers a Master of Divinity degree program of three years, integrated with field experiences. These activities include professionally supervised social work, counseling, and parish internship. The College staff is augmented with visiting lecturers. In 1974 it had a library of 31,000 volumes and 570 periodicals. It offers continuing education for the clergy, the Master of Divinity degree, pastoral workshops, and short courses in theology. There are programs for the religious and the laity. The College has a broadcast and instructional program operated by a full-time staff. It supplies videotapes for instructional use, programs for marriage preparation courses, Confraternity of Christian Doctrine teacher-training tapes, and self-administered seminars.

Michael made his final profession of vows on 7 September 1961 and was ordained Deacon on 30 May 1964. The Reverend Mister Pfeifer was ordained to the priesthood by Auxiliary Bishop Stephen A. Leven of San Antonio in the Oblate Major Seminary chapel in San Antonio on 21 December 1964. Father Pfeifer received the degree of Master of Divinity from the Oblate College of the Southwest in 1965.

At first assigned to Mexico City, Mexico, from July 1965 to August 1967, Father Pfeifer served as director of primary grades at the Colegio Vista Hermosa and was bursar at La Purisima Seminary. From September through December 1967 he was Associate Pastor of St. Patrick's Parish in Houston, Texas. He served his first term as Mission Procurator for the Mexico Delegation of Oblates of Mary Immaculate in January 1968. After serving as Associate Pastor of Our Lady of Guadalupe Parish in Brownsville, Texas, from February through July 1968, he was again Mission Procurator for Oblates in Mexico from August 1969 through May 1975. He was stationed at J. G. Icazbalceta College in San Rafael, Mexico.

For the month of June 1975 Father Pfeifer was Director of the Mary Immaculate League in Mexico City. From July 1975 through June 1981 he was Vicar Provincial of the Mexico Delegation of the Oblates of Mary Immaculate in Mexico City. He then became Provincial of the Southern United States Province of the Order from July 1981 to July 1985. This province includes the Southern United States, Mexico, and Zambia.

On 1 January 1984 the Very Reverend Pfeifer was assisted by a Vicar Provincial, seven consultors, a bursar, and an administrative assistant and secretary to the Council. The Southern Province with headquarters in San Antonio included 220 priests, ten brothers, six novices, and six scholastics, with sixty-one parishes and 121 missions attached. Three religious houses and fifty-two religious residences served the Archdioceses of Denver, Mexico City, New Orleans, and San Antonio, as well as the Dioceses of Austin, Baton Rouge, Beaumont, Brownsville, Galveston-Houston, San Angelo, Corpus Christi, and Dallas. The Provincial was also Chairman of the Board of Trustees of the Oblate College of the Southwest.

On 4 January 1984 the Southern Province began mission activities in Lukulu Province of the Republic of Zambia. Although Zambia enjoys full diplomatic relations with the Vatican, only about thirty percent of its population are Catholics, according to the *Statistical Yearbook of the Church, 1986*. Animism is the predominant faith of the people with Hindu, Protestant, and Muslim minorities. Catholicism was introduced into the country by Portuguese priests in the sixteenth century, but most advances in conversions have come after the Second World War.

The mission area chosen by the Oblates was thirty-six villages covering territory about 100 miles long and 100 miles wide on the eastern side of the Zambezi River to the border of Angola. According to Father Pfeifer, who visited in 1985, the Lozi people have a native religion which is a mixture of "spiritualism and superstition in which witches play an important part in the life of the village." Of the four original missionaries one died. The remaining priests learned to say Mass and prayers in the Lozi dialect to seven or eight thousand Christians among 52,000 people.

Father Pfeifer noted the poverty and illnesses of the people of Lukulu Province, who are particularly subject to malaria, tuberculosis, and leprosy. Weather problems affect life, and the people need help in medicine, agriculture, and education. Huge snakes and crocodiles take their toll of the people as well.

On 4 June 1985 Pope John Paul II appointed Father Pfeifer Bishop of San Angelo. The new bishop stated:

> I feel overwhelmed, very humble. I do feel it a call from the Lord to serve His people in this ministry as bishop. I do appreciate the trust and confidence the Holy Father has placed in me by naming me to be the principal shepherd of the Diocese of San Angelo.

In a statement reported in Spanish in *El Visitante Dominical* of San Antonio on 23 June 1985, a month before his ordination, Bishop Pfeifer expressed his trust in God, his thanks for the kindness and support of Archbishop Flores and for the good example of leadership and dedication set by his immediate predecessor, Bishop Joseph Fiorenza.

> He expressed his intention to all within the Diocese of San Angelo to collaborate with you all in building and extending the Kingdom of Christ through participation and dialogue and in a spirit of beginning, trust and love. [I hope] that all together we can work with our civic and governmental leaders on all levels, to promote one society built upon truth, justice and peace.

The Bishop wanted to work with those most in need, the poor, the neglected, the unemployed, the homeless, the stranger, and the refugee.

In a special greeting to the Hispanic people of the Diocese he expressed his pleasure in being among them and being allowed to serve them as bishop. He thanked his family, relatives and friends for their love and support, as well as his religious community. "In my heart I shall always be an Oblate Missionary priest. I have found my greatest fulfillment in the mission." He regretted leaving his position of Provincial of the Southern Province of the Oblates of Mary Immaculate. "But I accept this as the will of God and as the call of the Church." He concluded by praying for patience, understanding, support, and wisdom and asked for the prayers of the people.

Bishop Pfeifer was ordained bishop by Archbishop Patrick F. Flores of San Antonio in the San Angelo Coliseum in San Angelo on 26 July 1985. His co-consecrators were Bishops Joseph Fiorenza of Galveston-Houston and John Fitzpatrick of Brownsville. Archbishop Pio Laghi, the apostolic pro-nuncio to the United States, attended the ordination and bilingual Mass, as did more than twenty-one American bishops and more than 200 priests in a congregation of over 4,000 people.

At 11:30 A.M. that day the new bishop was installed in Sacred Heart Cathedral in San Angelo by Bishop Fiorenza, Father Timothy Murphy, administrator of the Diocese since 18 February 1985, and the diocesan consultors. Father Larry Droll, Diocesan Chancellor and Cathedral Rector, read the mandate of appointment and Father Murphy gave an official welcome. Bishop Pfeifer made a profession of faith with promises of loyalty to the Holy See, and his mitre, crozier, and ring were blessed. Midday prayer followed with the new bishop speaking. Luncheon was served at the Sheraton Hotel where Archbishop Laghi was greeted and spoke briefly.

On 1 January 1985 the Diocese of San Angelo had twenty-nine counties in a 37,433 square mile area. It had fifty-eight diocesan priests, thirty-four religious order priests, fifty permanent deacons, forty-eight women religious, forty-eight parishes, twenty-five missions, sixteen seminarians, three elementary schools, and a general hospital among its personnel and institutions. There were 72,000 Catholics of 604,958 in the total population.

On 10 October 1985 Bishop Pfeifer with Revs. Maurice Voity and Robert Kelly travelled to Mexico City. The Bishop presented Auxiliary Bishop Ricardo Watty Urquidi, MSpS, of Mexico City with a check for $26,000 from the Diocese of San Angelo and another check for $16,000 from the Diocese of Lubbock. He presented a check to the Oblate community for $26,000 from the people of the Diocese of San Angelo. These funds were given to church leaders in Mexico to aid the victims of a devastating earthquake in Mexico City.

On 26 October 1986 Bishop Pfeifer was invested as a Knight of the Equestrian Order of the Holy Sepulchre of Jerusalem in Corpus Christi Cathedral in Corpus Christi, Texas. Five days later he issued a pastoral letter titled "The Freedom of Catholics and Official Church Teaching," published in the *West Texas Angelus*, the official diocesan newspaper for the Diocese of San Angelo.

The letter urged Catholics to seek answers by listening carefully to church teaching on moral questions. The Bishop stated that the official teaching of the Pope "in union with the other bishops is without a doubt the best guidance for arriving at truth." Teachings from Vatican congregations are official in that they are addressed to the whole church and should be part of the formation of conscience of any member of the Church.

Official teaching can not lead Catholics astray. Until the teaching is final, it should be open to ongoing exploration and revision of the teaching. When the work of theologians leads in seemingly contradictory directions to the stated teachings, church authorities can demand the theologian in question cease to publish views for the sake of unity and peace of the Church. This does not resolve the question in making a final judgment. The Bishop advised prayer, study, reflection, and consultation in seeking aid for moral dilemmas.

Like many other bishops Bishop Pfeifer concerns himself with the shortage of vocations for the priesthood and its effect on ministry. On 18 February 1992 he presented a seminar on "Priestless Sundays" attended by some 350 people at Holy Angels Parish in San Angelo. Bishop Pfeifer presented Bishop Sheehan of Lubbock, chairman of a special task force of the national bishops' conference to deal with priestless Sunday celebrations. Stress was placed on regular Sunday worship, with the importance of the prayer community taking part with a ritual book for such services. The selection and training for such ministry was deemed important, in keeping with its substitutional nature. If a Eucharistic celebration is not possible, it is still necessary to provide the ministries of religious education, youth, and care of the sick and elderly. The book featured two types of celebrations: 1) Morning and Evening Prayer with reception of Holy Communion and 2) The Service of the Word of God with reception of Communion, which Bishop Sheehan felt was an integral part of the service.

In another situation Bishop Pfeifer was glad not to be chosen in 1992 as the bishops' conference chairman of the Women in Society and in the Church Committee. Bishop John J. Snyder of St. Augustine, Florida, was chosen instead. After nine years of effort the pastoral letter on women had reached the fourth draft. It was rejected by a vote of 163 to 110. Bishop Pfeifer felt that such issues as patriarchy, sexism, and feminism were not being properly addressed. He agreed with the Pope concerning the ban of priestly ordination for women but wanted a "frank and open discussion" of the issues in the progress toward ultimate unity.

In 1994 the Bishop issued a sexual abuse policy concerning all church personnel. He had developed a written procedure for priests as early as 1987. The new policy covered sisters, deacons. employees and volunteer workers in the Diocese of San Angelo as well. Though the policy was being implemented in pre-need, it made clear that sexual misconduct by any person working for the Church would not "under any circumstances be tolerated." All to whom the policy applies are to obey church law and those of community, state, and federal government in such matters. The Diocese will work with civil authorities to inform and to cooperate with them. Bishop Pfeifer had previously conducted seminars and workshops on child abuse and the issue of celibacy among Roman Catholic priests.

In early 1995 the Diocese of San Angelo had thirty-one active diocesan priests and twenty-three Religious order priests, thirty-nine permanent deacons, and forty-eight women Religious. There were forty-nine parishes and twenty-four missions, with thirty-nine parishes having resident pastors. There were three elementary schools and a diocesan total of 14,427 students under Catholic instruction. In this diocese of twenty-nine Texas counties with an area of 37,433 square miles, the Catholic population was 78,850 in a total population of 674,500, or 12 percent.

Also in 1995 the Diocese of San Angelo established its own web site on the Internet, an expanding computer network, with information about the location of the Diocese, Bishop Pfeifer, and a list of diocesan parishes and missions, complete with location, telephone numbers, and Sunday Mass schedules. With an on-line edition of the *West Texas Angelus* diocesan newspaper, subscribers can access the site using this address: http://home.navisoft.com/sanangelo. The electronic edition is to be updated with each new printed edition. Future listings will contain names of priests, religious and pastoral ministers, a diocesan calendar and perhaps special divisions for diocesan ministries. The *NC Catholic* for the Diocese of Raleigh, North Carolina, is thought to be the first such paper to be accessed by Internet subscribers.

The bilingual bishop of San Angelo is a modern missionary who keeps fit by jogging. His German name means "piper" and his episcopal motto is "*Christo Et Populo Per Mariam*" ("For Christ and His People Through Mary"). After almost 150 years in Texas the oblates have a native Texan in its hierarchy.

Most Reverend Bernard F. Popp, DD
Titular Bishop of Capsus and
Auxiliary Bishop of San Antonio

Born in Nada, Colorado County, Texas, Bernard F. Popp is the second native of this city to become an auxiliary bishop of San Antonio. The first was Hugo M. Gerbermann, MM, born on 11 September 1913. Both men attended St. John's Seminary and were ordained only seventeen days apart.

Born on 6 December 1917 Bernard is the son of Ferdinand, Jr. and Anna (Staff) Popp. A second generation German-American, he was the third child in a family of three boys and four girls. He was educated in St. Mary School (Nada), Nada High School, and Draughton's Business College. From 1936 to 1943 he attended St. John's Seminary in San Antonio. He also received the degree of Master of Arts in Theology from St. Mary's University in San Antonio in 1974.

The Reverend Mister Popp was ordained by Archbishop Robert E. Lucey, for the Archdiocese of San Antonio, in San Fernando Cathedral in San Antonio, on 24 February 1943. For the first thirteen years of his priesthood he was an associate pastor in San Antonio churches. He served in St. Agnes Parish (1943-1945), St. Joseph's Parish (1945-1948), St. Patrick's Parish (1948-1949), and St. Mary Magdalen Parish (1949-1956).

Father Popp was Secretary to Archbishop Lucey from 1945 to 1967. Pope Pius XII appointed him a Papal Chamberlain, with the title of Very Reverend Monsignor, on 10 May 1954. Monsignor Popp. became Pastor of St. Mary Magdalen Parish in 1956 and held this appointment until 1964. On 28 April 1961 Pope John XXIII appointed him a Domestic Prelate, with the title of Right Reverend Monsignor.

St. Mary Magdalen Parish in San Antonio began in the Los Angeles Heights area with territory taken from St. Ann's Parish in 1940. During Father Popp's association with the Parish a new rectory and school structure were erected in 1949. In 1954 the present convent was built. Later a three-story classroom structure was added to the school. The present church was dedicated in 1960. Territory was taken from St. Mary Magdalen's in 1954 to establish St. Gregory's Parish. Ten years later Monsignor Popp was appointed to establish the new Parish of the Holy Spirit.

Holy Spirit Parish in San Antonio was formally erected by Archbishop Lucey on 12 August 1964. It was formed from territory taken from St. Mary Magdalen and Blessed Sacrament parishes. Monsignor Popp was Pastor from 1964 to 1967. He arranged with the Sisters at Mount Sacred Heart to offer services in the convent chapel during the early days of the parish. The first structure on the eight-and-one-half acre tract was an all-purpose building dedicated on 22 November 1964. There were five hundred families in the congregation. Holy Spirit School opened in August 1965 with Sisters of St. Benedict of Boerne as the nucleus of the staff. In August 1966 Auxiliary Bishop Stephen A. Leven blessed the new rectory and new school building.

In 1967 Monsignor Popp became an Archdiocesan Consultor and moved to Victoria, Texas. There he was Pastor of St. Mary's Parish and Dean of the

Victoria Deanery. This historic parish dates from a log church ordered built by Don Martin de Leon, a Mexican colonizer of Texas, in 1824. The building was completed in 1830 but, as most Mexican families in the area, returned to Mexico after 1836, the chapel served as a barracks, a courthouse, and as a Presbyterian church.

In 1840 Father Jean-Marie Odin, CM, reclaimed the chapel and installed Father Eudaldus Estany, CM, as its first resident pastor under the name of Our Lady of Guadalupe. After awhile it became known as St. Mary's. It is the first Catholic church canonically erected in the Republic of Texas. A new brick church was built in 1863 at the corner of Bridge and Church Streets on land donated by the widow of Don Martin de Leon.

Father Augustus Gardet, pastor from 1856 to 1891, brought Sisters of the Incarnate Word and Blessed Sacrament from Brownsville in 1866. He gave them his house at Main and Church Streets for their convent and girls' school. In 1868 Father Gardet founded St. Joseph's School for boys and in 1880 expanded it to include a short-lived seminary. The present church was begun in 1902 and dedicated in 1904 at the corner of Main and Church Streets. Monsignor Frederick O. Beck, pastor from 1941 to 1967, built St. Mary's Hall in 1949, completely remodeled the church in 1954, and built the present rectory in 1959.

Back in San Antonio in September 1968 Monsignor Popp was a Pro-Synodal Judge of the Archdiocesan Tribunal and was Pastor of St. Paul's Parish until June 1978. St. Paul's was formed from the northwest section of St. Ann's Parish at the intersection of St. Cloud Road and Sutton Drive. Permission was given to build a combination chapel-school structure with the promise of the Brigidine Sisters in Ireland to staff the school. The Brigidine convent began in 1953, the year the Sisters arrived. There were a new church and a school in 1954. Four new classrooms were built in 1955 and in that year St. Paul's became a separate parish. In 1958 a new church and school were built on Callaghan Road, known as St. Luke's Parish from 1959.

A new church for 750 people and a rectory with office space and conference rooms was dedicated on 8 March 1964, after almost two-and-a-half years in construction. A four classroom unit was approved in October 1965. The convent was air-conditioned and the parish council and school board established in 1967.

Monsignor Popp converted the library into classrooms and a new unit with library and science room was constructed for $98,000. New restrooms and a new gym floor were added and dedicated on 23 August 1970. Properties were purchased along John Adams Drive for future parking. A counseling center began at 420 Sutton Drive to serve people in northwest San Antonio. By 1974 there were 1,600 families in the parish.

On 6 February 1975 Monsignor Popp became Vice-Officialis and on 20 December 1976 Officialis of the Archdiocesan Tribunal. He was appointed its Judicial Vicar in 1977. From 1978 to 1983 Monsignor Popp was Rector of San Fernando Cathedral. The origin of this historic church was its founding on 2 July 1738 by a few families from the Canary Islands. Construction from 1738 to 1748 was made possible with a $5,000 donation from the Spanish Royal Treasury and $12,000 from the Viceroy of New Spain. It was blessed and opened for services on 6 November 1749.

Designated the Cathedral Church of the Diocese of San Antonio on 28 August 1874, San Fernando was severely damaged by fire in 1828 and completely repaired in 1841. An addition to the Cathedral was built from 1863 to 1868.

In the twentieth century Claretian Fathers staffed the Cathedral from 1902 to 1978. The South Belfry was added, the cupola reinforced, and stained glass windows, marble altars, and communion rails were installed. The sanctuary floor was tiled and the nave was covered with terrazzo. A rectory was built at the rear of the structure in 1923.

A parish school operated from 1930 to 1967. The gymnasium built in 1948 was taken over by the Urban Renewal Agency in 1973. A second cemetery began in 1919, and both San Fernando cemeteries were taken over by the Archdiocese in 1942. The cathedral parish now shares facilities with Immaculate Heart of Mary Parish.

San Fernando was renovated in 1974. The rectory and office built around the old apse in the 1920s was reconstructed into new priests' quarters to the South of the main structure. A small park, stone pavement, and iron fencing were added.

Monsignor Popp established the San Fernando Catechetical Center to aid the families of the three barrios. He was a volunteer on the Christian Assistance Ministry program, an ecumenical effort to assist the indigent and homeless. His organization "The Pillars of Our Cathedral" concerned itself with maintenance and continued restoration. His establishment of an Endowment Fund made possible a legal corporation for continued support of the Cathedral. The "Volunteers for Tourism" act as hosts to the tourists who visit San Fernando. His successor Father Virgilio Elizondo made a $750,000 project to renovate the Cathedral and to make it again a center for Hispanic traditions and culture. During his term as cathedral rector Monsignor Popp was Archdiocesan Director of Cemeteries (from 1981), Dean of the Central City Deanery (1982), Chairman of the Archdiocesan Presbyteral Council, and Chairman of the Central Urban Vicariate.

Pope John Paul II appointed Monsignor Popp Titular Bishop of Capsus and Auxiliary Bishop of San Antonio on 7 June 1983. Archbishop Patrick F. Flores ordained him bishop in San Fernando Cathedral on 25 July 1983. Soon afterward he was named Director of Archdiocesan Personnel Services. He served a term as member of the United States Catholic Conference Region X Ad Hoc Committee for Human Development beginning in 1984.

On his seventy-fifth birthday in 1992 Bishop Popp tendered his resignation for age as required. He retired on 23 March 1993. At this time he was a Consultor, a member of the Presbyteral Council, Director of Archdiocesan Cemeteries, and Director of the Department of Personnel Services. The Bishop, whose name means "messenger," traces his descent from Heinzendorf in Moravia, later known as Hyncice in Czechoslovakia. Even after retirement Bishop Popp assisted the Archdiocese by maintaining a Confirmation schedule while awaiting the appointment of an auxiliary bishop. A valued and experienced administrator of the Archdiocese of San Antonio, he continues, as of mid-1995, to make his home in that city.

Most Reverend Ricardo Ramirez, CSB, DD
Titular Bishop of Vatarba and
Auxiliary Bishop of San Antonio
First Bishop of Las Cruces

Bishop Ricardo Ramirez, CSB, is the first member of the Congregation of the Priests of St. Basil (Basilians) to enter the hierarchy of Texas. Founded in Annonay, France, in 1822, its general motherhouse is in Toronto, Ontario, Canada. It is represented in the United States in the Archdiocese of Detroit and the Archdiocese of Santa Fe and in the dioceses of Galveston-Houston, Gary, Las Cruces, Phoenix, Rochester, and Oakland. It is noted for its educational and parochial work.

Born to Natividad and Maria (Espinosa) Ramirez in Bay City, Matagorda County, Texas, on 12 September 1936, young Ricardo was educated in the public elementary and high schools of Bay City. He received the Bachelor of Arts degree from the University of St. Thomas in Houston, Texas, in 1959.

In 1988 Bishop Ramirez would recall the influence of Father Vincent J. Guinan, CSB, the first president of the University of St. Thomas, upon his future life. He said of the former university president, who died in 1973:

> Father Guinan left some mighty big boots to fill. He was a recruiter and a promoter. He raised money, he taught and he was an administrator. He is a person who lives on in our memories and we who have had the privilege to have known and to be touched by him consider ourselves very blessed.

The guidance of Father Guinan seems to have helped the young man set his course. Henceforth he would follow the religious life. Ricardo Ramirez entered the Basilian Novitiate in Pontiac, Michigan, after college graduation and took his first vows in the Congregation of the Priests of St. Basil there on 12 September 1960. From 1960 to 1963 he taught English, history, and religion at St. Thomas High School in Houston and at Catholic Central High School in Detroit, Michigan. Thereafter he attended St. Basil's Seminary in Toronto, Canacla, from 1963 to 1965 and the Seminario Conciliar in Mexico City, Mexico, from 1965 to 1966.

On 10 December 1966 in St. Ann's Church in Houston, Texas, Ricardo Ramirez was ordained a priest of the Basilian order by Bishop John L. Morkovsky of Galveston-Houston. He was assigned to parish duties first in Owen Sound, Ontario, Canada, and then in Detroit, Michigan, from 1966 to 1968. He received the degree of Master of Arts in religious education from the University of Detroit in 1968. Father Ramirez was assigned to Centro Cultural of San Juan de Aragon in Mexico City as Chaplain from 1968 to 1970. While in Mexico he taught at the Regional Seminary of Tehuacan in the State of Puebla from 1970 to 1976. He founded the program, "Cateqiuisas Familiar," on the idea that the family is the basic evangelizing agent of the individual. This concept spread quickly throughout the country and soon became international. He obtained a leave of absence in 1973 and received the Diploma in Pastoral Studies from the East Asian Pastoral Institute in Manila, The Philippines, in 1974.

On his return to the United States he was Executive Vice-President and Director of the Mexican American Cultural Center in San Antonio, Texas, from 1976 until 1981. He lectured on the church history of the southwest, and on anthropology, evangelization, and liturgy.

Pope John Paul II appointed Father Ramirez Titular Bishop of Vatarba and Auxiliary Bishop of San Antonio on 27 October 1981. Archbishop Patrick Flores of San Antonio ordained him bishop in the Convention Center Arena in San Antonio on 6 December 1981. His co-consecrators were Bishops Rafael Ayala y Ayala of Tehuacan, Mexico, and John Morkovsky of Galveston-Houston.

The ordination ritual stressed the Hispanicism of the new bishop. At 2:30 P.M., thirty minutes before the ceremony, there was a Guadalupana Procession during which the following songs were sung: "Manañitas A La Virgen De Guadalupe," "Buenos Dias Paloma Blanca," and "Guadalupanas." The ceremony began at 3:00 P.M. with Rev. Virgilio Elizondo of the Mexican American Cultural Center as homilist and Msgr. (later Auxiliary Bishop) Bernard Popp giving the welcome.

Archbishop Flores celebrated Mass, during which the hymn "Me Alegre" was sung and the "Gloria" was sung in Spanish. The first reading was from Isaiah 40:1-5, 9-11 ("Comfort, give comfort to my people, says our God. . . In the desert prepare the way of the Lord!"). The second reading was 2 Peter 3: 8-14 in Spanish ("We hope for the new skys and the new land that God has promised, in which all will be just and good.") The Gospel was Luke 1:46-55 ("My being proclaims the greatness of the Lord, my spirit finds joy in God my savior. . .").

The Rite of Episcopal Ordination began with the hymn, "Veni Creator Spiritus." It was followed by the presentation of the Candidate for ordination, the Reading of the Apostolic Mandate of his appointment, and the homily by the Archbishop on the duties of the bishop. Then came the examination of the Candidate by the Archbishop before the people, the Litany of the Saints, the laying on of hands, and the prayer of consecration. Bishop Ramirez was then anointed, presented with the Gospels, invested with his insignia, and formally seated upon his throne.

During the Liturgy of the Eucharist these hymns were sung: "El Buen Pastor," "Virgencita Bendice Estos Dones," and "Cordero De Dios," "Gift of Finest Wheat," and "Aleluya." The hymn of thanksgiving was "Pescador de hombres" and the exit songs were "Santa Maria del Camino" and "Adios O Virgen de Guadalupe."

The new bishop's coat of arms carried out these themes, symbolizing family origins, priestly vocation, and devotion to the causes of justice and peace. The shield was partitioned horizontally with a black background and a red and black chevron. In the top division a silver eagle in motion armed with an olive branch symbolizes the Mexican-American heritage of the Ramirez family, the Bishop's association with the Mexican American Cultural Center, and with the civil rights of his people. The eagle represents daring and strength and being in flight portrays the Bishop as a man of action. The olive branch ("rama" in Spanish) represents his name and his desire for peace through justice.

On the bearer's right a silver book from the coat of arms of the Basilian Fathers symbolizes a dedication to learning and teaching, especially the Word of God. In the bottom division there is a white rose, barbed in green and seeded in gold, showing that the Bishop places himself under the patronage of Mary under the title of Our Lady of Guadalupe, Patroness of Americas. On the left of the bearer a silver star indicates the State of Texas, where the Bishop was born, reared, and served.

During his time in San Antonio Bishop Ramirez wrote *Fiesta, Worship and Family* in 1981. He was also a consultant for the National Conference of Catholic Bishops (NCCB) Committee on the Liturgy and Hispanic Affairs.

Pope John Paul II appointed Bishop Ramirez first bishop of Las Cruces, New Mexico on 31 August 1982. He was installed in the Cathedral of the Immaculate Heart of Mary in Las Cruces on 10 October 1982. The Diocese of Las Cruces is a ten-country area of 44,483 square miles. At the time of its founding it had 120,000 Catholics in a total population of 360,000. Bishop Ramirez was installed a Knight of the Equestrian Order of the Holy Sepulchre of Jerusalem at an installation presided over by Cardinal John Carberry in Tulsa, Oklahoma, on 23 October 1983.

On 4 June 1988 Bishop Ramirez returned to his alma mater for an All Classes Reunion. The University of St. Thomas in Houston proclaimed him a distinguished alumnus and presented him with the Father Vincent J. Guinan, CSB Distinguished Alumnus Award. He celebrated Mass in the Crooker Center and spoke of St. Thomas and his writings on the Eucharist.

Bishop Ramirez attended the National Workshop on Christian Unity in Denver, Colorado, 4-7 May 1992. There he called for a Hispanic summit of Protestant and Catholic leaders in the best interests of both churches. In October 1993 he took a stand with Bishop Peña of El Paso and Bishop Sandoval Iniguez of Ciudad Juarez in an attempt to aid workers having a difficult time during an Immigration and Naturalization Service blockade of the Rio Grande border between El Paso and Ciudad Juarez.

The Bishop has had an active membership in the National Conference of Catholic Bishops. He has served as Chairman of the Committee on the Church in Latin America and as a member of the subcommittee on Hispanic Liturgy, the Committee on Women in Society and in the Church and on the Ad Hoc Committee on Nomination of Conference Officers. As a liturgist he called for services to energize, encourage, and enliven the worshipper. He felt that only by true community and true worship is true promotion of justice achieved. He suggested that in a community with linguistic diversities, the use of Latin in worship might be appropriate.

In July 1995 Bishop Ramirez returned from the State of Chiapas in Mexico in an effort to promote peace in that region. He feels strongly that the Church must exercise efforts to "promote justice and peace." But such a conclusion should be brought about through political, social and economic reform. He led a delegation of bishops to the Diocese of San Cristobal de las Casas in Chiapas as a member of the United States Catholic Conference Committee for International Policy on Social Development and World Peace.

In early 1995 the Diocese of Las Cruces had nineteen active diocesan priests and forty-four Religious order priests, twenty-five permanent deacons, four male Religious and eighty-five women Religious. There were forty-four parishes with the same number of missions. There were five elementary schools and a total of

11,673 students under Catholic instruction. The Catholic population was 125,300 in a total population of 455,000 pr 28 percent.

Bishop Ramirez, whose Spanish surname means "mighty counselor" and "wise protector," takes for his motto, "*Hazme un Instrumento de Tu Paz*" ("Make me an instrument of your peace"). His daily concern is to serve people by seeking peace through justice.

He has served as chairman of the North American Acsdemy of Liturgy and is a member of the American Board of Catholic Missions and Liturgy, the Hispanic Liturgy Institute, the New Mexico Humanities Council, PADRES, and the Knights of Columbus. He has been active as coordinator of Hispanic Affairs Input and as a member of the Comite de Estudios de la Historia de la Iglesia Latina-America (CEHILA) and the National Catholic Council for Interracial Justice. He has contributed articles to *Worship* and to the *New Catholic World.* On 14 November 1995 the Bishops of the United States, during their regular yearly meeting in Washington, DC, elected Bishop Ramirez chairman of the Campaign for Human Development Committee of the United States Catholic Conference. The Bishop shows daily what one determined man from Bay City, Texas, can accomplish for the betterment of his church and for the larger society.

Most Reverend Louis Joseph Reicher, DD
First Bishop of Austin

The most controversial member of the Catholic hierarchy in Texas is Louis Joseph Reicher. Known as the "Builder Bishop" for the more than 200 churches and institutions put into new or renewed service during his tenure, he spent more than fifty years in financial matters. Yet as author of the Reicher trust he helped bring about a situation in which the trust became a matter for litigation. Hoping to avoid a public controversy, Reicher's successor, Bishop Vincent M. Harris, wrote to Ruben Johnson, James Nash, Bert Maloney, and E. Barham Bratton, the trustees, in October 1973:

> I consider your total cooperation equally urgent in accounting for and returning those properties that belong to the Diocese of Austin. If such action is not forthcoming I shall be forced to take the regrettable step of seeking redress in the courts. In such a case I shall be forced to seek not only recovery. . . of properties which belong to the Diocese. . .but also compensation from the Trustees. . . .Gentlemen, I earnestly appeal to you as loyal Catholics and in the name of justice to help your Bishop ameliorate this present situation and to avoid litigation which would cloud the many fine years of service that you have collectively given the Church and would cause wonderment and disedification to our faithful Catholic people.

It was not always thus.

Louis Joseph Reicher was born to Jacob and Marie (Krebsbach) Reicher in Piqua, Miami County, Ohio, on 14 June 1890. After study in the local parish school he graduated from St. Jerome's College in Kitchner, Ontario, Canada, in 1911. He then entered St. Mary's Seminary in Cincinnati, Ohio. Soon thereafter he wrote to Bishop Nicholas Gallagher of Galveston, expressing his wish to become a missionary in Texas. This request was approved. But Reicher worked for the United States Steel Corporation from 1912 to 1916 before coming to Texas in November 1916. He enrolled in St. Mary's Seminary in La Porte and finished his course in 1918.

On 6 December 1918 Christopher Byrne, the new Bishop of Galveston, ordained the Reverend Mister Reicher for that diocese in St. Mary's Cathedral in Galveston. Seeing in the young priest a man of promise, Bishop Byrne made him Diocesan Chancellor, a position he held until his appointment as Bishop of Austin almost thirty years later.

At first assigned to the Cathedral in Galveston, Father Reicher performed his priestly duties and was chaplain of the Dominican Sisters from January 1919 to July 1945. As Chancellor he was a model of efficiency in planning parishes and in building churches, missions, and schools. Reicher made possible the acquisition of the episcopal residence known as the "Bishop's Palace" in 1923. He also built a new diocesan chancery.

While living in Dickinson and working in Galveston, Father Reicher was asked to establish a parish in Houston. The parish began through the work of the Park Place Catholic Association, founded in the home of R. Henry Langdon. Mister Langdon became its chairman of the board of directors on 17 January

1922 to form a parish in the Park Place Addition.

The Land Committee of the Association recommended a five homesite tract of land in Park Place. It was purchased on 17 January 1923. Rev. Peter Tonson, OMI, said Mass on Sundays in the Park Place School Auditorium, while Srs. Mary Eugenia and Mary Paula of the Sisters of the Incarnate Word and Blessed Sacrament taught there on Sunday afternoons.

Vincent Harris, Father Reicher's parishioner and later his successor as bishop, would remember in 1986 how his pastor would ride the old interurban railroad to Park Place on Sundays and Holy Days to say Mass at St. Christopher's. But only after Reicher's appointment as Pastor was L. R. Bond chosen to design plans for a church building and meeting place.

Bishop Byrne approved the plans, suggested names, but in the end allowed the Parish to be named for himself. On 27 March 1924 the contract to erect the first unit of the building to be used as a church was let. This one-story brick veneer building measured thirty by fifty feet and was located on the corner of Broadway and Moline. On Sunday, 31 August the Bishop dedicated the first unit of a parish school building. In Fall 1924 Dominican Sisters succeeded the Sisters of the Incarnate Word and Blessed Sacrament as teachers of the Sunday school.

By 1939 some sixty-five families attended the Parish regularly together with some thirty families more. The church was enlarged and a wing added, which was used as a school. A new church building was erected and the Dominican Sisters staffed the school with fifty students. By 1941 St. Christopher's Parish had grown to 125 families. Bishop Byrne now needed a regular pastor and appointed Rev. (later Msgr.) E. K. Fulkerson to replace Monsignor Reicher on 6 July 1941.

During his years as Chancellor and Pastor Father Reicher served at various times as Vicar for Religious and as a member of the Diocesan Administrative Council. He was appointed Domestic Prelate, with the title of Right Reverend Monsignor, by Pope Pius XI on 2 March 1935. Pope Pius XII appointed Monsignor Reicher Pronotary Apostolic on 9 July 1940.

Pius XII created the Diocese of Austin on 15 November 1947 by the Bull *Ad Animarum Bonum.* It was formed from the Archdiocese of San Antonio and the Dioceses of Galveston and Dallas. From San Antonio came the counties of McCulloch, San Saba, Mason, Llano, Blanco, Hays, Caldwell, and parts of Burnet, Travis, and Bastrop south of the Colorado River. The counties of Lampasas, Coryell, McLennan, Limestone, Bell, Falls, Robertson, Williamson, Milam, Brazos, Lee, Burleson, Washington, Austin and parts of Colorado, Burnet, Fayette, Bastrop, and Travis north of the Colorado River came from the Diocese of Galveston. From the Diocese of Dallas came the counties of Coleman, Brown, Mills, and Hamilton. This was an area of approximately 22,000 square miles.

The papal Bull made Austin the see city of the new diocese with the Church of St. Mary as its cathedral. This church was designed by the Galveston architect Nicholas J. Clayton, the first professional architect in Texas, and built by Rev. Daniel J. Spillard, CSC. Ira A. Correl put in a new altar and several sculptures and Professor of Architecture Raymond Everett of the University of Texas designed the episcopal throne and made the wood carvings.

Monsignor Reicher was appointed Bishop of Austin by Pope Pius XII on 29 November 1947. The Pope stated in the Bull of appointment:

> Today, We, with the advice of Our Venerable Brethren the Cardinals of the Holy Roman Church in charge of Consistorial Affairs, do choose by Apostolic Authority for the Church of Austin. . .Our beloved son Louis J. Reicher, Pronotary Apostolic *ad instar,* and Chancellor for the Episcopal Curia of the Galveston Diocese, him do We appoint Bishop and Shepherd of this Church.

Bishop Reicher's good works had gone before him. Among other projects he had built were the seminary at La Porte with the Kirwin memorial chapel and helped raise an endowment to support it. He improved the Catholic Cemetery in Galveston, providing a perpetual care system. It was he who increased the value of the Diocese of Galveston and who made it financially independent. Bishop Reicher's consecration took place on 14 April 1948 in St. Mary's Cathedral in Galveston. Bishop Byrne, who had ordained him almost thirty years before, was his consecrator. His co-consecrators were Bishop Joseph H. Albers of Lansing, Michigan, and Coadjutor Bishop Mariano S. Garriga of Corpus Christi. Two archbishops, an abbot, and fourteen bishops attended the ceremony. Auxiliary Bishop William D. O'Brien of Chicago preached the sermon, saying of Bishop Reicher that

> the devotion to his office [as chancellor] and to his bishop. . .has hardly been surpassed in the history of the Church in Texas. . . .It entitles him to any honor that the Holy See can confer upon him.

On 13 May 1948 Archbishop Robert E. Lucey of San Antonio installed his suffragan bishop in St. Mary's Cathedral in Austin. This was a great occasion for church and state. The Bishops of Galveston, Dallas, Corpus Christi, El Paso, and Amarillo were present. So were Governor and Mrs. Beauford Jester, former Governor Dan Moody, several justices of the state Supreme Court, state representatives and senators, and the Mayor of Austin Tom Miller. Bishop Garriga of Corpus Christi addressed his new brother bishop in these words:

> We bring you earnest prayers and sincere wishes that your ministry may be long in years, fruitful and successful; and that you may be happy as you walk into the future in the steps of Odin, the Sower of the Seed, who loved Austin dearly; and that in spirit you will follow Dubuis, the Apostle on Horseback, and walk in step with Gallagher, the Master Builder, in his quiet, unostentatious and efficient manner.

Bishop Garriga, who died in 1965, did not live to see the working out of the "Reicher Trust". If he had he might not have compared the ''Builder Bishop" with his illustrious predecessors. Instead he might have put Bishop Reicher in a class all his own.

At the evening reception held in the Union Building of the University of Texas, government officials showered additional praise upon the Bishop and his church. Governor Jester said: "I want to congratulate your Church in its staunch fight against Communism." James E. Kilday, assistant to Tom C. Clark, the Attorney General of the United States, brought a letter from President Harry

S. Truman. The President noted, "In times such as this our country and the whole world are desperately in need of spiritual leadership. It is heartening to know that strong men are being called to that leadership in our country."

James Kilday added:

> As with you of the Catholic Hierarchy and priesthood, so with us of the Justice Department our common aim is to give each what is his due. . . .Through all of two thousand years of the Church's history it has loved justice and hated iniquity.

The President of the University of Texas, Mayor Miller, and many other public officials congratulated the Bishop in person and extended their good wishes to him. To this tribute Bishop Reicher replied: "I pledge to give my all toward the advancement of Christian culture in this area."

The Bishop did much to advance the Church in his diocese. In the course of the next twenty-three years he built or restored more than 200 churches and institutions. Among these are the chancery office in Austin, Holy Cross Hospital there, the Newman Apostolate on five college campuses, and six low-rent housing projects under church sponsorship. The Church in Central Texas was well served and the Bishop implemented the decrees of the Second Vatican Council. He supported religious freedom and strongly supported the ecumenical movement. And he encouraged Catholic participation as citizens. He did much to advance the cause of civil rights in diocesan affairs.

Bishop Reicher bought an 800-acre ranch west of the City on Lake Austin. On 5 June 1964 it had rained all day. Driving to his ranch from downtown Austin, he found the gate open. When he got out of his car to shut it, he slipped. The car moved forward and he fell, crushing his foot in the process. He was in no danger of death, but he was almost seventy-four years old and considered his mortality.

Some years before the Bishop had met a young Catholic layman named Ruben Hartwell Johnson in Cameron, Texas, through Dr. Edward Rischar, an owner of the Cameron Hospital. Johnson's mother Marie was a nurse at this hospital. At first an X-ray technician, Johnson later became Chairman of the Board of the United Bank in Austin and a member of the Finance Commission of Texas, appointed by Governor Mark White.

According to Ken Case, writing for the magazine *Third Coast*, Ruben Johnson wished to buy the Bessie Mae Radford Trust for one million dollars. Johnson made a written agreement with Bishop Reicher as guarantor. Case says:

> On May 9, 1964, the transaction was consummated. Supposedly, [Jimmy] Radford received a check for $500,000. The remaining $500,000 was placed in certificates of deposit at City National Bank of Austin. That money would be held until 1971, 20 years after Bessie Mae Radford's death, as a guarantee that the trust would be turned over to Johnson and Reicher. If the body of the trust was released on schedule, then Radford would get the other $500,000. Until 1971, Radford would receive only the interest on those certificates of deposit.

> The written agreement between Johnson and Reicher was equally straightforward. Income from the Radford trust would be used to pay off the million-dollar loan. Then the remaining Radford bank stocks, bonds, oil leases, hotels, and other real estate would be divided between Johnson and Reicher. The bishop would get a third; Johnson would get the rest.

It was to Ruben Johnson the Bishop turned in helping to form his own trust.

In June 1964 four men created the Louis J. Reicher, First Bishop of Austin, Trust. They were James P. Nash, honorary chairman of the board of Capital National (later Texas Commerce) Bank; A. J. "Bert" Maloney, senior vice-president and director of City National (later First City) Bank; Monsignor Maurice Deason, chancellor of the Austin Diocese; and Ruben Johnson, owner of the Bessie Mae Radford Trust. Bishop Reicher was trust manager and Ruben Johnson bought, sold, and invested. With the acquisition of money, property, stocks, and bonds, by 1974 the value of the trust was estimated to be thirty million dollars.

Profits of the trust were to aid various institutions of the Catholic Church in Texas. The Bishop claimed that the basis of the trust was his own money and that after buying his ranch his personal assets were used for investments. Bishop Reicher wrote to Austin priests in 1973 concerning the composition of trust funds:

> Let me briefly give you some facts. I started accumulating these funds over 50 years ago while a priest in the Diocese of Galveston. Before coming to Galveston I worked in a steel mill in Ohio and saved approximately $3,000. This personal money is in this trust, along with gifts given to me. . . .From this meager beginning I was successful in investing and reinvesting these funds. . . . Never were the funds of any diocese used in creating this trust. . . . Let me assure you that I have not alienated Diocesan property.

Although the Reicher trust claimed credit for such projects as underwriting the Cancer Treatment and Research Center and the Rebekah Baines Johnson Geriatric Center in Austin and the Regis Retirement home in Waco, Ken Case states:

> But for the first eight years, from 1964-72, Reicher and his trustees did not make a single charitable grant. Instead Reicher-trust profits were used to buy such things as blue chip stocks, a drilling company, 23 nursing homes in Boston, a community in Florida called Lehigh Acres, and a twin-engined airplane for the use of Ruben Johnson and Bishop Reicher.

Provisions of the *motu proprio* (administrative document) *Ecclesiae Sanctae* issued by Pope Paul VI requested voluntary retirement of all bishops attaining seventy-five years of age. This regulation covered the situation of Bishop Reicher, aged eighty-one, who submitted his resignation on 15 November 1971. His successor was Vincent M. Harris, former Bishop of Beaumont and Coadjutor Bishop of Austin.

At the time of the formal announcement of Reicher's resignation in Rome in 1971, he and Bishop Harris were attending a bishops' conference in Washington, DC. Bishop Harris received a call at his hotel. As he later testified, he was told that Sister Marie Therese, Reicher's housekeeper and secretary, was

> raiding the vault, taking things out by the boxful. I instructed the chancellor to get her out. And because she had the combination to the vault and the key to the chancery building, I instructed him to have the combination changed and the door lock changed.

This effective removal of Reicher trust records, stocks, and bonds was preceded a few weeks earlier by the visit of Monsignor Deason, a Reicher trustee, to Bishop Harris. As Harris remembered the visit:

> He [Deason] told me that he had just found out that the [Reicher trust] funds were not for the benefit of the diocese. He was very much distraught. He was in tears. He wanted to resign from the trust, and I begged him to stay on. . . . I said that I need a friend on the trust. It wasn't many weeks after that that he died from a massive heart attack.

On their return from Washington, Bishop Reicher went to his ranch on Lake Austin and continued to manage the Reicher trust. Bishop Harris attempted to see Bishop Reicher, only to be told by Sister Marie Therese that he was not available. Bishop Harris also asked to see diocesan ledgers of church assets and liabilities. He was told they did not exist.

Bishop Harris next hired an accountant named Lin Lorette to create a diocesan bookkeeping system. The Reicher trustees did not offer to help. Ken Case quotes Lorette as saying: "Reicher took everything when he left. All that he left Bishop Harris was the ability to borrow money." Nor did Bishop Reicher return the money to Bishop Harris. In mid-1972 Bishop Reicher suffered a stroke. E. Barham Bratton, an attorney and Monsignor Deason's replacement as a Reicher trustee, voted with the other trustees to make Ruben Johnson the new manager of the Reicher trust. Bishop Reicher recovered from his stroke but no longer dealt directly with his trust.

Matters came to a head in April 1973 when the Internal Revenue Service (IRS) sent the Reicher trustees a bill for six million dollars, including four million for unpaid taxes and a two million dollar penalty for alleged tax fraud. The IRS maintained that the Reicher trust's tax-exempt status should be revoked, as the IRS claimed that the trust had been operated as a business making profits. The IRS letter to the Reicher trustees said in part:

> Based on an analysis of its limited accounts, the income generated by the alleged Trust and not accumulated was used primarily for the personal living expenses of the Grantor/Manager [Reicher]. . . . An infinitesimal amount was used for charitable purposes.

Lawsuits generated by some Reicher trust business deals were filed in Massachusetts, Rhode Island, New York, and Florida. The IRS submitted another tax bill for sixteen million dollars. Bishop Harris had tried months before to enlist the cooperation of the Reicher trustees, but to no avail. The Catholic bishops of Texas requested the dissolution of the trust and that the money be returned to Bishop Harris. The trustees refused. An appeal by Vatican authorities to the trustees had the same result.

On orders from Rome Bishop Harris sued the Reicher trustees on 16 May 1973, alleging mismanagement of Catholic monies, claiming the Reicher trust for the Catholic Church, and requesting its return to the Austin Diocese. The case was tried before Judge Herman Jones in the 98th District Court of Travis County, Texas. Judge Jones ordered a complete audit of the Reicher trust, which would be performed by the accounting firm of Price Waterhouse.

Bishop Reicher in a letter of 24 September 1973 to Price Waterhouse declined to grant an interview concerning the Reicher trust, stating he had told Donald S. Thomas, attorney for the trustees, all pertinent information. Price Waterhouse confirmed independently that most of the Reicher trust stock portfolio was purchased with church money. The firm calculated that only $200,000 worth of real estate and $47,000 in securities belonged to Bishop Reicher. The remaining trust money was composed of Church assets.

Price Waterhouse also discovered an entity called West Texas Properties. It had been known previously as the Bessie Mae Radford Trust. The accounting firm discovered the written agreement between Ruben Johnson and Bishop Reicher. More than $900,000 was still owed on the Reicher loan to Johnson. The audit showed Reicher used church money to guarantee the loan and that Reicher trust money was used to pay interest on the loan. The Reicher trust paid Jimmy Radford's two sons $200,000 in settlement of a lawsuit filed by them against Ruben Johnson after Jimmy Radford's death in December 1969. The Price Waterhouse audit showed Ruben Johnson owed the Reicher trust $473,127 and that real estate, oil-and-gas leases, stocks, and bonds from the Radford Trust still remained in the name of Ruben Johnson.

The Attorney General of Texas, John L. Hill, became a defendant in Bishop Harris's lawsuit. As Harris was challenging the Texas Trust Act, the Attorney General's office, in particular its Charitable Trust Division, would have to defend Bishop Reicher if the Court found he had properly managed his trust.

In February 1974 the Charitable Trust Division informed the Attorney General in a memorandum that it would not defend Bishop Reicher nor any of the trustees due to improper management by present [1974] trustees. The Division alleged nonfeasance, misfeasance and lack of loyalty in performance of fiduciary duty. It found abuse of discretion in "virtually ignoring the beneficiaries of the Trust" and that the trustees "have violated the spirit and charitable nature of the Trust by placing their own personal interests above those of the beneficiaries."

The memorandum continued:

> The instance which gives us the most concern is the one where the trustees allowed one trustee [Ruben Johnson] to personally borrow large sums from the trust with the apparent intent not to pay the same. I think it can safely be stated that if an audit had not been conducted in this case the trust would have been depleted by the sum of $388,876. . . . Arguably, the language of Section 32.45 (a)(2)(A) [criminal misapplication of funds, a second-degree felony] would constitute the continuing failure of Ruben Johnson to deal with the property he holds as a fiduciary in the manner spelled out in an agreement under which he holds such property, as an 'ele-

> ment' of the crime prohibited under this section. Specifically, his continuing two-thirds ownership and management of West Texas Properties [Jimmy Radford's inheritance] and his outstanding accounts receivable owing to the Reicher Trust fall in this category.

The attorneys of the Charitable Trust Division made three recommendations to the Attorney General: (1) to amend the suit to remove the trustees, (2) to hold the trustees accountable by punitive damages for their culpability, and (3)

> that before litigation proceeds further, the Attorney General seek an opinion from the State Bar Grievance Committee or the Court concerning the ethical conduct and conflict of interest questions which are present in the case by virtue of the representation by one law firm [Clark, Thomas] of the Trust and Trustees.

Donald Scott Thomas, a senior partner of Clark, Thomas, Winters & Shapiro, an Austin law firm, was born in Bogata, Red River County, Texas, on 10 June 1920. A law graduate of the University of Texas, he had been in practice for thirty years before 1974. He had served on the National Commission on Reform of Federal Criminal Laws from 1967. He was a member of the Travis County and American Bar Associations, the State Bar of Texas, and was a Fellow of the American College of Trial Lawyers and of the American Bar Foundation.

Donald Thomas at different times had represented Jimmy Radford, Ruben Johnson, the Reicher trust, Bishop Reicher, and the Reicher trustees. But Thomas did not withdraw from the case and Attorney General Hill chose to take no action concerning it. Thomas has since suffered a stroke.

The case of Bishop Harris against the Reicher trust finally went to trial in June 1974. It ended a few days after it began with "an indefinite recess." According to a contemporary issue of the *Abilene [Texas] Reporter-News*:

> [Ruben] Johnson had told the court he would testify to 'extremely sensitive' matters concerning the inner workings of the church, and revealed that he had files given to him by Reicher on condition that they not be made public unless ordered by the court.
>
> Those files could prove 'extremely embarrassing,' Johnson said, and involved the appointment of Bishop Harris, Reicher's successor to the Austin diocese. But the recess Thursday blocked that testimony.

Johnson did not testify further and the files were not revealed.

The settlement of the trial came on 11 November 1974. Ruben Johnson would not be held liable for any violations of the Texas Trust Act. It was agreed on both sides that the Reicher trust was the property of the Catholic Church from its inception. Bishop Harris would control the trust until the death of Bishop Reicher. At that time Harris would dissolve the trust. Ruben Johnson agreed to repay all the money he owed the Reicher trust, plus six per cent interest. Johnson would also sign over one-third of the Radford Trust (now known as West Texas Properties) to the Church.

As late as 1985 Monsignor Lonnie Reyes, then Chancellor of the Austin

Diocese, was asked if Ruben Johnson repaid the $473,127 Price Waterhouse said Johnson owed. Reyes answered, "If he owed it, I assume he paid it."

Bishop Reicher continued to live out his retirement on his Lake Austin Ranch. He entrusted his care to the Dominican Sisters. As late as 1 January 1984 the "Louis J. Reicher, First Bishop of Austin, Trust, A Fund of the Diocese of Austin" was listed in *The Official Catholic Directory Anno Domini 1984* (39). Bishop Harris was listed as Executive Director, and the trustees were Rev. Msgr. Lonnie Reyes, and Messrs. Ruben H. Johnson, Mike W. Butler, and Ben F. Vaughan, III. Bishop Reicher died at his ranch on 23 February 1984, at the age of ninety-three, and was buried four days later in Assumption Cemetery in Austin, Texas.

Bishop Vincent M. Harris retired on 19 December 1985. His successor Bishop John E. McCarthy was installed on 25 February 1986. Ruben Johnson remained a trustee of the August J. and Sadie L. Henck Memorial Fund, which was started in 1960, and was once part of the Reicher trust. On 6 October 1987 the Roman Catholic Church in Texas received a $1,502,000 check. The gift was announced at a news conference in Austin attended by Bishop McCarthy, Ruben Johnson, and state Attorney General Jim Mattox. The office of the Attorney General reviewed the Henck trust and made final disbursements from it. The Roman Catholic bishops of Texas had approached the trustees in 1986 about disbursing the trust funds. From October 1972 through 1986 the Henck trust disbursed $2.26 million to churches, schools, hospitals, and adoption centers.

On the present occasion the Dioceses of Austin and of Galveston-Houston received approximately half-a-million dollars each. Bishop McCarthy explained that "We wanted to do some rapid development, especially in the Austin area." He said also that the money for Galveston-Houston would be for student scholarships to Catholic schools in Galveston, the former home of the Hencks. Other Catholic dioceses would equally divide the remainder of the check.

There was also an additional amount of $250,000 in real estate, securities, and notes, from the vested assets from the Henck Memorial Fund for distribution to Catholic dioceses in Texas. Bishop Vincent M. Harris died in Houston, Texas, on 31 March 1988. As of 1 January 1988 *The Official Catholic Directory Anno Domini 1988* (41) did not list the position of Chancellor of the Austin Diocese. Bishop Reicher's name lives on in the name of Reicher High School in Waco, Texas.

Most Reverend Placido Rodriguez, CMF, DD, LLD
Titular Bishop of Fuerteventura and
Auxiliary Bishop of Chicago
Second Bishop of Lubbock

Those who know Bishop Placido Rodriguez see his ready and sincere smile as a key to his personality. His warmth and humor are gifts he brings to the daily concerns of his office. But he is most serious in his respect for the dignity and worth of the individual, in his special concern for the poor and those who seek his aid, and in his love and dedication for his personal and spiritual heritage. He works well with others. Yet he knows that the plans and policies he proposes will be his own. His first name in Spanish means "calm," with the connotations of "patient" and "serene." He has attained these qualities through his own inner strength and his perspective from his origins.

Born in Celaya, State of Guanajuato, Mexico, on 11 October 1940, the eleventh of fourteen children, he is the eighth son of the eleven sons and three daughters born to Eutimio Rodriguez Cardenas (1898-1965) and Maria Concepcion (Rosiles) Rodriguez (1904-1960). His father was a skilled cabinet maker and the owner of a furniture factory in a city with then about 40,000 population, some 125 miles from Mexico City. Eutimio was a staunch defender of the Catholic Church in Mexico and of the rights of workers during the government persecution (1926-1940). His devotion to these causes was so great that at times he was in actual fear of his life. Maria cared for her growing family, the couple's extended family of relatives, and the many visitors who came to see them. As a boy Placido remembered the priests of his city, the marketplace, and visits to his beloved grandmother "Maraquita." He was a good student who grew up helping around the house, playing with his brothers and sisters, and playing baseball with the team called "El Carmen".

Placido's family made him aware that each person's dignity is holy and is a part of God's plan and design. His sense of belonging increased his feeling of community and of God's providence working within his own life. He developed inside a home in which love of God and of the Church was paramount, respecting his father's strong views of justice and his mother's quiet piety. The Rodriguez family was one in which religion was part of daily life and of intrinsic interest. Of the ten surviving children Antonia became Sister Ancilla, MEF, and Simon took orders as a permanent deacon of the Archdiocese of Chicago.

In December 1952 Placido graduated from the Colegio Vasco de Quiroga, a grammar school in Celaya. On 13 January 1953 he moved to Chicago with his parents, a younger sister, and four young brothers. His father wanted to begin anew in a country which he felt would have more respect for the virtues he held dear. Such a move was not without its consequences. The family was forced to adopt English as a primary language and came to realize that the United States was a largely Protestant country. There were few Hispanics in Chicago at that time, no bilingual education, and only one tortilla factory.

But Placido accepted the challenge and came to look upon the move to Chicago as God's plan for him. His childhood physician Dr. Jorge Prieto would many years later remember the young man to whom he gave polio shots in those days. Placido's refreshing smile, invariable courtesy and good humor made a deep impression upon the doctor. He saw his former patient grow into one he considered a man of the people and a diplomat. With enrollment in St. Francis of Assisi School at 813 West Roosevelt Road in Chicago, Placido began a journey of discovery which would lead him one day to Lubbock, Texas, as its bishop.

The new student at St. Francis would soon become a part of an institute which began on 16 July 1849. On that day in Vich, Spain, a diocesan priest Anthony Mary Claret (1807-1870), with five of his fellow priests, founded the Missionary Sons of the Immaculate Heart of Mary (CMF), more commonly known as Claretians after the principal founder. Claret later became archbishop of Santiago, Cuba (1851-1857) and was canonized a saint eighty years after his death by Pope Pius XII.

By 1904 Claretians, known for their missionary, parochial, educational, and retreat activities had established parish canters in Texas, Arizona, and California. Twenty years later Cardinal George Mundelein invited the order into the Archdiocese of Chicago to care for its growing Hispanic community. Rev. John Maitztegui, CMF, founded Our Lady of Guadalupe Parish at 3200 Ninety-First Street, the oldest Hispanic Catholic parish in the Midwest. One of its pastors would be the Rev. Placido Rodriguez, CMF.

Another Claretian institution in Chicago is St. Francis of Assisi Parish. Others are Holy Cross-Immaculate Heart of Mary Parish at 4541 South Wood Street and St. Paul Parish at 206 East Twenty-Fifth Street. The order has always placed emphasis on helping young children and the working poor, together with a strong devotion to St. Jude. The Claretian League of St. Jude maintains a branch for Chicago police officers to pray for police work. Claretians publish the magazines *The Voice of St. Jude* and *Salt*, operate several institutions of higher learning, and a ministry to the poor. Claret House is a part of the Catholic Theological Union. There is also a volunteer program for missionaries to work in clinics and schools in Guatemala. This religious institute, with headquarters in Rome, has its Eastern Province of the United States in Oak Park, a suburb of Chicago.

At St. Francis of Assisi School Placido came to have a vocation for the priesthood while in the seventh grade. He had met priests in Mexico at an early age. Most of his brothers had attended the seminary and one had majored in theology. St. Anthony Claret became his ideal as a missionary and a model for spirituality and character content. He was later to recall that Claret had been a bishop as well, and was thus a further source of inspiration. As he states it: "I wanted to do something that differed from everyone else and something that I knew reflected God's plan for my life." Placido saw in the priesthood a chance to promote the healing of the human spirit. He was particularly influenced in his vocation by Rev. Richard Bartlett, CMF. When he informed his parents and they were certain that the young man was serious and wished to help others, they gave him their blessings.

After graduation from St. Francis of Assisi School on 5 June 1955, Placido enrolled in St. Jude's Seminary High School, a Caretian institution, in Momence, Illinois, in August of that year. Momence is fifty miles south of Chicago. He graduated in June 1959 and entered the Claretian Novitiate in Los Angeles, California. He made his First Profession of Vows in Compton, California, on 8

September 1960. And, as he says, ''I began to appreciate my vocation as a Claretian missionary."

The young seminarian attended the Claretian College Seminary at Calabasas, California, from 1960 to 1964, where he studied philosophy. His education was "a very intense program," stressing the importance of community life. At first only Latin was spoken for instruction with English coming later. During his stay Placido applied for American citizenship in the United States District Court for the Central District of California. It was granted on 5 March 1964. Graduating from college that year, he began his theological studies at the Catholic University of America in Washington, DC. While in that city, he made his Perpetual Profession of Vows as a Claretian and was ordained a deacon in 1967. He spent his deacon year (1967-1968) doing parish work in Silver Spring, Maryland. In 1968 he received the degrees of Bachelor of Sacred Theology (STB) and Licenciate in Sacred Theology (STL).

The Reverend Mister Rodriguez was ordained a priest on Ascension Thursday, 23 May 1968, in the St. Vincent De Andreis Seminary Chapel in Lemont, Illinois, by then Auxiliary Bishop (later Bishop of Orlando, Florida) Thomas J. Grady of Chicago. He was the only Claretian ordained that day, along with five others of the Vincentian order. Returning to Chicago, he said his First Mass at St. Francis of Assisi Church.

In August 1968 Father Rodriguez received his first assignment as associate pastor of Our Lady of Guadalupe Parish and the National Shrine of St. Jude in South Chicago, the oldest Hispanic parish in the Midwest. He became its pastor in 1972. During these years he was a consultor on the Claretian Provincial Council and traveled to its missions in Guatemala. He also visited England and Wales, Ireland, France, Spain, Italy, and Switzerland. From 1975 to 1981 he was Claretian Director of Vocations. In this position he was responsible for seminary formation programs, programs on spirituality, and spiritual direction. He traveled extensively East of the Mississippi River.

Father Rodriguez continued his studies at Loyola University of Chicago. He received the degree of Master of Arts in urban studies in 1971 and was awarded that university's honorary degree of Doctor of Laws in 1988. Becoming fluent in English did not change his Hispanic heritage. It added a new dimension to his pastoral and missionary capabilities. His favorite author is the late Rev. Anthony De Mello, SJ, whose books of short stories, such as *Song of the Bird* and *Taking Flight,* he treasures for their wisdom. His favorite reading deals with the life and history of the Mayans, Aztecs, and Incas, as well as Our Lady of Guadalupe. A particularly interesting subject for the Bishop is the relation of Aztec history, significance, meaning, and symbolism to the New Evangelism and its implications for today.

In the past many American seminaries were closed to Hispanics. Currently those in Mexico are full. But in 1994 only ten diocesan and ten religious order priests in the Archdiocese of Chicago were Hispanic, hardly one per cent of the total number. The bishop knows that the Hispanic people are religious and respond to the call of the Church. Their gifts enrich and rejuvenate it because ''They are a people rich in tradition, culture and faith and they come to contribute what they have to the church." For them pastoral attention is necessary. Bishop Rodriguez's greatest satisfaction as a priest is being able to help people who look for an Hispanic priest who speaks their language and appreciates their customs. He believes parents need to encourage vocations in their children.

Because he knows the importance of youth in the Church, he is painfully aware that urban youth may join gangs, have disintegrating families, use drugs, and have low self-esteem. He looks to adults to support young people and to offer them positive life opportunities. In increasing vocations among Hispanic Catholics, the Bishop would point to their experience, to their lack of vocations, to their cry to be understood, and to their desire to be ministered to by their own. Then they would see the need and plan for more priestly, religious, and seminary vocations.

Bishop Rodriguez knows that self-discipline and hard work yield good results. Though he found it difficult to learn the English language and culture to balance parish and student work, he became, at the age of thirty-one, the youngest pastor in the Archdiocese of Chicago, with only three years of experience as associate pastor. He realizes Hispanic people know who they are and what they want to be. They have the necessary skills and know their destiny. Their greatest need is "to learn how to integrate that identity into the American culture all around us." And to accomplish this good, they must assume a leadership role in society.

As a parish priest Father Rodriguez found his greatest joy in working with people. He touched them directly through the sacraments, prayed in their homes, consoled the bereaved, went to sick calls at most difficult times, preached, visited the Guatemala and Chilapa missions, and helped the needy and those looking for jobs. In turn, he found the Hispanic people of Chicago generous in receiving him. He could represent them in a way they had not been represented previously. And as their number grew to a million persons in Chicago he was a member of the Council of Religious Leaders of Metropolitan Chicago for ten years. He asked each parishioner to live the life of a Christian and to remain faithful to traditions and customs.

On 6 September 1981 Father Rodriguez became pastor of Our Lady of Fatima Parish in Perth Amboy, New Jersey, at that time the oldest Hispanic community in the Diocese of Trenton. Here the Pastor guided eighteen different parish organizations and activities at the same time. He ministered to Hispanics of the East Coast, including Puerto Ricans, Dominican Republicans, and others from the Antilles, Central and South America. Here he helped immigrants find jobs and visited Puerto Rico and the Dominican Republic. When Perth Amboy became a part of the new Diocese of Metuchen, its bishop Theodore E. McCarrick, later archbishop of Newark, appointed him Diocesan Director of Hispanic Ministry.

On 18 October 1983 Father Rodriguez received a telephone call which changed the direction of his life. The call came from Washington, DC, and the caller was Archbishop Pio Laghi, then Apostolic Delegate to the United States. Laghi informed him of his impending appointment as Titular Bishop of Fuerteventura and Auxiliary Bishop of Chicago by Pope John Paul II. The news came as "a big surprise. . . . I was not prepared in the seminary to be a bishop." Members of religious orders do not strive for these positions. He was also unprepared for the great contributions Hispanics would make to the American

Church, for all the *Encuentros* (meetings) and their effects upon them, and for the outlook on Latin America and on liberation theology, which would affect the mission of the Church.

But these matters were in the near future. And Father Rodriguez was aware of the good he could achieve as a bishop. He knew that parishioners want to be loved and have their faith affirmed. He knew from his celebration of daily Mass that prayer with the celebrant leads them closer to the Church and to Christ. He would be approachable and open and listen to their concerns. And his earlier life in Chicago had prepared him for this extension of his ministry. The formal announcement of his elevation to bishop took place on 31 October 1983.

Placido Rodriguez was ordained an auxiliary bishop of the Archdiocese of Chicago in Holy Name Cathedral in Chicago by Cardinal Joseph Bernardin, assisted by auxiliary bishops Nevin W. Hayes, O.Carm. (died 1988) and Alfred L. Abramowicz (retired 1995) of Chicago. Also ordained as auxiliary bishops of Chicago at the same time were Timothy J. Lyne (retired 1995), John G. Vlazny (later bishop of Winona, Minnesota), and Wilton D. Gregory (later bishop of Belleville, Illinois). Bishop Rodriguez was the first Hispanic bishop for Chicago, the first in the Midwest, and the first Claretian bishop in the United States and Mexico. The date was 13 December 1983.

In January 1984 he was assigned Vicariate III with its Deaneries 5, 6, and 7, containing in 1994 fifty-six parishes of the Archdioceses of Chicago. There are six vicariates and twelve deaneries in the Archdiocese. On 28 February 1984 Bishop Rodriguez moved into St. Mark's Parish at 1048 North Campbell Avenue. The parishes and institutions of Vicariate III include downtown Chicago, Little Village ("La Villita"), the West Side, Humboldt Park, Logan Square, and West Town. There are many Mexican, Puerto Rican, and Central American communities, with many African-American and Polish Catholics. Each vicariate team has a support system including the vicar (an auxiliary bishop), deans, the Hispanic coordinator, the vicariate administrative consultant and the bishop's administrative assistant. Bishop Rodriguez early on had regular meetings with his deans and structured monthly meetings to gather information and plan initiatives.

In 1994 Bishop Rodriguez had for his deans Revs. Robert Coleman, James Flynn, and Joseph Peplansky, CMF. Mr. Robert Heineman, an employee of the Department of Financial Services working with the vicar and the deans on parish financial administrative matters, was his administrative consultant. Heineman remembers the Bishop as patient, punctual and willing to see difficult tasks through to their conclusions. He thought him to be a strong believer in social justice, aiding people to become educated, a hard worker, and a good listener. The Bishop's kind and gentle manner, Heineman felt, indicated respect for all people and their dignity. Cardinal Bernardin said of the Bishop: "He brings heart to the decisions of the archdiocese. . . . and no matter what, I know I can count on him to be personally supportive and say a kind word."

As an auxiliary bishop of Chicago, Bishop Rodriguez would awake at daybreak and pray for daily guidance. After a quick look at the morning newspaper, he attended to his office work and correspondence. Each ninth of April he would lead the Way of the Cross in the Pilsen section of Chicago. While spending much time in religious activities and in preaching, he did not neglect youth groups in an attempt to instill qualities of respect and obedience to lawful authority. Sometimes he would hold interviews with the media concerning his administrative activities.

As a good communicator, Bishop Rodriguez offered a Mass for the Virgin of Guadalupe for four consecutive years. The Mass was telecast on Channel 44 (WSNS-TV) in Chicago. Every Thursday at noon he would broadcast a talk on religion and the family on Radio Station WIND. Yearly in October he attended a special banquet to collect funds for scholarships for Hispanic seminarians. In his honor it was named the "Claretian Bishop Placido Rodriguez Scholarship". He also served as president of *Consejo Pastoral*, the Hispanic Archdiocesan Pastoral Council. He was a board member of the SAFER Foundation and of St. Mary of Nazareth Hospital in Chicago. On its one hundredth anniversary, Weber High School presented the Bishop with its Archbishop Joseph Weber, CR Award, on 17 February 1990. Three months later, on 18 May, he was given the President's Award of Montay College in Chicago.

As a member of the National Conference of Catholic Bishops (NCCB), Bishop Rodriguez served on its committees on Ecumenical and Interreligious Affairs and on Laity (1984-1990) and on Hispanic Affairs (1990). For the United States Catholic Conference (USCC), the operational secretariat and service agency of the NCCB, he was a member of its Campaign for Human Development (1988), the Liaison Committee with the Conference of Mothers Superiors (1986-1988), and was director of the Midwest Hispanic Catholic Commission, a regional office for the Secretariat for Hispanic Affairs of the USCC, in South Bend, Indiana. The Commission serves twenty archdioceses and dioceses in Ohio, Indiana, Illinois, Michigan, and Wisconsin.

Hispanic ministry in large American cities involves bilingual churches, centers and agencies. Its services may include legal aid, job placement, language instruction, recreation and social facilities, and counseling. By 1990 twelve or more dioceses had a Hispanic population of more than 50 percent, with twenty-seven others having between 25 and 50 percent. Fifty-five percent of 152 dioceses and archdioceses had Hispanic apostolates. Ministries to Hispanics included those for youth, small Christian communities, the Cursillo movement, Catholic charities and social ministry, lay leadership formation, and charismatic renewal. Most Hispanics are twenty-five years old or younger, and as many as 100 thousand a year convert to fundamentalist and pentecostal churches.

With such a background three *Encuentros* or national meetings took place in 1972, in 1977, and in 1985. Bishop Rodriguez took part in *Encuentro* III, which was held in Washington, DC, in August 1985. This meeting produced a master pastoral plan for Hispanic ministry approved by the NCCB in 1987. Its main features consist of collaborative ministry, evangelization, a missionary option regarding the poor, the marginalized, the family, women and youth, and the formation of lay leadership.

During these years Bishop Rodriguez was an active missionary, making a number of trips abroad. In July 1989 he traveled to Chilapa, State of Guerrero, Mexico, to bring a missionary and to receive one assigned to Chicago. In 1990 he visited Owerri in Nigeria, meeting with the Ibo tribe and ordaining fifteen Claretian priests and eight deacons in the Cathedral of the Assumption. In August 1991 he went to Guatemala on a peace mission. While there he met the

Apostolic Delegate to Guatemala, the President of the Republic, and visited the Mayas and the K'ekchis.

On 5 April 1994 Pope John Paul II appointed Bishop Rodriguez bishop of Lubbock, along with Bishop Joseph A. Galante as bishop of Beaumont. In Lubbock that day during a press conference, Bishop Rodriguez said: "I accept this appointment graciously and consider it as a blessing and as a divine calling to come and serve as Pastor of this local Church [diocese] in order to shepherd it in the name of the Lord." He thanked the Pope and recalled the founder of the Claretian order. He cited his own motto: "*Caritas Christi Urget Nos*" ("The love of Christ impels us" from 2 Corinthians 5:14). He added, "I come as one who serves among you. I am anxious to serve you, and to express to you my full commitment and dedication with religious fervor."

To the priests, deacons, religious, and laity of the Diocese of Lubbock, he said:

> As a missionary and Shepherd, I come with open arms, and mind, with openness to your friendship, to your love and affection in order to surrender to you my dedication, my energies and talents, my prayer and faith, in this wonderful and lovable people of this Diocese, whom God has entrusted to my pastoral care.

Praising his predecessor, Archbishop Michael J. Sheehan of Santa Fe, the bishop asked for preparation to begin his ministry with prayer, particularly directed toward an increase in "priestly, Diaconal, Missionary vocations, religious life, and all sorts of lay ministries." In Spanish he added:

> With this announcement of His Holiness, John Paul II, of whom I am his servant, Bishop Placido Rodriguez, CMF, to be his bishop, or Shepherd of this Diocese, I come with you as your servant to journey together as a diocesan family to come near to the Heavenly Father. I ask your prayers to prepare for the day of the beginning of this apostolic concern (translation mine).

Bishop Rodriguez thanked Cardinal Bernardin, the auxiliary bishops, and people of the Archdiocese of Chicago, saying: "I want to put into practice his [the Cardinal's] wonderful example of faith and steadfastness." He also thanked Msgr. Curtis T. Halfmann, the administrator of the Diocese of Lubbock, as well as its people. He ended his remarks by saying:

> Finally, I would like to invoke the intercession of Mary, the Mother of Jesus, and the Mother of the Disciples of Jesus. I would like to have Mary as Pope Paul VI would call her: *The Star of Evangelization*, and ask Mary for her protection. May we all grow spiritually under her maternal care.

On the same day Cardinal Bernardin issued his own statement in Chicago. He was pleased at the Bishop's appointment and observed that the new bishop of Lubbock had "a wealth of pastoral experience." He said Vicariate III was "a large, complex and ethnically and racially diverse area," He added that the bishop "was of great help to me in the pastoral oversight [as episcopal vicar] of 56 parishes and 40 elementary and five high schools. He was also very active in many other archdiocesan activities." He said the Bishop was known for "prayerfulness, kindness and pastoral sensitivity." Also:

> I wish Bishop Rodriguez well as he assumes his new responsibilities. We will miss him very much but rejoice that the Holy Father has recognized his qualities and named him a diocesan bishop. I know that I speak for the entire archdiocese when I assure him of our continued prayers and support.

Now came the time for leave-taking and for summing-up. The Bishop toured his vicariate for the last time as its bishop in late April 1994. There were many highlights. In Deanery 5 he noted the good works of St. Elizabeth Hospital, the community kitchen of St. Stanislaus Kostka Parish, feeding 270 people daily, thirteen schools with 4,731 students, religious education programs, and ministries to prisoners and to the infirm. Among the parishes in Deanery 6 were those of St. Agatha, Presentation of the Blessed Virgin Mary, and the Holy Family. He found flourishing ministries of justice and peace and education and parishes aiding others through the sharing of resources. Blessed Sacrament and Holy Family parishes had programs of alphabetization, and St. Agatha worked for family support. Fourteen primary schools had 4,289 students. And there was an education program for deaf-mutes and assistance for the elderly.

He came to Deanery 7 on 27 April. At St. Ann's Parish he remembered the completed work in Pilsen, La Villita, and Heart of Chicago. The schools of St. Ann, St. Paul, St. Michael, St. Stephen, St. Agnes of Bohemia, Epiphany, Good Shepherd, St. Procopius, and Our Lady of Tepeyac had 2,960 students. The Bishop inspected the works of the Resurrection program, which helped the community renovate homes. The *El Valor* mission office encourages people to value themselves and to grow in self-estimation and in personal dignity. He also inspected Kolbe House (the prison ministry), Alivio [Comfort] Medical Center, and the Interfaith Organization.

At last the time to say goodbye came. The bishop said it in Spanish:

> I carry away all of you in my heart. I do not say goodbye, but until I see you again. I leave my home, as do many other Hispanics. I have lived in Chicago for twelve years and now, as a good missionary, ought to go out to seek another obligation (translation mine).

He raised his hand in blessing, saying: "May you have simplicity. . .patience. . .peace. . .joy. . .and God in the Trinity. . .be always with you."

On Sunday, 1 May 1994, the Day of Farewell was at hand. Bishop Rodriguez celebrated Mass in Holy Trinity Polish Mission, together with priests of Vicariate III. He told those assembled, "I am very grateful for all and each of you for the work we have done together. You welcomed me with open arms. I shall remember always the many good things the Catholic Church has done here." A reception followed.

The Bishop hoped his flock would remember him as an auxiliary who tried to serve them all. As an episcopal vicar in an inner-city vicariate he "tried to live at the same level of pastoral service as others in the vicariate." He had tried to make known the importance of vocations. And he identified himself with all parishioners who looked for harmony and peace, and who advocated justice and racial harmony.

In his years of service in Chicago the Bishop had witnessed many changes.

Growth was an undeniable fact. The Hispanic population grew five times faster than the overall population. There were more volunteers in the parishes and an increase in Hispanic vocations. The leaders were coming. There was a Mexican-American Police Organization, local chambers of commerce, business groups, Hispanic civic organizations. And there were groups to serve Hispanic athletes, lawyers, and firefighters, to name a few. There was an amnesty program available through Catholic Charities.

In the Archdiocese of Chicago the people were taking hold. New leadership developed through workshops, institutes, and diaconate programs. There were more "*communidades de base*," groups for ongoing faith formation. Each vicariate now had its own Hispanic ministry coordinator and the newspaper *Chicago Catolico* was a vehicle for evangelization. There was a Hispanic-American consultant for the Archdiocese. *Conseio Pastoral*, the principal consulting body, was established in 1988. The Second Archdiocesan *Encuentro* took place during Easter Week 1994. Hispanics were now being included in every level of archdiocesan life and Bishop Rodriguez enhanced identification of the Hispanic community. And the City of Chicago had given back. It was home, family, and church. As the Bishop said, "I will miss all as a friend would miss a friend. Chicago has formed me for what I am."

What would await him in Lubbock, Texas? He knew the meaning of service and his physical capacity to serve. He would take time to adapt. He would organize his schedule so as to leave time for proper amounts of rest and recreation.

He had been a runner; so he might include some jogging. He enjoyed sports, plays, and opera (including that other Placido, named Domingo), but had little time for television. His greatest hope in moving to Lubbock was to serve the people entrusted to him and to perform the work the Pope required. He would try to live in such a way as to involve all people with Christ. He would develop all cultural groups in the Diocese of Lubbock to work and to worship better together by working for understanding among them and by affirming their work in the sight of God. Finally he would get to know his priests, co-workers and parishes and develop a cohesive plan of action by focusing pastoral attention on people and priests.

When Bishop Rodriguez began his work with Vicariate III in the Archdiocese of Chicago in 1984, the Archdiocese consisted of 1,411 square miles and occupied two counties in Illinois. There was a total population of 5,693,562, of which 2,368,316 were Catholic, or 42 per cent. One thousand two hundred fourteen diocesan priests and 1,441 religious order priests, 407 male religious, 446 permanent deacons, and 5,162 women religious served the people, along with five other auxiliary bishops, all led by the cardinal-archbishop. There were 444 parishes (all with resident pastors) and eight missions. There were eight colleges and universities, four seminaries with 1,211 diocesan seminarians, fifty-nine high schools, and 375 elementary schools with 129,862 elementary school students. Twenty-nine thousand nine hundred eighty-six high school students and 116,003 elementary school students were under religious instruction. In the past year of 1983 38,164 people were baptized Catholics and 14,108 marriages took place.

By contrast, as a diocese, Lubbock had neither archbishop nor cardinal, and there were no auxiliary bishops. There were no male religious. It consisted of twenty-five North Texas counties, with 23,382 square miles. It had no Catholic colleges and universities, seminaries, and high schools. The first church in the present diocese was constructed at Hermleigh in Scurry County in 1907. Germans, Polish, Czech and Irish farmers, and Irish and Mexican Catholics came to build railroads. Mexican immigration increased significantly in 1911, and the Sisters of Mercy opened a parochial school in 1920. The growth of oil fields and agriculture stimulated parish development. And the Diocese of Lubbock, with its four deaneries, was formed 80 percent from the Diocese of Amarillo and 20 percent from the Diocese of San Angelo in 1983. The new diocese was 80 per cent Hispanic and prayer groups ("*catequesis familias*") and other small faith communities are popular in parishes.

The prospects for a Hispanic bishop here were excellent. The majority of Hispanic Catholics have family stability, a sense of community, a sense of joy, respect for life, and respect for the elderly. Their bishop had all of these qualities. His one cardinal rule: "Be as helpful as you can to everyone regardless of their origin or capabilities" would stand him in good stead with all his people. His good works had gone before him. In an editorial in the *West Texas Catholic* Bishop Leroy Matthiesen of Amarillo would describe him as:

> A tranquil man with vision and complete trust in the guidance of the Holy Spirit, coupled with friendly accessibility and an unassuming manner, is the way those who have worked with him describe the bishop.

The installation of Bishop Rodriguez as second bishop of Lubbock took place on 1 June 1994 in the Lubbock Municipal Auditorium, Fourth and Boston Streets, at 7:00 P.M. A reception followed after the ceremonies at the Christian Renewal Center, Fourth and Toledo Streets, in Lubbock. Archbishop Patrick F. Flores was the installing prelate, with the assistance of Cardinal Joseph Bernardin, Archbishop Michael J. Sheehan, and some forty bishops. Altogether some 3,000 people attended on a very hot evening.

Father Ron Kinsman, formerly executive director of the United States Bishops' Committee on the Liturgy, headed the committee for the installation. Father Lawrence Hemp was master of ceremonies. The planning committee had representatives of the Diocesan Council of Catholic Women, the Knights of Columbus (of which the Bishop is a member), and the Lubbock Serra Club. The 150-voice diocesan choir lent its talent to the proceedings.

After introductory remarks by Archbishop Flores and Cardinal Bernardin, Archbishop Sheehan of Santa Fe (the Bishop's predecessor) read the Apostolic Mandate appointing his successor, first showing the Mandate to the diocesan consultors. After Archbishop Flores questioned Bishop Rodriguez about his willingness to accept his new office and the Bishop accepted, he was escorted to his *cathedra* or chair by Archbishop Flores and Cardinal Bernardin. Archbishop Flores earnestly wished that the new bishop would remain in that chair for the next twenty years. Here Bishop Rodriguez received his pastoral staff or crozier and was greeted by representatives of diocesan, ecumenical, and civic communities.

Said the Bishop:

> I consider this appointment as a commission, as a mandate to tend to the needs of this local church. It has been one of my lifelong dreams to fulfill a missionary calling. Today, I find a special calling and grace for fulfilling this missionary vocation.

He remarked in Spanish: "*Viva la Dioceses de Lubbock; Viva la Virgen de Guadalupe; Viva Cristo Rey*" ("Long live the Diocese of Lubbock; Long live the Virgin of Guadalupe; Long live Christ the King").

The Bishop spoke of Hispanic values and gifts:

> We are known for our profound respect for the dignity of each person, for family life, for a marvelous sense of community that celebrates life through 'fiesta,' for a loving appreciation of God's gift of life, for a sense of time that allows us to savor life, and for an authentic and consistent devotion to Mary, the Mother of God.

When the ceremonies were over, Bishop Rodriguez placed a bouquet of roses before an image of Our Lady of Guadalupe.

After he had been in office for seven months and greeted the New Year of 1995, Bishop Rodriguez found he had 39,818 Catholics in a total population of 448,640, or nine percent. There were thirty-three diocesan priests and eleven religious order priests, twenty-four permanent deacons, and thirty-six women religious. His thirty-six parishes had thirty-two resident priests. He had twenty-seven missions. Two thousand three hundred thirty high school students and 5,752 elementary school students were under Catholic instruction. There were seven diocesan seminarians and two Catholic elementary schools with 405 students. There was one Catholic hospital. During the past year of 1994 there were 1,976 baptisms and 350 marriages in the Diocese of Lubbock.

True, the Diocese of Lubbock is much different from the Archdiocese of Chicago. But given the gifts of Bishop Placido Rodriguez it has every opportunity for continued growth, in institutions and in the Spirit of Christ. The Claretian missionary from Mexico seems to be the right man in the right place at the right time. On the 14 November 1995 the Bishops of the United States, at their annual meeting in Washington, DC, elected Bishop Rodriguez a member of the United States Catholic Conference Campaign for Human Development committee.

Most Reverend Enrique San Pedro, SJ, STD, SSL
Titular Bishop of Siccesi and
Auxiliary Bishop of Galveston-Houston
Coadjutor Bishop of Brownsville
Fourth Bishop of Brownsville

Enrique San Pedro was a man of many parts. Cuban by birth and an American citizen by choice, he was a member of the Society of Jesus and a worldwide traveler. A scholar and a speaker of uncommon talents, he used his knowledge and his linguistic skills as a missionary. By the Grace of God his humanism was Christ-centered. Classicist, philosopher, and theologian, his learning always employed the Bible. A truly wise man, he used his education and his abundant intelligence to spread the Word of God. A true citizen of the world he wore his wisdom with humor and wit. He loved people and was happiest when among them. Humble to the point of being self-effacing, he sought to exalt others and to advance his flock with his administrative abilities. Neither a liberal nor a conservative in his own eyes, he expressed himself in this way: "In theoretical matters I try my best to find the truth and, in practical matters, I try my best to do good." In this endeavor he was particularly successful. Those who greeted his living presence knew they had been in the company of a holy man.

Felipe San Pedro of Havana, Cuba, married Esperanza Xiques of the same city when she was only sixteen in 1886. Of their thirteen children eleven survived to maturity. When Esperanza died in 1921, her grieving husband followed shortly thereafter. Their son Enrique (died 1984) married Maria Antonia Fornaguera (died 1976), whose father died in 1920 and whose mother died in 1932. Enrique and Maria San Pedro had four children, Silvia (Mrs. Alberto Camacho), Enrique the future bishop, Bertha, and Javier.

To one who valued the lives of his grandparents as the younger Enrique did, it is sad that he had only distant memories of his paternal grandmother. A visit to Merida, Yucatan, Mexico, the birthplace of Esperanza Xiques to Cuban parents, prompted this statement:

> Grandparents are custodians of tradition, family traditions, religious traditions, cultural and national traditions. They are the roots of families and therefore not only of their own children, but especially of their grandchildren. These roots of which Chesterton wrote: 'There is strength in striking root' (*BH*, 23 February 1994).

Enrique San Pedro, the future bishop of Brownsville, was born in Havana, La Habana Province, Cuba, on 9 March 1926. At the age of ten he attended Belen Jesuit Preparatory School and two years later Sagua la Grande Minor Seminary. The young seminarian enrolled in the Society of Jesus at the Jesuit novitiate in Cienfuegos, about 120 miles from Havana, on the momentous day of 7 December 1941. The Society of Jesus (Jesuits) was founded in 1534 at Paris by the former Spanish soldier St. Ignatius of Loyola (1491-1556), whose order was approved by Pope Paul III (1540) and who was canonized (formally declared a saint) by Pope Gregory XV (1622). Jesuits are known primarily for their missionary, educational, and literary works. After two years at Cienfuegos

Enrique left Cuba for studies in Spain. Hereafter he would visit his homeland for brief periods in 1950, in 1957, and in 1987.

San Pedro received the degree of Master of Arts in Classics from the College of St. Estanislao (Stanislaus) in Salamanca, Spain, in 1947. Thereafter he received the degree of Licentiate in Philosophy (Ph.L.) from the Pontifical University "Comillas", then at Santander, in 1950. At this point he made the decision to enter the China Province of the Jesuits as a missionary. This preference became an impossible dream because the Communist government of China closed its borders to all foreign missionaries. Before leaving Spain he taught at a theologate (or major seminary in Barcelona.

So after a brief visit to Cuba, the twenty-four year old seminarian was sent instead to the Philippines. Beginning in November 1950 he attended a Jesuit language school in Manila, which was originally established in Peking (Beijing), China. In 1952 San Pedro was sent to the Jesuit Ateneo de Manila to teach high school students. In 1954 he began his theological studies in Baguio, Benguet Province, in the St. Robert Bellarmine Faculty of Theology, relocated there form Shanghai, China.

Because Jesuit formation is long and thorough, Enrique's theological studies were shortened by one year. He was ordained a deacon on 12 March 1957. Six days later, along with fifteen other Jesuit scholastics, the Reverend Mister San Pedro was ordained a priest in the cathedral church in Baguio City by Bishop William Brasseur of the Mountain Province. One month later Father San Pedro left the Philippines for Europe.

For the rest of his life Bishop San Pedro would remember his stay there and the people of the Islands:

> As a young man, in my late twenties and early thirties I spent seven happy years in the Philippines. It was from 1950 through 1957. . . .Those years in the Philippines taught me to love the Filipino people and to appreciate their many talents. I greatly admire also their devotion and attachment to the Catholic faith. This last quality, which reminds me of a similar one among Mexicans, makes the Filipinos eminently qualified to evangelize their Asian brothers and sisters (*BH*, 14 March 1994).

The outgoing, optimistic bishop did not choose to recall here that in the Philippines he encountered a close brush with death in 1951. Stricken with typhoid fever, he received the last sacraments of the Church. His complete recovery seemed to baffle his doctors. It became clear to him that God had spared his life.

The study of Semitic languages brought Father San Pedro back to Europe. He received the degree of Licentiate in Sacred Theology (STL) at Leopold-Franzens University in Innsbruck, Austria, in 1958. He continued in residence there, while taking time from 1960 to study at the Pontifical Biblical Institute in Rome and also in Jerusalem. He received the degree of Licentiate in Sacred Scripture (SSL) from the Institute in 1963, with permission to pursue doctoral studies (never completed) in that subject matter field. While in Rome in the year of 1963- 1964 he lectured for one semester at Loyola University of Chicago (Rome). The following semester found him lecturing in the Hebrew School of Theology at the Colegio de San Francisco de Borja in Barcelona, Spain. He completed his graduate studies with the degree of Doctor of Sacred Theology (STD) from Leopold-Franzens University in 1965.

Superbly educated, Father San Pedro was as well-equipped for teaching and missionary work by his study of languages. He could speak fluently English, French, German, Italian, Latin, Spanish, and Vietnamese, with a reading knowledge of biblical Hebrew and Greek. In addition he could make sense of about ten more languages, or some twenty in all. His next assignment was professor of Old Testament at the Pontifical National Seminary of St. Pius X at Da Lat, Vietnam. In addition he was assistant dean of studies and secretary to the theological faculty (1967-1972) and editor of the theological digest (1968-1971). When Communist forces from the North invaded, San Pedro was forced to leave the country on 3 September 1975.

With Miami, Florida, as home base for the next eleven years, San Pedro held a number of teaching positions. He was a visiting professor at the Seminario de Santo Tomas in Santo Domingo, Dominican Republic, in 1976-1977 and again in 1980-1981. From 1978 to 1980 he was a professor of Holy Scripture at the Pacific Regional Seminary (Suva, Fiji) and its head librarian from 1978 to 1979. He was guest lecturer at the Pacific Theological College there from from 1978 to 1980. Between 1978 and 1985 he taught seminars and courses in Fiji, French Polynesia, American Samoa, and Haiti. Back in Miami, he was both professor of Holy Scripture and Homiletics at St. Vincent De Paul Seminary in Boynton Beach, Florida, and instructor for the permanent deacon program for the Archdiocese of Miami.

An associate pastor in St. Raymond's Parish in Miami from 1983 to 1986, San Pedro was professor of Sacred Scripture at the Belén Jesuit Preparatory School in Miami in 1986. He had attended the same school fifty years before when it was located in Havana.

On 1 April 1986 Pope John Paul II appointed Father San Pedro Titular Bishop of Siccesi and Auxiliary Bishop of Galveston- Houston. Reactions to his appointment were unqualified praise. Bishop Joseph A. Fiorenza of Galveston-Houston stated:

> I am deeply grateful to Pope John Paul II for giving the Diocese of Galveston-Houston a magnificent Easter gift in the person of Bishop San Pedro. In the name of the clergy, religious and laity, I warmly welcome him to the diocese and to Texas. I am confident that this gifted and zealous man will be an enormous help in serving all the people of our diocese.
>
> This area has an international flavor with the many nationalities represented here. Bishop San Pedro is especially qualified by an international experience and as a linguist to minister to the variety of people who enrich our community with their cultures and traditions.
>
> While all of his duties have not been identified, I will name him the Vicar for Hispanics and the episcopal Vicar for the Central Vicariate. I look forward to having him as a brother- bishop and a coworker.

Priests of the Galveston-Houston diocese were equally pleased by the appointment. Monsignor Teodoro de la Torre of Cuban descent said:

> Although I have not met him, I have heard a lot about him. He is definitely a priest of the church. Also, he is specially qualified because such a tremendous sector of our diocese is Hispanic or Vietnamese and he can minister to both. Something that greatly impresses me is the fact that coming from a very prominent Cuban family he gave up everything to serve God.

Monsignor Lawrence Peguero, a Mexican-American priest then pastor of Holy Name Parish in Houston, thought: "He is very qualified and very friendly. If he is *carinoso* [affectionate], the Mexican-Americans will love him."

Rev. (and Later Monsignor) Philippe Le-Xuan Thuong, then associate pastor of St. Jerome Parish in Houston, was a former seminary student of Bishop San Pedro's in Vietnam. He said of his former professor: "He is a great teacher and a great man. I am extremely happy." And the Cuban seminarian (later Rev.) Norberto Conde felt that nothing but good could come from the appointment:

> I am delighted. The fact that he has been a professor of scriptures for so many years and that he taught seminarians will make him particularly sensitive to the needs of seminarians. Also, the fact that he is an international man will make him understanding of all the nationalities of our diocese.

In 1986 the Diocese of Galveston-Houston had about 50,000 Vietnamese, over half of whom were Catholic. There were about 200,000 or more Hispanics, mainly from Mexico, Central America, and Cuba. About fifteen parishes in the Diocese, including St. Vincent De Paul in Houston, had one or more Masses in Vietnamese each Sunday. Two Vietnamese parishes in the Diocese were Our Lady of Levang in northern Harris County and Vietnamese Martyrs in southeastern Harris County.

Monsignor de la Torre writing in Spanish for *The Texas Catholic Herald* for 27 June 1986 indicated the new bishop's academic credentials and the time and place of his episcopal ordination. He noted that the Bishop was a man of brilliant academic promise who offered himself as a missionary for China. Although he was defeated in this purpose by Chinese communists, he served as a missionary in other lands and always deferred to his superiors. Monsignor de la Torre then said in part:

> And not only did he teach marvelously. Taking his rest time, he devoted himself body and soul to the apostolate: to marriage encounters, youth, prisons, parish service, pastoral care of Hispanic and Vietnamese populations.
>
> In my twenty years of priestly life in Houston, I have seen our diocese grow, above all the Hispanic Apostolate. I believe that, if God grants me life, I shall see even more happy days in our local church, because Bishop San Pedro seems to have exceptional qualities for this position. He did not display personal ambition, which greatly helps the work of a priest, above all when his work is as auxiliary to another pastor.

> He is a tireless worker. He lavishes his energies happily upon those most in need of spiritual attention.
>
> This especially endows the ministry among Hispanics and Vietnamese, both very important apostolates in our diocese. He distinguishes himself by a great prudence, a quality which will help him much in the delicate mission to which he has been entrusted.
>
> He smiles much and has good humor, but he also knows not to speak to those who seek to manipulate him.
>
> But above all, he is a son of the Church, Bishop San Pedro said of the Vietnamese:
>
> 'The Vietnamese are charming people, industrious, tenacious, well-mannered. I have known of villages that were destroyed and rebuilt three times over. Vietnamese Christians are reliable. I learned from them that there are many forms of laughter. They are very happy people, very loyal as friends' [translation mine].

Bishop Fiorenza appointed Bishop San Pedro a vicar general of the Diocese, Episcopal Vicar of the Central Vicariate, and Vicar for Hispanics. In 1986 the Central Vicariate consisted of the Central Deanery (fourteen churches, including the co-cathedral, the Northeast Deanery (twelve churches), and the Southeast Deanery (fourteen churches), all in Houston.

Bishop San Pedro's ordination took place in the Albert Thomas Convention Center in Houston on 29 June 1986. Bishop Joseph A. Florenza of Galveston-Houston was his consecrator, with Archbishop Edward A. McCarthy and Auxiliary Bishop Agustin A. Roman, both of Miami, as co-consecrators. Bishop Roman, like Bishop San Pedro, was born in Cuba. Archbishop Patrick F. Flores of San Antonio was homilist.

Fifteen bishops of Texas and twelve others attended. There were many Hispanics and Vietnamese in the audience of approximately 6,000. Readings, prayers, and songs were in English, Spanish, and Vietnamese. Hispanics, Vietnamese, Chinese, and African-Americans sang. Archbishop Flores had Matthew 9:36-38 as his text. He stated that, although the flock had a shepherd, the task of caring for it was so great because of the problems of the flock. The appointment of an auxiliary was God's way of showing mercy.

Bishop San Pedro recalled his press conference in Houston on 1 April 1986. He said, "I have no plans. I have been appointed auxiliary bishop and I will obey and help." He told the Vietnamese present in the audience that he understood exile, for he himself was a refugee and knew of divided families and of being part of a strange culture. But in Catholicism, he said, God is the father and the Church is the mother.

To the Spanish-speaking he promised "to plan together the work of the Kingdom of God." To the 300 Miamians who attended, he offered thanks for their good Christian examples. He also remembered his family: "On other occasions we have been further away from each other. But where there is love, distances mean nothing."

On the first of July 1986 he became pastor of Sacred Heart Co-Cathedral in Houston, a position in which he would later be succeeded by his former pupil

Msgr. Philippe Le-Xuan Thuong. He was the third Jesuit and the eighteenth Hispanic bishop in the United states. On 10 January 1987 Bishop San Pedro ordained twin brothers who were also former Anglican priests. David and Bruce Noble became Catholic priests in St. Mary's Seminary Chapel and studied to become hospital chaplains. The Bishop was here as lecturer in St. Mary School of Theology, the University of St. Thomas in Houston, during the academic year 1986-1987.

Bishops Roman and San Pedro issued a joint statement which appeared in *The Texas Catholic Herald* in English and Spanish in the issue of 9 January 1987. They sought "mercy and understanding" for mentally ill Cubans in federal prisons as a result of the *Mariel* migration in 1980. They asked for a resolution of the issue and said in part:

> The cases of those who committed crimes in Cuba should be reviewed to determine if they were duly judged.
>
> Those who committed crimes in this country but who have already served their sentences should be freed if it is determined that they do not constitute a threat to our society.
>
> Those who are still serving their sentences should do so in adequate facilities.

The two bishops requested rehabilitation for the imprisoned Cubans and that individual prisoners be heard to put an end "to the inhumane situation of uncertainty and indefinite incarceration".

On 28 January 1987 Bishop San Pedro spoke to the Annual Diocesan Congress of Continuing Christian Education during the Spanish language session in the Albert Thomas Convention Center in Houston. His subject involved challenges and opportunities of the Hispanic Catholic. He presented three challenges. The first was that Hispanic Catholics would become a majority within a few years and should begin to act the part despite the lack of a native clergy in the United States. The second challenge was the scarcity of Hispanic priests and the need to foster vocations among the Hispanic peoples. The third challenge was to avoid going from an oppressed minority to an oppressor majority.

> If we have taken into account this challenge of being a majority already, we ought to unite for the true majority can realize its Christian agreement in the Church in Galveston-Houston and in the United States.

In March 1987 the Bishop announced that a Mass in Spanish at 1:00 P.M. was added to the Sunday schedule at Sacred Heart Co- Cathedral. There was one on weekdays at 5:15 P.M.

On 29 March 1987 there was a Diocesan Committee on Girl Scouting recognition dinner held in conjunction with the Catholic Committee on Scouting at the St. John Vianney parish activity center in Houston. Bishop San Pedro, assisted by Msgr. Thomas A. Wendland, the diocesan chaplain for scouting, presented awards. The Bishop presented the St. Anne Medal, the highest Catholic national recognition for outstanding services of adults who contribute to the spiritual development of Catholic young people in girls' organizations and further Catholic adult leadership. He also presented the St. Elizabeth Ann Seton

Medal, a national recognition that affirms the work of those who help youth develop their spiritual lives within the context of girls' organizations. He then presented the Diocesan Family Award, an appreciation placque, and a framed United States Commemorative Girl Scout Stamp "First Issue" for 12 March 1987.

On 3 May 1987 the Bishop addressed Hispanic parish delegates. He discussed the function of the laity within the Church. But the month of August that year had a special importance. For Bishop San Pedro returned to visit his homeland after thirty years. His mother had died in 1976 and his father in 1984. He kept their memories alive. For on his hand his episcopal ring was made up of his mother's wedding band and one of the gold coins given to him and to his brother and sisters by his paternal grandparents.

He was met on arrival by air by the local Jesuit superior, by retired Auxiliary Bishop Fernando Azcarate of Havana, and by a representative of the Cuban government Ministry of Religion. His first stop was the Jesuit residence of Villa San José where he met some old friends. He went next to the Jesuit parish and residence at Reina. On 9 August he said Mass there in the parish church. He had entered the Jesuit order there on 30 November 1941, before enrolling as a Jesuit a week later, and donning his first cassock on the twelfth of December.

On the next day the Bishop went by car to Matanzas and the Yumuri Valley. Then he went to Southern Cuba, to the port city of Cienfuegos, where he had spent time as a seminarfan. The Castro government took over the novitiate at one time and used it as a school. The Jesuits now occupied one small area of the four-story building. The chapel was open and abandoned. Bishop San Pedro flew to Santiago de Cuba to visit the shrine of Our Lady of Charity of E1 Cobre, the patroness of Cuba. He met the bishop of Santiago and six of the ten priests remaining in that city and said Mass there.

In Havana memories crowded in at the Church of the Passionists where he said Mass. It was across the street from the house where he was born and lived until the age of five. He met an old lady of eighty-five years. She remembered his parents and had seen him as a newborn. Of his home in Cuba the Bishop said:

> I would have wanted to stay. The needs there are enormous; even the need for human warmth among the clergy itself. And I want to return.

But other work called him.

On the first and second of October he was in San Jose, Costa Rica, a participant in the Central American Conference for Peace. On 25 October he was invested as a Knight of the Equestrian Order of the Holy Sepulchre of Jerusalem at St. Michael's Church in Houston.

Bishop San Pedro served on the national scene in the National Conference of Catholic Bishops (NCCB) and the United States Catholic Conference (USCC). He was chairman of the Committee on Hispanic Affairs (1990-1993), and a member of the Committee on Priestly Formation, a consultant on the Committee on the Liturgy and its subcommittee on Hispanic Liturgy. He was also on the NCCB executive board for Interracial Justice and the national advisory committee, the Liaison Committee for Vietnamese Catholics in the United States (immigration and refugee services), and the Advisory Council to the NCCB/USCC.

In Houston he was a member of the Hispanic AIDS Coalition, the Greater Houston Coalition for Education Excellence, the University of Houston's President's Advisory Council, the Houston Area HIV Health Services Planning Council, the Houston Independent School District Crackdown education committee, the Asia Society, and the National Trust for Historic Preservation of the Vatican Library. Bishop San Pedro was also a board member of the Greater Houston AIDS Alliance, of the Institute of Religion, of the Institute of Hispanic Culture, of Vocational Guidance Services, of the CASA-Child Advocates, and of the Texas Medical Center.

Over the years he was a participant in the First International Catholic Congress on Biblical Studies in Louvain, Belgium, and in international congresses on the student of the Old Testament held at Oxford, Bonn, and at Uppsala, Sweden. He found time to write *Introduccion a la Literatura Profetica (Introduction to Prophetic Literature)* (1982), and *Diez Años Dialogando (Ten Years Dialoging)* (1989), as well as a number of professional articles and book reviews.

On 13 August 1991 Pope John Paul II named Bishop San Pedro Coadjutor of Brownsville with right of succession to Bishop Fitzpatrick. At his press conference that day San Pedro called his new assignment "a pioneer diocese and a model of pastoral work". He expressed admiration of Bishop Fitzpatrick, whose guidance, he said, would help him. The four-county diocese was 80 percent Hispanic, with 560,701 Catholics in a total population of 710,888, with sixty-one parishes and forty-seven missions.

Some troubles were anticipated. The new bishop thought the socio-economic situation in Brownsville was "a problem and a serious challenge for the Church". Young people left school at an early age, an increase in Catholic education needed implementation, and a sense of hopelessness at the inability to find jobs had to be abated. The need for more vocations was an immediate problem. Bishop Fitzpatrick projected one priest for every 13,000 Catholics as a certainty. San Pedro concluded by praising Bishop Fiorenza for his friendship and outstanding leadership and Auxiliary Bishop Guillory for his friendship and support.

Bishop Fiorenza said of Bishop San Pedro:

> The Diocese of Brownsville will have a tireless and dedicated servant of the gospel. His zeal and love of people will endear him to the wonderful people of the Rio Grande Valley. He has worked with the bishops of Mexico on common difficulties among the United States and Mexican border due to the continuing immigration of people. He is very sensitive to the human tragedy of the people who have to leave their homeland to seek a decent living or to flee civil strife.
>
> I am grateful to bishop San Pedro for the five years that he served the Church of Galveston-Houston as an auxiliary bishop. As my Vicar for Hispanics he was implementing the National Pastoral Plan for Hispanics which is a concerted program of evangelization.

> He also served on many civic and educational organizations for Hispanics. His intelligence, talents and dedication will be sorely missed.

Bishop Fitzpatrick developed parishes as small Christian communities and parish-based social action programs. He had the sponsorship of the Campaign for Human Development, the Bishops' anti-poverty program. As head of the Bishops' Committee on Hispanic Affairs, Bishop San Pedro met with United States Trade Representative Carla Hills, along with five other United States bishops and seven Mexican bishops, regarding negotiations for free trade with Mexico.

On 26 September 1991 San Pedro was installed as Coadjutor Bishop of the Diocese of Brownsville at the Virgen De San Juan Del Valle Shrine at San Juan, Hidalgo County, Texas. Bishop Fitzpatrick presided. Archbishops Agostino Cacciavillan, the Vatican Pro-Nuncio to the United States, and Patrick Flores of San Antonio took part, along with some sixteen other bishops. Priests, deacons, and laypeople made up the rest. There were lectors from the dioceses of Galveston-Houston and Brownsville, ceremonial masters such as Rev. Adrian Correa and other diocesan priests, deacons, Religious, and lay ministers. Deanery representatives from the Brownsville, Harlingen, McAllen, Mission, Rio Grande City, and Weslaco deaneries offered general intercessions (prayers on behalf of the people).

Bishop San Pedro's sisters, brother, brother-in-law, and sister-in-law presented the Gifts of bread and wine for the Celebration of the Eucharist. The diocesan choir was directed by Eduardo Arguelles and Gilda Keith. Ministers of hospitality were ushers of the Shrine and members of the Diocesan Pastoral Council.

Ceremonies began with several hymns, primarily in Spanish, followed by the processional "All Creatures of Our Lord and King," by St. Francis of Assisi, translated by Williams Draper and arranged by Noel Goemanne. Archbishop Flores greeted the audience, and Bishop San Pedro presented his papal mandate (or letter of appointment) to the College of Consultors. After the letter was read by Archbishop Cacciavillan, the new bishop was formally seated and received the consent of the people as their shepherd. The singing of the "Gloria"' in Spanish was followed by the first reading from Deuteronomy 3:1-18.

This passage concerns Joshua's appointment as Moses' successor. the injunction that the Law be read every seven years, and the Lord's last instructions to Moses. The psalm response was the singing of Psalm 23 ("The Lord Is My Shepherd") in Spanish, followed by the second reading of 1 Peter 5:1-4, concerning shepherds of the flock of God. A sung "Alleluia" preceeded the Gospel, John 15:1-17, on "I am the Vine and You are the Branches."

Bishop San Pedro offered the homily, after which deanery representatives offered the general intercessions. The presentation of the Gifts brought on the hymn, "*Envia Tu Espiritu*" ("Send Forth Thy Spirit") by Bob Hurd. After prayers came "*Padre Nuestro*" ("Our Father") in a setting by Carlos Rosas. There were two communion hymns in Spanish.

The ceremony ended after communion with the hymns "Holy God, We Praise Thy Name" by Jonaz Franz and the postlude, "*Cantale*" ("Sing to the

Lord") by José M. Marmol. There was a reception on both sides of the Shrine building with an opportunity for the people to greet their new coadjutor bishop.

An eyewitness to the event was struck by Bishop San Pedro's personality (which "shines forth"), his facility with languages, his graceful way of instructing others, and his general affability. "He thanked everyone, right and left for whatever reason, adding his personal touch where it fitted." Speaking primarily in Spanish, San Pedro told Bishop Fitzpatrick that he was here to serve and to follow his directives, to serve him, and to do everything he was told to do, if he could do it conscientiously. For example, he promised to continue to support the work of Casa Oscar Romero and Valley Interfaith, if their missions remained meaningful. There were many people from Houston making up the "diocesan" choir and many priests, with close to twenty bishops on the altar. "All in all," thought the observer, "I would say he endeared himself to his people." Soon after his installation, Bishop San Pedro left for Rome to participate in a workshop on refugees worldwide to which he was invited.

On 30 November 1991 Bishop Fitzpatrick's resignation as bishop of Brownsville was accepted and Bishop San Pedro took his place. The following day was the First Sunday of Advent, a beginning of the church year and a new beginning for the Diocese of Brownsville. As in the case of his predecessor, some of Bishop San Pedro's decisions were considered controversial.

For example, the Bishop took the side of immigrant Ricardo Aldape Guerra in pleading for a stay of execution. There was some doubt that Aldape actually killed Houston police officer James Harris in July 1982. There was interest in the case in Mexico, Italy, and Japan. San Pedro thought it would be best if Aldape got another appeal in order to prove his innocence. He did not wish to overturn established law. As one writer put it, "While he [San Pedro] feels that the death sentence is not needed in modern society, he does see the need to ensure laws are obeyed."

The Bishop represented the Pope during a United Nations Round Table discussion on refugees on 9 and 10 March 1993. As did many other clergymen, the Bishop had visited the Immigration and Naturalization Service detention center in Bayview, Cameron County. A Mass he said there for Haitian detainees and an interview about his forthcoming appearance at the Round Table prompted this insight:

> Perhaps we would be more sensitive to the plight of our brothers and sisters, and more open to come to their help. If we would take more seriously the admonitions of the Scriptures that remind us that we do not have here a lasting city (see Hebrews 13:14), because our citizenship is in heaven (see Philippians 3:20) and therefore, we are all aliens and sojourners (see 1 Peter 2:11) (BH, 6 February 1993).

The Bayview center also housed Chinese nationals. Bishop San Pedro invited priests who spoke Chinese and Haitian French to help the Bayview detainees. In New York he told the Round Table participants that refugeeism is "one of the greatest human tragedies of modern times". He also attended the meeting of the United Nations Council on Refugees. He deplored policies of ethnic cleansing, destruction of homes and property, and economic strangulation.

About the beginning of 1993 the Bishop undertook to write a weekly series of brief articles to appear in the *Brownsville Herald.* Partly personal essay and partly meditation, these pieces fulfilled the classical ideal of mixing instruction and delight. Continued for some sixteen months until illness made their continuation impossible, they form a record of San Pedro's thoughts and concerns. They deal with the Bishop's life, his judgments on current events, and record pastoral matters. Most of them contain pointed references to the Bible. As a whole they are concise, interesting, and thought-provoking. The following is characteristic:

> I remembered that in spite of all the sadness, sorrows and miseries that are the normal fare of our daily news, we are still the holders and bearers of the 'Good News'. The good and great news of the love of God for each and every one of us; the good news of the victory of our risen Lord over sin and death; the good news of the Christian hope that God 'will wipe every tear from [our] eyes, and there shall be no more death or mourning, wailing or pain, for the old order has passed away!' (Revelation 21:4) (*BH*, 22 May 1993).

The acceptance of the pastorate of Our Lady of Guadalupe Parish by the Jesuit Mexican Province on 7 March 1993 was a joyous occasion. The Feast of Pentecost, the birthday of the Church, on 30 May provoked this response from the Bishop: "St. Paul admonishes us to live according 'to the law of the spirit of life in Christ Jesus' (Romans 8:2), for it is this 'spiritual life' that should identify the Christian, as it is written in the letter to the Galatians: 'If we live in the Spirit, let us also follow the Spirit' (5:25) (*BH*, 29 May 1993). His column on "Universal Health Care" reminded him of his closeness to death in the Philippines (1951) and his dangerous illness in Vietnam (1967). "Reasons for Being Thankful" included the dates of his baptism (18 May 1926), of his confirmation (31 May 1927), of his First Communion (19 March 1933) and of his ordinations as deacon, priest, and bishop.

For 1994 the Bishop had a wish: "May we begin this New Year 1994 under the sign of God's blessing so beautifully expressed in the Lord's Prayer!" (*BH*, 4 January 1994). In February he observed:

> It is a sad reflexion on the human condition the fact that racism is such a widespread phenomenon. I have been privileged to live at least a short period of time in every continent and in a large number of different countries. I have thus experienced first hand that racist tendencies are to be found everywhere (*BH*, 9 February 1994).

On Sunday, 13 February the Bishop celebrated Mass at the Shrine of Our Lady of San Juan del Valle in neighboring Hidalgo County for couples in the diocese celebrating silver and golden wedding anniversaries. He said of this occasion:

> Holy Scripture teaches us in unmistakable terms that matrimony is an institution based on human nature (the duality and complementarity of sexes), as well as on God's plan for us (see Genesis 2:18-24). The dignity and beauty of marriage is based on these premises; however Christian marriage has a beauty and dignity that greatly

> surpasses that of the natural institution. For this reason St. Paul sums up a beautiful passage on wives and husbands with these words: 'This is a great mystery, but I speak in reference to Christ and the Church' (Ephesians 5:32; see Ephesians 5:21-33) (BH, 16 February 1994).

The recollection of the Winter Olympic Games held at Lillehammer, Norway, on 12 through 27 February 1994, and athletic competition in general influenced this thought:

> This aspect of exercise and discipline together with the exultation of the triumph inspired St. Paul to compare the asceticism demanded of Christian living to the sports of his time in a famous passage of his first letter to the Corinthians. 'Do you not know,' he wrote to the Christians of Corinth, well acquainted with the Isthmian games celebrated nearby, 'that the runners in the stadium all ran in the race, but only one wins the prize? Run so as to win. Every athlete exercizes discipline in every way. They do it to win a perishable crown, but we an imperishable one. Thus I do not run aimlessly; I do not fight as if I were shadow-boxing. No, I drive my body and train it, for fear that, after having preached to others, I myself should be disqualfied' (1 Corinthians 9:24-27) (BH).

The sight of kindergarten children singing and dancing in costumes for their families, sponsored by the Headstart program "*Ninos, Inc.*" and the parental involvement needed to advance these children, brought about these thoughts:

> It is important to remember in this context [adult assistance of children to reach their full potentials] the very special relationship that Jesus had with children; His words taught us clearly the value in His eyes of each and every one of those tender lives, while His actions showed unmistakably His love for them (*BH*).

One of Bishop San Pedro's last unalloyed joys in his life was to say Mass in his cathedral at the invitation of The Cameron County Filipino Catholic community on Sunday, 13 March 1994. In his column in the *Brownsville Herald* for the following day, he recalled his stay in the Philippines and that his last view of those beautiful islands was a three-day stopover on his way to Vietnam in 1964.

Near the end of March the usually vigorous bishop found himself in a hospital bed. Characteristically, he recalled that Christ's suffering and death brought about mankind's redemption:

> The positive value of suffering, although arguable from a strictly material analysis of reality, coincides in the popular saying 'no pain, no gain,' however, it becomes a comforting certitude when seen through the eyes of faith the beautiful and moving fourth oracle of 'the Servant of the Lord' in the book of Isaiah (see Isaiah 52:13; 53:12) underscores the redemptive value of suffering; speaking of the suffering Messiah it says: 'It was our infirmities that he bore, our sufferings that he endured. While we thought of him as stricken, as one smitten by God and afflicted. But he was pierced for our offenses, crushed for our sins; upon him was the chastisement that

> makes us whole, by his stripes we were healed (Isaiah 53:4-5) (*BH*, 23 March 1994).

And again:

> The quest for immortality, the deep desire for eternal life that nests in the human heart, finds its most perfect answer in the mystery of Our Lord's resurrection and in the promise of eternal life for us that it contains. By Christ's resurrection we receive, through our baptism, that 'newness of life,' (see Romans 6:1-4), that is a pledge of our sharing in the glory of his resurrection (*BH*, 29 March 1994).

For almost a year past, the Bishop had enjoyed the "tranquility and solitude" afforded him by residence in a house in nearby San Pedro in Cameron County. Just off the Military Highway and not too far from his office, he found it was "quite simple, unpretentious, comfortable, but above all a quiet country house". He had learned of its existence by chance. A lady from Brownsville sitting next to him on an airplane trip from Harlingen to Houston told him of its being bequeathed to the Diocese. On his return to Brownsville San Pedro verified the lady's story, secured title to the property, and began to enjoy the house in a town which bore his own name (*BH*, 4 April 1994).

But even such mild pleasures were coming to an end. The diagnosis of prostate cancer in April 1994 led to eight weeks of therapy in McAllen in Hidalgo County. Treatment included thirty-seven radiation treatments and minor surgery in Brownsville on 26 April. The prospect was for a recovery of five to seven weeks.

In May Bishop San Pedro appointed the fifty-four year old priest, Rev. Robert DaVola, his vicar general, to be temporary administrator of the Diocese. DaVola was a New Yorker and a former Oratorian, dedicated to the formation of lay people in becoming spiritual leaders faithful to the Church. He had come to the Rio Grande Valley as a superior of his order in 1974. He was later incardinated (affiliated) into the Diocese of Brownsville as a diocesan priest to assist the Bishop and the Diocese. On the day after the Bishop's death (18 July 1994) Father DaVola was elected administrator of the Diocese of Brownsville by its college of consultors, pending the selection of a new bishop.

Although a CAT scan taken on 15 June showed no spread of the cancer and treatment ended on 24 June, the Bishop did not feel well enough to carry on his duties. If he could only return to Miami, walk its beach and meditate, he was sure his strength would be restored and he could return to Brownsville invigorated in September. For a time he stayed in Miami, where his younger sister was a staff member in a local hospital. But weakness and loss of appetite prompted the Bishop to check into Mount Sinai Hospital in Miami on 10 July.

At Mount Sinai the bishop's health continued to decline. Apparently his treatment had weakened him to the extent that recovery became impossible. He received the last rites of the Church on 14 July. His sisters in Miami and his brother from California, together with some nieces and nephews, came to his bedside. On Friday, 15 July Father DaVola and Sr. Esther Dunegan, IWBS, the diocesan chancellor, flew to Miami from Brownsville, in an effort to be of assistance. The Bishop asked for prayers and for forgiveness if he had offended anyone by his decisions. On the following day he lost the ability to recognize his visitors. His kidneys failed that night and he died a few minutes past 6:00 A.M., on Sunday, 17 July 1994.

Word of the Bishop's death came to Brownsville early Sunday morning. Parishioners at St. Luke's, where he had said his first Mass as bishop, were holding their annual bazaar to raise funds to improve their parochial school. The first reaction was shocked surprise, followed by a moment of silence and prayer at his passing.

In his two-and-a-half years in Brownsville, the Bishop had shown considerable promise. He had managed to visit and to say Mass in each of his parishes and had begun to tour his missions. He dissolved the Casa Oscar Romero, converting it into Ozanam Center, a homeless shelter. He put priests in charge of parishes in Progreso and in San Juan, created a Council of Deacons, and bolstered the Office of Vocations in its efforts to interest more people in pursuing careers as priests, religious, and deacons. He founded the Office of Planning and Development. At the time of his death he was working to improve education and the seminarian program and to create a foundation to provide funding for diocesan projects. That he was able to accomplish these things, given his commitments outside his diocese, showed him to be a worthy leader.

Archbishop Edward A. McCarthy of Miami said of Bishop San Pedro:

> He was a brilliant and holy bishop. Exiled from his native Cuba, he preached the gospel from many parts of the world and in many languages, including Vietnamese. He enriched the Archdiocese of Miami by teaching in our seminary and at Belen [Jesuit] High School, and by administering pastorally to our people.

The Bishop's body was brought back to the Valley, to Miller International Airport at McAllen, at 4:45 A.M., on Monday, 18 July. His simple wooden coffin was taken to the Shrine at San Juan, the scene of his installation as coadjutor bishop. Here he would lie in state on Tuesday from 9:00 A.M. to 9:00 P.M., guarded at all times by an honor guard of Fourth Degree Knights of Columbus in full dress. A funeral Mass followed on Wednesday morning at 10:30 A.M.

On Tuesday, 19 July, the *Valley Morninq Star* of Harlingen, Texas, wrote in its editorial that Bishop San Pedro was one of the Rio Grande Valley's "primary torchbearers for progress". He made "structural changes designed to improve the diocese's financial outlook" but also tried to get more Valley people to pursue religious careers. The Bishop was "a highly educated man, holding many degrees and speaking more languages than the average person can name." The newspaper praised his commitment to education, feeling that his "humanity" went beyond "his brilliance, his expertise and his familiarity with the world." He was a man "eminently approachable and excellent at putting others at ease."

On the same day the *Brownsville Herald* printed a letter from a fifteen year old student at Hanna High School in Brownsville named Nicholas J. Elizondo. Recalling the Bishop, Elizondo said in part: "I thank God for giving us Bishop San Pedro; he enlightened so many. When I met him and we shook hands, I felt a warmth go through my body. I knew this man was touched by God and he was a great man." He concluded by saying, "Every time I see a sunrise, I'll know he started the day with me." The young student felt the Bishop shared his hopes and dreams.

At 10:30 A.M., Wednesday, 20 July, at the Virgen De San Juan Del Valle Shrine in Hidalgo County, Archbishop Patrick Flores celebrated Mass. There were twelve bishops, many clergymen, and about 3,000 people altogether. Srs. Ester Dunegan, IWBS, and Dolorette Farias, SSND, director of Christian Formation and Education for the Diocese of Brownsville, were lectors. Rev. Edward T. deLeon, OMI, the director of the Shrine, was master of ceremonies, assisted by diocesan priests. Seminarians further assisted and priests, deacons, religious, and lay ministers were eucharistic ministers. Hernan Gonzalez, Charles E. Frankhauser, Jr., and Pamela G. Downing presented the Gifts of bread and wine. Jesse Garza directed Our Lady of Sorrows Choir from McAllen.

The first reading was from Daniel 12:1-3 about the time of the end of the world. The psalm response was Psalm 27 ("The Lord Is My Light"). The second reading was in Spanish, 1 Corinthians 15:51-57 concerning final victory over death. After the sung "Alleluia," the Gospel was Luke 23:44-49 and 24:1-6, the death of Jesus and His resurrection.

Archbishop Flores began his homily by saying: "I could only enumerate a few of the many graces that God bestowed upon Bishop San Pedro. We thank God that he was a blessing for all of us." The Archbishop remembered that, when he heard Bishop San Pedro was ill, he called him from California. The Bishop said, "I've reached the end. Pray to God that I will be faithful until death." The Archbishop told the people, "Because he said what he said, I honestly believe that he's in the hands of God."

Bishop Ricardo Ramirez, CSB, of Las Cruces, New Mexico, also spoke. He said, in part, that the Mass showed the solidarity of the Catholic Church and the people's appreciation to God for Bishop San Pedro. He added, "I think it was a beautiful expression of gratitude to this man who was so gifted and gave his gifts to the church." Among those attending were about twenty members of the late bishop's family, including his two sisters.

Father Bernard Doyon, OMI, celebrated Mass for Bishop San Pedro in the Cathedral of the Immaculate Conception in Brownsville for about eighty people. There was a special memorial service there on July 20 at 7:00 P.M.

On the following day, Thursday, 21 July, Bishop San Pedro's body was returned to Miami for viewing at the Belén Jesuit Preparatory School, where he had taught, from 7:00 P.M. until Midnight. On Friday, 22 July, the Bishop lay in state in St. Mary's Cathedral from 9:00 A.M. to 10:45 A.M., followed by Mass celebrated by Archbishop Edward McCarthy of Miami at 11:00 A.M. Bishop San Pedro was buried that day in Our Lady of Mercy Cemetery in Miami.

On the following Wednesday, 27 July 1994, a memorial Mass in honor of the late bishop was held at Sacred Heart Co-Cathedral in Houston, where San Pedro had served as pastor. Said Bishop Joseph A. Fiorenza:

> The untimely death of Bishop San Pedro is an enormous loss to the Diocese of Brownsville and to the Church in Texas. He was an outstanding Churchman and a totally dedicated servant of the gospel. I treasure the five years that he served as auxiliary bishop and vicar for Hispanics in the Diocese of Galveston- Houston. His zeal, intelligence, love for the Church and sense of humor, was a great gift to us. He was intimately involved in the Hispanic community

> and his leadership was invaluable. He also made significant contributions to the civic community during his service here. I mourn his death and offer my prayerful condolences to his family, the Diocese of Brownsville and to his Jesuit brothers for whom he had a special allegiance and affection.

A classicist by training and inclination, Bishop San Pedro had the balance in life one would expect from the scholar. When his prodigious knowledge was combined with the missionary's desire to spread the Word of God, it made him an outstanding priest and bishop. The harmony of his life is made manifest in his coat of arms. Its colors are red, white, and blue, the components of the Cuban, American, and Texan flags.

The upper portion has a red field with a dragon, symbolizing the Bishop's Asian missionary service, together with "I.H.S.," the emblem of his order, the Society of Jesus. The sinister impalement on a white field displays three ears of wheat and a key taken from the arms of the San Pedro and Xiques families. The wheat represents the Eucharist and the key the Sacrament of Penance or Reconciliation. These symbols are also found in the coats of arms of Cuba and of Havana. The dexter side has a blue field with a crescent representing Mary, the Mother of Jesus, and a single star, representing both Texas and Cuba.

The Bishop took for his motto a passage from 2 Corinthians 12:15: "*Libentissime impendam et superimpendar*" ("Most gladly will I spend myself and be spent for your sakes"). For Bishop San Pedro it was the standard of his ministry and of his work on earth. Like a comet, this brilliant figure passed through the Texas sky and left a trail for all to wonder.

Most Reverend Anthony J. Schuler, SJ, DD
First Bishop of El Paso

A missionary priest of the American West, Anthony J. Schuler was born in Pennsylvania and grew up in Colorado. To him was given the task of helping to settle a frontier. As the first bishop of El Paso, he established and built Church institutions. And he left a solid foundation for his successors.

Anthony was the son of Joseph and Albertina (Algeier) Schuler, born in St. Mary's, Elk County, Pennsylvania, on 20 September 1869. He moved with his parents and five brothers and sisters to Georgetown, Clear Creek County, Colorado, in 1876. Here his father worked as a miner. Father Nicholas C. Matz, the French-born priest who became coadjutor bishop (1887-1889) and bishop of Denver (1889-1917), was a friend to young Anthony and taught him Latin and Greek. The student became interested in religion and decided to enter the Society of Jesus in 1886.

Founded by St. Ignatius of Loyola in France in 1534, the Society of Jesus (Jesuits) won papal approval in 1540. The order came to the United States of America to Baltimore in 1833 and opened its second province in St. Louis, Missouri, in 1863. Anthony Schuler entered St. Stanislaus Seminary and Jesuit Novitiate in Florissant, Missouri, on 7 December 1886. He made his first vows as a Jesuit on 8 December 1888. From 1890 to 1893 he studied science and philosophy at St. Louis University in Missouri, an institution founded by Jesuit priests in 1818.

Anthony Schuler returned to Colorado in 1893 as Professor and Prefect of Regis College in Denver, an institution founded by the Jesuits six years before. Here he remained until 1898 when he undertook theological studies at Woodstock College in Maryland. He was ordained a priest of the Society of Jesus by Archbishop (later Cardinal) Sebastiano Martinelli, OSA, the Apostolic Delegate to the United States, in the Woodstock College chapel on 27 June 1901. From 1902 to 1903 he was again Professor and Prefect of Regis College. After receiving the degree of Doctor of Divinity from Woodstock College, he was President of Regis College from 1903 to 1906.

A brief assignment to St. Stanislaus Seminary in Missouri (1906-1907) was followed by parish work in El Paso, Texas. Between 1907 and 1910 he was Assistant Pastor and Pastor of Sacred Heart Parish, Pastor of Holy Family Parish, and Chaplain of Hotel Dieu. For the next five years Father Schuler was again President of Regis College in Denver. He was Assistant Pastor of Sacred Heart Parish in Denver (1910-1913) and Pastor (1913-1915). From 1914 to 1915 he was also Diocesan Director of the Apostleship of Prayer.

From the turn of the twentieth century the more than 10,000 Catholics of the El Paso, Texas, area began to have churches of their own. Due to the work of the Jesuit priest Carlos Pinto, the Parishes of the Holy Family, Immaculate Conception, and Sacred Heart came into being. Father Pinto next laid the foundations for the parish church of St. Patrick's. Changes were taking place at such a rate in Arizona and southern New Mexico that the bishops of the ecclesiastical province of Santa Fe met in 1913.

Bishop Henry Granjon of Tucson wished to separate the southern part of

New Mexico from his diocese so that he might better serve the spiritual needs of his people in the State of Arizona. The problem was that the detached portion was too small to become a diocese but too large to be added to adjoining dioceses. Bishops Joseph P. Lynch of Dallas and John W. Shaw of San Antonio were glad to cede portions of their territories, however.

The Sacred Consistorial Congregation of the Vatican found this agreement acceptable. Pope Pius X issued a Bull of erection on 3 March 1914 creating the Diocese of El Paso. To the detached New Mexico counties of Grant, Luna, Dona Ana, Otero, Eddy, and part of Sierra, he added the Texas counties of El Paso and Culberson from the Diocese of Dallas and Presidio, Jeff Davis, Reeves, Brewster, Terrell, Pecos, Crane, Ward, Loving, Winkler, Ector, Andrews, and Gaines from the Diocese of San Antonio. The Church of the Immaculate Conception in El Paso became the temporary cathedral for the Diocese.

Although Rev. John J. Brown was announced as Bishop in 1915, he failed to take office and later resigned. On 17 June 1915 Pope Benedict XV appointed Father Schuler Bishop of El Paso. Bishop Schuler would have preferred to have the aged Bishop Matz of Denver as his consecrator. It was he who had guided the first steps of the young man into the religious life. Although he attended, he was too ill to perform the ceremony.

Archbishop John P. Pitaval of Santa Fe consecrated Bishop Schuler in the Cathedral of the Immaculate Conception in Denver on 28 October 1915. Bishops Patrick McGovern of Cheyenne and Henry Granjon of Tucson were co-consecrators. Bishop Schuler was formerly installed as Bishop of El Paso in November 1915 by Archbishop Pitaval and by Bishop Shaw of San Antonio in the pro-Cathedral of the Immaculate Conception in El Paso.

On his return to El Paso the people of the City remembered Bishop Schuler from his days as a pastor there. Children strew flowers before him and women offered bouquets, as the crowd cheered. He gave his first episcopal blessing to the children whom he asked to pray each day for him "that I may measure up to the demands that will be made upon me."

He was given a banquet by the Knights of Columbus, who declared that the new bishop was the first member of the Council to be a member of the hierarchy. Rev. Edward Barry, SJ, presented him with a check for $58,000 for his new Cathedral of St. Patrick's which Father Pinto had been building for two years. Bishop Schuler dedicated it on 29 November 1917.

At this time the Diocese of El Paso had an area of more than 64,000 square miles. There were more than 50,000 Catholics with some thirty priests to serve them. Four priests were stationed in Marfa. They covered, on horseback, all of Brewster and Presidio counties, an area of more than 10,000 square miles. Twenty-six days after they left their rectory they returned for three days of rest. Then they went on their circuit again, caring for eight missions and twenty-three Mass stations.

Jesuits of Sacred Heart Parish in El Paso cared for missions as far as Van Horn, about 110 miles away. Three Franciscans cared for all the churches and missions in Eddy County, New Mexico. Four priests served all of Dona Ana County. Many Mexicans crossed the border because of revolution and religious persecution.

The City of El Paso had four parishes, with nine others in Texas and eleven in New Mexico. There were about fifty missions with three academies, nine parochial schools, and three hospitals. Bishop Schuler rolled up his sleeves and went to work. He built St. Patrick's Cathedral, St. Joseph's School, the Catholic Community Center, the Guardian Angel School, Sacred Heart and St. Margaret's orphanages, and St. Joseph's Sanatorium in El Paso. He sponsored and patronized the erection of Loretto Academy by the Sisters of Loretto. He also helped found the newspapers *Catholic Weekly* and *Western American.* And he lent his voice in persuading the Jesuits of Las Vegas, New Mexico, to move their offices of *Revista Catolica* to El Paso.

Bishop Schuler was a force for every movement to improve El Paso and his diocese, including the cleaning up of public dance halls. To the poor and needy he was a faithful friend and a founder of Associated Charities and the Community Chest. When his golden jubilee as a member of the Society of Jesus occurred in 1936, the citizens of El Paso named him their outstanding citizen.

Bishop Sidney M. Metzger was appointed Coadjutor Bishop to the seventy-two-year-old Bishop Schuler in 1941. When the aged bishop retired on 22 November 1942, he thanked those who helped him in his ministry. He said in part:

> My heart is filled with deepest gratitude to God for the unfailing loyalty and devotion of my priests, religious and laity . . . and the gracious helpfulness of those citizens of El Paso who are not of my flock but to whom I am also a debtor.

A week later his resignation became effective and Bishop Metzger became Bishop of El Paso.

Bishop Schuler left 118 priests in charge of fifty parishes, ninety-seven missions, five academies, twelve parochial schools, four hospitals, six orphanages, and three day nurseries. There were also a maternity clinic and two large Catholic centers.

The Bishop, whose German name means "scholar", lived up to that designation. But more than that he was a builder of churches and institutions whose outstretched hand grasped the hands of others of similar good will and worked together in pursuit of the moral and physical well-being of others. He retired to Regis College where he lived out his life. He died at St. Joseph's Hospital in Denver, Colorado, on 3 June 1944.

The citizens of El Paso mourned their former bishop, who had shown his love of God in his love for his people. At his funeral on 13 June 1944 his successor Bishop Metzger said of him: "His charming simplicity, gentleness, kindness, all radiated from a soul that lived in union with God." Bishop Schuler was buried in Concordia Cemetery in El Paso, Texas. In 1983 his remains were transferred to a vault in Mount Carmel Cemetery in that city.

Most Reverend John William Shaw, DD
Titular Bishop of Castabala and
Coadjutor Bishop of San Antonio
Fourth Bishop of San Antonio
Eighth Archbishop of New Orleans

In the person of John William Shaw history repeated itself. He was the second priest to come as a bishop to San Antonio from the Diocese of Mobile and the second bishop to go from Texas to become archbishop of New Orleans. He followed in the footsteps of Bishop Pellicer in 1874 and Bishop Odin in 1861. But the path he took was his own.

John William was one of six children of Patrick and Elizabeth (Smith) Shaw, who were natives of Ireland. He was born in Mobile, Mobile County, Alabama, on 12 December 1863. His early education took place at St. Vincent de Paul parochial school and at the Academy of Brothers of the Sacred Heart in Mobile. He began his clerical studies at St. Finian's Diocesan Seminary in Navan, County Meath, Ireland. From 1882 until 1888 he attended North American College in Rome.

The Reverend Mister Shaw was ordained by Cardinal Lucindo Parochi, the vicar general of Rome, in the Basilica of St. John Lateran in Rome on 26 May 1888. From September 1888 to February 1889 he was assigned to the Cathedral of the Immaculate Conception in Mobile, pending his first regular parish assignment. From 1889 to 1891 he was Assistant Pastor of St. Peter's Parish in Montgomery, Alabama, and became Assistant Pastor of St. Vincent de Paul Parish in Mobile in 1891. In 1892 Father Shaw became Rector of Immaculate Conception Cathedral in Mobile and was made Chancellor of the Diocese four years later.

He held these appointments until Pope Pius X appointed him Titular Bishop of Castabala and Coadjutor Bishop of San Antonio (with right of succession) on 7 February 1910. Bishop Shaw was consecrated by Archbishop James H. Blenk of New Orleans in the Cathedral of the Immaculate Conception in Mobile on 14 April 1910. His co-consecrators were Bishops Edward P. Allen of Mobile and Cornelius Van de Ven of Alexandria, Louisiana. On 18 May 1910 the ailing Bishop John Forest appointed Bishop Shaw Administrator of the Diocese of San Antonio.

Bishop Shaw wished to help the condition of the Mexican people of his diocese. He wrote to Archbishop Blenk on 20 January 1911, describing the condition of

> these poor souls, who are full of faith, wonderfully responsive to kindness and generous as far as their slender means permit. . . . We have at least 20,000 Mexicans in the city yet we have only eight fathers and of these some are always absent on the country missions. . .If you happen to know of any really zealous, unselfish priests who speak Spanish I need not say how grateful I should be if you would recommend them to come here.

On 11 March 1911 Bishop Forest died and Bishop Shaw became Bishop of San Antonio. The Catholic population at that time was approximately 95,000 with 128 churches and thirty-nine schools in the diocese. The Bishop wrote to Rev. Joseph Rose, OMI, on 8 May 1911 concerning the arrival of two Spanish priests in the Diocese. He wanted Father Rose to tell them that the work is

> hard and ill paid, they will indeed be fortunate if they get an assistant's salary of $25.00 a month and they will have no chance of a settled parish for some years.

Bishop Shaw wrote to an applicant for parochial duties in his diocese on 28 March 1912:

> I find myself unable to accede to your request as I am well supplied at present with German priests and have no need of English speaking priests: what I chiefly need being Poles, Bohemians, and Spaniards.

Work for the clergy grew apace as Catholic Action groups enlarged their activities. In 1911 the Gibbons Literary Club began in San Antonio, as did the Laymen's Retreat Movement at St. Mary's University. On 30 October 1912 a fire destroyed St. John's Orphanage with the loss of five sisters and three boys. Many friends, particularly Peter Kuntz, enabled Bishop Shaw to replace the ruined building with a new structure on Mission Road, named St. Peter's Home. It is now St. Peter's-St. Joseph's Home.

The Catholic Daughters of America established their first court in the Diocese in Yoakum on 1 June 1913. They founded a second court that year in San Antonio. By 1974 there were five courts in San Antonio and twenty-six in the Archdiocese. The Catholic Women's Association began in San Antonio to provide a residence for students and working girls in 1916.

San Antonio parishes of Holy Redeemer, St. Gerard's, Immaculate Heart of Mary, Our Lady of Guadalupe, St. Ann's, Our Lady of Perpetual Help, St. Philip of Jesus, and Our Lady of Sorrows started between 1910 and 1915. In the Diocese there were new parishes of St. John Nepomocene in New Taiton, St. Anthony's in Palacios, Assumption of the Blessed Virgin Mary in Ganado, St. Anthony's in Runge, Sts. Cyril and Methodius in Shiner, Our Lady of Grace in La Coste, and Our Lady of the Gulf in Port Lavaca.

By 1913 Bishop Shaw had become Texan enough to speak up to the Vatican concerning jurisdictional matters. The Vatican proposed a plan to make the San Antonio Diocese a part of the Province of Santa Fe. Though this would be the fate of the Diocese of El Paso for almost seventy years, Bishop Shaw wrote to Archbishop (later Cardinal) Giovanni Bonzano, the Apostolic Delegate to the United States, recommending the autonomy of Texas as an ecclesiastical entity.

He said in part:

> This is in my opinion especially true of Texas for Texas is of all our states most proud of her history. Texans never forget that the state was one time an independent Republic; even to this day you may hear people speaking of 'Texas' *and* the 'United States'.

The San Antonio Diocese remained attached to the Province of New Orleans until 1926. Then Archbishop Shaw of New Orleans saw his former diocese become an archdiocese and a metropolitan see as the Province of San Antonio.

Asked to report to the Vatican on mixed marriages in his diocese, Bishop Shaw felt record-keeping was in a poor state and that the migratory pattern prevented him from knowing the outcome of these marriages between persons of different faiths. On 18 September 1913 he wrote to Archbishop Blenk of New Orleans:

> The Sacred Congregation must think we are wonderful statisticians here, and that we missionary bishops find time to hang heavily on our hands. I wish some of these good cardinals had a taste of missionary life in our Southland. It would not hurt some of those monsignori secretaries who are all the time looking up work for us to do, to have a few months of real missionary life.

Bishop Shaw considered travel no small part of his missionary duties in a period when missionaries traveled throughout the Diocese and the Trans-Pecos and Big Bend regions in covered wagons, enduring hardship and privation.

When the Diocese of El Paso was created on 3 March 1914, the Diocese of San Antonio ceded the counties of Terrell, Brewster, Presidio, Jeff Davis, Pecos, Reeves, Loving, Ward, Winkler, Crane, Ector, Andrews, and Gaines, losing 29,000 square miles in the process. Andrews, Crane, Ector, Pecos, and Terrell were lost to the Diocese of San Angelo on its formation in 1961 and Gaines to the Diocese of Lubbock in 1983.

Ever mindful of the need to foster native vocations, Bishop Shaw opened St. John's Diocesan Seminary in 1915. It closed in June 1970, its work replaced by Assumption Seminary. Bishop Shaw had another project, one which involved the diocesan chancellor, Rev. William Hume. From 1911 to 1919 Father Hume was in charge of the old Spanish missions around San Antonio.

Mission Concepcion served as St. John's Seminary chapel for a time. Mission San Francisco De La Espada had the interior walls repaired and plastered, a brick floor laid, and a wood ceiling, metal roof, and new doors and windows installed in 1911. The Mission became an active parish, and the Sisters of Charity of the Incarnate Word established a parish school from 1915 until 1967. Mission San Juan Capistrano, an active parish again since 1909, received additional repairs in 1915.

The era of Bishop Shaw was turbulent. In Mexico the Carranza and Villa revolutions drove refugees into Texas, World War I started in Europe, and the United States entered that war in 1917. The Bishop's aid of Mexican refugees and his efforts on behalf of his Mexican-American laity won him recognition from the Vatican. Pope Benedict XV appointed him an Assistant to the Pontifical Throne on 25 September 1916. In that year the Diocese had 141 priests with about two hundred churches and seventy schools. By 1918 the Catholic population of the Diocese numbered 165,440.

On 11 January 1918 the creation of the Diocese of Lafayette, Louisiana, reduced the Archdiocese of New Orleans by about 11,000 square miles, forty parish churches, and a population of about 300,000. Pope Benedict XV appointed Bishop Shaw Archbishop of New Orleans and Administrator of the Diocese of Lafayette on 25 January 1918. He served as Administrator until the consecration of its first bishop, Jules B. Jeanmard, on 8 December 1918. On that date Archbishop Shaw received the Pallium, the insignia of his archepiscopal office.

In 1919 Archbishop Shaw invited the Missionary Oblates of Mary Immaculate to administer St. Louis Cathedral in New Orleans. In that same year the Sisters of Charity of the Incarnate Word were brought in to teach at St. Francis de Sales parochial school, which is now defunct. He had known the work of both orders from his days in San Antonio.

The Archbishop convoked the sixth synod for New Orleans in 1922, the first since 1889. Between 1920 and 1923 he started a fund drive with the aid of Chancellor August J. Bruening. It collected almost one million dollars for the building of Notre Dame Major Seminary, located at 2901 South Carrollton Avenue in New Orleans. In 1923 the Sisters of St. Francis of Calais opened Our Lady of the Lake Hospital in Baton Rouge. It is now Mercy Hospital operated by the Sisters of Mercy in that city on 301 North Jefferson Davis Parkway.

Monsignor Peter M. H. Wynhoven reorganized the social services and charities of the Archdiocese, setting up Associated Catholic Charities in 1924. In 1925 Monsignor Wynhoven established Hope Haven as a boys' home and opposite Madonna Manor, a school for boys, replaced St. Mary's and St. Joseph's orphanages.

Franciscans came to take charge of the new parish of St. Mary of the Angels in New Orleans and the missions of the Lower Coast on 21 July 1925. The Sisters of the Holy Ghost and Mary Immaculate arrived in September 1926 from San Antonio to teach Black children in St. Luke's School, now not in operation. Archbishop Shaw encouraged the endeavors of Catharine Bostick and Zoe Grouchy in establishing the Missionary Servants of the Most Holy Eucharist of the Third Order of St. Dominic for the religious instruction of children in public schools and social relief work.

The Society of the Divine Word took over mission stations on the east and west banks of the lower Mississippi River in 1928. Nor was the campus apostolate neglected. Rev. (later Bishop) Maurice Schexnayder began the Newman Club on the Louisiana State University campus in Baton Rouge in 1929 at a time when Catholic students numbered about one-third of the total. In 1983 about seventy per cent of these students were Catholics.

The Great Depression of 1929 froze some archdiocesan funds and high interest rates on monies borrowed in the 1920s and made it difficult for parishes to meet their payments. Jesuits purchased Jefferson College in Convent, Louisiana, in 1931 and converted it into Manresa House of Retreats. In 1932 the Archbishop established *Catholic Action of the South* as the official archdiocesan newspaper to replace *Morning Star*, which filled that function from 1878 to 1930. The present New Orleans archdiocesan paper is called the *Clarion Herald*. Between 1919 and 1934 thirty-three new parishes were established in the Archdiocese.

Archbishop Shaw, whose name means "grove of trees" and whose episcopal motto was "God provides," died in New Orleans, Louisiana, on 2 November 1934. He is entombed there in St. Louis King of France Cathedral.

Most Reverend Michael Jarboe Sheehan, STL, JCD
First Bishop of Lubbock
Apostolic Administrator of Santa Fe
Eleventh Archbishop of Santa Fe

One does not become the youngest Roman Catholic archbishop of the United States of America by accident. Positive qualities are required and being in the right place at the right time is not in itself sufficient. In the case of Michael Sheehan a graduate education in Rome, an ability to speak Spanish and pastoral experience with Hispanics, administrative ability, and ten years as a diocesan bishop just may have determined his selection. When personal qualities of devotion to the Church, intelligence and a sense of humor, and involving people in decision-making add to the mixture, one begins to see that youth is not the most important attribute. Many elements go into the making of an archbishop, and the process takes many years to complete.

Michael Jarboe Sheehan was born to John Edward and Mildred (Jarboe) Sheehan in Wichita, Sedgwick County, Kansas on 9 July 1939. He was part of a family of four, including brothers John and Joseph and a sister Mary. Reared in Texarkana, Texas, Michael attended Sacred Heart Parish School there. After high school graduation in 1957, he attended St. John's and Assumption seminaries in San Antonio, Texas. Completing the course of study in 1961, he proceeded to the North American College in Rome.

The North American College was founded by American bishops in 1859 and the first ordination of an alumnus took place in 1862. It was granted pontifical status by Pope Leo XIII in 1884. It is a residence and house of formation for American seminarians and graduate students. Many students pursue theological and related studies at the Pontifical Gregorian University. Such was the case of Michael Sheehan, who was ordained a deacon (1963). His ordination to the priesthood took place in the Church of St. Agatha in Rome on 12 July 1964.

The Pontifical Gregorian University was founded in 1552 in Rome. The Pontifical Biblical Institute and the Pontifical Institute of Oriental Studies are associated with it. Father Sheehan completed his theological studies at the Gregorian and was awarded the degree of Licentiate in Sacred Theology (STL) in 1965.

Having been ordained for the then Diocese of Dallas-Fort Worth, its bishop Thomas K. Gorman appointed the young priest Assistant Pastor of the Church (later Cathedral) of the Immaculate Conception in Tyler, Smith County. He was given responsibility for its mission at that time, St. Edward's Church in Henderson County. From 1965 to 1967 Father Sheehan also taught at Gorman High School in Tyler and was chaplain at the East Texas Chest Hospital (now known as The University of Texas Health Center in Tyler). He was Catholic Youth Organization moderator for East Texas (1965-1975) and served as Newman Chaplain for Henderson County Junior College (now Trinity Valley Community College) in Athens (1966-1967). Father Sheehan was also a member of the Priests' Senate for the Diocese of Dallas-Fort Worth (1966-1968).

Leaving Tyler in 1967, Father Sheehan was secretary to Bishop Gorman until 1968, when he returned to Rome to complete his graduate studies, this time in canon law. While in Rome he served as an auxiliary Navy chaplain and received the degree of Doctor of Canon Law (JCD) from the Pontifical Lateran University (founded 1773) in 1971.

Thereafter Sheehan's rise in church affairs was rapid. He was Assistant General Secretary of the National Conference of Catholic Bishops (NCCB) in Washington, DC (1971-1976), and also acted as liaison or coordinator between the United States Catholic Conference (USCC) and the Texas Catholic Conference (1971-1976). He was Executive Secretary of the Bishops' Advisory Conference (1973-1976) and received the National Association of State Catholic Conferences Director's award in 1974.

Father Sheehan's association with the NCCB was productive over many years. He was a member of the Hispanic Affairs, Evangelization, and Proselytism committees, and in 1993 he chaired the Nominations committee. He gained valuable experience in establishing ministries to Hispanic communities, in pastoral research and practices, in immigration services, and as liaison with Catholic Charismatic Renewal. This movement reflects

> the personally experienced actualization of grace already sacramentally received, principally in baptism and confirmation.
>
> The experience of baptism of the Holy Spirit is often accompanied by the reception of one or more charismatic gifts. A characteristic form of the renewal is the weekly prayer meeting, a gathering which includes periods of spontaneous prayer, singing, sharing of experience and testimony, fellowship and teaching (1995 *CA* 303).

On his return to Dallas in 1976 Father Sheehan was made Rector of Holy Trinity Seminary there. Founded in 1965 as a theologate or major seminary, Holy Trinity occupied its present facilities adjacent to the main campus of the University of Dallas in Irving in 1967. Possessing complete religious, dining and athletic facilities, it is now a minor seminary for undergraduate students in formation for the diocesan priesthood and attending classes at the University. Leaving the rectorship in 1982, Father Sheehan became Pastor of Immaculate Conception Parish in Grand Prairie and was also a Diocesan Consultor.

Pope John Paul II appointed Father Sheehan Bishop of Lubbock on 29 March 1983. Archbishop Patrick F. Flores of San Antonio performed his episcopal ordination and installation in the Lubbock Memorial Civic Center on 17 June 1983 at 7:00 P.M., on the day the new Diocese of Lubbock came formally into being. On 23 October 1983 Bishop Sheehan was installed a Knight of the Equestrian Order of the Holy Sepulchre by Cardinal John Carberry in Tulsa, Oklahoma.

As of mid-November 1981, the Bishop of Amarillo, Leroy T. Matthiesen, was reported to be in favor of making a division of his forty-six county diocese, covering the entire Texas Panhandle from the Oklahoma-Texas boundary line south to Dawson and Gaines counties. In March 1983 it was decided that the Diocese of Amarillo would contribute twenty of its counties, together with five counties from the Diocese of San Angelo, to form the Diocese of Lubbock.

On the day of his appointment (29 March 1983) Bishop Sheehan appeared at a press conference held at Christ the King parish house in Lubbock at 2:00 P.M., on the site of the new cathedral. He said in part:

> I am honored and humbled that the Holy Father has chosen me as the first Bishop of Lubbock. I look forward with real enthusiasm in working with the clergy, religious and laity of the South Plains in creating the new Church of Lubbock where Franciscan missionaries first brought the faith nearly 450 years ago.

Bishop Sheehan said of himself: "I try to avoid extremes." When asked if he owned a pair of cowboy boots for his new assignment, he replied, "No, but I'm ordering some."

The realignment left the Diocese of Amarillo with twenty-six counties populated by 40,000 Catholics in thirty-five parishes and twelve missions. It would be served by forty priests, twenty-six permanent deacons, and 128 women religious. There were seven elementary schools and a high school with an enrollment of 1,421 students.

The twenty-five counties of the Diocese of Lubbock (approximately 23,382 square miles) would begin with a Catholic population of about some 50,000 people, about 80 per cent of them Hispanic. The new bishop spoke Spanish, had been the pastor of a largely Hispanic congregation in Grand Prairie, and was well- versed in the policies and practices of Hispanic ministry. As of 1 January 1984 he had thirty-nine priests, thirty permanent deacons, and thirty-seven women religious to assist him in the operation of thirty-four parishes, twenty-seven missions, two chapels, one general hospital, three elementary schools and a private high school (subsequently closed due to financial loss), with 12,706 students under Catholic instruction. There were 51,817 Catholics in the general population of 451,330.

Over the years Bishop Sheehan continued to pursue his various interests. He had contributed articles to the *New Catholic Encyclopedia* and was the author of *Shared Responsibilities at Work* (1975). In 1983 he became a trustee of St. Mary's Hospital in Lubbock (to 1989) and chaplain (to 1993) of the local Serra Club. He was a member of the board of directors of the Mexican American Cultural Center in San Antonio and of the Texas Conference of Churches. He was a papal vistor of American seminaries, a member of the Canon Law Society of America, and a member and past chairman of the American Board of Catholic Missions. In 1992 he would become a trustee of Catholic Relief Services, visiting Kenya to deliver food in August of that year. When time and temperature permitted, there could be racquetball and snow skiing.

By January 1988 two more priests were active in the Diocese, as well as eight additional women religious. There were one less parish and one more mission with neither chapels nor high schools listed in the *Official Catholic Directory* for that year. Thirteen seminarians studied for the priesthood. Other institutions included a pastoral center, a retreat house, and fifteen convents and residences for women religious. Two foundations aided the Diocese and Christ the King School. There were 10,407 students under Catholic instruction with 51,657 Catholics in a total population of 501,000.

Also in the same month of January 1988 one of two incidents occurred which would bring Bishop Sheehan national attention. Parishioners of St. John Neumann Parish in Lubbock began to report unusual occurrences taking place in the church during the regular Monday night Mass and rosary service. Some said the Blessed Virgin Mary delivered messages during the recitation of the rosary. Attendance was sometimes as high as 1,000 as word of the happenings spread.

During the rosary parishioners Mike Slate, Mary Constancio, and Theresa Werner knelt at the altar and wrote on note pads. Afterward they read the messages they said Mary had sent. Other parishioners reported they were physically healed, felt the Virgin's presence, and smelled roses throughout the service.

Mike Slate, a retired air force officer, publicly read the message from his notebook. He had written:

> My dear little children, listen to me your mother, I want to help you. I want you to be in heaven, where we can pray and serve our Father for all eternity. Yes, my dear ones, you must have signs and you will have these signs. . .but it will be up to you to believe.

Mary Constancio, a former hospital therapist, and Mrs. Werner, a housewife and mother, also read their messages. Mrs. Constancio's was in Spanish. The English translation said:

> My children, do not be sad. Have joy in your hearts, have peace. Listen to the prayer that you ask for the Lord will give it to you.

After the readings some members of the congregation sought out the visionary messengers for blessings. They responded by laying their hands upon those with physical or personal problems.

Bob Golec came to the devotions from Midlothian in June with chronic knee problems. But he said they disappeared when Mrs. Werner gave him a message from Mary and Msgr. Joseph W. James, the pastor of St. John Neumann's, offered a prayer of blessing in his behalf. Mr. Golec considered this remedy was a sign to strengthen his faith.

The fifty-six-year-old Monsignor James seemed to give some credence to the messages. He and other parishioners of St. John Neumann's had gone to Medjugorje, Yugoslavia. In this city six young people claimed to see apparitions of Mary starting in June 1981. They said they had seen, heard and touched Mary in visions and were given ten sacred messages about world events. They were urged to seek peace through prayer, penance, and personal conversion. Bishop Pavao Zanic of Mostar-Duvno appointed a commission to investigate. It reported in March 1984 that the authenticity of the apparitions was not established and that reported healings had not been verified. Bishop Zanic termed the sightings "collective hallucination" exploited by local Franciscan priests.

Archbishop Frane Franic of Split-Makarska had a different view. He said in December 1985 that "my personal conviction is that the events at Medjugorje are of supernatural inspiration." He saw a manifestation of spiritual development in the six young people, in increased Mass attendance and sacramental practice at the scene of the apparitions, and in reconciliation among people.

The Roman Catholic Church considers miracles as

> observable events or effects in the physical or moral order of things, with reference to salvation, which cannot be explained by the ordinary operation of laws of nature and which, therefore, are attributed to the direct action of God. They make known, in an unusual way, the concern and intervention of God in human affairs and for

> the salvation of men (1988 *CA* 317).

God as the Creator and Master of the laws of nature, so claims the Church, may occasionally set them aside and produce effects beyond their power. The Church admits miracles when the events bear upon grace and no natural explanation can be found for them.

Bishop Zanic instituted a diocesan commission in conformity with canon law concerning discernment of alleged apparitions and private revelations. The Vatican Congregation of the Doctrine of the Faith approved the Bishop's work and encouraged its continuance at the national episcopal level.

Pending the determination by the commission and judgment of the Church, a communique published in the official bulletin of the Archdiocese of Zagreb on 29 January 1987, withdrew permission for pilgrimages to be organized motivated by the supernatural character attributed to the facts of Medjugorje. It recommended instead legitimate devotion to Mary according to the *magisterium* (teaching authority) of the Church and especially to those directives in the apostolic exhortation *Marialis Cultus* of 2 February 1974. This communique was reprinted in the 22 February 1987 English edition of *L'Osservatore Romano* and was signed by Cardinal Franjo Kuharic, Archbishop of Zabreb and President of the Yugoslav Episcopal conference, and by Bishop Zanic of Mostar-Duvno.

Bishop Zanic was so incensed by disregard of the instruction to end pilgrimages to Medjugorje that he banned Masses in his diocese by priests leading pilgrimages until the commission of the bishops' conference completed its work. This action was reported by the Italian magazine *Jesus* in August 1987. But pilgrimage Masses continued to be celebrated at the site of the alleged apparitions.

By early 1988 it was estimated that 8,000,000 people had visited Medjugorje in the past seven years. The Yugoslav National Tourist Office in New York reported 235,000 persons from the United States visited Yugoslavia in 1987 and assumed most had made the trip to Medjugorje. Father Peter M. J. Stravinskas, editor of *The Catholic Answer*, visited Medjugorje in the summer of 1988. He found Christ-centered devotion, a greater increase in sacramental reception, and generally solid preaching and teaching. But he found negatives as well.

In the opinion of Father Stravinskas the messages of the apparitions add nothing to other revelations, the visions appear too frequently (at least daily for seven years), too "programmed" (sometimes two daily, with Mary changing locations), and too talkative (thousands of transcript pages). He observed that the visionary messengers were kept apart during interviews and that illnesses are "too easily attributed to diabolic possession."

He concludes:

> This pilgrimage brought home to me the Church's wisdom in delaying her response to alleged apparitions, because time is a critical factor in discerning the truth. When there finally *is* an official pronouncement, my own guess is that it will be neither a condemnation nor an approval.
>
> Instead, the Church may reiterate Gamaliel's counsel to the people of Israel concerning the Apostles: 'Have nothing to do with

> these men, and let them go. For if this. . .activity is of human origin, it will destroy itself. But if it comes from God, you will not be able to destroy them; you may even find yourselves fighting against God!' (Acts 5:38-39).
>
> In the meantime, we all should heed the basic message of Medjugorje, which is nothing other than that of the Gospel.

As late as 1995 the authenticity of the Medugorje message was not resolved by the Church. In a statement published on 2 January 1991 the bishops of Yugoslavia stated (19 to 1) that, "On the basis of research conducted so far, one cannot affirm that supernatural apparitions are involved." Interest in Medugorje and devotion to Mary in the area remain intense. But after the dissolution of Yugoslavia into its constituent states, the location of Medjugorje in Boenia-Herzegovina has made pilgrimages less frequent due to civil war there.

The importance of Medjugorje for the Church and for events in Lubbock is that it has sparked a debate and tightened criteria for belief in alleged apparitions. Hence there is no official statement on their validity. The happenings in that city have, however, produced a framework for action and demonstrated a process for attempting to resolve such matters.

Back in Lubbock, Monsignor James, when interviewed by the Associated Press, said in part: "I think we're going to see some beautiful, beautiful thing - experience her [Mary's] presence." He interpreted the messages as indicating a miraculous occurrence on 15 August, the Feast of the Assumption of the Blessed Virgin Mary. The Parish worked with Lubbock city officials on crowd control, transportation and parking, and a public address system for those coming to St. John Neumann's.

Bishop Sheehan returned from his vacation in late July 1988. On 26 July he cautioned the faithful not to presume that "anything spiritual is happening." He took a "cautious attitude" about the messages and added, "I neither encourage people to participate in the events nor do I discourage them."

A crowd estimated from 12,000 to more than 15,000 converged upon the Church of St. John Neumann in Lubbock on 15 August 1988. Diane Winston, the religion editor of the *Dallas Times Herald*, attended the ceremony. Some people claimed to have seen figures in the clouds and others claimed to have a photograph showing the door to heaven. There were reports that some rosaries turned from silver to gold. Ms. Winston quoted Rev. Albert Meyer, a Benedictine monk from New Mexico, as saying: "The biggest miracle I've seen here is all the people saying the rosary and praying for the Lord."

Bishop Sheehan waited a few days and issued an announcement through his office:

> I am asking the National Conference of Catholic Bishops [NCCB] to assist me in preparing an investigation of the event, and a panel of specialists will be appointed shortly for this task.

Joe Lipovsky, speaking for the NCCB, said of Bishop Sheehan's efforts in this matter:

> He is free to set up his own investigation and ask experts in on his own but the national organization has nothing to do with that.

Bishop Sheehan made his investigation known to the Apostolic Nunciature in Washington, DC. He requested Monsignor James "not to promote or print the rosary Messages" until the conclusion of the investigation.

Rev. Frederic Jelly, OP, of Mount St. Mary's Seminary in Emmittsburg, Maryland, headed the committee. Other members were Msgr. Robert C. Rehkemper, Vicar General of the Diocese of Dallas; Rev. James J. Gill, SJ, a psychiatrist at the Jesuit Educational Center for Human Development in Cambridge, Massachusetts; Rev. George Montague, a scripture scholar from St. Louis, Missouri; and Sister Patricia A. Smith, RSM, Professor of Theology at St. Mary's Seminary and University in Baltimore, Maryland.

The committee rejected the happenings in Lubbock on 15 August as miraculous, deciding that God did not "suspend the law of nature to cause unnatural phenomena" and thought the Marian messages "appear to come out of a normal prayer life." The committee members attended Sunday Mass at St. John Neumann's Church in Lubbock and the Monday night rosary service and interviewed many of the clergy, the visionary messengers, and others who came to church services. The investigation disclosed no signs of anyone seeking monetary or personal gain, but that some messages "presented an angry God in a language that is strident and makes one question the claim to divine inspiration."

The committee reported many positive aspects including a deeper devotion to Mary, a spiritual reconciliation within families, and many people returning to church. The conclusion was that the "supernatural grace of Christ may be operative in the lives of many people without such events being miraculous" and that private revelations deepen people's devotions. But it went on to say that private revelations "never become part of the dogma of the church." Recommendations were that rosary devotions at the church continue but that visionary messages be submitted to the bishop prior to printing and distribution.

By keeping his head and proceeding calmly while others rushed to various conclusions, Bishop Sheehan showed he could be tested in a different situation and emerge in a way which reflected credit on himself and on the Church. The second incident which would bring him to national attention occurred about four years later.

On 2 December 1992 a television report out of New Orleans identified the Rev. Rodney C. Howell, a priest of the Lubbock diocese and dying from cancer at age sixty in a hospice, as a molester of children during his priestly career. Reverend Howell was identified as the brother of Reverend Gerard J. Howell, a priest church authorities in New Orleans said abused children in the New Orleans Center for Deaf Studies and barred from priestly duties since 1980.

Rev. Rodney Howell, now semi-comatose and dead within a few weeks after the announcement, was pastor of St. Pius X Parish in O'Donnell, Texas, for more than ten years. It seems a family had complained that Rodney Howell had abused two of their children in 1986 and was later treated for alcoholism.

Although charges of these incidents in Texas do not seem to have been made previously, the response of Bishop Sheehan was forthright and unambiguous. On hearing the television report, he announced he would not tolerate sexual abuse and urged those victimized to call the Diocese or two counselors agreeing to help. He said, "I am shocked to hear the allegation that this sexual abuse may have taken place in our diocese." He held a press conference on 7 December 1992 and convened a team of experts and liaisons with public officials. "Our highest priority is helping such victims [of verifiable sexual misconduct by priests or church employees] find healing and wholeness," observed the Bishop.

Bishop Sheehan's style of problem-solving is rooted in calmness, a desire for fairness, and seeks to reach conclusions satisfactory to reasonable people. One supposes that the bishop had in mind the adage, "Justice delayed is justice denied." His directness and attempt to do the right thing does much to relieve and assure all parties involved in difficult situations. An effective speaker on human rights, his proven abilities would soon do much to dispel trouble festering within the Archdiocese of Santa Fe, New Mexico from years past.

Robert Fortune Sanchez was the Archbishop of Santa Fe. At his appointment in 1974 he was the first Hispanic archbishop in the United States of America. He was chosen by Pope Paul VI without prior episcopal experience, at the rather early age of forty. On 8 March 1993 the Archdiocese of Santa Fe confirmed that five women alleged that Archbishop Sanchez had had sexual relations with them in the 1970s and early 1980s. One woman involved was Judy Maloof, member of a prominent New Mexican Catholic family.

It was further alleged that Archbishop Sanchez paid $25,000 to a woman who contended he assaulted her a year before he became Archbishop in 1973. The CBS television program "60 Minutes" reported on 21 March 1993 that Sanchez paid the woman the money in 1991 when she confronted him about the alleged assault. The sum was reportedly paid for her therapy and to secure her silence. Archdiocesan attorney Chuck Reynolds said, "There has never been a claim of rape by anybody." On 22 March "60 Minutes" spokesman Ron Brunett said, "We stand by the report based on the information we have."

Archbishop Sanchez submitted his letter of resignation on 19 March and went into seclusion. Later that month he issued a statement seeking forgiveness for any pain caused by the allegations. But he neither confirmed nor denied them. On Monday, 5 April 1993 the Archbishop called Bishop Sheehan to offer him support and prayers. On the following day Pope John Paul II officially appointed Bishop Sheehan Apostolic Administrator of Santa Fe, to retain the administration meanwhile of the Diocese of Lubbock.

Bishop Sheehan said: "I am deeply grateful for the ministry of Archbishop Sanchez throughout the years. He's a friend. I grieve with him and the church of Santa Fe during these distressing times. . . .I promise to do everything I can to bring healing and peace." Sadly the situation in which the Bishop found himself was much worse than it seemed.

The healing of the Archdiocese would have to happen over time. It was not merely a case of losing a native son to an outsider. It was much deeper than that. For some thirty years past a number of priests already in the Archdiocese or sent there from across the United States came to a treatment center in Jemez Springs, in Sandoval County, New Mexico. Here an order of priests known as the Servants of the Paraclete (founded 1947) had its generalate (or headquarters). Its ministry was the treatment of priests, who had various types of problems.

When such priests were pronounced "cured", they sometimes were assigned parish ministries in the Archdiocese. Some of them were child abusers or pedophiles. At one time it seems that church authorities believed that transferrals to other parishes or dioceses would end the problem. But the Church came at last to realize that some illnesses are not curable by ordinary means and do not respond to treatment. The best option for all concerned, it was at last realized, was to remove the priest from ministry and to prevent him from being in any situation involving the pastoral care of minors.

Archbishop Sanchez had appointed a commission to look into the question of problem priests. But little had been accomplished and Bishop Sheehan knew that a definite set of commission proposals would have to be implemented. A rash of lawsuits from the former victims of abuse made it imperative that policies be in place and action taken.

For the indefinite future the Bishop would divide his time between administering the Diocese of Lubbock and the Archdiocese of Santa Fe. In ten years he had capably developed the Diocese and its institutions. It was both spiritually and financially sound. His pastoral letter of 1985 identified evangelization (the preaching of the Gospel and the development of the life of faith) as the "most important item on the agenda" of the Church. He realized that the necessary time he spent in Santa Fe would not seriously detract from his duties in Lubbock. He would be spending the majority of his time in Santa Fe for the indefinite future.

Bishop Sheehan brought a reservoir of good will with him. He had a plan to deal with his main problem. It consisted of removing priests accused of sexual misconduct, helping victims of abuse to seek counseling, asking for forgiveness on behalf of the Church, and pledging to try to keep abuses from happening again. In working with Archbishop Sanchez's commission, he was able to set a new archdiocesan policy to deal with issues of sexual improprieties. It included forming a permanent review board to investigate allegations of wrongdoing, establishing a "counseling fund" to promote the mental welfare of victims and a hot line telephone number for the use of those feeling themselves victims, removing from ministry any guilty priestly child abuser, and tightening screening processes for seminarians.

The Bishop knew that part of the problem involved a lack of confidence in the Archdiocese by the laity. He would have to "put the household of faith in order" and would need help in that undertaking. His presence needed to be felt and it would be necessary to put that household through a public cleaning.

After five days on the job (11 April 1993) he felt well enough to attempt some humor: "I feel very much at home here. I love the green chile." On 1 July 1993 he could combine humor with more serious purposes. He admitted to hiding nothing. His closet, he said, contained nothing but his belongings, consisting mainly of tennis shoes, skiis, and ski boots. He added: "Every church is like a family. Every family has its painful moments. Some people in the family get over their pain more quickly. For some people it takes longer." On 13 August 1993 he reassured the people: "Even though sometimes humans fall, like how we've had some bad priests, it doesn't mean the church will fall. If this church was built only on men, it would have fallen years ago." He attempted to balance the ledger in his statement to the *People of God*, the official archdiocesan newspaper, for August 1993: "It is true that some members of the clergy have failed to live up to their promises. Most of them, however, have also done much good and brought the love of Christ and his peace and forgiveness to many."

Bishop Sheehan said of his administration of the Archdiocese of Santa Fe:

> Mainly I've tried to be a pastor. . . .The people have been hurt deeply. . . . I've been making the rounds of the parishes, asking their pardon in the name of the church. I've focused especially on the needs of the priests. The priests are hurting because a number of their group have been accused of misconduct with minors.

He added: "The loss of their archbishop is a terrible blow. He is much loved and a native son." By mid-August of 1993 he had visited every deanery in New Mexico, rallying his priests and ensuring that the people felt a spirit of continuity.

Pope John Paul II appointed Bishop Sheehan Archbishop of Santa Fe on 17 August 1993. The position he had undertaken was now permanent. He had done his job well and would be permitted to carry out the policies he had suggested. He would formally retain the title of bishop of Lubbock until his installation as archbishop. On the morning of the announcement Archbishop Sheehan said Mass, held a press conference in the Lubbock Catholic Center, and flew to Albuquerque for a meeting with Santa Fe consultors and deans. He would be joined by bishops Ricardo Ramirez, CSB of Las Cruces and Donald E. Pelotte, SSS of Gallup, his New Mexican suffragans.

In Lubbock the Archbishop thanked the clergy, women religious and laity for helping to create the Diocese:

> I am very grateful for the support and love I have known as Bishop of Lubbock; from the Catholic community and from the rest of West Texas, too. I can truthfully say I have received 100 times more than I have given. I will miss Lubbock very, very much.

When Archbishop Sheehan left Lubbock there were forty-five priests, twenty-five permanent deacons, and 41 women religious, serving thirty-six parishes, twenty-seven missions, two pastoral centers, a Catholic hospital, a special center for social services, two elementary schools, and 10,227 students under Catholic instruction. There were 48,194 Catholics out of a total population of 448,312, or 11 percent.

At the press conference in Albuquerque, the Archbishop designate said in part:

> I am deeply humbled to be asked by the Holy Father to serve as the Archbishop of Santa Fe. It is, indeed, an historic diocese; rich in Native American and Hispanic cultures, blessed with a long tradition of Catholic heritage. I will work diligently with the priests, religious and laity of the archdiocese to deal with the painful problems that presently afflict the church of Santa Fe and to move the Church forward in the years ahead.
>
> I have felt warmly welcomed in the Archdiocese of Santa Fe. I have come to know many people through visits to all eight deaneries and many parishes, pueblos and groups. I trust that the grace of Jesus Christ and the power of the Holy Spirit will help me be a faithful

> shepherd for the people, a good co-worker with the ministers of other faiths and a productive citizen in the State of New Mexico.

The "painful problems" of which Archbishop Sheehan spoke were those brought on by at least nineteen priests of the Archdiocese accused of sexual misconduct, together with a number of lawsuits alleging that the Archdiocese had not made its best efforts to handle these matters.

The Archdiocese of Santa Fe is one steeped in historic tradition. Franciscans discovered this land in 1539 and called it "The New Mexico" in 1581. And they were its sole Catholic ministers from 1598 when the first Spanish colony and Indian missions were established under their custody until Santa Fe became a diocese in 1853, three years after the creation of the Vicariate Apostolic of New Mexico. Today the Franciscans are joined in the Archdiocese by sixteen other orders of men religious and by sisters from forty-seven orders of women religious.

At present, the ecclesiastical province of Santa Fe covers the geographical area of the States of Arizona and New Mexico, including the Archdiocese itself, the Dioceses of Phoenix and Tucson in Arizona and the Dioceses of Gallup and Las Cruces in New Mexico. The cathedral of San Francisco de Asis (St. Francis of Assisi) was first established in Santa Fe in 1610, while the first church in Albuquerque dates from 1706. While the cathedral is in active use, the Archdiocese is governed from Albuquerque. The Archdiocese of Santa Fe was created in 1875 and now covers 61,142 square miles and is spread across nineteen New Mexican counties. Michael J. Sheehan would be its eleventh archbishop.

On Monday, 20 September 1993, on the evening before his installation the Archbishop took canonical possession of his cathedral. Priests, deacons, deans, and the college of archdiocesan consultors led the procession there, flanked by the Vicar General (Very Rev. Leo Lucero) and the Chancellor (Very Rev. Ron Wolf).

The Archbishop struck the bronze doors of the Cathedral, which record the history of the Archdiocese from 1539 to 1986 in their sixteen panels, with a wooden mallet. In this manner of symbolically seeking admission, the Rector Father Crispin Butz, OFM opened them to admit the archiepiscopal party. He led them to the vestibule where the Archbishop received the archiepiscopal Cross, recalling Christ's redemption of mankind. Here Archbishop Sheehan put on his cope and miter, while the Senior Consultor (Father Ramon Aragon) presented the crozier, saying: "Accept the pastoral staff used by your predecessors in this holy temple. With it, keep watch over the flock now entrusted to you, making sure that none who are given over to your shepherding may ever be lost."

Father Johnny Lee Chavez, a dean, offered Archbishop Sheehan holy water, with which he blessed himself, while Father Chavez prayed that the new ministry of the Archbishop would renew all priestly commitments to the glory of God. The Rector then enjoined the Archbishop, "Enter now into the Mother Church of our Archdiocese, making it your own." The organ played "*Ecce Sacerdos Magnus*" ("Behold the High Priest") and the cathedral bells pealed forth.

The Archbishop offered a response to the greeting of dignitaries present, including Governor Bruce King and Mayor Sam Vick. After remarks in English and in Spanish to the effect that, speaking of the cathedral "*Mi casa y tu casa son nuestra casa*" ["My house and your house are our house"], he said in part:

> I wish to direct much of what I have to say this evening to my brother priests but indirectly I speak to all of you. We observe the Vespers [Evening Prayer] of the Feast of St. Matthew, Apostle and Martyr - one of the twelve Jesus chose. The reading from Paul's second letter to the Corinthians, Chapter 12, describes the life of Paul. It is an intensely personal even intimate account of Paul's ministry. He speaks of the difficulties of being an Apostle. I am content with weakness, with distress with mistreatment for the sake of Christ - for when I am powerless, Paul says, that's when I am strong. He tells us for those who serve Jesus will know suffering but will always have his help.
>
> Earlier in the Epistle, Chapter 1, St. Paul speaks about his troubles. They had troubles in the early Church just as we do today. His trouble was so great that, 'he was crushed beyond his strength, even to the point of despairing of life itself.' But then he says that God comforts others with the same consolation we have received. We have suffered in the Church, the scandal of sexual abuse by several members of the clergy. Victims have been hurt. The pain that comes from it all has been difficult. Yet we have the promise of consolation - God's strength and inner peace. Why? So that we can console the others who need us. The others who have been hurt by these problems or by any other concerns in their lives and in their families. Paul's letter contains rich and meaningful teachings for us tonight.
>
> I promise to be a good shepherd to you and to give my life in service of you. I promise to be a productive citizen of Santa Fe and of our state. . . . We face some problems. I really need your help and support. But with God's grace and with our mutual collaboration we will move on into the future. Purified and stronger than ever.

The Vicar General read the papal letter of appointment, and the Chancellor presented it to the Consultors to witness. The Archbishop made a profession of faith, after which all present applauded to signify their consent to the papal choice. The profession of faith, an act publicly affirming the authentic teachings of the Church and the willingness to defend them, was followed by the oath of fidelity. The Archbishop was then escorted to his chair and then the people sang the "Magnificat". The ceremony closed with prayers of intercession and a final blessing by Archbishop Sheehan. Afterwards he greeted those present in Clare Hall.

The installation of the Archbishop began promptly the following day (21 September 1993) at the Albuquerque Convention Center at 7:00 P.M. The Red Road Crossing Drum and Singing Group began the call to assemble. The first procession was made of banner bearers representing parishes and missions of the Archdiocese, followed by the Knights of Columbus, Knights of the Holy Sepulchre, and young people with colored banners. Priests and deacons, bishops and archbishops preceded the cardinals, the Apostolic Pro-Nuncio representing the Pope, and Archbishop Sheehan.

Among the hierarchy, in addition to the pro-nuncio and Archbishop Sheehan, were cardinals from Chicago and Los Angeles, archbishops of Louisville, New Orleans, and San Antonio, the former archbishop of Newark, twenty-six present and former bishops, six auxiliary bishops, the administrator of St. Thomas, The Virgin Islands (who would become a bishop), and representatives of the National Conference of Catholic Bishops and the United States Catholic Conference, of the Archdiocese of Denver, and of the Diocese of Beaumont. Governor Bruce King of New Mexico and Mayor Louis Saavedra were among the civil dignitaries and Dr. Wallace Ford represented the New Mexico Conference of Churches. Family members included brother John and sister-in-law Sue from Columbia, Missouri, brother Joseph and sister-in-law Frances from Kansas City, Missouri, two cousins from Tulsa, Oklahoma, and a nephew from Seattle.

Archbishops Sheehan and Cacciavillan (the pro-nuncio) wore red vestments for the Feast of St. Matthew, Apostle and Martyr. The other clergy wore white albs and stoles made for this celebration. The stoles, personal gifts of Archbishop Sheehan, featured a cross design taken from a cross in the courtyard of San Lorenzo Church at the Picuris Indian Pueblo in northern New Mexico. It was typical of many Spanish and Indian folk art crosses carved for churches and cemeteries in the state. Each stole had a turquoise stone, regarded by the Pueblo Indians as possessing the quality of soothing vision for the mind and guarding against all external dangers and accidents. The stones are said to bring peace and prosperity to the wearer, serving as a symbol of harmony and of well-being.

When the Red Drum ended its processional chant, the choir and the assembly sang the opening hymn. Vicar General Lucero welcomed the audience and Archbishop Sheehan presented the pro-nuncio, who presented the Consultors with the letter of appointment from Pope Paul II. After reading this mandate, Archbishop Sheehan received questions on his willingness to accept his new office and its responsibilities. The pro-nuncio concluded the interrogation with prayer.

Then Archbishop Cacciavillan escorted Archbishop Sheehan to his chair, brought from the cathedral in Santa Fe, assisted by Bishops Pelotte and Ramirez. Here the pro-nuncio presented the crosier to Archbishop Sheehan with the applause of the people. Then representatives of the Archdiocese, clergy, religious, laity, ecumenical and civic groups greeted the new archbishop in the name of the community.

At the homily Archbishop Sheehan welcomed all in English and in Spanish. In Spanish he said:

> *Mi nombre no es hispano pero mi corazon es muy hispano!. . . .Me gusta sus costumbres, su musica, su comida, sus fiestas. Ustedes son un tesoro precioso par la Iqlesia y para la comunidad* [My name is not Hispanic but my heart is very Hispanic!. . .I like your customs, your music, your food, your celebrations. You are a valuable treasure for the Church and for the community].

He pledged to work together with all people and told them he loved them. A particularly important part of his message was:

> I come to you at a painful moment in the history of the Archdiocese. There has been scandal. Some priests have been guilty of sexual abuse of minors during the past thirty years. But I repeat what I have said before. The Church will not tolerate the abuse of minors by priests or any other churchworkers. No priest guilty of such misconduct will be allowed to return to regular parish ministry. I have established a permanent review board to investigate any allegations of such misconduct.
>
> My heart reaches out to any victims and their families. In the name of the Church I apologize to you for the harm that has been done. I have established a Counseling Fund to help you receive the necessary care. I plan to visit every victim in the Archdiocese and ask for reconciliation.
>
> The process for accepting seminarians for studies and priests for ministry from other places has been tightened up. We can't change the past but we can do a great deal about the future. I made you a promise. I will do everything I can to see that no child is ever again put in harm's way!
>
> Now I speak to those who have been scandalized by the problems and tempted to go away from the church. Stay with us! It was individuals not the Church that was at fault. Any place you go there will be human weakness. Stay with us!

And later:

> I am deeply grateful for the ministry of Archbishop Sanchez. For many years he served as priest and Archbishop here. He has been a friend of mine for a long time. We must not let the tremendous good that he did be forgotten in the midst of the problems we face. He is with us in prayer today.

Noting the presence of the pro-nuncio, he remarked:

> Let me say that this local church is committed to the Holy Father, to sound Catholic teaching, to following the liturgical regulations of the Universal Church and to a happy Catholic way of life.

In conclusion:

> I am happy to accept my new ministry. But I can't do it alone. I need you - clergy, religious and laity to work with me. I promise to serve you with all my energy and with all my heart. With the help of Jesus and with the intercession of Our Lady of Guadalupe and all the Saints we begin the journey tonight. God has promised to be with his Church forever. Let us with joy, lift our hearts and our voices. *Elevamos nuestras voces con el grito, 'Que Viva Nuestra Senora de Guadalupe! Que Viva Cristo Rey! Que viva Santa Fe!'* [We lift our voices with the shout, 'Long live Our Lady of Guadalupe! Long live Christ the King! and Long live Santa Fe!'].

After a prayer for blessings and guidance, ninety-one eucharistic ministers representing the parishes of the Archdiocese provided Communion to the multitude. The recessional closed the ceremonies.

Although the installation formally relieved Archbishop Sheehan of his duties in Lubbock, it was not until two days later (23 September 1993) that the Consultors of the Diocese of Lubbock elected Msgr. Curtis T. Halfmann, pastor of St. John Neumann Parish, as the diocesan administrator, pending the selection of a new bishop. The Archbishop traveled thirty miles South of Rome "to pray for all the victims of child sexual abuse" at the tomb of St. Maria Goretti (1890-1902) in Nettuno on 29 September. Maria had chosen death at the hands of her would-be attacker rather than physical violation by him. The Archbishop concelebrated Mass, met and had lunch with the Pope on 30 September. He had come to report on Lubbock but he also talked about Santa Fe. Concerning Archbishop Sanchez's resignation and allegations of sexual abuse against other priests: "I told him [the Pope] I am committed to dealing with the scandal and to restoring the faith of the people. He promised his prayers and support."

The Archbishop sent a letter to his parishes and missions dated Sunday, 19 December 1993, expressing his fear of archdiocesan involuntary bankruptcy and the seizing of financial assets and properties due to the threat of lawsuits involving clerical sexual abuse. He estimated that lawsuits and claims ranging over a thirty-year period would eventually cost $50 million. The allegations were that priests were inadequately supervised in their ministries by archdiocesan officials. All parishes were involved as they were considered one corporation in civil law. Bankruptcy would force the courts to seize parish savings and all nonoperating cash and property. Therefore the Archbishop asked each parish and each mission to start a fund to handle settlements from savings and nonoperating cash and property, as well as reports on property not needed for parish activities.

As of 16 December 1993 eighteen abuse-related cases were settled out of court, leaving forty-one lawsuits. The Archdiocese sold some of its property in Santa Fe and tried to sell forty acres North of the Catholic Center in Albuquerque. The Archbishop announced he received a salary of $550 monthly plus expenses. He hoped to have a pool of $3 million. As he said, "I had nothing to do with this problem. I am just trying, together with God's grace and the help of my advisers, to solve the problem and keep the church going forward."

On 9 January 1994 the Archbishop told parishioners at Our Lady of Fatima Parish in Albuquerque that nine additional cases involving sexual abuse had been settled on the previous Friday (7 January 1994). He now had thirty-two lawsuits to resolve and had been paying claims out of an archdiocesan fund of $2 million. He asked parishes for help to defray costs and sent letters asking help from ten parishes in states that had sent priests with sexual abuse problems to New Mexico for treatment.

On 7 February 1994 Archbishop Sheehan announced the settlement of a total of forty-six sexual abuse lawsuits in the past two months. Two main insurance carriers agreed to help pay for the settlements without liability for the sexual abuse charges. Archdiocesan Catholics contributed more than $1 million to a fund to help pay the settlements. Insurers were in court trying to be absolved from paying claims but stated they would continue to do so until the courts found in their favor. Lloyds of London and the Interstate Fire and Casualty Company had sued the Archdiocese for relief from liability on the sexual abuse claims in federal court in 1993. The insurers noted that their policies required that injuries be unexpected and that companies should have received notice of incidents as they took place.

Compounding the problem was the treatment center for problem priests run by the Servants of the Paraclete in Jemez Springs, New Mexico. The center accepted priests from around the country and some went from there to parish ministry in New Mexico. The Archbishop stated: "We now know you can't cure pedophilia. We're being judged by 1990 standards for things that happened in 1960." The Archdiocese hired Paul Bardacke, a former state attorney general, around the first of 1994. He settled nine cases in January and seventeen in February. Forty-six cases were settled, with thirteen more in litigation and about fifty other people notifying the Archdioceses of their claims against it.

By March 1994 all except one parish in the Archdiocese offered to help. One-and-a-half million dollars had been gathered by 12 February. About this time Archbishop Sanchez was reported living at "a religious house in this country where he helps as a chaplain for the sisters." By the middle of February the Archdiocese announced it was garnishing funds from offending priests. A former priest from another diocese "sent $2,500 and promised to send a total of $20,000" to help settle claims against himself. The National Conference of Catholic Bishops provided legal assistance and donated land owned near Las Vegas, New Mexico.

On 3 October 1994 there was a settlement between the Servants of the Paraclete treatment center and seventeen men who alleged that they were sexually abused as boys in Almagordo, New Mexico, by Father David Holley. Holley was sentenced to a 275-year prison term in 1993 for abusing children at St. Jude Mission Catholic Church in Almagordo between 1971 and 1976. He had been sent to the center from the Diocese of Worcester, Massachusetts, and released to parishes on weekends. The Massachusetts diocese was named a defendant and also the Diocese of El Paso, to which Almagordo belonged in the 1970s. Another defendant was Lovelace Health Systems, Inc., which provided counseling services under contract with the Paraclete order. The Holley case was one of about seventy-five lawsuits filed in Albuquerque alleging molestations by present and former Roman Catholic priests.

Throughout this ordeal Archbishop Sheehan has drawn upon his faith in God and on his own sense of compassion. While the burden on himself is severe, his perspective allows him to take his work very seriously and to put others at ease. That his work is taking the right direction is indicated by the adoption of twenty-eight recommendations and suggestions for sexual abuse policies by the National Conference of Catholic Bishops during their annual meeting (14 to 17 November 1994) in Washington, DC (see 1996 *CA* 52- 53).

As of 1 January 1995 the Archdiocese of Santa Fe consisted of 61,142 square miles in a Catholic population of 260,129 within a total population of 926,635 or 28 per cent. It contains an abbot, 110 diocesan priests, ninety-one religious order priests, 129 permanent deacons, ninety-four brothers, and 300 sisters. There are ninety-one parishes, 216 missions, six pastoral centers, four Catholic hospitals, one health care center, three homes for the aged, a day care and extended day care center, three specialized homes, three specialized centers for social services, and a residential home for care of the disabled. There are a diocesan seminary, a college, three high schools, eighteen elementary schools, and 31,471 students under Catholic instruction. As metropolitan Archbishop Sheehan is head of the Province of Santa Fe with the Archdiocese and the suffragan sees of Phoenix and Tucson in Arizona and Gallup and Las Cruces in New Mexico.

The scholarly and bilingual Archbishop Sheehan, whose Irish name means "peaceful" and whose episcopal motto is "Love One Another Constantly," adapted from 1 Peter 1:22, quarters his arms with those of the Archdiocese of Santa Fe. On the dexter side (left facing the viewer) the Archdiocese shows a gold cross of the Faith on a red field, signifying the City of Santa Fe (Holy Faith). In the upper left quarter created by the cross is a triple tower of Castile in Spain. The red and gold colors signify the New Mexican association with that country. In the base are the crossed hands of St. Francis of Assisi and of Jesus Christ in gold, recalling the labor of the Franciscans and that St. Francis is patron of the Archdiocese.

On the sinister side (right facing the viewer) is a blue field with a gold parallel section in the center. In the upper field is a white dove holding an olive branch of peace in its beak, symbols of the Sheehan family. In the middle is a gold bar with a conjoined circle and triangle to represent Holy Trinity Seminary, of which the Archbishop was Rector. In the lower blue field is the silver white dome of St. Peter's Basilica in Rome with the golden Roman numeral "II" in the left-hand corner to signify that the Archbishop was in St. Peter's on the day that Vatican Council II opened in 1962. And the travels of Archbishop Sheehan, which have taken him from Wichita, Kansas to the Archdiocese of Santa Fe, continue.

Most Reverend James Anthony Tamayo, DD
Titular Bishop of Ita and
Auxiliary Bishop of Galveston-Houston

On the evening of 10 March 1993, more than 5,500 people gathered into Sam Houston Coliseum in Houston, Texas, for the ordination of James Anthony Tamayo, the new auxiliary bishop for the Diocese of Galveston-Houston. Bishop Fiorenza of Galveston- Houston was his consecrator, with Bishop Gracida of Corpus Christi, where he had grown up and served, and Bishop San Pedro of Brownsville, his birthplace, as his co-consecrators. Archbishop Patrick Flores delivered the homily.

Twelve bishops who had been or were ministering in Texas were also there. So were the present and former archbishops of Oklahoma City, as well as bishops from Louisiana, California, and Mexico. Bishop Tamayo's parents, his sister and brother-in-law were there, along with many family, friends, and wellwishers. In this two-and-a-half hour ceremony the liturgy and music were recited and sung in Spanish. When the ceremony was concluded, a Mariachi band played festive airs.

During the homily Archbishop Flores recalled the words of Christ to his apostles. They were to remind the new bishop of his special relationship as a bishop of the Church. He is the servant, not the ruler, of those committed to his care. Yet he is more than a servant. Christ said:

> And you are my friends if you do what I command you. I do not call you servants any longer, because a servant does not know what his master is doing. Instead, I call you friends, because I have told you everything I heard from my Father. You did not choose me; I chose you and appointed you to go and bear much fruit, the kind of fruit that endures (John 15:14-16).

This message was the appropriate one for a life already filled with service to others, the love of family and friends, and devotion to God and country.

Bishop Tamayo is a man who understands his priorities. He has said: "God called me to serve the people and be among the people." Born in Brownsville, Cameron County, Texas, along the Mexican border, on 23 October 1949, he grew up bilingual and bicultural. His father is Antonio Peña Tamayo of Port Isabel, one of twelve children whose family stressed the importance of education. And Antonio studied at Texas Southmost College, a junior college in Brownsville.

During his naval service as a petty officer at Chase Field in Beeville during World War II, Antonio met a high school graduate named Maria Guadalupe Borrego. He married this young lady of a deeply religious Catholic family. Their older child was a daughter, Maria Mercedes (now Mrs. Jesse Barrera and the mother of two daughters and a son). The birth of James Anthony followed two years later.

Seeking better opportunities, the Tamayos moved to Corpus Christi in 1955. Antonio found employment in a civil service position at the Naval Air Station. Maria waited until her children started to school and began work as a telephone operator at J. C. Penney's. She retired as a cashier in 1983. Mrs. Tamayo was a devoted mother. Her father, George Borrego, a retired widower, was a part of the family and cared for her children from the time they left school each day until their parents returned.

Maria Mercedes and James attended Christ the King School in Corpus Christi. The little boy was inclined toward the religious life because of the example of his first grade teacher, Sr. Mary Lila Aguilar, IWBS, who was his father's second cousin, and Fr. Gregory Deane, an outgoing young priest, whose friendliness and piety impressed him.

After high school James first attended Del Mar, a state- supported junior college in Corpus Christi. He later attended the University of St. Thomas in Houston, where he earned the degrees of Bachelor of Arts and Master of Arts and completed major studies at its School of Theology (also known as St. Mary's Seminary). He spent his deacon year at Our Lady of Guadalupe Church in Houston. On 11 June 1976 he was ordained a priest for the Diocese of Corpus Christi at Corpus Christi Cathedral in Corpus Christi by its bishop, Thomas J. Drury.

Father Tamayo's early assignments as parochial vicar (assistant pastor) were all in Corpus Christi. These were St. Patrick's (1976-1981), the Cathedral parish (1981-1982), and St. Pius X (1982-1985). During these years he served the Diocese as moderator of ecumenism (1977-1984), assistant chancellor (1980-1985), secretary to Bishop Gracida (1984-1985), diocesan consultor, and chairman of the priests' personnel board (1984-1993).

In 1985 Pope John Paul II appointed Father Tamayo to the rank of Monsignor. That same year he became episcopal vicar for the clergy and for the Hispanic apostolate, a position he held until 1990. He became Pastor of St. Andrew's in Corpus Christi in 1986 and Priest-in-Charge of St. Joseph's Mission in Port Aransas in 1988. He left these positions on being named to the pastorate of Blessed Sacrament Parish in Laredo, where he served from 1990 to 1993.

In Laredo he was chaplain for Court Isabella No. 683 of the Catholic Daughters of the Americas, a member of St. Augustine's School Board, and chairman of Calvary Catholic Cemetery. For the city he took part in Graduate Leadership (1991) and was a member of Mi Laredo Image Committee and the Gulf Coast Council Advisory Board of the Boy Scouts of America. During this period he was episcopal vicar for the Western Vicariate of the Diocese of Corpus Christi. During his years in the Corpus Christi diocese Monsignor Tamayo was also defender of the bond for the diocesan tribunal and was a member of the Permanent Diaconate Board, the Presbyteral Council, the Diocesan Liturgical Commission, and the Diocesan Board of Education.

He had long felt the need for military chaplains and requested the permission of Bishop Gracida to go on active duty. On 12 April 1985 Tamayo began as a Category B Chaplain at Lackland Air Force Base near San Antonio. He was commissioned First Lieutenant in the Air Force Reserve eleven days later. His original duties were to serve as Unit Catholic Chaplain to the permanent personnel at Lackland. That year he transferred to the 433rd Military Airlift Wing, Kelly Air Force Base, also near San Antonio, a command of General John Sullivan. Here he served 3,500 wing personnel, a majority of whom are Catholics. As the wing's only Catholic chaplain, he became a Class A reservist, ministering one weekend a month. Active in Operation Desert Storm, he won promotions to Captain and to Major by 1993. He is a life member of the Reserve Officers Association and the Air Force Association.

Appointed an auxiliary bishop of the Galveston-Houston diocese on 26 January 1993 by Pope John Paul II, Tamayo stated: "As an auxiliary bishop I am first of all a servant in the Person of Christ the High Priest." Appointed Episcopal Vicar for Hispanics by Bishop Fiorenza, he realizes the significance of his position:

> As a bishop of Spanish descent, my voice can carry leadership and authority within the community and the Church. I will use my voice after hearing the voices of the Hispanic Catholics and support and guide them in achieving education, health, and economic gains.

He also serves as a diocesan consultor and as a member of the Presbyteral Council.

Bishop Tamayo's philosophy of service is well-illustrated by his coat of arms. The shield with its red field depicts an open chalice, from which a host issues. It radiates five golden rays beneath a golden (or yellow) rose. The colors red and gold are traditionally Hispanic. As the Mass is at the center of the priest's life, the Sacred Species of the Body and Blood of Christ produced at Mass radiate grace to all. The rose is a symbol of natural beauty and the beauty of inner grace. As it radiates beauty, so, too, believers radiate the grace of Christ within them.

Bishop Tamayo's motto is "Todo con Amor" ("All with Love"), words made famous by Pope John XXIII, who requested the council fathers of the Second Vatican Council to perform all their duties in this manner. To the Bishop, these words are not just a duty but his own way of life.

Most Reverend Thomas Tschoepe, DD
Second Bishop of San Angelo
Fifth Bishop of Dallas

One of nine children born to Louis and Catherine (Sloan) Tschoepe in Pilot Point, Denton County, Texas, on 17 December 1915, Thomas Tschoepe attended St. Thomas Grade School there from 1922 to 1930. After seminary study at the Pontifical College Josephinum in Worthington, a suburb of Columbus, Ohio (1931-1943), the Reverend Mister Tschoepe was ordained for the Diocese of Dallas on 30 May 1943.

For the next ten years he was engaged in pastoral work in the Diocese as Assistant Pastor of St. Patrick's Parish in Fort Worth (1943-1946), of St. Mary's Parish in Sherman (1946-1948), and of Sacred Heart Cathedral in Dallas (1948-1953). Father Tschoepe became Administrator of St. Patrick's Parish in Dallas in 1953 and was Pastor of St. Augustine's Parish there in 1956. He was Rector of Sacred Heart Cathedral in Dallas from 1962 through 1965.

Appointed Bishop of San Angelo by Pope Paul VI on 12 January 1966, Bishop Tschoepe received episcopal ordination on 9 March 1966. Pope Paul VI transferred him to Dallas on 27 August 1969 following the resignation of Bishop Gorman for age.

As Bishop of Dallas Tschoepe emphasized Catholic education and continued to strengthen further the Confraternity of Christian Doctrine programs throughout the Diocese. He established parish councils and initiated the Permanent Diaconate program, as well as seeking to expand services for Hispanics and the young.

By 28 October 1980 Bishop Tschoepe had served as past president of the Texas Conference of Churches and was state chaplain for the Knights of Columbus and the Catholic Daughters of the Americas. In November 1982 there were 225 priests in the Diocese and almost 350 women religious to serve sixty-four parishes, thirteen missions, and thirty-four diocesan institutions among others. Shortly before he became Bishop of Dallas Tschoepe witnessed the establishment of the Diocese of Fort Worth. In late 1986 another division with the Diocese of Tyler lost twenty-one counties to the new diocese.

As of 1 January 1988 the Diocese of Dallas, with nine counties and 7,523 square miles, had an abbot, seventy-eight active diocesan priests, seventy-four religious order priests, and nineteen extern priests. There were also ninety-six permanent deacons, three male religious, and 229 female religious, with twenty-two seminarians. Many of these served in the fifty-five parishes, eight missions, six pastoral centers, a hospital, an orphanage and child welfare center, ten nurseries, four protection of life and family centers, and two other institutions. There were a collegiate seminary, a university, seven high schools, twenty-eight elementary schools, and 37,271 students under Catholic instruction. Over 200,000 Catholics lived in a population of about 2,500,000.

With the appointment of Bishop Charles V. Grahmann as Coadjutor of Dallas in 1989 and his commencement of duties in February 1990, it was expected that Bishop Tschoepe's resignation would be accepted on his seventy-fifth birthday, 17 December 1990. On 8 June 1990 he was honored at Sabbath services of

Temple Shalom for his help in organizing the St. Rita-Temple Shalom dialogue group and for his commitment to Jewish-Catholic relations. The group was formed about 1975. Bishop Tschoepe and Rabbi Besser announced the formation of the Dallas Commission on Catholic-Jewish relations and of the first intercongregational dialogue group.

Bishop Tschoepe had hoped to retire formally on 15 July 1990, the one hundredth anniversary of the establishment of the Diocese of Dallas and the fifty-ninth birthday of Bishop Grahmann. As this date fell on a Sunday, however, the resignation by which Bishop Grahmann would become Bishop of Dallas was moved up one day to 14 July 1990 so that it could be officially printed in *L'Osservatore Romano,* the official publication of the Vatican.

So it was that Msgr. Rene Passigato of the Apostolic Nunciature in Washington, DC, made the official announcement on 14 July 1990. At a press conference in Dallas on that day Bishop Tschoepe stated that he never asked nor wanted to become a bishop and was glad his tenure was over. "I'm glad to get rid of it. It used to be called the onus, or burden, of the priesthood. I am glad to give it to my successor."

On 15 July 1990, the one-hundredth anniversary of the creation of the Diocese of Dallas, Bishop Tschoepe was homilist at a Mass commemorating the anniversary. About 1,000 people attended the ceremony in the Cathedral with Bishop Grahmann and about eighty diocesan priests. The retiring bishop recalled his earlier service as assistant pastor and his consecration as bishop in the Cathedral.

Bishop Tschoepe, whose episcopal motto is "Paratum Cor Meum" ("My Heart Is Ready"), began the Catholic Community Appeal and contributed meaningfully to programs in communications and evangelization, refugee resettlement, and family life and the deaf apostolates. After his retirement as Bishop of Dallas, he moved to Waxahachie in Ellis County, a city of about 19,000, where he continued to serve as Associate Pastor of St. Joseph's Parish on East Marvin Street.

Right Reverend Peter Verdaguer, DD
Titular Bishop of Aulon and Vicar Apostolic of Brownsville

This son of Spain was one of the last missionary bishops of the formative period of the Texas Catholic hierarchy. He spent many years away from his own country in pursuit of his obligations. Devoted to his flock, he died while actively engaged in their service.

Born in San Pedro de Torello, Catalonia, Spain, on 10 December 1835 to Francisco and Maria (Prat) Verdaguer, Peter studied in the Vich and Barcelona seminaries in the Barcelona Province. He completed his education in the United States at St. Vincent's Seminary in Cape Girardeau, Missouri.

Bishop Thaddeus Amat, CM of Monterey-Los Angeles ordained Peter Verdaguer in San Francisco, California, on 12 December 1862. After completing a pastorate in Turupa, San Salvador, he was Pastor of the Old Mission in San Gabriel, California, in 1867. He became Pastor of St. Bernardine Parish in San Bernardino (1872) and Rector of Our Lady of the Angels Parish in Los Angeles (1874). Father Verdaguer was a member of the Bishop's Council (1875-1881) and Judge of the Tribunal (1879-1883) for the Diocese of Monterey-Los Angeles.

Pope Leo XIII appointed Father Verdaguer Titular Bishop of Aulon and Vicar Apostolic of Brownsville on 3 July 1890. Thereafter the Bishop returned to Spain. Bishop Jaime Calala y Albora consecrated him in Barcelona on 9 November 1890. He was assisted by Bishops José Morgades y Gili of Vich and Tomas Costa y Forraguera of Lérida, who were his co-consecrators.

Bishop Verdaguer was installed in Brownsville, Texas, on 21 May 1891. Following the death of Bishop Manucy in 1885 the Brownsville vicariate had come under the administration of Bishop Neraz of San Antonio. Because the obligations of the Diocese were pressing, Neraz turned to Rev. Claude C. Jaillet, the Vicar General of the Vicariate. Father Jaillet performed episcopal duties until the arrival of Bishop Verdaguer.

As did Bishop Manucy, neither did Bishop Verdaguer find in Brownsville a suitable See city. At this time the Lower Rio Grande Valley needed to develop new towns and greater trade opportunities. Although the Celaya Brothers constructed a railroad from Brownsville to Port Isabel (a distance of twenty-two miles) in 1871, it was not until 7 June 1904 that the St. Louis-Brownsville and Mexican Railroad reached Brownsville, connecting it with Robstown near Corpus Christi. A western extension of this railroad led to the development of the City of Mission in 1908. Bishop Verdaguer moved his residence to Laredo, one of the most populated cities in his vicariate. His immediate tasks were to build up the Church and to spread the faith. To this end he made complete visitations of the Vicariate in 1892, in 1896, and in 1907.

Through 1895 various congregations of women religious had labored in Texas more than forty years. Their efforts were important in fulfilling the pastoral and educational missions of the Vicariate. Sisters of the Incarnate Word and Blessed Sacrament came to Texas from Lyon by way of New Orleans in 1852. By the end of that year they were in Brownsville. Here they constructed a convent and boarding school for girls in early 1853.

With Brownsville as their headquarters the Sisters survived tropical storms, epidemics, Civil War skirmishes, and Indian attacks. By 1900 the Congregation opened a school in Rio Grande City, which lasted more than twenty years. By the twentieth century women religious were much in evidence throughout Texas.

Ursuline Nuns established convents and schools in Galveston in 1847 and in San Antonio in 1852. Bishop Dubuis asked them to come to Laredo in 1868, and they opened a convent school there on 30 March 1869. When the railroad came to Laredo, the nuns constructed the Ursuline Academy there.

Sisters of Mercy came to Refugio in 1875 and built their first permanent convent. They opened a school for children there, a school in Peñitas in 1897, and a later one in Laredo. Invited to teach in the public school system in Mercedes, they did so from 1909 to 1915. Part of the public school faculty in Roma for over twenty-five years, they also taught in Catholic schools and in Christian doctrine programs in Mission, McAllen, Edinburg, and Harlingen.

Bishop Verdaguer constructed St. Peter's Church in Laredo for English-speaking Catholics in 1896. For Mexican Americans he built Our Lady of Guadalupe Church in 1899 as a mission of St. Augustine Parish. St. Anthony's, the first Catholic Church in Raymondville, was dedicated on 2 February 1908. Our Lady of Mercy was the first Catholic Church in Mercedes in 1909. The Church in Mercedes had Harlingen, La Feria, Lyford, La Jarita, Raymondville, and San Benito as dependencies, and Weslaco, Donna, Alamo, and Edcouch as mission territories. On 16 October 1910 Sacred Heart of Mary Immaculate, the first Catholic Church in Harlingen, was dedicated. Railroads and industry helped build up the towns, mission centers and chapels.

The development of irrigation and sugar growing promoted the agricultural industry and led to greater land development and a new interest in living in the Rio Grande Valley. To the Bishop, whose care extended to the present-day dioceses of Corpus Christi and Brownsville combined, it was necessary to travel constantly. He felt his presence needed everywhere, but he saw in it a life of material poverty despite spiritual richness.

Bishop Verdaguer wrote to a priest who wanted to come to the Vicariate as a missionary:

> Should you. . .be willing to submit yourself to a poor mission life, in my most poor Vicariate, you may come. . . . But the Vicariate is poor, very poor, so much so that even in Laredo, the best parish, the priests do not have a regular monthly salary. Some months they get ten dollars, some eight, some five, but never more than ten.

But he had done better than he thought.

By 1911 he had sixteen secular and sixteen religious order priests, fifteen churches with resident pastors, and sixty chapels and stations. Nine of the parishes had parochial schools with an estimated total enrollment of more than 1,200 students. The Brothers of Mary Immaculate opened St. Joseph's College for Boys in Brownsville and religious communities established five academies for young ladies in the Vicariate.

This well-liked bishop made himself known as a missionary on horseback throughout the length and breadth of his vicariate. He died in his carriage between Santa Maria and Mercedes, Texas, while on a confirmation tour on 26

October 1911. Because of his work and that of his committed followers the Vicariate was converted into a Diocese within six months following his death. Bishop Verdaguer lies buried in the St. Augustine Church cemetery in Laredo, Texas.

Most Reverend John Walter Yanta, DD
Titular Bishop of Naratcata and Auxiliary Bishop of San Antonio

For John Yanta it all began with the faith and the church. The faith was Roman Catholic and the church was a special one, the Immaculate Conception of the Blessed Virgin Mary in Panna Maria, Karnes County, Texas. Now a center for agribusiness and tourism Karnes County has dark soils and rolling hills traversed by the San Antonio River. Oak and mesquite trees are notable features of its landscape. It is a beautiful area of South Texas, and the faith of its people, like the roots of the oak tree beside the church, runs deep.

In this Church of the Immaculate Conception, on 15 June 1920, John Andrew Yanta married Mary Magdalen Pollok. They were both descendants of Polish immigrants from the Opole area of South Poland, small farmers who left a part of the world occupied by Prussians, who challenged their right to practice their own religion. Although Poland had disappeared from the map of Europe by partition to Russia, Prussia, and Austria in 1795, no one could erase the language, the culture, and the Catholicism of these people. Even in this century, after the dark night of Nazi and Soviet tyranny lasting fifty years, the country remains more than 95 per cent Catholic. And when it comes to being Catholic, Poles yield to no other people in the strength and devotion of their beliefs.

John Andrew was an army veteran of World War I. He tried automobile sales for a time and then became a farmer and rancher. Mary Magdalen's family was among the first groups of 100 families settling in Panna Maria on 24 December 1854. It was the first Polish colony and Polish Catholic church in the United States. For these people who journeyed overland from the Gulf of Mexico to reach their new home in Texas, it was a fortunate choice. Like them, Texas values its independent ways very highly. The settlers had come to the right place.

The Yantas had eight children, a daughter Valeria (now Mrs. Ebeier), and seven sons, Edwin, Ernest, Wilfred, John Walter the future bishop, Fabian (now deceased), Joseph James, and Vernon. The first four children were baptised in the church in Panna Maria and the last four in St. Anthony's Church in Runge, a short distance to the southeast.

John Walter Yanta was born six miles northwest of Runge, now a small city of about 1200 inhabitants, in Karnes County, Texas, on 2 October 1931, the fifth child and fourth son of John Andrew and Mary Magdalen (Pollok) Yanta. With paternal grandparents living with his family, John's sister Valeria spoke only Polish when she started school. With the deaths of these grandparents about this time, the family turned to English as the dominant household language. The Bishop himself speaks English, German, Polish, and Spanish. Growing up in the country, the Yantas worked hard at chores and leisure time was spent in fishing, swimming, and hunting. While hunting and fishing are still interests, Bishop Yanta has taken up golf and tarocks, a European card game. He learned to cook growing up and has kept up his practice over the years.

Despite his position as a middle child, his family early noted his leadership qualities. He was an apt student and had an early vocation for the priesthood.

Yet during the serious illness of his father (who died in 1971) in 1950 and 1951, John temporarily discontinued his studies and helped operate the family farm and ranch.

Looking back over the first twenty-five years of his priesthood in 1981, Father Yanta remarked:

> To whom do I owe my vocation? After God, of course, my parents - especially my mother. Her prayer life - especially her lengthy time in morning and evening prayer - made a deep impression on me. I am grateful for my vocation to the priesthood of Jesus, first of all, to Our Lord Who called me. I thank the many who helped form me on the road to the priesthood and to this day, my parents, family, and relatives, Confraternity of Christian Doctrine teachers, former pastors, Brothers and priests of the Society of Mary, Vincentian Fathers of St. John's and Assumption Seminaries, my brother priests, religious Sisters, and the many good people I have worked with over the twenty-five years of my priesthood.

Two people who made an impression on the future bishop were Father Charles J. Drees (died 26 September 1968), the pastor of St. Anthony's Parish in Runge, and Msgr. Erwin A. Juraschek, who he first knew as a seminarian and with whom he was associated in the Archdiocesan Catholic Youth Organization (CYO). By 1990 Monsignor Juraschek was pastor of the Nativity of the Blessed Virgin Mary Parish in Cestohowa in Karnes County.

John Walter Yanta completed the first seven grades in public schools in Runge. In 1943 he enrolled in Central Catholic High School in San Antonio, where he completed the eighth and ninth grades. Central Catholic is the successor of an institution begun by Marianist priests on Military Plaza in San Antonio on 25 August 1852. The present building on North St. Mary's Street opened on 17 January 1932. It instructs about 800 students yearly. He entered the postulate of the Society of Mary at Maryhurst Normal Seminary at Kirkwood, Missouri. There he completed the tenth grade. But he returned to San Antonio the following year, deciding instead to become an archdiocesan priest.

He enrolled in St. John's Seminary in San Antonio and completed his high school course in 1948. He finished his college studies in 1952, after taking a year (1950-1951) out to aid his family in Runge. He spent summers from 1951 to 1953 teaching cathechism in Cotulla, Camp Wood, and Rocksprings. Entering Assumption Seminary in San Antonio in the Fall of 1952, he graduated in 1956. Archbishop Robert E. Lucey ordained him for the Archdiocese of San Antonio in San Fernando Cathedral in San Antonio on St. Patrick's Day, 17 March 1956. The Reverend Messrs. Louis Fritz, Charles V. Grahmann, Alton A. Rudolph, and Emil Wesselsky were ordained with him, though none of the five young men were anyways Irish. Charles Grahmann was later an auxiliary bishop of San Antonio, and afterward Bishop of Victoria in Texas and of Dallas.

Father Yanta began his priestly career as associate pastor at St. Ann's Parish in San Antonio from 1956 until 1962. In 1962 he became moderator of the Archdiocesan Catholic Youth Organization (CYO). For the next six years he was successively district youth director, assistant director, and, finally, director of the entire Archdiocesan program. From 1964 to 1972 he was director of the

National Council of Catholic Youth for Texas and Oklahoma. During these years he also served as associate pastor of Our Lady of Grace Parish (1962-1963), Holy Name Parish (1963-1964), and St. Pius X Parish (1964-1965), all in San Antonio. And he was chaplain at St. Benedict's Hospital and Nursing Home from 1965 to 1973.

On 6 April 1965 Father Yanta founded a singularly successful enterprise for the Archdiocese of San Antonio. It was the San Antonio Neighborhood Youth Organization (SANYO). He would continue to develop it, as its executive director, until the end of 1971. The project got underway in the Summer of 1965 with a federal contract of $440 thousand and 962 high school students. By 1990 the program helped more than 90,000 young people and adults increase their expertise and love for education, culture, health, recreation, and work. It developed many budding careers and instilled a work ethic that has benefitted its grantees and the citizens with whom these people have become involved in their professional and personal capacities.

As youth director for the Archdiocese Father Yanta saw an advertisement in a national Catholic magazine about the Neighborhood Youth Corps, sponsored by the Department of Labor. He wanted poor youth to acquire skills and to make some money. Writing off for a Youth Corps brochure to gain some insight into that agency, he saw an opportunity to help young people learn responsibility. He had met the late president John F. Kennedy in the White House Rose Garden in 1963. Both men felt that such a system would aid school dropouts. As Father Yanta said of Kennedy, "When I heard him speak, I felt this was God's call in a special way."

SANYO helped form the Greater San Antonio Federation of Neighborhood Councils and preceded Communities Organized for Public Service (COPS), both of which aided to empower leadership for social betterment. By 1990 SANYO was the premier job training organization in terms of longevity and the largest funded through the Job Training Partnership Act. Since 1965 SANYO has received more than $80 million in federal grants and has assisted more than 90,000 persons with remedial education, training and employment assistance. All grantees were at the time aided economically disadvantaged. Thirty-two centers were set up on the West Side, South Side and East Side of San Antonio for referral services for public assistance to adults and families. SANYO sponsored additionally recreational programs at centers and after school tutorials promoting the growth and development of people.

Father Yanta said of SANYO: "There was such an enthusiasm and great optimism among the participants. This was a new freedom for them - a new vision of what their lives would be." One man caught up in this movement was Julian F. Rodriguez, a reporter on the San Antonio *Express-News*. Father Yanta met him in 1967 and he became administrative assistant in charge of personnel. When Father Yanta left SANYO, Rodriguez became its executive director. By that time Yanta had educational, training and employment programs in place with more than $18 million in federal funds.

There was an awards banquet at the Marriott Rivercenter in San Antonio on 22 May 1990. It recognized friends, businesses, government and social service agencies which had helped SANYO by support and encouragement. It also honored Father Yanta's founding vision and those thousands whose lives he had helped build. Among the honorees were Julian Rodriguez, Mary N. Lopez, an economics research associate at the University of Texas at San Antonio, City Manager Alex Briseno, Gilbert Vasquez, Larry Johnson, Vera Ivy, the Mexican American Legal Defense and Educational Fund, Kelly Air Force Base, and the United States Automobile Association. On his appointment as bishop, Rodriguez said of Yanta:

> My immediate impression was of a highly intelligent, warm and loving person. He was a hard worker, a 'driver' with high expectations of himself and those around him. . . .Throughout a busy schedule he has always made time for those around him as he did in officiating at the recent baptism of our newly adopted child.

In 1970 Father Yanta organized the Polish American Priests' Association (PAPA) and has served as Secretary-Treasurer (1970-1980), Treasurer (1980-1984), and President (1986-1988), as well as national president (1990-1994). It now numbers more than 4000 Catholic priests of Polish descent. In 1971 and 1972 he studied briefly at the Jagellonian University in Poland. Since then he has gone to Poland a second time to study and has led two pilgrimages to that country. He founded the Texas Division of the Polish-American Congress and was its president (1971-1976). It began with forty people and by 1990 its members numbered 167,000 Polish Texans. Father Yanta was a national vice president of the Polish-American Congress in 1990.

In 1973 Father Yanta became director of the Archdiocesan Council of the Laity and on 12 September of that year pastor of Sacred Heart Parish in San Antonio. Sacred Heart Parish, in the Prospect Hill area of the City, dates from 1899. Originally German-American, today it is primarily Mexican-American. By 1974 it had seen the construction of three church buildings, the last dedicated on 22 December 1963. The Sacred Heart Civic Center for the area was dedicated on 22 June 1973, and the parish also had a school, which closed in 1968. Auxiliary Bishop Stephen A. Leven served as pastor of this parish in 1969, immediately preceding his appointment that year as bishop of San Angelo. With Father Yanta's arrival the parish had been served by fifteen priests, sixty Sisters and hundreds of lay workers. At least twenty vocations to the priesthood and religious life came from this parish. During this period Father Yanta was president of the Archdiocesan Senate of Priests (1977-1979) and of the Texas Conference of Priests' Senates (1978-1981).

By 1981 Yanta's organizational and managerial talents pointed his abilities within the Archdiocese in a new direction, that of the communications media. Relieved temporarily of parish duties to concentrate on his new work he was appointed Editor-in-Chief of *Today's Catholic*, the archdiocesan newspaper. He took up this duty on 25 January and became Archdiocesan Director of Communications in May.

Today's Catholic is a biweekly publication of the Archdiocese of San Antonio. Catholic journalism in San Antonio began with the *Monthly Journal* (1889) of St. Mary's Parish. It developed into the *Southern Messenger* (1892), which was published by the Menger family until 1957. It had statewide circulation. In that year the *Southern Messenger* was merged with the *Alamo Register* (begun by Archbishop Lucey in 1942) to become the *Alamo Messenger*. In 1972 the

Alamo Messenger became *Today's Catholic*. During the two years of Father Yanta's editorship circulation jumped from 11,000 in 1981 to 38,000 in 1983.

As Director of Communications, Father Yanta founded Catholic Television of San Antonio (CTSA) and was its first executive director. It was the first Catholic noncommercial public access station in the United States. On 28 November 1981 the station began operations on Channel 36, UA Columbia. CTSA became affiliated with the Catholic Telecommunication Network of America (CTNA, also founded in 1981), a private satellite network operated by United States Catholic bishops. It currently provides video and computer resources for parish religious education programs and has headquarters in Washington, DC (1995 *CA* 595). CTSA soon moved its studios to the Archdiocesan Chancery. Father Yanta praised the work of others, saying of CTSA:

> I am grateful to the Archbishop [Flores], Father Dan Hennessy who served as finance chairman, Father Larry Stuebben as program director, the pastors, benefactors, staff, and volunteers who have made CTSA a reality. Praise God!

On 28 April 1983 Father Yanta resigned his communications position pending the appointment of a new executive director and also concluded his editorship of *Today's Catholic* that same year. His new assignment was as pastor of St. James the Apostle Parish in San Antonio. The parish began officially on 20 July 1954. The present church was dedicated on 19 July 1959 and was renovated in 1972. By 1974 the parish had produced three religious vocations and one priestly vocation. The parochial school opened in 1957 and a new rectory was completed in 1970. The parish has continued to expand its facilities. Plans in 1994 called for building a new school and a convent for the religious Sisters. Groundbreaking was held for El Jardin de (The Garden of) St. James, a thirty-four unit retirement center, and there were plans to expand the church.

Father Yanta enjoys parish work. Sunday is the high point of the week for him. His interest is always in helping others and being the pastor of a large Mexican-American parish reminds him of similarities with the Polish community. "Both have love for family, a strong Catholic faith, great devotion to Mary, are celebrating people, demonstrative of their emotions and have large families." He is also very proud of his six parishioners pursuing religious vocations in the seminary and the convent.

On the unforgettable day of 13 September 1987, the day Pope John Paul II visited San Antonio, Father Yanta waited at the Chancery Office on the Seminary grounds in San Antonio to greet him, together with 1,000 people of Polish descent. It was the first visit by a Pope to San Antonio. And more than this impressive number, Father Yanta represented 167,000 Polish Texans, who as one wished to greet, even symbolically, not only the Head of the Roman Catholic Church on Earth but also the first Polish pontiff.

John Paul and his entourage returned to the Seminary grounds around 8:00 P.M., having witnessed a long day of formal events. It seemed for awhile that the Pope would not meet with the group after all. As the Vatican official explained, His Holiness was tired. The Pope had been invited to Panna Maria but could not come. Even 300 letters were unavailing. So the people had come here to see him. But Father Yanta held his ground. He felt that he had arranged for the Pope to meet his people here. That was the way it was going to be. Father Yanta won over the Vatican bureaucracy. His people did see their pope.

At 8:30 P.M. John Paul II met with the people of the Panna Maria area. The determination of one Polish Texan priest had won out over all. In a larger sense the meeting was also fitting and proper. The Polish American priest from Karnes County had at the very least a sentimental claim upon the Pope from Wadowice, Poland. The spirit of Panna Maria had overshadowed all.

So here in San Antonio, on the night of 13 September 1987, history had come full circle. The religious liberty Father Leopold Moczygemba realized in Texas was about to return after many years to Poland. Pope John Paul II had worked long and hard in that vineyard. That a Polish pope could not meet with those who spoke the language of his heart was unthinkable. The spirit of Panna Maria prevailed. Just as the original settlers of Panna Maria planted Polish life and culture in Texas and stood their ground, so did Father Yanta. His Texas roots were as deep as the oak tree in Panna Maria. He would see the Pope - and the Pope did see him. It was again Christmas Eve of 1854, when the first Polish immigrants came to Texas, and more than a hundred years of history dissolved in this night.

One thousand people of all ages had come to see the Pope. But they were united in heritage and in faith. The spirit of Father Moczygemba was present ninety-six years after his death and thirteen years after his posthumous return to Texas from Detroit in the presence of his great-great-nephew, the aged priest Henry Moczygemba.

John Paul II addressed the group in Polish and led them in a hymn to Our Lady of Czestochowa. He received flowers from two children, one a descendant of the Moczygemba family. Father Henry Moczygemba, pastor of Immaculate Conception Parish in Asherton, Dimmit County, presented a bust of Father Leopold his ancestor to John Paul. At last Canon Goebel of Panna Maria presented a miniature replica of his church. Father Yanta's people had kept the faith. And because Father Yanta was of the same blood and spirit as those who had overcome bigotry, poverty, a long sea voyage, Indian attacks, snakes, and unfriendly terrain to reach Panna Maria, he was able to vanquish the impeding Vatican bureaucracy. After his meeting with the Pope and its conclusion by Archbishop Flores, John Paul II could then, and only then, eat a light supper and retire for the night.

Father Yanta was appointed Monsignor by Pope John Paul II on 29 November 1989. He continued to perform useful services for the Archdiocese in addition to his parish duties. Between 1992 and 1994 he was chairman of the Priests' Personnel Committee and coordinator of the Archbishop's Appeal. During his tenure the Appeal was oversubscribed, for the funds collected exceeded the stated goal.

To indicate actively his beliefs on the evils of abortion Monsignor Yanta began to demonstrate in March 1992 against the New Women's Clinic in San Antonio. In January 1993 he took part in a demonstration at the Clinic which led to a brief term of imprisonment and to his conviction of trespassing in April 1994. County Court-At-Law Judge Bonnie Reed ordered him to stay away from the site, which the Monsignor promised to do but stated he would continue demonstrating at other abortion clinics. In this case he was given a six-month probated sentence and fined $300. He appealed the conviction.

Pope John Paul II appointed Monsignor Yanta Titular Bishop of Naratcata and Auxiliary Bishop of San Antonio on 27 October 1994. At his press conference that day the Bishop-elect began his statement with thanks, "Praised be Jesus Christ!" and followed it up in Polish with *Niech Bedzie Pochwalony Jezus Chrystus!* He praised God for the call to become bishop and said he was honored by the confidence of the Pope:

> I have always had a great admiration and respect for his strong leadership, his untiring zeal, his bold proclamation of God's truth to teach as Jesus did, and his great wisdom.

He noted that he and Archbishop Flores both came from small Texas towns, attended Texas seminaries, were both ordained priests in 1956, and were the first ethnics of their types to be ordained bishops. "To you, Archbishop, I pledge my love, loyalty, and obedience to serve you and all the members of our beautiful Archdiocesan family."

Bishop Yanta thanked God for his family, noting that his father and brother Fabian were now deceased. He had twenty-nine nieces and nephews "and their many recent arrivals." He also mentioned his grandparents and great-grandparents who had come from the province of Silesia in southwestern Poland to Panna Maria in 1854 and 1855. He added:

> I am very proud to be a priest of the Archdiocese of San Antonio. Our priests are dedicated, hardworking, loyal, zealous, and Christ-centered.

To deacons, religious and the laity:

> Thanks for your life-giving faith, for your sacrificing love, and for making Jesus truly present in your parishes, communities, marriages, and families.

Finally:

> I dedicate my ministry of Bishop to Mary, Virgin and Mother, under all her titles, especially to Our Lady of Guadalupe, Our Lady of Czestochowa, and Mary, Help of Christians.

He concluded his statement with English and Spanish blessings and the Spanish Sign of the Cross prayer. Archbishop Flores presented Bishop Yanta with the pectoral cross and purple cap of his new office.

Speaking of his work, the Bishop has said, "You could say I give 101 percent to any project I undertake." He hoped he could retain his parish and that his new position "will make me more intimate with Christ, help me live the Gospel and bring unity to the church as I work with my fellow priests." He desired "to help Archbishop Flores and all the people of the archdiocese. That has to be my number one priority."

Many tributes poured in from those who approved the promotion. Bishop Grahmann of Dallas said:

> Bishop Yanta is a classmate of mine - the Class of 1956. He is a very dedicated, hardworking priest, loyal to the church. His zeal has always been filled with great compassion for people. He al-

> ways has time for his people. He will be an excellent pastoral bishop.

Another classmate, Fr. Emil Wesselsky, pastor of Sacred Heart Parish in San Antonio, observed:

> I am one of five seminarians ordained with John Yanta in 1956. Even then, seeing his faithfulness to prayer, coupled with his abilities for 'let's get the job done' when we had work orders, I always knew deep within myself that he could be a bishop since he had all those leadership qualities.

Another voice from Sacred Heart Parish wished the new bishop well. Belinda Cruz stated:

> Many years ago Father Yanta as pastor of Sacred Heart Parish hired me as a cook/housekeeper. I'm still there today. May God bless you, Auxiliary Bishop Yanta!

Retired Auxiliary Bishop Bernard Popp of San Antonio said simply:

> Bishop John Yanta is a dedicated priest, a pastoral person . . . . He will serve the church of this archdiocese for a long time and he will do it well.

Louise Janysek Jurgajtis, the Executive Secretary of the Polish American Priests' Association, declared:

> Auxiliary-bishop John Yanta follows the principles set down by the Ten Commandments, the code of canon law and the church laws.
>
> Having been associated with him for many years in his work with PAPA (Polish American Priests' Association) of Texas, I have seen a certain charisma that attracts people to him. He is a loving and caring person who relates to all of God's family, from the unborn to the octogenarian. He is not afraid to stand up for what he believes is right.

The place for the episcopal ordination of the first Polish-American bishop of Texas was Panna Maria. The event would occur on Friday, 30 December 1994 (The Feast of the Holy Family) at 1:00 P.M. The pastor of the Immaculate Conception of the Blessed Virgin Mary Parish in Panna Maria was Fr. Franciszek (Frank) Kurzaj. He said:

> Auxiliary Bishop Yanta brought me to America, introduced me to the wonderful people of Texas and gently guided my first steps in the new country.
>
> I consider him not only my mentor but my most reliable friend. I wish and pray that the new responsibility may not distance him from the people but bring him even closer to the least fortunate and those rejected by society.

As a concession to the expected crowd, so that everyone could be seated comfortably, the ceremony was held outside the church.

The three-hour ordination was in English, Polish, and in Spanish. The facade of the church featured tapestries honoring the Holy Family, Our Lady of

Czestochowa, and Our Lady of Guadalupe. Choral music was supplied by the St. James's children's choir, Holy Redeemer children's choir, school children of St. Gregory the Great Elementary School, Holy Name Parish, the Vietnamese Choir of San Antonio, and the Sisters of Our Lady of Sorrows Seraphic Franciscans. Darnell Waun of Holy Trinity Church and Leticia Hernandez of St. Paul's Parish in San Antonio were the cantors, offering prayers on behalf of the people. High school bands from Falls City, Karnes City, Kenedy, Poth, and Runge played instrumental music. Mary Katherine Pollock of Holy Trinity Parish in Falls City was the organist, while Henry Guerra acted as master of ceremonies.

There was a procession of Catholic organizations, including the Knights of Columbus, the Catholic Daughters of America, and Knights and Ladies of the Holy Sepulchre. They were followed by priests and about twenty-five bishops from Texas, New Mexico, Oklahoma, Illinois, Tennessee, Michigan, and Wisconsin. Bishop-elect Yanta was escorted by young people wearing traditional Polish costumes and carrying flowers and greenery. The Bishop's chaplains were Monsignor Henry Moczygemba and Father Thomas Kavanaugh, CM, the Bishop's seminary teacher. This was one of the last appearances of the venerable Father Moczygemba, who died at the age of eighty on Texas Independence Day, 2 March 1995.

On this occasion the consecrator was Archbishop Patrick F. Flores of San Antonio, with co-consecrators Bishop Alfons Nossol of Opole, Poland and Bishop Charles V. Grahmann of Dallas. Msgr. Patrick J. Murray, Chancellor of the Archdiocese of San Antonio, read the papal letter of appointment. The homilist was Cardinal Adam Maida, Archbishop of Detroit, who had received the red hat of a cardinal only a few weeks before.

The Cardinal noted there were twenty-eight different heritages present at this ordination. He saw in this celebration a "special moment in time that linked back to the Lord and his Apostles and now with the worldwide faith of all people of every ethnic and racial background." He charged Bishop Yanta to be "a faithful minister of God's peace and love. The role of bishop is a special vocation to celebrate the sacraments and to bless all the moments of human life." Cardinal Maida encouraged the new bishop to be the

> Shepherd of the hearts and minds of the people of Christ including the unborn, the undocumented and to help people understand how to live daily life in and with the family. Uphold the dignity of all human life and encourage a deeper respect for one another in this life.

The Bishop's family presented him with a ring made of his parents' wedding bands. His miter was the gift of the Polish American Priests' Association, which he had founded. His crozier was made of wood from the oak beside the Church in Panna Maria, a pecan tree from the parish grounds of St. Anthony's Church in Runge, and a mesquite tree from the Yanta family farm.

When he spoke, Bishop Yanta recalled his ancestors with their hopes, hardships, and adversities. He thanked those who attended and pledged loyalty and support to Archbishop Flores. He asked prayers that he might be of help to the Archbishop and to love and aid his people and to remember his own motto,

"Bear Witness to the Truth." He dedicated his ministry as bishop to Our Lady of Czestochowa and to Our Lady of Guadalupe. He thanked all who made the day possible including Delores Martinez, tine: head of the Archdiocesan Liturgy Office, Louise Janysek Jurgajtis, Fr. Frank Kurzaj, his parishioners, and his own family members.

He spoke most memorably about the "eternal truths" of Jesus and the Church's purpose, which is "to see that Jesus' teachings are held intact until the end of the world." And condemning the violence of killers, Bishop Yanta added:

> Certainly, it's a terrible crime that someone would kill and say it was in the interest of preserving life. We don't condone anything like that. It bothers me that people don't react to what's going on inside abortion clinics.

After the conclusion of the ceremonies, the women of the deanery, the Archdiocesan Council of Catholic Women, and other womens' organizations hosted a reception in Bishop Yanta's honor.

Bishop Yanta's coat of arms is a summary of his life. In the top left corner or dexter side the open book of Sacred Scriptures lies on a blue field. It represents the Word of God proclaimed by St. Paul, and it is superimposed upon the keys of St. Peter, symbolizing the authority of the Church. Both men were prisoners and martyrs for their faith.

On the top right corner or sinister side the Opole lies on a red field. The Opole is a cross made of half an eagle (dexter) joined to half a Christian cross (sinister). The Polish eagle is a symbol of the Bishop's ancestors who came from the Province of Silesia in 1854 and 1855 from the Opole area. It also represents St. John the Evangelist, the Bishop's patron saint. The Cross of Christianity represents the cross Christ died upon for the redemption of mankind and the Bishop's pastoral love and concern for youth, the future of the Church.

In the base on a green field is the facade of the church in Panna Maria colored gold. Dexter, there is an "M" upon a crescent and sinister, two feet. The church is that of the Immaculate Conception of the Blessed Virgin Mary, home to the Bishop's great-grandparents. It is the first Polish settlement and first permanent Polish parish in the United States. The letter "M" is taken from the Pope's coat of arms and symbolizes devotion to Mary, the mother of Christ. The quarter moon represents the Immaculate Conception, patroness of the United States of America and of the church of Panna Maria. The feet (sinister) represent the feet of an unborn person of ten weeks of age, and is the international pro-life symbol. They symbolize the Bishop's respect for life from conception to natural death. They also recall the words of Isaiah 52:7, quoted by St. Paul in Romans 10:15. The Bishop's motto, "Bear Witness to the Truth," recalls the words of Christ to Pilate in John 18:37.

On 22 October 1995 Bishop Yanta received a particular mark of esteem from the Church he has always served. That day he became a Knight of the Equestrian Order of the Holy Sepulchre in St. Michael's Church in Houston, Texas. One would expect no less from a bishop whose priestly life is a daily exemplification of his motto, "Bear Witness to the Truth."

List of Abbreviations

AAS	*Austin American-Statesman*
BH	*Brownsville Herald*
c.	Number of canon in 1983 Code of Canon Law in Paulist Press edition (1985).
CA	*Catholic Almanac* (various editions)
cann.	Plural of canon [supra]
CAT	Catholic Archives of Texas, Austin (diocesan and/or personal files)
CET	*Catholic East Texas* (Tyler diocese)
DMN	*Dallas Morning News*
DTH	*Dallas Times Herald*
ETC	*East Texas Catholic* (Beaumont diocese)
EVD	*El Visitante Dominical*
Giles	Robert C. Giles, *Changing Times: The Story of the Diocese of Galveston Houston in Commemoration of Its Founding* (Dallas: Taylor for John L. Morkovsky, 1972).
HC	*Houston Chronicle*
HP	*Houston Post*
HT	W. P. Webb and E. S. Branda, eds. *The Handbook of Texas,* 3 vols. (Austin: Lakeside and U of Texas P for the Texas State Historical Association, 1952-1976).
NCE	*New Catholic Encyclopedia*
NCR	*National Catholic Reporter*
OCD	*Official Catholic Directory* (various editions)
PHP	*Palestine [TX] Herald-Press*
SAE	*San Antonio Express-News*
SAL	*San Antonio Light*
TA	*Texas Almanac and State Industrial Guide* (various editions)
TCH	*Texas Catholic Herald* (Galveston-Houston diocese)
TCHS	*TCHS [Texas Catholic Historical Society] Newsletter*
TCTT	*Tyler [TX] Courier-Times-Telegraph*
TdC	*Today's Catholic* (San Antonio archdiocese)
TMT	*Tyler [TX] Morning Telegraph*
TxC	*Texas Catholic* (Dallas diocese)
VCW	*Valley Catholic Witness* (Brownsville diocese)
Wangler	Msgr. Alexander C. Wangler, ed. *Archdiocese of San Antonio 1874-1974* (N.p.: Newsfoto Yearbooks for Francis J. Furey, 1974)
WTA	*West Texas Angelus* (San Angelo diocese)
WWA	*Who's Who in America* (various editions)
WWSS	*Who's Who in the South and Southwest* (various editions)
WWW	*Who Was Who in America*

Notes

Introduction

A. The Province of San Antonio: An Overview

[1]*OCD 1992* (Wilmette, IL: Kenedy, 1992), 911.

[2]*1992 CA* ed. Felician A. Foy, OFM and Rose M. Avato (Huntington, IN: Our Sunday Visitor, 1991), 152-153, 169, 210-212, 413-414. On 1 March 1994 Pope John Paul II established the eparchy of Our Lady of Lebanon, Los Angeles (Maronite Rite) for Lebanese Maronite Rite Catholics in California, Texas, and thirty-one other western American states.

[3]*NCE*, 1981 rpt. s.v. "Archbishop." by S[tephen] E[dward] Donlon [SJ, STD].

[4]*The Code of Canon Law: A Text and Commentary*, ed. James A. Corriden, Thomas J. Green, and Donald E. Heintschel (Mahwah, NJ: Paulist Press £or the Canon Law Society of America, 1985), 353- 354. This is the English text of the 1983 *Code of Canon Law*; in Latin, *Codex Iuris Canonici* (*CIC*). All future such references are to this edition (unless otherwise noted), hereafter referred to as *CIC*.

[5]1992 *CA*, 437-440.

[6]*CIC*, 354-355

[7]*CIC*, 355.

[8]*1992 CA*, 216.

[9]*OCD 1992* ("1992 General Summary," 34). See also *NCE*, 1981 rpt., s.v. "Metropolitan (Canon Law)," by L[awrence] G[regory] Wrenn [JCL].

[10]*1986-1987 TA*, ed. Mike Kingston and Ruth Harris, Sesquicentennial Ed. (Dallas: *The Dallas Morning News*, 1985), 629.

B. The Foundation of the Office of Bishop

[1]*CIC*, 265.

[2]1992 *CA*, 195-197. All scriptural quotations (unless otherwise noted) are from *Good News Bible: The Bible in Today's English Version*, Catholic Study Edition (New York: Sadlier, 1979). The basic text for the Old Testament is the Masoretic Text printed in *Biblia Hebraica* (3rd ed., 1937), ed. Rudolf Kittel. The basic text for the New Testament is *The Greek New Testament* published by the United Bible Societies (3d ed., 1975).

[3]"Apostle," Karl Rahner and Herbert Vorgrimler, *Dictionary of Theology*, 2nd ed., trans. Richard Strachan et. al. (Freiburg: Herdes, 1976; rpt. New York: Crossroad, 1985), 23-24.

[4]*NCE*, 1981 rpt. s.v. "Bishop (in the Bible)." J[ohn] J[ames] O'Rourke [STL, SSL].

[5]Klaus Berger, "Bishop: I. New Testament," *Encyclopedia of Theology*, ed. Karl Rahner (New York: Crossroad, 1982), 142-144. For a discussion of the historical development of the office of bishop, see Wolfgang Beinert, "Bishop: II. Church History," 144- 146 in this work. See also *NCE*, 1981 rpt. s.v. "Bishop (in the Church)" by S[tephen] E[dward] Donlon [SJ, STD], a more readable (and less diffuse) presentation.

[6]1992 CA, 143-144. For a discussion of the Synod of Bishops established

by Pope Paul VI on 15 September 1965, its purpose, function, and assemblies through September 1991, see this work, 145-146.

C. Formative Education of a Bishop of Texas

[1]*1992 CA*, 148.

[2]Joseph Nathan Kane, *The Kane Book of Famous First Facts and Records in the United States* (New York: Charter Communications; Ace Books, 1974), 147, 149.

[3]*OCD 1993* (New Providence, NJ: Kenedy, 1993; "1993 General Summary," 1847).

[4]*OCD 1993* ("1993 General Summary," 1880).

[5]Franklin C. Williams, Jr., "Bicentennial Papers: Reflections on the Catholic Experience in America, Texas, and Palestine [Texas]." 1976, p. 43.

[6]Wangler, 60-62 and *Assumption Seminary: San Antonio, Texas*. San Antonio: Assumption Seminary, n.d. [4,5].

[7]*Assumption Seminary*, [2,5,14] and *1988-90 Catalog: Oblate School of Theology*, San Antonio: Oblate School of Theology [1988], 28-29.

[8]Giles, 230-232.

[9]*University of Dallas: General Bulletin 1990-1991* 32, no. 1 (August 1990): 3, 8, 10, 69, 173-175, 178-180, 191, 195, and *OCD 1993*, 267.

[10]Jean Evangelauf, "Tuition for 1993-94 Climbs Sharply, Doubling or Tripling Pace of Inflation," *The Chronicle of Higher Education*, 29 September 1993, A33.

[11]*The Chronicle of Higher Education*, 25 August 1993, 107.

[12]The other five institutions with their undergraduate tuitions and fees (same prices for non-residents of Texas) are the University of Saint Thomas in Houston ($8,162), Saint Edward's University at Austin ($8,902), and three at San Antonio, Our Lady of the Lake Uniyersity ($8,180), Incarnate Word College ($8,325), and Saint Mary's University ($8,536). "Fact File: 1993-94 Tuition and Fees at More Than 3,000 Colleges and Universities," *The Chronicle of Higher Education*, 29 September 1993, A40.

Dioceses and religious orders no longer finance the complete costs of seminary education for high school, college, and theological studies. More lay instructors need larger salaries and health care and other benefits. Rev. James Walsh, director of the Seminaries Department of the National Catholic Education Association (NCEA) in Washington, DC, estimates most seminaries now charge between $8,000 to $11,000 per year for tuition, room and board, with the real cost for education being $15,000 to $16,000 per year per student. The Center for Applied Research in the Apostolate (CARA) at Georgetown University estimates that there were 6,698 seminarians in the United States of America during 1992-1993, with one-half in theology studies.

Payment plans range from full cost, students paying back part of their tuition, to students paying entirely for themselves. Many college seminarians take out student loans from the government. Serra International has raised $674,000 in grants to seminaries for student aid since 1983. The Knights of Columbus gave a total of $4.5 million directly to candidates for the priesthood and Religious life in 1993. Their Refund Support Vocations Program (RSVP) provided $1.5 million to seminarians, postulants, and novices in 1993. A Vocations Scholar-

ship Fund of $3 million begun in 1991 supplies forty seminarians nationwide with need-based grants of $2,500, as they attend thirty-four different schools of theology.
Students may also work at jobs on campus and outside jobs during summer breaks. Some seminarians, as do those in the Archdiocese of Los Angeles, receive funds from the Estelle Doheny Foundation (starting 1986) for major seminary expences. They receive free tuition, free room and board, a book allowance up to $300 per year, medical insurance, car insurance up to $600 per year, and a monthly stipend of $125.
Religious orders pay for seminarians when they are in vows and are canonically and legally responsible for them, according to Rev. Michael Rock, 0. de M., vocations director for the Mercedarians in Philadelphia. Many orders have their own universities. Some orders require people to pay room and board if they have not taken vows. Mercedarians require their men to sign a release promising not to attempt to collect back wages, from time spent in Religious orders, if they leave. Members of Religious orders usually take vows of poverty, barring them from keeping inheritances, company retirement or profit-sharing plans, while diocesan (secular) priests are merely supposed to live "simply". Robert J. Hutchinson, "Soaking Seminarians: The High Cost of Seminary Studies," *Catholic Twin Circle*, 22 May 1994, 10-11.

[13]Southwestern at Georgetown ($11,000), Trinity at San Antonio ($11,720), and Southern Methodist at Dallas ($13,580). "Fact File: 1993-94 Tuition and Fees at More Than 3,000 Colleges and Universities," *The Chronicle of Higher Education*, 29 September 1993, A40.

[14]*OCD 1993*, 372.

[15]*University of St. Thomas School of Theology at St. Mary's Seminary 1989-1990*. Houston: University of St. Thomas, 1989.

[16]*OCD 1993*, 932.

[17]*Assumption Seminary* [6-15] and *1988-90 Catalog: Oblate School of Theology*, 4-16, 22-27, 32-50.

[18]*CIC*, 323.

[19]*CIC*, 323.

[20]*CIC*, 575.

[21]*CIC*, 577.

[22]*CIC*, 576.

[23]*CIC*, 571-572.

[24]*1992 CA*, 534-537

[25]The pontifical degrees of Bachelor of Sacred Scripture (S.S.B.), Licentiate in Sacred Scripture (S.S.L.), and Doctor of Sacred Scripture (S.S.D.) are offered only through the Institute (7 May 1909) and the Commission, a non-curia! institute founded by Leo XIII (30 October 1902) and restructured by Paul VI (27 June 1971). It is attached to the Congregation for the Doctrine of the Faith. *1992 CA*, 152, 537. See also *The Catholic University of Amerlca: The School of Religious Studies 1986-1987 Announcements* 72, no. 2 (15 March 1986): 74-75.

[26]*The Catholic University of America: The School of Philosophy 1985-1987 Announcements* 71, no. 5 (15 April 1985): 18, 32-44, 52-55, 68-86.

[27]*The Catholic University of America: The School of Religious Studies 1986-*

1987 Announcements 72, no. 2 (15 March 1986): 18, 32-44, 51-54, 69-71, 79-87, 112-114, 124-142. See "Licentiate Programs in Canon Law," *TCH*, 25 March 1994, 6.

D. The Theology and Authority of the Episcopate

[1]*CIC*, 319.

[2]Joseph Lécuyer, "Bishop III. Theology," *Encyclopedia of Theology*, 147-148.

[3]The Documents of Vatican II, gent ed. Austin P. Flannery, OP, trans. Father Cornelius Williams, OP (New York: Pyramid Communications; Pillar Books, 1975), 371.

[4]Ibid., 374.

[5]Ibid., 375.

[6]Ibid., 374.

[7]Ibid., 376.

[8]*NCE*, 1981 rpt. s.v. "Hierarchy. In The Bible." by J[ohn] J[ames] O'Rourke [STL, SSL].

[9]Ibid., s.v. "Sacramental Theology of Bishops." by A[ugustine] Rock [OP, STLr,STD] and *The Documents of Vatican II*, 382-384.

[10]Ibid., s.v. "Hierarchy. In Theology." by S[tephen] E[dward] Donlon [SJ, STD].

[11]Ibid., s.v. "Canon Law of Hierarchy." by J[ohn] W[iley] Goeke [JCD] and *1992 CA*, 229. See also *Ministeria Quaedam* ["Concerning Certain Ministries"], "An apostolic letter, from Paul VI, given *motu proprio*, by which the discipline of first tonsure, minor orders and subdiaconate in the Latin Church is reformed." 15 August 1972, trans. Austin P. Flannery, OP, *The Documents of Vatican II*, 427-432.

[12]Ibid., "Canon Law of Hierarchy." See also Ibid., s.v. "Ecclesiastical Ordinaries." by M[ichael] J. Keene [OSB, JCD]. In Ibid., s.v. "Hierarchy" by D[avid] N. Power [OMI] Power notes that the term "hierarchy" usually refers to the episcopacy. It sometimes includes three degrees of the ordained ministry. It underlines the powers of bishop and distinguishes between clergy and laity. Today the mission of a bishop is considered one of service. The powers of order and jurisdiction are equally affirmed. The bishop is charged to use his powers for the good of the Church by men endowed with the Holy Spirit. His official position guarantees his authority.

[13]Lécuyer, 148-150 and Ibid., "Sacramental Theology of Bishop."

[14]*The Documents of Vatican II*, 373.

[15]"Sacramental Theology of Bishop."

[16]Lécuyer, 150-151.

[17]1992 CA, 123-124.

[18]*NCE*, 1981 rpt. s.v. "Bishop." by J[ames] Provost [STD].

[19]*1992 CA*, 145.

[20]Ibid., 368, 437-438 and *CIC*, 368.

[21]"Bishop." by J. Provost.

E. The Designation of Bishops

[1]*CIC*, 323.

[2]Ibid.

[3]Ibid., 320-321.

[4]For instructive discussion on this point see *1992 CA*, 409-412 and Thomas J. Reese, SJ, *Archbishop: Inside the Power Structure of the American Catholic Church* (New York: Harper & Row, 1989), 11-12.

[5]Those who know the candidate's work history and habits render more valuable information than do those whose contact with the candidate is purely social.

[6]I have found Reese's *Archbishop*, "Chapter 1. The Selection of Bishops," 1-52 so useful that I have used his discussion as my outline for this section. It contains much recent information, though I have added and updated material here and there. Reese's notes are also generally excellent, especially notes 2 and 3, which provide a compact reading list on this subject.

[7]Note particularly Section 5 of Canon 377 above. The Council for the Public Affairs of the Church known as the Section for Relations of States within the Vatican Secretariat of State is still concerned in some jurisdictions with bishop selection. See especially the article by Jean-Louis Harouel, "The Methods of Selecting Bishops Stipulated by Church-State Agreements in Force Today," *Electing Our Own Bishops*, ed. Peter Huizing, Knut Walf, and Marcus Lefebure (New York: Seabury P.; Edinburgh: T.&T. Clark, 1980), 63-66.

[8]Reese, *Archbishop*, 4-5.

[9]*1992 CA*, 174-175. The *1992 CA*, 173 gives Cacciavillan's birthdate as 14 August 1926, while *OCD 1992*, A-61 gives it as 14 August 1925.

[10]*OCD 1993* ("1993 General Summary," 1878).

[11]Reese, *Archbishop*, 16. If Reese refers to Bishop Bernard F. Popp, he is definitely mistaken. Popp is an ethnic German, the son of Ferdinand Popp, born in Hinzendorf (now Hyncice) in Moravia. See Joe Michael Feist, "German-Texans Assume Leadership Positions of Church in Lone Star State," *CET*, 13 April 1990, 16. The article originally appeared in *TxC*.

[12]Canon Law Society of America, *Procedure for the Selection of Bishops in the United States* (Hartford: Canon Law Society of America, 1973), 20, quoted in Reese, *Archbishop*, 18.

[13]Reese, *Archbishop*, 31-34. See also Peter Hebblethwaite, "'Secret' Criteria Set Bishops' Appointments," *NCR*, 4 February 1994, n.p. Hebblethwaite, *NCR*'s Vatican affairs writer, is apparently unaware of Reese's publication of this material in 1989. I have preferred Reese's version, though Hebblethwaite's differs very little. Hebblethwaite says his source is "*Golias*, a French Catholic satirical magazine published in Lyons."

[14]*1992 CA*, 158 and personal knowledge.

[15]Ibid., 147.

[16]Ibid., 393, 148-149 and Reese, *Archbishop*, 37.

[17]*1992 CA*, 147.

[18]Hebblethwaite, n.p.

[19]"Editorial," by Peter Huizing and Knut Walf, trans. David Smith, in *Electing Our Own Bishops*, vii.

[20]Jean Gaudemet, "Bishops: From Election to Nomination," trans. Iain

McGonagle, in Ibid., 10-15.

[21]John Cogley, *Catholic America* (Garden City, NY: Doubleday; Image Books, 1974), 16-27. See also Annabelle Melville, "American Catholic," and Katharine Bird, "Laying a Foundation for the Future," *CET*, 14 October 1988, 8-9 and Rev. James Vanderholt, "First U.S. Bishop Was Elected to Office by Priests," *ETC*, 8 April 1994, 4. Franklin's *Private Journal* quoted in Cogley, 21.

[22]*OCD 1993* ("1993 General Summary," 1847).

[23]Quoted by John Tracy Ellis, "The Appointment of Bishops and the Selection of Candidates in the United States since Vatican II," in *Electing Our Own Bishops*, 81 and note 1, 84.

[24]An Account of the Consecration by One Bishop of the *First Romish Bishop in the United States*, in Kane, *Famous First Facts*, 147.

[25]Reese, *Archbishop*, 49-52. See also John Thavis, "The Pope's Bishops: Shaping the World's Hierarchy in His Image," *TCH*, 22 January 1988, 20.

F. Types and Duties of Bishops

[1]*1992 CA*, 143-144, 152-153. *1979 CA* ed. Felician A. Foy, OFM (Huntington, IN: Our Sunday Visitor, 1978), 182-183, 195-196 covers the same material in more detail. Canons 349 to 359 of the 1983 *Code of Canon Law* concern cardinals.

[2]*1979 CA*, 182, 184, 364.

[3]*The Riverside Chaucer*, gen. ed. Larry D. Benson. 3d ed. (Boston: Houghton Mifflin, 1987), 28. See also the explanatory note on "The Clerk" by Warren S. Ginsberg, 810-811.

[4]Ibid., "Glossary," 1229.

[5]*Webster's New Collegiate Dictionary* rev. ed. (1975) s.v. "clergy,' "clergyman," "cleric," "clerical," "clerk."

[6]*1979 CA*, 183, 356, 387 and 1992 CA, 144, 304, 331. Yet another type is the monastic bishop. For an account chiefly concerned with medieval Ireland, see *NCE*, 1981 rpt. s.v. "Bishop, Monastic." by [Rt. Rev.] J[ohn Joseph] Ryan [STL].

[7]*1979 CA*, 184 and 1992 CA, 144.

[8]My discussion closely follows *CIC*, 324-348, treating bishops in general, diocesan bishops, coadjutor and auxiliary bishops, the impeded see, and the vacant see. I have presented some editorial commentaries in terms of their particular usefulness in illuminating some of the canons.

[9]"Dogmatic Constitution on the Church," 27 in *The Documents of Vatican II*, 382.

[10]"Decree on the Pastoral Office of Bishops in the Church," 8(a) in Ibid., 567.

[11]"As examples of areas withdrawn from the competency of the bishop, one might note certain irregularities for orders (c. 1047) or marriage impediments whose dispensation is reserved to the Holy See (c. 1078, §2). Furthermore, in the structuring of pastoral ministry the bishop may introduce a system of limited tenure for pastors only after authorization by the conference of bishops (c. 522). Finally, in the tribunal arena, the bishop may authorize tribunals with one clerical judge in first instance (c. 1425, §4) or lay judges ([c.] 1421, §2) only with the permission of the conference of bishops." *CIC*, 325, note 45.

[12]"See also c. 755 on the bishop's responsibility to foster the ecumenical movement and to formulate appropriate norms. Among other canons pertinent to the bishop's ecumenical responsibilities are the following: 844 (sacramental sharing), 933 (celebration of the Eucharist in a non-Catholic church), 1124-1129 (ecumenical marriages), and 1183 (burial of a member of another Christian church). See also [J.] Alesandro ["Law and Renewal: A Canon Lawyer's Analysis." *CLSAP* (1982)], 6-8. One should especially note the responsibility of bishops individually and the conference of bishops to consult with hierarchs of other churches before policies on sacramental sharing are finalized (c. 844, §5). The principle should be operative in other areas as well, e.g., norms on ecumenical or mixed marriages." Ibid.,326, note 47.

[13]*The Documents of Vatican II*, 14-15.

[14]"Technically speaking, whenever the law refers explicitly to 'diocesan bishop' and not to 'local ordinary' or 'ordinary' simply, the vicar general or episcopal vicar needs a special mandate or authorization from the bishop to act (c. 134, §3). This usually refers to especially significant administrative acts such as incardinating or excardinating a cleric (cc. 265-272), establishing a parish (c. 515, §2), permitting the alienation of church property (c. 1292, §1)." Ibid., 330, note 57.

[15]"Judicial processes are structured theoretically according to a contentious or conflict of rights model whereas practically speaking most cases in church courts are marriage cases, which do not really involve such conflicts of rights for the most part. . . ." Ibid., 331, note 59.

[16]"At times it may be pastorally advisable to dispense from church law in a given instance. See c. 87 on dispensations from universal laws and c. 88 on dispensations from diocesan laws, laws of provincial or plenary councils, or laws of the conference of bishops. for the most significant postconciliar document in this area, see Paul VI *m*[otu] *p*[roprio] *De episcoporum muneribus*, June 15, 1966, in *AAS* 58 (1966), 467-472." Ibid., 331, note 60.

The apostolic letter of 15 June 1966 referred to in the paragraph above may be translated "The Power of Diocesan Bishops". It contains regulations for granting the dispensations by bishops in accordance with the "Decree on the Pastoral Office of Bishops in the Church," 8. See *The Documents of Vatican II*, 567.

[17]*The Documents of Vatican II*, 573-574.

[18]Ibid., 584-586 and 608-609.

[19]This form originated from the Congregation for Bishops in 1975. "Among the areas of inquiry in the S[acred] C[ongregation for] B[ishops] form are the following: pastoral and administrative organization of the diocese; general religious situation; economic situation of the diocese; liturgy; clergy; religious and secular institutes; cooperation with the missions, seminaries, and universities; Catholic education; the laity; ecumenism, social assistance, and various other pastoral questions. There is also a section of the form that seeks statistical information about some of the above areas of inquiry." *CIC*, 335, note 73.

[20]*The Documents of Vatican II*, 597.

[21]Ibid., 578-579 and 598-599.

[22]These bishops are required to attend meetings of the conference of bishops and might attend the synod of bishops. *CIC*, 340. "As regards the role of coadjutor and auxiliary bishops outside the diocese, one might note their right

and duty to be present at an ecumenical council with a deliberative vote (c. 339, §1), their participation in particular (plenary or provincial) councils with a deliberative vote (c. 443, §1, 2°), and their membership in the conference of bishops, the coadjutor with a deliberative vote (c. 454, §1) and the auxiliaries with a deliberative or consultative vote depending on the statutes (c. 454, §2). However, only the diocesan and coadjutor bishops and not the auxiliary bishops enjoy a deliberative vote in the drawing up of or modifying of the conference statutes (c. 454, §2)." *CIC*, 340, note 84.

[23]"At times the administrator is barred from acting at all. For example, he may not establish public associations of the faithful (c. 312, §1, 3°). He may not convoke a diocesan synod (c. 462, §1). He may not grant dimissorials [discharges or dismissals] to a candidate who has been denied them by the bishop (c. 1018, §2). At times he may function but subject to restrictions not normally binding the bishop. He may remove the chancellor or the notaries only with the consent of the college of consultors (c. 485). He may permit the secret diocesan archives to be opened but only in case of necessity (c. 490, §1). He may issue dimissorials but only with the consent of the college of consultors (c. 1018, §1, 2°).

"At times he may act only after the see has been vacant for a year. With the consent of the college of consultors, he may grant letters of excardination [a formal document releasing a priest from his membership in a diocese] or incardination [a formal document incorporating a priest into a diocese] or permit a cleric to migrate to another particular church [diocese] (c. 272). He may name pastors on his own whereas during the first year of the vacancy he can only install or confirm pastors who are presented (e.g., religious pastors) or elected in virtue of special legal provisions (c. 525, 1°-2°)." Ibid., 346-347, note 94.

[24]*OCD 1993*, 1074 lists the office hours for the Chancery of the Diocese of Tyler as Monday through Friday 8:00 A.M. to 4:30 P.M. *CET* lists closings (besides weekends) as follows: 1 January for New Year's Day (1 January 1993, 3), 8 April for a half-day on Holy Thursday and 9 April all day for Good Friday (9 April 1993, 3), 5 July for Independence Day observance (2 July 1993, 3), 16 August for Assumption Day observance (13 August 1993, 3), 6 September for Labor Day and 10 September for Chancery moving day (27 August 1993, 3, from 1920 Sybil Lane in Tyler), 1 November for All-Saints Day (22 October 1993, 3), 25 and 26 November for Thanksgiving holidays (19 November 1993, 3), 8 December for the Feast of the Immaculate Conception (3 December 1993, 3), 24 December for Christmas Eve, 27 December for the Christmas Holiday and 31 December for one half-day on New Year's Eve (17 December 1993, 3). Open house and the blessing of the new headquarters of the chancery took place on 5 December 1993 between 2:00 and 4:00 P.M. (CET, 19 November 1993, 3). It is now located at 1015 ESE Loop 323 in Tyler.

[25]*CET*, 1 January through 12 December 1993, 3. Details of the individual events and reactions of the bishop may be found in individual issues.

[26]*OCD 1993*, 1074-1076 and Diocese of Tyler, *Diocesan Directory: October 1992-1993* (Tyler: Diocese of Tyler, 1992).

[27]*CET*, 1 January 1993, 3.

G. Episcopal Style: Address, Heraldry, and Vesture

[1]"Ecclesiastical Forms of Address Recognized in the United States," *OCD 1984* (Wilmette, IL: Kenedy, 1984), vii. Christopher W. French, ed., *The Associated Press Stylebook and Libel Manual*, rev. ed. (Reading, MA: Addison-Wesley for The Associated Press, 1987), 185 makes no titular distinction.

[2]*OCD 1992*, A-46.

[3]*OCD 1984*, vii. Under "Rev." *The Associated Press Stylebook* suggests using the word "the" before an individual's name with this description because "the abbreviation *Rev*. does not stand for a noun," 183. Further the *Stylebook* observes that the words "curate," "father," and "pastor" should not be used routinely before an individual's name unless they appear before a name in a quotation, in which case they should be capitalized, 182. *Webster's New Collegiate Dictionary*, rev. ed. (1975), hereafter referred to as *Webster's Dictionary* s.v. "Forms of Address," suggests "Reverend Father" or "Reverend" with the salutation "Father" with surname, or only "Father".

[4]*OCD 1992*, A-48 and *OCD 1984*, vii. The *1992 CA*, 144 also agrees. *The Associated Press Styiebook* prefers "Monsignor" to "Reverend" and states that the title should not be abbreviated, 182. Nor does the *Stylebook* distinguish between "Right Reverend" and "Very Reverend" monsignors, recognizing implicitly that such post-Vatican II distinctions are "no longer" made, 185. In *Webster's Dictionary* all monsignors are "Right Reverend" with the salutation of "Monsignor".

[5]Charles Kidd and David Williamson, eds., *Debrett's Peerage and Baronetage 1990* (London: Debrett's Peerage and Macmillan London, 1990; New York: St. Martin's Press, 1990), in the section entitled "Forms of Addressing Persons of Title," 31, indicate the distinction between "Most Reverend" for archbishops and "Right Reverend" for bishops generally. This form of address is more proper here for hierarchy of the Church of England. See also OCD 1992, A-45 and 1992 CA, 296.

[6]*OCD 1984*, vii. *Webster's Dictionary* prefers the salutation "Right Reverend and Dear Father" for the abbot.

[7]*OCD 1984*, vii. *Whitaker's Almanack 1994*, 126th ad. (London: Joseph Whitaker, 1994), 426-427 shows that the titles of "Most Reverend" and "Right Reverend" are used by archbishops and bishops of England and Wales and of Scotland, respectively. In the case of the Irish hierarchy the title of "Most Reverend" is used for both archbishops and bishops, as is the American practice. This reference is for Roman Catholic hierarchy.

Concerning cardinals, *The Associated Press Stylebook*, 182 prefers to use the title immediately before the individual's name. On page 184 it notes that the title used between the Christian name and surname is "a practice traceable to the nobility's custom of identifications such as *William, Duke of Norfolk*, is still used in formal documents but otherwise is considered archaic."

[8]*Webster's Dictionary*.

[9]On this subject the best guide is Bruno Bernard Heim, *Heraldry in the Catholic Church* (Gerrards Cross: Van Duren, 1978). Archbishop Heim, a Vatican diplomat and former Apostolic Delegate to Great Britain and Gibraltar, is an active practitioner of the heraldic art. He often illustrates the text and his knowl-

edge of these matters is comprehensive. While I have defined most terms throughout, the reader may find useful basic information on the general subject in Peter G. Summers, *How To Read A Coat of Arms* (London: The National Council for Social Service for The Standing Conference for Local History, 1967). For a thorough discussion of the entire subject, see A[rthur] C[harles] Fox-Davies, *A Complete Guide to Heraldry* rev. by J[ohn] P[hilip Brooke] Brooke-Little (London: Thomas Nelson, 1969; reprint, New York: Crown Publishers, Bonanza Books, 1985). Page references are to this reprint edition.

[10]Heim, 9-11, 18, 29, 31-32, 43.

[11]Ibid., 21, 45-46.

[12]Ibid., 23. Because Archbishop Heim published his book on heraldry five years before the revised Code of Canon Law was promulgated, all his references to the canons are to the 1917 version. Although I have changed the 1917 references to those of 1983, the reader may use the "Table of Corresponding Canons: 1917 Code with 1983 Code" in *CIC*, 1069-1092.

[13]Heim, 24-25.

[14]Ibid., 35-39.

[15]Ibid., 83-84.

[16]Ibid., 86-89.

[17]Ibid., 45. It is an interesting historical anomaly that the chief herald of England, His Grace the Duke of Norfolk, while deciding heraldic matters and organizing state occasions for the Church of England as Earl Marshal and Hereditary Marshal of England, is himself a Roman Catholic.

[18]Ibid., 78.

[19]For the range of papal documents on the subject of heraldry, see Ibid., 154-164, which Archbishop Heim presents in the original Latin Text.

[20]Ibid., 49-53, 59-64. Fox-Davies observes that ecclesiastical heraldry in England consists "exclusively of the official arms assigned to and recorded for the archiepiscopal and episcopal sees, and the mitres and crosiers which are added to the shields, and a certain number of ecclesiastical symbols which occur as charges" (465). Brooke-Little in Note 271 to this page states the following:

"As the law stands, it seems that arms cannot be granted to Roman Catholic Sees, as the bishops are not recognized as corporations sole and their use of territorial titles is contrary to certain provisions contained in the 'Catholic Emancipation' Act 1829. Arms can, however, be granted to most Roman Catholic institutions, and to prelates and clergy as individuals.

By an Earl Marshal's warrant dated 17 July 17 1967, certain insignia was approved for use in connection with the personal arms of Roman Catholic prelates and clergy. The approved insignai is as follows: 1. Cardinals place over their arms a red hat having thirty red tassels interlaced with gold thread. 2. Archbishops place over their arms a precious mitre (*mitra pretiosa*) and/or a green hat having twenty tassels, and a doubled traversed cross in pale behind the shield. 3. Bishops and Abbots Nullius Dioceseos place over their arms a precious mitre and/or a green hat having twelve tassels, and a single traversed cross or crosier either in pale or in bend behind the shield. 4. Abbots place over their arms a simple mitre (the white *mitra simplex*) or a black hat having six tassels, and a crozier either in pale or in bend behind the shield. 5. Protonotaries

Apostolic, Vicars, and Prefects Apostolic place over their arms a crimson hat having twelve tassels. 6. Religious Superiors General or Provincial and Honorary or Titular Protonotaries Apostolic place over their arms a black hat having twelve tassels. [7. Omitted in text.] 8. Privy Chamberlains and Chaplains to the Pope place over their arms a black hat having twelve violet tassels. 9. Canons of Cathedral Chapters place over their arms a black hat having six tassels. 10. Priests place over their arms a black hat having two tassels. If any prelate or clergyman is also a Cardinal, he will substitute the Cardinal's hat for the hat belonging to his degree and use it in conjunction with such other insignia as may be appropriate." So far as heraldic rules for Roman Catholic clergy who exercise powers beneath those of bishop, see Heim, 114-128.

In Chapter VII of *Heraldry in the Catholic Church* Archbishop Heim discusses heraldry in the Church of England. Archbishops and bishops of the Church of England ensign their shields with the *mitra pretiosa* and do not employ the ecclestical hat over unadorned arms of their sees. They may impale their personal arms with those of their sees. Two croziers in saltire can be behind such shields.

Prior to 1976 helms and crests might have been used in lieu of ecclesiastical hats, which were sometimes used. In Scotland a clergyman has a black hat with a single black tassel on each side. But if he is a royal chaplain, the tassels and cords they hang from are red. The Dean of the Chapel Royal has three red tassels on either side of his hat. Bishops have green hats with six and archbishops with ten tassels on either side of their hats. An Earl Marshal's warrant for 1967 established matters affecting insignia for Roman Catholic clergy (see above).

The Earl Marshal did the same service for Church of England clergy in his warrant of 21 December 1976. It prescribes "appropriate Ecclesiastic Hats"which might be used in place of helms and crests. The Schedule of Ecclesiastical Hats includes those for deans (black hat with three red tassels pendent from purple cords on each side), archdeacons (black hat with three purple tassels pendent from purple cords on either side), canons, honorary canons, canons emeritus and prebendaries (black hat having three red tassels pendent from black cords on either side), priests (black hat having one black tassel pendent from a black and white cord on either side), doctors of divinity (hat appropriate to their degree, the cord being interlaced with a skein of red), members of the sovereign's ecclesiastical household (hat appropriate to their degree charged on the front of the crown with a Tudor Rose proper [correctly drawn and colored]), and deacons (black hat without cords or tassels) (134-135, 139-142).

[21]Heim, 67-70.

[22]Ibid., 70-73.

[23]Ibid., 54-55, 58-59.

[24]Ibid., 64-67, 73-75, 79

[25]Ibid., 75-78, 80-81.

[26]Ibid., 93-95, 96-98.

[27]For a discussion of the armorial bearings of those ecclesiastical prelates, priests, religious, and entities allowed to bear arms, see Ibid., 92-93, 114-128. Thsee subjects include abbots and provosts with mitre and crozier, major religious superiors, prelates "di fiocchetto" (with tassels), protonotaries apostolic,

prelates of honor, chaplains to His Holiness, canons, deans and minor superiors, priests, abbesses and lay religious, and corporate ecclesiastical bodies.

[28]Ibid., 91-92, 98-113. See also *1979 CA*, 347.

[29]Heim, 111-113.

[30]Ibid., 129-133.

[31]See "Escudo de Armas de Monseñor Plácido Rodríguez, C.M.F., D.D., Obispo Auxiliar de Chicago," *El Chicago Católico*, Mayo 1993, *Suplemento Especial de XXV Aniversario Ordenacion Sacerdotal 1968-1983 de Monseñor Plácido Rodríguez, C.M.F., D.D., Obispo Auxiliar de Chicago*, 24; Paul J. Sullivan, "Escudo de Armas del Obispo Plácido Rodríquez, Segundo Obispo de Lubbock, Texas," *El Chicago Católico*, Mayo 1994, *Obispo Rodrlguez: Suplemento Especial*, 21A; "The Coat of Arms," *South Plains Catholic* (Diocese of Lubbock), 8 May 1994, *Supplement*, 32; and Paul J. Sullivan, "Coat of Arms Reflects Bishop Rodriguez's Heritage," *The New World* (Archdiocese of Chicago), 20 May 1994, *Bishop Rodriguez: A Special Supplement*, 10B. (All translations from the Spanish are mine.)

[32]*NCE*, 1981 rpt. s.v. "Clerical Dress," by N[icholas] Halligan[, OP, STD]; *NCE*, 1981 rpt. s.v. "Liturgical Vestments," by M[urray Allen] McCance; *Encyclopedia Americana*, 1991 ea., s.v. "Costume, Religious," by Wayne Dynes; *1992 CA*, 215-216.

[33]Dynes, "Costume, Religious."

[34]*1992 CA*, 215. Prior to 1970 gold and blue vestments were sometimes used: gold particularly in place of white (but never violet or black) and blue, for feasts commemorating the Blessed Virgin Mary. The present writer remembers an occasion on which blue vestments were worn. It was a Mass for the one hundredth anniversary of the dogmatic definition of the Immaculate Conception, celebrated by Bishop Thomas K. Gorman in his cathedral in Dallas, Texas, on 8 December 1954.

[35]Dynes, "Costume, Religious." See also *1992 CA*, 273 for a more complete listing of Byzantine liturgical vestments and appurtenances.

[36]*NCE*, 1981 prt. s.v. "Episcopal Ceremony and Vesture," by [Rt. Rev.] J[oaquin] Nabuco[, A.P.].

[37]Sometimes a prelate may be in charge of several different jurisdictions during his lifetime. In the case of the late Vincent Harris, bishop of Beaumont and Austin, he was buried in the churchyard of his cathedral in Beaumont. Bishop Harris was native neither to Beaumont nor to Austin.

[38]Nabuco, "Episcopal Ceremony and Vesture." See also *1992 CA*, 296-332 passim.

H. How the Province of San Antonio Developed Within Texas

[1]See Paul J. Foik, CSC, James P. Gibbons, CSC, and William H. Oberste, eds., *Our Catholic Heritage in Texas, 1519-1936, with Supplement 1936-1950*, by Carlos E. Castañeda. 7 vols. (Austin: von Boeckmann-Jones, 1936-1958). Volume 7 entitled *The Church in Texas Since Independence, 1836-1950* is hereafter cited as *OCHIT*. The period from 1836 is being supplanted by James Talmadge Moore. His projected two-volume study includes *Through Fire and Flood: The Catholic Church in Frontier Texas, 1836-1900* (College Station: Texas A&M Press, 1992). A good recent and compact history of Texas may be

found in *1986-1987 TA*, 167-227, the bibliography of which makes an excellent reading list.

[2]Jerry Sadler, *History of Texas Land* (Austin: General Land Office of the State of Texas, 1961), 3-7. Mr. Sadler was Commissioner of the General Land Office from 1961 to 1971. In 1994 the office of commissioner was a four year, statewide elective office, paying a salary of $79,247 per year. The commissioner "manages state funds from which the state receives revenue; supervises the leasing of the state's minerals and tidelands; [and] directs the environmental division in the General Land Office." Christy Hoppe, "Land Agency Race Focusing on Integrity: Mauro, Greytok at Odds; Libertarian Also Running," *DMN*, 6 November 1994, 10-11 (Q).

[3]Sadler, 12.

[4]See the map showing claimed and present boundaries of Texas in *1986-1987 TA*, 193.

[5]Under the Republic and State of Texas there have been twenty-eight commissioners of the General Land Office since it was created in 1837. The present incumbent (1994) is Garry Mauro.

[6]Sadler, 8-10.

[7]Ibid., 10-11.

[8]*1988-1989 TA*, 378-379.

[9]Mike Kingston and Mary G. Crawford, eds., *1994-1995 TA* (Dallas: *DMN*, 1993), 47.

[10]Sadler, 16.

[11]Ibid., "Table A: Disposition of the Public Domain of Texas under the Republic and the State," 24.

[12]Ibid., 16-17, 24. Page 17 contains a misprint of the number of acres appropriated for San Jacinto veterans. It should read 1,169,382 and *not* 1,169,832.

[13]Ibid., 17,24. On page 17 the words "Legislation of 1889" apparently refer to the Sales Scrip Act of 1887.

[14]Ibid., 24.

[15]Ibid, 15-16, 24.

[16]Ibid., 17, 24. The Sixteenth Legislature set aside land for state capitol construction in 1879, not 1882 as stated on page 17. The legislation is entitled "An Act to provide for designating, surveying and the sale of 3,050,000 acres of the unapprorpiated public domain, for the erection of a new State Capitol and other necessary public buildings at the seat of government, and to provide a fund to pay for surveying said lands." (Chapter XIII, General Laws, 16th Legislature, Approved 20 February 1879). See Texas Legislative Council, *The Texas Capitol: Symbol of Accomplishment*, 4th ed. (Austin: Texas Legislative Council, 1986), 29-30.

[17]Ibid., 16, 24.

[18]Ibid., 24 and 1994-1995 TA, 496. The *Texas Almanac* article "The Public Lands of Texas," 495-496 is a summary of "a longer history of the Texas public domain in the General Land Office," revised for the *Texas Almanac* by Commissioner Mauro and the staff of the General Land Office. It is recommended to the reader in search of additional details. There is a statistical table entitled "Public Lands of Texas," with information taken from the records of the General Land Office, following this article on page 496. It seems current to about

the first part of the year 1993.

[19]Sadler, 18, 24 and *1994-1995 TA*, 496.

[20]Sadler, 18-19, 24 and *1994-1995 TA*, 496.

[21]*1994-1995 TA*, 496.

[22]Ibid.

[23]Ibid.

[24]Other authorities disagree. The "1991 Statistical Abstract of the United States" (revised) gives the area of Texas as 262,017 square miles of land and 4,790 square miles of inland water, *1994-1995 TA*, 109. The *Hammond Citation World Atlas* gives the Texas land area as 267,339 square miles (Maplewood, NJ: Hammond, 1973), v, as does the *NCE* in its article on Texas (1981 rpt.). Sadler in his *History of Texas Land* gives the area of Texas as 173,682,674 acres. According to the information supplied, this was a typographical error for 173,582,674 acres, which converts to 271,222 square miles (page 24). In this "area" of speculation one may choose his own authority.

[25]*OCHIT*, 7:38-40.

[26]Ibid., 7:36-37.

[27]Ibid., 7:37 and note 4.

[28]Ibid., 7:56-57.

[29]Ibid., 7:58-61.

[30]Ibid., 7:75.

[31]Ibid., quoted 7:107-109.

[32]Ibid., 7:109.

[33]*1988-1989 TA*, 95.

[34]Jean Marie Odin, CM, letter to Cardinal Barnabo, 18 September 1851, *OCHIT*, 7:110-111.

[35]Ibid., 7:111.

[36]Ibid., note 8.

[37]Ibid., 7:111. In 1994 the Province of New Orleans includes only the State of Louisiana, the Province of Mobile includes the states of Alabama and Mississippi, and the Province of Oklahoma City includes the states of Oklahoma and Arkansas.

[38]For E1 Paso to 1981 see Ernest J. Burrus, SJ, "A Brief Account of the E1 Paso Diocese," *TCHS* Jan. 1987: 1-3.

[39]*1994-1995 TA*, 160-285 passim and *OCD 1993*, 366.

[40]*OCHIT*, 7:129-130.

[41]Ibid., 7:130-131 and notes 51-54, 133-134. See also Gilberto Rafael Cruz and Martha Oppert Cruz, A Century of Serv*ice: The History of the Catholic Church in the Lower Rio Grande Valley* (Harlingen, TX: United Printers & Publishers, 1979), 16-17.

[42]*OCHIT*, 7:155.

[43]*1994-1995 TA*, 160-295 and *OCD 1993*, 926. *OCD* states that the Diocese of San Antonio was "Established August 28, 1874". Castañeda gives the date as 27 August in *OCHIT*. This position is confirmed by Wangler, the archdiocesan history of San Antonio, which reprints the translation of Pius IX's decree of Erection," "Given at Rome, at St. Peter's, under the seal of the Fisherman, on the 27th day of August in the year 1874, the 29th of Our Pontificate," ii. Wangler states that the "Decree" is a copy of the Vatican original "Given from

the Vatican, 15th June, 1949," ii.

[44]*OCHIT*, 7:139-140.

[45]*1994-1995 TA*, 179-264 passim and *OCD 1993*, 264.

[46]*OCHIT*, 7:145-146 and Cruz and Cruz, 28-29.

[47]*1994-1995 TA*, 158-295 passim and *OCD 1993*, 251.

[48]*OCHIT*, 7:150-151.

[49]*1994-1995 TA*, 168-292 passim and *OCD 1993*, 318.

[50]*OCHIT*, 7:157-158.

[51]*1994-1995 TA*, 159-288 passim and *OCD 1993*, 30.

[52]*OCHIT*, 7:161.

[53]*1994-1995 TA*, 161-291 passim and *OCD 1993*, 46.

[54]Thomas H. Drury, "The Diocese of San Angelo," *TCHS* June 1985: 1-2.

[55]*1994-1995 TA*, 157-282 passim and *OCD 1993*, 923.

[56]Cruz and Cruz, 35.

[57]*1994-1995 TA*, 173-290 passim and *OCD 1993*, 141.

[58]"New Diocese of Beaumont Established," *ETC* 27 June 1986: A3.

[59]*1994-1995 TA*, 175-282 passim and *OCD 1993*, 71.

[60]Patrick Foley, "The Diocese of Fort Worth," *TCHS* June 1986: 1-3.

[61]*1994-1995 TA*, 159-294 passim and *OCD 1993*, 354.

[62]*OCD 1984* (Wilmette, IL: P. J. Kenedy, 1984), 901.

[63]*1994-1995 TA*, 172-288 passim and *OCD 1993*, 1081.

[64]*OCD 1984*, 462.

[65]*1994-1995 TA*, 160-294 passim and *OCD 1993*, 550.

[66]Tom Pratt, "Tyler Site of New Diocese," *TMT* 17 December 1986, sec. 1:1,6.

[67]*1994-1995 TA*, 157-293 passim and *OCD 1993*, 1074.

[68]*1994-1995-TA*, 157-295 passim and *OCD 1993*, 30-1081 passim.

I. The Bishop and His Diocese

[1]In this section I have relied heavily on Reese, *Archbishop*, as a general national outline. I have also tried to bring definitions of terms into conformity with the "Official Catholic Directory Glossary," *OCD 1992*, A-45 through A-51 passim.

[2]Cf. Reese, v-xii and 349-365.

[3]Ibid.

[4]"Official Catholic Directory Glossary" and personal knowledge.

[5]*NCE*, 1981 rpt. s.v. "Diocese (Eparchy)" by H[enry] G[eorge] Bowen [JCD, STL] and *1995 CA* ed. Felician A. Foy and Rome M. Avato (Huntington, IN: Our Sunday Visitor, 1994), 144-146.

[6]"Official Catholic Directory Glossary" and Bowen, "Diocese (Eparchy)".

[7]Reese, xi.

[8]*OCD 1994* (New Providence, NJ: Kenedy, 1994; "1994 General Summary," 1958-1960).

[9]Reese, xi.

[10]Ibid., 53-59. But see Susan De Matteo, "Bishop Appoints First Chancellor; New Deacon Head," *CET*, 9 October 1992, 1: "Father Gavin Vavarek has been appointed chancellor of the Diocese of Tyler by Bishop Edmond Carmody. The appointment, which took effect Sept. 23 [1992], marks the first time the diocese has had a chancellor, a position required by canon law, the bishop said." For whatever reason, Bishop Herzig, the founding bishop of the Tyler diocese, chose not to make such an appointment.

[11]Reese, 63 and *OCD 1994*, 933.

[12]Reese, 66.

[13]Reese, 85.

[14]Reese, 76-126 and *The Documents of Vatican II*, 876-877.

[15]*The Documents of Vatican II*, 579.

[16]Congregation for Bishops, *Directory on the Pastoral Ministry of Bishops* (Ottawa: Canadian Catholic Conference, 1974) no. 203, p. 104, quoted in Reese, 117.

[17]Reese, 117-120. Chapter 6 of *Archbishop* (192-258) deals with the bishop's relationship to his priests, expecially the appointment of pastors. The conclusion (256-258) may be summarized as follows: The size of an archdiocese (or diocese) affects the degree to which an archbishop (or bishop) is involved in personnel issues. He is involved in all priestly assignments and gets complaints from employees and hears about problems from his top administrators. In an attempt to make decisions easier and better, personnel offices and boards, tenure policies, open hiring, and other procedures meet with varying success. Consistency and equity are two very important principles in personnel matters. Personnel boards are often overworked and their members can suffer from burnout.

Chapter 7 of *Archbishop* (259-306) deals with the related subject of archdiocesan (or diocesan) governance of Catholic schools and Catholic social services, two of the biggest ministries in the Church. The conclusion (305-306) may be summarized as follows: Instead of direct involvement the archbishop (or bishop) may act through the superintendent of schools, the director of religious education, or the director of Catholic Charities. These people must have his trust because he must approve major changes in policy affecting their programs. This is especially true of policies involving archdiocesan (or diocesan) funds, those that impact on pastors, or on other important constituencies. He can use the budgetary process to set priorities. All programs involve issues of governance, finances, and Catholicity. Unlike secular agencies all Catholic archdiocesan (or diocesan) agency programs "must be in keeping with the teachings of the church and reflect gospel values."

[18]*The Documents of Vatican II*, 580.

[19]Reese, 120-123. The Archdiocesan Synod for the Archdiocese of San Antonio opened officially in San Fernando Cathedral on 27 November 1994. During 1995 the Synod Office works on the parish level to gather input on the strengths and needs of the archdiocese. On 12 January 1995 parish facilitators were appointed to work with their pastors. Workshops will enable the facilitators to conduct surveys and listening sessions.

The facilitators have these basic tasks: 1) "to help the discussion group perform effectively by bringing out the potential of every participant, creating a climate in which all feel comfortable to speak openly and honestly;" 2) "to model a respect for all members of the group, showing openness, sensitivity and a willingness to listen;" 3) "to not [sic] dominate the group, but instead to encourage members to accept their own responsibility to engage with one another in open dialogue;" 4) to allow the opinions and feelings of the group to develop naturally and to focus on clarifying, synthesizing or keeping order as necessary;" and 5) "to make sure that the group accomplishes its task in a timely manner, focussing on the discussion and formulating recommendations as expected." Sr. Janet Marie Abbacchi, SSND, serves as synod coordinator. Julie Rohmer, "Synod Update: Parish Facilitators Appointed," *TdC*, 20 January 1995, 9.

[20]James Provost, "Diocesan Synods," [National Pastoral Life Center] *Center Papers* 1 (September 1984): 2, quoted in Reese, 124.

[21]Provost, "Diocesan Synods, n 1-2, quoted in Reese, 125.

[22]Reese, 125-127.

[23]Ibid., 128-149.

[24]*OCD 1994*, 30-1089 passim and "1994 General Summary," 1958-1960.

[25]Ibid., 369-370, 1959.

[26]"New Vicar General, Episcopal Vicars Named," *TCH*, 7 February 1986, 2. This article contains a map showing the division of the vicariates before the diocesan cessions to Tyler and Beaumont.

[27]Diocese of Galveston-Houston, *The Official Catholic Directory of the Diocese of Galveston-Houston* (Houston: Chancery Office of the Diocese of Galveston-Houston, 1991), 27. The section entitled "Description of diocesan Departments and Ministries," 18- 23 is a helpful guide. See also *OCD 1994*, 370.

[28]"Five Secretariat Directors Named in Chancery Office Reorganization," *TCH*, 25 July 1986, 1, 21. This article contains the organizational chart mentioned in the text.

[29]For various changes and assignments see relevant issues of *TCH*.

[30]Photocopies of pages 1-2 entitled "Diocesan Statistics," published by the

Diocese of Tyler (April 1987) and in the author's possession. Cf. *OCD 1987* (Wilmette, IL: Kenedy, 1987), 971, which agrees in most particulars. But it lists the number of diocesan priests as twenty-three, does not list the hermit priest (at present included as a diocesan priest), and gives the number of missions in the diocese as fourteen. See also "Number of Catholics in Tyler Diocese Put at 28,774," *CET*, 8 January 1988, 2. This figure was given to Ms. Kathy Ladd, Diocesan Programs Director of the *Official Catholic Directory* in 1988.

[31]Tom Pratt, "Monsignor Joseph New Vicar General," *TMT*, 25 February 1987, sec. 1, p. 4. See note 10 supra.

[32]Personal recollection. "Diocesan Statistics," 1 shows enrollment for the four Catholic elementary schools is 601, for the middle school 143. and for the high school 140, as of April 1987.

[33]For useful summaries on the Tyler diocese, see the following articles in *CET*: Robert Plocheck, "1990: In Diocese and the State," 21 December 1990, 8-9; Robert Plocheck, "1991: A Sad Year for the Church in East Texas," 3 January 1992, 8; Robert Plocheck, "1992: New Bishop Is Major Change of Transitional Year for Catholics in East Texas," 1 January 1993, 8; Susan De Matteo, "1993: New Chancery, New Parishes in Formation, Priests Move into Diocese," 31 December 1993, 8; and Susan De Matteo, "Diocese Celebrates Year of Growth," 30 December 1994, 1, 6. For details on the Tyler diocesan presbyteral council revision, see Susan De Matteo, "Presbyteral Council of Ten To Replace Group of 45," *CET*, 20 November 1992, 3. Two *TMT* articles by Religion Editor Tom Pratt in the 9 July 1993 issue, sec. 5, p. 1 are worth notice. "Pastoral Networking: Tyler Pastor Oversees Diocese's Ministry Program" concerns Rev. Randy Martin's work in this connection. Under "Tribute Made to Ed Luman" in Editor Pratt's column "Religion Scene," Pratt notes that the late Tyler diocesan financial officer (1987-1993) began with $25,000 and raised diocesan funds to $3.1 million. See also *OCD 1994*, 1081-1083 for recent information on the Tyler diocese.

[34]"Deaneries of the Diocese of Tyler," *Diocesan Directory: October 1992-1993* (Tyler: Chancery Office of the Diocese of Tyler, 1992), I-II.

[35]The remainder of this section relies heavily on Reese, *Archbishop*, "Chapter 8. Beyond the Archdiocese," 307-348, which I have used primarily in outline form.

[36]See "Statement of the Catholic Bishops of Texas Opposing Casino and/or Riverboat Gambling," *TdC*, 20 January 1995, 13.

[37]*1995 CA*, 443-446.

[38]Texas Catholic Conference, "Legislative Memo: 74th Legislature Began January 10," *TdC*, 20 January 1995, 19.

[39]*1995 CA*, 443-444 and "Texas Bishops in National Posts," *CET*, 11 December 1987, 6.

[40]National Catholic News Service, "Texas Bishops Tell Human, Spiritual Sides of Ad Limina visit," 13 May 1988, in Reese, *Archbishop*, Chapter 8, note 20.

[41]John Paul II, "Developing a Pastoral Vision for the Year 2000," *Origins* 17 (28 April 1988) 801, in Reese, *Archbishop*, Chapter 8, note 22.

[42]On the Vatican intervention in the Archdiocese of Seattle (1983), its causes and its aftermath, see Reese, *Archbishop*, 337- 344. On the Catholic pressure

group situation in the Archdiocese of Newark, see Reese, *Archbishop*, 344-345.

J. Some Notes on Finances

[1]Catholic News Service, "Protestants Giving More Than Catholics," in *CET*, 10 March 1995, 3.

[2]*1995 CA*, 198.

[3]Geoff Williams, "Why Generation X Needs to Support the Church," *Catholic Twin Circle*, 5 June 1994, 9.

[4]Glenn Ellen Duncan, "Why We Give to Our Church," *Catholic Twin Circle*, 24 October 1993, 3.

[5]Thomas J. Murphy, "The Parish: Riding on Spare Change," interview by Glenn Ellen Duncan, *Catholic Twin Circle*, 5 June 1994, 10-12.

[6]Florence Wedge, How Much Should I Give to My Parish? (Liguori, MO: Liguori Publications, 1978), 3-23. See also 1995 CA, 331

[7]*NCE*, 1981 rpt. s.v. "Cathedraticum," by J. W. Goeke. The definition of "cathedraticum" in *1995 CA*, 301 does not distinguish between the two meanings of the term.

[8]*1995 CA*, 317.

[9]*Ibid.*, 330.

[10]*CIC*, 156-157, 864-870. The reader would do well to examine the entire Book V of this edition, entitled "The Temporal Goods of the Church," 857-890, including canons 1254 through 1310. As John A. Alesandro states in the "General Introduction" on page 18, this book "includes norms on the acquisition and administration of goods, on contracts, in particular the alienation of ecclesiastical property; and on pious wills and foundations."

[11]Richard P. Garrigan, "Helping Parishes Finance Their Future," interview by Glenn Ellen Duncan, *Catholic Twin Circle*, 24 July 1994, 10-11.

[12]David Briggs, "Clergy Salaries Rising Slower Than Inflation, Study Says," *DMN*, 14 March 1992, 43A.

[13]*The Catholic Answer*, 12 November 1988, 13-14.

[14]Michael Miesch, "How Much Do Priests Earn?," *CET*, 10 May 1991, 2.

[15]See Jackson W. Carroll, Dean R. Hoge, and Francis K. Scheets, OSC, "Costs of Professional Parish Leadership: A CrossDenominational Study," (Washington, DC: Catholic University of America, 13 January 1988,Mimeographed). In 1983 the range of pay for Catholic priests per year (excluding room and board but including benefits) went from $4512+ to $14,149 for newly ordained priests to $4512+ to $16,040 for a priest who has performed forty years of service. Priests with various societal problems (such as alcoholism, drugs, gambling, crime) can cost heavily on the diocesan level. See Reese, *Archbishop*, n. 1, p. 380 and 199-202. It is fair to say that since the publication of this book a number of these concerns are being addressed with increasing effectiveness.

[16]Reese, *Archbishop*, 259-260.

[17]Ibid., 260-261 and *1995 CA*, 532-533. Reese notes the existence of two offices is common, one for schools and the other for religious education programs. For their operations see his discussion, 261-266.

[18]Reese, *Archbishop*, 267-277.

[19]Ibid., 281-284.

[20]Ibid., 284.

[21]*OCD 1994*, "1994 General Summary," 1959. For the Province of San Antonio (State of Texas) the totals may be found on page 1960. These include 25 Catholic hospitals treating 1,547,102 patients, 16 health care centers with 275,239 patients, 49 specialized homes with 253,440 patients, 8 orphanages with 997 assisted, 38 day care centers with 5,088 assisted, 51 special care centers for social services with 1,083,663 assisted, and 3 schools for the handicapped with 433 students.

[22]Reese, *Archbishop*, 284.

[23]*1995 CA*, 545.

[24]Reese, *Archbishop*, 285-288, 291-304.

[25]Ibid., 150-158.

[26]For the 1994 composition of the Tyler diocesan building board, see *OCD 1994*, 1081.

[27]The Catholic Church Extension Society began in 1905 with papal approval. It aids the American church and its dependencies in home mission areas. During its existence it has collected and expended some $230 million for seventy-six designated dioceses. Its twelve-member board of governors includes the archbishop of Chicago as chancellor, a priest as president, five bishops, and five lay people. The permanent address of the Society is 35 East Wacker Drive, Chicago, IL 60601. See *1995 CA*, 527.

In 1990 the Catholic Church Extension Society awarded the Diocese of Tyler $35,000 in grants, of which $19,000 went to the Student Center at Stephen F. Austin State University in Nacogdoches, $7,000 to the church at Pittsburg, $6,000 to the church at Mt. Pleasant, and $3,000 to organize a Newman Center at Kilgore College. See "$35,000 in Grants," *CET*, 18 August 1989, 3.

[28]Reese, *Archbishop*, 159-163 and Michael Miesch, "So, You Want To Build A Church," *CET*, 29 April 1988, 1.

[29]Reese, *Archbishop*, 163-168.

[30]Ibid., 169-172 and these articles from *CET*: "Diocesan Insurance Deductibles Increase," 29 September 1989, 3 and "Diocese Adopts Medical Insurance Policy for 145," 27 October 1989, 3. Such articles illustrate how a diocese adopts plans and policies in its formative years. *CET* is rich in articles on developing decisions and the reader is encouraged to pursue its issues for instructive follow-ups on such matters.

[31]Reese, *Archbishop*, 172-173 and "Palestine, Mount Vernon Become Twin Parishes," *CET*, 7 July 1989, 2.

[32]Reese, *Archbishop*, 173-175.

[33]*1995 CA*, 414-418.

[34]Peter Feuerherd, 'U.S. Bishops Re-Examine 'Tax' System," *National Catholic Register*, 26 July 1992, 1,6.

[35]Reese, *Archbishop*, 175-181. Assessments are needed for social services, education, and popular programs. Insurance, utilities, the finance office, the tribunal, and the chancery office are often paid for by assessment. Popular programs and the number of assessments made for them vary with dioceses and their constituent groups.

[36]Diocese of Tyler, *Diocesan Annual Appeal* (Tyler: Diocese of Tyler, 1995).

[37]Diocesan Services Fund '95 in *TCH*, 10 February 1995, 28. See also *OCD*

1994, 370, 1081.

[38]*TCH,* 27 January 1995, 14-15. Catholic diocesan newspapers frequently print balance sheets for the calendar or fiscal year. These detailed statements have a format prepared by a bookkeeper or CPA.

For the Tyler diocese, this type of report, together with an inspiring message by the Bishop, may be found in *CET*, 24 March 1995, 8-9. The preparer, Ernest M. Negem, CPA, under date of 8 March 1955, addresses Bishop Carmody as follows:

> The accompanying balance sheet of the Diocese of Tyler- Chancery Office as of Dec. 31, 1994, and the related statements of support and revenue, expenses, capital additions, and changes in fund balances, and changes in cash for the period then ended, and the accompanying supplementary schedule of functional expenses, which are presented only for supplementary analysis purposes, have been compiled by me, in accordance with Statements for Accounting and Review Services issued by the American Institute of Certified Public Accountants.
>
> A compilation is limited to presenting in the form of financial statements information that is the representation of management. I have not audited or reviewed the accompanying financial statements and, accordingly, do not express an opinion or any other form of assurance on them.

Negem appends nine notes with the following headings: Summary of Significant Accounting Principles, Receivables, Changes in Deferred Restricted Amounts, Property and Casualty Insurance, Health Care Plan, Post Retirement Employee Benefits, Lay Tax Deferred Annuity Plan, Priests Pension Plan, and Transfers involving Foundation.

A particular type of diocesan fund is the "burse," the purpose of which is to pay for the education of men who wish to become priests but lack the necessary financial means.

In the Galveston-Houston diocese the Catholic Clerical Student Fund began in 1933 and is a project of the Diocesan Council of Catholic Women (DCCW). Burses comprise freewill offerings and are named for Catholic individuals or organizations. A burse is considered complete here when it reaches the amount of $15 thousand. This sum is invested to benefit the individual student from the interest. The principal is untouched. The bishop receives the interest alone every April at the DCCW Convention. He uses the amount to aid the cost of a seminarian's education. At ordination the burse works for another candidate. See Patricia G. Mainka, ''Burses Assist Those Preparing To Serve in the Priesthood," *TCH*, 18 September 1987, 11.

In the Tyler diocese as of 30 March there were fifteen burses ranging from $1,459.34 to three burses of $25 thousand each, for a total of $237,119.51. "Seminary Burses," *CET*, 16 June 1995, 15.

[39]"Mother Dioceses Divide Resources with Tyler Diocese," *CET*, 27 November 1987, 3; Michael Miesch, "Dallas, Tyler Settlement Nears," *CET*, 24 June 1988, 3; "Final Check Received from Dallas Diocese," *CET*, 8 July 1988, 3. The last two articles supply rounded figures.

[40]*1995 CA*, 322. For an idea of why papal visits and other such matters must be provided for on such a lavish scale, these representative articles on Vatican finances may be informative:"Vatican's Budget Deficit: Dioceses, Bishops Asked To Increase Contributions," *TCH*, 12 June 1987, 2; "Vatican Deficit Persists," *TCH*, 13 November 1987, 6; "Annual Financial Report from Vatican," *CET*, 27 November 1987, 10; Shawn Tully, "The Vatican's Finances," *Fortune*, 21 December 1987, 28-40; "Vatican Deficient at $56.7 Million," *CET*, 4 March 1988, 10; "Vatican Projects Record Deficit" and "Vatican Unveils Bank Reform," *CET*, 17 March 1989, 10; "Vatican Bank Scandal," *Catholic Twin Circle*, 7 November 1993, 17.

[41]"Pope To Receive $105,000 from Catholics of State, TCH, 8 April 1988, 10; "Only Texas Ahead on Papal Trip Fund," *CET*, 15 April 1988, 6.

[42]"Archbishop Flores Reports on Papal Visit Contributions," *TCH*, 13 November 1987, 11.

[43]Joel Williams, "The Papal Visit Sept. 13, 1987: Officials Report Raising 75% of Texas Papal Visit Funds," *DMN*, 29 August 1987, A41.

[44]"Momentous Year for East Texas Catholics: New Diocese, Bishop," *CET*, 25 December 1987, 1.

[45]Joel Williams, A41, and Helen Parmley, "The Papal Visit Sept. 13, 1987: Special Collection Set To Pay for Papal Visit," *DMN*, 22 August 1987, A35.

[46]"Videotape Helps Pay Pilgrimage Costs," *ETC*, 28 August 1987, 6.

[47]Juli R. Branson, "Who's Going To Pay for the Papal Guard?" *SAL*, 31 July 1987, A1+. See also Robert C. Giles, "Texas Guardsmen Train Locally for Papal Visit Security Mission," *TCH*, 28 August 1987, 11.

[48]David McLemore, "The Papal Visit: Traffic Jams Expected for Texas Mass," *DMN*, 9 August 1987, A39+; "Papal Parade Route Released," *TCH*, 28 August 1987, 17. See also David Real, "Security Airtight for Pope: All Bases Covered in San Antonio," *DMN*, 7 September 1987, Al+.

[49]Deborah Martin, "Painting of St. Anthony Presented to the Pontiff," *TCH*, Papal Supplement, 18 September 1987, 7.

K. Roman Catholic Bishops in Texas: A Processional

The last section to the "Introduction" is an introduction to the bishops in Texas themselves. Material for this summary is derived from material taken from the biography of each bishop.

Roman Catholic Bishops in Texas

In this section, unlike the Introduction, I have listed my sources informally. Many sources repeat the same information. So here a simple listing seems sufficient.

Most Reverend Warren Louis Boudreaux, DD, JCD, LLD

Information on Bishop Boudreaux is from the 1995 *CA* and the *OCD* for 1994, and the *CAT* individual file included in the Diocese of Beaumont files. For his dissertation topic see the *Comprehensive Dissertation Index, 1861-1972*, 37 vols. (Ann Arbor, MI: Xerox University Microfilms, 1973), 33:471. For a discussion of matter raised by the dissertation, see James A. Coriden, Thomas J. Green, and Donald E. Heintschel, eds., *The Code of Canon Law: A Text and Commentary* (Mahway, NJ: Paulist Press for The Canon Law Society of America, 1985). Descriptions of the positions of vice-chancellor and officialis may be found in Diocese of Galveston-Houston, *The Official Catholic Directory of the Galveston-Houston Diocese 1986-87* (Houston: Diocesan Chancery, 1986), 11-12. Recent information on Bishop Boudreaux may be found in *WWSS, 1993-1994*, 23rd, ed. (1992), 79 and *WWA 1995*, 49th ed. (1994), 1:395.

Name derivations of bishops throughout are from various sources and principally from Elsdon C. Smith, *New Dictionary of American Family Names* (New York: Harper, 1973).

Right Reverend Thomas Francis Brennan, DD

For information on Bishop Brennan see the 1995 CA, page 473, and *WWW* (4:115), which lists his date of birth as 1853 and not 1855 as in some other accounts. The 1995 *CA* also gives the bishop's title as Usula. See too the *OCD* for 1984. A good source is Paul J. Foik, CSC, James P. Gibbons, CSC, and William H. Obereste, gen. eds., *The Church in Texas Since Independence, 1836-1950*, by Carlos E. Castañeda (Austin: Von Boeckmann-Jones, 1958) 136-145, 477, vol. 7 of *Our Catholic Heritaqe in Texas, 1519-1936, with Supplement, 1936-1958*, hereafter referred to by volume and page as *OCHIT*. I have also examined the *CAT* individual file included in the Diocese of Dallas file. There is an article by Sr. M. Claude Lane, OP, in *HT* (3:109), which is heavily indebted to Casteñada. Other articles of interest are those by bishop of Dallas-Fort Worth Thomas K. Gorman, "Diocese of Dallas-Fort Worth," *NCE*, 1981 ed, and Rev. Thomas P. Cloherty, "The History of the Diocese of Dallas," *TCHS* Nov. 1982: 1. Gorman notes the subdivision of the Dallas diocese into other dioceses^: 1914 (E1 Paso), 1926 (Amarillo), 1948 (Austin), 1961 (San Angelo), and 1969 (Fort Worth). It also lost twenty-one counties to Tyler in 1986. See also John J. Delaney, *Dictionary of American Catholic Biography* (Garden City, NY: Doubleday, 1984) 61, hereafter cited as *DACB*.

Most Reverend Christopher Edward Byrne, DD, LLD

The best general account of the life of Bishop Byrne may be found in Giles, 56-59. A good short biographical account is in Sam H. Acheson, Herbert P. Gambrell, Mary Carter Toomey, and Alex M. Acheson, Jr., eds., *Texian Who's Who: A Biographical Dictionary of the State of Texas* (Dallas: Texian, 1937),

72. There is additional information in *OCHIT*, 7:477 and in the *CAT* individual file of the Diocese of Galveston-Houston. The *OCD* for 1994 and the 1995 *CA* provide some information, particularly dates, and there are brief biographical articles in *WWW*, 3:123 and in HT, 3:129- 130. The damage assessment of the Texas City explosion and fire of 1947 may be found in the 1988-1989 *TA* 42, 397. For a brief summary of Bishop Byrne's career see Sr. M. Gerard, OP, "A Brief Sketch of the Diocese of Galveston-Houston, Texas," *TCHS*,Nov. 1981, 2. See also *DACB*, 77.

Most Reverend Edmond Carmody, DD

For general information on the life of Bishop Carmody, see the 1995 *CA* and the *OCD* for 1994. Bro. Edward J. Loch, SM, archivist of the San Antonio archdiocese, supplied the documents, "Press Conference. . . Appointment of Rev. Msgr. Edmond Carmody Auxiliary Bishop of San Antonio, Nov. 8, 1988" and the Bishop's Statement of Acceptance in English and in Spanish. These documents contain useful background information.

Ms. Margaret Schattel, circulation director of *Today's Catholic*, the official publication of the Archdiocese supplied a number of articles from that publication. There are two articles by Maura Ciarrocchi, "First Irish-born Bishop for San Antonio, 18 Nov. 1988, 1+ and "San Antonio Welcomes Bishop Carmody," 16 Dec. 1988, A1. Also three articles dated 16 Dec. 1988: "Key Events in Bishop Carmody's Life," A2; Rev. Peter McKenna, "Reflections on Our Journey to the New World," A4+; and "The Carmody Family Name," A9.

For local reporting, see *SAL*: John Tackett, "Flores Gets More Assistance: New Auxiliary Bishop Is Ready To Pitch In with Bishop Popp," 9 Nov. 1988, E1+ and Juli R. Branson and Mack Sisk, "Bishop Makes Catholic History: Ordination Marks San Antonio's First Irishborn Prelate," 16 Dec. 1988, A1+ J. Michael Parker has written a number of articles on Bishop Carmody for *SAE*, including, "S.A. Priest Named Auxiliary Bishop," 9 Nov. 1988, B2; "Third World Experience Prompts Bishop's Motto," 12 Nov. 1988, F1; "Next Step for Priest: Auxiliary Bishop," 10 Dec. 1988, n.p.; "Irish Family Sheds Tears of Joy for Soon-to-Be Ordained Bishop," 15 Dec. 1988, n.p.; "Carmody Ordained during Two-Hour Mass," 16 Dec. 1988, n.p.; "Auxiliary Bishops' Stays Short," 17 Dec. 1988, n.p.; and "Law Hails Feats of U.S. Bishops," 19 Dec. 1988, n.p. See also "Boston Cardinal To Assist in S.A. Ordination Rites," 5 Dec. 1988, n.p.

Wangler's archdiocesan history of San Antonio is useful for information on the parishes in which Bishop Carmody served, as is the *OCD* for 1984, 775, 777, which lists Bishop Carmody's archdiocesan activities just prior to his missionary service in South America. For information on the exact date of the Bishop's degrees from Our Lady of the Lake University in San Antonio, see its publication, *Lake Alumni* for the article "Alumnus Named Auxiliary Bishop," Feb. 1989, 2.

As Bishop of Tyler, Bishop Carmody's activities appear in *CET*, the official newspaper of the Diocese of Tyler. These articles are representative: By Susan De Matteo: "Bishop Carmody To Head Tyler Diocese," 27 March 1992, 1, 14; "Missionary Zeal Defines Bishop Carmody," 10 April 1992, 16; "'Bishop's Mother Thought It Was Just A 'Phase'," 8 May 1992, 1, 16; "Papal Decree To

Be Read at Celebration for Second Bishop of Diocese of Tyler," 22 May 1992, 1; "'New Relationship, A New Covenant'," 5 June 1992, 1, 9; "Carmody Family Impressed by Texas Hospitality," 5 June 1992, 16; "Gathering of Catholics, Installation Bring Media Focus to East Texas Church," 5 June 1992, 8; "Bishop Appoints First Chancellor: New Deacon Head," 9 Oct. 1992, 1+; "Diocese Signs Papers To Buy New Chancery," 4 June 1993, 1, 3; "'Diocesan Handbook Applies to Some 200 Employees," 4 June 1993, 3; "Annulment Process Eased for Diocesan Petitioners," 24 Sept. 1993, 1, 3; "Pilgrim Bishop Travels in Footsteps of Christ," 20 May 1994, 1+. By Michael Miesch: "New Bishop To Be Installed Memorial Day: Tyler's Oil Palace Slated for Ceremony," 27 March 1992, 1; "New Bishop Plans To Lead by Serving Local Churches," 10 Apr. 1992, 1-2; "Bishop Recalls Profound Lessons from Missions," 24 Apr. 1992, 1, 16; "'As Is Quite Plain To See I Was Born in Ireland'," 8 May 1992, 1, 13; "Installation Set for Shepherd of East Texas," 22 May 1992, 1, 16; "More Than 3,500 Attend Oil Palace Ceremony," 5 June 1992, 1, 9; "Bishop's Installation Made Up of Various Events," 5 June 1992, 16; "Diocese, Parishes Get $60,000 from Extension Society," 9 Oct. 1992, 3; "Bishop Carmody Sees Need in Liturgy, Small-Town Presence," 12 Feb. 1993, 1-2; "When Pope Spoke There Was A Calmness, A Peacefulness," 27 Aug. 1993, 3; "Pope, Bishop Carmody To Discuss Diocese," 10 Sept. 1993, 1, 3; "Bishop Carmody, Pope Talk about Bible Belt," 22 Oct. 1993, 1-2. By Jo Anne Flores Embleton, "Father Brennan to Assume Post of Vicar General," 16 June 1995, 1+. By Sr. JoAnn Niehaus, OP, "Coat of Arms: Bishop Edmond Carmody," 22 May 1992, 2. By Edmond Carmody, "For You I Am A Bishop, But with You I Am A Christian," 5 June 1992, 3 [Installation homily, selected remarks].Unattributed articles: "Edmond Carmody," 22 May 1993, 2 [biog.]; "Prospective New Chancery on Tyler Loop," 21 May 1993, 1, 3; ''Birthright of Tyler: Ten Years of Maternity Service to Needy Women, 500 Babies," 21 May 1993, 16; "Presbyteral Council Opens Discussion of Priests' Salaries, Considers Radio Time," 24 Sept. 1993, 3.

For local Tyler reporting, see these articles by Tom Pratt in *TMT*: "Bishop Named for Diocese: Tyler-Based Prelate Will Be 'Shepherd' for Forty-two East Texas Parishes, 25 March 1992, 1, 6; "3,000 Expected for Catholic Ritual," 25 May 1992, 1, 8; "Tyler Catholic Diocese Gets New Bishop: Bishop Urges Flock To Work toward Unity," 26 May 1992, 1, 5; "Pope Hears Report on Tyler Diocese," 8 Oct. 1993, sec. 2, pp. 1,5. The following articles by Tom Pratt appeared in *TCTT*: (with Sr. JoAnn Niehaus, OP), "New Tyler Bishop's Personal Crest Highlights Family Life, Mission Work," 15 May 1992, sec. 5, p. 1; "In Tyler,Installation Service Slated Monday for Bishop-Designate Edmond Carmody," 22 May 1992, sec. 5, p. 1; "New Bishop To Be Installed," 24 May 1992, 1, 10; "Bishop in All Seasons: Irish-born Carmody Celebrates First Year in Tyler," 21 May 1993, sec. 5, p. 1; "Religion Scene: Tyler Bishop To Be Honored by Gorman," 8 Oct. 1993, sec. 5, p. 1. By Edmond Carmody: "Tyler Bishop Recounts Holy Land Pilgrimage," 13 May 1994, sec. 5, p. 2. Unattributed: "Bishop Names Longview Pastor New Vicar General for Diocese," 16 June 1995, sec. 5, p. 1.

Representative articles on Bishop Carmody from Dallas, Houston, Palestine [Texas], and San Antonio: By Dorothy Neville: "Tyler Bishop Sees Mission in Reaching Area Newcomers," *DMN*, 2 May 1993, A47, A62. By Susan

DeMatteo: "Bishop Carmody Installed in Tyler," *TCH*, 5 June 1992, 21. Unattributed *TCH* articles: "Bishop Carmody Named To Head Diocese of Tyler," 5 June 1992, 1, 12; "Southwest Liturgical Conference in Tyler," 8 Oct. 1993, 21; "Collection Reminds All To Aid Missions, Carmody," 21 Oct. 1994, 7. "Tyler Diocese Installs Its New Bishop," *PHP*, 26 May 1992, 1, 12. By J. Michael Parker in *SAE*: "Carmody One of Fading Group of Irish-born Bishops," 16 May1992, D13; "Carmody Installed As Bishop of East Texas Diocese: Former San Antonio Auxiliary Assumes Post at Tyler Ceremony," 26 May 1992, A7.

See also *WWSS*, 24th ed., 1995-1996, 133; Jo Anne Flores Embleton, "Unity Stressed as 163 Knights Join 4th Degree," *CET*, 22 Sept. 1995, 1, 10.

Most Reverend John Joseph Cassata, DD

Bishop Cassata himself supplied me with an outline of his life at my request in October 1987. I have preferred this information as correct over all other sources when a conflict of dates has arisen concerning appointments, consecration, and installation. Editions of *WWA* yield inadequate information and, according to Bishop Cassata's outline, accounts of his life in *CA* and *OCD* are not entirely accurate. There is some information about him available in the individual *CAT* file on Fort Worth.

I have consulted the Catholic University of America, *Announcements: School of Religious Studies 1986-87* (Washington, DC: Catholic U of America P, 1986) 124-128 for specific requirements of pontifical degrees. Robert C. Giles in *Changing Times* discusses diocesan institutions familiar to Bishop Cassata. See also his "Bishop Cassata Served Many Years As A Priest in Galveston-Houston," *TCH*, 22 Sept. 1989, 1, 20, a comprehensive account of the late bishop's life. Most of the same information is available in "Retired Bishop Cassata Dies at Eighty," *DTH*, 10 Sept. 1989, A26. For a summary of the bishop's administration in Fort Worth see Patrick Foley, "The Diocese of Fort Worth," *TCHS*, June 1986, 1-3. The 1979 *CA*, 691 provides information on the Order of the Holy Sepulchre.

Most Reverend Augustine Danglmayr, DD, LLD

Ms. Estelle Metzger, Archivist of the Diocese of Dallas, supplied valuable photostatic materials from her files. Two typewritten fact sheets were supplied by Bishop Danglmayr. The collection also shows holy cards (obverse and reverse) depicting Joseph and Theres[i]a Dangelmayr [sic], the translation of the warrant of appointment of Bishop Danglmayr as Domestic Prelate, dated 15 January 1937, and a page of the program for the civic reception of the Bishop following his episcopal ordination in 1942. The materials also include five articles: "Coat of Arms of Bishop Danglmayr," *The Southern Messenger*, 8 Oct. 1942, n.p.; "Retired Bishop Honored," *TxC*, 11 June 1982, 7; "Bishop Danglmayr Honored on Dual Anniversary," *The Muenster Enterprise*, 18 June 1982, 2-3; "Highlights in the Biography of Bishop Danglmayr," *The Muenster Enterprise*, 18 June 1982, 3; and "Jewels for Danglmayr Rites Recall Dallas Church History," n.d., n.p.

There is some additional information on Bishop Danglmayr in the CAT individual file of the Diocese of Dallas, in the 1992 *CA*, the *OCD* for 1992, and in Carlos E. Castañeda, *OCHIT* 7:478. See also "Ninety-three-Year-Old Texas

Bishop Dies at Home," *TMT*, 19 Sept. 1992, sec. 1, p. 5; Eric Garcia, "Ex-Chancellor of Catholic Diocese of Dallas Dies," *DMN*, 19 Sept. 1992,A29; and "Oldest U.S.Bishop Dies," *TdC*, 16 Oct. 1992, 21.

Most Reverend Lawrence Michael DeFalco, DD

Information on Bishop DeFalco may be found in standard sources, such as the 1979 edition of the *CA*, the *OCD* for 1994, various editions of *WWA*, and in the individual file of the *CAT* for the Diocese of Amarillo. See also *WWW* 7:148. For information on the degree of Licentiate in Canon Lau (JCL) see The Catholic University of America, *Announcements: School of Religious Studies 1986-1987* (Washington, DC: Catholic U of America P, 1986) 79-82. For a summary of Bishop DeFalco's activities as bishop of Amarillo see Sr. Nellie Rooney, OSF, "History of the Diocese of Amarillo," *TCHS* June 1984, 2. See also *DACB* 137.

Most Reverend Joseph Patrick Delaney, DD

Information on Bishop Delaney may be found in the 1995 *CA* and in the *OCD* for 1994. The *OCD* has recent information on the Diocese of Fort Worth. The individual file of the *CAT* for the Diocese of Fort Worth is useful, as are articles on Bishop Delaney in *WWSS, 1995- 1996*, 24th ed. 212 and in *WWA, 1995*, 1: 902. See also *Who's Who in Religion, 1992-1993*, 4th ed., 122. See also "Texas Bishops in National Posts," *CET*, 11 Dec. 1987, 6. For information on the Theological College, see The Catholic University of America, *Announcements: School of Religious Studies 1986-87* 143-145. For more recent developments in the Diocese of Fort Worth, see these articles in *DMN*: Sherry Jacobson, "Pastor Admits Sex Abuse, Resigns, FW Officials Say: Church Says [19]57 Incidents Involved 12-Year-Old," 4 July 1995, A23 and Linda Stewart, "Parishioners Stand by Priest in Sex-Abuse Case: Mass Held at FW Church Preaches Love, Forgiveness," 5 July 1995, A15. See also "Fort Worth Priest Resigns in Abuse Case," *CET*, 14 July 1995, 3.

Most Reverend Arthur Jerome Drossaerts, DD, LLD

The individual file in *CAT* for the Archdiocese of San Antonio is the best primary source on Archbishop Drossaerts. The best general account is Wangler 27-30. Information about the events of 15 and 16 February 1927 and quotations from participants in the municipal reception, installation, and investiture of the Archbishop are from the Installation Edition of *The Southern Messenger* for 17 February 1927, as quoted by Castañeda in *OCHIT* 7:154-157. In the same publication Castañeda gives a brief life of the Archbishop 7:478. Other biographical sketches are available in *WWW* 1:340 and in HT 1:520. Editions of the CA and the *OCD* give minimal accounts. See also *DACB* 153.

Most Reverend Thomas Joseph Drury, DD, LHD

The best primary sources of information on Bishop Drury are the *CAT* individual files of the San Angelo and Corpus Christi dioceses. *WWA*, 44th ed. (1985-1986), 1:753 contains a biographical scketch as does the 1992 CA. Although the OCD for 1992 (248) indicates that Bishop Drury received the degree of Doctor of Laws (LLD), I have not found any record of its reception.

For recent information on Bishop Drury, see the following articles: in *TCHS*: Bishop Thomas J. Drury, "The Diocese of San Angelo," June 1985, 1-2 and John W. Meany, "The History of the Diocese of Corpus Christi," June 1983, 2; in *TCH*: "Bishop Drury Honored," 28 October 1983, 20; ''Incarnate Word Honors Irish in Texas," 27 Feb. 1987, 17; and "Bishop Drury Served Corpus Christi Diocese," 14 Aug. 1992, 10; in *CET* for 14 Aug. 1992: "Bishop Drury's Age 90, Not 84," 6 and Joe Michael Feist, "Newspaperman Reminisces about Bishop Drury," 6.

The particular meaning of Bishop Drury's name is from La Reina Rule and William K. Hammond, *What's In A Name?: Surnames of America* (1973; New York: Jove-Harcourt Brace Jovanovich, 1977) 147.

Right Reverend Claude Marie Dubuis, DD

The best primary source of Bishop Dubuis is the *CAT* individual file on the Diocese of Galveston-Houston. The best general account is Giles, 24-27,and Wangler, 9-13, describes the bishop's life. Castañeda in *OCHIT*, 7:122-129 describes Dubuis's administration as Bishop of Galveston and outlines his life in the same work, 7:123- 124 n. 35 and 7:478. The *CA* and *OCD* are standard sources, as are *WWW* (H:226) and *HT* (1:522). See also James Talmadge Moore, *Through Fire and Flood: The Catholic Church in Frontier Texas, 1836-1900* (College Station: Texas A&M P, 1992), designed to update Castañeda. as well as Sr. M. Gerard, OP, "A Brief Sketch of the Diocese of Galveston-Houston," *TCHS*, Nov. 1981, 1.

For an assessment of Bishop Dubuis's historic contribution to the Church in Texas, see the remarks by his successor Bishop Joseph A. Fiorenza, "Together in His Name: Reporting to the Pope," *TCH*, 8 Apr. 1988, 3. For a description of the bishops of Texas visiting France in April 1988, see Susan De Matteo, "Bishop Herzig Sets Out on Pilgramage to France, Visit to Rome," *CET*, 1 Apr. 1988, 3. Susan De Matteo has also written a report on the trip to France with the assessment of Bishop Herzig of Tyler in an untitled article appearing in *CET*, 13 May 1988, 3. See also *DACB* 155-156. For the present writer's attempt to ascertain the date of Bishop Dubuis' episcopal appointment, see "The Appointment of Bishop Dubuis: A Crux for Castañeda," *East Texas Historical Journal* 28, no. 2 (1990), 35-38.

Right Reverend Peter Dufal, CSC, DD

The best information on Bishop Dufal may be found in the individual file of the Diocese of Galveston-Houston in the *CAT*. Castañeda provides an extremely brief sketch in *OCHIT* 7:479. See also Moore's *Through Fire and Flood* (1992). *CA* and *OCD* are standard references.

Right Reverend Edward Joseph Dunne, DD

As in most instances, the best primary source on Bishop Dunne is the individual file in the *CAT* file on the Diocese of Dallas. Castañeda provides a brief outline of the bishop's life in *OCHIT* 7:479. See Also Moore's *Through Fire and Flood* (1992), editions of *CA* and *OCD* and brief accounts in *WWW* 1:348 and *HT* 1:526.

See also articles by Rev. Thomas P. Cloherty, "The History of the Diocese of Dallas," *TCHS* Nov. 1982, 1-2 and by the late Bishop T[homas] K[iely] Gorman. "Diocese of Dallas-Fort Worth (Dallasensis-Arcis Vorthensis)," *NCE*, 1967 ed., 4:619. See Moore also in connection with Dunne's predecessor Brennan. On the development of the Dallas diocese generally, see James Tucek, *A Century of Faith: The Story of the Diocese of Dallas* (Dallas: Diocese of Dallas, 1990).

Most Reverend David Eugene Fellhauer, PHD, JCD

Standard outlines of Bishop Fellhauer's life may be found in the *1995 CA*, 452 and the *OCD 1994*, 1088. For basic details, see "Rev. David E. Fellhauer: Biographical Data," "Curriculum Vitae: David E. Fellhauer" [Rev. 10-2~81], and "Statement: Rev. David E. Fellhauer" [on being named bishop of Victoria, 19 Apr. 1990]. From the Diocesan Archives, Diocese of Dallas, supplied by Ms. Metzger, the diocesan archivist. For reactions in Dallas, see Kathleen Reese, "Dallas Diocese Judicial Vicar Chosen Bishop of Victoria," *DTH*, 20 April 1990, n.p. and these articles in *TxC*: Joe Michael Feist, "Dallas Priest Named Bishop of Victoria," 27 Apr. 1990, 3; Carol Luker, "On to Victoria," 25 May 1990, 3,7; and Joe Michael Feist, "Bishop Fellhauer Ordained, Installed as Bishop of Victoria," 1 June 1990, 3.

Reportage from Victoria in *The Catholic Lighthouse* includes: "New Bishop To Be Installed on Memorial Day," 18 May 1990, 1; David E. Fellhauer, "Getting To Know the New Bishop," interview by Lea Villareal, 18 May 1990, 6-7; articles by Lea Villareal in the 22 June 1990 issue: "Episcopal Ordination Draws over 1,000 People," 5; "Bishop Brings Knowledge, Skill and Experience to the Diocese," 5,7; "'He Was Just A Regular Little Boy,' Remembers The Bishop's Mom," 11; and "Tribunal Staff Experiences Mixed Emotions about Fellhauer Leaving," 12. See also Sr. JoAnn Niehaus, OP, "The Coat of Arms of Bishop Fellhauer," 22 June 1990, 16.

Other sources: *TCH*"New Bishop Named for Victoria Diocese," 27 Apr. 1990, 1,3 and "Bishop Fellhauer Ordained, Installed for Victoria Diocese," 8 June 1990, 21. John DeMers, "Bishops Take Action on a Tough, Varied Agenda," *National Catholic Register*, 4 July 1993, 1, 10. Susan De Matteo, "The Bishop's Dad: Gun Barrel City Couple Taught by Example," *CET*, 17 June 1994, 1, 16.

Most Reverend Joseph Anthony Fiorenza, DD

The best primary sources for Bishop Fiorenza are the individual *CAT* files for the dioceses of San Angelo and Galveston-Houston. The installation issues of the diocesan newspapers of San Angelo and Galveston-Houston provide much information. These are: "The Episcopal Ordination and Installation of Joseph A. Fiorenza Bishop of San Angelo," *Texas Concho Register*, 26 October 1979, 1-64 and "Joseph Fiorenza: The Man, The Priest, The Bishop," *TCH*, 8 February 1985, 1-8. A summary of his career may be found in the article "Bishop Fiorenza Named Kelly Distinguished Alumnus," *ETC*, 30 October 1987, 3. Brief biographies are available in current editions of the *CA* and the *OCD*. See also *WWA*, 1995 ed., 1172, as well as *Who's Who in Religion*, 1992-1993 ed., 159. For recent information on the Diocese of Galveston-Houston see *OCD* 1995, 380.

These articles are of particular interest: *TCH*: "Cardinal O'Connor Elected To Head Pro-Life Committee," 24 November 1989, 20; Marion Zientek, ''Bishop Fiorenza Completes Five Years: Sees A Dynamic Diocese; Gives His Vision of the Church," Interview with Bishop Joseph A. Fiorenza; interview by Marion Zientek, 23 February 1990, 24; Bishop Joseph A. Fiorenza, "To: The Catholic People of Galveston," 25 June 1992, rep. 24 July 1992, 28; Marion Zientek, "Reorganization of Parishes in Galveston," 24 July 1992, 1, 28; Bishop Joseph A. Fiorenza, ''Together in His Name: Remembering and Celebrating Our First Bishop," 25 Sept. 1992, 3; Bishop Joseph A. Fiorenza, "Together in His Name: A Visit with the Pope," 8 October 1993, 3; and "Bishop Fiorenza Observes 10th Jubilee of Installation," 10 February 1995, 2. See also "'Houston Bishop Named to NCCB Committee,"CET, 28 Feb.1992, 6. Bishop Fiorenza writes a regular column in the *TCH* under the general heading "Together in His Name'' and his activities are fully reported in this diocesan newspaper for the Diocese of Galveston-Houston.

Most Reverend John Joseph Fitzpatrick, DD

Information on Bishop Fitzpatrick may be found in the individual *CAT* file on the Diocese of Brownsville. Standard accounts of his life may be found in such sources as *WWA*, 44th ed., 1:900; *WWSS*, 23rd ed., 255; and *Who's Who in Religion*, 4th ed., 160. See also any recent edition of *CA* or *OCD*.

The four pages of the *Valley Catholic Witness* for 23 May 1971 comprise the installation edition for Bishop Fitzpatrick in Brownsville. The program "Celebration of Installation of The Most Reverend John J. Fitzpatrick, D.D. as Third Bishop of Brownsville and Eucharistic Celebration" for 27 May 1971 is useful, as is the program "Eucharistic Celebration on the Forty-fifth Anniversary of the Bestowal of Priestly Orders upon John Joseph Fitzpatrick Third Bishop of Brownsville" for 13 December 1987. Gilberto Rafael Cruz and his wife Martha Oppert Cruz provide an account of Bishop Fitzpatrick's diocesan activities in *A Century of Service: the History of the Catholic Church in the Lower Rio Grande Valley* (Harlingen: United Printers & Publishers, 1979) 38-42.

Bishop Fitzpatrick's 1985 speech on the Sanctuary Movement, from which I have quoted liberally, is entitled "Sanctuary for Latin American Refugees: Biblical Values and the Politics of Repression," and is Chapter 16 of Dennis M. Corrado and James F. Hinchey, eds., *Shepherds Speak: American Bishops Confront The Social and Moral Issues That Challenge Christians Today* (New York: Crossroad, 1986) 180-190.

These articles provide some perspective on Bishop Fitzpatrick: *Brownsville Herald*: "Bishop Celebrates Forty-fifth Anniversary as Priest," 11 December 1987, n.p. and Lisa Baker, "Fitzpatrick Plans Exit after Years of Service," 13 December 1987, D1. Laurie Hansen, "Brownsville Bishop Urges Church To Fight Status Quo on Borders," *TxC*, 23 February 1990, 9. "Bishop Best Known for His Defense of the Poor and Immigrants Retires," *TCH*, 6 December 1991, 1, 24. *CET*: Laurie Hansen, "Bishop Retires after Twenty Years in Brownsville," 6 December 1991, 1, 16 and "Brownsville Shelter Ceases Operation as Refugee Center, 14 August 1992, 6.

Most Reverend Laurence Julius Fitzsimon, DD

Information on Bishop Fitzsimon may be found in the individual file for the Diocese of Amarillo in the *CAT*. Castañeda in *OCHIT* 7:480 provides a biographical sketch, as does *WWW* 3:286. See also any recent edition of the *CA* or *OCD*. For accounts of the Floresville and Seguin deaneries see Wangler 166-185 and 232-248. For a discussion of Bishop Fitzsimon and the Diocese of Amarillo, see Sr. Nellie Rooney, OSF, "History of the Diocese of Amarillo," *TCHS*, 1 June 1984, 1-2.

Most Reverend Patrick Fernandez Flores, DD, LLD

Information on Archbishop Flores may be found in the *CAT* individual files on El Paso and San Antonio. *WWA*, 49th ed. 1:1198 contains a brief biographical sketch, as does *WWSS*, 23rd ed., 258. Basic accounts are available in any recent edition of *CA* and *OCD*, as well as *Who's Who in Religion*, 4th ed., 162.

Martin McMurtrey has written a biography entitled *Mariachi Bishop: The Life Story of Patrick Flores* (San Antonio: Corona, 1987). See also Matt S. Meier, *Mexican-American Biographies 1836-1987* (Westport, CT: Greenwood P, 1988). The Archbishop's continuing story is reported in *Today's Catholic*, the newspaper of the Archdiocese of San Antonio.

The following articles are of recent interest: "Cardinal O'Connor Elected To Head Pro-Life Committee," *TCH*, 24 Nov. 1989, 20; "Archbishop Flores Named to Bishops' Committee," *TxC*, 25 May 1990, 7; and "Hispanic Ministers Told To Use Language, Culture in Catechesis," *CET*, 14 July 1995, 6. See also these accounts by J. Michael Parker in *SAE*: "Archdiocese Calls First Synod Involving Laity: Multiyear Conference Starts with Education Phase," 27 Nov. 1994, B1, B5; "Catholics' Synod Is To Spotlight Laity: Archbishop Officially Calls Meeting," 28 Nov. 1994; A7-A8; "Religion: Art Exhibit Unusual Story of Year," 31 Dec. 1994, n.p.; "Archbishop Raises Funds for UTSA Student Center," [ca. 1995, n.p.]; "Flores Receives Salutes: Bishop Honored on Anniversary," 6 May 1995, A1, A14; "Hispanic Meeting Affirms Church's Commitment to Poor," 1 July 1995, B9; and "Catholic Bishops Commission Medal in Honor of Flores," 1 July 1995, B9. See also Deborah Menger, "Archbishop Saluted on 25th Anniversary," *SAE*, 6 May 1995, H2. Recent statistics for the Archdiocese may be found in the 1995 *OCD* 979.

Right Reverend John Anthony Forest, DD

Information on Bishop Forest is available from a variety of sources. The *CAT* individual file in the Archdiocese of San Antonio files is useful, as are the accounts in *WWW* 1:413 and in *HT* 1:618. Castañeda in *OCHIT* 7:480 has a brief sketch, as does *DACB* 199. Wangler 21-24 has a biography of Bishop Forest and traces the institutions of the Diocese of San Antonio throughout. Any recent edition of the *CA* or the *OCD* mentions Bishop Forest.

Most Reverend Francis James Furey, STD, PHD

Information on Archbishop Furey may be found in the *CAT* individual file on San Antonio, in *DACB* 199, in Wangler 34-36, and in *WWA* prior to his death in 1979. Recent issues of the *CA* and the *OCD* contain the essentials of his career, as they do for statistics on the Archdiocese of San Antonio.

Most Reverend Joseph Anthony Galante, DD, JCD

Information on Bishop Galante may be found in the 1995 *CA*, 453 and in the 1995 *OCD*, 74.

For primary materials from the Chancery Office, Archdiocese of San Antonio, see the following: Patrick F. Flores, *Msgr. Joseph Galante, Bishop Elect-San Antonio* and Joseph A. Galante, *Remarks at Press Conference*, both 13 October 1992. See also, Janie Montez, "*Despedida* [Leavetaking] Luncheon from Chancery Staff: Well Wishes." TMs, 4 May 1994.

The Catholic News Service has issued these pertinent dispatches: Jerry Filteau, *Galante: Philadelphia Priest Named to Vatican Post for Religious*, 9 December 1986; Maura Rossi, John Thavis, Sister Mary Ann Walsh, and Jerry Filteau, *Cloistered Nuns' Standoff Continues*, 17 October 1988; *Barricaded Carmelite Nuns Sue for Control of New Jersey Monastery*, 25 October 1988; Cindy Wooden, *et al., New Nashville Bishop, San Antonio Auxiliary Named*, 13 October 1992; and *Bishops Named: Two to Texas Dioceses*, 5 April 1994.

The Catholic Standard and Times, the publication of the Archdiocese of Philadelphia, provides much useful background: Father Paul S. Quinter, "Philadelphia Priest Named A Bishop for San Antonio," 15 October 1992, 1, 11 and *Bishop Joseph A. Galante: Episcopal Ordination Supplement*, special issue, A1-A12.

For the San Antonio reaction, see the following articles in *TdC*: Martha Brinkmann, "New Auxiliary Bishop Named for San Antonio," 16 October 1992, 1, 19 and "San Antonio Welcomes Bishop Galante," 11 December 1992, 1; *Bishop Galante Installation*, special issue, 11 December 1992, Al-A16; Julie Rohmer, "Bishop Joseph A. Galante Installed As Auxiliary Bishop," 25 December 1992, 16 and "Two New Bishops for Texas: Bishop Joseph Galante," 15 April 1994, 1, 4; *Bishop Joseph A. Galante*, special supplement, 29 April 1994, B1-B8; and Carolyn Martinez, "Bishop Galante Installed in Beaumont," 27 May 1994, 7. See also Gilberto Reyes, Jr., "New Bishop for City Announced." *SAL* 13 October 1992, A1. J. Michael Parker has written these articles for *SAE*: "Vatican Priest Becomes Flores' Auxiliary Bishop," 14 October 1992, G2; "S.A. Assignment Surprises Catholics," 17 October 1992, D13; "Pope Names Galante Bishop of Beaumont," 6 April 1994, D1, D9; "S.A. Bishop To Head Diocese of Beaumont," 9 April 1994, n.p.; "S.A. Comrades Get Last Laugh on Departing Bishop," 7 May 1994, D11.

ETC has published these articles: "Diocese Receives Its Fourth Bishop," 8 April 1994, 1,3; *Bishop Joseph A. Galante: Fourth Bishop of the Diocese of Beaumont*, special supplement, 29 April 1994, A1-A28; and *Welcome Bishop Galante*, special supplement, 13 May 1994, B1-B4. It continues to publish articles of interest concerning Bishop Galante on a regular basis. See also these articles, from *TCH*: Martha Brinkmann, "Auxiliary Named for San Antonio," 23 October 1992, 1, 8; "Auxiliary Ordained in San Antonio Ceremonies," 8 January 1993, 15; "Pope John Paul II Names Bishops To Lead Two Vacant Texas Dioceses," 8 April 1994, 1; and "Installation for Bishop Galante," 22 April 1994, 25; and from *CET*: "Vatican Priest Named Auxiliary in Texas," 23 October 1992, 1, 14 and "Vatican Monsignor Installed as Auxiliary in San Antonio," 18 December 1992, 6.

Right Reverend Nicholas Aloysius Gallagher, DD

Information on Bishop Gallagher may be found in the *CAT* individual file on the Galveston-Houston Diocese, and in *WWW* 1: 1436, *HT* 1:661, *DACB* 202, and Richard Henry Clarke, *History of the Catholic Church in the United States from the Earliest Period to the Present Time, with Bioqraphies of the Living Bishops*, 2 vols. (Philadelphia: Gebbie, 1889-1890) 2:86. Castañeda provides a brief biographical sketch in *OCHIT* 7:480 as does Giles, 28-31. Recent editions of the *CA* and the *OCD* contain brief references to Bishop Gallagher.

Although Giles gives the date of the Bishop's birth as 9 February 1846, Castañeda and other accounts give 19 February 1846 as that date.

Most Reverend Bernard Jacques Ganter, DD, JCD

Information on Bishop Ganter may be found in the *CAT* individual file of the Diocese of Beaumont. The present writer has in his possession an Information Page concerning Bishop Ganter's biographical data and activities and the typewritten article by Rev. James D. White, "The Coat of Arms of the Most Reverend Bernard J. Ganter, Bishop of Beaumont," 26 October 1977. 2 pp., both furnished by the *ETC* from diocesan sources. For the subject of Bishop Ganter's doctoral dissertation see the *Comprehensive Dissertation Index, 1861-1972* 34:565. Any recent edition of *CA* or of *OCD* gives basic information, as do standard reference works like *WWA* and *WWSS*. See also *Who's Who in Religion*, 4th ed., 1992-1993, 175.

Of many articles in *ETC*, the following are especially recommended: 22 August 1986: "Bishop Ganter Named Third Bishop of Beaumont," A1- A2, "New Chancery Staff Added," A3, and "Health Care Facilities in Diocese," A4; 26 September 1986: "Diocese Is 20 Years Old," A1 and the entire Section B; "Diocese of Tyler," 13 February 1987, 10-11. See also 22 October 1993: Carolyn Martinez, "Bishop Ganter Laid To Rest beside Cathedral," 1, A9, "Msgr. Enderle Elected Administrator for Diocese," 1, and *Bishop Ganter Remembered*, special supplement, A1-A-12.

See the Catholic News Service, *Bishop Ganter's Brain Tumor Recurs; Further Surgery Ruled Out*, 7 July 1993. Coverage by *CET* and *TCH* is also informative. *CET*: "Bishop Ganter Rests, Works at His Home," 9 October 1992, 6 and Carolyn Martinez, "Bishop Ganter Dies from Cancer; Served East Texas Parishes," 22 October 1993, 1, 6. *TCH*: "Bishop Ganter Undergoes Surgery for Brain Tumor," 28 August 1992, 1 and "Bishop Ganter Happy To Be Home; Taking Walk Daily," 25 September 1992, 1. Also, "Two Clergymen Plagued by Illnesses" [Ganter, Fos], 23 July 1993, 20 and Bob Giles, "Funeral Services for Bishop Ganter Conducted at St. Anthony Cathedral," 22 October 1993, 1, 28.

Most Reverend Mariano Simon Garriga, DD, LLD

Information on Bishop Garriga may be found in the *CAT* individual file on the Diocese of Corpus Christi. See also *WWW* 5:262, *HT* 3:327, and *DACB* 207. Castañeda has a brief sketch in *OCHIT* 7:481. See also Cruz and Cruz, *A Century of Service* 32-34, Wangler 96, and John W. Meany, "The History of the Diocese of Corpus Christi," *TCHS* June 1983: 1-2. There is a brief notice on the

Bishop in Meier, *Mexican-American Biographies*, 85-86. Mr. Meier is apparently unaware that Archbishop Patrick F. Flores is generally considered to be the "first Mexican-American bishop" (1995 *CA* 453). Bishop Garriga would most likely have considered his heritage Spanish, though definitely Hispanic. Mr. Meier errs also in having Pope Gregory XVI, who reigned from 2 February 1831 to 1 June 1846 (See 1995 *CA* 126), appoint Bishop Garriga to the hierarchy of Texas.

Most Reverend Hugo Mark Gerbermann, MM, DD

Information on Bishop Gerbermann may be found in the individual *CAT* file on the Archdiocese of San Antonio, earlier issues of *WWA*, and recent editions of the *CA* and the *OCD*. The present writer acknowledges gratefully the kind assistance of Bro. Edward J. Loch, SM, Archivist of the Archdiocese of San Antonio, and of Mr. Paul Joly of Maryknoll Media Relations in New York. They each provided useful materials, of which some are: File Cards Numbers 1 and 2 on Bishop Gerbermann, Archdiocese of San Antonio; "Guatemala Bishop Returns To Celebrate Nada Mass," *Alamo Messenger* 21 September 1962, n.p.; "Bishop Gets Post in S.A.," *SAE* 23 July 1975, n.p.; and Joe Fohn, "Bishop's Resignation Accepted," *SAE* 1 July 1982, A2. See also *Bishop Hugo M. Gerberman, M.M.: Maryknoll Missioner from Garwood To Celebrate 40 Years of Priesthood*, Maryknoll Media Relations (Maryknoll, NY: Media Relations, 1983).

Most Reverend Rudolph Aloysius Gerken, DD

Information on Archbishop Gerken may be found in the *CAT* individual file on the Diocese of Amarillo, as well as *WWW* 2:207, *HT* 3:335, and *DACB* 210. Castañeda in *OCHIT* 7:157-161 and 481-482 gives an account of the establishment of the Amarillo diocese, as does any recent edition of the *CA* or the *OCD*. See also Sr. Nellie Rooney, OSF, "'History of the Diocese of Amarillo," *TCHS* June 1984: 1-2 and A[ngelico] Chavez, OFM, "Archdiocese of Santa Fe," *NCE*, 1967 ed.

Most Reverend Roberto Octavio Gonzalez, OFM,DD

While there are notices of Bishop Gonzalez in recent editions of *CA* and *OCD*, the best sources may be found in the Boston area. From the Archdiocese of Boston, these "Communication Releases" were of particular help: Biog. 3 pp., *Boston's Auxiliary Bishops* 1 p., *West Region of the Archdiocese of Boston* 1 p., *Coat of Arms* 3 pp. and a photocopy of the Formal Invitation to the Episcopal Ordination of Bishop Gonzalez. See these articles from *The Pilot* (Archdiocese of Boston): for 22 July 1988: Philip F. Lawler, "Hispanic Auxiliary Bishop Appointed," 1, 10 and Bernard Cardinal Law, "From the Cardinal: To Welcome A New Bishop," n.p.; "Boston's Sixth Auxiliary: Record Throng Expected for Ordination of Bishop Gonzalez in Holy Cross Cathedral," 30 September 1988, A1; and for 19 May 1985: Rev. Robert O' Grady, "'Bishop Gonzalez Named Corpus Christi Coadjutor," 1, 3, "Declaracion de Obispo Gonzalez," 2, "Statement by Bishop Gonzalez," 3, and "Cardinal Law's Statement," 3. See also *Tablet* (Diocese of Brooklyn): "Boston's New Prelate Has Ties to Diocese," 23 July, 1988, n.p. and these articles from Texas newspapers: "Gonzalez Named

Coadjutor: To Succeed Bishop Gracida," *TxC* 19 May 1995, 15; "Bishop Gonzalez Welcomed As Coadjutor in Corpus Christi," *CET* 14 July 1995, 6; and "Bishop Gonzalez Welcomed to Corpus Christi Diocese," *TCH* 11 August 1995, 21.

Most Reverend Thomas Kieley Gorman, DD, DScHist

Information on Bishop Gorman may be found in the individual file of the *CAT* for the Diocese of Dallas, in *DACB* 220, and in Castañeda, *OCHIT* 7:482. See also older editions of *WWA* and most recent editions of the *CA* and the *OCD* for basic accounts. Bishop Gorman wrote an article "Diocese of Dallas-Fort Worth (Dallasensis-Arcis Worthensis)" in the *NCE*, 1967 ed. See also Rev. Thomas F. Cloherty, "The History of the Diocese of Dallas," *TCHS* Nov. 1982: 1-3.

Most Reverend Rene Henry Gracida, DD

Information about Bishop Gracida may be found in the *CAT* individual file on the Diocese of Corpus Christi and in any recent edition of the *CA* and the *OCD*. Any recent edition of *WWSS* and *WWA* gives a full outline of Bishop Gracida's life. See also *Who's Who in Religion* for 1992-1993, 4th ed., 191. Information on the Diocese of Corpus Christi may be found in the 1984 and 1995 editions of the *OCD*. The text of the Bishop's remarks on capital punishment is reprinted as Chapter 11 of *Shepherds Speak: American Bishops Confront the Social and Moral Issues That Challenge Christians Today*, ed. Dennis M. Corrado and James F. Hinchey (New York: Crossroad, 1986) 108-125. Some articles of interest are "Hispanic Leaders in Catholic Church," *DTH* 31 August 1987, A8, "Bishop Gracida among Non-Signers of Statement," *TxC* 25 May 1990, 7, and "Corpus Bishop Links Abortion to Racism," *CET* 28 February 1992, 6. Bishop Gracida's current activities are printed in *South Texas Catholic*, the diocesan newspaper for the Diocese of Corpus Christi.

Most Reverend Charles Victor Grahmann, DD

Details concerning dates of some appointments and installations of Bishop Grahmann seem to vary in recent issues of *CA* and *OCD*. Therefore, I have tried to sort a clear and consistent chronology based upon various other sources. There are standard references such es editions of *WWSS*, *WWA*, and in *Who's Who in Religion*, 4th ed. (1992-1993), 192. Various issues of *CA* explain organizations in the Church with which the Bishop has been associated. *OCD* provides past and current statistics on the Victoria in Texas and Dallas dioceses. Wangler provides excellent information to 1974 concerning religious institutions in the Archdiocese of San Antonio and in the Diocese of Victoria in Texas which have in some way involved the Bishop. The reader will find the *Catholic Lighthouse* of the Diocese of Victoria in Texas from its inception and *TxC* of the Diocese of Dallas, especially from 1989 on, useful in following the day-to-day career of Bishop Grahmann.

I devote some space in the "Introduction" section on finances to details of the Bishop's service as state treasurer for Catholic bishops of Texas for the expenses of the Pope's brief visit to Texas and for other related expenses.

The most detailed accounts of the Bishop's life appear in *Charles V.*

Grahmann: The Man. . .The Priest: On the Occasion of the Installation of Bishop Charles V. Grahmann as Coadjutor Bishop Of Dallas February 21, 1990, special supplement of the *TxC*, 16 Feb. 1990, 1-16. Some articles of particular interest in *TxC* are by Joe Michael Feist, "Diocese Welcomes A New Shepherd: Bishop Charles V. Grahmann Installed As Coadjutor Bishop of Dallas," 23 Feb. 1990, 3 and by Eva Opiela, "Bishop Grahmann Cites 'Contempt' for Church," 27 Apr. 1990, 3.

See these articles from the *Catholic Lighthouse*, for 5 Jan. 1990: "Bishop Grahmann Announces His Appointment to Diocese of Dallas," 1-2; "Strategic Planning Committee Offers History of Diocesan Funding," 1, 5; and "Diocese of Victoria Gains New Parishes," 3; for 16 Feb. 1990: "Bishop Grahmann's Farewell Message," 1; "Honoring Our Beloved Bishop Grahmann," 5; for 16 Mar. 1990: Joe Michael Feist, "People of Dallas Welcome New Coadjutor Bishop," 1; Lea Villareal, ''Msgr. McLaughlin Administrator Named for Diocese of Victoria,'' 1, 3; and Lea Villareal, ''A Special Gift Made for a Special Man: Handcrafted Crozier Made for Bishop Grahmann," 3.

See also *TCH*: "Bishop Spends Time Aboard Navy Ships," 24 Aug. 1987, 17; "Bishop Grahmann Named Coadjutor for Dallas," 22 Dec. 1989, 1-2; and "Pope Accepts Resignation of Dallas Bishop," 27 July 1990, 21; and in *ETC*: "Bishop Grahmann Serves at Sea," 28 Aug. 1987, 6.

For the Dallas press see *DTH*: by Scott Sunde, 20 Dec. 1989: "Dallas Catholics Welcome Bishop: Pope's Decision Puts Grahmann in Line To Head Diocese," A1, A21 and "New Bishop Seen As Man of All People: Service to the Church Runs Deep in Family," A20; and Kathleen Reese, "S[outh] Texas Bishop Installed As Tschoepe's Successor," 22 Feb. 1990, A13. See also these articles in *DMN*: Helen Parmley, for 20 Dec. 1989: "Bishop's Successor Announced: South Texas Cleric Is Named Coadjutor," A1, A23 and "Grahmann Is Man of Diversity: Bishop Says Fluency in Spanish Helped Him Win Dallas Post," A29; Sylvia Martinez, "Catholics Plan $22 Million Drive: Dallas Diocese Seeks Money for Education Fund, Projects," 4 June 1992, A29; "Catholics Buy Building As Site for New Chancery," 19 Sept. 1992, A37; Gayle Reaves, "Bishop To Join Protestors at Doctor's Home," 9 Jan. 1993, A38; Pete Slover, "'This Is My Job,' Bishop Says of Abortion Protest," 10 Jan. 1993, A29-A30; Daniel Cattau, "Inquiry on Priest Under Way: Diocese Launched Probe before Molestation Suit," 20 May 1993, A29, A36; Judith Lynn Howard and Daniel Cattau, "Officials Say Diocese Erred in Not Reporting Abuse Fears: They Say Failure To Inform Officials Possibly Illegal," 21 May 1993, A1, A18; Judith Lynn Howard, "Diocese Says It Reported Abuse Charge: Agency Cites Complaint; Police Deny Knowledge," 22 May 1993, A1, A9; Brooks Egerton and Judith Lynn Howard, "Priest Accused of Abuse Often Befriended Boys: Sex Allegations Shock People Who Respect Him," 23 May 1993, A1, A11; Judith Lynn Howard, "Allegations Upset Cleric's Mother: Abuse Charges 'Just Not True', She Says," 23 May 1993, A11; Daniel Cattau, "Bishop Defends Diocese in Sex Case," 28 May 1993, A32; Todd J. Gillman and Craig Flournoy, "Diocese Hid Abuse, Court Records Say: Church Lawyer Denies Coverup Allegations," 5 Aug. 1994, A1, A28.

Most Reverend Curtis John Guillory, SVD, DD

Besides notices in current *CA* and *OCD*, see *Who's Who in Religion*, 4th ed. (1992-1993), 200. I am grateful to Very Reverend Borgia Aubespin, SVD, Provincial of the Southern Province of the Society of the Divine Word, for providing me with a copy of Bishop Guillory's official notice of appointment sent to him by Archbishop Pio Laghi, dated 23 December 1987. The Southern Province has an article in its publication on the Bishop: "Our 12th Black Bishop," *In A Word* Jan. 1988, 3. The Society of St. Joseph of the Sacred Heart, Baltimore, Maryland, has published "Editorial," *The Josephite Harvest* Spring 1988, 1.

The *Clarion Herald* of the Archdiocese of New Orleans published these articles: "New Orleans Priest Named Auxiliary Bishop," 31 Dec. 1987, 1+; Florence L. Herman, "Becoming Bishop 'Overwhelming' Experience," 4 Feb. 1988, 1+; and Florence L. Herman, "Bishop Curtis Guillory Ordained Nation's 12th Black Bishop," 3 Mar. 1988, 8-9.

The following articles in *TCH* are of special interest: By Bob Giles: "Sharecropper's Son Named Auxiliary Bishop of Diocese," 8 Jan. 1988, 1; "New Auxiliary Bishop Remembers Home Life in 'the Old Country'," 8 Jan. 1988, 20; *Auxiliary Bishop-designate Curtis John Guillory,* spec. sec., 12 Feb. 1988, 1-4; and "Auxiliary Bishop Guillory Urges Journalists To Reconcile Ethnics," 22 Jan. 1993, 16. By other writers: "National Consultation Meeting of Black Catholics," 8 Jan. 1988, 2; "Office of Black Ministries Prepares for Three Activities," 8 Jan. 1988, 2; "Ordination Ceremonies Scheduled at Coliseum for New Auxiliary Bishop," 12 Feb. 1988, 1; "Seven from the [Galveston-Houston] Diocese Invested Knights, Ladies of the Holy Sepulchre," 25 Nov. 1988, 13. The obituary for Wilfrid Guillory appeared in the issue for 10 Sept. 1993. See also "Bishop Guillory Elected To Head NCCB Committee," 26 Nov. 1993, 28. There is "New Orleans Priest Named First Black Bishop in Texas," *CET* 8 Jan. 1988, 1.

For the Houston secular press, see in HC: Julia Duin, "City's First Black Bishop Ordained," 20 Feb. 1988, sec. 1, p. 27 and "Bishop Curtis Guillory," 5 Jan. 1992, G3. For HP: Richard Vara, "Sharecropper's Son Ordained As Bishop," 20 Feb. 1988, A10.

Most Reverend Vincent Madeley Harris, DD, LHD

Information on Bishop Harris may be found in *CAT* individual files of the dioceses of Beaumont and Austin. Editions of *CA* and of *OCD* provide outlines of his career as well as recent statistics for the years covered by them. Giles 134-135 discusses St. Christopher's Parish in Houston. A number of articles in *ETC* for 27 June 1986, A1-A4 relate to the early days of the Beaumont diocese. These are: "New Diocese of Beaumont Established," A1; "Fame Spread from His East Texas Roots," A2+; "Bishop Harris Named Founding Bishop of Beaumont," A3; and "DPO Building Had Varied History," A4. Some more recent information is provided by Rev. James Vanderholt in his article "History of the Diocese of Beaumont," A23, A25-A26, which appeared in *Bishop Joseph A. Galante: Fourth Bishop of the Diocese of Beaumont*, spec. supplement of the *ETC* 29 Apr. 1994, A1-A28.

See also Bob Giles, "Bishop Harris Remembered for His Service to the

Church," *TCH* 8 Apr. 1988, 1+. Additional information may be found in *WWA*, 44th ed., 1:1202 and in *WWSS*, 20th ed., 260. Issues of *TCH* for 15 July 1966, *ETC* for 22 Apr. 1988, and *The Catholic Spirit*, the official newspaper of the Diocese of Austin, for Apr. 1988 are also useful as is Kevin L. Baseaux, "A Short History and Description of the Beaumont Diocese," *TCHS* Dec. 1985, 1-5. For recent family information see the obituary for "George Malcolm Harris, Jr., Brother of Late Bishop Harris," *TCH* 9 Aug. 1991, 10.

Most Reverend Charles Edwin Herzig, DD

Various standard sources provide minimal information on Bishop Herzig. These are editions of *CA, OCD*, and reference works such as *WWA*, 45th ed. 1:1403 and *Who's Who in Religion*, 4th ed. 226. Wangler is useful for tracking down the archdiocesan institutions in San Antonio with which Bishop Herzig was connected. Information concerning the Diocese of Tyler at its inception is taken from the *Diocesan Directory* of April 1987 (photostatic copy in the author's possession). See also "Funeral Services Held in San Antonio for Bishop's Father," *CET* 29 Apr. 1988, 2.

I am indebted to Bro. Edward J. Loch, SM, Archivist of the Archdiocese of San Antonio for the following materials relating to Bishop Herzig: Curriculum Vitae of "Reverend Charles E. Herzig" (one typed sheet), "From a form from 1974," additional biographical information (one sheet), a photostat of Charles Herzig's ordination invitation, 1955 (one sheet), "Press Conference December 16, 1986 Tyler Diocese Bishop-Elect-Herzig," Press Release, Archdiocese of San Antonio (two pages), Press Release of Bishop-Elect Herzig on appointment as Bishop of Tyler (three typed pages, in English), and "Press Release of Bishop- Elect Herzig on appointment as Bishop of Tyler" (one typed page, in Spanish), translation mine.

Ms. Margaret M. Maher, Librarian of the National Catholic (now Catholic) News Service in Washington, DC, supplied me with a press release, "New Diocese Established in Texas, First Bishop Named," 16 Dec. 1986.

San Antonio newspaper accounts are of interest. See Steve Schlather, "Bishop elect Blessed with Achievement: Herzig Is Well-prepared for Duties Awaiting him," *SAL* 21 Dec. 1986, B1+, J. Michael Parker, "Bishop-elect Recalls 1968 Priests' Revolt," *SAE* 21 Feb. 1987, n.p., "Tyler's Bishop-elect Greets Supporters" (captioned photograph) *SAE* 25 Feb. 1987, A1, J. Michael Parker, "Rose Blooms Greet New Tyler Bishop," *SAE* 25 Feb. 1987, A10.

See also "Invitation to the Ordination of Bishop Charles E. Herzig" in Tyler, Texas, 24 Feb. 1987 (English and Spanish) and in the programs "Vespers and Service of Commitment Celebrating the Ordination of Bishop-Designate Charles E. Herzig As First Bishop of the Diocese of Tyler Texas," 24 Feb. 1987 (twelve pages) and "The Ordination of Charles E. Herzig as First Bishop of the New Diocese of Tyler, Texas," 24 Feb. 1987. Wendy Lane, "New Tyler Diocese Praised: Bishop-designate Seeks To Build Faith," *DMN* 25 Feb. 1987, A17. "Tyler's Bishop Herzig Dead at Age 62," *PHP* 10 Sept. 1991, 2.

For area diocesan newspapers see Bob Giles, "Bishop-designate Herzig Brings Strong Family Ties to Tyler Diocese," *TCH* 9 Jan. 1987, 10, "Ordination of New Bishop in Tyler Slated," *TCH* 13 Feb. 1987, 17, James Vanderholt, "Tyler Diocese Begins," *ETC* 13 Feb. 1987, 1, *Bishop Charles E. Herzig: Dio-*

cese of Tyler, spec. ed. of *TC* 20 Feb. 1987, Joseph A. Fiorenza, "Welcome to the Diocese of Tyler," *TCH* 27 Feb. 1987, 3, Silvia Novo Pena, "Bishop Herzig Receives Warm Tyler Welcome," *TCH* 13 Mar. 1987, 11, and "Bishop Herzig Served in Tyler Diocese Four Years," *TCH* 13 Sept. 1991, 10.

For Tyler newspaper coverage, see: Tom Pratt, "Tyler Site of New Diocese," *TMT* 17 Dec. 1986, A1+, Tom Pratt, "The Man Who Will Be Bishop: bishop-Designate of New Tyler Diocese A 'Laid-Back' Gospel Apostle," *TCTT* 11 Feb. 1987, sec. 1, p. 1+, "Ceremonies Today To Create Tyler Diocese, Install Bishop," *TMT* 24 Feb. 1987, sec. 1, p. 7, Tom Pratt, "Bishop Ordained: New Diocese in Tyler," *TMT* 25 Feb. 1987, A1+, Donna M. Lestage, "Bishop Greeted by Church Illuminaries [sic]," *TMT* 25 Feb.1987, A4, Paul Buck and John Harrison, photogs., "The Ordaining of A New Bishop (three photographs)," *TMT* 27 Feb. 1987, sec. 4, p. 6, Tom Pratt, "One-on-One Interview: Bishop Reflects on OneYear Anniversary," *TMT* 26 Feb. 1988, sec. 5, p. 1, Tom Pratt, "Bishop of Tyler Diocese Charles Herzig, 62, Dies," *TCTT* 8 Sept. 1991, sec. 1, pp. 1, 6, and Tom Pratt, "Overflow Crowd Bids Farewell to Tyler Diocese Bishop Herzig," 13 Sept. 1991, sec. 1, pp. 1-2.

CET is the best authority on Bishop Herzig since he founded it in late 1987. It kept a bimonthly record of his activities and during his tenure provided full details and in-depth coverage. While there are many excellent articles quoted throughout the "Introduction" to this work and elsewhere concerning the Bishop and the development of the Tyler diocese, I found these items most useful for biographical purposes: Susan De Matteo, "Bishop Herzig Sets Out on Pilgrimage to France, Visit to Rome," 1 Apr. 1988, 3, Susan De Matteo, "Bishop Herzig, Pope Discuss East Texas," 13 May 1988, 1, 3, Susan De Matteo, [Untitled Article on Texas Bishops Visiting France], 13 May 1988, 3. On Bishop Herzig's last months, see "Bishop Herzig To Undergo Care for Tumor," 12 Oct. 1990, 1, "Bishop Herzig To Return for Chemotherapy," 26 Oct. 1990, 1, "Bishop Herzig Gets Good Report on Health Condition," 7 Dec. 1990, 1, 3, "Bishop Herzig Views His Health, That of Diocese," 15 Feb. 1991, 1-2, 6, Michael Miesch, "Bishop Herzig Begins Radiation Treatment Anew," 19 July 1991, 1, 3, and "Bishop Returns after Phlebitis Treatment," 24 May 1991, 1, 3. The issue of 13 Sept. 1991 appearing immediately after Bishop Herzig's death contains ten articles (three with bylines by Michael Miesch, four with bylines by Susan De Matteo, two staff reports, and a tribute by the editor, Robert Plocheck) concerning Bishop Herzig. Other articles of special interest are the following: Michael Miesch, "Bishop Herzig Was 'Servant Leader,' Awed by God's Love," 27 Sept. 1991, 1, 10, Susan De Matteo, "Cathedral Filled with Mourners As East Texas Buries Its First Bishop," 27 Sept. 1991, 7, "Kenneth Herzig, Brother, Retired from Military-Civilian Service," 27 Sept. 1991, 8, Michael Miesch, "Bishop Wills Estate to Diocese for Parish Development," 22 Nov. 1991, 3, "Bishop Herzig, Diocesan Markers To Be Blessed," 27 Aug. 1993, 3, and Michael Miesch, "Bishop Recalls Predecessor as 'Sing-Along Pastor'," 24 Sept. 1993, 3.

Most Reverend Emmanuel Boleslaus Ledvina, DD

Information on Bishop Ledvina is available in the *CAT* individual file on the Diocese of Corpus Christi. See also Castañeda *OCHIT* 7: 482-483, *WWW* 5:421, and *DACB* 321-322. In the same work Castañeda also describes the work of the Catholic Church Extension Society 7:178-205. The *CA* gives yearly updates on the Society. See also Gilberto Rafael Cruz and Martha Oppert Cruz, *A Century of Service: The History of the Catholic Church in the Lower Rio Grande Valley* (Harlingen, TX: United Printers & Publishers, 1979) 29-31 and John W. Meany, "The History of the Diocese of Corpus Christi," *TCHS* June 1983, 1-2.

Most Reverend Stephen Aloysius Leven, DD

Information on Bishop Leven may be found in the *CAT* individual files on the Archdiocese of San Antonio and the Diocese of San Angelo. Brief accounts of his life are given in a number of editions of the *CA* and of the *OCD*. See also a brief sketch by Castañeda *OCHIT* 7:483 and by *DACB* 325. For information on Bishop Leven's activities in San Antonio see Wangler. The *Texas Concho Register* of 26 Oct. 1979 gives an account of Bishop Leven during his tenure as bishop of San Angelo.

Most Reverend Robert Emmet Lucey, STD

For primary information on Archbishop Lucey see the *CAT* individual files of the Diocese of Amarillo and the Archdiocese of San Antonio. For Amarillo see Sr. Nellie Rooney, OSF, "History of the Diocese of Amarillo," *TCHS* June 1984, 1-2 and for San Antonio see Wangler.

Saul E. Bronder in *Social Justice and Church Authority: The Public Life of Archbishop Robert E. Lucey* (Philadelphia: Temple UP, 1982) describes the Archbishop as a social liberal and an ecclesiastical conservative. At various phases in his career Bronder finds Lucey a labor organizer, a migrant farmworker advocate, and a voice for racial integration and social justice. Castañeda has a biographical sketch in *OCHIT* 7:483. Wangler 30-33 supplies a thorough treatment, as does *DACB* 331 for the basic facts. See also editions of the *CA* and the *OCD*.

Most Reverend Joseph Patrick Lynch, DD, LLD

Information about Bishop Lynch may be found in the *CAT* individual file of the Diocese of Dallas, as well as in Castañeda *OCHIT* 7:484, *WWW* 3:538, and *HT* 3:547. Notices may be found in various editions of the *CA* and the *OCD*. For information about Bishop Lynch's administration, see T[homas] K[ieley] Gorman, "Diocese of Dallasensis-Arcis Vorthensis (Dallas-Fort Worth)," in *NCE*, 1967 ed., as well as Rev. Thomas P. Cloherty, "The History of the Diocese of Dallas," *TCHS* Nov. 1982, 1-3 and *Texas Catholic Directory: Diocese of Dallas 1986-1987*, Sesquicentennial ed. (Dallas: Diocese of Dallas, 1986), 11.

Most Reverend John Edward McCarthy, DD

Primary materials on Bishop McCarthy may be found in the *CAT* individual files of the dioceses of Galveston-Houston and of Austin. There are yearly references in the *CA* and in the *OCD*. See also *Who's Who in Religion*, 4th ed. (1992), 335, *WWSS*, 24th ed. (1994), 570, and *WWA*, 49th ed. (1995), 2:2438. Statistics on the Diocese of Austin may be found in the *OCD*. My source for the date of Bishop McCarthy's appointment to Austin is 1995 *CA* 459, rather than 1995 *OCD* 47, which lists 24 Dec. 1985. These articles are of particular interest: "Fire Destroys Home of Bishop McCarthy," *TCH* 24 June 1988, 17, "Diocesan Goals Set for Annual Peter's Pence Collection," *CET* 8 June 1990, 6, "Bishop McCarthy Observes Fifth Anniversary in Austin," *TCH* 22 March 1991, 15, "Bishop McCarthy Receives UST's Guinan Award," *TCH* 7 June 1991, 12 and "Bishop McCarthy Recovers from Heart Surgery," *TCH* 13 Aug. 1993, 28. The Bishop's career may be followed in the pages of *The Catholic Spirit*, the official newspaper of the Diocese of Austin.

Right Reverend Dominic Manucy, DD

For primary information on Bishop Manucy see the *CAT* individual file for the Diocese of Corpus Christi, the successor of the Vicariate Apostolic of Brownsville. There are references in the *CA* and and in the *OCD*. For a nearly contemporary account see Rev. Richard H. Clarke, *Lives of the Deceased Bishops of the Catholic Church in the United States*, 2nd ed., 3 vols. (New York: Clarke, 1888) 3:388-396. For a more recent account, see James Talmadge Moore, *Through Fire and Flood: The Catholic Church in Frontier Texas, 1836-1900* (College Station: Texas A&M P, 1992). See Also Castañeda, *OCHIT* 7:132-136, 484-485, *DACB* 343, and *WWW* H:402.

The Vicariate Apostolic of Brownsville is discussed in Gilberto Rafael Cruz and Martha Oppert Cruz, *A Century of Service: The History of the Catholic Church in the Lower Rio Grande Valley* (Harlingen, TX: United Printers & Publishers, 1979), 16-21. See also John W. Meany, "The History of the Diocese of Corpus Christi," *TCHS* June 1983: 1-2.

Most Reverend Adolph Marx, DD, JCD

Primary information about Bishop Marx may be found in the individual *CAT* files on the dioceses of Corpus Christi and of Brownsville. See also Castañeda, *OCHIT* 7:485 and recent editions of *CA* and of *OCD*. His dissertation topic is in *Comprehensive Dissertation Index, 1861-1972*, 35:926. I have used Cruz and Cruz, 35 (cited above) for the date of the Bishop's appointment to Brownsville, rather than 1995 *OCD* 145, which lists 19 July 1965.

Most Reverend Leroy Theodore Matthiesen, DD, LittD

Primary information on Bishop Matthiesen may be found in the *CAT* individual file on the Diocese of Amarillo. See also *WWSS*, 24th ed. (1995), 564 and *WWA*, 49th ed. (1994), 2:2417, as well as *Who's Who in Religion*, 4th ed. (1992), 331. See also A. E. P. Wall, ed., *American Catholic Who's Who*, Bicentennial ed., vol. 21 (Washington, DC: National Catholic News Service for the United States Catholic Conference, 1975). Biographical and statistical references may be found in editions of *CA* and of the *OCD*. On the Bishop's German ancestry see Joe Michael Feist, "German-Texans Assume Leadership Positions of Church in Lone Star State," *CET* 13 Apr. 1990, 16, rptd. from an article in *TxC*. These articles are of particular interest: "Bishop Matthiesen Receives Award in Amarillo," *TCHS* Nov. 1982, 4; Sr. Nellie Rooney, OSF, "History of the Diocese of Amarillo," *TCHS* June 1984, 1-2; "Woman Named Amarillo Chancellor," *ETC* 27 June 1986, 2; "Bishop Leads Anti-Nuke Protest at Pantex Plant," *SAL* 9 Aug. 1987, A20; Thom Marshall, "Report Adds to Fears of Pantex Protesters," *HC* 11 Dec. 1988, E1; Bob Drummond, "Pantex Weak on Radiation

Safety Points," *DTH* 7 Dec. 1989, A27; "Amarillo Catholic Schools Forced To Reorganize," *TxC*, 23 Feb. 1990, 9; and "Pacifist Bishop Nears Retirement," *DMN* 17 June 1995, G4. Regular coverage of Bishop Matthiesen's administration in Amarillo may be found in *West Texas Catholic*.

His Eminence Cardinal Humberto Sousa Medeiros, STD

Primary information about Cardinal Medeiros is available in the *CAT* individual file of the Diocese of Brownsville. Some recent information is provided by J. Gordon Melton, *Religious Leaders of America: A Biographical Guide to Founders and Leaders of Religious Bodies, Churches, and Spiritual Groups in North America* (Detroit, Gale Research, 1991), Entry 625, 312. His dissertation topic is listed in *Comprehensive Dissertation Index, 1861-1972*, 36:6. See also WWA, 41st ed. (1980), 2:2271, *DACB* 385, and various editions of *CA* and *OCD*. *DACB* stresses the Cardinal's role in providing social services in Brownsville and his advocacy of pro-life activity and parish reform in Boston. Cruz and Cruz, *A Century of Service* 35-37 describes the Brownsville administration, as does the *OCD* for 1984 concerning the Archdiocese of Boston about the time of the Cardinal's death. Dr. Saverio Pisani, *A New Guide to Rome and Its Environs* (Rome: Verdesi, 1954) 142 describes the Church of Santa Susanna and the 1989 *CA* 149-150 relates the functions of the curial congregations of which Cardinal Medeiros was a member.

Most Reverend Sidney Matthew Metzger, STD, JCD

Primary information on Bishop Metzger may be found in the *CAT* individual files on the Archdiocese of San Antonio and the Diocese of El Paso. Castañeda, *OCHIT* 7:485 is useful, as are the 1979 *CA* 534 and Wangler 278. The Bishop was well-written about in such standard reference works as *WWA* during his lifetime. See also Steve Jacobs, "The History of the Diocese of El Paso," *TCHS* Nov. 1983, 1-2.

Most Reverend John Louis Morkovsky, STD

CAT individual files of the dioceses of Amarillo and Galveston-Houston contain primary information on Bishop Morkovsky. In addition to recent editions of the *CA* and of the *OCD*, see also standard reference works such as *WWA*, 45th ed, 2:2206. Giles 62-63 and Wangler 279 are useful on institutional, as well as biographical, information for the Diocese of Galveston-Houston and for the Archdiocese of San Antonio throughout.Castañeda, *OCHIT* 7:486 has a brief notice. *TCH* from its inception in 1964 through 1990 is a chronicle of the Bishop in Houston. See also these articles: Sr. M. Gerard, OP, "A Brief Sketch of the Diocese of Galveston-Houston," *TCHS* Nov. 1981, 1-2, Sr. Nellie Rooney, OSF, "History of the Diocese of Amarillo," *TCHS* June 1984, 1-2; "Bishop Morkovsky: Named Vice Postulator in US for Margil," *TCH* 27 May 1988, 13; Bob Giles, "To Observe 80th Birthday on Aug[ust] 16: Bishop Morkovsky Admits That He Has 'A Real Thirst for Life'," *TCH* 11 Aug. 1989, 24; and *Bishop John L. Morkovsky, S.T.D.: August 16, 1909 - March 24, 1990*, spec. supplement of *TCH* 13 Apr. 1990, 1- 4.

Right Reverend John Claude Neraz, DD

Primary information on Bishop Neraz may be found in the *CAT* individual file on the Archdiocese of San Antonio, in *DACB* 419, *HT* 2:270, and in *WWW* H:447. See also Clarke, *Deceased Bishops* 2:91 and Wangler 18-20. Notices also appear in recent editions of the *CA* and the *OCD*. For more recent scholarship see Moore, *Through Fire and Flood.*

Most Reverend Wendelin Joseph Nold, STD

Primary information on Bishop Nold may be found in the *CAT* individual file on the Diocese of Galveston-Houston. See also Castañeda, *OCHIT* 7:486, *DACB* 423, and Giles 60-61. There are references in recent editions of the *CA* and the *OCD*.

Right Reverend Paul Joseph Nussbaum, CP, DD

Primary information on Bishop Nussbaum may be found in the *CAT* invividual file on the Diocese of Corpus Christi. References are in Castañeda, *OCHIT* 7:146-149, 487; Cruz and Cruz, *A Century of Service* 28-29; *DACB* 425-426; *HT* 2:296; and *WWW* 1:908. See also John W. Meany, "The History of the Diocese of Corpus Christi," *TCHS* June 1983, 1-2 and "Diocese of Marquette (Marquettensis)," *NCE*, 1967 ed.

Right Reverend Jean-Marie Odin, CM, DD

Much has and much more will be written about the first Catholic bishop of Texas. The *CAT* individual file of the Diocese of Galveston and the Archives generally are good starting points. For recent scholarship see Patrick Foley, "Jean-Marie Odin, C.M., Missionary Bishop Extraordinaire of Texas," *The Journal of Texas Catholic History and Culture* 1:1 (March 1990): 42-60 and other related works, as well as Moore, *Through Fire and Flood.* See also Clarke, *Deceased Bishops* 2:203-239, Castañeda, *OCHIT* 7:40-129, 487, *DACB* 439-440, *HT* 2:302, and *WWW* H:455, as well as "John Mary Odin" and "Archdiocese of New Orleans (Novae Aureliae)," *NCE*, 1967 ed. Giles 22-23 and Wangler 7-12 provide biographical sketches.

Other useful accounts are Jean-Marie Odin,CM, letter to the Society for the propagation of the Faith, 14 May 1849, in *TCHS* June 1978, 1-2; Bro. William H. Dunn, CSC, "Bishop Jean-Marie Odin," *TCHS* June 1980, 1-3; and Sr. M. Gerard, OP, "A Brief Sketch of the Diocese of Galveston-Houston, Texas," *TCHS* Nov. 1981, 1-2. See also recent editions of *CA* and *OCD*.

Right Reverend Anthony Dominic Ambrose Pellicer, DD

Primary information on Bishop Pellicer may be found in the *CAT* individual file of the Archdiocese of San Antonio. For other notices of his life and ministry see Castañeda, *OCHIT* 7:129-133, 488, Clarke, *Deceased Bishops*, 3:404-411, Wangler 14-17, *DACB* 460-461, *HT* 3:717-718, and *WWW* H:474.

Most Reverend Raymundo Joseph Peña, DD

Primary information on Bishop Peña may be found in the *CAT* individual files on the Archdiocese of San Antonio and the Diocese of El Paso. There are biographies in *WWA*, 49th ed., 2:2872 and in *WWSS*, 24th ed., 679. See also *The*

Rio Grande Catholic for the E1 Paso Years. These articles are of interest: Steve Jacobs, "The History of the Diocese of E1 Paso," *TCHS* Nov. 1983, 1-2; Rev. Ernest J. Burrus, SJ, "A Brief History of the El Paso Diocese" *TCHS* Jan. 1987, 1-3; "Holy Sepulchre Knights, Ladies To Be Invested," *TCH* 23 Oct. 1987, 20; "Texas bishops in National Posts," *CET* 11 Dec. 1987, 7; Lynwood Abram, "Sister Act: Feisty Nun Still Battling Church Leaders," *HC* 30 May 1993, D1, D6; "El Paso Bishop Seeks Moratorium on Border Blockage, Cites Hardship," *CET* 22 Oct. 1993, 7; "Longtime Bishop of El Paso Is Transferred to Brownsville Diocese," *DMN* 24 May 1995, A18; Lisa Marie Gomez, "Peña Serves Brownsville As Its Bishop," *BH* 24 May 1995, 1, 10; Lisa Marie Gomez, "Bishop Peña Brings Activism to Brownsville: New Bishop Takes Heat for Moral Commitment," *BH* 4 June 1995, A1, A12; "Peña Named to Pre-Synod Council," *CET* 16 June 1995, 7; Lisa Marie Gomez, "'*Haz Todo con Amor*': Valley's Fifth Bishop Installed," *BH* 7 Aug. 1995, 1, 8; Lisa Marie Gomez, "Bishop Conducts First Mass," *BH*, 8 Aug. 1995, 1, 8; "Installation Ceremonies for Brownsville Bishop," *TCH* 11 Aug. 1995, 21.

Most Reverend Michael David Pfeifer, OMI, DD

For primary information I have used the "Curriculum Vitae" and "Clergy Biographical Data for *Today's Catholic*," kindly supplied me by Ms. Mary Louise Anderson, Secretary to the Provincial of the Southern Province of the Missionary Oblates of Mary Immaculate in San Antonio, Texas. Brief biographies of Bishop Pfeifer may be found in such standard reference works as *Who's Who in Religion*, 4th ed., 404, *WWSS*, 24th ed., 686, and *WWA*, 49th ed., 2:2902.

EVD of San Antonio, Texas, has the following useful articles: "*Oblatos de Texas in Zambia 'Porque Primero Todos Somos Misioneros'*," 24 Feb. 1985, 1, 4-5; Fernando Piñon, "Mike Pfeifer *Nombrado Opisbo de San Anqelo*" 23 June 1985, 1, 8; and "*Texto Completo del Padre Mike* [Statement of Acceptance on Appointment as Bishop of San Angelo]" 23 June 1985, 1, 8.

The *TCH* prints "Oblate Father Named Bishop of Diocese of San Angelo" 14 June 1985, 24 and "San Angelo Welcomes Its New Bishop" 9 Aug. 1985, 10. See also the *WTA*: "Fifth Bishop Ordained at Coliseum Rite As 4,000 Sing and Pray for His Ministry" 9 Aug. 1985, 2-3 and Fr. Maurice Voity, "Bishop Brings Our Prayers, Gifts to Mexico City" 1 Nov. 1985, 1. Wangler supplies information about San Antonio institutions and the *OCD* gives statistics for the San Angelo diocese.

Ms. Margaret M. Maher, Librarian of the National Catholic (now Catholic) News Service, kindly supplies a bulletin "Catholics Told To Accept Responsibility for Seeking Answers on Own" dated 6 Nov. 1986. More recently there are: Maurice J. Voity, "Facing Priestless Sundays: A Bishop's How-To Seminar," *CET* 28 Feb. 1992, 2; J. Michael Parker, "Bishop Relieved at Not Being Elected," *SAE* 21 Nov. 1992, C9; and "W[est] Texas Bishop Develops Policy on Sexual Abuse: He Says Statement Is Effort To Take More Active Stance on Clergy Abuse," *DMN* 19 Oct. 1994, A29, A34. Bishop Pfeifer's activities are reported in the *West Texas Angelus*, the official diocesan newspaper for the Diocese of San Angelo.

Most Reverend Bernard F. Popp, DD

I am indebted to Bro. Edward J. Loch, SM, Archivist of the Archdiocese of San Antonio, Texas, for kindly supplying me with a three-page biography of Bishop Popp, entitled "Bernard F. Popp" and dated August 1987. See also A. E. P. Wall, editor-in-chief, *American Catholic Who's Who, 1976-1977*, bicentenial ed., vol. 21 (Washington, DC: NC News Service of the USCC, 1975), *WWA*, 45th ed. 2:2483 and *Who's Who in Religion*, 4th ed. 410. For his retirement date, see 1995 *CA* 464. Wangler describes various archdiocesan institutions associated with Bishop Popp. See also Mary Ann Noonan-Guerra, *San Fernando: Heart of San Antonio* (San Antonio: Artes Graficas for the Archdiocese of San Antonio, 1977) and David Fritze, "Crumbling Cathedral Thrives in San Antonio," *DTH* 31 Aug. 1987, A7. The *OCD* and *Today's Catholic* provide details of his service. On Bishop Popp's German ancestry see Joe Michael Feist, "German-Texans Assume Leadership Positions of Church in Lone Star State," *CET* 13 Apr. 1990, 16, rptd. from *TxC*.

Most Reverend Ricardo Ramirez, CSB, DD

Information on Bishop Ramirez is available in standard sources, such as *Who's Who in Religion*, 4th ed., 421 and *WWA*, 49th ed., 2:3016.Much information is available through the program: "The Episcopal Ordination of His Excellency The Most Reverend Ricardo Ramirez, C.S.B., D.D. Auxiliary to the Archbishop of San Antonio." Convention Center Arena. 6 December 1981. San Antonio, Texas. See also issues of the *CA* and of the *OCD*. These articles are of special interest: Mike Arellano, "Bishop Ramirez Receives UST Distinguished Alumnus Award," *TCH* 10 June 1988, 15; "Bishop Ramirez Calls for Hispanic Summit of Protestant, Catholic Leaders," *CET* 5 June 1992, 7; "El Paso Bishop Seeks Moratorium on Border Blockage, Cites Hardship," *CET* 22 Oct. 1993, 7; Susan De Matteo, "Sunday Mass Has To Be Good to Be 'Welcoming'," 17 Dec. 1993, 1-2; "Catholic Bishop Urges Reforms," *TCTT* 14 July 1995, sec. 5, p. 2.

Most Reverend Louis Joseph Reicher, DD

Primary information on Bishop Reicher may be found in the *CAT* individual file of the Diocese of Austin. Castañeda, *OCHIT* 7: 161-164, 488, discusses his life to the time of his consecration as bishop of Austin. Additional information appears in the *TCH* Supplement for 24 May 1968, in the *AAS* for 17 Nov. 1971, and in *The Catholic Spirit*, the Diocese of Austin newspaper, Special Supplement for March 1984. There are brief biographies in the *CA* and statistical material in the *OCD*. Of particular interest is the article by Ken Case, "The Secret Life of Ruben Johnson, Part One: Friendship Based on Trust," which appeared originally in *Third Coast Magazine* for April 1986, especially valuable for its explanation of the workings of the Reicher trust. For information on the Austin diocese see Stephen V. Jacobs, "History of the Diocese of Austin," *TCHS* Dec. 1984, 1-2.

Giles 134-135 discusses St. Christopher's Church in Houston. "Fame Spread from His East Texas Roots," *ETC* 27 June 1986, A2 is an interview with retired (now deceased) Bishop Vincent Harris, Former bishop of the dioceses of Beaumont and Austin. A brief biography of Donald Scott Thomas may be found in *The Texas Legal Directory 1981: Official Directory of the State Bar of Texas*, 2 vols. (Dallas: Legal Directories Publishing, 1981) 2:56. Concerning the Henck Memorial Trust see "Texas Dioceses To Share $1.5 Million," *DMN* 7 Oct. 1987, A21 and "Catholic Dioceses in State Receive $1.7 Million," *TCH* 23 Oct. 1987, 17.

Most Reverend Placido Rodriguez, CMF, DD, LLD

The goodwill and aid of the following people helped me gather information about Bishop Rodriguez: Rev. Theodore Cirone, CMF, Provincial Superior of the Eastern Province of Claretian Missionaries in the United States, Oak Park, Illinois; Ms. Nancy Sandleback, Assistant Archivist of the Archdiocese of Chicago; the staffs of *The New World* and *Chicago Catolico*, official publications of the Archdiocese of Chicago; and Ms. Pat Behnke, Communications Office Manager, *South Plains Catholic*, the official publication of the Diocese of Lubbock.

Bishop Placido Rodriguez, CMF, "*Curriculum Vitae*," three typewritten pages undated and the "Press Conference," Diocese of Lubbock, 11:00 A.M., 5 April 1994, on two typewritten pages.

"*Una vida dedicada a servir a Dios y a sus hermanos; Monseñor Placido Rodriguez, CMF, DD, Obispo Auxiliar de Chicago: XXV aniversario ordenacion sacerdotal 1968-1993*," *Chicago Catolico, suplemento especial de aniversario* (Mayo 1993), 1-28 and "*Obispo Placido Rodriguez de Lubbock: Monseñor Placido Rodriguez sera insatado el 1° de junio, 1994, como segundo obispo de la Dioceses de Lubbock, Texas*," *Chicago Catolico, suplemento especial* (Mayo 1994), A1-A28. Also, "Bishop Placido Rodriguez, Diocese of Lubbock in Texas: *El amor de Cristo*," *The New World*, special supplement for 20 May 1994, B1-B32.

"Pope Names Bishop Placido Rodriguez, CMF, New Bishop of Lubbock, *South Plains Catholic*, 10 Apr. 1994, 1; "*Bishop Placido Rodriguez, CMF, DD: 'A Warm, Gentle Listener' to Shepherd the Diocese of Lubbock*," *South Plains Catholic*, supplement for 8 May 1994, 1-32; and "Most Rev. Placido Rodriguez, CMF, Installed as Bishop of Lubbock," *South Plains Catholic*, 12 June 1994, 1, 12, and supplement, 1-4.

See also *Bishops Named: Two to Texas Dioceses*, Catholic News Service, 5 Apr. 1994; "Pope John Paul II Names Bishops To Lead Two Vacant Texas Dioceses," *TCH*, 8 Apr. 1994, 1; and Leroy Behnke, "Bishop Rodriguez Welcomed to Lubbock Diocese," *TCH*, 17 June 1994, 25.

Various issues of *CA* and *OCD* for information on Hispanic ministries and for statistical summaries of the Archdiocese of Chicago and of the Diocese of Lubbock.

Most Reverend Enrique San Pedro, SJ, STD, SSL

Ms. Agnes Browne of Brownsville, Texas kindly provided me with numerous articles from Valley newspapers, as well as a number of clippings from Bishop San Pedro's weekly column in BH. Ms. Pamela Downing, Director of Public Relations of the Diocese of Brownsville provided other articles, additional columns by Bishop San Pedro, and other information.

There are standard accounts in such publications as *CA, OCD, Who's Who in Religion*, 4th ed. (1992-1993), 451, and *WWA*. *WWA* is particularly useful for listing the bishop's affiliations and other information. It takes precedence over other accounts as the information was supplied by the bishop himself. I have also noted information written by him from a file of some thirty articles by him written for the *BH* (1993-1994) in my possession. See also "Biographical Sketch: Most Rev. Enrique San Pedro, S.J.," Diocese of Brownsville. 2pp. Typed; "The Celebration of the Eucharist and Installation of Bishop Enrique San Pedro As Coadjutor Bishop of the Diocese of Brownsville." Brownsville: Diocese of Brownsville. 20 pp.; Agnes Browne, Brownsville, Texas, to Franklin C. Williams, Jr., Palestine, Texas, TLS, 10 Oct. 1991. In possession of author; *News Release*, Diocese of Brownsville, 19 July 1994; "Mass of Resurrection of Most Reverend Enrique San Pedro, S.J.: Bishop of the Diocese of Brownsville." 20 July 1994. 10:30 A.M. Virgen de San Juan del Valle Shrine, San Juan, Texas. 10 pp.

Besides articles written by Bishop San Pedro for *BH*, see these articles from the same publication: Robert C. Gonzalez, "Brownsville Catholic Bishop Supports Death Row Inmate Ricardo Aldape Guerra," undated; Larry Clubb, "Formally Seated." Photograph of McAllen *Monitor* in *BH*, 27 Sept. 1991, 3; Diane Smith, "San Pedro Becomes Bishop," 1 Dec. 1991, A1-A5; Tim Lopes, "Brownsville's Bishop To Address U.N.: San Pedro To Speak for the Pope on the Plight of Refugees," 6 Feb. 1993, 1, 6; "'Bishop Stands Up for Refugees: Talks to U.N. for Holy See," n.p., n.d., 1, 8; Cecilia Balli, "Bishop Gets Last Rites," 15 July 1994, A1, A10; Cecilia Balli, "Bishop Still Ill, But Less in Pain," 16 July 1994, 3, 10. "Bishop Near Death, Kidneys Failing," 17 July 1994, A1, A12; Cecilia Balli, "Bishop Enrique San Pedro Dies in Miami," 18 July 1994, 1, 12; Cecilia Balli, "Bishop Taken to San Juan Shrine," 19 July 1994, 1; Nicholas J. Elizondo, "Letter to the Editor," 19 July 1994, n.p.; Cecilia Balli, "Valley Pays Respects to Bishop," 20 July 1994, 1; Cecilia Balli, "Thousands Attend Mass for Bishop San Pedro," 21 July 1994, A1, A8.

"Houston Auxiliary Named Bishop in Brownsville," *CET*, 16 Aug. 1991, 1, 3; "Bishop-Elect Consecration Sunday," *ETC*, 27 June 1986, 3; "Valley Catholic Leader Dead at 68: Bishop San Pedro Succumbs to Prostate Cancer in Miami Beach," *SAE*, 18 July 1994, A7; "Bishop of Brownsville Undergoing Cancer Treatment," *TxC*, 13 May 1994, 15.

From *The Monitor* of McAllen, Texas: Patty Sandoval Bazzini, "Bishop's Successor Installed: Coadjutor To Stay Active in Causes," 27 Sept. 1991, A1, A14; Brenda Rodriguez, "Bishop San Pedro Gravely Ill: Valley Catholic Leader Suffering from Cancer, Receives Last Rites," 15 July 1994, A1, A12; Caitlin Francke, "Valley Catholics Praying for Bishop," 16 July 1994, 1; Caitlin Francke, "Bishop's Condition Worsens," 17 July 1994, 1; Tim Hoover, "Bishop Enrique San Pedro Dies: Funeral Mass Scheduled for 10:30 A.M. Wednesday at San Juan Shrine," 18 July 1994, A1, A8; Brenda Rodriguez, "Thousands Pay Respects to Most Rev. San Pedro," 20 July 1994, D1-D2.

From *TCH*: Rev. Virgilio Elizondo, "*Como llegar al corazon hispano*," 28 Oct. 1983, 19; "Cuban-born Jesuit Named Auxiliary Bishop for Diocese," 11 Apr. 1986, 1; Special Edition, 27 June 1986, 1-4; "Ordination Scheduled for Auxiliary Bishop," 27 June 1986, 1; Msgr. Teodoro de la Torre, "*El Obispo Enrique San Pedro*," 27 June 1986, 17; Sylvia Novo Pena, "Bishop San Pedro's Ordination Filled with Joy and Pageantry," 11 July 1986, 12-13; Special Edition, 9 Jan. 1987, 1-4; "Twin Brothers Ordained," 23 Jan. 1987, 2; Sylvia Novo Pena, "*Mons. Enrique San Pedro discute los retos del hispano en la Iglesia,*" 27 Feb. 1987, 15; "Sunday Mass in Spanish Announced," 13 Mar. 1987, 14; "Names and Faces," 10 Apr. 1987, 8; Sylvia Novo Pena, "*Mons. San Pedro habla del laicado,*" 8 May 1987, 15; Bishop Enrique San Pedro, "*Juan Pablo II y el jubileo mariano,*" 22 May 1987, 15; Sylvia Novo Pena, "Bishop San Pedro's Return to Cuba A Journey Abounding in Memories," 4 Sept. 1987, 14; Sylvia Novo Pena, "One Day's Journey on the Road to Peace," 9 Oct. 1987, 1, 24; "Holy Sepulchre Knights, Ladies To Be Invested," 23 Oct. 1987, 20; Marion Zientek, "Bishop San Pedro Named Coadjutor for Brownsville," 23 Aug. 1991, 1, 7; Bob Giles, "Bishop San Pedro Dies in Miami," *TCH*, 22 July 1994, 1-2.

See also *Valley Morning Star* of Harlingen, Texas: C. R. Leal, "Bishop Speaks." Photograph, 27 Sept. 1991, 1; Randy Davidson, "Bishop San Pedro 'Gravely Ill' Following Radiation Treatment," 15 July 1994, A1, A8; Randy Davidson, "San Pedro's Condition Unchanged," 16 July 1994, 1; Allen Essex, "Bishop San Pedro Near Death," 17 July 1994, A1, A12; Randy Davidson and Jennifer Huckabay, "Death Cuts Short Bishop's Legacy: San Pedro's Vision Draws Praise As He Falls to Cancer at 68," 18 July 1994, A1, A10; "Editorial: In Memoriam - Bishop San Pedro," 19 July 1994, n.p.; Jennifer Huckabay, "Catholics Mourn Leader's Loss: Service for Bishop To Be Wednesday," 19 July 1994, A1, A12; Brenda Rodriguez, "Bishop's Life Celebrated: Valley Catholics Pay Last Respects to Spiritual Leader," 21 July 1994, A1, A8.

Most Reverend Anthony J. Schuler, SJ, DD

Primary information on Bishop Schuler may be found in the *CAT* individual file of the Diocese of El Paso. Castañeda, *OCHIT* 7: 149- 154, 488-489 gives a good account to which that of Sr. M. Claude Lane, OP, in *HT* 3:862 is much indebted. See also *WWW* 2:473 and Steve Jacobs, "The History of the Diocese of E1 Paso," *TCHS* Nov. 1983: 1-2, together with *DACB* 515.

Most Reverend John William Shaw, DD

Primary information on Archbishop Shaw may be found in the *CAT* file on the Archdiocese of San Antonio. Wangler has a good discussion in his archdiocesan history 25-27. Castañeda, *OCHIT* 7: 489, *HT* 3: 873, and *WWW* 1:1111 provide sketches. For information on the New Orleans period, see "Archdiocese of New Orleans (Novae Aureliae)," *NCE*, 1967 ed.

Most Reverend Michael Jarboe Sheehan, STL, JCD

Basic information on Archbishop Sheehan may be found in standard reference works, such as the 1995 *CA* and the 1995 *OCD*. See also *WWA*, 49th ed. (1994), 2:3135, *WWSS*, 23rd ed. (1993-1994), 739, and *Who's Who in Religion*, 4th ed. (1992-1993), 469. One particularly good source for the Archbishop's early career is A. E. P. Wall, ed.-in-chief, *American Catholic Who's Who, 1976-77*, Bicentennial ed., Vol 21 (Washington, DC: National Catholic News Service for the United States Catholic Conference, 1975), 35. For statistics on the Diocese of Lubbock and on the Archdiocese of Santa Fe, see *OCD* for the appropriate years. For information on Medjugorje see any recent edition of the *CA*.

For area coverage of the Lubbock years, see: Mary Alice Robbins, "New

Diocese Sought for South Plains," *Lubbock Avalanche-Journal* 16 Nov. 1981, 1, 14; Mary Alice Robbins, "Lubbock Considered As Diocesan Center," Lubbock *Avalanche-Journal* n.d.; Janey Joyce, "New Catholic Diocese Formed," *Amarillo Globe-Times* 29 March 1983, 1; "Lubbock Catholic Diocese Established," *Lubbock Avalanche-Journal*, 29 March 1983, 1; Pat Graves, "Sheehan Named Bishop of New Lubbock Diocese," *Evening Journal* (Lubbock), 29 March 1983, 1; "Establishment of Catholic Diocese of Lubbock Announced," *Amarillo Daily News*, 30 March 1983, D4; Kenneth May, "One Man's Opinion: Practice It, Teach It," *Evening Journal* (Lubbock), sec. 4, p. 4; Beth Pratt, "Sheehan To Take Santa Fe Post: Bishop Caps 10-year Lubbock Stint," *Lubbock Avalanche-Journal*, 18 Aug. 1993, A1.

See also: "Diocese of Lubbock Formed: 13th in Texas," *TCH* 8 Apr. 1983, 1; "Worshipers at Rosary Report Peace Messages," *TCTT* 22 July 1988, sec. 5, p. 2; Wendy E. Lane, "Bishop Urges Scepticism over Virgin Mary Messages," *DMN*, 27 July 1988, B12; Diane Winston, "With Those Smiles, You Know They Still Believe in Miracles," *DTH*, 30 Aug. 1988, B5; "Bishop Orders Investigation of Miracle Reports," *DTH* 23 Aug. 1988, B1; Helen Parmley, "Catholic Panel Rejects Lubbock 'Miracles'," *DMN* 8 Oct. 1988, A33; Peter Stravinskas, "But Good Reasons To Be Wary," *National Catholic Register* 9 Oct. 1988, 5; Jean Pagel, "Bishop Assails Sexual Abuse: Sheehan Urges People Accusing Priest To Tell Lubbock Diocese," *DMN* 8 Dec. 1992, A17, A24; "Lubbock Bishop Urges Sexual Abuse Victims To Seek Counseling," *CET* 18 Dec. 1992, 6; "Payment A Surprise, Priest Says: Ex-Archbishop's Lawyer Denies Report of Rape," *DMN*, 23 March 1993, A12; "Bishop To Head Archdiocese: NM Archbishop's Resignation Accepted after Sex Allegations," *DMN*, 7 Apr. 1993, A37; "Pope Accepts Resignation of Archbishop," *TCH* 9 Apr. 1993, 1, 24; "Lubbock Bishop Named to Santa Fe Post," *CET*, 9 Apr. 1993, 1, 3; "Acting Head of NM Diocese Draws Praise," *DMN* 12 Apr. 1993, A19, A24.

On the Santa Fe period, see: Jerry Filteau, *Bishop Sheehan Named Archbishop of Santa Fe*. Catholic News Service. 17 Aug. 1993; The Roman Catholic Diocese of Lubbock, *Press Release (Revised)*, 17 Aug. 1993; Brent Hunsberger, "Acting Archbishop To Stay," *Albuquerque Tribune*, 17 Aug. 1993, A1, A5; Art Geiselman, "New Archbishop To Bind Wounds," *Albuquerque Journal*, 18 Aug. 1993, A1, A5; Colleen Heild and Tom Sanchez, "'A Real Shot in the Arm': N.M. Parishioners Embrace Anglo, Non-Native's 'Definitive Leadership'" *Albuquerque Journal*, 18 Aug. 1993, A1, A5; "Special Commemorative Issue," *People of God* Oct. 1993, 1-48 [particularly valuable]; "Archbishop Sheehan Heartened by Response to Fund-Raising Appeal," *South Plains Catholic*, 10 Apr. 1994, 10.

See also: "Archbishop Named for Santa Fe: Bishop Sheehan of Lubbock Chosen," *DMN* 18 Aug. 1993, A29, A34; "Lubbock Diocese is Saddened by Bishop's Departure," *DMN* 18 Aug. 1993, A34; "New Archbishop Has Broad Experience," *DMN* 18 Aug. 1993, A34; "New NM Archbishop Close to Hispanics, Says Leader of Group," *DMN* 20 Aug. 1993, A29; Jerry Filteau, "Bishop Sheehan Named Archbishop of Santa Fe," *CET* 27 Aug. 1993, 6; "Bishop Sheehan of Lubbock Named As The New Archbishop of Santa Fe," *TCH* 27 Aug. 1993, 1; "Archbishop of Santa Fe Is Installed," *TCH* 8 Oct. 1993, 21; "Lubbock Pastor Elected Diocesan Administrator," *TCH* 8 Oct. 1993, 21; Cindy

Wooden, "Santa Fe Archbishop Prays at Shrine of St. Maria Goretti," *CET*, 22 Oct. 1993, 6; "Santa Fe Archbishop Warns of Bankruptcy," *CET* 31 Dec. 1993, 6; "Santa Fe Cleric Asks Catholics for Money To Resolve Lawsuits," *DMN* 11 Jan. 1994, A12; Michael Haederle, "Santa Fe Diocese Hopes Sex Abuse Charges Easing: Many Cases Being Settled, Insurers Helping Out," *DMN*, 13 Feb. 1994, A39, A41; Laura K. Trujillo, "Archbishop in New Mexico Uses Humor To Gain Congregation's Trust," *DMN* 25 Sept. 1994, A50; "New Mexico Priests' Center Settles Molestation Suits with 17 Men," *DMN*, 8 Oct. 1994, 1.

Most Reverend James Anthony Tamayo, DD

For basic information on Bishop Tamayo, see 1995 *CA* 468 and *OCD* 1994, 369-370. The following articles in *TCH* are informative: Bob Giles, "Hispanic Auxiliary Bishop Named for the Galveston-Houston Diocese," 12 Feb. 1993, 1, 12; Bob Giles, "Bilingual, Bicultural from Childhood Days," 12 Feb. 1993, 12-13; "Ordination Slated for Auxiliary Bishop," 26 Feb. 1993, 1; Paul Sullivan, "Coat of Arms of His Excellency, The Most Reverend James Anthony Tamayo, D.D. and Auxiliary Bishop of Galveston-Houston," 26 Feb. 1993, 24; Bob Giles, "Festive Ceremonies Mark Ordination of Auxiliary Bishop," 12 March 1993, 1, 28. See also the following article, which appeared originally in the *Valley Morning Star* (Harlingen, Texas): Randy Davidson, "Valley Family Turns Out To Welcome Young Bishop," *BH* 29 May 1993, 5.

Most Reverend Thomas Tschoepe, DD

For information on Bishop Tschoepe see the *CAT* individual file of the Dallas of Diocese and standard reference works such as the *CA*, the *OCD*, and *WWA*. I am grateful to Ms. Estelle Metzger, Archivist of the Diocese of Dallas, for a "Curriculum Vitae" of Bishop Tschoepe dated 27 Oct. 1980 and for information on the Bishop from the *Texas Catholic Directory, 1986-1987*, Sesquicentennial ed. (Dallas, Diocese of Dallas, 1986), 13. Statistics on the Dallas diocese reflect changes after the division of the Diocese of Tyler from the Diocese of Dallas and may be found in the *OCD* for 1988. See also Rev. Thomas P. Cloherty, "The History of the Diocese of Dallas," *TCHS* Nov. 1982, 1-3, "Dialogue Group To Honor Bishop," *TxC* 1 June 1990, "Pope Accepts Resignation of Dallas Bishop," *TCH* 27 July 1990, 21 and "Bishop Tschoepe Steps Down in Dallas," 20 July 1990, 1, 16.

Right Reverend Peter Verdaguer, DD

Primary information on Bishop Verdaguer may be found in the *CAT* individual file on the Diocese of Corpus Christi. See also Castañeda in *OCHIT* 7:137, 145, 489-490, *HT* 2:837, *WWW* 1:1277, Cruz and Cruz, *A Century of Service*, 22-28, and Michael E. Zilligen, "History of the Brownsville Diocese," *TCHS* March 1989, 5-9.

Most Reverend John Walter Yanta, DD

Aside from scant information contained in the 1995 *OCD* 979 and 1996 *CA* 473, I am heavily indebted to Bro. Edward Loch, SM, Archivist of the Archdiocese of San Antonio, who provided me with some pertinent information on Bishop Yanta from his files, and to Ms. Margaret Schattel of *Today's Catholic*, who provided me with some recent material concerning Bishop's Yanta's appointment and installation. I have also used Wangler's archdiocesan history of San Antonio extensively for background on archdiocesan institutions relating to Bishop Yanta.

From the file material (generally unpaged), see: "SA Priest Finds Unity at Tucson," *TdC*, 9 May 1980; "Father Yanta Assumes Additional Media Duties," *TdC*, 22 May 1981; "Fr. Yanta Resigns from CTSA," *TdC*, 29 Apr. 1983; "SANYO: 25 Years of Helping Youth," *SAE*, 13 May 1990; Veronica Salazar, "Dedication Rewarded," *SAE* 13 May 1990, M1, M6; and "SANYO Helps People Succeed," *SAE*, 18 May 1990. Two pages from a booklet in honor of the Bishop's twenty-fifth anniversary of priestly ordination headed "John W. Yanta" and dated 17 March 1981 are informative. A page marked *Press Conference* and dated 27 October 1994 by Archbishop Patrick F. Flores provides biographical information on Bishop Yanta. There is also Bishop Yanta's "Statement of Bishop-Elect John W. Yanta," dated 27 October 1994.

For additional material from *TdC*, see the following: Maura Ciarrocchi, "Msgr. John W. Yanta To Be First Bishop of Polish Descent for San Antonio Archdiocese," 11 Nov. 1994, 1, 3; "Bishop- elect Yanta Supplement," 23 Dec. 1994, A1-A20; Martha Brinkmann, "Bishop Yanta Installed in Panna Maria," 20 Jan. 1995, 1, 3; Archbishop Patrick F. Flores, "Focus: Looking Back and Looking Forward," 20 Jan. 1995, 2; and "Bishop: Expressions of Friendship and Appreciation from His Friends," 20 Jan. 1995, 4-5.

For information on Pope John Paul II's visit to San Antonio, see Rebecca Trounson, "No Time for Panna Maria: Tiny Polish Community Crushed That Pope Won't Be Visiting," *HC* 24 Aug. 1987, 1 and Marion Zientek, "'Our Hearts Are in the Old Country,' Pope Tells Polish," *TCH*, Papal Supplement, 18 Sept. 1987, 6. For more information on Bishop Yanta, see: "Priest Convicted in Abortion Protest Named San Antonio Auxiliary Bishop," *DMN* 28 Oct. 1994, A37; "Yanta Named Auxiliary Bishop for San Antonio Archdiocese," *CET* 4 Nov. 1994, 6; "New Auxiliary Bishop Appointed for San Antonio Archdiocese," *TCH* 11 Nov. 1994, 1; and J. Michael Parker, "S.A. Priest Yanta Ordained As Bishop," *SAE* 21 Dec. 1994, A1, A4.

Works Consulted

Note: To avoid unnecessary duplication, I have omitted listing articles, pamphlets, and brochures, which are documented in Notes.

Acheson, Sam H., Herbert P. Gambrell, Mary Carter Toomer, and Alex N. Acheson, Jr. *Texian Who's Who: A Biographical Dictionary of the State of Texas*. Vol. 1. Dallas: Texian, 1937.

Amarillo, Diocese of. File. Catholic Archives of Texas, Austin.

Assumption Seminary. *Assumption Seminary: A Theologate in Association with the Oblate School of Theology for the Education of Men for Service in the Priestly Ministry*. San Antonio: Assumption Seminary [1989].

Austin, Diocese of. File. Catholic Archives of Texas, Austin.

Bartlett, John. *The Shorter Bartlett's Familiar Quotations*. Ed. Kathleen Sproul. New York: Permabooks, 1953.

Bayard, CM, Ralph. *Lone-Star Vanguard: The Catholic Reoccupation of Texas (1838-1848)*. Saint Louis: Vincentian, 1945.

Beaumont, Diocese of. File. Catholic Archives of Texas, Austin.

Biographical Encyclopedia of Texas. New York: Southern Publishing, 1880.

Bishop Hugo M. Gerbermann, M.M.: Maryknoll Missioner from Garwood To Celebrate 40 Years of Priesthood, Maryknoll Media Relations. Maryknoll, NY: Media Relations, 1983.

Boston, Archdiocese of. "Communication Releases" Concerning Bishop Roberto O. Gonzalez, OFM. 9 pp. 1988.

Bronder, Saul Edmund. *Social Justice and Church Authority: The Public Life of Archbishop Robert E. Lucey*. Philadelphia: Temple UP, 1982.

Brownsville, Diocese of. Biographical Materials Concerning Bishop Enrique San Pedro, SJ [including programs relating to his installation as bishop and funeral services].

___. File. Catholic Archives of Texas, Austin.

Carmody, Edmond. "Press Conference. . .Appointment of Rev. Msgr. Edmond Carmody Auxiliary Bishop of San Antonio, Nov. 8, 1988." Archives, Archdiocese of San Antonio.

___. Statement of Acceptance As Auxiliary Bishop of San Antonio in English and in Spanish. 8 Nov. 1988. Archives, Archdiocese of San Antonio.

Cassata, John J. Letter to the Author. 7 October 1987.

Castañeda, Carlos E. *Our Catholic Heritage in Texas 1519-1936 and Supplement 1936-1950*. Ed. Paul J. Foik, CSC, James P. Gibbons, CSC, and William H. Oberste. 7 vols. Austin: Von Boeckmann-Jones, 1936-1958.

Catechism of the Catholic Church. Vatican City: Libreria Editrice Vaticana; Washington, DC: United States Catholic Conference, 1994.

Catholic University of America, The. *The School of Religious Studies: 1986-1987 Announcements*. 72.2 Washington, DC: The Catholic University of America, 15 March 1986.

___. *The School of Philosophy: 1985-1987 Announcements*. 71.5. Washington, DC: The Catholic University of America, 15 April 1985.

Celebrity Who's Who by the Editors of "Who's Who in America." New York: World Almanac, 1986.

Chaucer, Geoffrey. *The Riverside Chaucer.* Gen. Ed. Larry D. Benson. 3d ed. Boston: Houghton Mifflin, 1987.

Clarke, Richard Henry. *History of the Catholic Church in the United States from the Earliest Period to the Present Time.* 2 vols. Philadelphia: [Gebbie], 1889-1890.

___. *Lives of the Deceased Bishops of the Catholic Church in the United States.* 2nd ed. 3 vols. New York: Privately Printed, 1888.

"Coat of Arms of Bishop Danglmayr." *Southern Messenger* 8 Oct. 1942: N.P. Archives, Diocese of Dallas.

Cogley, John. *Catholic America.* 1973. Garden City: Image-Doubleday, 1974.

Comprehensive Dissertation Index, 1861-1972. 37 vols. Ann Arbor, MI: Xerox University Microfilms, 1973.

Connell, CSSR, Francis J. *The New Baltimore Catechism No. 3: Being the Text of the Official Revised Edition of the "Baltimore Catechism No. 2" Amplified with Supplemental Questions, Answers and a Glossary.* Study Helps and Exercises Thomas A. Chapman, CSSR. Father Kinkead Memorial Edition. 1943. New York: Benziger, 1954.

Corpus Christi, Diocese of. File. Catholic Archives of Texas, Austin.

Corrado, Dennis M., and James F. Hinchey, eds. *Shepherds Speak: American Bishops Confront The Social and Moral Issues That Challenge Christians Today.* New York: Crossroad, 1986.

Corriden, James A., Thomas J. Green, and Donald E. Heintschel, eds. *The Code of Canon Law: A Text and Commentary.* Mahwah, NJ: Paulist Press for the Canon Law Society of America, 1985.

Cruz, Giberto Rafael, and Martha Oppert Cruz. *A Century of Service: The History of the Catholic Church in the Lower Rio Grande Valley.* Harlingen, TX: United Printers and Publishers, 1979.

Dallas, Diocese of. File. Catholic Archives of Texas, Austin.

___. *Texas Catholic Directory: Diocese of Dallas 1986-1987.* Sesquicentennial ed. Dallas: Diocese of Dallas, 1986.

Dallas, University of. *General Bulletin 1990-1991.* 32.1. Irving, TX: University of Dallas, August 1990.

Danglmayr, Augustine. Biographical Information. 2 pp. Archives, Diocese of Dallas.

Danglmayr, Joseph and Theresia. Holy Cards [Photostats]. Archives, Diocese of Dallas.

Davis, Ellis A., and Edwin H. Grobe, comps. *The New Encyclopedia of Texas.* 3rd ed. 4 vols. Dallas: Texas Development Bureau, n.d. [ca. 1929].

Deck, E. M. *The Baltimore Catechism No. 2 with Explanations.* Buffalo: Rauch and Stoeckl, 1929.

Delaney, John J., and James Edward Tobin. *Dictionary Of Catholic Biography.* Garden City, NY: Doubleday, 1961.

Diamond, Wilfrid. *Dictionary of Liturgical Latin.* Milwaukee: Bruce, 1961.

Dictionary of American Biography. 20 vols. with index and 7 supps. to date. New York: Scribners, 1928- .

Dubuis, Claude Marie. Special Collection. Catholic Archives of Texas, Austin.

Ellis, John Tracy, ed. *The Catholic Priest in the United States: Historical Investigations.* Collegeville, MN: Saint John's UP for the United States

Catholic Conference., 1971.
El Paso, Diocese of. File. Catholic Archives of Texas, Austin.
Fitzsimon, Lawrence J. Special Collection. Catholic Archives of Texas, Austin.
Flannery, OP, Austin P., gen. ed. *The Documents of Vatican II*. Preface John Cardinal Wright. New York: Pillar-Pyramid, 1975.
Flores, Patrick F. Press Conference. *Msgr. Joseph Galante, Bishop Elect-San Antonio*. San Antonio. 13 Oct. 1992. Archives, Archdiocese of San Antonio.
___. Press Conference. "Tyler Diocese and Bishop-Elect Herzig." San Antonio. 16 Dec. 1986. Archives, Archdiocese of San Antonio.
Fort Worth, Diocese of. File. Catholic Archives of Texas, Austin.
Fox-Davies, Arthur Charles. *A Complete Guide to Heraldry*. Rev. by John Philip Brooke Brooke-Little. London: Thomas Nelson, 1969; reprint, New York: Crown Publishers, Bonanza Books, 1985.
Foy, OFM, Felician A., ed. *1979 Catholic Almanac*. Huntington, IN, Our Sunday Visitor, 1978.
___, and Rose M. Avato, eds. *1987 Catholic Almanac*. Huntington, IN, Our Sunday Visitor, 1986.
___. *1988 Catholic Almanac*. Huntington, IN: Our Sunday Visitor, 1987.
___. *1990 Catholic Almanac*. Huntington, IN: Our Sunday Visitor, 1989.
___. *1992 Catholic Almanac*. Huntington, IN: Our Sunday Visitor, 1991.
___. *1995 Catholic Almanac*. Huntington, IN: Our Sunday Visitor, 1994.
___. *Our Sunday Visitor's 1996 Catholic Almanac*. Huntington, IN: Our Sunday Visitor, 1995.
French, Christopher W., ed. *The Associated Press Stylebook and Libel Manual*. Rev. ed. Reading, MA: Addison-Wesley for The Associated Press, 1987.
Galante, Joseph Anthony. *Remarks at Press Conference* [on his appointment as Auxiliary Bishop of San Antonio]. 13 Oct. 1992. Archives, Archdiocese of San Antonio.
Galveston-Houston, Diocese of. File. Catholic Archives of Texas, Austin.
___. *The Official Catholic Directory of the Galveston-Houston Diocese 1986-87*. Houston: Diocesan Chancery, 1986.
___. *The Official Catholic Directory of the Diocese of Galveston- Houston 1991*. Houston: Diocesan Chancery, 1991.
Giles, Robert C. *Changing Times: The Story of the Diocese of Galveston-Houston in Commemoration of Its Founding*. Dallas: Taylor for John L. Morkovsky, 1972.
Good News Bible: The Bible in Today's English Version. Catholic Study Edition. New York: Sadlier, 1979.
Greeley, Andrew M. *Confessions of a Parish Priest: An Autobiography*. 1986. New York: Pocket-Simon and Schuster, 1987.
Harter, John Michael. "The Creation and Formulation of the Roman Catholic Diocese of Amarillo 1917-1934." MA Thesis. West Texas State U, 1975.
Heim, Bruno Bernard. *Heraldry in the Catholic Church: Its Origin, Customs and Laws*. Garrards Cross, Bucks.: Van Duren, 1978.
Herzig, Charles Edwin. Biographical Information. Archives, Archdiocese of San Antonio.

___. Invitation to Episcopal Ordination. Tyler, TX, 24 Feb. 1987 [In English and Spanish].
___. Invitation to Priestly Ordination. San Antonio, 31 May 1955. Archives, Archdiocese of San Antonio.
___. Press Release on Appointment As Bishop of Tyler. San Antonio. 16 Dec. 1986. Archives, Archdiocese of San Antonio [In English and Spanish].
Hoffmann's Official Catholic Directory. Milwaukee, Hoffmann, 1888.
Huizing, Peter, Knut Walf, and Marcus Lefébure, eds. *Electing Our Own Bishops.* Spec. Issue of *Concilium* 137.7 (1980): 1-101. Edinburgh: T. & T. Clark, 1980.
International Who's Who, 1987-88, The. 51st Ed. London: Europa, 1987.
"Jewels for Danglmayr Rites Recall Dallas Church History." N.p. N.d.: N. pag. Archives, Diocese of Dallas.
Kane, Joseph Nathan. *The Kane Book of Famous First Facts and Records in the United States.* New York: Charter Communications; Ace Books, 1974.
Kemp, Louis Wiltz. *The Signers of the Texas Declaration of Independence.* Salado: Anson Jones, 1944.
Kidd, Charles, and David Williamson, eds. *Debrett's Peerage and Baronetage 1990.* London: Debrett's Peerage and Macmillan London: New York: St. Martin's P, 1990.
Kingston, Mike and Ruth Harris, eds. *1986-1987 Texas Almanac and State Industrial Guide*. Sesquicentennial Edition. Dallas: *The Dallas Morning News,* 1985.
___, and Mary G. Crawford, eds. *1988-1989 Texas Almanac and State Industrial Guide.* Austin: Texas Monthly Press for *The Dallas Morning News*, 1987.
___. *1990-1991 Texas Almanac and State Industrial Guide.* Austin: Texas Monthly Press for *The Dallas Morning News,* 1989.
___. *1992-1993 Texas Almanac and State Industrial Guide.* Houston: Gulf Publishing for *The Dallas Morning News,* 1991.
___. *1994-1995 Texas Almanac and State Industrial Guide.* Dallas: *The Dallas Morning News,* 1993.
Laghi, Pio. Letter to the Author. 17 Nov. 1986. Number 4944/86/6 from Apostolic Nunciature, Washington, DC.
___. Letter to Very Reverend Borgia Aubespin, SVD. 23 Dec. 1987. Number 4795/87/4 from Apostolic Nunciature, Washington, DC [released 18 Jan. 1988].
Lane, OP, Sister Claude. "Catholic Archives of Texas: History and Preliminary Inventory." MA Thesis. University of Texas, Austin, 1961.
Leven, Stephen A. Special Collection. Catholic Archives of Texas, Austin.
Lubbock, Diocese of. Biographical Materials Relating to Bishop Placido Rodriguez, CMF. 5 pp. 1994.
McMurtrey, SM, Martin. *Mariachi Bishop: The Life Story of Patrick Flores.* San Antonio: Corona, 1987.
Meier, Matt S. *Mexican-American Biographies: A Historical Dictionary 1836-1987.* Westport, CT: Greenwood Press, 1988.
Melton, J. Gordon. *Religious Leaders of America: A Biographical Guide to*

Founders and Leaders of Religious Bodies, Churches, and Spiritual Groups in North America. 1st ed. Detroit: Gale Research, 1991.

Metzger, Estelle. Letter to the Author. 6 May 1987.

Michaud, Stephen G., and Hugh Aynesworth. *Ted Bundy: Conversations with a Killer.* New York: Signet-NAL, 1989.

Moore, James Talmadge. *Through Fire and Flood: The Catholic Church in Frontier Texas, 1836-1900.* No. 42 of *The Centennial Series of the Association of Former Students, Texas A&M University.* College Station: Texas A&M P, 1992.

National Catholic News Service. *New Diocese Established in Texas, First Bishop Named.* Washington, DC. 16 Dec. 1986: 15.

National Encyclopedia of American Biography. New York: James T. White, 1891-

National Opinion Research Center. *The Catholic Priest in the United States: Sociological Investigations.* Dir. Andrew M. Greeley. Washington, DC: United States Catholic Conference, 1972.

New Catholic Encyclopedia. 18 vols. Palatine, IL: Heraty for The Catholic University of America, 1967-1989.

New Schaff-Herzog Encyclopedia of Religious Knowledge, The. Ed. Samuel Macaulay Jackson. 13 vols. 1907. Grand Rapids: Baker, 1977.

Noonan-Guerra, Mary Ann. *San Fernando: Heart of San Antonio.* Artes Graficas for the Archdiocese of San Antonio, 1977.

Oblate School of Theology. *1988-1990 Catalog.* San Antonio: Oblate School of Theology, 1988.

Odin, CM, Jean-Marie. Letter to Officers of the Propagation of the Faith. Lyon, France. 14 May 1849. Trans. Carmen Kelly. *TCHS Newsletter* June 1978: 1-2.

___. Special Collection. Catholic Archives of Texas, Austin.

Official Catholic Directory, The. Various edns. Wilmette, IL and New Providence, NJ: Kenedy, 1984-1995.

Oram, James. *The People's Pope: The Story of Karol Wojtyla of Poland.* San Francisco: Chronicle, 1979.

Pacelli, Cardinal Eugenio. Letter to Very Reverend Monsignor Augustine Danglmayr. 15 January 1937. Archives, Diocese of Dallas.

Pfeifer, OMI, Michael David. "Clergy Biographical Data for *Today's Catholic.*" Office of the Southern Province, Missionary Oblates of Mary Immaculate, San Antonio, TX.

___. "Curriculum Vitae." Office of the Southern Province, Missionary Oblates of Mary Immaculate, San Antonio, TX.

Pisani, Saverio. *A Week in Rome: A New Guide to Rome and Its Environs.* Rome, It.: Enrico Verdesi, 1955.

Privett, SJ, Stephen A. "Robert E. Lucey: Evangelization and Catechesis among Hispanic Catholics." Diss. Catholic University of America, 1985.

Rahner, Karl, ed. *Encyclopedia of Theology: The Concise "Sacramentum Mundi."* New York: Crossroad, 1982.

___, and Herbert Vorgrimler. *Dictionary of Theology.* 2nd ed. New York: Crossroad, 1985.

Ramos, Mary G., and Robert Plocheck, eds. *1996-1997 Texas Almanac and*

State Industrial Guide. Dallas: *The Dallas Morning News*, 1995.
Reese, SJ, Thomas J. *Archbishop: Inside the Power Structure of the American Catholic Church*. San Francisco: Harper and Row, 1989.
Reicher, Louis Joseph. Special Collection. Catholic Archives of Texas, Austin.
"Rev. Curtis Guillory, SVD." *Black Catholic Men of God*. N.p.: n.p., 1976.
Riding, Alan. *Distant Neighbors: A Portrait of the Mexicans*. 1984. New York: Vintage-Random House, 1986.
Rosten, Leo, ed. *Religions of America: Ferment and Faith in an Age of Crisis*. New York: Simon and Schuster, 1975.
Rule, La Reina, and William K. Hammond. *What's In A Name?: Surnames of America*. 1973; New York: Jove-Harcourt Brace Jovanovich, 1977.
Ryan, W. M. *Shamrock and Cactus: The Story of the Catholic Heroes of Texas Independence*. San Antonio: Southern Literary Institute, 1936.
Sadler, Jerry. *History of Texas Land*. Austin: General Land Office of the State of Texas, 1961.
St. Thomas, University of. *The School of Theology at St. Mary's Seminary 1989-1990*. Houston: University of St. Thomas, 1989.
___. *Undergraduate Catalog 1989-1991*. Houston: University of St. Thomas, 1989.
San Angelo, Diocese of. File. Catholic Archives of Texas, Austin.
San Antonio, Archdiocese of. File. Catholic Archives of Texas, Austin.
Schraner, Anthony. *New. . .Saint Joseph Annotated Catechism: A Full and Clear Explanation of the Catholic Faith in Question- and-Answer Form with Copious Informative and Historical Notes: With Many Citations from the Bible, the Second Vatican Council, and the Papal Documents*. New York: Catholic, 1981.
Smith, Elsdon C. *New Dictionary of American Family Names*. New York: Harper, 1973.
Summers, Peter G. *How To Read A Coat of Arms*. London: The National Council for Social Service for The Standing Conference for Local History, 1967.
Texas Legal Directory 1981: Official Directory of the State Bar of Texas, The. 2 vols. Dallas: Legal Directories Publishing, 1981.
Texas Legislative Council. *The Texas Capitol: Symbol of Accomplishment*. 4th ed. Austin: Texas Legislative Council, 1986.
Tschoepe, Thomas. Biographical Information. 28 Oct. 1980. Archives, Diocese of Dallas.
Tucek, James. *A Century of Faith: the Story of the Diocese of Dallas*. Dallas: Diocese of Dallas, 1990.
Tyler, Diocese of. *Diocesan Directory*. Tyler: n.p., April. 1987.
___. *Diocesan Directory: October 1992-1993*. Tyler: Diocese of Tyler, 1992.
Vanderholt, James F. *Called to Serve: The History of St. John's and Assumption Seminaries, San Antonio, Texas, 1915-1990*. San Antonio: St. John's and Assumption Seminaries Alumni Association, 1990.
___, Carolyn B. Martinez, and Karen A. Gilman. *The Diocese of Beaumont: The Catholic Story of Southeast Texas*. Beaumont: Catholic Diocese of Beaumont, 1991.
Wall, A. E. P., ed. *American Catholic Who's Who*. Bicentennial ed. Vol 21.

Washington, DC: National Catholic News Service for United States Catholic Conference, 1975.

Wangler, Alexander C., ed. *Archdiocese of San Antonio 1874-1974.* N.p.: Newsfoto Yearbooks for Francis J. Furey, 1974.

Webb, Walter Prescott, and Eldon Stephen Branda, eds. *The Handbook of Texas.* 3 vols. Austin: Lakeside and U of Texas Press for the Texas State Historical Association, 1952-1976.

Webster's New Collegiate Dictionary. Rev. ed. Springfield, MA: G. & C. Merriam, 1975.

Wedge, Florence. *How Much Should I Give to My Parish?* Ligouri, MO: Ligouri Publications, 1978.

Whitaker's Almanack 1994. 126th ed. London: Joseph Whitaker, 1994.

Who's Who in America. Chicago and New Province, NJ: Marquis, 1899-

Who's Who in Religion, 1992-1993. 4th ed. Wilmette, IL: Marquis, 1992.

Who's Who in the South and the Southwest. Chicago and New Providence, NJ: Marquis, 1947-

Who's Who in the World. Chicago and New Providence, NJ: Marquis, 1974-

Who Was Who in America, 1607-1981. 8 vols. Chicago, Marquis, 1967-1981.

Williams, Franklin C., Jr. "Bicentennial and Beyond: The Catholic Experience in Texas." University of Texas at Austin. 1984.

___. "Bicentennial Papers: Reflections on the Catholic Experience in America, Texas, and Palestine [Texas]." 1976.

Index

Lubbock, Diocese of, 2, 44-45, 92, 106, 137, 163, 174, 177, 231, 255, 303, 430, 454-458, 480, 483-490, 496

Addenda

Most Reverend Edmond Carmody, DD:

On 25 March 1996 Bishop Carmody was awarded the honorary degree of Doctor of Humane Letters (L.H.D.) by the University of the Incarnate Word (formerly Incarnate Word College), San Antonio, Texas. He was cited "for his lifetime of loving commitment and dedication to Incarnate Word College, to San Antonio, to Texas, and to God."

Most Reverend Hugo M. Gerbermann, MM, DD:

Bishop Gerbermann died of respiratory complications at the Czech Catholic Home in Hillje, Texas (his residence since 1989), on 19 October 1996. After a funeral Mass on 22 October he was buried in St. Mary's Cemetery at Nada, Texas.

Most Reverend Armando X. Ochoa, DD:

Born Oxnard, California, 9 April 1943. Son of Angel M. and Mary (Barba) Ochoa. Educated Santa Clara schools, Oxnard, California (1948-1961); Ventura (California) College (1961-1962); St. John's College (BA, 1966) and Seminary (Camarillo, California). Ordained for Los Angeles Archdiocese, 23 May 1970. Associate Pastor, St. Alphonsus Parish (Los Angeles, 1970-1975); St. John the Baptist Parish (Baldwin Park, 1975-1981); St. Teresa of Avila Parish (Los Angeles, 1981-1984). Appointed Monsignor by Pope John Paul II, 1983. Administrator (1984) and Pastor (1986-1987), Sacred Heart Parish, Los Angeles. Appointed Titular Bishop of Sitifi and Auxiliary Bishop of Los Angeles by Pope John Paul II, 23 December 1986. Episcopal Vicar of the San Fernando Pastoral Region, 1 February 1987. Ordained Bishop, 23 February 1987. Appointed Bishop (5th) of El Paso, 1 April 1996. Installed, 26 June 1996. Associate Director (1975) and Co-Director (1976-1987), Spanish-speaking Permanent Diaconate program for Archdiocese of Los Angeles. Director, Secretariat for Ethnic Ministry program (1986). Boy Scouts of America (Order of the Arrow). Avocations: tennis, racquetball, basketball, snow skiing, and bicycling. Office: 499 St. Matthews Street, El Paso, Texas 79907.

About the Author

Franklin Cadmus Williams, Jr. was born in Palestine, Texas, on 30 July 1941. He is the son of the late Franklin Cadmus and Cathryn Lucille (Pessoney) Williams. His father, an attorney, served as county attorney and county judge of Anderson County, Texas. Judge Williams was a fourth-generation Texan, whose great-grandfather Felix Cadmus Grundy Williams, M.D., emigrated from Monroe County, Georgia.

Franklin Williams was educated in local schools and graduated from Palestine High School in 1959. He received the degree of Bachelor of Arts with a double major in English and history from Baylor University in 1963. His graduate degrees are Master of Arts from Stephen F. Austin State University (1965) and Doctor of Philosophy from the University of Wisconsin-Madison (1975). During his studies he was granted membership in Sigma Tau Delta, the international English honor society.

Between 1964 and 1981 Doctor Williams taught at Stephen F. Austin State University, the University of Wisconsin-Madison, Austin Peay State University, East Texas State University, and Jarvis Christian College. Since 1981 he has been an independent scholar and the owner and bibliographer of one of the largest collections of biographical and critical materials relating to Oliver Goldsmith, the eighteenth-century British author.

A member of the Modern Language Association of America, the Texas State Historical Association, and the Texas Catholic Historical Society, Doctor Williams has been actively engaged in the study and writing of Texas Catholic history for a period of twenty years. The late bishop John L. Morkovsky of Galveston-Houston appointed him to the Parish Historical Project of that diocese and he has done research on the lives of Roman Catholic bishops who have served in Texas for some time past.

Franklin Williams now makes his home in Palestine, Texas. His biography appears in *Who's Who in the South and Southwest, Who's Who in the World,* and *Who's Who in America.*